Police Leadership and Administration

This innovative text adapts the strategic management process to the police organizational environment, illustrating how to tailor responses to the unique problems and issues that professionals are likely to face in the field of law enforcement. The authors cover pioneering management techniques for leaders facing the challenges of today's complex environment, offering police executives guidance on planning, setting direction, developing strategy, assessing internal and external environments, creating learning organizations, and managing and evaluating the change process. The book also tackles how to handle the political, economic, social, and technical considerations that differ from one community to the next.

Providing a foundation with which to adapt to an ever-changing criminal justice climate, this book trains leaders to search for solutions rather than relying on old formulas and scientific management principles. It is an essential resource for forward-thinking police leadership courses in colleges and professional training programs.

Gennaro F. Vito is a Professor in the Department of Criminal Justice at the University of Louisville. He also serves as a faculty member in the Administrative Officer's Course at the Southern Police Institute. He holds a Ph.D. in Public Administration from The Ohio State University. Active in professional organizations, he is a past President and Fellow of the Academy of Criminal Justice Sciences and recipient of its Bruce Smith Award in recognition of outstanding contributions to criminal justice as an academic or professional. He has published on topics including capital sentencing, police consolidation, police traffic stops, policing strategies for drug problems in public housing, attitudes toward capital punishment, and the effectiveness of criminal justice programs, such as drug elimination programs, drug courts, and drug testing of probationers and parolees. He has made more than 100 presentations at professional meetings, including the American Correctional Association, the International Community Corrections Association, and the Kentucky Bar Association. He is the co-author of nine textbooks in criminal justice and criminology.

Anthony G. Vito is Assistant Professor of Criminal Justice and Criminology at Ball State University. He also served on the faculty of the University of West Georgia where he received the Outstanding Research Award. He holds a Ph.D. in Justice Administration from the University of Louisville. In 2015, he was recognized as the Outstanding Graduate Student by the Southern Criminal Justice Association. Dr. Vito has published articles in various journals, including *Policing: An International Journal of Police Strategies & Management*, *Deviant Behavior*, and the *American Journal of Criminal Justice*. Dr. Vito's research interests include policing (traffic and stop-and-frisk results), drug use, criminological theory, capital sentencing, and issues surrounding race/gender in the criminal justice system.

William F. Walsh is the former Director of the Southern Police Institute and Professor Emeritus in the Department of Criminal Justice at the University of Louisville. He holds a Ph.D. in Sociology from Fordham University. A former Lieutenant with the New York City Police Department with 21 years of service, he has conducted research on police and security issues, and authored several articles in scholarly journals, monographs, book chapters and books on police administration, supervision, and management. Before joining the University of Louisville, he served on the Administration of Justice Faculty at The Pennsylvania State University, where he received the National Continuing Education Association Faculty Service Award in 1988. In 2006, he was named the first recipient of the James J. Fyfe Award for a lifetime of service and scholarship to the law enforcement profession by the Police Partnership of New York City. In 2008, Mayor Jerry E. Abramson of the city of Louisville, Kentucky presented him with the Community Partnership Award for his services to the Louisville Metro Police Department.

Police Leadership and Administration

A 21st-Century Strategic Approach

Second Edition

Gennaro F. Vito, Anthony G. Vito
and William F. Walsh

Routledge
Taylor & Francis Group

NEW YORK AND LONDON

Designed cover image: © Getty Images

Second edition published 2025
by Routledge

605 Third Avenue, New York, NY 10158
and by Routledge
4 Park Square, Milton Park, Abingdon, Oxon, OX14 4RN

Routledge is an imprint of the Taylor & Francis Group, an informa business

© 2025 Gennaro F. Vito, Anthony G. Vito & William F. Walsh

The right of Gennaro F. Vito, Anthony G. Vito & William F. Walsh to be identified as authors of this work has been asserted in accordance with sections 77 and 78 of the Copyright, Designs and Patents Act 1988.

All rights reserved. No part of this book may be reprinted or reproduced or utilized in any form or by any electronic, mechanical, or other means, now known or hereafter invented, including photocopying and recording, or in any information storage or retrieval system, without permission in writing from the publishers.

Trademark notice: Product or corporate names may be trademarks or registered trademarks and are used only for identification and explanation without intent to infringe.

First edition published by Routledge 2019

Library of Congress Cataloging-in-Publication Data
Names: Vito, Gennaro F., author. | Vito, Anthony Gennaro, author. | Walsh, William F., author.
Title: Police leadership and administration : a 21st-century strategic approach / Gennaro F. Vito, Anthony Gennaro Vito, William F. Walsh.
Description: Second edition. | New York, NY : Routledge, 2025. | Includes bibliographical references and index.
Identifiers: LCCN 2024007912 (print) | LCCN 2024007913 (ebook) | ISBN 9781032604336 (hardback) | ISBN 9781032604305 (paperback) | ISBN 9781003459095 (ebook)
Subjects: LCSH: Police administration—United States. | Police—United States. | Leadership.
Classification: LCC HV8141 .W348 2024 (print) | LCC HV8141 (ebook) | DDC 363.2068—dc23/eng/20240327
LC record available at https://lccn.loc.gov/2024007912
LC ebook record available at https://lccn.loc.gov/2024007913

ISBN: 978-1-032-60433-6 (hbk)
ISBN: 978-1-032-60430-5 (pbk)
ISBN: 978-1-003-45909-5 (ebk)

DOI: 10.4324/9781003459095

Typeset in Minion Pro
by Apex CoVantage, LLC

Access the Support Material: www.routledge.com/9781032604305

Dedication

We dedicate this work to all our police students who during the last two decades and a half at the Southern Police Institute have freely shared their knowledge and experiences with us in the dynamics of the classroom and as a result enriched their professors and profession.

The Professors Vito dedicate this text to the memory of Officer Ronald D. Vito of the Niagara Falls (NY) Police Department.

Contents

Preface

This book provides a primer on strategic management in policing. Policing is currently going through a period of tumultuous change and challenge. Rapid transformations in technology, community demographics, individual rights, cultural values, economics, social unrest, violent crime, transnational terrorism, and challenges to their legitimacy and government regulations have created a challenging world that is experiencing a variety of legal and social problems.

For the last three decades, police executives and criminal justice scholars have been rethinking what constitutes effective policing. It takes a special type of organizational leadership to position a police department to deal with these forces. This challenge has led to the selection of strategic management as the defining concept of this book.

The purpose of this book is to addresses current trends and strategies in police leadership and administration. Specifically, it focuses on the evolution of professional policing, the leadership role of the police executive, and the strategic management of the police organization. In addition, it examines the latest in management techniques that are directly related to the emerging role of the police executive as they face the challenges of today's complex environment.

Written from the perspective of the chief executive, it begins with an examination of the history and development of professional police administration and leadership. It defines, discusses, and identifies the concepts, techniques, and issues relating to managerial authority, leadership, administration, and command. It explores police leadership and administration through an examination of the issues and challenges of setting organizational direction, managing change, and strategic analysis. It examines the process of strategic management through the development of organizational strategy, strategic planning, operations, and human resource management. It discusses performance measurement, organizational integrity, and professional standards. This book also functions as a guide for the development of police organizations as learning organizations. Lastly, it covers the issues related to creating safe communities, police legitimacy, and preparing for the future.

1 The Evolution of Police Leadership and Administration

Learning Objectives

1. To describe the evolution of policing.
2. To identify the police functions.
3. To describe the types of police departments in the United States.
4. To define the administrative challenge of today's policing environment.
5. To identify the relationship between the learning organization and strategic policing.
6. To understand the impact of Peel's London police model on professional policing.
7. To describe the relevance of *The Nine Principles of Law Enforcement*.
8. To define the different paradigmatic shifts in 20th-century American policing.
9. To identify the characteristics of the Community Problem-Solving Paradigm.
10. To be able to list the characteristics of the top suburban police departments.
11. To describe the difference between an open and closed management system.
12. To identify the characteristics of strategic policing.
13. To define the CompStat management system.
14. To describe Intelligence-Led Policing.

Introduction

The "**Police**" are an organized body of individuals that represent the civil authority of a government. The origin of the word "police" can be traced to the Greek word *politea*, which refers to the internal administration and government of the city (Fyfe, Greene, Walsh, Wilson, & McLaren, 1997, p. 4). Since the emergence of professional policing in the 1830s, the word has come to define the personnel and organizations whose principal concern is the maintenance of order and the enforcement of law. Members of the police profession may be referred to as police officers, troopers, sheriffs, constables, agents, rangers, and peace officers. Police departments are products of their

DOI: 10.4324/9781003459095-1

political, historical, and community environments. In the United States, policing has evolved into a local governmental function responsible for public order and safety within a defined political jurisdictional area such as a city, town, county, and borough or state. The police in the many municipalities are the only public service who will respond when called 24 hours per day, seven days a week. As a result, police officers are the most visible representatives of local governmental authority. As such, their enforcement activities determine the limits of public safety, the level of governmental service, and individual freedom. Since American police departments are primarily local institutions, they are influenced by and responsive to pressure and politics of the community within which they serve.

Our nation has developed from an agrarian-based group of former English colonies into a complex technological society that is interconnected to the entire world. The strains and pressures created by this transformation have brought about economic and social changes that affect all aspects of our society, including public safety. The effective use of police resources is essential to the maintenance of community safety and security. However, the events of 9/11 and the resulting national emphasis on homeland security have accelerated the need for police departments to understand and effectively respond to the shifting demands and uncertainty of these times. Changing economic systems, multiculturalism, demographics, community confidence, family structures, limited resources, technology, and transnational crime are increasingly placing greater demands on police services. As these demands have expanded, public expectations of what the police should be doing and how they should do it have also changed. Today's police organizations are expected to take responsibility for traditional order-maintenance functions as well as many new ones, requiring different skills and ways of working (Flanagan, 2008).

United States Policing System

The United States has one of the more decentralized and complex policing systems in the world. This system is an outgrowth of the nation's founders' fear of a strong centralized government. This fear made them emphasize local autonomy over centralized authority while delegating policing powers to state and local governments. A Bureau of Justice Statistics survey conducted in 2020 found nearly 708,000 full-time sworn law enforcement officers serving in 14,700 agencies that provide protective services to 329.5 million people in the United States. These departments consist of:

- 14,726 General-Purpose Local (municipal) Police Departments.
- 2,889 Sheriff's Offices.
- 49 State Police Departments.

Descriptions of American police organizations include:

- **Urban—multilevel departments**: These are large bureaucratic hierarchical organizations with a high degree of task specialization. They are usually staffed with over a thousand sworn and non-sworn employees. Their service areas are characterized by diverse socioeconomic urban communities consisting of high-density zones of crime and human service demand.

- **Suburban departments**: These are medium-sized organizations of less than a thousand sworn employees. They usually have a strong resource base with limited task specialization. Suburban police departments are presently experiencing an increase in service demand. Most departments with 100 or more officers had full-time specialized units to address child abuse, juvenile crime, gangs, and domestic violence.
- **County police/full service sheriff's office**: These organizations have a variety of organizational structures, service demand and development. Structural change is occurring in which smaller municipal police departments are being merged with the countywide agencies or contracting with them to provide police services.
- **Small community**: These departments have a small number of personnel, usually less than 25 officers, lack resources but have a close relationship with the communities they serve. Their operational officers are expected to perform all police tasks. About half (48 percent) of police departments in the United States employed fewer than 10 officers.
- **State and highway—state-wide jurisdiction**: These are large bureaucratic organizations that either perform full-service policing state-wide or are restricted to the enforcement of highway safety regulations and laws. They are noted for their traditional military-style culture and high levels of integrity. In states where they have full state-wide police powers they support local police in serious or complicated cases and help to coordinate multijurisdictional task force activity. There are 49 State Police Departments in the United States. The state of Hawaii is the one exception.
- **Special function**: These are organizations whose authority is limited to enforcing special laws, control areas, and specific functions. Campus and Fish, Game, and Wildlife police organizations are typical examples of these agencies.

Our policing system is responsible for three distinct functions: crime control, order maintenance, and service provision (Glensor, Correia, & Peak, 2000). Noted police scholar Herman Goldstein (1977, p. 23) identified the complex multiple objectives of policing as follows:

1. To prevent and control conduct widely recognized as threatening to life and property (serious crime).
2. To aid individuals who are in danger of physical harm, such as the victim of a criminal attack.
3. To protect the constitutional guarantees, such as the right of free speech and assembly.
4. To facilitate the movement of people and vehicles.
5. To assist those who cannot care for themselves: the intoxicated, the addicted, the mentally ill, the physically disabled, the old, and the young.
6. To resolve conflict, whether it be between individuals, groups of individuals, or individuals and their government.
7. To identify problems that have the potential for becoming more serious problems for the individual citizen, for the police, or for the government.
8. To create and maintain a feeling of security in the community.

Police departments seek to fulfill these objectives by responding to emergency calls for service, preventing crime, enforcing laws and ordinances, rendering first aid, resolving disputes, regulating traffic, investigating crimes, and arresting violators. However, the way police departments administer and deliver their principal programs and services has evolved over the last two centuries.

Administrative Challenge

As one might imagine, administering a police organization today is a challenging task. The modern police agency is expected to take responsibility for traditional order-maintenance functions as well as many new ones, which require different skills and ways of working. The complex nature of today's policing and the economic climate in which police organizations operate has fundamentally changed the leadership expectations of police executives (Flanagan, 2008). Every day, police leaders face issues of complexity, uncertainty, and sensitivity that require a different level of thinking and decision making. Police executives are challenged to create effective organizations that are adaptable and proactively responsive to changing public safety needs and community relationships. Conventional ways of thinking, analyzing data, solving problems, making decisions, and responding to organizational demands are changing. Few situations are easily resolved with methods developed to address issues in the past. Today's challenges require thinking at different analytical and strategic levels.

Geller (1997) assessed this challenging administrative environment by asking, "Can our police and sheriff departments find ways to work smarter, not just harder?" He answered by suggesting that police departments should become "*learning organizations*" just as many of our nation's most successful business organizations have. Geller believes that this development will allow police departments to innovate and create new strategies to provide public safety. In this manner he believes that they will serve their communities more effectively, efficiently, and legitimately. A **learning organization** is one that enhances its effectiveness by adapting to the needs of its environment (Senge, 1990). It actively engages, evaluates, and adapts by continually assessing its environmental demands and operational methods. It learns from its own and the similar experiences of other organizations to adjust and respond to the environmental demands it faces.

Managers in learning organizations actively seek to expand their capacity to understand the environmental pressures they are facing by consistently gathering and analyzing information. The knowledge gained from this process forms the basis for the creation of data-driven strategies and tactics that are designed to respond to changing operational demands. In learning organizations, information collection is a constant process, along with ongoing verification and analysis. In order for police organizations to become learning organizations they must develop the ability to restructure their operational tactics to meet both current and changing needs of their communities (Silverman, 1999). In these departments the development of operational tactics and strategies is an information data-driven analytical process. Operational success and sustainability are maintained through an ongoing process of information gathering, analysis and sharing, strategy and tactical development, implementation, and continuous assessment.

Managerial decisions in learning organizations are influenced by a diverse set of factors that are derived from without and within these organizations. Externally, these factors include, but are not limited to, changes in government, community demographics, cultural values, economic conditions, both local and transnational crime, global terrorism, and the degree of community confidence in the police organization and its officers. Internally, clarity of an organization's mission and goals, recruitment and retention of personnel, organizational values, internal politics, accountability, training, unions, and managerial ability affect police organizational performance. These forces place increased pressure on how police executives and administrators plan and decide their organization's response to the community's needs.

This challenge has led to the selection of strategic management as the unifying theme of this book. **Strategic management** is the art and science of formulating and implementing strategies to accomplish organizational goals and objectives (David, 2009). The primary purpose of strategic management is to achieve an organization's mission by matching its strengths and capabilities with the demands placed upon it by its environment (Dessler, 2004). Strategic management is the process by which learning organizations are created. It is currently being practiced in police departments whose executives are developing management systems that are operating under a variety of mega-strategies such as **CompStat, Intelligence-Led Policing**, Predictive Policing, and Evidence-Based Policing. Strategic management and the variety of ways in which it has been adapted in policing is the primary focus of this book.

In policing, strategic management involves the development of innovative strategies whose characteristics involve information analysis and technology, strategy and tactics development, managerial accountability, creativity, and continuous assessment to control crime and provide public safety. Strategic management requires that a police department's chief executive and his or her administrative team create a "*strategic vision*" for the department that consists of clear, measurable goals that are focused on integrating organizational elements such as information gathering, computer information systems, patrol, specialized units, and staff support systems to respond to the public safety needs of the community. At the unit level, strategic management refers to the managerial integration of information, strategy, tactics, personnel, and evaluation to achieve organizational goals and objectives. This is a proactive instead of a reactive approach to organizational leadership that is appropriate for responding to changing environmental demands. The first adaptation of this form of management in United States policing occurred in 1994 in New York City when then Police Commissioner William Bratton and his command staff reengineered the police department through the development of the CompStat process (Bratton and Knobler, 1998).

This chapter will identify and explain the historical events that have led to the development of contemporary police administration and strategic management in policing. Many students tend to think of history as just a dry recitation of "facts": dates, names, and places from the hoary past. Although a chronology of events is an important part of the process, the study of history offers much more. Examining the development of an important societal institution like the police explains the basis for its current practices as well as provides answers to pertinent questions such as the following: How has the police mission developed over time? How have police organizations evolved? Where are the police going as an institution? In today's world, how can police departments provide public safety? Naturally, before we can consider these, we must understand where the police (as an organization) have been. History provides a starting point for the understanding of police organizational leadership and administration as well as enhances our understanding of the present.

Professional Policing: The Early Years

Policing has always existed in some form or another in every society. Tribal groups practiced self-policing through the enforcement of behavioral standards by their leaders, councils of elders, religious leaders, and adult members. As societal groups became more complex and industrialization occurred, governing groups and national states saw the need to develop a more structured and organized form of policing. France established a police department for the city of Paris as early as 1544 (Palmer, 1988, p. 69). Urban police forces founded on the French model were created in Russia's St. Petersburg (1718), Prussia's Berlin (1742), and in the capital of the Austro-Hungarian Empire, Vienna (1751). European police forces were armed military-style organizations whose purpose was to serve the national state and maintain public order. These departments acted as both a social and political control system which drew their power from and gave their service to the government that created them (Critchley, 1972, p. 52; Bayley, 1975). Reaction to the pervasive nature of the continental policing systems is the basis upon which rests the Anglo-American belief that excessive centralization of police power should be avoided. However, the origins of what is known today as "Professional Policing," a department of individuals specifically created, trained, and empowered to enforce the law and maintain public order, can be traced to the creation of the London Metropolitan Department in 1829.

In the late 18th and 19th centuries English society was transformed from an agrarian to an urban, industrialized one. This brought about mass migrations of people from rural areas to urban centers in search of employment. One outcome of this process was a breakdown of both civil and social control that necessitated a change in public order control methods. The traditional English fragmented policing system based on watch and wards, constables, and justices of the peace became overwhelmed and ineffective. London, the capital of the British Empire, was a violent, crime-ridden city policed by a fragmented antiquated public safety system.

London Metropolitan Police Model

After many years of debate on the subject of policing the city of London, the English Parliament in 1829 passed the Metropolitan Police Act. It authorized the creation for the city of London of a 3,000-member full-time, uniformed police department. The **London Metropolitan Police** transformed London into one of the safest cities in the world at that time and as a result its police department became a model for the development of urban police departments worldwide (Lee, 1901, p. 228). Sir **Robert Peel**, the Home Secretary of England, is credited with the Act's passage as well as providing the organizational vision and direction for the new police force (Fyfe et al., 1997, p. 7). Peel, in his wisdom, knew that a police force created by the government would be rejected by many English citizens as a foreign form of coercion that would usurp their traditional rights. There was considerable public and parliamentary suspicion of Peel's efforts. The new department met with fierce opposition both before and immediately after its creation (Lee, 1901, p. 245).

From a developmental perspective, it is important to understand why this department succeeded and became the model for so many police organizations. The answer lies in its executive leadership, vision, clarity of mission, organizational strategy, accountability system, administrative practices, and the appropriateness of these for that society's demands at that time. Peel understood that gaining the support of the people was a necessary factor in achieving both acceptance and legitimacy for his "New Police." Current community unrest and protest against police departments in the United States reflects that this factor is as important today as it was in Peel's time. The Metropolitan Police Department from its beginning was based upon the principle that "the people are the police, and the police are the people." From its origin Peel designed the London Metropolitan Police Department as an organization that drew its authority from the legal system and the people it served. He envisioned that his police officers would do things that any citizen would do to make the society safe if they had time to do so (Moore & Braga, 2003, p. 13).

To implement his vision and achieve its acceptance by citizens, Peel and his associates selected men who were even-tempered and reserved; chose a uniform that was unassuming (navy blue rather than military red); and insisted that officers be restrained and polite in their dealings with the public (Uchida, 2010). Peel's police constable constitutionally had original authority and personal responsibility for his actions. However, he was beholding to the law, not a national or local government.

A key factor in Peel's achieving his objectives was the department's executive leadership. He appointed jointly two Commissioners of Police to administer and lead the department. Richard Mayne (1796–1868), an Irish barrister, was selected because of his legal experience and Lieutenant Colonel Charles Rowan (1782–1852), a military officer, for his experience with military organization and discipline. These joint-commissioners combined Peel's strategic vision, executive power, administrative knowledge, and organizational strategy with the strong application of discipline to instill a department-wide cultural value system based on impersonal public service into the structure and practice of the department (Klockars, 1985, p. 42). The "Prevention of Crime and the Maintenance of Order" was established as the department's primary mission. Peel and his commissioners decided that the "true test of the department's effectiveness would be the absence of crime and disorder, and not the visible evidence of police action in dealing with them" (Lee, 1901, pp. 228–244).

The operational strategy used to achieve this mission was a visible uniformed patrol system based on interlocking foot patrol beats that covered the city's streets. These foot beats were designed so that each officer should be able to see every part of his beat at least once in 10 minutes or a quarter of an hour; and this he was expected to do. The objective of this tactic was to have a highly visible uniformed patrol force guarding the streets to prevent crime and ensure citizen safety. The patrols were expected to prevent street robberies, vandalism, and disorder as well as control juveniles, street prostitutes, and drunks. The officers were unarmed except for a small hardwood truncheon that they kept concealed.

The department was a military-style bureaucracy with a hierarchical staffing structure based on a ranking system. A set of rules and regulations guided the performance of all ranks. Merit determined promotions, but improper behavior or poor performance would receive harsh discipline. "Between the years of 1830 and 1838, there were nearly five thousand dismissals, and more than six thousand resignations from the department" (Lee, 1901, p. 240). The *Nine Principles of Law Enforcement* guided the use of the department's policing powers, operations, and interaction with citizens. These "General Instructions" were issued to every new police officer beginning in 1829.

The Nine Principles of Law Enforcement

1.   The basic mission for which the police exist is to prevent crime and disorder, as an alternative to their repression by military force and severity of legal punishment.
2.   The ability of the police to perform their task is dependent on public approval of their existence, actions, behavior, and/or ability of the police to secure and maintain public respect.
3.   The police must secure and maintain the respect and approval of the public; means also the securing of the willing cooperation of the public in the task of observance of laws.
4.   To recognize always that the extent to which the cooperation of the public can be secured diminishes proportionately, the necessity for the use of physical force and compulsion for achieving police objectives.
5.   To seek and to preserve public favor, not catering to public opinion, but by constantly demonstrating absolutely impartial service to law, in complete independence of policy, and without regard to the justice or injustice of the substance of the individual laws; by ready offering of individual service and friendship to all members of the public without regard to their wealth or social standing; by ready offering of sacrifice in protecting and preserving life.
6.   To use physical force only when the exercise of persuasion, advice, and warning is found to be insufficient to obtain public cooperation to an extent necessary to secure observance of the law or to restore order; and to use only minimum degree of physical force which is necessary on any particular occasion for achieving a police objective.
7.   To maintain at all times a relationship with the public that gives reality to the historic tradition that the police are the public and that the public are the police; the police only being members of the public who are paid to give full-time attention to duties which are incumbent on every citizen, in the interest of community welfare and existence.
8.   To recognize always the need for strict adherence to police executive functions, and to refrain from even seeming to usurp the powers of the judiciary or avenging individuals or the State, and of authoritatively judging guilt and punishing the guilty.
9.   To recognize always that the test of police efficiency is the absence of crime and disorder, not the visible evidence of police action in dealing with them.

(Lee, 1901)

However, there is no direct evidence that Sir Robert Peel authored these nine principles, but they were developed by several British police intellectuals (i.e., Jeremy Bentham, Patrick Colquhoun, Henry Fielding) and the first commanders of the British police (Richard Mayne and Charles Rowan) (Lyman, 1964; Grieve, 2015). They were first published by Charles Reith (1975) and subsequently repeated in American textbooks on policing (Germann, Day, & Gallati, 1968; see Lentz & Chaires, 2007). Yet, there is no doubt that the nine principles have profoundly influenced policing in Britain and the United States (Williams, 2003).

Pocock and Poole (2021, p. 5) note that the *Nine Principles of Law Enforcement* fall into "four core categories"—Mission (Principle 1); Professionalism (Principles 2–6); Cohesion (Principles 3, 7, and 8); and Measurement (Principle 9). Therefore, they define the organization's core mission, relationship with citizens, and operational standards, including using force. The absence of crime and disorder became the hall-mark of police effectiveness (Lee, 1901, p. 243). Former New York City Police Com-missioner William J. Bratton believes that many of today's police problems can be resolved by these principles (Goldstein & Goodman, 2014). The London police offi-cers' authorization to control citizens was drawn from the social authority and power of the institution of which they were a part (Klockars, 1985, p. 49). The centrally administered, disciplined, semi-military organized police department eventually won the respect and support not only of the citizens they policed but also the world. During the mid- to late 19th century, similar professional police departments based on this model were established throughout England and beyond (Repetto, 1978).

Development of Professional Policing in America

In the United States, policing evolved from the responsibility of the 17th- and 18th-century colonial sheriff, volunteer posse, slave patrols, constables, and civilian night watch to an organized, 24-hour governmental function. In the early 19th century, industrialization, immigration, socioeconomic conditions, riots, and pervasive urban crime created social unrest, disorder, and fear among citizens. Urban riots, sensational murders, fear of immigrants, and unsafe conditions in American cities resulted in many municipalities creating police departments that were modeled after Peel's Lon-don force. The police departments created in New York City (1844), Chicago (1851), Cincinnati and New Orleans (1852), Philadelphia (1854), Boston (1855), Newark and Baltimore (1857), and Kansas City and St. Louis (1861) adopted the London depart-ment's organizational structure and patrolling system but not its guiding principles and organizational culture. As a result, these departments did not develop an efficient, respected, or ethical police service or create safer cities (see Lane, 1967; Repetto, 1978).

In 19th-century America, local governmental authorities were evolving, and as a result organized policing began as a decentralized, partisan, politically controlled, and corrupt function in most major cities of the day (Repetto, 1978). Police chiefs and offi-cers owed their loyalty to the local political bosses responsible for their appointment. They used their police powers to serve the objectives of these individuals (Kelling & Moore, 1988). This development ensured that politics would be a major factor in developing professional policing in the United States.

The Boston Police Department, led by Stephen James O'Meara from 1906 to 1918, was the one department that was an exception to this practice. Raymond Fos-dick, in *American Police Systems* (1915, pp. 121–122), identified Boston as the best police department in the United States. O'Meara's appointment in 1906 resulted from the municipal reform movement that began at the end of the 19th century and extended into the 1920s. O'Meara's leadership abilities and how he used his office's power contributed to his success. Under O'Meara's leadership, the Boston Police came closest to implementing that administrative ideal of both Peel and America's municipal reformers. The following characteristics led to his successful administration:

1. O'Meara was appointed police commissioner for a five-year term.
2. He had full authority over personnel matters, including hiring, firing, and pro-moting virtually at will.
3. The officers were selected from the working class of Boston.
4. Like in London, they were recruited from the people they policed.

5.   The department maintained a relatively high ratio of police to population, which permitted full utilization of a beat patrol system similar to that used in London.
6.   Management and supervision ensured a high integrity and legality standard was maintained.

(Fyfe et al., 1997, p. 12)

O'Meara employed a strong authoritarian leadership style not unlike that used to administer the London Police. This example of a strong chief executive using coercive power to create and sustain a positive police organization has been repeated throughout the history of modern police administration, beginning with Rowan and Mayne. Unfortunately, the impact of strong police chiefs usually lasts only during their tenure in office. O'Meara died in 1918. The following year the officers of the Boston Police Department conducted an unsuccessful strike to gain recognition for their trade union and improve their working conditions. The city of Boston dismissed the striking officers and hired a new force of 1,000 officers. Police officer attempts to unionize nationally were set back for 20 years, and the achievements of O'Meara's administration were destroyed (Repetto, 1978, pp. 97–105).

Kelling and Moore (1988) analyzed the organizational development of American professional policing by dividing it into three eras: political, reform, and community policing. They identified each era with a specific policing strategy or paradigmatic view that structured the way police managers viewed their leadership role, administered their departments, and responded to the problems of the time. A **paradigm** is "a mental screen or cognitive filter through which information passes before it can be integrated into human thought processes and behaviors" (Kuhn, 1962; More, Vito, & Walsh, 2012, p. 139). Paradigms serve as a basis and guide for decision-making. They also limit a decision-maker's ability to recognize and develop new ways of doing things by restraining their thought processes to existing methods that have proven to be successful in the past (Covey, 2004, p. 26; More et al., 2012). According to Kelling and Moore's perspective, the organizational development of professional policing in the United States is a product of the issues, thinking, values, and beliefs of a specific historical era. It is also a tale of resistance to new ideas before accepting them in the face of crises (Wadman & Allison, 2004). The impact of the Boston police strike described earlier is an example of this process.

The period in which the development of American urban police departments began in the 1840s and lasted into the early part of the 20th century Kelling and Moore identified as the *Political Era*. Local political powers controlled city departments. Police officers served their public and political bosses by maintaining public order through a watchman style of policing. They were more deeply involved in the community through the provision of a variety of social services. The 19th-century police officer performed more as a street social worker than police officers today (Whitehouse, 1973).

Toward the end of the 19th century and the beginning of the 20th century, municipal reformers and police administrators sought to end political control and corruption by professionalizing the police. This **Reform Era** lasted in varying degrees until the 1980s, when **community problem-solving policing** emerged. During the reform period, several influential police chiefs and police scholars redefined the police function and organization. The primary police mission changed from the 19th-century focus on maintaining the peace and providing social services to a narrow emphasis on crime-fighting through law enforcement and managerial control by a bureaucratically administered police department. The reformers believed that the administration of police departments should be separated from the influence of politics and its values (Conser, Russell, Paynich, & Gingerich, 2005). They theorized that an administratively controlled police department commanded by a strong independent police chief with powers similar to that of Stephen James O'Meara of Boston was the ideal administrative model. These beliefs dominated police administration until the 1960s, when increases in crime, the civil rights movement, anti-war protests, riots, and Supreme Court decisions seriously challenged them and created an intense examination of the practice of policing in the United States (Fyfe et al., 1997, pp. 3–27).

During the 1980s, the **Community Problem-Solving Policing Era** emerged out of the desire to create a more effective, responsive, and just police service that would have a closer relationship with the citizens and community they served. The central precept of community problem-solving policing is creating public safety through forming partnerships between police and citizens to solve safety problems.

The authors of this text believe a fourth era, the **Strategic Policing Era**, should be added to this schema. This era began with the adoption of strategic policing strategies by urban police departments in the last decade of the 20th century and continues today. As a result of these efforts, a shift in the basic methods of policing marked by the development and adaptation of data-driven police operational strategies is now occurring (Kelling & Bratton, 1993).

Each of these eras has left its mark on today's police organizations. These paradigmatic shifts' legacy drives how police departments define their primary mission, articulate their operational philosophy, structure their organization, interact with the community, and provide service delivery. During the 20th century, the police profession changed the focus of its organizational and operational strategies three times.

Paradigmatic Shifts of the 20th Century

Reform Paradigm

As policing emerged in the 19th century, corrupt politicians and political machines controlled many local and city governments. Corruption and inefficiency were rampant. Municipal policing provided a source of patronage that regulated businesses, operated election machinery, and exercised power over the daily life of citizens (Repetto, 1978). Politics influenced personnel hiring, while standards for hiring and training were almost non-existent. Most officers were native-born citizens with limited education and skills who learned their craft on the job. Only the largest municipal police departments formally trained new officers in a police academy. Officers often responded to the problems they confronted on their patrol beats with brute force. Most police executives administering local police departments were appointed and removed for political reasons. Positional qualifications, leadership training, and development for police managers did not exist.

In response to these conditions, civic reformers began efforts to change the administration of police departments in the United States. The reformers included scholars like Leonhard F. Fuld, Raymond Fosdick, Bruce Smith, and Elmer D. Graper and police executives such as Orlando W. Wilson, J. Edgar Hoover, and Los Angeles Police Chief William Parker. The reformers' ideal was a politically neutral police organization centrally administered and controlled by professionally trained managers and a tenured police chief. They sought to create a new legitimacy for policing based on law, scientific methods of investigation, and crime control operations. Their efforts helped to create a nationwide effort to transform politically dominated police departments into rational-legal, bureaucratically controlled organizations focused on crime control and criminal apprehension as their primary mission (More et al., 2012).

The reformers advocated:

1. Elimination of political interference.
2. Specialization of police duties.
3. Clearly defined duties.
4. Constant supervision of duties.
5. Strong executive leadership.
6. Constant auditing by inspectors.
7. Maintenance of internal discipline.
8. Comprehensive training of police officers.
9. Careful selection of personnel based on merit and qualifications.
10. Elimination of police duties not associated with crime control and law enforcement.

(Fuld, 1910; Graper, 1921; Fosdick, 1969)

Between 1930 and the 1980s, this reform movement's efforts resulted in a bureaucratic command-and-control style of administration dominating policing. Police departments were administered through an integrated and coherent semi-military organizational control structure that sought authority in criminal law enforcement; emphasized bureaucratic organizational structure; relied on motorized preventive patrol, rapid response to calls for service, and reactive criminal investigation as crime control tactics. Departments measured their effectiveness in crime reports, arrest, and clearance data. Unfortunately, as Sir Robert Peel foresaw, these are measures of police response to crime but not how effective police were in preventing crime.

The first great visionary of this reform movement was **August Vollmer**, who served as chief of police in Berkeley, California, from 1905 to 1932. He envisioned the creation of a professional police service through the adaptation in policing of theories and concepts drawn from management, sociology, psychology, and social work. Vollmer was the first police executive to advocate business management principles, ethical standards, and a sense of professionalism for policing. He was also the first police chief to hire college-educated police officers, many of whom went on to command other police departments (Oliver, 2017). The administrative architect of Vollmer's vision, **Orlando W. Wilson**, was one of Vollmer's college-educated officers and his protégé. Wilson originated this movement's organizational strategy (Fyfe et al., 1997, p. 13). He had a great influence on police managers across the United States through his authorship of the first published texts on police administration, such as *Police Records* (1942), *Police Planning* (1957), and several editions of *Police Administration* beginning in 1951, all of which became mandatory reading for police managers. Through his writing, Wilson successfully laid the foundation for a professional police management and service delivery strategy that governed policing until the 1980s.

These reform efforts produced an administrative-oriented police leadership that transformed many departments into bureaucratically controlled organizations emphasizing crime control (Guyot, 1991). The major operational strategy of the reform era included: (1) a motorized patrol force dispatched by radio to create an impression of omnipresence and rapid response to incidents of crime and (2) investigative units trained in methods of criminal investigation, such as automated fingerprint identification and the use of criminal histories (Moore & Trojanowicz, 1988, p. 5).

The basic principles of the Reform model of policing are:

1. The primary function of policing is crime control.
2. Police departments should be independent of politics.
3. A highly centralized command structure and standardized operating procedures can produce an effective and efficient police service.
4. The police organization should be hierarchical and subdivided according to a division of labor and task specialization.
5. Officers should be selected based on established recruitment standards.
6. Officers should be well-trained and disciplined.
7. Preventive random motorized patrol deters crime.
8. Policing should use modern technology.
9. Police officers should enforce laws impartially.
10. Scientific investigative methods solve crimes.

(Goldstein, 1990, pp. 23–25)

Many of these principles still influence police organizational administration today.

In support of this administrative perspective, O.W. Wilson developed nine tenets of organizational administration to guide police organizational development during this era. He advised that:

1. Tasks similar in purpose, method, or clientele should be grouped into one or more units under the control of a single person.
2. Duties should be defined precisely and known to all organization members to determine responsibility.
3. Communication channels should be established so that information can flow up and down the organization to delegate authority.
4. The principle of unity of command that states that an employee should only be answerable to one person must be applied.
5. Span of control, which is the number of employees that a supervisor or manager can control, should be limited.
6. Each task should be assigned to a member of the organization.
7. Line personnel must be supervised around the clock.
8. Each assignment of responsibility must carry a commensurate authority to accomplish the task.
9. Persons to whom authority is delegated are held accountable for its use.

(Wilson & McLaren, 1977, pp. 73–74)

These tenets helped to create administratively controlled bureaucratic police departments whose primary functions were random patrol, crime control, and criminal investigation. A shift had occurred from the 19th-century politically controlled order-maintenance policing to a highly structured reactive crime-fighting model (Bratton & Kelling, 2012). The political era's order maintenance and social services were not actual police work. Police organizational principles emphasized the division of labor and unity of command. Task specialization was implemented along with hierarchical control of employees (Fayol, 1992, pp. 37–43). Attempts were made to standardize and control officer discretion, decision-making, and behavior by developing policies and procedures. The desire to control the discretionary activities of officers led to structural changes such as a shorter span of control for closer supervision of officers and the creation of additional hierarchal layers of management. Meticulous record-keeping was emphasized, and following the chain of command was the desirable channel of communication (Harring, 1982, pp. 25–32; Fyfe et al., 1997).

O.W. Wilson also developed the theory of preventive patrol. He advocated that if motorized police officers drove conspicuously marked cars randomly through city streets and gave special attention to certain "hazards" (bars and schools, for example), a feeling of police omnipresence would be created. In turn, this sense of omnipresence would both deter criminals and reassure good citizens. Moreover, vigilant patrol officers moving rapidly through city streets would happen upon criminals in action and be able to apprehend them (Kelling & Moore, 1988).

The reform era's approach to organizational administration paralleled the concepts suggested by the works of the classical organizational theorists that dominated managerial thinking into the 1930s and that remain influential today in policing. Classical theorists emphasized stable, clearly defined machine-like organizational structures and procedures to control employees and effectively attain goals and objectives. They envisioned organizations working like well-constructed machines with carefully designed interrelated parts. People are a part of this machine, but the organization and its mission took priority over people (Morgan, 1997).

The organizational model that exemplifies this theoretical perspective is the **bureaucracy**. German sociologist **Max Weber** (1864–1920) described the bureaucracy as a centralized managerial authority system based on a logical hierarchical ordering of positions from the top to the bottom of the organization (Weber, 1947, pp. 329–341). He believed that the characteristics of the bureaucracy made it capable of achieving a higher level of efficiency and effectiveness than other organizational forms.

The police department that emerged during this reform period used structure to centralize administrative control of the department—laws, policy, rules, and procedures defined performance expectations. Individual initiative, enterprise, judgment, and creativity were controlled through the command staff's application of policies and procedures. The foremost example of this model of policing during this era was the Los Angeles Police Department during the administration of Chief William Parker (1950–1966). Parker took over a corrupt police department and transformed it into the nation's leading model of police bureaucratic professionalism (Walker & Katz, 2011, p. 44).

During the reform era, police operational tactics became grounded in random motorized preventive patrol, rapid response to calls for service, and reactive investigation of crime. O.W. Wilson's emphasis on the omnipresence and invulnerability of motorized patrol led to most of a department's patrol officers being assigned to motor units (Fyfe et al., 1997, p. 540). This process required patrol units always to roam the streets randomly. Citizens were expected to call the police to activate officer response. The 911 emergency systems developed in the 1960s made it easier for the public to contact the police and obtain a quick response. As a result, the unintended consequence of this strategy is that answering calls for service became the most time-consuming patrol task. Patrol workloads increased to such an extent that operational units found it difficult to perform preventive patrol (Kessler, 1993). At the same time, the citizen's obligation for crime prevention was reduced, and the police department's responsibility for community safety increased. Citizens turned into passive recipients of crime control services. Patrol became a reactive function activated by crises instead of a crime-preventive function.

The reform-era police organizations became closed bureaucratic systems that emphasized internal control and adherence to policy and procedures. Department policy and procedures covered every conceivable aspect of organizational life. Officers were discouraged from becoming too friendly with the people they served because policing was the responsibility of professionally trained officers only. The total motorization of patrol further enhanced this separation. In some departments, uniform patrol officers were discouraged from making drug arrests to control corruption. The effort to prevent corruption and control officer behavior shaped every aspect of the police organization, administration, and tactics (Kelling, 1995).

In the attempt to free policing from political influence, it became separate from and unresponsive to the communities it served. A technical form of professionalism developed based on skills and values associated with crime control, rather than focus on crime prevention and community respect. Instead of creating safer communities through crime prevention, the era's reactive patrol strategy emphasized responding to crime but did little to prevent crime (Kelling, Pate, Dieckman, & Brown, 1975). A powerful administrative orthodoxy emerged rooted in the traditions of military command and bureaucratic management that became the foundation for the theory and practice of police management (Moore & Stephens, 1991).

Table 1.1 summarizes the characteristics of the reform era. This era dramatically changed police administration by creating closed organizations isolated from political and community influences. As a result, law enforcement agencies became the most autonomous and isolated public departments in urban government (Goldstein, 1990). In the final analysis, however, the reform movement failed in every conceivable way: it did not prevent crime, it did not solve crimes, and it lost the consent of the public, especially the minority community (Bratton & Kelling, 2012).

The concepts and principles of the reform era swept the country. The conclusion that crime fighting was the primary police task had a commonsense appeal. In attempting to avoid the pitfalls of the political era, this movement successfully reduced political influence and replaced it with managerial control. However, the era's dominant leadership style resulted in police managers becoming increasingly autocratic and remote from their operational personnel. While professionalism was the ideal of this era, it did not extend to the lower level of the organization, the patrol officer. Management maintained the fiction that the total organization is designed to support patrol, but this was not the case. Management continually tried to control and structure the behavior of patrol officers. This administrative style stifled officer initiative and communicated that management did not trust them to think independently. Everything had to follow the methods outlined in the procedural manual. These efforts even extended to the personal conduct of the officer when off duty. Specific rules and

TABLE 1.1 Reform Paradigm: 1930–1980s

- **Mission**—crime control and rapid emergency response
- **Strategy**—random preventive patrol, response to calls for service, and after-the-occurrence crime investigation
- **Organizational system**—closed, command and control bureaucracy
- **Structure**—hierarchical organization defined by rank, policy, standards, rules, and task specialization
- **Authority**—criminal law—technological expertise—command authority independent of politics and community control
- **Service tactics:** 3 Rs—random motorized preventive patrol, rapid response to calls for service, and reactive investigations

procedures supported by disciplinary punishments ensured strict departmental policy and values compliance.

The emphasis on managerial control and decreased officer discretion produced a **deprofessionalization syndrome** that weakened the professional status of the patrol officers (see Sharp, 1982; Stokovic, Kalnich, & Klofas, 2012). As a result, in large urban police departments, any assignment except patrol was eagerly sought after, and over time patrol was performed by the newest, most inexperienced officers and those who had been reassigned back to patrol as punishment for rule violations. Patrol became the dumping ground of many departments (Sparrow, Moore, & Kennedy, 1990). Thus, the "best and brightest" officers were often absent from the front line of police service delivery.

Another product of this command and control system with its deprofessionalization syndrome is the creation of two separate organizational cultures—the **street cop** and the **management cultures**. In response to the command and control management style, the working officers (street cops) developed a self-protective culture of beliefs, values, and norms that reinforced solidarity and support with fellow officers above professional standards of conduct and organizational integrity. Once officers were socialized into this culture, it shaped how they performed their duties and viewed community members, their department, and their managers. Street cops believed that their managers' only concern is advancing their careers and that these managers will not protect them from politicians, the media, civilians, and others who do not understand "real" police work, with its constant ambiguity and relentless pressure to "do something, now." Officers adopted the belief that they were on their own, forced to do society's dirty work, but received little understanding and support from the public and their department's administrators (Reuss-Ianni, 1983; Kelling, 1995). The reform era's attempts at controlling officer discretion through its command-and-control administrative practices undermined the goals of police professionalization.

Crises and Paradigm Shift

During the 1960s and 1970s, the United States underwent social changes that altered the government's relationship with its citizens. The civil rights movement and the due-process decisions of the United States Supreme Court impacted police practices, and this, followed by the anti–Vietnam War protests, challenged the methods police used to handle demonstrations, riots, marches, rallies, and citizens' constitutional rights. Television viewers saw minorities and demonstrators gassed, clubbed, and attacked by dogs. Supreme Court decisions found police investigative tactics and interrogation methods unconstitutional. It led to a comprehensive examination of police practices and the justice system, resulting in two national studies, the President's Commission on Law Enforcement, and the Administration of Justice in 1967 and the National Advisory Commission on Criminal Justice Standards and Goals in 1973. These studies focused on the organization, personnel, education, training, and management of police departments. However, they also raised serious questions about police accountability and their relationship with the communities they served (Goldstein, 1990, p. 10). A paradigm shift had begun that challenged the basic conception of how policing should be conducted and organized in the United States.

The issues and questions raised at this time sparked scholars' interest in police research. Funding for much of this research came from the Safe Streets Act created by Congress in 1968 and private sources such as the Ford, Guggenheim, and Charles Stewart Mott Foundations. These efforts disclosed that police officers used a great amount of discretion in their work and that the majority of their calls for service were not crime-related. It became evident that policing was more complex than originally perceived by those within and outside of the profession. Lastly, a series of studies conducted during the 1970s found that the police operational strategies of random motorized preventive patrol, rapid response to calls for service, and reactive investigation were not the effective crime control tactics the police claimed. These conclusions added to a controversy associated with police strategies and tactics (see Kelling et al., 1975; Greenwood, Petersilia, & Chaiken, 1977; Spelman & Brown, 1981).

Research conducted during the 1980s determined that citizens' view of their safety and fear of crime was more closely correlated with community disorder than crime (Kelling & Moore, 1988). Unfortunately, order maintenance had been all but eliminated as a police tactic by the reform movement. Few departments collected data on disorder offenses or trained officers to handle such activities. Nor did they encourage and reward officers for successfully performing order-maintenance activities. The primary police focus was on serious crime, especially felonies, not on offenses that created disorderly neighborhoods (Wilson & Kelling, 1982, pp. 29–38). A shift in police strategy occurred during the reform era, moving policing away from crime prevention and order maintenance to after-the-fact reaction to crime (Bratton & Kelling, 2012). Community problems became compartmentalized into unrelated single-incident responses, and crime prevention and Peelian policing ideals were forgotten.

The Community Problem-Solving Policing Paradigm

The 1980s marked the beginning of another paradigmatic shift in policing. The events of the previous two decades, along with the impact of research findings and the unprecedented rising of crime rates beginning in 1965, created more questions than answers for police administrators about the effectiveness of their organizations. In addition, during this period, a new breed of officer who differed greatly from those in the past entered policing and began moving up the ranks to positions of authority. The "**new breed**" started entering policing in 1968 with the employment of the first of the "Baby Boomer" generation (born between 1943 and 1960) (Zemke, Raines, & Filipczak, 2000). This employment cohort was better educated than past recruits and included increased numbers of women and minorities, and veterans of the Vietnam War. Minority and women officers earned equal treatment in hiring and promotion after numerous legal challenges to past discriminatory practices that eliminated them from police employment and advancement. These "new breed" officers began to question the management practices, policies, and procedures they were subjected to daily. Also, during this period, several police departments began experimenting with different operational tactics to create safer cities that included foot patrol and decentralization of patrol units, emphasizing community outreach and problem-solving. These experiments were conducted by police departments in Boston, Massachusetts; Flint, Michigan; Houston, Texas; Newark, New Jersey; New York City; and Santa Ana, California. The neighborhood-oriented policing philosophy developed by the Houston Police Department defined its approach to public safety as follows:

> an interactive process between police officers assigned to specific beats and the citizens who either work or reside in these beats to develop ways to identify problems and concerns mutually and assess viable solutions by providing resources from both the police department and the community to address the problems and concerns.
>
> (Oettmeier & Bieck, 1987, p. 5)

At this time, one of the foremost authorities on policing, Herman Goldstein (1979), articulated and later expanded on the concept of problem-oriented policing (POP). Goldstein suggested that the police should analyze a wide range of information to identify the cause of the problems that affect communities and create crime, then construct and implement responses uniquely suited to each particular problem. He urged police managers to consider implementing this approach to solving community crime rather than relying solely on rapid response to individual calls for service and arrest-oriented practices. Goldstein's suggestion challenged traditional police practice and the reform movement's claim to police crime control expertise. He disclosed that police seldom systematically analyzed the underlying substantive community problems that generate the major proportion of a police department's service demand. He asserted that the police cannot resolve isolated community problems one incident at a time. He claimed that successful problem control requires community members with a stake in the problem to be included in its analysis and solution.

Police departments experimented with problem-oriented policing in Baltimore County, Maryland; Madison, Wisconsin; San Diego, California; and Newport News, Virginia. A unique aspect of the problem-oriented approach is that it does not require total organizational redirection by a department in its operational methods. Instead, it can be a process practiced by a specific unit or department. Many departments adopted these processes as part of their Community Policing programs (Reitzel, Piquero, & Piquero, 2005).

In less than two decades following the initial community-oriented experiments, Community Policing (COP) evolved as the new organizational orthodoxy of policing (Eck & Rosenbaum, 1994; Rosenbaum, 1998; Cordner & Bibel, 2005). In 2015, the Bureau of Justice Statistics found that nearly 70 percent of local police departments include Community Policing in their mission statement. That includes nine out of ten departments serving populations of 25,000 or more. Trojanowicz and Bucqueroux (1994, p. 2) define Community Policing as:

> a philosophy and an organizational strategy that promoted a new partnership between people and their police. It is based on the premises that both the police and the community must work together to identify, prioritize, and solve contemporary problems such as crime, drugs, fear of crime, social and physical disorder, and overall neighborhood decay, to improve the overall quality of life in the area.

James Q. Wilson and George L. Kelling provided theoretical support for this new community-oriented paradigm published in a 1982 *Atlantic Monthly* seminal article entitled "Broken Windows: The Police and Neighborhood Safety." They argued that police departments focused solely on detecting serious crimes are not truly helping communities survive. In addition, Wilson and Kelling claimed that it was community disorder in the form of broken windows, trash, street prostitution, and drug dealing that attracted criminals and bred fear among citizens. This fear created citizen apathy and insecurity, leading to community abandonment and even more crime in marginal communities. They concluded that fighting crime is important; however, fighting fear is essential for communities to survive.

A major impetus for the adoption of Community Policing occurred in 1994 when Congress passed the *Omnibus Crime Bill, 18 U.S.C.A. § 1033(e)*, that provided funding for the hiring of 100,000 new police officers. The act specified that these new officers must engage in Community Policing. As a result, thousands of local governments directed their police to adopt Community Policing as an organizational strategy to gain additional police officers through federal funding.

At the heart of the community-oriented philosophy is a broad view of the police function that involves the creation of a partnership between the police and the residents of the communities they serve. Hopefully, this partnership will improve the quality of community life by creating problem-solving strategies to enhance neighborhood safety. However, some early proponents of this form of policing have claimed that it returns policing to the original principles of Sir Robert Peel (Braiden, 1986). Operationally, Community Policing moves beyond incident-driven reactive policing by directing patrol officers' attention to the conditions underlying disorder and criminal incidents. Officers must work closely with neighborhood residents to identify and address crime and disorder issues by using the resources and capabilities of the department and the local community. With community cooperation, the police would obtain valuable information and support that will assist them in solving crimes, creating order, and sometimes identifying unknown problems (Trojanowicz & Bucqueroux, 1994). This perspective envisions policing with an expanded purpose that combines crime control with the responsibility to prevent crime and promote and maintain community order.

The operational strategy of Community Policing contains the following key elements:

- Decentralization of patrol units by geographical assignment. Officers are assigned to foot beats, substations, and community-policing zones to be closer to the community.
- Selection of several officers as community policing officers to liaise with the community and patrol and manage specific beats, zones, and/or substations.
- Selection of a line supervisor, usually a sergeant or lieutenant, to oversee the community patrol officers.
- Directed and structured patrol activities designed to develop a closer interpersonal relationship between citizens and community patrol officers.
- Citizen-police engage in joint efforts in problem identification, analysis, and resolution.
- Problem response strategies developed at the operational level.
- Enhancement of communication between the department, community, and other agencies within and outside of city government.

(Fyfe et al., 1997, p. 541)

Community Policing encourages departments to develop a close bond between the patrol officer and the community. Officers should get to know the citizens on their beats and understand their needs, habits, and wishes (Farrell, 1988). The underlying belief is that the police must relate to and understand a community to identify its problems and develop creative responses to public safety issues. Community Policing is the actualization of the concept that police in a democracy is not a closed organization that is insular, self-contained, or cut off from the communities from which their power truly derives—an actualization of the Peelian concept that "the police are the people and the people are the police." An initial evaluation of the community foot patrol program in Flint, Michigan, found that citizen fear of victimization declined, citizen satisfaction with the police was enhanced, and the attitudes of the police toward the public improved. In addition, many officers found foot patrols personally and professionally rewarding (Trojanowicz, 1982).

Advocates of Community Policing encouraged police departments to adopt pro-active decentralized strategies designed to address issues of crime, fear, and disorder within neighborhoods. In return, community members take a proactive role in help-ing the police and other government entities set and implement community-oriented policies. Citizens would have input in setting organizational goals and objectives and establishing priorities for action. Ideally, policing in each community or neighbor-hood would follow neighborhood needs and values (Kelling & Coles, 1996). In its ideal form, Community Policing foresees police assignments and strategies following local needs, norms, and values. This decentralized approach to operational strategy is assumed to provide citizens with protection tailored to diverse communities' needs (see Table 1.2).

In contrast to the reform era, Community Policing expands the function of polic-ing beyond crime to the resolution of community problems (Peak & Glensor, 2012). In essence, Community Policing places more responsibility on the police department. Agencies committed to Community Policing must perform their traditional duties of law enforcement, order maintenance, and service and attempt to identify and solve local problems. The police function is expanded to include a proactive response to maintaining order, dealing with quality-of-life offenses, problem-solving, and fixing community "broken windows."

Community Policing represents a major transformational change that redefines how the police organization understands its function, operations, and relationship to the community. It is a program, an operational strategy, and an organizational philos-ophy designed to promote police-citizen, community-based problem-solving. Ana-lytical community problem-solving beyond the resolution of specific incidents is a strategic redirection that contrasts previous efforts by reform-era police management to limit officer discretion and standardize their administrative control. However, while this community problem-confronting approach contradicted many of the reform era's key features, it retained its bureaucratic organizational structure. Lastly, relying on citi-zen endorsement of order-maintenance activities (to justify police activities) acknowl-edges dependence on the political process and the broadening of the police function.

During the 1990s, adoption of Community Policing methods increased mark-edly as many departments devoted a proportion of their patrol resources to Com-munity Policing. In 1996, *Good Housekeeping*, a popular monthly magazine that is subscribed to by millions of American households, published a special report on a year-long survey that identified America's best suburban police forces. The survey focused on the suburbs because this is where a sizable portion of the country's pop-ulation lived. The article claimed, "Today's top departments do more than just arrest

TABLE 1.2 Community Problem-Solving Policing 1980s–Today

- **Mission**—community safety, stabilization, and problem-solving
- **Strategy**—decentralized service delivery based upon community needs identified through community police problem-solving partnerships
- **Organizational system**—open system
- **Structure**—hierarchical with decentralized, programmatic, and place-based officers and units
- **Authority**—philosophy—community partnership and engagement focused on problem identification and -solving
- **Service Tactics**—line officer-based, foot patrol, bikes, teams, neighborhood police stations

criminals—they help neighborhoods solve problems and stop crime before it starts." *Good Housekeeping* identified the following characteristics as those that each of the top police departments had in common:

- Excellent leadership is epitomized by a police chief with vision and the skills to carry it out.
- An ability to identify trouble spots and act before making arrests is needed.
- Quick and thorough response to citizens' calls for assistance, complaints, and concerns.
- Innovative programs, often technology-based, fight crime more quickly and effectively.
- Officers who see policing as a career of choice and who are personally accountable for community stability.
- Intolerance of brutality and corruption within the ranks.
- Creative solutions to address traditional hard-to-handle crimes such as domestic violence and drug abuse in schools.
- Citizens who are active auxiliaries of the crime-fighting team and who are encouraged to critique the department's performance.

(Domanick, 1996, pp. 82–92)

The significance of this article is that it reflects the extent to which the operational dimensions of Community Policing and problem-solving have become the standard by which mainstream America judges police organizational excellence. The Office of Justice Programs in 2000 reported that 65 percent of departments serving 50,000 or more residents indicate that they have a full-time Community Policing unit (Reaves & Goldberg, 2000). It also reflects the emphasis on using technology-based innovation to address crime which has emerged as a defining characteristic of strategic policing.

Ideally, Community Policing is a bottom-up strategy that emphasizes the police officer's use of information, judgment, wisdom, problem-solving abilities, and expertise to solve community public safety issues. At the same time, it supports a strategic redirection in policing because it encourages police departments actively to engage their external environment and develop strategies to address public safety needs instead of just responding to single incidents. Thus, Community Policing represents a significant shift in organizational power and control from administration to operations.

This type of organizational shift requires police administrators to adopt a flexible leadership style different from the traditional "command and control" methods that departments had developed in the reform era (Moore & Stephens, 1991). Community Policing challenges police executives to be aware of their interdependence with the community and understand the factors that affect public safety. It provides a viable frame of reference and calls for integration between the department and its community. Unfortunately, research has determined that the organizational change process needed to support this philosophy and make community-oriented strategies work is incomplete (Zhao, He, & Lovrich, 2003).

Despite financial support from the federal government, Community Policing has never fully become a complete organizational strategy. In many police departments, Community Policing is a programmatic function that is the responsibility of an organizational subunit. Police departments operating this way are divided into a closed and open system organizational model. Most of the department's officers are still subjected to traditional reform-style management, and their primary operational strategy is random patrol and single-incident response policing. Today, almost every specialized program developed by a police department is labeled Community Policing. Stand-alone Community Policing units tend to evolve into operational ghettos whose officers are considered not engaging in real police work (Toch & Grant, 1982). Departments that claim to be Community Policing organizations are still bureaucratically structured and functioning with operational service delivery strategies similar to that developed in the reform era of policing (Greene & Mastrofski, 1988; Skogan, 1990). However, the central philosophy of Community Policing, emphasizing listening to and working more closely with the community, has become the dominant tenet of 21st-century police administration.

Strategic Policing: A Developing Paradigm

During the three decades before the 1990s, the United States experienced its highest recorded crime rates. At the beginning of the 21st century, changing societal conditions and fear of crime created greater demands on police services, testing the limits of the traditional operational strategies that developed during the reform era. As the demands on policing expanded, public expectations of what the police should be doing also diversified and grew. The events of 9/11 created a national emphasis on homeland security. However, fiscal difficulties further enhanced by the financial crisis of 2008 affected the ability of local governments to provide services such as policing. A national survey of police departments conducted by the Police Executive Research Forum in 2010 found that 51 percent of the respondents' departments had experienced significant cutbacks in personnel and staffing levels. Thus, the police were expected to address increasingly demanding public safety needs and be more effective, but had fewer personnel resources to accomplish these demands.

As they responded to these environmental demands some police administrators sought to change their operational methods and develop more effective responses to the challenges they were facing (Moore & Stephens, 1991; Kennedy, 1993; Bratton & Knobler, 1998; Maple, 1999). Executives within this group began to experiment with new ways of policing. They sought to use their resources more effectively and resolve public safety problems while innovating their operational response strategies. New strategies such as CompStat, Hot Spots, Focused Deterrence, Intelligence-Led, and Evidence-Based Policing emerged as part of these new data-driven approaches to policing labeled by some as "Predictive policing" (Pearsall, 2010). The operationalization of these new strategies created another paradigm shift as they engaged an open-system organizational information perspective that was based upon the adaptation of data-driven strategic problem-solving tactics for their organizations. This form of management prevalent in the corporate world emphasized the linkage between the organization and the environment in which it existed and the outcomes it desired to achieve (Moore & Stephens, 1991).

An evolution of thought began to take place within the police profession. Police executives who learned from their own experiences were now generating new ideas about how to police the nation's communities. The strategies they developed paralleled organizational techniques drawn from the corporate world that used data analysis to anticipate trends in market conditions to drive sales strategy. Police departments began to use data analysis to anticipate and identify trends in community safety and crime and develop strategic responses to these conditions. These new strategies shared common elements that included developing information from various sources, analyzing these data, and using the intelligence that was produced to anticipate and respond to crime and problem conditions.

The idea of the strategic management of policing was initially discussed during the Executive Session on Policing 1985–1988 conducted at Harvard University's Kennedy School of Government. In a monograph developed during this session, Moore and Trojanowicz (1988) defined it as a strategy that increased police capacity to deal with crimes that are not well controlled by traditional methods. In 1991, Mark H. Moore and Darrel W. Stephens co-authored a text for the Police Executive Research Forum that made a strong case for policing to move beyond the administrative practice of command and control and adopt the practices of strategic management. David Kennedy (1993), however, warned that strategic policing, with its wider range of tactics, new responsibilities, and roles for officers and managers, would require hard choices for managers especially regarding resource allocation to be successful.

For the purposes of this discussion, **strategic policing** is defined as the art and science of developing, implementing, and evaluating data-driven cross-functional strategies to accomplish organizational goals and objectives (David, 2009). It involves the integration of information analysis, strategy development, managerial accountability, operational tactics, and continuous evaluation. It represents a significant shift from the way managers traditionally conceive of their departments and how they conduct the process of policing. A central facet of this process is the alignment of a department's strengths and capabilities with the demands placed upon it by its external and internal environments. Operational managers are expected to formulate, implement, and evaluate cross-functional strategies and tactics that respond to the demands of their department's environment to achieve organizational goals and objectives. Departments engaging in strategic policing function as open learning systems that actively interact and understand and learn from the environment in which they exist and respond to its demands as proactively as possible.

All organizations interact with their environment; it is the degree in which they do and understand the demands the environment makes of them that varies. **Closed systems** such as the ones that emerged in policing during the reform era interacted minimally on an incident-by-incident basis. These organizations were perceived to be administratively self-regulating closed structures that were complete unto themselves, not affected by external forces. This is not an accurate view of the police organizational reality in today's world. Today police organizations are viewed as complex structures subjected to a variety of environmental influences and driving forces.

Strategic policing envisions police departments as **open system learning organizations** that acknowledge their dynamic interrelationship with their external environment. This concept of policing emphasizes the understanding and use of external environmental inputs (information about driving forces such as crime and community safety problems) and internal processes (organizational capability to respond to and manage demands) to create outcomes and services that are valued by the communities they serve (More et al., 2012, p. 10).

Open system police organizations engage with and understand their community and its problems. They engage in a continual process of transforming inputs (intelligence data, citizen complaints, governmental mandates, problems, safety issues, police observations) into a coordinated response by managing internal subsystems (calls for service processing, crime analysis, developing operational strategy, tactical deployment, investigation, arrests) that produce outcomes (e.g., public safety, crime control, traffic control, dispute resolution, fear reduction, community survival, and justice). Effectiveness is based upon the adaptation of their operational practices and resources to community needs and expectations (Roberg, Kuykendall, & Novak, 2002, pp. 35–36).

Strategic policing involves the integration of information analysis, strategy, managerial accountability, operational tactics, and performance evaluation within the daily functioning of the police department. It is designed to create a more proactive police response to crime prevention and public safety through intelligence analysis, the identification and management of problems, and the deployment of department resources. In strategically managed departments intelligence becomes the basis for operational decisions about deployment of resources, tactics, impact assessments, performance outcomes, and community safety. Through strategic analysis departments are able to identify potential and current crime patterns and persistent offenders. This intelligence provides departments with the ability to anticipate crime trends and threats instead of just reacting to them incident by incident.

A central facet of strategic policing is the development and utilization of a contingency process to plan and develop tactics to respond to public safety demands. Contingency theory holds that the most effective organizations possess a degree of adaptability and flexibility that enables them to respond to the changing and contradicting demands they confront (Banner & Gagné, 1995). Strategic policing provides police operational managers with the discretionary flexibility to initiate and reshape operational tactics to meet changing demands. The department's response to crime and community safety becomes broader, more proactive, and more sophisticated. Strategic management organizes policing as an information-intensive learning endeavor (Pearsall, 2010). However, departments that engage in strategic policing still employ a centralized bureaucratic structure and an administrative style that controls intelligence and operational strategy.

Operational managers are responsible for using intelligence gained from community engagement and analysis to develop tactics and focus their attention on current and potential crime patterns as well as threats to community safety. The benefit of understanding, engaging, and building relationships with the community is one tactic learned by police managers during the community problem-solving policing era. As new intelligence data arise, commanders are expected to adjust their tactics to respond effectively. This process provides the department with the means to develop the capacity to initiate and reshape operational behavior to meet changing demands. As a result, the police department is functioning as a learning organization.

Strategic policing represents the adaptation of the learning organization concept to policing by consistently expanding a department's capacity to restructure its operational tactics to meet both the current and changing needs of their communities (Silverman, 1999). Strategically managed departments continually evaluate and adapt to their environment instead of simply trying to maintain the status quo and operate in a reactive mode such as traditionally managed police organizations. Learning organizations analyze the forces that affect them, continually assess their ability to respond to these forces, and learn from their own and similar experiences of other organizations. They are working smarter, not harder (Geller, 1997).

Major examples of strategies currently in use during this developing era in policing that will be discussed in this text are CompStat, Hot Spots, Focused Deterrence, Intelligence-Led, and Evidence-Based Policing. As part of this chapter, we will briefly discuss CompStat and Intelligence-Led Policing because of their significant impact on changing the course of police administration and leadership. Table 1.3 summarizes the organizational strategy of the strategic policing era.

Strategic policing is not one form of policing (i.e., traditional, community, or problem-solving) but a blend of all these, plus an organizational management process that is based upon ongoing analysis of the department's data drawn from the external

TABLE 1.3 Strategic Policing 1994–Today

- **Mission**—prevent, control, and reduce crime; improve quality of life and community safety
- **Strategy**—combines information gathering, crime and problem data analysis with a geographic focus and tactical development
- **Organizational System**—open system mission-driven outcome-focused adaptive learning system
- **Structure**—bureaucratic and geographically decentralized
- **Authority**—knowledge-based—system thinking—managerial accountability system
- **Service Tactics**—information gathering, timely and accurate analysis, incident mapping, community partnerships, intelligence-based development of operational strategies and tactics, and continual follow-up and assessment. Data analysis and public safety needs focuses and drives operational units' tactics.

---

environment and the evaluation of its operational tactics. It builds on the past and present to engage the future of policing.

 ## CompStat

The first adaptation of strategic management in policing occurred in 1994, when the New York City Police Department (NYPD) developed an organizational management and operational service delivery process entitled CompStat. CompStat employs a comprehensive, continuous analysis of current crime patterns, with the development of tactics based upon this data analysis, identification, and evaluation of results, and redirection of operational personnel to meet changing conditions (Silverman, 1999; Walsh, 2001). Once a police manager had monitored and analyzed the intelligence data, he or she could deploy their resources to reduce crime in the "hot-spot areas" in a logical data-driven manner. It was not a one-shot, incident-driven approach but a continuously updated daily accounting of data keyed to localities that held supervisors up and down the chain of command accountable for solving problems and preventing them from reoccurring. The NYPD executive team's organizational strategy set clear performance outcomes that concentrated on crime prevention and suppression and on managerial accountability based on real-time information analysis, integrated problem-solving, and tactical development. CompStat also set a premium on monitoring, accountability, and maintaining managerial oversight of the entire organization (Silverman, 1999; Henry, 2002). Through this process NYPD used information technology, operational strategy, and managerial accountability to focus the Department's resources on crime and quality-of-life problems that were affecting the entire city. It was the first development of the learning organization concept in policing. CompStat's emphasis on crime prevention and suppression, and on supervisorial accountability, would have a profound impact on increasing the effectiveness and efficiency of NYPD and other large city police departments that would adopt it (Domanick, 2015).

Operationally, CompStat is radically different from the accepted concepts and practices that have guided police administration through most of its existence from the reform era. It utilizes methods and strategies like those used by corporate managers to achieve their mission (Henry, 2002). CompStat is based upon and emphasizes the vital link between timely intelligence information, operational decision-making, and crime control objectives (McDonald, 2002). As a management tool, its utility rests in the fact that it is adaptable to constantly changing conditions and any organizational setting. The underlying principle of CompStat is the belief that police officers and police agencies can have a substantial positive impact on crime and quality-of-life problems (Bratton & Knobler, 1998).

The New York City Police Department's CompStat process is credited with turning the city from a place that once represented the ultimate in urban lawlessness into a city safer than many other cities in the United States. Police statistics for New York City indicate that serious crime has decreased by double digits since NYPD developed CompStat in 1994. Since then, serious felony crime in New York City has dropped by 80.07 percent and murder by 86.4 percent (see NYPD website: www.nyc.gove/html/nypd). CompStat has been adopted by most of the larger police departments in the United States as well as police organizations in other countries.

Intelligence-Led Policing

Intelligence-Led Policing is a business model and managerial philosophy in which data analysis and crime intelligence are pivotal to an objective, decision-making framework that facilitates crime and problem reduction, disruption, and prevention through both strategic management and effective enforcement strategies that target prolific and serious offenders (Ratcliffe, 2016, p. 63). This process is based upon the fact that the police during the normal course of their work gather a great amount of data about crime and offenders. Community and problem-solving policing enhanced this informational gathering. At the same time, problem-oriented policing supports the belief that analysis of this data is useful in determining responses to crime and community problems.

Intelligence-Led Policing, like CompStat, employs a top-down hierarchical administrative control system like the one advocated during the reform era. Operationally it combines crime analysis and criminal intelligence to focus police resources on serious crimes and offenders (Tilley, 2003). In 1995, the Chief Constable of Kent, England, Sir David Phillips, pioneered the first use of Intelligence-Led Policing in a systematic manner. He positioned intelligence at the heart of his department operational decision-making. The Kent Intelligence Unit directed aspects of daily police activities (Maguire & John, 2006). This policing strategy has been adopted by police departments in the United States, New Zealand, Australia, India, and Europe. The Bureau of Justice Assistance issued a report on Intelligence-Led Policing in 2005, noting that policing cannot function without collecting, processing, and using intelligence. The report emphasized that intelligence is vital for decision-making, planning, strategic targeting, and crime prevention (Peterson, 2005).

Analysis

Emerging out of the development of strategic policing is a new police leadership model similar to that found in corporate organizations. This model represents a change in how police administrators conceive of their department's organizational strategy as they analyze and convert information, prioritize resource allocation, develop tactics to prevent and respond to public safety demands. Police executives who practice this managerial approach are expected proactively to develop and implement an organizational direction based upon current intelligence that allows their departments to initiate and reshape their activities to meet the changing demands of their operational environment. Through a process of data collection and analysis, they are expected to align the capabilities of their internal organization with the demands and needs of their external environment. Properly implemented, strategic policing turns the police organization into an open, adaptive, learning organization.

The extent of the adaptation of strategic policing and its effect on community safety remains to be empirically tested. While knowledge about the effect of these developing strategies is still emerging, there is optimism about the future of policing (Braga & Weisburd, 2006). Strategic policing will require organizational changes that demand more than quick adaptations and limited structural changes. A properly designed organizational strategy must establish command accountability and integrity at all levels of the department or this process has the potential to degenerate into a numbers game without lasting impact (Eterno & Silverman, 2012). Ideally, it should focus the entire organization on its primary public safety mission. Strategic policing is a blend of the old and the new, retaining an organizational leadership style and structure similar to that employed by the Peelian Reform of 1829 and the Professional Reform of 1930 to the 1980s (Willis, Mastrofski, & Weisburd, 2004). Time will tell the extensiveness of strategic policing's impact on police administration.

Conclusion

This chapter began with a quote from Thomas Repetto (1978) describing police administration as a living, breathing organism shaped by the political, social, and economic trends of time and place. Our descriptive history of the development of professional policing supports his position. In the 19th century, executive leadership and strong administrative practice were the critical elements in the success and acceptance of the London Metropolitan Police as a worldwide model of professional policing. The police paradigm shifts of the last century were also products of efforts by strong police leaders as they responded to the challenges they faced. August Vollmer in Berkeley, California, O.W. Wilson in Kansas City and Chicago, J. Edgar Hoover of the FBI, and William Parker of Los Angeles were the developers and disseminators of the professional police reform movement. Lee Brown of Houston, Texas, Hubert Williams of Newark, New Jersey, Neil Behan of Baltimore County, Maryland, and Darrel Stephens of Newport News, Virginia, are but a few of the police chief executives who were responsible for the community problem-solving paradigm shift (Sparrow et al., 1990). William J. Bratton, twice Commissioner of the NYPD and former Chief of the Los Angeles Police Department, along with the 1994 NYPD executive team, are the creators and implementers of the CompStat process.

William Bratton is an example of a strong strategic leader whose leadership style energized the bureaucratic structures of the police organizations under his command. These organizations were changed through the introduction of strategic management practices and the establishment of accountability measures that accurately determined levels of both production and performance. They became police learning organizations.

Today's police departmental structure, management, and service delivery strategies are the result of three organizational redirections that occurred during the 20th century. Disenchantment with political control of the police and widespread corruption at the beginning of the century led to the reform era. The ultimate goals of this reform were to free policing from political influence and professionalize the occupation. Services that could be described as social work were eliminated, and the primary mission of the police became crime control through enforcement of the law. Administrative control established through bureaucratically structured organizations became the dominant objective of the reformers, and every effort was made to reduce officer discretion. This movement established the bureaucracy as the dominant police organizational model. The vast majority of police organizations in the United States are still organized and managed in this manner.

In the 1960s, a series of societal changes and civil unrest in American cities challenged police legitimacy. In reaction to these external driving forces, unanswered questions were raised by critical research on the effectiveness of police operational practice. The desire by many police executives for a change from the traditional police practices developed in the past led to the emergence of the community problem-solving policing models.

During the community problem-solving era, departments began to adopt a more open-system approach that involved customer engagement and service philosophy. Crime control remained as one of the primary functions of law enforcement, but attempts were made to broaden police objectives to include order maintenance, conflict resolution, and problem-solving, and engaging in community partnerships. Input from members of the community was actively sought. Policing attempted to decentralize along programmatic lines, employing community-based substations and geographically based teams. Line officers were assigned to a specific beat for an extended period to conduct crime control meetings, engage in problem-solving activities, and work diligently to improve the relationship between the police and the public. However, the dominance of the reform era's bureaucratic organization with its control-oriented management culture resulted in a limited adaptation of Community Policing by many police departments.

Perhaps the challenge of police reform is not to "banish bureaucracy" but to return it to functionality (Osborne & Gaebler, 1993; Osborne & Plastrik, 1997). In many police departments today, bureaucratic values still define their relationship with the public, shape organizational goals, and set performance standards. However, many managers are pragmatists who understand they must temper bureaucratic values with genuine empathy (for employees and clients) if they are to accomplish the department's mission, goals, and objectives effectively (More et al., 2012).

Strategic policing addressed the schism between bureaucracy and Community Policing. While many of the creators of strategic policing reject Community Policing as an effective organizational strategy, they retain its central philosophy—to work closely with the community to identify and address crime and disorder issues. Strategic policing is an attempt to reengineer police administration by blending the best of both the bureaucratic and community problem-solving organizational processes to develop proactive instead of reactive organizations.

Strategic policing provides police administrators with a way to retain the lessons of the past while constantly reassessing, learning, and redirecting the organization to meet future needs. It is not bureaucracy, or Community Policing, or problem-solving policing alone, but a combination of all of these that are being used by strategic administrators as they direct their organizations to meet the needs of public safety in United States. Lastly, it should be remembered that in a democracy policing should always respond to the needs of the people. It is a work in progress shaped by the political, social, human, organizational, and economic trends of time and place.

KEY TERMS

Bureaucracy	London Metropolitan Police	Reform era policing
Closed system	New Breed	Strategic management
Community problem-solving policing	*Nine Principles of Law Enforcement*	Strategic policing
CompStat	Open system	Street cop culture
Deprofessionalization syndrome	Paradigm	Types of police organizations
Intelligence-Led Policing	Peel, Robert	Vollmer, August
Learning organization	Police	Weber, Max
	Political era policing	

References

Banner, D., & Gagné, T. Elaine (1995). *Designing effective organizations: Traditional & transformational views.* Thousand Oaks, CA: Sage.

Bayley, D. (1975). Police and political development in Europe. In C. Tilly (Ed.), *The formation of national states in Western Europe* (pp. 328–379). Princeton, NJ: Princeton University Press.

Braga, A., & Weisburd, D. (2006). Police innovation and crime prevention: Lessons learned from police research over the past 20 years (2015, July 20). This review draws upon material available in David L. Weisburd & Anthony A. Braga (Eds.), *Police innovation: Contrasting perspectives.* New York: Cambridge University Press. Hebrew University of Jerusalem Legal Research Paper.

Braiden, C. (1986). Bank robbers and stolen bikes: Thoughts of a street cop. *Canadian Police College Journal, 10,* 1–30.

Bratton, W., & Kelling, G.L. (2012, December). Counts count, police matter: Of tactics and strategy. *The Police Chief, 79,* 54–59.

Bratton, W., & Knobler, P. (1998). *Turnaround.* New York: Random House.

Conser, J., Russell, G., Paynich, R., & Gingerich, T. (2005). *Law enforcement in the United States.* Sudbury, MA: Jones and Bartlett.

Cordner, G., & Bibel, E. (2005). Problem-oriented policing in practice. *Criminology & Public Policy, 4,* 155–180.

Covey, S.R. (2004). *The seven habits of highly effective people.* New York: The Free Press.

Critchley, T. (1972). *A history of police in England and Wales.* Montclair, NJ: Patterson Smith.

David, F.R. (2009). *Strategic management,* 12th ed. Upper Saddle River, NJ: Prentice Hall.

Dessler, G. (2004). *Management: Principles and practices for tomorrow's leaders.* Upper Saddle River, NJ: Prentice Hall.

Domanick, J. (1996, November). America's best suburban police forces. *Good Housekeeping,* 82–92.

Domanick, J. (1996, 2015). *Blue: The LAPD and the battle to redeem American policing.* New York: Simon & Schuster.

Eck, J., & Rosenbaum, D. (1994). The new police order: Effectiveness, equality and efficiency in community policing. In D. Rosenbaum (Ed.), *The challenge of community policing* (pp. 3–23). Thousand Oaks, CA: Sage.

Eterno, J.A., & Silverman, E.B. (2012). *The crime numbers game: Management by manipulation*. Boca Raton, FL: CRC Press.

Farrell, M. (1988). The development of the community patrol officer program: Community policing in the New York City police department. In J. Greene & S. Mastrofski (Eds.), *Community policing: Rhetoric or reality?* (pp. 73–88). New York: Praeger.

Fayol, H. (1992). General principles of management. In J. Shafritz & J. Ott (Eds.), *Classics of organizational theory* (pp. 37–49). Long Grove, IL: Waveland Press.

Flanagan, R. (2008). *The review of policing: Final report*. London: Home Office.

Fosdick, R. (1969, reprint of 1915 original). *American police systems*. Montclair, NJ: Patterson Smith.

Fuld, L.F. (1910). *Police administration*. New York: Putnam.

Fyfe, J.J., Greene, J.R., Walsh, W., Wilson, O., & McLaren, R. (1997). *Police administration*. New York: McGraw-Hill.

Geller, W. (1997). Suppose we were really serious about police departments becoming learning organizations? *National Institute of Justice Journal, 234,* 2–8.

Germann, A., Day, F., & Gallati, G. (1968). *Introduction to law enforcement and criminal justice*. Springfield, IL: Charles C. Thomas.

Glensor, R., Correia, M., & Peak, K. (2000). *Policing communities: Understanding and solving problems*. Los Angeles: Roxbury.

Goldstein, H. (1977). *Policing a free society*. Cambridge, MA: Ballinger.

Goldstein, H. (1979). Improving policing: A problem-oriented approach. *Crime and Delinquency, 25,* 236–258.

Goldstein, H. (1990). *Problem-oriented policing*. New York: McGraw Hill.

Goldstein, J., & Goodman, J.D. (2014, April 16). A London guide for 1 Police Plaza. *New York Times,* A20.

Graper, E. (1921). *American police administration*. New York: Palgrave Macmillan.

Greene, J., & Mastrofski, S. (1988). *Community policing: Rhetoric or reality?* New York: Praeger.

Greenwood, P., Petersilia, J., & Chaiken, J. (1977). *The criminal investigation process*. Lexington, MA: Heath.

Grieve, J. (2015). Historical perspective: British policing and the democratic ideal. In P. Wankhade & D. Weir (Eds.), *Police services: Leadership and management perspectives.* (pp. 15–28). Switzerland: Springer International.

Guyot, D. (1991). *Policing as though people mattered*. Philadelphia: Temple University Press.

Harring, S. (1982). The Taylorization of police work: Prospects for the 1980s. *The Insurgent Sociologist, 4,* 25–32.

Henry, V. (2002). *The CompStat paradigm: Management accountability in policing*. New York: Looseleaf Press.

Kelling, G.L. (1995). How to run a police department. *City Journal, 5*(4), 1–13.

Kelling, G.L., & Bratton, W.J. (1993). Implementing community policing: The administrative problem. *Perspectives on Policing, 17,* 1–11.

Kelling, G.L., & Coles, C. (1996). *Fixing broken windows: Restoring order and reducing crime in our communities*. New York: The Free Press.

Kelling, G.L., & Moore, M. (1988). The evolving strategy of policing. *Perspectives on Policing, 4,* 1–4.

Kelling, G.L., Pate, T., Dieckman, D., & Brown, C. (1975). *The Kansas City preventive patrol experiment*. Washington, DC: Police Foundation.

Kennedy, D.M. (1993). The strategic management of police resources: *Perspectives on Policing, 14,* 1–9.

Kessler, D. (1993). Integrating calls for services with community- and problem-oriented policing: A case study. *Crime & Delinquency, 39*, 485–508.

Klockars, C.B. (1985). *The idea of police.* Beverly Hills, CA: Sage.

Kuhn, T.S. (1962). *The structure of scientific revolutions.* Chicago: University of Chicago Press.

Lane, R. (1967). *Policing the city—Boston, 1822–1825.* Cambridge, MA: Harvard University Press.

Lee, W. (1901). *A history of the police in England.* London: Methuen.

Lentz, S., & Chaires, R. (2007). The invention of Peel's principles: A study of policing "textbook" history. *Journal of Criminal Justice, 35*, 69–79.

Lyman, J. (1964). The Metropolitan Police Act of 1829: An analysis of certain events influencing the passage and character of the Metropolitan Police Act in England. *Journal of Criminal Law & Criminology, 55*(1), 141–154.

Maguire, M., & John, T. (2006). Intelligence led policing, managerialism and community engagement: Competing priorities and the role of the National Intelligence Model in the UK. *Policing & Society, 16*(1), 67–85.

Maple, J. (1999). *The crime fighter.* New York: Doubleday.

McDonald, P.P. (2002). *Managing police operations: Implementing the New York crime control model—CompStat.* Stamford, CT: Thomson.

Moore, M., & Braga, A. (2003). *The bottom line of policing: What citizens should value and measure in police performance.* Washington, DC: Police Executive Research Forum.

Moore, M., & Stephens, D. (1991). *Beyond command and control: The strategic management of police departments.* Washington, DC: Police Executive Research Forum.

Moore, M., & Trojanowicz, R. (1988). Corporate strategy for policing. *Perspectives in Policing, 6*, 1–8.

More, H.W., Vito, G.F., & Walsh, W.F. (2012). *Organizational behavior and management in law enforcement.* Upper Saddle River, NJ: Prentice Hall.

Morgan, G. (1997). *Images of organization.* Thousand Oaks, CA: Sage.

Oettmeier, T., & Bieck, W. (1987). *Developing a policing style for neighborhood oriented policing.* Houston: Houston Police Department.

Oliver, W. (2017). *August Vollmer: The father of American policing.* Durham, NC: Carolina University Press.

Osborne, D., & Gaebler, T. (1993). *Reinventing government.* New York: Plume.

Osborne, D., & Plastrik, P. (1997). *Banishing bureaucracy.* New York: Addison-Wesley.

Palmer, S. (1988). *Police and protest in England and Ireland, 1780–1850.* New York: Cambridge University Press.

Peak, K., & Glensor, R. (2012). *Community policing & problem solving: Strategies and practices.* Upper Saddle River, NJ: Prentice Hall.

Pearsall, B. (2010). Predictive policing: The future of law enforcement? *NIJ Journal 266* (May), 16–19. Washington, DC: National Institute of Justice.

Peterson, M. (2005). *Intelligence-led policing: The new intelligence architecture.* Washington, DC: Bureau of Justice Assistance.

Pocock III, E., & Poole, L. (2021, January 10). Peel's nine principles—A misnomer. Unpublished manuscript, 130.

Police Executive Research Forum (2010). *Is the economic downturn fundamentally changing how we police?* Critical issues in policing series. *Washington*, DC: PERF.

Ratcliffe, J. (2016). *Intelligence-led policing*, 2nd ed. New York, NY: Routledge.

Reaves, B., & Goldberg, A. (2000). *Law enforcement management and administrative statistics, 1997.* Washington, DC: Bureau of Justice Statistics.

Reith, C. (1975). *The blind eye of history: A study of the origins of the present police era.* Montclair, NJ: Patterson Smith reprint (1952).

Reitzel, J., Piquero, N., & Piquero, A. (2005). Problem-oriented policing. In R. Dunham & G. Alpert (Eds.), *Critical issues in policing* (pp. 419–431). Long Grove, IL: Waveland.

Repetto, T.A. (1978). *The blue parade.* New York: Free Press.

Reuss-Ianni, E. (1983). *Two cultures of policing: Street cops and management cops.* New Brunswick, NJ: Transaction Books.

Roberg, R., Kuykendall, J., & Novak, K. (2002). *Police management.* Los Angeles, CA: Roxbury.

Rosenbaum, D. (1998). The changing role of the police: Assessing the current transition to community policing. In J. Brodeur (Ed.), *How to recognize good policing: Problems and issues* (pp. 3–29). Thousand Oaks, CA: Sage Publications.

Senge, P. (1990). *The fifth discipline: The art & practice of the learning organisation.* New York: Doubleday.

Sharp, E. (1982). Street-level discretion in policing: Attitudes and behaviors in the deprofessionalization syndrome. *Law and Policy Quarterly, 4,* 167–189.

Silverman, E. (1999). *NYPD battles crime: Innovative strategies in policing.* Boston: Northeastern University Press.

Skogan, W. (1990). *Disorder and decline: Crime and the spiral of decay in American neighborhoods.* New York: The Free Press.

Sparrow, M., Moore, M., & Kennedy, D. (1990). *Beyond 911: A new era for policing.* New York: Basic Books.

Spelman, W., & Brown, D. (1981). *Calling the police: Citizen reporting of serious crime.* Washington, DC: Police Executive Research Forum.

Stokovic, S., Kalnich, D., & Klofas, J. (2012). *Criminal justice organizations: Administration and management.* Belmont, CA: Wadsworth.

Tilley, N. (2003). Community policing, problem-oriented policing and intelligence-led policing. In T. Newburn (Ed.), *Handbook of policing* (pp. 311–339). Portland, OR: Willan.

Toch, H., & Grant, J. (1982). *Reforming human services.* Beverly Hills, CA: Sage.

Trojanowicz, R. (1982). *An evaluation of the neighborhood foot patrol program in Flint, Michigan.* East Lansing, MI: Michigan State University.

Trojanowicz, R., & Bucqueroux, B. (1994). *Community policing: How to get started.* Cincinnati, OH: Anderson.

Uchida, C. (2010). The development of American police: An historical overview. In R. Dunham & G. Alpert (Eds.), *Critical issues in policing* (pp. 17–36). Long Grove, IL: Waveland Press.

Wadman, R.C., & Allison, W.T. (2004). *To protect and to serve: A history of police in America.* Upper Saddle River, NJ: Prentice Hall.

Walker, S., & Katz, C.M. (2011). *The police in America.* New York: McGraw Hill.

Walsh, W. (2001). CompStat: An analysis of an emerging police managerial paradigm. *Policing, 24*(3), 347–362.

Weber, M. (1947). *The theory of social and economic organization.* New York: The Free Press.

Whitehouse, J. (1973). Historical perspectives on the police community service function. *Journal of Police Science and Administration, 1*(1), 87–92.

Williams, K. (2003). Peel's principles and their acceptance by American police: Ending 175 years of reinvention. *The Police Journal: Theory, practice and principles, 76* (April), 97–120.

Willis, J., Mastrofski, S., & Weisburd, D. (2004). CompStat and bureaucracy: A case study of challenges and opportunities for change. *Justice Quarterly, 21*, 463–493.

Wilson, J., & Kelling, G. (1982, March). Broken windows: Police and neighborhood safety. *Atlantic Monthly* (March), 29–38.

Wilson, O.W. (1942). *Police records—Their installation and use.* Chicago: Public Administration Service.

Wilson, O.W. (1957). *Police planning.* Springfield, IL: C.C. Thomas.

Wilson, O.W., & McLaren, R. (1977). *Police administration.* New York: McGraw Hill.

Zemke, R., Raines, C., & Filipczak, B. (2000). *Generations at work.* New York: American Management Association.

Zhao, S., He, N., & Lovrich, N. (2003). Community policing: Did it change the basic functions of policing in the 1990s? A national follow-up. *Justice Quarterly, 20*, 697–724.

2 Administration, Authority, and Command

Learning Objectives

Learning Objectives

1. To be able to define the terms "administration," "authority," and "command" in policing.

2. To know the attributes of managerial authority.

3. To identify the critical responsibilities of the three command levels.

4. To be able to discuss the managerial functions.

5. To identify the elements of different styles of supervision.

6. To be able to explain the changing nature of police management.

Introduction

The **administration** of a police department involves the logical coordination and arrangement of people, tasks, and resources in a manner designed to achieve its mission. Department managers accomplish this responsibility by using their authority to command and manage the organization's employees and assets. The goals of the administrative process are to ensure organizational effectiveness, enhance its potential, and organize it to achieve desired outcomes. It is important to note that all department successes and failures are products of human behavior. Historically, organizations have sought to ensure behavioral compliance and reduce uncertainty in employee performance through the establishment of an administrative system that involves a hierarchical authority structure; scalar levels of command; delineation of tasks, policy, rules, procedures, and processes; and managerial accountability (Swanson, Territo, & Taylor, 2011). The organization's hierarchical structure delineates lines of authority tasks and sets responsibilities. The majority of the police departments in the United States distribute command authority and responsibility through three distinct organizational levels: executive, middle management, and supervisory. The higher the administrative level, the greater the responsibility, authority, and power. The bureaucratic organization continues to dominate policing because it is designed to ensure control and accountability in the uncertain, complex, and often hostile environment faced by many police departments.

Organizational administration and management involve the exercise of command authority to control, direct, and coordinate the department's personnel, resources, and activities (Fyfe, Greene, Walsh, Wilson, & McLaren, 1997). The department's direction, policy and procedures, internal structures, mission, values, and

DOI: 10.4324/9781003459095-2

practices define command authority and responsibility. Managers at all levels of the organization are expected to achieve performance objectives and provide performance control, feedback, and assessment of the areas of responsibility under their command authority. Managerial and organizational effectiveness, however, depends on the willingness and capabilities of the department's employees to support and follow managerial direction. Employees do not always achieve what their managers expect, because of differences in their knowledge, skills, abilities, and commitment to organizational objectives. As a result, the performance response to managerial direction is an uncertain variable requiring oversight and direction. Understanding the complexity of the relationship between organizational objectives, command levels, and employee performance requires critical analysis and comprehension of the concepts of **managerial authority** and command and human behavior. This chapter helps the reader understand the police organization's administrative levels, authority at each level, and command responsibilities. So, as Drucker (1998) advised, they know what is important and will focus on that instead of wasting their time on things irrelevant to their organization's effectiveness.

Managerial Authority

Max Weber (1864–1920), the originator of the study of complex organizations, argued the **bureaucracy** constitutes the most efficient and rational way to organize and that systematic processes and organized hierarchies were necessary to maintain order, maximize efficiency, and eliminate favoritism (Weber, 1947, pp. 329–341). Police departments are bureaucratic organizations not unlike that described by Weber. They are centralized managerial authority systems with task responsibilities based on a logical hierarchical ordering of positions. **Organizational structure** defines positional roles, departmental interdependences, and communication channels. It assigns authority, accountabilities, and responsibilities. It determines who is empowered to make decisions and the depth and extent of their authority. Management is accorded legitimate authority and power to direct and control a group of employees assigned to accomplish specific tasks. Each manager is responsible for the employees' accomplishments under their command and should have the authority to achieve this responsibility. The exercise of managerial authority involves the interaction of two organizational elements, the managerial (superior) and the employee (subordinate). Weber (1947, p. 324) defines **authority** within the bureaucratic system as "the probability that a given group of persons will obey certain specific commands from sources." In policing, these concepts were structurally developed to achieve tighter managerial control, better performance, and more accountability to combat political **influence**, corruption, and lack of confidence that the political era of policing had created in American policing in the 19th and early 20th centuries (Goldstein, 1990).

Managerial authority within a bureaucracy is legal and rational when attached to an individual's position and exercised through a system of rules and procedures. A common element for an authority relationship to exist and be effective is voluntariness on the part of a subordinate (employee). **Voluntariness** involves a choice made by the free will of the employee, as opposed to being made as the result of managerial coercion or duress. The department's effectiveness is thus inseparable from the accomplishments of its personnel (Covey, 1997). Using coercion or duress involving the threat of punishment or sanctions may gain an employee's unwilling, limited compliance. True authority and respect for command derive from employees who will-ingly follow managerial directives and accomplish tasks at the required performance level without direct supervision. It is important to remember that police patrol officers function the greater proportion of their tour of duty without the immediate direction of their managers. The internal motivation of the officer is directly affected by how they are managed and influenced by their manager. Good managers understand that using influence and respect instead of directing employees is an important managerial technique. Employees who are respected and feel good about themselves and how they are treated will produce good results (Blanchard & Johnson, 2003). Additionally, legal and social constraints have restricted the ability to use coercive power in the current organizational world. Laws and regulations such as the Fair Labor Standards Act, Title VII of the 1964 Civil Rights Act, Civil Rights Act 1991, and the Age Discrimination in Employment Act, Equal Employment Opportunity Act, and rulings by federal courts have resulted in restricting and limiting the power of managers (Dessler, 2012).

Command Levels

As noted in the previous chapter, police departments vary in size, complexity, and diversity of their mission, from small organizations with fewer than 25 officers to large urban organizations employing 1,000 or more people. However, almost all of these departments are internally divided by **levels of command** authority. As departments grow in size and complexity of tasks, the number of individuals serving at these levels will increase. In a small police department, there will always be a chief of police, but there may only be one lieutenant or one or two sergeants. In large urban police depart-ments, there can be ten or more individuals at the executive level alone. The majority of police organizations have three distinct but overlapping command levels: the exec-utive level, the middle management level, and the supervisory.

Executive Level

Individuals at the **executive strategic level** have various titles, such as commissioner, director, chief, sheriff, colonel, or superintendent. The chief executive's position is a demanding, high-profile position that often is expected to maintain availability 24 hours a day, seven days a week. The **administrative functions** of the executive stra-tegic level involve human resource development, maintaining organizational integrity and respect, and the creation of a positive organizational culture.

The qualifications required for the police chief's position differ depending on the size of the department and the region of the country. Small departments may have minimum requirements for the position, while larger departments will have educational and experiential levels that will vary with the department size (Peak, 2012). For exam-ple, the International Association of Chiefs of Police, in its nationwide search for a chief of police for Leesburg (103 employees), Virginia, described the ideal candidate as being:

CHIEF OF POLICE

Leesburg Police Department

- A strong leader, both internally and externally.
- Able to demonstrate the effective use of modern organizational leadership practices.

- Engaged with the community and have a visible presence.
- Committed to a Community Policing philosophy.
- Able to communicate well to build trust and transparency.
- Politically savvy and adept at working with and through political processes.
- Dedicated to building and maintaining collaborative partnerships, internally and externally.
- Focused on youth issues.
- Concerned with seeking solutions to mental health and domestic violence issues.
- Experienced in a growing and diverse community.
- Familiar with 21st-century policing concepts, including procedural justice and the guardian vs. warrior perspective.
- Committed to building diversity within the department.

The police chief's principal responsibility is administering the department and ensuring it effectively carries out its mission. At the same time, the chief must gain the approval and support of the political structure and community for the department. They are expected to be able to conceptualize and define their department's role in the communities they serve. Chiefs of police are praised for their department's achievements and held accountable for their failures. Recent events such as that in Ferguson, Missouri, in 2014 disclosed that a split-second decision by an unsupervised police officer to use deadly force could eventually lead to the dismissal or resignation of a police chief. The chief executive's most critical function is meeting their department's organizational needs and the community's current needs while simultaneously preparing it to meet future departmental demands (Reiss, 1985). Creating an effective department to meet future demands requires ensuring that the department's knowledge, skills, diversity, systems, and technology are ready for the task (Colvin, 2015). The responsibilities of the chief's position differ with the size and functions of their department. Chiefs of large departments are assisted by a command staff of other executives whose titles include assistant chief, deputy chief, assistant director, deputy commissioner, colonel, or lieutenant colonel.

Leading a police department is a complex, demanding task. Police executives provide their organizations with direction and performance oversight to achieve maximum use of their assets and capabilities (Moore & Trojanowicz, 1988). They must inspire and organize the activities of the department's employees. Police chiefs must also establish cooperative relationships externally with federal law enforcement agencies, surrounding jurisdictions, and related services such as Fire and Emergency Medical Transportation (Cunningham, Jones, & Behrens, 2011). They accomplish this through personnel management, budgeting, operational management, and community relations. The police chief executive, with the assistance of their command team, is required to establish a strategic direction for the department that unleashes the power and potential of the organization to impact the public safety demands facing the community it serves. They accomplish this by creating an organizational strategy that sets performance priorities for the department that meets the requirements of the government and community.

The diversified and complex nature of today's public safety environment has fundamentally changed the leadership expectations of police executives. Every day, law enforcement executives face complexity, uncertainty, and sensitivity issues that require a different level of thinking and decision-making. Before the August 2014 fatal shooting of Michael Brown, in Ferguson, Missouri, the effectiveness of most police chiefs was determined by crime rates and response to 911 calls (Williams, 2015). Now police executives must be astute in dealing with their community's safety demands and complex issues involving race, class, ethnicity, gender, and sexual orientation, not only in the context of the public served but also within their police organizations. They must understand the importance of diversity from its broadest perspective, such as education, training, career development, personal values, differing ages, race, color, creed, religious affiliation, nationalities, and sexes. Conventional ways of thinking, analyzing data, solving problems, making decisions, dealing with the public, and responding to organizational demands are obsolete. Few situations are easily resolved with old methods, and today's challenges require critical thinking at different levels.

For example, when Ray Kelly was appointed New York City's Police Commissioner for the second time in 2002, the public safety challenges he was confronted with involved a consistent possibility of terrorist activity because of the events of 9/11 and the city's high value as a terrorist target. This factor demanded a fundamental rethinking of the role of the New York City Police Department. As a result, he set into motion a complete reordering of the department's priorities, including a focus on counterterrorism and intelligence (Kelly, 2015, p. 143). The department developed a counterterrorism unit that is considered one of the more sophisticated in the world, complete with sea, land, and air capabilities.

Police chief executives are accountable for the following administrative activities:

1. Development of a departmental mission, vision, goals, and operational objectives.
2. Creation of strategic, operational, procedural, tactical, and budgetary plans.
3. Creation of an organizational structure and division of labor focused on ensuring fulfillment of mission and performance objectives.
4. Establishment of guiding principles, values, policy, and procedures that support an organizational culture that upholds its legitimacy in the eyes of the community and the department.
5. Employment of a leadership direction and style that, while focused on mission fulfillment, will also achieve willing compliance and support from employees of the department and members of the community.
6. Creating adequate resource levels, budget, personnel, and technological capability.
7. Controlling and assessing departmental activities for integrity, efficiency, and effectiveness through measurement, evaluation, and, when necessary, redirection.
8. Ensuring that all department members are competent and adhere to the highest standards of integrity and ethics.

(More, Vito, & Walsh, 2012, p. 38)

An assistant chief is usually the second in command of a department and normally functions as the alter ego of the police chief executive. Generally, deputy and assistant chiefs supervise major functional subdivisions such as operations, investigations, or support services. For example, the city of Mesa, Arizona, Police Department has three assistant chiefs: one in charge of operations, another administration, and one in the community engagement and employee services section. Assistant chiefs are central figures in the management team, with operational and administrative responsibilities. They may assist the chief executive in developing the department's goals and objectives, and assist in administration. The executive's management team is responsible for creating a quality, high-performance work environment through planning, directing, and coordinating activities in the department. Their duties involve problem-solving at the highest level and technical nature, formulating departmental policies, planning, staffing, developing and maintaining a positive organizational culture, and sustaining accountability for operational efficiency and effectiveness.

Wolfe and Nix (2016) suggest that police administrators can accomplish the above functions by practicing **organizational justice** during management activities. Organizational justice is a leadership philosophy that focuses on three key issues.

- Managers ensure *procedural fairness* when dealing with employees. Their decisions do not unfairly favor one employee over another; the reasons are clearly explained to relevant parties, and employees are given a reasonable voice in the decision-making process.
- Managers must practice *distributive fairness*. They ensure that promotions, salary increases, and discipline are fairly distributed throughout the organization. Positive outcomes should not only fall on those with friends in high places. Likewise, negative outcomes should not manifest only among certain groups.
- Lastly, managers must strive for *interactional fairness*. Employees should be treated with respect and dignity. Supervisors should maintain an honest and open relationship with their subordinates.

Administrative Paradox

While reform-era police change agents sought to remove the influence of politics from policing, it is a fact that today police chief executives still serve at the pleasure of the mayor or city manager. As a result, the chief executive's role is inherently political because the controlling governmental authority appoints them. However, the role of the executive also requires that the police chief balance external and internal environmental demand pressures that can conflict with the political expectations of their position. The external environment involves changing crime patterns, homeland security, numerous and variable demands for service, changing public safety conditions, demands for accountability, directives from the judiciary and legislature, and state- and federal-mandated training. The internal environment involves managing the department, planning, setting direction, maintaining organizational integrity and transparency, creating goals, developing policies, ensuring fiscal accountability, supervision, workload efficiency, and budget (Cordner, 2013). Police chiefs often find that the demands from these two environments are conflicting and difficult to address (Timoney, 2010). These issues have resulted in the police chief executives of Chicago (Illinois), Baltimore (Maryland), Ferguson (Missouri), Suffolk County (New York), and Cincinnati (Ohio) either resigning or being removed from their positions. One egregious act of misconduct by a police officer can lead to the firing of a police chief (Williams, 2015).

In the early years of the development of professional policing, organizational development was created by strong autocratic leaders such as London's Sir Richard Mayne (1796–1868) and Lieutenant Colonel Charles Rowan (1782–1852); Berkeley's August Vollmer (1876–1955); Boston's Stephen James O'Meara (1854–1918); Wichita and Chicago's O.W. Wilson (1900–1972); and LAPD's William Parker (1905–1966). Since the millennium, a shift has occurred in police organizational management from traditional autocratic systems to open strategic organizations that engage with the environments within which they operate. Through the emphasis on Community Policing and police legitimacy, police chief executives are now, more than ever, coming to understand the community's role in police policy-making. Traditional notions of command and managerial authority are no longer relevant to the day-to-day realities of today's police organization. They proved inadequate to prevent or respond to the 1992 riots in Los Angeles (Domanick, 2015). Today's police executives are expected to be transformational leaders who can identify and understand the needs of the community, its agency, its political environment, and the motivations of each. To do so, many forward-thinking police executives seek to form a collaborative partnership model of policing. This model seeks to unite the police, the community, and political and business leaders in a unified vision of police mandates and service.

In 1999, the International Association of Chiefs of Police held the organization's first president's Leadership Conference, comprising carefully selected teams of nationally recognized and accomplished practitioners brought together to examine the roles of the contemporary police executive. The conferees sought to identify how the police executive role was changing and how police executives can manage current and changing community and organizational environments to satisfy the objectives of the many complex constituencies that police must serve. They concluded that police executives must possess an extraordinary range of capacities. At the core of the executive's role, they identified the following areas of responsibility:

- The community.
- The governing body.
- The department and its workforce.
- The profession.

The chief executives' responsibilities to their community involve prioritizing communication, collaboration, partnership development, and understanding and responsiveness to community needs. Less frequently cited by the conferees but identified as important were efficient service, freedom from fear, improved quality of life, equal protection and service, integrity of the police agency, and trust-building. Responsibilities to the governing body involved demonstrating integrity, trust, truthfulness, openness, and commitment. Two sets of responsibilities to the department and the workforce demanded the highest priority. The first focused on inspiring and procreating leadership, and the second provided a vision, a clear mission, goals, and objectives, along with developing the department to manage present and future workloads successfully. The participants noted that the executive was obligated to advance the profession of policing by mentoring and developing new leadership, helping to develop a common body of leadership knowledge, and raising professional standards (IACP, 1999).

Recently, policing has been challenged by a growing protest movement accompanied by acts of civil disobedience after the deaths of several African Americans at the hands of police officers. In response to waves of protest and demands for reform on December 18, 2014, President Barack Obama issued an Executive Order appointing an 11-member Task Force on 21st Century Policing to respond to the number of serious incidents between law enforcement and the communities that have occurred. The president wanted a quick but thorough response that would begin the healing process and restore community trust by identifying best practices and otherwise make recommendations on how policing practices can promote effective crime reduction while building public trust.

The task force noted that trust between law enforcement agencies and the people they protect and serve, is essential in a democracy. It is key to the stability of our communities, the integrity of our criminal justice system, and the safe and effective delivery of policing services, as well as the foundational principle underlying their inquiry into the relations between law enforcement and the communities they serve (President's Task Force on 21st Century Policing, 2015). Today, building trust and nurturing legitimacy on both sides of the police/citizen divide has become a fundamental responsibility of all police executives and the basis for personnel evaluation.

Improving Police-Minority Relations

Several issues surround the improvement of police-minority relations. A literature review of police activities and race carefully delineates the methodological differences in determining racial disparities and racial bias in operational outcomes—traffic stops, arrests, and stop, question, and frisk. While the research findings indicated that minorities were more likely to be subjected to police authority, it is difficult to ascertain the source of these outcomes. Racial disparity occurs when there are aggregated differences among racial groups subjected to police intervention. Racial bias is an attempt to infer that such differences are due to officers' or their agencies' conscious or unconscious decision to treat one racial group differently (Smith, Rojek, Petrocelli, & Withrow, 2017, p. 175). The authors concluded that most of the studies reviewed lacked the methodological rigor and statistical precision to prove cause and effect in such studies (Smith, Rojek, Petrocelli, & Withrow, 2017, p. 176).

However, research findings show that Blacks harbor distinct feelings about police legitimacy. Research based in Milwaukee, WI, documented that Blacks were less likely to report crimes to the police via 911 calls after a well-publicized police beating of a suspect (Frank Jude). The results demonstrated that Blacks are likely to evidence "legal cynicism" when confronted with news of police brutality (Desmond, Papachristos, & Kirk, 2016). Interviews with 50 young Black men in Southwest Philadelphia revealed their attitudes toward the police based on their personal experience. They felt that officers were more likely to engage in misconduct when they feared patrolling "unfamiliar and dangerous neighborhoods" (Henson, 2022, p. 20). They felt more comfortable with officers who did not fear or hold such misperceptions.

The National Initiative for Building Community Trust and Justice attempts to improve police-community relations through training and joint meetings. The John Jay College of Criminal Justice led this effort in six cities: Birmingham (AL), Fort Worth (TX), Gary (IN), Minneapolis (MN), Pittsburgh (PA), and Stockton (CA). The program features training and technical assistance for police officers in engaging citizens in a procedurally just manner, helping them mitigate their biases, developing model departmental policies, and conducting reconciliation meetings with community members. Preliminary evaluation research results found that pairing the six sites with their communities and focusing on procedural justice facilitated success and that training and reconciliation improved relationships (Jannetta, Esthappan, Fontaine, Lynch, & LaVigne, 2019). The reconciliation process featured fact-finding regarding past harms caused by the department, the acknowledgment of that harm, sustained listening, and collecting community narratives of police perceptions (Jannetta, Esthappan, Fontaine, Lynch, & LaVigne, 2019). These efforts led to policy changes in five of the six departments.

Middle Management Level

Individuals at the **middle management level** in policing are majors, captains, lieutenants, watch commanders, or civilian managers in administrative positions. The primary responsibilities of their role vary with the department size but usually involve the oversight and direction of one or more of an agency's divisions or functional units responsible for Patrol, Investigations, Traffic, Communications, Personnel, or Special Operations. Administratively they command a budget, personnel, planning, internal affairs, training, or public information unit or serve in a senior staff position for the chief or other senior executives (Geller & Swanger, 1995). Their activities may range from actual operational work to largely administrative review.

Middle managers are critical in aligning their department's mission, goals, and objectives with its operational accomplishments. They are primarily responsible for organizational effectiveness and efficiency. These managers interpret and operationalize departmental goals, objectives, policies, and procedures into the day-to-day tasks of their units. The chief executive's vision and direction are converted into operational reality at their organizational level. Stamper (1992, p. 153) claims that their responsibilities also involve keeping the promises made by higher-ups. What the chief or mayor, city manager, or city council claims will occur, these managers ensure it will happen through their authority, planning, directional activities, and allocation of resources. As a result, they manage the day-to-day operations of police departments by standardizing and controlling organizational procedures and officer performance. They balance what is desired and what must be done and the organization's operational capability. Thus, they are the leading edge of centralized control over a department's internal environment and organizational operations (Kelling & Bratton, 1993, p. 9). They can either accept or reject them as interpreters of the chief executive's strategic decisions. When they communicate their vision to employees, it can either be positive or negative (Charrier, 2004). As a result, they have also been identified in the research as the major source of subversion, resistance, and sabotage of change efforts in policing. They are described as the lagging edge of resistance to innovation (Sherman, Milton, & Kelly, 1973; Goldstein, 1990; Sparrow, Moore, & Kennedy, 1990; Kelling & Bratton, 1993; Vito, Walsh, & Kunselman, 2005).

Middle managers accomplish their responsibilities by planning, organizing, commanding, coordinating, and controlling departmental resources and personnel (Fayol, 1992). In exercising these functions, they activate the department's strategy and tactics by setting objectives, planning and implementing operations, and evaluating the performance of supervisors and units under their control. These managerial functions are activities engaged in by all managers; the time spent on each activity varies with each managerial level. They are critical middle management activities because they operationalize the department's organizational direction and strategy.

Planning involves identifying the activities necessary to translate a department's mission, vision, and organizational goals into specific unit objectives and identifying resources needed to accomplish these objectives. Since police departments exist in an ever-changing environment, middle managers must be aware of and monitor the changing demands created by the department's external and internal environments. Their planning activities involve setting objectives, developing strategies, and identifying operational tactics for addressing these environmental demands (Kelly, 2015). Planning allows the manager to identify what should be done, when, by whom, and what needs to be accomplished. However, middle managers must also be able to implement their plans, communicate, and inspire the various units and personnel under their command to achieve desired objectives. They also must be flexible and ready to change their plans when conditions change. All middle managers are held accountable for the quality of their plans, the quality of their efforts, their accomplishments, their managerial oversight of operations, and the results obtained (Haneberg, 2005).

Organizing involves structuring an organization and deploying resources necessary to establish accountability, workload and resource distribution, and a unified organizational effort. It involves aligning strategy, structure, process, information systems, reward systems, employees, and operational service delivery. Organizing considers the major purpose of a unit, the tasks required to fulfill this purpose, the nature and authority of the people involved, their geographical distribution, and time constraints. A well-organized department acts as a unified team, supporting each other and the department's strategy with a desire to achieve maximum effectiveness (More et al., 2012).

Police departments usually display their functional structure by a scalar chart. Organizational charts identify the department's chain of command, each managerial position, and the units commanded by each position. They also depict what each position is accountable for and whom each is responsible for. These charts identify the organization's official lines of command, authority, and communication. However, they should not be etched in stone. Middle management problem-solving and performance analysis will often result in repositioning units and personnel to align with the development of new strategic objectives.

Commanding involves setting direction through leadership, authority, motivation, and **empowerment**, The purpose of command is to achieve the optimum performance from all employees. Command success rests on personal qualities and knowledge of general management principles (Fayol, 1949, p. 97). Middle managers are accountable for achieving desired outcomes through the performance of the units under their command. The command function empowers managers with the authority to direct their units by developing clear, effective operational strategies and tactics to achieve objectives. It is not a numbers game of achieving output statistics. Operational commanders have the authority, but must also be able to implement their tactics and inspire their command to achieve desired objectives. They are accountable for overseeing their unit's operations and the results obtained. Command is exercised through a thorough knowledge of personnel; by eliminating the incompetent; by balancing the interests of the organization and its employees through a "strong sense of duty and of equity" (Fayol, 1949, pp. 98–103). Successful commanding officers are capable of motivating employees and encouraging employees to take the initiative. They engage in critical thinking, have integrity, communicate clearly, and base their decisions on regular evaluations and inspections. Their most important attribute is to be a complex problem-solver.

Coordination is the process of achieving unity of action through synchronizing the efforts of independent unit activities. It aims to integrate several units into an orderly whole to achieve its mission. An ideal way of conceiving this management principle is to think of the police department as comprising one large team, not individual power centers competing for resources and glory with each other. It requires that organizational managers engage in systems thinking, teamwork, and breaking traditional administrative barriers. Thus, middle managers should be proficient at networking and building relationships within and without the agency. They must think beyond their control areas and consider the department an integrated team supporting each other and its mission. Coordination is accomplished by the combined action of executive management, which supervises the whole, plus middle managers whose efforts are directed toward the successful working of each particular part (Fayol, 1949, p. 106). Coordination is the essence of management and is implicit and inherent in all management functions. It requires clear communication and good leadership.

Controlling involves all those activities undertaken to ensure that actual operations conform to the planned operations (David, 2014). All managers must fix accountability, set standards, compare performance with these standards, and take corrective action where needed (Dessler, 2004). It is the managers' responsibility to know what is happening with the technical and human resources entrusted to them by their organization. The essence of management thus involves the continual assessment of performance and accomplishments. The control function involves the following activities:

1. Identifying goals and objectives.
2. Establishing and maintaining standards.
3. Continual communication with subordinates.
4. Monitoring individual and organizational performance.
5. Evaluating personnel by comparing actual to desired performance.
6. Rewarding when appropriate.
7. Taking corrective action when necessary.

The primary objective of the control function is to certify that employee performance is at the desired level to accomplish organizational objectives and goals. However, managers must also ensure that their employees have the knowledge, skills, and ability to perform their duties at the desired level of performance. Organizational objectives will never be achieved if those responsible for task accomplishment are improperly informed, ill-trained, or ignorant of expected performance levels. Effective managers obtain and share the information needed to achieve operational progress with their subordinates. When conditions change or deviations from previously agreed-upon standards are identified, evaluation should identify what must be done and corrective action should be taken.

The five managerial functions just discussed are highly interrelated. They do not necessarily occur as listed but can happen simultaneously. It is important to remember that the performance of these functions is continually modified by any or all of the following factors:

• Changing environmental demands.
• Managerial knowledge and competence.
• Organizational level.
• Nature and type of activity.
• Knowledge, competence, and commitment of employees.

(More et al., 2012, p. 41)

Kelling and Bratton (1993) analyze administrative problems associated with implementing strategic change in policing and contend that middle managers became the main proponents of centralizing control during the reform era. Drucker (1998) asserts that middle managers' positional authority allows them to slow the decisional process to a crawl and make the organization increasingly incapable of adapting to change. For example, failure to win middle management's support is a primary contributor to the demise of team policing in the 1970s (Sherman et al., 1973). Geller and Swanger (1995), in their study of middle managers for the Police Executive Research Forum, also identified this command level as the most daunting obstacle to efficient and meaningful organizational change.

Sparrow and colleagues (1990, pp. 213–214) identified several ways middle managers influence their organizations. First, middle managers operate at the department's boundary between knowledge and power. Their positional authority empowers them to translate the executive's vision and direction into operational strategies. Second, middle managers largely control the department's professional environment. The processes they develop and their actions in dealing with subordinates define and reinforce the core cultural values of the department. These core values tell the officers what operational behaviors are unacceptable. Third, middle managers are the ones who can determine how employees view the department's procedural manual—to justify strict bureaucratic discipline or as a source of knowledge, guidance, and inspiration. Fourth, middle managers can quash new ideas (and they've been routinely accused of doing so, especially ideas they believe challenge their authority). Fifth, middle managers can define work in a way that encourages their officers to tackle harder, broader problems: they can empower their officers by letting them know that the organization values their knowledge and expertise. Finally, middle managers control the extent to which positive discretion, legitimacy, and procedural justice are built explicitly into the department's value system and address the new leadership demands of the 21st century.

However, middle management's power to affect change can be harnessed positively by including those managers in planning, acknowledging their legitimate self-interests, and motivating their investment in long-range solutions that enhance community safety and security (Travis, 1995). Geller and Swanger (1995) suggest that chief executives can positively engage middle managers by providing them with support and authorization to devise strategies and modify systems and procedures to support strategic change. Such delegation of authority would involve middle managers in planning for change to increase their credibility with subordinates. Chief executives can maintain consultative relationships with middle managers to motivate ongoing thinking about effectively meeting strategic goals and objectives and developing a clear linkage of rewards to performance in implementing desired changes. Chief executives can seriously commit to training middle managers well in the skills they need in their adjusted roles. In summary, the middle managers' organizational position gives them the power to choose what they will do: passively resist, tolerate, or lend their support and lead in reengineering their organizations. Thus, the skills and abilities of these managers are imperative to the department's successful service to the community.

Supervisory Level

Individuals at the **supervisory level** hold the rank of sergeant, corporal, or civilian supervisor except for integrated police-fire organizations, where supervisors hold the title of lieutenant. They are responsible for achieving departmental objectives by directing and overseeing operational activities. Supervisors are the department's first level of command authority and the primary contact officers have with their department's administration. They are accountable for their subordinate employees' performance on a day-to-day basis. Supervisors are the link between the department's executive and middle management levels and operations and are a principal factor in the day-to-day control and accomplishments of the department. The quality of an officer's daily life and perception of their department depends heavily on how well the officer satisfies the expectations and demands of their supervisor (Goldstein, 1990).

Supervisors are accountable for ensuring the department's employees perform according to law, departmental policy, procedures, and ethical values. Line supervisors in patrol and investigative units make important decisions regarding the utilization of their officers to meet workload demand and management of their subordinates

(Cordner, 2013). Their decisions are key in converting mission and policy into day-to-day practice (Willis, 2011). These decisions affect the quality and manner of police operations, the service provided to a community, and the commitment and competence of the employees who provide that service. Supervisors serve as a nexus of information gathering and distribution within the organization and as a point of legitimate contact for the community (Crank & Langworthy, 1992; Haberfeld, 2006). As the department's principal quality-control agents, supervisors significantly impact the effectiveness and financial liability of the police organization (Walsh & Donovan, 1990). The ability to command depends on how effectively they build a positive relationship of mutual respect and trust within their work unit (More et al., 2012). However, they must also understand that their workgroup's dynamic, problem-solving process and culture affect their subordinate's performance.

Individuals seeking the supervisor position must complete a qualifying process set forth by the municipality's civil service regulations. Testing is usually established when supervisory vacancies exist or on a regular schedule. The promotional process normally requires establishing a period between the announcement and the test to give candidates time to prepare for the exam. These announcements usually contain the job classification, qualifications, dates and times of the process, location of each phase, description of the assessment, if used, and the duties and responsibilities of the position. Each candidate is then given a bibliography listing testing materials the examination process will cover. The testing weights, methods, time limits, and cut-off scores are also provided and will vary by department and civil service regulations. For example, to qualify to test for the position of sergeant in the Pinellas Park Police Department, Florida, candidates must:

1. Be a currently employed full-time Florida certified police officer.
2. Have three years with the Pinellas Park Police Department as of the testing date.
3. Have five years of total police experience.
4. This five years' experience must be within the last five years before the testing date.
5. Have an AA degree from an accredited school.

(PPPD Directive Manual, Standard Operating Procedure,
Promotion SOP #32, 2006)

The process also may involve oral boards, chief's interview, in-basket exercises, and writing ability tests. Once completed, a rank-order list of the candidates is created. The chief of police, depending on the municipality, has the authority to select the candidate to be promoted from the top three or five on the list. The list will usually remain valid for a period established by local civil service regulations. Success in this process requires a great deal of preparation and commitment by the officer to achieve a high ranking on the candidates list. Thus, it is a valuable tool for enhancing officers' knowledge of their department's policies, procedures, and the law.

Newly promoted supervisors are usually required to complete a one-year probationary period in which their suitability to supervise officers is evaluated. In most police departments, the newly promoted supervisor will be assigned to uniform patrol and supervise officers on a patrol shift almost immediately. In most states, new supervisors must attend a mandatory basic supervision course within one year of promotion. However, this course may only be available months after functioning in their role. As a result, the primary way many supervisors learn the requirements of their position is through trial and error or mentoring by other supervisors. Unfortunately, this is not always adequate preparation for such an important and demanding role.

When promoted to supervisory rank, an individual becomes part of the department's management team. They enter a new phase of their career requiring a transition to a different role and mindset (Van Maanen, 1984; More & Miller, 2014). This transition will necessitate a significant change in their operational philosophy and outlook. They will now be held accountable for their unit's performance, and their supervisor's evaluation will be based on their subordinates' accomplishments. On a day-to-day basis, they must consider how organizational objectives and issues impact their and their officers' performance. It necessitates a personal and intellectual transformation that will change their organizational perspective, basic concepts of work, and relationships with others in the department. This transformational adjustment is further complicated because new supervisors are inadequately prepared for their roles in many departments. They are often required to exert authority over individuals who are their social and professional colleagues. In the majority of medium to small police departments, new supervisors manage work units whose members represent a peer group whom they have befriended, identified with, and worked closely with for years. It is a challenging task.

One can easily conclude that the supervisor's position is a unique and somewhat conflicting role. It intersects two organizational worlds: administration and operations, management and the street (Reuss-Ianni, 1983). In some departments, these two worlds view each other with hostility and animosity; in others, there is mutual respect and cooperation. In departments with negative organizational dynamics, this places the supervisor in an in-between position that can be a continual source of conflict and stress. If not understood and responded to correctly, the differing expectations of the two sides can develop into contradictory pressures that create conflict and role ambiguity for supervisors (More et al., 2012). Supervisors must spend significant time identifying employee needs and expectations and using interpersonal techniques with their officers to be effective. They must develop skills and abilities that will allow them to manage the variety of people and performance challenges that occur daily in policing. They engage in directing, mentoring, training, coaching, team-building, and counseling to enhance their subordinates' knowledge, skills, and capabilities (More & Miller, 2014).

The department's executive and middle management levels expect supervisors to:

1. Manage day-to-day operations.
2. Work for the attainment of organizational objectives.
3. Maintain a well-trained, motivated work unit.
4. Create a positive work environment.
5. Use authority responsibly and legally.
6. Adhere to and administer the department's policies and procedures.
7. Keep superiors, employees, and peers informed.
8. Prevent problems, as well as solve them.
9. Be creative, innovative, and flexible.
10. Provide leadership and use initiative.
11. Be accountable.

(More et al., 2012, p. 48)

Employees will expect their supervisor to:

1. Be accessible.
2. Be a role model.

3. Assist them in attaining individual and organizational needs.
4. Assist in integrating them into the organization.
5. Create a work environment that provides job satisfaction.
6. Let them know what is expected.
7. Use authority appropriately.
8. Be fair in their personnel evaluations.
9. Help in developing new skills.
10. Identify and maximize their talents that result in growth.
11. Provide information needed to accomplish tasks.
12. Support in becoming a productive employee.

(More & Miller, 2014, p. 26)

Styles of Supervision

Styles of supervision refer to the different behavioral approaches supervisors use to influence their employees' commitment and performance. It is the way by which supervisors manage and work with their subordinates. Some supervisors make the task of supervision look easy: they are efficient, competent, and respectful of their subordinates and motivate their officers to high performance levels with minimum effort. Others constantly complain about the quality of their officers and how they perform the given tasks. They spend most of their time attempting to control their officer's work performance. However, their subordinates never seem to please them or accomplish what they expect. These are two different examples of supervisory styles.

How patrol officers perform their day-to-day operational tasks is the basis for achieving the department's mission and the community's cooperation with the department. It can also be a source of tension within the community, resulting in the dismissal of the police chief and civil unrest (Williams, 2015). Operationally, conflicts arise as police officers fail to fulfill the requests and orders of their supervisors. How proficiently an officer performs day-to-day tasks will be influenced by the interpersonal skills of their supervisor. How a supervisor interacts with subordinates, communicates responsibilities and expectations, motivates them, and gains their trust and respect determines the influence and compliance they will achieve with their subordinates. The ability to influence subordinates is an important element of the supervisor's role, because an integral part of the patrol officer's job involves autonomy. Unlike other organizational managers, police supervisors are accountable for subordinates who work independently outside their immediate control (President's Task Force on 21st Century Policing, 2015). Officers are involved in countless situations daily that demand quick decisions and action without immediate supervisory direction. As a result, supervisors usually participate in an event after an officer has taken action. The officers they command perceive them as after-the-fact "Monday Morning Quarterbacks."

Thus, their supervision directly affects an officer's motivation to perform properly (Engel, 2003). How supervisors interact with their officers and communicate their direction is critical in achieving willing compliance, but can also create hostility and resistance. Developing successful and productive work teams is a function of the supervisor's ability to cultivate mutual respect, competence, and commitment in their command officers. Research confirms that officers who feel respected by their supervisors and peers are more likely to accept departmental policies, understand decisions, and comply voluntarily (More & Miller, 2014).

Successful supervisory leadership occurs when subordinates willingly comply with their direction. Supervisors must understand and be concerned with their impact on others if they truly wish to enhance their leadership ability. Their function is to accomplish tasks through the performance of their subordinates. Formal authority may be enough to effect limited changes in performance. Still, to gain commitment or lasting changes in attitude and behavior, supervisors must be able to influence others to perform willingly without using fear or coercion. It is the true essence of leadership. Influence is the process of altering, affecting, or changing others' attitudes, behaviors, values, and beliefs.

One way to convert positional authority into influence is for the supervisor to be willing to empower those whose performance they depend upon. **Empowerment** involves sharing leadership and is a sign of respect for others. It is more than a delegation task; it is an attempt to open and tap the creative power of the officers. Empowerment is based on the belief that organizations frequently underuse their employees' abilities. However, employees will contribute if given the chance and the responsibility. Empowerment provides unit members with positional and personal power sources to handle situations without always seeking supervisory approval. It helps to develop a sense of shared leadership and a sense of creative decision-making. Empowerment develops a belief in unit members that they are all in it together and that their success depends on each team member's contribution.

Empowerment sends a message of trust from the supervisor to those they empower. It is an essential ingredient for teamwork to take place. Empowerment does not guarantee that others will or should exercise their influence in all circumstances. Thus, empowerment requires that supervisors, through different behavioral actions, establish boundaries within which the empowered employee has the freedom to operate. These boundaries establish decisional guidelines and accountability. Supervisors can empower others by:

1. Letting others decide the methods they use for accomplishing tasks.
2. Creating an environment of cooperation, information sharing, discussion, and shared ownership of unit goals and objectives.
3. Encouraging their officers to take initiative, make decisions, and use their knowledge.
4. Letting others put their ideas and solutions into practice.
5. Building morale and confidence by recognizing successes and encouraging effectiveness.

Empowerment promotes trust and respect, which enhances a supervisor's ability to exercise influence. By sharing their power and not being critical or second-guessing their subordinates, supervisors can build relationships with their officers to motivate and inspire them to pursue mutually agreed-upon goals. One of the authors, on a visit to the Hungarian National Police, observed a detective supervisor in a city of 65,000 people holding a bi-weekly meeting with his seven subordinates. The agenda for the meeting was a review of the unit's unsolved cases. He encouraged the officers to make suggestions on how these cases should progress. The group analyzed these suggestions, and the supervisor empowered his detectives to employ their suggestions. As a result, they had an extremely high solvability rate. The meeting we observed displayed high officer commitment, mutual trust, respect for the contributions of each member, and a willingness to try new approaches. Instead of a power-based supervisory style, the unit's commander employed a team-centered approach grounded upon respect for each detective's contribution, talent, and commitment. A winning style of supervision achieved a high solvability rate for the unit. Interestingly, the detectives all were older and had more police experience than their supervisors.

Factors Affecting Supervisory Style

Police supervisors, by their role and occupational experience, are task-oriented. They must respond to situations in which their department and subordinates expect them to take charge and handle. These factors reinforce the task orientation of the role. A supervisor's management style also reflects their beliefs, values, and attitudes about what they think of their subordinates and how they should be managed. These psychological constructs contain the standards upon which supervisors judge themselves and others. They often select a supervision style because their mindset and on-the-job experiences tell them this is how supervisors should act. These factors raise the question of what supervision style is appropriate for supervisors. How do supervisory styles influence officer behavior? Do successful supervisors have a personal outlook or vision that makes them successful leaders?

The Project on Policing Neighborhoods addressed these questions, a systematic observational study of patrol officers and first-line supervisors in two metropolitan police departments in 1996 and 1997 (Engel, 2002, 2003). It examined the influence of 64 sergeants' supervisory styles on the behavior of 239 patrol officers, having identified the sergeant-supervisor of each officer. A review of prior research identified ten attitudinal dimensions that potentially shape supervisors' styles:

- How they make decisions.
- How they distribute power.
- The extent to which they attempt or avoid exerting leadership.
- The priority they place on aggressive enforcement.
- The priority they attach to Community Policing and problem-solving.
- How they view subordinates.
- Whether they engage in inspirational motivation.
- How task-oriented they are.
- Whether they focus on building friendships and mutual trust with subordinates.
- Whether they focus on protecting subordinates from unfair criticism and punishment.

Factor analysis of these dimensions identified four distinct supervisory styles: traditional, innovative, supportive, and active supervisory styles. The influence of these different supervisory styles on patrol officer behaviors was assessed. The findings confirm that supervisory styles can influence patrol officer behavior when making arrests, issuing citations, using force, and engaging in Community Policing. The study's most important finding was that style or quality of field supervision can significantly influence patrol officer behavior, apart from quantity of supervision. Front-line supervision can influence patrol officer behavior, but the study found that this influence varies according to the supervision style. None of the styles identified by the study are ideal, because each has benefits and disadvantages (Engel, 2003).

Traditional supervisors are direct, task-oriented, command-and-control supervisors. Their ultimate concern is to control subordinate behavior and achieve task completion. They expect their officers to produce measurable activity such as field interrogation reports, arrests, citations, and the accompanying paperwork and documentation. They exert their authority in most encounters with officers by taking charge, making on-the-spot decisions, and telling their officers what to do. They are less likely to reward, but more likely to punish, subordinates. Their primary concern is task completion, not people. More than 60 percent of traditional supervisors in the study strongly agree that "enforcing the law is the patrol officer's most important responsibility." They strongly believe in the importance of bureaucratic values, such as adherence to the chain of command and the department's rules and regulations. These individuals are examples of the command-and-control authoritarian style of management that emerged during the reform era of policing in the 20th century. This supervisory style seeks to simplify the supervisor's control of their unit and enhance their authority over their officers while leaving no room for independent thought on the part of the officers. Some believe this supervisory style is required in emergencies that demand strict control and rapid decision-making. Unfortunately, it stifles employee initiative, development, and independent problem-solving. These supervisors create dependants out of their subordinates because they restrict their officers' ability to innovate and use their intellect creatively.

Innovative supervisors are characterized by their tendency to form positive relationships with their officers, low task orientation, and more positive views of their subordinates. They are considered innovative because they encourage their officers to support and use Community Policing and problem-solving strategies. They accomplish this through coaching, mentoring, and facilitating these strategies. For example, Engel (2002) found that 96 percent of these supervisors agree strongly with the statement "a good patrol officer will try to find out what residents think the neighborhood problems are," as compared to 48 percent of traditional supervisors, 68 percent of supportive supervisors, and 68 percent of active supervisors. They empower their subordinates by delegating decision-making, refraining from telling officers how to handle a situation, and seldom interceding and taking over an incident. They also spend more time working with the public or other officers per shift than supervisors using a different supervision style.

This style represents a consensus-seeking approach to supervision. Supervisors who use it will decide after they obtain suggestions and advice from work unit members. The supervisor is still accountable for the final decision, which is arrived at after consulting the staff. This supervision style requires an individual to be open and candid with their employees. However, it also requires work unit members who are competent and committed to the department's goals and objectives.

Supportive supervisors use praise and encouragement to motivate subordinates, their willingness to be a personal counselor, and their desire to protect. They are less concerned with enforcing rules and regulations and ensuring that officers produce. These supervisors are likelier to encourage their subordinates through praise and acknowledgment, counsel officers as needed, and consistently show concern for subordinates. Just over two-thirds of these supervisors in the study believe that one of their most important functions is their duty to protect officers from unfair censure or punishment. Sometimes, supportive supervisors do not have strong ties or positive relationships with management. This working relationship results in the supervisor functioning as a protector rather than a supporter. These supervisors have not transitioned to the different roles and mindsets their supervisory position demands.

Active supervisors embrace a philosophy of leading by example. They aim to be heavily involved in the field alongside subordinates while controlling patrol officer behavior; they act as street officers and supervisors. Almost all active supervisors (95 percent) report they often go on their initiative to incidents their officers handle. Supervisors with an energetic style are characterized by directive decision-making, a strong sense of supervisory power, and a relatively positive view of subordinates. Although active supervisors believe they have considerable influence over subordinates' decisions, they are less likely to encourage team building, coaching, or mentoring. The study proposes one possible explanation: they are reluctant to become so involved that they alienate subordinate officers. A fine line separates an active supervisor from being seen as over-controlling or micromanaging.

Compared with the other supervisory styles, the active supervisor influences police officer actions greatly. It is especially true regardless of the style; when a supervisor is present at the scene of an incident, the more likely an officer will make an arrest. The longer the supervisor is present, the more likely there is to be an arrest. Also, patrol officers with active supervisors spend more time in proactive activities. However, patrol officers with active supervisors are more likely to use force against suspects. The study found that the mere presence of a supervisor significantly influenced the use of force. Active supervisors promote greater use of force and proactivity (which could expose the officer to greater risk if things go wrong) by taking precisely the risks they want them to take (Engel, 2003).

The study's findings identified the active style as more likely than the others to influence officer behavior. This influence can be positive or negative; for example, it can inspire subordinates to engage in more problem-solving activities or result in more frequent use of force. The active supervisory style was also conducive to implementing Community Policing goals (Engel, 2001).

In another supervisory study, Willis (2011) used focus-group data from six police departments to analyze first-line supervisors' strategic decision-making and how they operate within the context of CompStat and Community Policing. He noted that in the typical bureaucratic and reactive departments that existed before implementing these strategies, patrol supervisors were expected to exert internal control that was "essentially negative, relying primarily upon sanctions for non-compliance with police rules" (Engel, 2002, p. 52; see also Kelling & Moore, 1988; Weisburd & McElroy, 1988). A critical element of strategic and Community Policing is decentralizing decision-making authority to make police organizations more flexible and responsive to local conditions. Willis noted that implementing these strategies would require significant changes in how first-line supervisors learn about crime and disorder problems and exercise their judgment in ways most likely to produce desired results.

These studies disclose that how officers are supervised impacts their behavior. Unfortunately, supervision styles are more likely to develop because of experiential learning rather than through the limited training offered by many police departments. Strategic policing properly implemented will change the role and decision-making of operational supervisors (Willis, 2011).

To address the preparation of new supervisors, the Kentucky Department of Criminal Justice Training developed a three-week (120-hour) training program for newly promoted sergeants or officers on their agency's promotion lists. The course is designed to assist in understanding and developing supervision styles by individuals taking a leadership position for the first time. The instruction emphasizes the importance of the sergeants' ability to identify their leadership strengths and style while maintaining a high standard of expectation both for themselves and those under their supervision. A central feature of this course is the Situational Leadership Model developed by Hersey and Blanchard (1993). This model focuses on two central concepts: leadership style, and the individual's or group's maturity level. Students are taught to adjust their leadership styles based on the task they confront and assess their subordinates' abilities. In the course, students take part in classes focusing on the role of a supervisor, leadership, resolving conflict, managing diversity, monitoring officer performance, professional image, legal issues for supervisors, ethics, interpersonal communication, effective written communication, making decisions, solving problems, managing critical incidents, public speaking, emotional survival, budgeting, and media relations.

The above supervisory styles discovered by the research can serve as models for supervisors to measure themselves against. However, the question remains whether there is one best way to supervise. Blake and Mouton (1994), developers of the "Managerial Grid", assert that there is, and it is a supervisor who combines a deep concern for employees and relationships with a high concern for task performance. Effective supervisors manage themselves and their units' people to give the organization and its employees a meaningful experience. Supervisors who can balance both concerns are more effective. However, supervisors must understand their needs and their environment's situational and human dimensions.

The Changing Nature of Police Management

Traditional methods of police administration, authority, and command are currently being challenged by substantial demands for change (President's Task Force on 21st Century Policing, 2015). Since the latter part of the 20th century, police departments have been restructuring their organizational strategies to respond more effectively to these demands. The emergence of Community Problem-Solving, CompStat, Intelligent-Led, Smart Policing, issues concerning police legitimacy, and Procedural Justice has resulted in a new set of expectations for police managers at all levels of the organization. These efforts challenge traditional beliefs about police administration, command, and authority. In this current climate of demand and change, police managers are expected to be more effective by becoming strategic thinkers who engage in systematic problem-solving while achieving desired operational outcomes through a variety of analytical and data-driven tactics and strategies instead of using traditional command-and-control processes based upon rules and procedures and statistical counting of outputs instead of outcomes.

Effective organizations are ones in which people work at their full potential to achieve the organization's mission (Drucker, 2004). Senge (1990) identified effective organizations as ones skilled at creating, acquiring, and transferring knowledge and modifying their performance to reflect this new knowledge and insights. Organizations that do this are known as "**learning organizations**." Learning in these organizations reflects the willingness to question basic operating assumptions, use different tactical approaches, and experiment with different strategies to achieve desired outcomes. Managers in these organizations are expected to be system thinkers and self-confident learners open to new information. They are concerned with how their current operational demands affect their department's ability to provide public safety to its community and how their tactics gain citizen respect and support.

The "learning organization" construct appropriately describes the **strategic management** process emerging as the new paradigm of police organizational management. Various departmental adaptations occur throughout policing in the United States, Canada, and Europe. Each of these involves developing a strategic accountability system and philosophy of crime control that considers identifying and tracking emerging crime or quality-of-life trends and disseminating information to promote the development of a proactive, preventative approach to reduce crime and disorder. With goals to stimulate productivity, performance, and effectiveness, these police departments are using information technology and organized problem-solving to turn police officers into problem-solvers and to leverage their intellectual capital to pre-empt crime and neighborhood deterioration (Brown & Brudney, 2003).

This process requires all management levels to support and develop best practices in crime trend evaluation and response. In these departments, organizational strategy is the lynchpin that unites the decisions and actions of executives, operational commanders, line supervisors, and front-line officers into a coordinated and consistent pattern. As a result, the crafting, implementation, and execution of operational strategies and tactics become critical managerial functions. Another critical management requirement in this type of organization is to develop, engage, and apply the intellect and skills of employees to strategic organizational activities (Walsh, 1998).

For strategic management to be successful and for police departments to become effective learning organizations, the empowerment of middle managers and line supervisors is critical. They must be empowered with the authority to develop clear, effective tactics to address crime and quality-of-life conditions in their operational areas. These managers must be ready to change their plans when crime conditions change or desired results go unachieved. They must also be held accountable for the quality of their plans, their efforts, and their oversight of operations and results obtained. Executives and middle managers must constantly follow up on what is being done and evaluate results. Evaluation makes it possible to assess individual tactical responses' viability and incorporate the knowledge gained into subsequent strategy development efforts. By knowing how well a particular tactic worked on a problem and which elements worked most effectively, departments can better construct and implement effective responses for similar problems. The follow-up and assessment process also permits the redeployment of resources to meet newly identified challenges once a problem has abated. Managers in this process must receive training in critical thinking, problem-solving, tactic development, and implementation.

Strategic policing forces all managers at all levels of the department to be concerned with how they and their units contribute to the department's mission and goals. This strategic redirection requires developing a managerial skill set that involves information management and analysis, problem-solving, planning, strategy development, measurement, and communication. Chief executives are critical to this process because they must sponsor and champion this adaptation. The department's executive team must empower middle managers to develop strategies and tactics to meet objectives. The executive level must be able to accept failure and view it as an opportunity to create change. They must learn from failure and adjust by changing or replacing tactics rather than punishing for it. The ability and willingness to reallocate resources, support creative solutions to problems, track progress, and integrate functions within the agency require a strategic management orientation similar to that found in successful business organizations.

Conclusion

Most police departments in the United States are bureaucratic organizations with centralized managerial authority systems based on a logical hierarchical ordering of positions. This structural arrangement defines positional roles, departmental interdependences, and communication channels. It assigns authority, accountabilities, and responsibilities. It determines who makes decisions and the depth and extent of their authority and power. Managers use their authority to command and manage their organization's employees and assets. Command authority is structured through three distinct organizational levels: executive, middle management, and supervisory. The higher the administrative level, the greater the command responsibility, authority, and power. Understanding the complexity of the relationship between organizational objectives, administrative levels, and employee performance requires comprehending the concepts of authority, power, and command.

Management is accorded legitimate authority and power to direct and control a group of employees assigned to accomplish specific tasks. Management develops the capacity to achieve its objectives by organizing and staffing, creating organizational structure, and identifying sets of job functions, staffing jobs with qualified people, delegating responsibility for carrying out strategy and tactics, and devising systems to monitor operations and accomplishments.

A new managerial era is emerging in policing because of the adaptation of different problem-solving, data-driven operational strategies. These strategies represent a significant change in the way the police conceive of their departments, manage, and respond to operational demand. Police executives using these strategies are proactively developing organizational processes that allow their departments to initiate and reshape their activities to meet changing public safety demand. They are transforming their departments into proactive, strategically managed departments instead of reactive organizations (Wexler, Wycoff, & Fischer, 2007). Police departments that use strategic management techniques are aligning their external and internal environments through decisions based upon intelligence analysis. They are creating open-system adaptive-learning organizations. Crime and public safety are problems to be analyzed and resolved, not something to which to react.

This strategic transformation involves restructuring organizations and utilizing new outcome-based performance systems. Core functions, operational strategies, managerial accountability, distribution of power, and culture are reorganized to achieve a more effective impact. A properly designed strategic management process should establish accountability at all managerial levels of the organization under the direction of the executive staff and focus the entire organization on the department's mission. Time will tell whether strategic policing is the appropriate model that police executives should adopt to govern their departments and provide public-safety services. Last, it should be remembered that, in a democracy, policing should always respond to the needs of the people. Policing is a work in progress shaped by time and place's political, social, organizational, and economic trends.

KEY TERMS

Active supervisors	Coordination	Organizational structure
Administration	Empowerment	Organizing
Administrative functions	Executive strategic level	Planning
Administrative paradox	Influence commanding	Strategic management
Authority	Innovative supervisors	Styles of supervision
Bureaucracy	Learning organizations	Supervisory level
Command levels	Managerial authority	Supportive supervisors
Commanding	Middle management level	Traditional supervisors
Controlling	Organizational justice	Voluntariness

References

Blake, R.R., & Mouton, J.S. (1994). *The managerial grid III: The key to leadership excellence*. Houston, TX: Gulf Publishing.

Blanchard, K., & Johnson, S. (2003). *The one minute manager*. New York, NY: William Marrow.

Brown, M.M., & Brudney, J.L. (2003). Learning organizations in the public sector? A study of police agencies employing information and technology to advance knowledge. *Public Administration Review, 63*(1), 30–43.

Charrier, K. (2004). Strategic management in policing: The role of the strategic manager. *Police Chief, 71,* 60–70.

Colvin, A. (2015, April). Mapping the future of policing: Developing capabilities and partnerships. *The Police Chief,* 30–31.

Cordner, G.W. (2013). *Police administration,* 8th ed. New York, NY: Elsevier.

Covey, S.R. (1997). The habits of effective organizations. In F. Hesselbein & P.M. Cohen (Eds.), *Leader to leader* (pp. 215–216). San Francisco, CA: Jossey-Bass.

Crank, J.P., & Langworthy, R. (1992). Institutional perspective on policing. *Journal of Criminal Law & Criminology, 83,* 338–363.

Cunningham, M.R., Jones, J.W., & Behrens, G.M. (2011). Psychological assessment of chief of police candidates: Scientific and practice issues. *Journal of Police and Criminal Psychology, 26,* 77–86.

David, F.R. (2014). *Strategic management: A competitive advantage approach, concepts & cases*. Upper Saddle River, NJ: Prentice Hall.

Desmond, M., Papachristos, A., & Kirk, D. (2016). Police violence and citizen reporting in the black community. *American Sociological Review, 81*(5), 857–867.

Dessler, G. (2004). *Management: Principles and practices for tomorrow's leaders*. Upper Saddle River, NJ: Prentice Hall.

Dessler, G. (2012). *Human resource management*. Upper Saddle River, NJ: Prentice Hall.

Domanick, J. (2015). *Blue: The LAPD and the battle to redeem American policing*. New York, NY: Simon & Schuster.

Drucker, P. (1998). *On the profession of management*. Boston, MA: Harvard Business Review.

Drucker, P. (2004). What makes an effective executive? *Harvard Business Review, 82*(6), 58–62.

Engel, R.S. (2001). Supervisory styles of patrol sergeants and lieutenants. *Journal of Criminal Justice, 29*, 341–355.

Engel, R.S. (2002). Patrol officer supervision in the community policing era. *Journal of Criminal Justice, 30*, 51–64.

Engel, R.S. (2003). *How police supervisory styles influence patrol officer behavior*. Washington, DC: National Institute of Justice.

Fayol, H. (1949). *General and industrial management*. London: Pitman.

Fayol, H. (1992). General principles of management. In J. Shafrits & J. Ott (Eds.), *Classics of organizational theory*. Pacific Grove, CA: Brooks/Cole.

Fyfe, J.J., Greene, J.R., Walsh, W., Wilson, O., & McLaren, R. (1997). *Police administration*. New York, NY: McGraw-Hill.

Geller, W.A., & Swanger, G. (1995). *Managing innovation in policing: The untapped potential of the middle manager*. Washington, DC: Police Executive Research Forum.

Goldstein, H. (1990). *Problem-oriented policing*. New York, NY: McGraw Hill.

Haberfeld, M.R. (2006). *Police leadership*. Upper Saddle River, NJ: Prentice-Hall.

Haneberg, L. (2005). *High impact middle management*. Avon, MA: FW Publications.

Henson, A. (2022). "Dickheads" and "cool cops": The impact of officers' perceived and contextual competence on black men's appraisals of police. *Journal of Research on Crime and Delinquency*, 1–31. doi:https://doi.org/10.1177/00224278221 137340

Hersey, P., & Blanchard, K. (1993). *Management of organizational behavior—Utilizing human resources*. Englewood Cliffs, NJ: Prentice Hall.

International Association of Chiefs of Police. (1999). *Police leadership in the 21st century: Achieving and sustaining executive success*. Alexandria, VA: IACP.

Jannetta, J., Esthappan, S., Fontaine, J., Lynch, M., & LaVigne, N. (2019). *Learning to build police-community trust: Implementation assessment findings of the National Initiative for Building Community Trust and Justice*. Washington, DC: The Urban Institute.

Kelling, G.L., & Bratton, W.J. (1993). Implementing community policing: The administrative problem. *Perspectives on Policing, no. 14*. Washington, DC: National Institute of Justice.

Kelling, G.L., & Moore, M.H. (1988). From political to reform to community: The evolving strategy of police. In J.R. Greene & S.D. Mastrofski (Eds.), *Community policing: Rhetoric or reality* (pp. 3–26). New York, NY: Praeger.

Kelly, R. (2015). *Vigilance: My life serving America and protecting its empire city*. New York, NY: Hachette.

Moore, M.H., & Trojanowicz, R.C. (1988). Corporate strategy for policing. *Perspectives on Policing*, no. 6. Washington, DC: National Institute of Justice.

More, H.W., & Miller, L.S. (2014). *Effective police supervision*, 7th ed. Burlington, MA: Elsevier.

More, H.W., Vito, G.F., & Walsh, W.F. (2012). *Organizational behavior and management in law enforcement*. Upper Saddle River, NJ: Prentice Hall.

Peak, K. (2012). *Policing America: Challenges and best practices*. Upper Saddle River, NJ: Prentice Hall.

Pinellas Park Police Department (2006). *Directives manual, standard operating procedure, no. 32, Promotions*. Pinellas Park, FL: Pinellas Park Police Department.

President's Task Force on 21st Century Policing. (2015). *Final report of the President's task force on 21st-century policing*. Washington, DC: Office of Community Oriented Policing Services.

Reiss, Jr., A.J. (1985). Shaping and serving the community: The role of the police chief executive. In W.A. Geller (Ed.), *Police leadership in America: Crisis and opportunity* (pp. 61–69). New York, NY: Praeger.

Reuss-Ianni, E. (1983). *Two cultures of policing: Street cops and management cops.* New Brunswick, NJ: Transaction Books.

Senge, P. (1990). *The fifth discipline: The art & practice of the learning organization.* New York, NY: Doubleday.

Sherman, L.W., Milton, C.H., & Kelly, T.V. (1973). *Team policing: Seven case studies.* Washington, DC: Police Foundation.

Smith, M., Rojek, J., Petrocelli, M., & Withrow, B. (2017). Measuring disparities in police activities: A state of the art review. *Policing: An International Journal of Police Strategies & Management., 40*(2), 166–183.

Sparrow, M.K., Moore, M., & Kennedy, D. (1990). *Beyond 911: A new era for policing.* New York, NY: Basic Books.

Stamper, N.H. (1992). *Removing managerial barriers to effective police leadership: A study of executive leadership and executive management in big-city police departments.* Washington, DC: Police Executive Research Forum.

Swanson, C.R., Territo, L.J., & Taylor, R.W. (2011). *Police administration: Structures, processes, and behavior.* Upper Saddle River, NJ: Prentice Hall.

Travis, J. (1995). Managing innovation in policing: The untapped potential of the middle manager. *Research in Brief.* Washington, DC: National Institute of Justice.

Timoney, John F. (2010). *Beat cop to top cop.* Philadelphia, PA: University of Pennsylvania Press.

Van Maanen, J. (1984). Making rank: Becoming an American police sergeant. *Urban Life, 13,* 155–176.

Vito, G.F., Walsh, W.F., & Kunselman, J. (2005). Community policing: The middle manager's perspective. *Police Quarterly, 8*(4), 490–511.

Walsh, W.F. (1998). Policing at the crossroads: Changing directions for the new millennium. *Policing: An International Journal of Police Science and Management, 1*(1), 17–25.

Walsh, W.F., & Donovan, E.J. (1990). *The supervision of police personnel: A performance-based approach.* Dubuque, IA: Kendall Hunt.

Weber, M. (1947). *The theory of social and economic organization.* New York, NY: The Free Press.

Weisburd, D., & McElroy, J. (1988). Enacting the CPO role: Findings from the New York City pilot program in community policing. In J.R. Greene & S.D. Mastrofski (Eds.), *Community policing: Rhetoric or reality* (pp. 89–102). New York, NY: Praeger.

Wexler, C., Wycoff, M.A., & Fischer, C. (2007). *Good to great policing: Application of business management principles in the public sector.* Washington, DC: Department of Justice Office of Community Oriented Policing Services and Police Executive Research Forum.

Williams, T. (2015, December 9). Under fierce scrutiny, police chiefs shift focus. *New York Times,* A23.

Willis, J.J. (2011). First-line supervision and strategic decision-making under Compstat and community policing. *Criminal Justice Policy Review, 24*(2), 235–256.

Wolfe, S., & Nix, J. (2016). Managing police departments post-Ferguson. *Harvard Business Review,* https://hbr.org/9/13.

3 Police Leadership

Learning Objectives

1. To define leadership in policing.

2. To identify the elements of leadership styles.

3. To define the attributes of transformational leadership.

4. To identify the elements of the Leadership Challenge Model.

5. To identify the elements of servant leadership.

6. To identify the elements of situational leadership.

Introduction

Leadership is the key force behind the creation of effective organizations. In policing, leadership can energize and become a dynamic force in the agency—invigorating change and sponsoring professionalization. Leadership motivates individuals to perform the tasks that can move the organization forward. Effective leaders motivate their followers to do what is best for the organization. They accomplish this by creating a sense of purpose that both motivates and directs followers so they voluntarily make meaningful contributions to the department. Thus, a leader is a source of both guidance and inspiration. In this chapter, we will provide a review of relevant theories of leadership that apply to policing.

The elements of police leadership are a vital concern and provide a sign of what is important. Leadership is not found only at the executive/administrative level of the police organization. It can be exercised at any level of the department. For example, Haberfeld (2006, p. 3) defines police leadership as "the ability to make a split-second decision and take control of a potentially high-voltage situation that evolves on the street." She also asserts that line officers are "the true leaders on the streets, using their leadership skills in daily encounters with the community, and police executives and policy makers need to realize it" (Haberfeld, 2006, p. 3). Baker (2006, p. 41) contends that effective leadership is exercised by police managers in different ways, depending upon their rank in the department. Senior executive leadership should develop and share their vision for the organization, charting the path to accomplishing this vision by establishing strategic objectives, practicing collaboration, and delegating tasks. Police middle managers operationalize the vision by coordinating and planning, mentoring and coaching, building teams, and empowering and rewarding subordinates. First-line supervisors, the closest managers to the department's employees, provide

DOI: 10.4324/9781003459095-3

leadership by example, supervising, training, and developing teams while evaluating performance.

All department levels must be mobilized and involved to ensure successful police leadership. Coaching and mentoring the people doing day-to-day operations ensure the leader's vision for the department is realized, and the organization will succeed. Leadership is most effective when it is aware of the needs and expectations of subordinates. Villiers (2003, p. 33) notes that police leaders motivate their followers to:

- Transcend self-interest for the sake of organizational goals and values.
- Raise their need level from security and safety to self-esteem or autonomy.
- Share with the leader a common vision of the importance of the leader's goals or values to the organization's future.

Motivated followers can achieve more than they thought possible, strengthen their commitment to, and raise, departmental performance.

There are three related ideas about administration that guide our definition of leadership. First, leadership is a process that cannot be conceptually separated from achieving organizational objectives. Second, leadership can be learned by people in administrative positions in organizations. Much of the leadership literature assumes that effective leadership can be taught. Third, the leadership process is a group process. To accomplish organizational objectives, leaders must identify and influence a significant number of people who must do the work necessary for success. According to Gladwell's (2006) Tipping Point Leadership theory, once the beliefs and energies of a critical mass of people are engaged, conversion to a new idea will spread, bringing about fundamental change quickly. The process of leadership must be examined in light of how leaders get people to achieve the tasks necessary for organizational existence and survival.

Effective leadership is grounded upon the direction and guidance the leader provides through four leadership styles. **Directive leadership** emphasizes the leader's expectations and the tasks to be performed by subordinates. The leader emphasizes important organizational rules and regulations and their relationship to task performance. The leader guides subordinates and motivates them to accomplish the tasks required by the organization. **Supportive leadership** is an employee-centered process. Supportive leaders are approachable and friendly with their employees. Their primary concern is to accomplish the organization's tasks while meeting their subordinates' needs. **Participatory leadership** emphasizes collaboration between the leader and the subordinates. The leader seeks to involve subordinates in decision-making while assuring their importance in the organization. **Achievement-oriented leadership** is concerned with producing results. The leader expects workers to attempt to do their best and is confident they will achieve stated goals. Each style can create an effective organization.

Traditional Styles of Police Leadership

Effective leadership is crucial to successful policing. It includes managing personnel, decision-making, and police-community relations. Police leaders must possess various skills, including managing personnel, making decisions in high-pressure situations, and communicating effectively with the community. The adoption of a leadership style depends upon several factors. However, it comes in several different forms. Here is an overview of traditional leadership styles in organizations.

Autocratic

Autocratic leadership is a function of the police organizational hierarchy. The leader attempts to control subordinates and makes decisions without their input (Wuestewald & Steinheider, 2012). Power is centralized through the rigid enforcement of procedural rules and regulations. Subordinates must follow directions without question (Silvestri, 2007).

Despite its authoritarian nature, there are some advantages to autocratic leadership. It can be effective when subordinates are inexperienced or unskilled and require direct supervision. Also, it can resolve risky situations to prevent harm promptly (Brandebo, 2020).

However, the autocratic style of leadership presents significant disadvantages. It sponsors subordinate dependency if they are not involved in decision-making, thus causing poor morale (Bao & Ge, 2019). Since they cannot suggest ideas, this style stifles subordinates' creativity.

Bureaucratic

The **bureaucratic leadership** style also emphasizes strict adherence to rules and regulations and standardized procedures and includes the rational analysis of data to guide operations. Here, decision-making is based on objective criteria, not personal preferences. It is a feature of a top-down organizational structure in which power and authority flow from the top of the hierarchy to the lower levels of the organization (Kelling & Moore, 1989).

The bureaucratic style can increase efficiency, consistency, and establish predictability in the organization. By establishing clear procedures and protocols, police leaders can ensure that officers follow best practices and that their actions align with the department's goals and values. This can help to reduce errors, improve quality, and promote accountability (Herrington & Schafer, 2019). In addition, it promotes fairness and equity in decision-making by avoiding favoritism and nepotism to build trust and confidence among officers and the community (Brunetto et al., 2017).

One crucial disadvantage of the bureaucratic style is its lack of flexibility, which hampers the ability to respond to change. Police leaders may need to be able to make decisions quickly and adapt to new situations. Bureaucratic structures can sometimes be too rigid to allow this flexibility. It can isolate the department from its community and retard citizen involvement in decision-making (Kelling & Moore, 1989). The bureaucratic style stifles creativity and innovation by subordinates due to its strict adherence to rules and regulations. It discourages officers from thinking outside the box or taking risks to solve problems. It can promote adherence to standard procedures that may not be effective or appropriate to the situation. Strict adherence to policy can also subject the community to questionable police actions and erode the public trust in law enforcement.

Democratic

The rise of Community Policing sponsored the development of a democratic style of police leadership. Community Policing aims to work collaboratively with the community to identify and address issues contributing to crime and disorder. The **democratic leadership** style was particularly well-suited to this new approach because it emphasizes collaboration, teamwork, and soliciting input from subordinates. Decision-making is based on building consensus. Police leaders act as facilitators (Wuestewald & Steinheider, 2012). This approach is particularly effective when there is a high degree of interdependence among team members and where the decision to be made significantly impacts the entire team.

Using the democratic leadership style promotes increased morale, job satisfaction, and commitment among subordinates (Hess & Bacigalupo, 2011). By involving subordinates in the decision-making process, leaders can help create a sense of ownership and investment in the outcomes of those decisions, leading to increased motivation and engagement among team members and better performance and outcomes.

One disadvantage is that it can slow decision-making because building consensus is time-consuming. Thus, it may be inappropriate in emergencies, where immediate action is necessary (Brandebo, 2020). It may also be less effective when team members have a high degree of conflict or disagreement. The leader may need a more directive approach to resolve the conflict and make decisions.

Laissez-faire Leadership

The laissez-faire leader engages in minimal influence and takes a "hands-off, let it ride" attitude toward followers. They are laid-back and make no effort to guide or motivate subordinates. It is the absence of leadership, featuring the avoidance of decision-making and the absence of feedback or rewards for subordinates (Skogstad, Einarsen, Torsheim, Aasland, & Hetland, 2007, p. 81). This style leads to negative outcomes: little organizational accomplishment and a lack of direction for subordinates as they become unmotivated and disheartened (Northouse, 2012, p. 57). Laissez-faire leaders procrastinate responses to critical issues, fail to complete duties, have poor productivity, and avoid involvement in solving conflict (Khan, Nawaz, & Khan, 2016, p. 6). Such avoidance can lead to high levels of psychological distress among subordinates that often sponsors bullying in the workplace (Skogstad, Einarsen, Torsheim, Aasland, & Hetland, 2007, p. 89). For all its weaknesses, laissez-faire leadership may be appropriate when subordinates are highly skilled, motivated, and have an excellent performance record (Khan, Nawaz, & Khan, 2016, p. 2; Jaafar, Zambi, & Fathil, 2021, p. 4).

Research Findings on Leadership Styles

The literature on police leadership reveals that distinct styles have been exercised differently. In an early study of 155 police managers, Kuykendall and Unsinger (1982) reported that "salesman" was the most commonly reported leadership style. The respondents noted that they viewed themselves as team managers who avoided "risky" styles. They avoided delegating high-level tasks to their subordinates. These police managers lacked trust and confidence in the abilities of their followers. However, in a similar study, Bruns and Shuman (1988) surveyed 365 law enforcement officers in 10 managerial training programs in Arizona from 1978 to 1982. They found that the respondents supported a highly participative management style for police leaders.

Girodo (1998) surveyed police chiefs from departments around the world, characterizing their leadership style under four categories: transformational leaders were considerate, charismatic, and personable; bureaucratic leaders identified with the management of a police organization structured by its rules; social contract leaders felt that their approach was professional. Most of the police chief respondents identified with the Machiavellian model that stressed manipulating subordinates to achieve management ends. Girodo felt that the paramilitary structure of police departments helped create an authoritarian leadership style.

The bureaucratic structure of police departments is another major source of police organizational authoritarianism. Mayo (1985, p. 411) asserts that police chiefs spend too much of their time directing the daily operations of their departments because they have little faith in the talents and loyalties of their subordinates and fail to pay attention to long-term, strategic issues facing their departments. Archambeault and Weirman (1983) contend that the bureaucratic model of police departments results in a work environment that discourages productivity, initiative, and commitment among its workforce members. Bureaucracy also promotes the pursuit of individual self-interest and adversarial relationships between police managers and their employees, encouraging "game playing," resulting in an impersonal work climate.

The competency and background of police executives influences their leadership reputation. Krimmel and Lindemuth's (2001) analysis of 205 municipal managers in Pennsylvania revealed that these managers ranked the performance of police chiefs who managed a union shop, had some college credits, who were graduates of the FBI National Academy, and who were promoted from within consistently higher than those who did not possess these attributes. Similarly, Rowe's (2006) ethnography of British police officers determined that superiors who had direct experience with and maintained their ties with the street where "real police work" was done were considered the best leaders. Those management supervisors who moved up the ranks without such experience were viewed with suspicion and were less likely to be accepted.

Several studies have analyzed assessments of the leadership attributes and performance of police managers. For example, Stamper (1992) surveyed 52 police chiefs and 92 of their immediate assistants and found that their self-assessments and those of their subordinates revealed a discrepancy between belief and practice among these chiefs. The chiefs felt they placed a premium on sharing their vision of the future, practicing openness and honesty, fostering teamwork by helping their employees get the work done, and recognizing excellence in performance. Externally, these chiefs said that they promoted questioning of agency policies while working closely with the members of their community. They professed the adoption of an intuitive and creative approach to their work while taking a stand against discriminatory practices. The chiefs also believed that their leadership functions were most deserving of their time and attention on the job. However, their immediate assistants did not perceive that the behavior of the chiefs was consistent with their expressed beliefs about leadership. In their opinion, the chiefs were much more involved in the technical and procedural aspects of management than their leadership functions. These findings led Stamper to conclude that leadership had been "structured out" of police administration. Like Mayo, he surmised that police chiefs spent too much time and attention to management concerns and failed to lead their departments.

Recent studies assessing the state of police leadership have been more positive. Densten (2003) surveyed 480 Australian senior police officials. He reported that the effectiveness of a police leader was a function of leader reputation and followers' satisfaction with job performance of their leaders; impression management and image building by leaders; how dependent followers are on direction and resources from the leaders and how dependent leaders are upon the follower's completion of activities to achieve success (Densten, 2003, p. 412).

Similarly, interviews with 150 British officers revealed that they wanted leaders to make them feel proud of their work and their contributions. Effective leadership involved offering high-quality service, maintaining high personal and professional standards, empowering staff, and possessing relevant knowledge and skills. The way officers feel about how they are treated by the organization affects both the quality of their performance and the service they provide to the community (Dobby, Anscombe, & Tuffin, 2004).

A case study examined the implementation of participatory management in a suburban police agency through the construction of a Leadership Team. The team established and enhanced collaborative relationships between all levels of the department and the community. Officers felt that the opportunity to take part in agency decisions increased and that their input and opinions were seriously considered. They noted increased pride in the agency—a zero officer turnover rate during the period in question. Noted empowerment factors included the participation of all ranks in the decision-making process, management seeking feedback from all levels of the department, and consistent and reliable support of employee decisions by management. Finally, the officers noted that they were motivated to implement Community Policing as they saw fit and they displayed greater motivation to engage in discretionary conduct (Steinheider & Wuestewald, 2008). The study documents how participatory leadership can improve introducing innovations by increasing the motivation of workers at all levels of the department.

Fischer's (2009) interviews with 25 American police chiefs determined that police leaders must be both honest and transparent in their dealings with their subordinates, set a good example of performance and integrity, be a change agent that moves the agency forward, support and honor the performance of their charges. They should be "consensus builders" who should follow a democratic leadership approach (Fischer, 2009, p. 10). Results from Isenberg's (2010) survey of 26 American police chiefs mirror these opinions. These chiefs also stressed the need for leaders to be optimistic role models who breed confidence in their agency and the community it serves. They should be unafraid to set goals that involve risk (Isenberg, 2010, p. 42). They recommended the use of a leadership style that is inclusive and seeks the support of all members of the organization (Isenberg, 2010, p. 44).

Support for the change to this police leadership style has grown. A survey of police managers attending the Southern Police Institute examined their attitudes concerning ideal leadership behavior. Andreescu and Vito (2010) found that gender and race played a significant role in structuring leadership preferences. Both males and females expressed a preference for task-centered and structured leadership. Yet, women and African Americans seemed to prefer transformational leaders who favored a democratic, work-oriented style and allowed subordinates freedom of action while responding to the concerns of followers.

Schafer (2010a) surveyed 1,000 police supervisors to determine their opinions regarding the traits, habits, and effective practices of police leaders. They ranked honesty and integrity as the most important characteristics. In addition, they noted that personality and interpersonal skills (caring, communication, and work ethic) were more significant than technical aspects (decision-making, competency, knowledge) in determining effective police leadership (Schafer, 2010a, p. 651; see also Schafer, 2013). While these officers considered the achievement of key goals as significant, they also gave weight to the "interpersonal dynamics of the workplace" including accessing the growth and development of subordinates, maintaining morale, and the leader's maintenance of positive standing within the agency (Schafer, 2010a, pp. 652–653).

These mid-level managers also suggested that the best way to achieve police leadership development was through a mixture of education, practical application, and constructive feedback. Young officers should be exposed to leadership via mentoring and observation of positive role models (Schafer, 2009).

These studies illuminate the strong consensus that police leadership should be democratic. Officers want their leaders to be positive role models who seek their opinions and wish to foster their improvement and development. There is strong sentiment for the abandonment of the "command and control" model of police management and its replacement with an inclusive style of leadership. These empirical findings provide a basis for our review of three influential theories of leadership that have been applied to policing—tipping point, transformational, and servant leadership.

Tipping Point Leadership

Tipping point leadership consists of a four-step process to bring about rapid, dramatic, and lasting change with limited resources. There are four "hurdles" that change agents must typically overcome in any organization (Kim & Mauborgne, 2003, p. 64). It can be applied to reveal the implementation problems that both Community Policing and CompStat have faced.

1. **The cognitive hurdle**: *Put managers face to face with problems and customers. Find new ways to communicate.*

   Community Policing faces a "model muddle." Hunter and Barker (1993, p. 157) define this muddle as layers of "BS" in that Community Policing "seeks to be all things to all people under the umbrella of community involvement." As a result, departments have great difficulty implementing the model because no one really knows whether it is a program, a philosophy, or both.

   In both New York and Los Angeles, Bratton (1988) perceived this as meaning that he had to get the department and its leadership to recognize that they were failing in their crime control mission and had been for several years.

2. **The resource hurdle**: *Focus on "hot spots" and bargain with partner organizations.*

   Departments implementing Community Policing have been hampered by resource limitations and the need to integrate handling high service demand resulting from calls for service with community problem-solving (Kessler, 1993).

   As Bratton notes, the public sector has never had a vast surplus of resources. At the LAPD, he removed all personnel from special duties and placed them back on the street. In the Lowell (MA) CompStat implementation study, it was noted that flexibility in reassigning personnel was not accomplished due to the department's responsibility to be fair to its employees, respond to unpredictable situations, and be equitable to its citizens while meeting political demands of powerful constituents (Willis, Mastrofski, Weisburd, & Greenspan, 2003, p. 482).

3. **The motivational hurdle**: *Put the stage lights on and frame the challenge to match the organization's various levels.*

   Despite all the attention given to Community Policing, performance measures based upon its delivery have not been developed by police departments. By retaining traditional measures (like arrests and citations), departments implementing Community Policing have violated a fundamental maxim of organizational development: *"What gets measured, gets done!"*

Bratton stresses that accountability is the key to CompStat. In particular, he feels that police officers must be controlled because of the vast power they hold over the citizenry. He also states that, while he often must "lead from behind," he stresses inspiration and positive motivational techniques in his change efforts. Despite this description, one of the "urban legends" surrounding CompStat is that accountability becomes confrontational, personal, and, ultimately, demeaning. Although they did not experience such treatment directly, Lowell line officers believed that CompStat sessions were forums where officers "had their balls ripped off," were "someone's punching bag," and were "sometimes kind of humiliated, or embarrassed in front of other people." Like Bratton, the Lowell chief noted that, while he did use CompStat sessions to reward or punish his officers, he was averse to humiliating them, preferring to ask questions and foster a supportive environment (Willis et al., 2003, pp. 477–478).

4. **The political hurdle**: *Identify and silence internal opponents; isolate external ones.*

Although Community Policing typically enjoys support among political leaders and local officials who wish to appear progressive and responsive to the needs of citizens, Community Policing has been relegated to "innovation ghettos"—specialized units who provide services (see Toch & Grant, 1982). It has rarely been implemented on a departmental basis. In the meantime, the majority of the police department's service delivery strategy continues to be a response to citizen-generated calls for service and pressures brought by civic and political leaders.

Bratton (1998) addressed this problem by downsizing one managerial level of NYPD between the executive staff and the operational precincts. He abolished divisional commands and placed the Inspectors and Deputy Inspectors assigned to these units in command of precincts. These are appointed ranks that serve at the pleasure of the Police Commissioner. If they failed to meet their outcome-based command leadership requirements, they could be demoted back to their civil service rank of Captain and removed from command by order of the Commissioner. Internally, he recruited a top NYPD commander, John Timoney, to audit the responses of the top staff toward Bratton's concept of order maintenance-policing and identify those who would support and those who would oppose the premise. Externally, support was provided for this organizational direction by then Mayor Rudolph Giuliani who had considerable influence in the courts, district attorney's office, and jail due to his reputation as an effective federal prosecutor (Kim & Mauborgne, 2003, p. 69).

Bratton's use of the tipping leadership style described above energized the bureaucratic structure of police organizations he commanded. These organizations were changed through the introduction of an entrepreneurial spirit and the establishment of accountability measures that accurately determine levels of both production and performance. Instead of abandoning their citizen partners as in the past, they also recognized that citizens are partners in policing with responsibilities to their communities for assisting in the solving of crime and disorder problems (see Osborne & Gaebler, 1993; Osborne & Plastrik, 1997).

Transformational Leadership

Burns (1978) argues that individuals in an organization may be influenced and motivated by leaders via two methods: transactional and transformational leadership. Each of these types of leadership has different ways to influence attitudes and motivation. Transactional leadership relies on the reciprocal and deterministic relationship between a leader and their subordinates (Bass & Riggio, 2006). Here, leaders engage in a bargaining process with subordinates to motivate them. The leader regulates the bargaining process so that benefits may be issued and received to continue positively valued behavior. Officers are rewarded by their supervisors when they engage in and perform their duties in the manner prescribed by the rules and regulations of the organization.

Transactional leadership is characterized in multiple ways. First, a transactional leader uses contingent rewards (e.g., work for pay or time off) to underlie the arrangements for explicit or implicit agreement on goals to be reached to get the desired rewards or behavior. Second, the transactional leader monitors subordinate performance to ensure effectiveness. Third, transactional leaders are passive and only take action when a problem arises. It results in a mutually beneficial exchange that leads to goal achievement. Unfortunately, this exchange may only garner short-term commitment. Instead of creating a more sustainable performance change in officers, it creates reward-seeking behavior that ceases when the rewards end.

Transformational leaders seek to change the organizational status quo and take the organization on a new and effective path. Instead of maintaining traditional forms of command and control and reacting to crime, transformational police leaders develop a proactive strategic vision of their department's operational performance. They recognize the fluid context in which their departments operate. They also understand that there are forces to which police organizations must adapt and evolve to remain effective in a changing world. It is these forces that are creating new models for conducting the business of policing (Batts, Smoot, & Scrivner, 2012). The strategic policing methods they practice involve the effective use of intelligence and developing flexible strategies to meet public safety needs. They seek to instill in their departments a set of organizational values focused on effectiveness, crime prevention, community engagement, information management, organizational and managerial accountability, ethics, and the control of crime (Moore & Trojanowicz, 1988).

Transformational leaders are present in today's police organizations. In his assessment of leadership in the Los Angeles Police Department, Reese (2005, p. 132) identified Chief William Bratton as a transformational leader due to his intellectual vision, empathy for his officers and the community, and personal charisma and communication skills. Empirically, transformational leadership has been a focus of studies on police leadership. Murphy and Drodge (2004) interviewed 28 Royal Canadian Mounted Police officers on their views of police leadership within the framework of transformational leadership theory. They describe that at the center of transformational leadership theory are the "Four I's" (Murphy & Drodge, 2004, pp. 2–3):

1. *Idealized influence*: The leader stands for something that followers aspire to.
2. *Inspirational motivation*: A sense of collective identity inspired by the leader's vision.
3. *Intellectual stimulation*: Challenge to followers to examine ways to enhance their productivity.
4. *Individualized consideration* to followers.

The RCMP officers stressed that leaders can emerge at all levels of the organization and that leadership skills can be learned. They stressed the significance of the "Four I's" and how leaders must be genuinely concerned with the needs of followers.

The impact of transformational leadership was the subject of an ethnographic study of one department. Through interviews and observations, Murphy (2008) found that officers stressed the linkage between leadership and shared values. Leaders must personify these values and demonstrate consistency, honesty, and fairness in their supervisory decisions. These officers felt an emotional attachment to leaders who inspired them by standing for their values, even when upper management blocked their attempts to implement change.

A study of German police officers found that transformational leaders exerted a direct, positive influence on shared leadership and an indirect, positive influence on follower job satisfaction through their capacity to clarify organizational goals (Masal, 2015).

In South Australia, Mazerolle, Darroch, and White (2013) examined the implementation of and outcomes of problem-oriented policing (POP) in South Australia. Using a time series design, they found that POP generated an overall drop in crimes per 100,000 population—particularly in property crime. These results were attributable to the transformational leadership style of Commissioner Mal Hyde, who drove the innovation by supporting those who attempted to create new operational ideas. Through his top-down approach to implementation, Commissioner Hyde oversaw the POP agenda and changed the police culture.

Sarver and Miller (2014) surveyed 161 Texas police chiefs with scales designed to measure their leadership attitudes and aptitudes. They found that the chiefs were evenly split across several leadership styles: transactional, transformational, and passive/avoidant. Several attributes were identified as strongly related to the transformational leadership style as compared to the others, including extra effort, effectiveness, satisfaction, extraversion, openness, and conscientiousness. In terms of performance, chiefs who adopted the transformational leadership style were more successful in motivating their subordinates to make the extra effort on the job. Their followers were more satisfied with their leadership style than chiefs in the other groups. They also received fewer formal complaints than their counterparts.

However, several studies have noted the limitations of transformational leadership. Cockcroft (2014) suggests that transformational leadership is incongruent with the culture of policing where street-level and management cops possess different and sometimes opposing views of their world of work (see also Niederhoffer, 1969; Reuss-Ianni, 1983). He argues that much of police work relies upon "the transactional demands of command" and that one form of leadership will not be appropriate for every set of organizational relationships (Cockcroft, 2014, p. 12). Research by Swid (2014) shows that transformational and transactional leadership are not mutually exclusive and that both can be practiced by the same individual. Both are necessary for organizational growth and maintenance, but subordinates preferred transformational leaders who provided opportunities for growth experiences (Swid, 2014, p. 590).

Yet, transformational leadership theory states that such leaders can convey a sense of vision and mission in a way that transforms the follower's sense of the possible. Transformational leaders motivate their followers to:

- *Transcend self-interest for the sake of organizational goals and values.*
- *Raise their need level from security and safety to self-esteem and autonomy.*

- *Share with the leader a common vision of the importance of the leader's goals or values to the future of the organization.*
- *Achieve more than they thought possible.*
- *Strengthen their commitment to the organization.*
- *Induce feelings of trust, admiration, loyalty, and mutual respect.*

(Villiers, 2003, p. 33)

Transformational leaders are change agents who renovate the organization by empowering their followers and getting their commitment to a new organizational vision. In Chapter 5, we further discuss transformational leadership and organizational change management.

 ## The Leadership Challenge Model

Transformational leadership is the basis for the **Leadership Challenge Model** (Kouzes & Posner, 2012). It comprises five practices that effective leaders demonstrate:

1. *Model the way* (setting a personal example).
2. *Inspire a shared vision* (envisioning, articulating, and sharing a new future).
3. *Challenge the process* (willingness to question and confront the status quo).
4. *Enable others to act* (nurture and empower the development of followers).
5. *Encourage the heart* (recognize and celebrate the accomplishments of followers).

Each of the Five Practices includes Ten Commitments that illustrate leaders' performance in their accomplishments.

For example, under "Model the way," Commitment 1 states that leaders find their voice by communicating their values. Leaders must express their values to empower and motivate others. Values are significant because they influence how leaders respond to followers. Genuine beliefs sponsor passion and strengthen moral principles among colleagues. Modeling the way is also linked to competence. Commitment 2 states that leaders must align their values with their actions. Successful leadership performance reflects their ability to act upon their stated values. It enables them both to set an example and to build consensus among followers. To reinforce these values among their followers, leaders not only teach and tell stories but they give them life through their personal example. Murphy (2008, p. 176) directly observed that officers admired transformational leaders who "walked the talk" but saw they invoked fear and insecurity among upper management who constrained them from getting results when it meant breaking the rules.

Inspiring a shared vision involves recognizing the organization's challenges and opportunities while working toward their realization. Thus, Commitment 3 finds that leaders envision the future by imagining exciting and ennobling possibilities via positive messages. Leaders enlist others to share their vision by articulating it and finding common ground with their followers by speaking from the heart (Commitment 4). There are three components of leadership vision: (1) The Past—where we have been, the tradition of the organization; (2) The Present—where we are now, colored by realistic optimism; and (3) The Future—where we are going, the promise of success.

Leaders challenge the process and move their followers to action. They proactively seize the initiative to improve organizational effectiveness in the long term. Commitment 5 is: leaders find innovative ways to bring change about. They create meaningful challenges for their followers and invite them to seek ways to make changes effectively. Leaders experiment and take risks, creating small wins that generate enthusiasm and support among followers. Individual initiative is rewarded, not punished, because mistakes are viewed as learning experiences that will help move the organization forward (Commitment 6).

Leaders enable others to collaborate and act through these practices. Collaboration is fostered by creating a climate of trust in the organization and the ability and competence of its personnel (Bratton & Tumin, 2012). They enable their employees by trusting their ability to complete assigned tasks successfully. Such leaders are servants of the organization who assume their roles and responsibilities to meet the needs of others—not through seeking power and status. They encourage their officers to seize the initiative and feel the need to do so. In Commitment 7, leaders build collaboration by promoting cooperative goals and building trust. By sharing their power with their employees, leaders increase their own. They train and mentor their employees so they can solve problems and implement solutions, thus inspiring confidence and building competence. Due to these actions, employees make ready to assume responsibility for their actions and performance. Leaders strengthen followers in this fashion, sharing power and discretion with followers (Commitment 8).

Leaders encourage the hearts of followers by recognizing and celebrating their accomplishments. They promote high standards and hold followers accountable for their performance. Recognition is personalized when individual performance is commendable and outstanding. Rewards are creatively constructed, personalized, and recognized in a public setting. Commitment 9 finds leaders recognizing contributions by showing appreciation for individual excellence. Celebrating successful performance reaffirms values and creates a community spirit within the organization (Commitment 10).

Kouzes and Posner (2012) assertively conclude that leadership is a skill that can be learned through the study of these practices and commitments. They have been demonstrated in the past by effective leaders. Leaders who learn and practice them can make a positive difference in their organization, its members, and its clients. The Leadership Challenge Model is a construct that reflects the ideals and practices of transformational leadership (Carless, 2001). Transformational leaders make organizations more effective and successful by defining the values that embrace the enduring principles of a people. Transforming values lie at the heart of transformational leadership (Burns, 2008, p. 307).

Fischer's interviews with police chiefs document evidence of the Five Practices of the Leadership Challenge Model in policing. Under "model the way," Fischer's respondents advised new chiefs to keep in mind that actions speak louder than words when trying to gain their officers' confidence (Fischer, 2009, p. 46). Chiefs must be open, honest, transparent, sincere, and have a strong work ethic. They should be accountable and acknowledge the mistakes they make. "The measure of the character of a police chief is the ability to exercise constraint in the use of the awesome power we have" (Fischer, 2009, p. 18).

Transparency means being honest and open about good and bad news in the police department. Accessibility means having mechanisms in place to ensure that reporters can get answers to their questions in a timely way (Fischer, 2009, p. 97). Particularly, these chiefs value "Management by Walking Around" (MBWA): "You have to get off your butt, get out of your office, ride the streets, go to meetings, and see for yourself what the situation is. This helps you identify problems before they occur" (Fischer, 2009, p. 84).

When "inspiring a shared vision," Fischer's police chiefs noted that it is likely to be popular—who would object to visionary goals, such as making a city safer and providing a responsive, committed police department? But the decisions a chief makes to *achieve* a vision can be controversial. Doing the right thing requires making difficult decisions that may be unpopular with politicians, the rank and file, or the public (Fischer, 2009, p. 6). It is important that a good leader makes it clear what their vision is and attracts those who believe in that vision to the leadership team (Fischer, 2009, p. 37). The chiefs also felt it was their job to sell their vision to their bosses. They advised that getting your bosses to buy into your vision for the department *before* you take the job is a key determinant in how you will fare as chief, and failing to get "buying in" should be a deal-breaker when you are considering a job as chief (Fischer, 2009, p. 80).

When "challenging the process," the chiefs remind us they are expected to be change agents. The test for a chief is to understand what changes to make, how much change is needed, and how much the department and elected officials can tolerate (Fischer, 2009, p. 5). They stressed the limited term of a police chief as cause for action: "You know the chief's job is not going to last forever. You must be up for that kind of challenge. If survival is an issue, you shouldn't be chief. If you can't take the risks, get out of the business" (Fischer, 2009, p. 22). Be tough, confident, and decisive in your role as a change agent. Get moving on your plans for change early in your administration, when the department and the community expect changes to happen (Fischer, 2009, p. 120).

"Enable others to act" is concerned with the empowerment of subordinates. Most chiefs said they were "consensus builders" and followed a democratic approach to leading their departments (Fischer, 2009, p. 10). "The real work is done by the young men and women who drive the radio cars, answer the phone, and talk to the public. Our job is to make their job possible. It's not about you; it's about the officers who do the real work" (Fischer, 2009, p. 13). The strategy for your vision "can't work unless the troops on the street do it" (Fischer, 2009, p. 39). "You can make mistakes here, but you can't lie, and you can't be dishonest. It's a tough job, but I want you to succeed, and you wouldn't be here if I didn't think you could succeed" (Fischer, 2009, p. 43). Chiefs are obligated to consult with and empower their command staff; give the staff members opportunities to show what they can do; and help them develop their leadership skills (Fischer, 2009, p. 51). "The chief needs to defend the department and its officers when they come under unwarranted criticism from elected officials. It sends the other elected officials a message that the chief is not afraid to strike back" (Fischer, 2009, pp. 79–80).

Finally, these chiefs acknowledged the significance of "encouraging the hearts" of subordinates. "A chief's focus should always be to make folks as good as they can be and then recognize them for their accomplishments" (Fischer, 2009, p. 24). "If you wanted everyone to like you, you should have been a circus clown, not a police supervisor. The job is about business" (Fischer, 2009, p. 35). Succession planning must include the encouragement of subordinates to undertake and complete difficult assignments. They are the future of the department.

Servant Leadership

Servant leaders provide direction, encourage participation, and sponsor mutual respect between leaders and followers while fostering their independence (Gardner & Reece,

2012). This treatment leads to the achievement of high-quality organizational results. Servant leaders put the needs of their followers before and above their concerns. They practice an ethical form of leadership that does not take advantage of followers. Jesus Christ was the first teacher of the concept of servant leadership. He set the example by washing his disciples' feet and taught that a leader's greatness is measured by a total commitment to serving fellow human beings (Sendjaya & Sarros, 2002, p. 59).

There are several distinct attributes attributed to servant leadership. For example, Greenleaf (1977) believed leaders should serve their followers and focus on satisfying their needs. Servant leaders are less concerned with their power and devoted to leadership by providing service to others. Servant leaders put the needs of their followers above their own. It is an ethical style of leadership. The organization's purpose is the welfare of its members, not to gratify the ego or reputation of the leader. The servant leader would never take advantage of followers.

Servant leadership has five basic principles:

1. *Concern for people.*
2. *Stewardship of the organization.*
3. *Equity (or justice).*
4. *Indebtedness* (the Rights of Followers), including the right to: be needed and involved, a covenantal relationship, to understand (the organization and its goals and objectives), affect one's destiny, be held accountable for performance, appeal decisions, and commit to the organization.
5. *Self-understanding (or awareness)*: creating an ethical climate for others by questioning the motives of organizational leaders and members.

One of the most crucial attributes of servant leaders is *agape'* —an unconditional love of others without regard for their due or desert. It is a love of behavior and choice, not a romantic feeling. The servant leader demonstrates it through the following attributes:

*   *Patience*: exercising self-control.
*   *Kindness*: giving attention, appreciation, and encouragement.
*   *Humility*: authentic feelings without pretense or arrogance.
*   *Respectfulness*: treating others as important.
*   *Selflessness*: meeting the needs of others.
*   *Forgiveness*: forgoing resentment when wronged.
*   *Honesty*: freedom from resentment of others.
*   *Commitment*: sticking to your choices and honoring your agreements.

(Hunter, 1998, p. 100)

As a result, the servant leader sets aside their wants and needs and seeks the greatest good for others (see also Russell & Stone, 2002, pp. 145–147; Spears, 2002, pp. 27–29). The servant leader is committed to the organization's growth and works to build community within them. In their research on police managers' attitudes toward leadership styles, Vito, Suresh, and Richards (2011) found that police managers attending the Administrative Officers Course at the University of Louisville's Southern Police Institute identified a marked preference for the principles of servant leadership. A study in a small Southwestern police department in the U.S. found that officers preferred the servant leadership style, because it provided opportunities for personal growth, commitment to the mental and physical health of officers, and built a culture of belonging (Russell, Broome, & Russell, 2018, pp. 86–87).

Advice from the Dalai Lama

In his book, *The Leader's Way*, the Dalai Lama (2009) offers examples of servant leadership that are especially relevant to police leadership. His advice on decision-making is pertinent to policing, where the use of deadly force is an issue. For every decision, the leader's goal is to consider the interests of the organization and all of the people affected by it. The benchmark for the decision is that it must cause no harm to others or, if harm is inevitable, reduce the harm as much as possible. Leaders should question their motives and recognize how their actions can affect others—both within and outside the organization. They should serve the needs of the entire organization and individual workers.

The Dalai Lama lists three stages of the decision-making process. First, make your initial decision and check whether there is harm to anyone, and if there is none, proceed. If harm is present, apply your creativity to find another solution that eliminates the harm. If the harm is impossible to avoid, make certain that it is justified, because it avoids a much greater harm or results in huge benefits to other people.

The Dalai Lama (2009, pp. 37–41) also lists "The Six Perfections" that mirror the attributes of servant leaders.

1. *Generosity*: A good leader is generous in giving credit where it is due.
2. *Ethical discipline*: Leaders must withstand temptation—greed, self-centeredness, lust, anger, hatred, fear, lack of self-confidence.
3. *Patience*: Must be cultivated. It allows the leader to deal with provocative circumstances (hostility, criticism, or disappointment) and improves judgment.
4. *Enthusiastic effort*: Displays your belief in the importance of the goals and motivation to achieve them.
5. *Concentration*: The ability to focus mental energy on one issue.
6. *Wisdom*: The ability to see things as they are.

Cultivating the Six Perfections can reap several benefits for the servant leader. They increase the ability to deal with a crisis. They improve decision-making and executing decisions. Other advantages are improved relationships with followers, heightened creativity, and increased enthusiasm for the job. Yet, the main theme is that the leader is a servant whose main concern is the welfare of others.

Good to Great

In *Good to Great*, Jim Collins (2001) led a team of researchers to examine 11 large companies that were particularly successful over a 15-year period.[1] Collins (2005) also showed how these ideas could apply to the public sector in a second monograph—*Good to Great and the Social Sectors*. The Police Executive Research Forum showed how Collins's business model applied to police management in a monograph—*"Good to Great" Policing: Application of Business Management Principles in the Public Sector* (Wexler, Wycoff, & Fischer, 2007).

One major finding was that charismatic and transformational leaders were not the norm in the rise of these companies. Instead, they were led by people who knew the business and rose from the ranks. They were characterized as "Level 5" leaders—executives who built greatness that endured, blending personal humility with professional will. Specifically, Level 5 leaders were quiet, reserved, shy, gracious, mild-mannered, and understanding. Their attributes revealed that:

- They were ambitious, but they put the needs of the organization first.
- They were modest, self-effacing, and understated in their style.
- They were driven by the need to produce sustainable results.
- They were concerned about the organization's future and set up successors for effectiveness.

(Collins, 2001, pp. 30–31)

While they were exceptionally modest, Level 5 leaders were determined to do what was necessary to make the organization great. They were disinterested in setting themselves up as heroes. Typically, they were ordinary individuals who let their company's results speak for themselves. In the PERF monograph, Level 5 leaders in policing believed in maintaining a "command presence" during a "defining moment"—a crisis where the police chief must speak to the public to maintain credibility with both the community and members of the department (Wexler et al., 2007, p. 17). Level 5 leaders exhibited the attributes of servant leadership.

Level 5 leaders used the "Window and the Mirror" to achieve results. They maintained humility in times of success, attributing it to good fortune or factors outside their control. Yet they took direct responsibility for failure, taking stock of problems by looking within the organization. Leaders succeed by attracting and keeping the right employees by following three practical rules:

1. When in doubt, do not hire—keep looking. You need the right people to implement change.
2. Act on the need to change personnel. The best people need guidance, not management. They are self-motivated and are driven to produce the best results.
3. Put your best people to work on the biggest opportunities, not the biggest problems. Opportunities allow people to become great.

(Collins, 2001, pp. 33–35)

Here, Collins uses the analogy of "getting the right people on the bus." The executives who ignited these transformations focused on getting the right personnel. The *Good to Great* leaders assembled their teams before deciding where the company should go. The PERF monograph recognized that this principle would be difficult to apply in policing, because almost all of the personnel are inherited by the chief upon assumption of the office (Wexler et al., 2007, p. 20).

Truth telling is a major component of the *Good to Great* process. The Level 5 leader is particularly adept at "confronting the brutal facts"—any bad news (hazards) facing the organization (Collins, 2001, pp. 65–69). A primary task in taking a company from good to great is to create a culture wherein people have a tremendous opportunity to be heard. "Red flag" mechanisms and other tools are present that highlight information too risky to be ignored. This leader takes care to tackle challenges without losing faith in the ability of the organization to overcome them. Here, the PERF monograph called attention to the CompStat process and problem-oriented policing (see Chapter 13) as examples of using data to confront the brutal facts in policing (Wexler et al., 2007, pp. 32–33).

The *Good to Great* companies were adept at determining just what they could be the best in the world at—what Collins termed "The Hedgehog Concept." Leaders must help organizations reflect on the following:

1. What the organization is passionate about. They did only those things that ignited the passion of organizational members, thus eliminating the need for motivation.

2. What the organization can be best in the world at. This recognition enables the organization to maintain a laser-like focus on its core competencies and reason for being.

3. What drives the organization's economic engine? What element is crucial to maintaining economic efficiency?

(Collins, 2001, pp. 94–97)

The Hedgehog Concept simplifies the organization's mission and provides a unifying principle to guide operations. The focus on crime reduction was identified as an example of this principle at work in police administration (Wexler et al., 2007, pp. 36–37).

The *Good to Great* companies had a "culture of discipline" (Collins, 2001, p. 124). The focus on implementing the Hedgehog Concept enabled employees to be diligent and intense in their thoughts and actions. Employees exercise self-discipline. They had greater freedom and responsibility to do their jobs. They were fanatical in the pursuit of excellence and greatness. Therefore, bureaucratic rules and authoritarian leadership for control were unnecessary. Again, the PERF monograph urged police leaders to "take a long, hard look at the facts about the organization, and then act on those facts" (Wexler et al., 2007, p. 39).

Technological fixes were not essential to the rise of these companies. They were not the key to success. The lesson is that leaders should not seize on every technological fad out of fear of being left behind. Avoid the tendency to overreact in such a fashion. Rather, they should use technology selectively to speed up the existing momentum, which is consistent with the Hedgehog Concept (Collins, 2001, pp. 152–153). In the PERF monograph, a new data management tool in the Chicago Police Department (Citizen Law Enforcement Analysis and Reporting—CLEAR) exemplifies how technology can speed change (Wexler et al., 2007, p. 41).

Organizations should avoid the trap of the "Flywheel and Doom Loop" (Collins, 2001, pp. 174–180). There was no single defining action, no grand program, no one killer innovation, no solitary lucky break, and no wrenching revolution or miracle that led to dramatic success. The *Good to Great* companies shunned the "Doom Loop"—the inconsistent and failed efforts resulting from chronic restructuring and management fads. Sustained momentum toward success was not the result of following an easy road. The PERF monograph described how crises in police agencies can become major catalysts for "widespread organizational change." Such change occurred in New Orleans in the mid-1990s when Chief Richard Pennington confronted severe and widespread corruption, implemented significant changes, and established problem-oriented policing and CompStat programs (Wexler et al., 2007, p. 45).

Finally, the *Good to Great* companies aimed high in their goals. They set "big, hairy, and audacious goals" (BHAGs). Their leaders exercised strategic thinking, setting extensive, comprehensive goals, and were able to sustain long-term success for their organizations. BHAGs were clear, simple, and united to the organization's core values (Collins, 2001, p. 203). In policing, Collins cited William Bratton's management of the New York City Police Department as an example of this concept—setting "audacious output goals, such as attaining double-digit annual declines in felony crime rates" via the CompStat process (Collins, 2005, p. 4). The PERF monograph noted that, in public sector organizations, "achieving greatness often is about 'overcoming obstacles'" (like the constraints imposed by budgets and labor agreements) (Wexler et al., 2007, p. 51). The inclusive methods used by the "*Good to Great*" companies, as identified by Collins, and the attributes of methods practiced by Level 5 leaders, support the premises of servant leadership.

Selecting a Leadership Style

The selection of a leadership style is affected by several factors. Tannenbaum and Schmidt (1958) developed a leadership continuum comprising seven different leadership styles, ranging from the full use of leadership authority to the allowance of complete freedom to subordinates to determine tasks and goals to follow. Under the first "autocratic" style, the leader makes a decision and announces it. In policing, this style is most appropriate when the leader wishes to maintain operational control, such as in an emergency (Walsh, 1983). With the second style, the leader takes the additional step of "selling" the decision (such as a new organizational policy) to subordinates with minimal involvement.

In the middle of their continuum, Tannenbaum and Schmidt (1958) cover the participative approach to leadership. The leader acts after getting suggestions and advice from followers. The leader still makes the final decision made in consultation with the staff. This interactive process builds trust, providing that the leader informs subordinates of the reasons behind the decision and provides feedback on whether their input was utilized. If not, this style may be viewed as manipulation. Collaboration is another step toward the empowerment of subordinates. The leader maintains control over the decision-making process by defining the limits of the situation and asking the group to make the final decision. Thus, the consultative process does not give complete control to the group. The leader still is the decisive factor.

A participatory style is more likely when the leader requires a qualified subordinate with valuable knowledge and skills. For example, a police supervisor may seek the advice of line officers before establishing a new patrol method in their area (Walsh, 1983). The recognition they know their beat and the resulting consultation by the supervision is a morale builder. Such inclusion leads to support for the policy they helped to establish. Other beneficial attributes include sharing responsibility, developing mutual trust, personal commitment, and developing the potential of subordinates. However, a participatory style requires mature subordinates and a leader willing to be candid with followers.

The selection of a style is affected by three forces: (1) within the leader; (2) within the group; and (3) within the situation. The forces in the leader include their value system and their confidence level in their subordinates. What are their leadership inclinations? Someone who feels they are the "Boss" is unlikely to engage in democratic leadership. What is their tolerance for ambiguity? Are you comfortable turning decision-making power over to subordinates when unsure of their decision? Overruling a democratic decision-making process after you permit to use it will have disastrous consequences.

The forces in the subordinates also help determine what type of style is in order. Participatory, democratic leadership is more likely when subordinates are independent, ready to assume responsibility for decision-making, have their own "tolerance for ambiguity," are interested in the problem faced, have a high level of knowledge and experience, and expect to be consulted and involved in decision-making.

The forces in the situation contribute to the selection of a leadership style in several ways. First, what is the type of organization under consideration? Police departments have typically been dominated by a "command and control" style that is not conducive to participatory leadership. In addition, what is the level of effectiveness of the group? A task force of experienced officers is more likely to be consulted than a group of newcomers to patrol. What is the nature of the problem itself and its level of complexity? Leaders seek help with complex problems. Subordinates are not interested in providing input to simple management decisions that do not affect their work life. Finally, the pressure of time itself is a crucial consideration. A consultation takes time. If a quick decision is required, the leader may not be able to seek time-rich consultation.

Tannenbaum and Schmidt (1958) conclude with the recognition that participatory, democratic leadership is a function of these factors and forces. It is not a matter of being strong or permissive, but of insight and flexibility. The successful leader knows the forces that are most relevant to decision-making. They know and understand the competency and commitment of their people. They are ready to call upon the talents of their subordinates and sponsor their growth and development. They are flexible and analyze the situation to determine the most appropriate style. If direction is in order, it is provided. If participatory management is called for, they can provide it.

Situational Leadership

Another variation on this question is by Hersey and Blanchard (1977) in their development of **situational leadership**. They describe leadership as composed of both a directive and a supportive dimension that should be applied appropriately in a given situation. The leader must evaluate subordinates and assess their competence and commitment to perform a task to determine an appropriate style. Leaders then adapt their style accordingly between directive or supportive methods to meet the changing needs of their subordinates. Leaders engage in directive behaviors by setting goals, establishing evaluation methods, setting time lines, defining roles, and showing how to meet goals. Supportive behaviors help subordinates feel comfortable about themselves, their colleagues, and their situation.

These methods are also presented along a continuum that parallels that provided by Tannenbaum and Schmidt that depends upon the talents and readiness of the followers along with the situation. Directing involves providing specific instructions and close supervision by the leader to achieve organizational goals. In the coaching mode, the leader explains their decision while providing the opportunity for questions about it to clarify meaning and purpose. Taking part gives subordinates control over decision-making, while the leader remains available to facilitate problem-solving. In delegation, the leader turns decision-making over to subordinates to implement the solution and take responsibility to achieve it.

The abilities, willingness, and readiness of followers are also determining factors in selecting a leadership style. Followers at Level 1 of readiness cannot engage in decision-making. Often, they are new to the work and inexperienced. Level 2 followers have gained confidence but lost some initial motivation for the work. At Level 3, followers have developed the skills to do the job but are uncertain and lack the confidence to do it independently. Level 4 followers are fully developed, committed, and motivated to complete work successfully. Leaders must adapt their style to these levels to be effective.

Again, this theory illustrates that leaders cannot use the same style in all situations. Their choice is constrained by their subordinates' competence level and experience and the situation they face. Therefore, leaders must be flexible in choosing and adopting their leadership style. No style is always relevant to meet the situation and the level of competence of both the leader and the followers.

Bad Leadership

Development of leadership ability can also benefit from negative examples—the mistakes that leaders make in temperament and execution. Kellerman (2004) offers seven ideal types of bad leadership. The first three are bad because they are ineffective, while the last four are examples of unethical behavior.

The first ineffective behavior is incompetent leadership. The leader lacks the will or skill to be effective and fails to create positive change. Some leaders fail due to the absence of practical, academic, or emotional intelligence. Instead, ineffective leaders are often careless, dense, distracted, and lazy, or they cannot deal with uncertainty and stress—unable to communicate, educate, or delegate.

The second category of ineffective leadership is rigid leadership. Here the problem is that the leader is stiff and unyielding. Although they may be competent, they are unable or unwilling to adapt to new ideas, new information, or changing times. They are "wooden-headed" and will not be moved by facts or logic.

Intemperate leadership is the third form of ineffectiveness. Here, the leader lacks self-control and is aided and abetted by followers unwilling or unable to intervene. Intemperate leaders fail to control their impulses and fall victim to lust and drug or alcohol abuse.

Their ethical lapses characterize the second group of ideal bad leadership types. The callous leader is uncaring or unkind. The needs, wants, and wishes of subordinates are ignored or discounted. Corrupt leadership is characterized by lying, cheating, or stealing and is typically motivated by power and greed. Unlike servant leaders, they put their self-interest ahead of the public interest. It features bribery, selling of favors, embezzlement, cutting corners, bending the rules, and breaking the law.

The insular leader minimizes or disregards the health and welfare of the organization's followers and persons. They ignore the needs of both groups. Evil leadership commits atrocities. Such leaders use pain as an instrument of power and commit acts of severe harm—physical, psychological, or both. Their intent is not only to terrorize but to prolong suffering.

Schafer's (2010b) analysis of police managers attending the FBI National Academy also identified the attributes of ineffective police leaders. They listed five acts of commission (conscious errors in leadership): (1) focus on self over others ("careerism"); (2) ego/arrogance; (3) closed-mindedness; (4) micromanagement (emphasizing autocratic control); and (5) capriciousness. They also recognized five acts of omission (failing to take appropriate leadership actions): (1) poor work ethic (loss of enthusiasm for and commitment to the job); (2) failure to act (due to fear of the consequences of their decision); (3) ineffective communication (inability to engage in a two-way dialogue with subordinates, refusal to explain key decisions, failure to accept input and criticism); (4) lack of interpersonal skills (failure to establish human relationships with members of the department and the community); and (5) lack of integrity (past actions that led to the loss of trust and respect). Thus, bad leaders showed behaviors that undermined the followers' sense of trust, legitimacy, and confidence.

Schafer (2010a) raised the interesting question that policing may be responsible for creating ineffective leaders due to the constraints upon the organization and failure to develop and sponsor true leaders. The five largest commissions charged with investigating and solving problems in American policing from 1931 to 1973 noted the lack of strong leadership and effective administrative practices as contributing factors tied to corruption, abuse of authority, use of force, police crimes, and civil rights violations (Schafer, 2009, p. 239).

Conclusion

This review of leadership theories and research findings documents the promise and productivity of forms of democratic leadership. Autocratic leadership is ineffective and harmful to subordinates. The transformational and servant leadership styles are the wave of the future. The needs and wishes of subordinates must be met, and their inclusion must be ensured to achieve organizational change.

In two literature reviews, the research on police leadership listed the following attributes of police leaders (Pearson-Goff & Herrington, 2014, pp. 17–18; Coelho de Moura, Borges, Morgado, & Ramalho, 2022, pp. 4–6):

1. Authoritative: the leader supervises and creates a positive climate based on communication and empathy.
2. Ethics: a sense of integrity and honesty.
3. Trust: generating a sense of trustworthiness among subordinates and community members.
4. Legitimacy: the need for leaders to be seen as "good coppers" so that the leader can pound a beat and do the job of a front-line officer.
5. Model the way: understanding their responsibility as role models to motivate and inspire subordinates and promote group cohesion.
6. Communication: at all department levels, with the community, in government. It is also crucial to provide informative feedback to subordinates and actively listen to what people say.
7. Effective decision-making: make decisions that lead to goal achievement. Involving subordinates in decision-making by articulating goals.
8. Investigative skill: basing decisions on facts and evidence, facilitating the ability to foresee critical threats to the organization and its community.
9. Effective thinking ability: critical, strategic, and creative. Balancing past and current knowledge.
10. Resilience: the ability to recover and overcome adversity.

These reviews also revealed that police leaders engaged in the following activities:

- **Create a shared vision**: creating a sense of purpose for followers.
- **Engendering organizational commitment**: supporting subordinates, promoting collaboration, and giving subordinates a voice in decision-making.
- **Care for subordinates**: seek and provide opportunities for staff, take responsibility for their well-being, coaching, and mentoring. Possessing emotional intelligence.
- **Driving and managing change**: managing the status quo while enacting change or reform.
- **Problem-solving**: proactive and collaborative to address interdependent and unforeseen, and complex issues.

In their reviews, these authors also note that leadership responsibilities differ across organizational levels. Executive-level leaders should focus on decision-making and strategic thinking while emphasizing ethical practices and fostering cooperation in the organization and with external forces. They must also create action plans while promoting and managing change. Middle managers should be concerned with the well-being of subordinates. These leadership competencies are based on officer perceptions rather than objective measures of police leadership performance.

A veteran police administrator and scholar, Robert Wasserman, has admonished police leaders to keep in touch with the lives of their subordinates, both on and off the job. They should be sought out—listen to what they say and think about their situation. Leaders must keep in touch with the needs of a changing workforce to understand their world and how they view it. Here, empathy will facilitate communication.

Wasserman also cautions police leaders (especially Chiefs and Sheriffs) to be aware and mindful of their political environment. When entering the job, they should be thoughtful and careful—"listen and learn." They should consider the "Issues of Complexity": race, homeland security, use of force, crime control strategy, ethics, public opinion, media, technology, and labor. They attempt to recognize and identify which issues will have "legs" and get out in front of certain key issues.

This advice and the leadership lessons provided in this chapter should help police leaders to be more effective. The autocratic "command and control" methods of the past are not relevant to all aspects of police administration. Followers need to be empowered, and a more inclusive style is necessary to practice strategic policing.

KEY TERMS

Achievement-oriented leadership
Autocratic leadership
Bureaucratic leadership
Cognitive hurdle
Democratic leadership

Directive leadership
Leadership Challenge Model
Motivational hurdle
Participatory leadership
Political hurdle

Resource hurdle
Servant leadership
Situational leadership
Supportive leadership
Tipping point leadership
Transformational leadership

Note

1. The 11 *Good to Great* companies were Abbott, Fannie Mae, Kimberly Clark, Nucor, Pitney Bowes, Wells Fargo, Circuit City, Gillette, Kroger, Phillip Morris, and Walgreens.

References

Andreescu, V., & Vito, G.F. (2010). An exploratory study on ideal leadership behaviour: The opinions of American police managers. *International Journal of Police Science and Management, 12*(4), 567–583.

Archambeault, W., & Weirman, C. (1983). Critically assessing the utility of police bureaucracies in the 1980s. *Journal of Police Science and Administration, 11,* 420–429.

Baker, T. (2006). *Effective police leadership: Moving beyond management.* Flushing, NY: Looseleaf Law Publications.

Bao, Y., & Ge, L. (2019). Linking transformational leadership and value congruence among Chinese police force: The mediating role of public service motivation. *Australian Journal of Public Administration, 78*(3), 373–395.

Bass, B., & Riggio, R. (2006). *Transformational leadership.* Mahwah, NJ: Lawrence Erlbaum Associates, Publishers.

Batts, A., Smoot, S., & Scrivner, E. (2006, July). Police leadership challenges in a changing world. *New Perspectives in Policing Bulletin.* Washington, DC: U.S. Department of Justice, National Institute of Justice.

Brandebo, M. (2020). Destructive leadership in crisis management. *Leadership & Organization Development Journal, 41*(4), 567–580.

Bratton, W. (1998). *Turnaround: How America's top cop reversed the crime epidemic.* New York: Random House.

Bratton, W., & Tumin, Z. (2012). *Collaborate or perish! Reaching across boundaries in a networked world.* New York, NY: Random House.

Brunetto, Y., Teo, S., Shacklock, K., Farr-Wharton, R., & Shriberg, A. (2017). The impact of supervisor–subordinate relationships and a trainee characteristic upon police officer work outcomes. *Journal of Management & Organization, 23*(3), 423–436.

Bruns, G., & Shuman, I. (1988). Police managers' perceptions of organizational leadership styles. *Public Personnel Management, 17*(2), 145–157.

Burns, J.M. (1978). *Leadership.* Mahwah, NJ: Lawrence Erlbaum.

Burns, J.M. (2008). The power and creativity of a transforming vision. In J. Gallos (Ed.), *Business leadership* (pp. 305–311). San Francisco, CA: Jossey-Bass.

Carless, S.A. (2001). Assessing the discriminant validity of the leadership practices inventory. *Journal of Occupational and Organizational Psychology, 74,* 233–239.

Cockcroft, T. (2014). Police culture and transformational leadership: Outlining the contours of a troubled relationship. *Policing, 8*(1), 5–13.

Coelho de Moura, R., Borges, A., Morgado, S., & Ramalho, N. (2022). Police leadership 2.0: A comprehensive systematic review of the literature. *Policing, 17*(1), 1–11.

Collins, J. (2001). *Good to great.* New York, NY: HarperCollins Books.

Collins, J. (2005). *Good to great and the social sectors.* New York, NY: HarperCollins Books.

Dalai Lama (2009). *The leader's way.* New York, NY: Broadway Books.

Densten, I. (2003). Senior police leadership: Does rank matter? *Policing, 26,* 400–418.

Dobby, J., Anscombe, J., & Tuffin, R. (2004). *Police leadership: Expectations and impact.* London: The Home Office.

Fischer, C. (2009). *Leadership matters: Police chiefs talk about their careers.* Washington, DC: Police Executive.

Gardner, B., & Reece, J. (2012, June). Revolutionizing policing through servant-leadership and quality management. *FBI Law Enforcement Bulletin,* 25–32.

Girodo, M. (1998). Machiavellian, bureaucratic, and transformational leadership styles in police managers: Preliminary findings of interpersonal ethics. *Perceptual and Motor Skills, 86,* 419–427.

Gladwell, M. (2006). *The tipping point: How little things can make a big difference.* New York, NY: Little, Brown.

Greenleaf, R.K. (1977). *Servant leadership.* Mahwah, NJ: Paulist Press.

Haberfeld, M. (2006). *Police leadership.* Upper Saddle River, NJ: Pearson/Prentice Hall.

Herrington, V., & Schafer, J.A. (2019). Preparing individuals for leadership in Australasia, the United States, and the UK. *Police Practise and Research, 20*(3), 240–258.

Hersey, P., & Blanchard, K. (1977). *Management of organizational behavior.* Englewood Cliffs, NJ: Prentice Hall.

Hess, J.D., & Bacigalupo, A.C. (2011). Enhancing decisions and decision-making processes through the application of emotional intelligence skills. *Management Decision, 49*(5), 710–721.

Hunter, J. (1998). *The servant*. New York, NY: Crown Books.

Hunter, R., & Barker, T. (1993). BS and buzzwords: The new police organizational style. *American Journal of Police, 12*, 157–168.

Isenberg, J. (2010). *Police leadership in a democracy: Conversations with America's police chiefs*. Boca Raton, FL: CRC Press.

Jaafar, S., Zambi, N., & Fathil, N. (2021). Leadership style: Is it autocratic, democratic, or laissez-faire? *ASEAN Journal of Management Studies, 3*(1), 1–7.

Kellerman, B. (2004). Thinking about leadership: Warts and all. *Harvard Business Review, 82*(1), 40–45.

Kelling, G. L., & Moore, M.H. (1989). The evolving strategy of policing. *Perspectives on policing, 4*, 1–14.

Kessler, D. (1993). Integrating calls for service with community and problem oriented policing: A case study. *Crime & Delinquency, 39*, 485–508.

Khan, Z., Nawaz, A., & Khan, I. (2016). Leadership theories and styles: A literature review. *Journal of Resources Development and Management, 16*, 1–7.

Kim, W., & Mauborgne, R. (2003, April). Tipping point leadership. *Harvard Business Review*, 60–69.

Kouzes, J., & Posner, B. (2012). *The leadership challenge*. San Francisco, CA: Jossey-Bass.

Krimmel, J., & Lindemuth, P. (2001). Police chief performance and leadership styles. *Police Quarterly, 4*, 469–483.

Kuykendall, J., & Unsinger, P. (1982). The leadership styles of police managers. *Journal of Criminal Justice, 10*(4), 311–321.

Masal, D. (2015). Shared and transformational leadership in the police. *Policing, 38*(1), 40–55.

Mayo, L. (1985). Leading blindly: An assessment of chiefs' information about police operations. In W. Geller (Ed.), *Police leadership in America* (pp. 397–417). New York, NY: Praeger.

Mazerolle, L., Darroch, S., & White, G. (2013). Leadership in problem-oriented policing. *Policing, 36*(3), 543–560.

Moore, M.H., & Trojanowicz, R. (1988). *Perspectives on policing—Corporate strategies for policing*. Washington, DC: National Institute of Justice.

Murphy, S.A. (2008). The role of emotions and transformational leadership on police culture: An autoethnographic account. *International Journal of Police Science & Management, 10*(2), 165–178.

Murphy, S., & Drodge, E. (2004). The four I's of police leadership: A case study heuristic. *International Journal of Police Science and Management, 6*(1), 1–15.

Niederhoffer, A. (1969). *Behind the shield: The police in urban society*. New York, NY: Anchor.

Northouse, P. (2012). *Introduction to leadership: Concepts and practice*. Thousand Oaks, CA: Sage.

Osborne, D., & Gaebler, T. (1993). *Reinventing government*. New York, NY: Plume.

Osborne, D., & Plastrik, P. (1997). *Banishing bureaucracy: The five strategies for reinventing government*. New York, NY: Addison-Wesley.

Pearson-Goff, M., & Herrington, V. (2014). Police leadership: A systematic review of the literature. *Policing, 8*(1), 14–26.

Reese, R. (2005). *Leadership in the LAPD*. Durham, NC: Carolina Academic Press.

Ruess-Ianni, E. (1993). *Two cultures of policing: Street cops and management cops*. New Brunswick, NJ: Transaction Publishers.

Rowe, M. (2006). Following the leader: Frontline narratives on police leadership. *Policing, 29,* 757–767.

Russell, F., Broome, R., & Russell, J. (2018). Servant leadership and the wellbeing of police officers: A case study. *Servant Leadership: Theory & Practice, 5*(2), 73–92.

Russell, R., & Stone, A. (2002). A review of servant leadership attributes: Developing a practical model. *Leadership & Organizational Development, 23*(3), 145–157.

Sarver, M., & Miller, H. (2014). Police chief leadership: Styles and effectiveness. *Policing, 37*(1), 126–143.

Schafer, J.A. (2009). Developing effective leadership in policing: Perils, pitfalls and paths forward. *Policing, 32*(2), 238–260.

Schafer, J.A. (2010a). Effective leaders and leadership in policing: Traits, assessment, development, and expansion. *Policing, 33*(4), 644–663.

Schafer, J. (2010b). The ineffective police leader: Acts of commission and omission. *Journal of Criminal Justice, 38,* 737–746.

Schafer, J.A. (2013). *Effective leadership in policing: Successful habits and traits.* Durham, NC: Carolina Academic Press.

Sendjaya, S., & Saros, J. (2002). Servant leadership: Its origin, development, and application in organizations. *Journal of Leadership & Organizational Studies, 9,* 57–64.

Silvestri, M. (2007). "Doing" police leadership: Enter the "new smart macho." *Policing and Society: An International Journal of Research and Policy, 17*(1), 38–58.

Skogstad, A., Einarsen, S., Torsheim, T., Aasland, M., & Hetland, H. (2007). The destructiveness of laissez-faire leadership behavior. *Journal of Occupational Health Psychology, 12*(1), 80–92.

Spears, L. (2002). Character and servant leadership: Ten characteristics of effective, caring leaders. *Journal of Virtues and Leadership, 1*(1), 25–30.

Stamper, N.H. (1992). *Removing management barriers to effective police leadership: A study of executive leadership and executive management in big-city police departments.* Washington, DC: Police Executive Research Forum.

Steinheider, B., & Wuestewald, T. (2008). From the bottom-up: Sharing leadership in a police agency. *Police Practice and Research, 9*(2), 145–163.

Swid, A. (2014). Police members' perception of their leader's leadership style and its implications. *Policing, 37*(3), 579–595.

Tannenbaum, R., & Schmidt, W. (1958). How to choose a leadership pattern. *Harvard Business Review,* 1–12.

Toch, H., & Grant, J. (1982). *Reforming human services: Change through participation.* Beverly Hills, CA: Sage.

Villiers, P. (2003). Philosophy, doctrine, and leadership: Some core beliefs. In R. Adlam, & P. Villiers (Ed.), *Police leadership in the twenty-first century: Philosophy, doctrine and developments* (pp. 15–33). Winchester, UK: Waterside Press.

Vito, G., Suresh, G., & Richards, G. (2011). Emphasizing the servant in public service: The opinions of police managers. *Policing, 34*(4), 674–686.

Walsh, W.F. (1983, November). Leadership: A police perspective. *The Police Chief,* 26–29.

Wexler, C., Wycoff, M.A., & Fischer, C. (2007). *"Good to Great" policing: Application of business management principles in the public sector.* Washington, DC: U.S. Department of Justice Office of Community Oriented Policing Services and Police Executive Research Forum.

Willis, J., Mastrofski, S., Weisburd, D., & Greenspan, R. (2003). *CompStat and organizational change in the Lowell police department.* Washington, DC: The Police Foundation.

Wuestewald, T., & Steinheider, B. (2012). Police managerial perceptions of organizational democracy: A matter of style and substance. *Police Practice and Research, 13*(1), 44–58.

4 Setting Strategic Direction

Learning Objectives

1. Identify the activities associated with setting organizational strategic direction.

2. Explain the difference between a reactive and proactive police organization.

3. Describe how to create an organizational strategy.

4. Explain the steps required to implement an organizational strategy.

5. Identify the issues relating to measuring the effectiveness of a strategy.

6. Understand what constitutes an effective police organization.

Introduction

The experiences since the millennium have emphasized that ever-changing events are constantly challenging policing. In this dynamic environment, law enforcement organizations are attempting to become more adaptive and effective in meeting the demands of the complex public safety arena in which they exist. Today, innovation is essential for police agencies in developing the strategies, tactics, and technologies they employ to prevent crimes and solve public safety problems (Stone & Travis, 2011). Concerned police administrators consistently seek to reinvent their organizational strategies and discover better ways to manage and meet their organizations' changing and complex demands. The operational strategies they are developing differ from those created in the past to address 19th- and 20th-century conditions. Once dominated by random patrol, rapid response to calls for service, and past event investigation, operational tactics are being replaced by strategic policing, CompStat, predictive policing, and Intelligence-Led Policing. Departments that employ these strategies use **data** to inform their crime control and operational decisions (Ratcliffe, 2016). This process is transforming police departments from **reactive organizations** that respond to complaints after they have occurred to **proactive** ones that seek to prevent wrongdoings before they take place (Wexler, Wycoff, & Fischer, 2007). Proactive crime prevention is a historical goal linked to the **Nine Principles of Policing**. It states that the true measure of police effectiveness is the absence of crime, not how it is responded to (Reith, 1956). Underlying the demand for innovation today is the belief that the traditional methods of policing are no longer effective and that police departments need to engage with and understand their environment and constituency base to appreciate their impacts on their work (Crank & Giacomazzi, 2009). As a result, a fundamental rethinking and questioning of how the police go about their day-to-day activities

DOI: 10.4324/9781003459095-4

and accomplish their mission is occurring (Weisburd & Braga, 2006). This process involves restructuring police departments' direction, mission, values, and operational systems by changing core functions, methods, incentives, accountability, distribution of power, and culture to achieve more effective organizations. This discussion's premise is that this transformation is more in line with the concepts associated with strategic management in the business sector instead of those associated with bureaucratic public administration that emerged in policing during the reform era. A redefinition of what constitutes an effective police organization is taking place. This new definition defines an effective police organization as one that has developed the ability to initiate and reshape its operational service delivery in a variety of ways that allow it to fulfill its public safety mission and prevent crime while increasing its value and legitimacy in the eyes of the community it serves (Stone & Travis, 2011; More, Vito, & Walsh, 2012) more effectively. Departments acquire, analyze, transfer, and use information (communication processes/technology/analysis) about their environment to structure their operational responses. This transformation of information into intelligence allows organizational managers to plan, initiate, reshape, and evaluate their operational strategies designed to increase their organization's effectiveness. As a result, departments are transforming into learning organizations as they become skilled at creating, acquiring, and transferring information and modifying their operational tactics to reflect new knowledge and insights gained from the intelligence data they have developed. **Learning organizations** identify and analyze the driving forces affecting them, evaluate their response to these forces, and adjust their operations based on this evaluation (DiBella & Nevis, 1998). According to this new emerging paradigm, the role of organizational leadership and management is to develop the capacity for their organizations to interact, understand, and respond to the needs of their external environment with their organization's internal resources and capabilities. It raises the following three specific challenges for police executives:

- Can their departments develop the capacity to obtain and analyze information and data about their environmental driving forces?
- Can their departments develop a flexible strategic response to these external driving forces?
- How do they accomplish this, given their department's current resources and operational capability?

Responding to these challenges requires organizations to develop the following:

- A shared sense of direction.
- A positive organizational culture.
- A culture of accountability.
- A desire for continuous improvement.

This chapter considers this perspective and identifies what police executives should do to set this new direction to develop their department's strategic renewal, transformation, and effectiveness.

Strategic Direction

Strategic direction is defined by a department's vision, mission statement, values, operational strategies, tactics, accountability systems, and measurement of performance outcomes. Effective organizations have a sense of direction (purpose), shared and supported throughout the organization. Their sense of direction is described in the organization's vision statement, is actively practiced by its employees, and serves as the foundation for developing a strong positive organizational culture that aligns the performance of everyone in the organization. Organizational direction defines what the organization wishes to become and accomplish.

The chief executive and their management team must establish a clear strategic direction for the department by implementing it and selling it to external and internal stakeholders. They also need to empower their employees to fulfill it while restructuring their organization to ensure that desired outcomes occur by intention, not by chance. To develop a sense of direction that is believed in and shared by all organization members, the executive team must clarify and share the department's vision and mobilize the entire organization. A shared sense of direction will focus and develop a committed workforce, mission fulfillment, and community support. For example, the 3,000-employee Illinois State Police Department's vision and mission statement states, "The Illinois State Police will strive for excellence in all we do — seeking to be one of the premier policing agencies in the country. The Illinois State Police will promote public safety to improve the quality of life in Illinois" (https://isp.illinois.gov/). This statement concisely describes what should happen and what the department desires to achieve.

Effectiveness is a shared core cultural value in the strategic organization because employees believe in and know the expectations and what they should do to be effective. This knowledge assists them in taking accountability for their performance and supporting their department's strategic direction. Developing a sense of direction will depend on the ability of the department's leadership to create meaningful direction, implement it, and achieve the willingness of its employees to accept it. The strategic organization is structured to employ its personnel and assets to maximum effect.

Developing a shared sense of direction requires:

- Creation of a clear, realistic strategic vision.
- Creating an organizational strategy that operationalizes the vision, mission, and core functions into action.
- Mobilization of the employees to support the vision.
- Identification of outcome goals that relate to the organization's strategic functions.
- Fixing accountability for achieving outcome goals.
- Establishment of ongoing assessment of accomplishment. A willingness to adjust and redirect when it is necessary.

Vision

Creating a realistic **vision** is the first step in setting the department's strategic direction. A department's vision should catalyze building trust, collaboration, interdependence, motivation, and mutual responsibility for success (Blanchard, 2007, p. 22). It is the foundation for developing an organizational **strategy** to set desired performance goals, objectives, the quality of service desired, and the means to achieve it. It should identify where the organization is presently and define where it should be in the future. A strategic vision should present a challenge that motivates and energizes employees to give their best and gives meaning to what they do. It should answer the question "What must the department do to enhance our effectiveness and prepare for future demands?" There is no standard formula for creating a vision; ideally, it should be collaboratively created. It has a greater chance of acceptance when developed through a process involving sworn and non-sworn personnel of all ranks, city leaders, other government agency partners, and a broad range of community representatives. It should define a sense of purpose that will be shared and accepted throughout the organization and the community. It should be an informed and forward-thinking statement of purpose that should guide the organization in all it does. However, the long-term challenge to the vision's development is not "how" the vision is created but the extent to which the vision is accepted and understood, and correctly aligns the department's internal capacity and culture with its external demands (More et al., 2012, p. 408). Its purpose is to identify a direction for the organization that should be compatible with the basic function (mission) for which the organization exists.

An organizational vision statement should:

- Focus on the organization's mission.
- Link the present to the future.
- Establish a standard for excellence.
- Be a guide for unit action and accomplishments.
- Be a yardstick by which to measure organizational efforts.
- Be a standard for judging individual effort and behavior.
- Reflect the organization's core positive values.

(Blanchard, 2007, pp. 21–36)

For example, the vision statement of the 560-employee Glendale, Arizona, Police Department accomplishes these objectives by stating:

> The men and women of the Glendale Police Department are committed to excellence and professionalism in delivering comprehensive law enforcement services. Our core responsibility is to prevent and reduce crime; we strive to create a community where everyone feels safe in their homes, businesses, schools, and neighborhoods. We will be the model of an innovative, community-oriented police department. Using current and developing technologies, we are committed to research and innovation. Technology will enhance our highly skilled workforce in the investigation of crime and the analysis of trends. We will continually strive to develop our members' skills and efficiently and effectively manage our resources to deliver the highest level of service to the public. Members of the Glendale Police Department will continue to form lasting and successful partnerships within the community and with law enforcement, government, faith-based and non-profit organizations. Everything we do, collectively or individually, will be done following our core values of Excellence, Integrity, Respect, Courage, Dedication, and Compassion.
>
> (www.glendaleaz.com/live/city_services/public_safety/
> police_department)

Glendale's vision statement clearly identifies the department's core responsibility, desired public safety outcomes, the means to achieve its vision, and core values to guide employee behavior.

It is important that, when developing a department's direction, its vision and mission be defined in terms of specific outcomes. This task requires that the chief executive and their command staff identify the performance outcomes that should be accomplished to achieve the department's vision. These outcomes should be communicated to those responsible for achieving them. This key activity translates the vision and mission of the department in operational terms. For example, the Idaho State Police (ISP) Strategic Plan (https://isp.idaho.gov/) identifies the following four focus areas as measurable outcomes for the department:

1. Excellence in law enforcement services.
2. Effective and efficient agency operations.
3. Collaboration and partnerships.
4. Workforce development.

During New York Police Commissioner William Bratton's first administration, the NYPD sought to maximize its potential for reducing crime and improving the quality of life by developing the following crime-control and quality-of-life goals:

*   Getting guns off the streets.
*   Curbing youth violence in schools and on the streets.
*   Driving drug dealers out of the city.
*   Breaking the cycle of domestic violence.
*   Reclaiming public spaces.
*   Reducing auto-related crime.
*   Bringing fugitives to justice.

(Henry, 2002, p. 227)

Establishing these strategic outcomes identified what the department expected of its officers. As a result, the NYPD became focused on crime and disorder problems, deployment of resources, disruption of criminal enterprises, and obtaining information from each arrest they made that would lead to other criminals and arrests (Bratton, 1999).

Creating Organizational Strategy

An organizational strategy aims to shape how the organization responds to the environmental demands challenging it in a coordinated manner. Strong directive leadership alone does not create an effective organization. The long-term challenge for the chief executive and the executive team is how their organizational vision is accepted, implemented, and correctly aligns the department's internal capacity with its external demands. Developing strategy requires the department's leadership and decision-makers to understand the organization's external driving forces, demands, and internal core values, resources, strengths, competencies, and weaknesses. The strategy sets organizational direction by translating its vision, mission, tactics, and values into action (Daft, 2002). A strategy defines the process a department will use to achieve its goals. Strategy is the means or process that integrates an organization's vision, mission, policies, operational sequences (tactics), and people into a cohesive whole. In some departments, it also defines how the department relates to its employees, stakeholders, and customers. Thus, an organization's strategy defines the agency's path to achieving its desired mission and vision (Moore and Trojanowicz, 1988). Moore (1995) has identified the following characteristics of a strategy:

1. It describes a purpose of value to the manager and the organization.
2. It is operationally feasible.

3.   It takes advantage of the competencies and capabilities of the individuals involved.
4.   It will attain the support of stakeholders.
5.   It achieves its purpose.
6.   It is ethical.

An organizational strategy should unite departmental operations, support units, or operational unit members into a unified effort. It should identify how the community will be served and how operational services will be delivered. It should address these questions:

1.   What is the department's mission?
2.   How will the department's mission be accomplished?
3.   How will the department relate to the community?
4.   How should the department be organized to achieve its mission?
5.   How should the department structure its service delivery?
6.   What core values should be adopted and supported?
7.   What performance outcomes should be accomplished?
8.   How will these outcomes be measured?
9.   Who is accountable for achieving these outcomes?

Strategy development begins with identifying, analyzing, and understanding the community's public safety needs and the department's present ability to fulfill these (Michaelson, 2001). Daily, police departments develop and record a wealth of data about every call for service, arrests, traffic stops, citations, crime complaints, and community safety conditions. Monitoring and analyzing the information in the department's crime and public safety demand database will provide the information necessary to complete this first step. The department's command team must also engage, interact, and dialogue with the community to understand its needs and how its core functions respond to these. This foundation provides a positive and realistic understanding of what the organization needs. The *President's Task Force on 21st Century Policing Implementation Guide* (2015, p. 18) recommends the following non-enforcement ways a police department and its community can engage and understand each other:

1.   Conduct community surveys, forums, and town hall meetings regularly, not just in crisis.
2.   Encourage regular officer participation in neighborhood or school meetings.
3.   Form community advisory groups (general or population-specific).
4.   Participate in positive interaction with the community that does not involve an enforcement action or investigation.
5.   Involve community members in discussing policing tactics and designing problem-solving efforts to reduce crime and improve quality of life.
6.   Adjust patrol schedules to allow time for interactions with the community.
7.   Measure and reward non-enforcement community contacts.

An organization-wide strategy should also respond to the critical leadership question "How does the department achieve desired outcomes in light of the organization's current situation and resources?" Outcomes are the ends, and strategy is the means for achieving them. However, a strategy is more than just a process developed in advance that contains a set of intended actions. New circumstances always emerge, and the future is not always what we expect. Therefore, it is appropriate for us to think of a strategy as being proactive (intended) and reactive (adaptive).

In this manner, strategy is best considered a combination of planned actions and on-the-spot adaptive reactions to developing information and circumstances. Strategy development is an interactive process that creates a game plan or intended actions and then adapts it as events unfold. A strategy is something managers must shape and reshape as new knowledge develops about events transpiring outside and inside the organization. It is why information analysis, monitoring work demand, creating feedback systems, and good communications within and without the department are important tools for the strategic manager. For example, the crime strategy meeting is a central part of the CompStat process. The communication process at these meetings accesses, evaluates, and adjusts the use of organizational resources, strategy, and tactics. Strategy and tactics become defined when the leadership team identifies the best ways to use organizational assets to meet challenges or exploit opportunities.

For example, suppose the department holds a commanding officer accountable for a given geographical area. In that case, all other department units within and without this command that function within this area should be aligned operationally to support the commander's strategies and tactical initiatives. The commanding officer should hold strategy meetings involving all these units so that the different commanders can work closely with each other, provide timely intelligence, and take part in the analysis and tactical planning and evaluation process. Thus, all units assigned in the area operate as a strategy-focused team instead of competing units seeking to achieve their agendas.

For example, Wiseman (2011, p. ii) offered the following suggestions for managing police budgets:

- Think long-term when facing a fiscal crisis by sticking to a strategic plan with a multiyear time frame.
- Do not just cut costs. Look for revenue opportunities.
- Invite innovation by considering privatization and selling public facility naming rights.
- Look outside for help and suggestions on improving operations at a reduced cost.
- Targeted layoffs are more effective than hiring freezes.

In traditionally managed police departments, executives often consider how to use their assets more narrowly. They assume that basic purposes and operating objectives were set long ago and now remain fixed in policy and procedures. They see their job as optimizing performance regarding these objectives, not considering new organizational challenges (Moore & Trojanowicz, 1988, p. 2). In these types of departments, police managers also assume that in conducting their organization's functions they are restricted to established policies and procedures. While they may institute a few innovative programs, these are rarely seen as part of a sustained effort to change the organization's basic operating methods. It is a prime example of what Barker (1993) identifies as "**paradigm paralysis**."

Paradigm paralysis develops over the lifespan of an organization as it encounters problems and resolves them. As more and more problems are resolved, the organization's leadership experiences a period of success. The success convinces organizational members that their way of "doing things" is correct, and a mindset develops whereby managers no longer solve new problems in any way other than what has worked in the past. Paradigm paralysis exists in police organizations that respond to the needs of a changing external environment with police methods created decades ago to address different issues. Strategic policing suggests departments should develop the capacity to step back and place threats and risks into a holistic analytical perspective that will allow policing to prevent crime across a wide area rather than addressing a single event that has already occurred in the past (Goldstein, 1990; Ratcliffe, 2016, p. 6).

The above discussion indicates that strategy development is an exercise in **outside-in thinking**. Thus, it is initially an externally driven activity. The challenge is for managers to keep their strategies closely matched to outside environmental driving forces such as crime, public safety threats, opportunities, work demand, changing community demographics, and socioeconomic needs. Indicators of these driving forces originate from analyzing changing crime patterns, social disorder, specific communities' needs, special events, external political initiatives, shifting demographics, and projections of future community demands. This process requires more proactive information gathering as an adjunct to traditional crime analysis (Ratcliffe, 2016, p. 176): "Crime analysis is the process of identifying patterns and relationships between crime data and other relevant data sources to prioritize and target police activity" (Cope, 2004, p. 194). It should summarize the data of crimes and public safety information, making it understandable for everybody, especially operational decision-makers. One crime map, for example, can explain hundreds of pages of information. The essential functions of police crime analysis operations are:

1.   To analyze the data of crimes to allocate resources and deploy personnel.
2.   To discover crime and suspect relationships and provide information for investigations.
3.   To identify the reasons and conditions causing criminality.
4.   To inform policy-makers about the reasons and conditions requiring further policy development.

(Timothy, O'Shea, & Nicholls, 2003, p. 235)

An organization's strategy will never effectively meet the demands of its environment unless managers actively engage their organization's external environment and gain up-to-date information through intelligence gathering, data analysis, community surveys, and communication networks. This method provides them the knowledge to identify threats and opportunities affecting the department and community's public safety. Strategy development depends on collecting accurate and timely information, data gathering and analysis, knowledge, and action. Ratcliffe (2016, p. 71) conceptualizes this process as a continuum that involves four critical elements, data, information, knowledge, and intelligence. He defines **data** as observations and measurements about crime, and **information** as data having greater relevance and purpose. **Knowledge** is data and information with a particular interpretation. **Intelligence** is the knowledge that generates a strategist's understanding and action. This continuum provides the basis for deciding what must be done, when, and by whom, to achieve the department's vision and mission. It also allows for identifying how the department responds to the driving forces that affect its public safety demand. This analysis should answer the following questions:

1.   What are the persistent patterns in our work demand?
2.   What threats and opportunities do these create?
3.   What are the critical areas we need to attend to now?
4.   What do we wish to accomplish?

This process generates the intelligence necessary to identify prolific and serious offenders, crime and disorder hot spots, and link series of crimes and incidents (Ratcliffe, 2016). These data will allow operational commanders to develop tactical measures to reduce and prevent crime.

The use of information and the development of intelligence as a basis for the direction of operational resources is the **critical difference** between proactive and reactive policing. Strategic departments constantly analyze their external environment, acquire information from it to develop intelligence, and utilize this knowledge in their strategy and tactical development. Reactive managers seldom prepare for the future but focus on responding to the current crises with their standard operation procedures. As a result, they become victims of the external driving forces they have failed to anticipate. The faster conditions change in a department's external environment, the more critical it becomes for that department to be proactive at gathering and diagnosing shifting external conditions and adjusting to these. In addition to traditional crime analysis, departments should place a high value on community engagement. By building community relationships and collaborative partnerships, departments can obtain current information about their external environment. This effort will allow them to be knowledgeable about potential changes in public safety issues and provide them with the information needed to respond to developing driving forces.

Creating strategy also depends upon **inside-out thinking**, because strategy development involves using internal resources and organizational strengths to respond to external conditions. Administrators must clearly understand their organization's strengths, capabilities, and weaknesses. Many traditional police executives try to improve organizational performance by pointing to the department's statistics and insist that their commanders achieve better ones—that is, more arrests and higher clearance rates. Goldstein (1979, 1990) identified this result as the "means over ends" syndrome. This syndrome emphasizes the department's operating methods and statistical counts of how they respond to crime rather than the substantive outcome of their work. This condition developed during the 20th-century reform era, concentrating on managerial control and the organization of police agencies. It is based upon that era's widely held assumption that improvements in the internal management of police departments will enable them to deal more effectively with community crime problems. In response to this paradigm, Goldstein (1979, 1990) suggests that if the police desire to improve they must concern themselves more directly with the product of their efforts, not how they respond to the forces affecting them. These efforts are seldom successful and fail to produce more substantive outcomes.

Instead of relying on numerical increases or decreases, it is more productive if managers understand the forces that create their operational problems and develop tactics and solutions to address these issues through strategy development (Kim & Mauborgne, 2003). For this process to function correctly, managers must understand how to use their people and the organization's core competencies and capabilities. Thus, to implement an organizational strategy, it may be necessary to adjust unit leadership, organizational structure, employee assignment, training, reward systems, accountability, budget allocations, policy, and procedures. These decisions should be based on understanding the department's current response to its work demand, how that demand changes, and where improvement is needed. Such decisions require knowledge of how the department presently handles these demands. It requires thinking and analyzing what operational steps to put the department's strategic response in operation, execute it proficiently, and produce good results. Strategy developers must also know the danger of exclusively engaging in inside-out thinking.

Traditional managers, cautious by nature, usually focus most of their time and energy inward on internal problems only, improving organizational processes and procedures and taking care of daily administrative duties. They are caught up in day-to-day organizational management. Standard policies and procedures dictate their actions. Their organizational direction and strategy often accommodate their fears, concerns, and desire for control. This style represents "CYA management." It is a "paradigm paralysis" that will lock the organization into maintaining the status quo. How boldly managers recognize and meet the challenge of new strategic opportunities and champion actions to improve organizational performance and proficiency are good indicators of their leadership ability and value to the department. Enlightened managers create strategic tactics by which they access, communicate, network, reinforce, or change the organization. They understand that if the organization suffers from paradigm paralysis, it will continue to do what it has always done and achieve what it always has.

McDonald (2002, p. 15) cites an old police adage: "What is counted is what is performed." This statement suggests that managers only do the expected. Additionally, she claims that if police departments are serious about crime control and enhancing the quality of life in communities, then police chief executives must focus on and reward their operational commanders for their ability to organize, create, implement, and execute strategies and tactics that successfully impact community crime and safety issues, not statistical counts of their response to crime incidents.

Implementing Strategic Direction

Implementing a department's strategic direction should be based on a logical set of connected activities. They define the organizational direction and identify performance targets and the operational tactics needed to transform the department into a new direction. **Strategy implementation** is central to the management process. Goal attainment by the department institutionalizes the strategy. A central part of implementing strategic direction is for each commanding officer to develop their unit's vision, objectives, strategy, and tactics based on the overall department's direction.

One way of accomplishing this objective is for the department's executive team to conduct regular department-wide strategy meetings with their operational commanders and support staff to align the department's operational demand, mission, strategic objectives, and tactics (Silverman, 1999).

The purposes of these meetings are to:

- Ensure operational commanders pay sufficient attention to crime and public safety issues in their geographical areas.
- Ensure the strategies and tactics designed to resolve a problem are creative and varied.
- Follow up on events from the previous meeting to demonstrate consistency, and stay focused on problems tied to the objectives.
- Ensure that all departmental and external resources brought to bear on the problem are available and coordinated.
- Provide an ongoing teaching/learning situation in which those who attend can learn about developing strategies and assess their impact.
- Review the impact of tactics and strategies that are developed and applied.

(McDonald, 2002)

In many departments, the chief of police directs these meetings, while in others it is the deputy chief of police or a designated member of the executive leadership team. It is important that, throughout these sessions, top management provides strong and consistent support for the department's strategic direction. The redirection will rarely succeed without it. In some cases, lack of executive support will result in strongly resisted implementation efforts and severely hindered chances for success. The presence of the chief or top executives establishes commitment and accountability and sets the tone for the organization and each commander's responsibility.

During these meetings, each operational commander should report on their problem identification process and analysis, tactical response action plans, projected outcomes, and results in responding to these issues. This executive should ask specific, precise, and well-focused questions. Commanders should be held accountable and responsible for the following:

- Identification of crime and public safety problems and trends.
- The quality of their efforts toward crime prevention and problem reduction.
- The quality of their tactical plans.
- Their managerial oversight of operations (including evaluation and feedback).
- The results they obtain.

(Bratton & Knobler, 1998)

Commanders' problem identification and response activities should be evaluated by all commanders and administrators present. Commanders must alter or eliminate failed tactics and continue successful ones. Reporting current intelligence, adapting tactics to changing conditions, and closely reviewing results should be a continual process at these meetings. This interchange serves as the basis for organizational learning about what is operationally successful and the detection and correction of errors. Former NYPD Deputy Police Commissioner for Crime Control Strategies Jack Maple (Maple & Mitchell, 1999, p. 93) describes these meetings as a live audit of overall police performance that constitutes the **first step to crime reduction**: the gathering and analysis of accurate, timely intelligence quickened by the heat of accountability. When something goes wrong, an initial response is often to look for another strategy or tactic to correct the error. However, if chosen goals, values, personnel use, plans, and tactic implementation are not questioned, then **single-loop learning** occurs.

A more effective response is for the executives and operational commanders present to question these elements and subject them to critical scrutiny. This method sets the stage for double-loop learning. **Double-loop learning** occurs when errors or problems are detected, analyzed, and corrected in ways that involve the modification of an organization's underlying norms, policies, strategic assumptions, and objectives (Argyris & Schön, 1974, pp. 18–19). The meeting's discussion should contain a two-way give-and-take analytical, communicative exchange in which all present can offer advice, support, and insightful analysis. It should be a dialogue involving the creative, free searching of complex issues and problem-solving techniques. Managers in a learning organization actively seek to expand their capacity to learn and adapt by consistently gathering and analyzing the information produced at these meetings. This knowledge assists them in creating problem-solving strategies that respond to changing environmental demands. These meetings should not consist of a blame game that embarrasses individuals, but instead be a **diagnostic**

dialogue that seeks to improve individual commanders, their operational capabilities, and results.

A free flow of information is critical to the success of this process. It should be maintained so that a process of organizational assessment and learning takes place. If not, the goals and strategies formulated at the meetings or follow-up sessions will be diluted or diverted as they go down to the rank-and-file officers (Dabney, 2010). Operational commanders should identify the crime and quality-of-life problems they focus on, the tactical action plan they have developed, and the projected and actual results from their past efforts. Successful tactics and results are shared with the other department managers present. Commanders should also be prepared to present alternative tactics to resolve the problem if their original strategy was unsuccessful. Failed tactics should be altered or eliminated, and successful tactics should continue and be replicated. At the end of these meetings, each commander should know what they have accomplished, what they must do to achieve their command objectives, and their evaluation by the department's executive staff (O'Connell & Straub, 2007, p. 62).

NYPD's CompStat strategy emerged out of that department's crime strategy meetings. The department's executive team created these meetings to focus their operational commanders' attention on the city's crime problems (Bratton & Knobler, 1998; Maple & Mitchell, 1999). CompStat evolved into a performance-based management accountability strategy radically different from the accepted concepts and practices that had guided police administration through most of its existence. The NYPD's department-wide strategy meetings became the vital link between information, intelligence development, strategic thinking, data-driven decision-making, command accountability, and double-loop assessment of the department's effectiveness. This process changed the department's flow of information, decision-making, and organizational culture while creating one of the more successful police organizational strategies in the police profession (Silverman, 1999).

Strategy implementation should involve all levels of the organization. For example:

Executive leadership team: The department's chief executive and leadership team are responsible for setting the department's strategic direction by framing a clear departmental vision and mission expressed in operational goals and objectives that define expected performance outcomes. It establishes priorities for the organization to address and measure. The chief executive must then empower operational commanders with the authority and resources to develop strategies and tactics to accomplish these objectives and establish who is accountable for what outcomes. Commanders must be supplied with accurate and timely intelligence upon which they can base their problem analysis and tactical plans. The operational commander's tactical plans and the results achieved become the basis for their evaluation at department-wide strategy assessment meetings. Tactical effectiveness and accomplishments are addressed at these meetings, and strategic adjustments are made where needed. The assessment aims to analyze, modify, or replace tactics rather than punish staff (absent evidence of serious incompetence). To assist operational commanders, the executive team must reallocate resources, support creative solutions to problems, track progress, and integrate functions within the agency to support their commanders (Bratton & Knobler, 1998; More et al., 2012).

Subdivision commanders: Operational subdivision commanders should establish their command's vision, set direction, and develop performance objectives that link these units to the department's direction. They should hold strategy meetings to analyze and share intelligence and empower, interview, and assess their unit commanders regarding problem-solving, plans, and desired outcomes. These meetings should develop teamwork, and accountability, establish unity of command, and implement the department's strategy. Group efforts should be focused synergistically to achieve their objectives (Covey, 1989).

Unit commanders: Unit commanders should be accountable for developing tactical action plans, the results they achieve, and the resources they use to achieve them. They should meet regularly with their line supervisors and officers, share intelligence and knowledge, set objectives, empower individuals to accomplish objectives, develop action plans, and assess operational outcomes. At this level, a critical point of analysis is the impact of the tactical deployment of resources to address specific conditions requiring attention in the areas for which the unit is accountable (McDonald, 2002; More et al., 2012).

Line supervisor: The line supervisor and their team are the department's basic functional unit (Maple & Mitchell, 1999). These individuals operate at the strategic execution level. Therefore, the first-line supervisors and their units ultimately decide the organizational and tactical success rate. Line supervisors (sergeants) daily communicate and work with their officers to obtain and share intelligence, define and implement street-level tactics and develop crime control measures for specific conditions. An important responsibility for these supervisors is sharing intelligence and analysis through all organizational levels. This task consistently informs upper managers of changing operational conditions at the point of service delivery. Therefore, they must be involved in this process because they are the individuals whose actions will produce the desired outcomes and maintain appropriate levels of organizational effectiveness.

The above-defined process is an operational mechanism to ensure the strategic direction flows throughout the department. The intent is that this flow of information will develop a **critical mass** of creativity, innovation, communication, and dedication throughout the organization (Gladwell, 2002; Henry, 2002). The department-wide strategy meetings should spawn and spread effective improvement methods while developing the dynamics for command accountability at all levels of the organization. They serve as an arena for testing each manager's ability and each unit's capabilities. It provides the executive team with a means to match positions with commanders with the skill, experience, expertise, and personality to manage proficiently. Organizational learning and strategic guidance should flow down to all department areas through this process while disseminating successful tactics throughout the organization. Engaging in this process to develop and enact crime control strategies can help agencies of all sizes to address hot spots, crime patterns, and trends. However, this process can be adjusted in less hierarchical organizations to fit a smaller organizational structure.

Strategy implementation should develop an organizational culture that supports the strategic transformation of the department and be incorporated into:

- Organizational policy and procedures.
- Decision-making and problem-solving processes.
- Accountability systems.
- Measurement and follow-up systems.
- Reward and discipline systems.
- Managerial communication systems.

- Selection and advancement systems.
- Organizational training.

The following activities will help a department develop the effectiveness of its directional-setting process:

Reward the doers and performers by celebrating and rewarding those who achieve performance objectives.

Conduct strategy review meetings where honesty prevails. The integrity of this process is critical. Without a true analysis of the facts and the resultant learning, effectiveness and learning are jeopardized.

Clarify responsibility and accountability. Do not assume everyone knows what they should do by when.

Controls require up-to-date performance information. The crime control strategy cannot depend upon guesswork. Real-time data and analysis are a constant requirement for success and changes in strategy.

Leadership must play an active role and use performance analysis effectively, avoiding all-or-nothing objectives. They must demand total honesty and integrity from subordinates and recognize and reward those who contribute to exceptional success.

Strategy review is the key to organizational effectiveness. A good review fosters discussion, clarifies strategy, helps set execution-related objectives, allows leaders to understand their people fully, and facilitates learning and organizational change (Hrebiniak, 2005, p. 16).

Strategy implementation and execution are always the product of organizational learning. If it is developed unevenly or too quickly in some areas, then follow-up and assessment and ongoing searches for ways to continuously improve and corrective adjustments are necessary.

Measurement of Progress

The department's executive team monitors the directional-setting process, decides when things are going well, and monitors changing events. Indications and analysis of inadequate performance, too little progress, and important new external circumstances are all part of the learning process and will require corrective action and adjustments. This process may involve modifications in vision, long-term direction, creating more realistic objectives, strategy, or implementation in light of actual operational experience(s), changing conditions, new ideas, and new opportunities. This process should be managed and adjusted continuously to provide the executive team with ongoing assessment of command accountability and organizational accomplishments. Chapter 10 provides a comprehensive discussion of measuring police performance.

As discussed earlier, the department's strategy meeting is an excellent management assessment tool, because it matches quantitative information on crime events, locations, and times with police deployment tactics and community public safety information. Operational commanders' tactics and accomplishments are reported, considered, and evaluated at these meetings. This process involves traditional managerial oversight, strategic assessment, outcome measurement, and problem-solving. A principal objective of these meetings should be assessing the department's reengineering efforts and their impact on its outcome measures. Continuous assessment is a central process to manage the department's strategic reengineering process. It creates information about the department's accomplishments and the data needed to improve performance. This process enables the executive team to hold managers accountable and to introduce correction or consequences for performance (Osborne & Plastrik, 2000, p. 247).

Managers should always measure what they are trying to accomplish. Outcomes are achieved through the identification and accomplishment of specific performance objectives. These must be spelled out clearly and communicated to those responsible for achieving them. Feedback systems and measurable objectives should always be part of organizational plans. Establishing appropriate quantitative and qualitative performance measures will help link strategic redirection activities to specific outcomes. Hard data is necessary for evaluating managerial strategies and outcomes. Administrators should avoid setting unrealistic and unattainable expectations by developing a strategy incorporating realistic and attainable goals as system elements. A **goal** is a general statement of purpose that should be related to the department's vision and mission. Goals and objectives (outcomes) should provide the manager with a way to measure progress, identify strategies that work, what are successful outcomes, and refocus resources as needed. Identifying baseline measures that record conditions before implementing change is necessary to compare relevant changes before and after.

Valid and reliable evaluation of police organizational performance requires:

1. **Identification of measurable outcomes (goals)**.
2. **Identification of measurable objectives (milestones, steps) to accomplish** the desired outcomes.
3. A data-**reporting system** for monitoring progress and maintaining **accountability**.
4. Assessment of actual accomplishments versus desired outcomes.

Lastly, all performance measures should relate to the agency, program, and operational unit mission and goals. They should be both legitimate and fair. The design and implementation of performance evaluations depend upon the intended purpose. Always measure what matters and what gives managers the information that they need. All else is a waste of time, budget, and organizational resources. According to McDonald (2002, p. 32), effectiveness comprises two measures.

Long-term measures are cumulative data comparisons, such as annual comparisons of serious crimes or crimes of serious concern to the community, such as youth homicides. Comprehensive measures might include the location and frequency of disorder complaints and measures of citizens' fear.

Short-term measures are assessments of tactics or strategies during operations. For example, if a solution to a set of problems is being implemented, progress should be tracked carefully to alter parts of the strategy. If the strategy fails, an analysis of its implementation, effects, and results will assist in designing a new approach. In this manner, organizational learning takes place.

Strategy implementation is an action-oriented activity. It involves decision-making, developing personnel competencies and capabilities, policy creation, motivating, culture-building, and exerting the leadership necessary to achieve desired outcomes and objectives. A department's vision, objectives, strategy implementation, and execution are never final; evaluating performance, monitoring changes in the surrounding environment, and making adjustments are normal and necessary parts of the strategic management process. Proficient strategy execution is always the product of organizational learning. Follow-up and assessment, ongoing searches for continuous improvement, and corrective adjustments are thus normal and necessary for a learning organization. Ideally, assessment should focus on the effectiveness and efficiency of the strategy. It should answer the following questions:

1. Did the strategy impact the problems or conditions it was created to address?
2. To what extent was the impact (percent decrease/increase)?
3. Was the process and service delivery consistent with strategy design specifications? Here a comparison is made between planned and actual events.
4. What is the cost-benefit analysis of expended resources to strategy outcomes?
5. Were organizational resources used properly?
6. Were targeted populations or neighborhood groups reached?
7. How did the officers perform?

(More et al., 2012)

Assessing the effectiveness of the department's directional-setting efforts should be concerned with outcome goals rather than outputs. It is not just the number of calls for service responded to, arrest data, and crime rates alone, but the condition of the community after implementing operational tactics. A primary concern should be whether the safety and security of the citizens in that community increased measurably by the department's efforts. Performance measurement should not be an end but a pathway to more effective service to the community. It is a feedback mechanism to help decision-makers focus on goals, strategies, and resource allocation to accomplish the department's mission.

Innovation Issues

Leading an organizational redirection is not without its difficulties. Public officials, community representatives, and department executives may support the new direction. Internally, department members may be against it because they wish to maintain the way things are now, the **status quo**. The department's internal environment comprises dynamic interrelationships among people who perform the functions and tasks necessary to implement organizational strategy and perform its day-to-day operations. They will not easily accept organizational reform. Executives seeking to establish a new direction for their organization must understand that they will face several formidable obstacles because of the difficulty of managing change in police agencies.

Based upon years of research in policing, Skogan (2008, p. 28) identified the following categories of resistance to transforming police organizations. These are:

- Resistance by mid-level and top managers.
- Resistance by front-line supervisors.
- Resistance by rank-and-file officers.
- Resistance by special units.
- Resistance by police unions.
- Competing demands and expectations.
- Inability to "measure what matters."
- Failure of interagency cooperation.

- Public unresponsiveness.
- Nasty misconduct diverting public and leadership attention.
- Reform may not survive the leadership transition.

Ultimately, the department's successful redirection depends upon the ability of the executive team to anticipate, identify, and manage the redirectional process, overcome resistance, and the willingness of their employees to support their efforts. Police managers need to understand how their organizational redirection efforts will affect their people, be aware of the indicators that signal resistance, and be prepared to resolve any resistance they may encounter. Skogan's (2008) identification of top managers, mid-level, front-line supervisors, and rank-and-file officers reveals that the individuals needed to implement the department's new direction will resist this effort. The executive team can overcome resistance by developing a critical mass of internal supporters—a tipping point used by Bratton with the NYPD (Henry, 2002; Kim & Mauborgne, 2003).

One way to accomplish this is to create dissatisfaction with the status quo and manage a process that coordinates events and changes to develop internal commitment and reduce resistance. Dissatisfaction with the status quo is a critical motivator. In many turnarounds, the hardest battle is getting people to agree on the causes of current problems and the need for change. Dissatisfaction with the organization's current state must be sufficient for them to develop an urgent desire to do things differently and overcome their resistance (Kotter & Cohen, 2002). Department-wide strategy meetings can expose the reality of the present state of the department and bring members face-to-face with operational problems. These meetings should:

1. Communicate information about potential crises or threats to the organization and its members.
2. Provide employees with factual data about organizational performance: what they are accomplishing instead of what they think they are.
3. Engage in frank discussion and dialogue about organizational problems and operational processes.
4. Set realistic performance expectations that will create the desire to change.

It is not sufficient to provide data or announce performance failures. There must be a real discussion and open communication about what is happening instead of what should or could be happening. The employees must understand the need for the department to transform and a sense of urgency to bring about this redirection. Employee motivation should then be directed into a focused organizational improvement effort. The department's new direction must be communicated as a response to the present state of the organization. This process will spark motivation, keep changes aligned, provide a means to evaluate how the organization is doing, and provide a rationale for the changes the organization will need to make.

Beer (1988) asserts that the organization's response to dissatisfaction with the status quo must address needed performance changes in structure and systems design to make the organization more effective. It should communicate purpose, provide answers to employees' questions, and gain their support. When people understand what is expected of them and why, they will often strive to achieve it.

Too often, efforts to improve organizations specify only one or two elements, such as structure and strategy, ignoring the behaviors and competencies required for change to take place. Ignoring the multiple elements of an organization is one of the primary reasons for failure. The directional-setting process will take time, and losing momentum and the onset of disappointment are real factors. However, developing a strategic redirection process cannot be developed in isolation. Those about to be affected by the change should have input into its implementation, or they will be a primary source of resistance. Identifying and putting together a guiding coalition (critical mass) empowered to lead this effort is critical (Kotter, 1996). These individuals need to work together as a team to make the change happen. Obstacles to the change process must be identified and eliminated. This process may mean changing strategies, structures, or people that will undermine the change effort. Recognizing and rewarding people for their efforts to support the new direction sends a powerful message supporting the redirection effort's credibility.

Goal Displacement

A persistent problem in assessing police performance is the difficulty in judging the outcomes resulting from the department's work. As a result, police departments frequently evaluate their performance based on the numerical outputs they produce. Operational commanders are usually evaluated on the outputs they produce during a specific period. Output measures such as the number of calls for service responded to, time in responding, reported crime complaints, arrests, stop and frisk reports, cases cleared, and reduced crime statistics are easier to measure. However, **goal displacement** occurs when these measures replace desired strategy outcomes, such as enhancing community safety, reduction of residents' fear levels, satisfaction with police services, development of problem-solving partnerships, and becoming ends in themselves. In many instances, monthly increases in these numerical outputs emerge as the primary objective for operational units. For example, a traffic unit is more concerned with producing increased citations and revenue from fines instead of addressing traffic safety issues.

When a department's performance is evaluated regarding numerical outputs, operational commanders are incentivized to maximize these outputs, regardless of whether maximizing outputs is the preferred strategy for achieving desired outcomes. This incentive to focus on statistical outputs can lead to organizational cheating, where unit commanders purposely manipulate output levels to portray their work in the best light possible. For example, in many traditionally managed departments using the CompStat strategy, crime strategy meetings have evolved into commander degradation ceremonies. Pressure on these commanders to produce desired numerical outputs is intense. This feeling leads to a greater concentration on producing output measures, transforming them into desirable ends. As a result, goal displacement occurs.

A commonly used example of goal displacement involves classifying crimes based on how well crimes are solved rather than the level of public safety. Reports of burglaries and break-ins are labelled unfounded because they are difficult to solve, rather than classified as real crimes. Whereas the probability of catching a burglar during or after the act is slight, the probability of catching drug dealers and prostitutes committing crimes is much greater. Thus, to ensure high clearance rates, a department may focus on relatively easy-to-clear crimes (Bohte & Meier, 2000). Another technique is to lower the value of the stolen property so that a misdemeanor crime is reported instead of a felony. These examples suggest how incentive structures can generate goal displacement.

Recent research into manufacturing artificial crime statistics based on interviews with 2,000 retired police officers from the NYPD reveals pervasive, system-wide manipulation of these statistics. Eterno and Silverman (2012) claim that concern with the department's reputation for reducing crime, much more than public safety, drives department policy. More evidence supporting this allegation has come forward because of several NYPD whistle-blowers. Officers Adrian Schoolcraft, Craig Matthews, Frank Polestro, Adyl Polanco, and Vanessa Hicks have talked openly to the media about the routine downgrading of crimes and the use of illegal arrest quotas by the NYPD.

The research and the statements by the whistle-blowers indicate that the manipulation of crime reports is a consequence of the misuse of CompStat. This innovative management accountability system was designed to reduce crime but has instead become a powerful mechanism to ensure that downgrading crime permeates the whole department. The researchers claim that their analysis found a clear message from the top commanders at police headquarters: make many stop-and-frisk actions, write many summonses, make many arrests for petty offenses, and downgrade serious crimes. These tactics have deeply alienated racial and ethnic minorities in New York City and revealed a broader dysfunction in the police department. The pressure on the officers to produce statistical output numbers and downgrade crime reports reflects the department's ineffective management and goal displacement deterioration. This unnecessary activity does not involve intelligence gathering, surveillance, or community involvement, nor does it use CompStat well. It alienates communities and hurts the NYPD's ability to fight serious and violent crimes (Silverman, Eterno, & Levine, 2012).

Conclusion

Setting and implementing a new organizational strategic direction is an action-oriented activity. It involves decision-making, developing personnel competencies and capabilities, policy creation, motivating, culture building, and exerting the leadership necessary to achieve desired outcomes and objectives. The executive team's responsible for staying on top of the strategy development and implementation process, monitoring changing events, and deciding when things are going well. They must provide the leadership needed to drive the strategic direction forward and monitor strategy execution. This effort entails assessing what it will take to make the strategy work and to reach the targeted goals and objectives on schedule. Success will depend upon the department's ability to use its existing personnel and resources effectively to produce favorable results. It is a critical step in strategy development, requiring identifying who is accountable for what objectives and setting that accountability. This activity aligns the organization with the strategy. It involves identifying who must achieve what, when, and using what resources. However, establishing accountability is only half the battle.

Outcome goals should be spelled out and communicated to those responsible for achieving them. Managers must be held accountable by the command staff for both their accomplishments and failures. Department-wide strategy meetings are critical because they provide information to reinforce execution methods, identify needed corrective mechanisms, and facilitate organizational learning and change. Corrective action and strategy adjustments are needed when assessments indicate inadequate performance or too little progress, or important new external circumstances have occurred.

The directional-setting process may involve modifications in the vision and creation of goals and objectives that are more realistic considering experience, changing conditions, new ideas, and new opportunities. The executive team must think through operationally what must be done to put the strategy in operation, execute it proficiently, and produce good results. Outcomes are achieved through the identification and accomplishment of specific performance objectives. This process is how strategy translates into operational terms. Reengineering isn't just about redesigning the organization. It requires the translation of a new direction into reality. Departments that undertake this process with understanding, commitment, and strong executive leadership will succeed by doing the following:

- Identifying and focusing on core function(s).
- Identifying the outcome(s) that these functions should achieve.
- Analyzing the way these outcomes are presently achieved (process).
- Identifying what you need to do to maximize the effectiveness of this process.
- Identifying and measuring everything that contributes to the outcome(s) desired.
- Designing the implementation process.
- Assessing and reassessing this process and its results.
- Adjusting where needed.
- Linking the reward structure to the achievement of targeted results.

KEY TERMS

Accountability	Identification of	Paradigm paralysis
Clarify	measurable objectives	Proactive organization
Conduct	(milestones, steps)	Reactive organization
Control	Identification of	Reporting system
Critical difference	measurable outcomes	Reward
Critical mass	(goals)	Short-term measures
Data	Implementing strategy	Single-loop learning
Diagnostic dialogue	Information	Status quo
Double-loop learning	Inside-out thinking	Strategic direction
Executive leadership	Intelligence	Strategy
team	Knowledge	Strategy implementation
First step to crime	Learning organization	Strategy review
reduction	Line supervisors	Subdivision commanders
Goal	Long-term measures	Unit commanders
Goal displacement	Outside-in thinking	Vision

References

Argyris, M., & Schön, D. (1974). *Theory in practice: Increasing professional effectiveness*. San Francisco, CA: Jossey-Bass.

Barker, J.A. (1993). *Paradigms: The business of discovering the future*. New York, NY: HarperCollins.

Beer, M. (1988). *Leading change*. Cambridge, MA: Harvard University Press.

Blanchard, K. (2007). *Leading at a higher level.* Upper Saddle River, NJ: FT Press.

Bohte, J., & Meier, K.J. (2000). Goal displacement: Assessing the motivation for organizational cheating. *Public Administration Review, 60* (March/April), 173–182.

Bratton, W.J. (1999). Great expectations: How higher expectations for police departments can lead to a decrease in crime. In R.H. Langworthy (Ed.), *Measuring what matters: Proceedings from the policing research institute meetings* (pp. 11–26). Rockville, MD: National Institute of Justice.

Bratton, W.J., & Knobler, P. (1998). *Turnaround.* New York, NY: Random House.

Cope, N. (2004, March). Intelligence-led policing or policing-led intelligence? *British Journal of Criminology, 44*(2), 188–203.

Covey, S.R. (1989). *The seven habits of highly effective people.* New York, NY: Free Press.

Crank, J.P., & Giacomazzi, A. (2009). A sheriff's office as a learning organization. *Police Quarterly, 12*(4), 351–369.

Dabney, D. (2010). Observations regarding key operational realities in a Compstat model of policing. *Justice Quarterly, 27*(1), 28–51.

Daft, R.L. (2002). *The leadership experience.* New York, NY: Harcourt.

DiBella, A., & Nevis, E. (1998). *How organizations learn: An integrated strategy for building learning capacity.* San Francisco, CA: Jossey-Bass.

Eterno, J., & Silverman, E.B. (2012). *The crime numbers game: Management by manipulation.* Boca Raton, FL: CRC Press.

Gladwell, M. (2002). *The tipping point: How little things make a big difference.* New York, NY: Hachette.

Glendale Police Department, www.glendaleaz.com/live/city_services/public_safety/police_department.

Goldstein, H. (1979, April). Improving policing: A problem-oriented approach. *Crime & Delinquency, 25(2).* DOI: 10.1177/001112877902500207.

Goldstein, H. (1990). *Problem-oriented policing.* New York, NY: McGraw-Hill.

Henry, V.E. (2002). *The Compstat paradigm: Management accountability in policing.* New York, NY: Looseleaf Press.

Hrebiniak, L.G. (2005). *Making strategy work: Leading effective execution and change.* Upper Saddle River, NJ: Pearson Education.

Kim, W., & Mauborgne, R. (2003, April). Tipping point leadership. *Harvard Business Review,* 60–69.

Kotter, J.P. (1996). *Leading change.* Boston, MA: Harvard Business School Press.

Kotter, J., & Cohen, D.P. (2002). *The heart of change.* Boston, MA: Harvard Business School Press.

Maple, J., & Mitchell, C. (1999). *The crime fighter.* New York, NY: Doubleday.

Moore, M. (1995). *Creating public value: Strategic management in government.* Cambridge, MA: Harvard University Press.

Moore, M.H., & Trojanowicz, R.C. (1988). *Corporate strategies for policing: Perspectives on policing.* Washington, DC: National Institute of Justice.

More, H.W., Vito, G.F., & Walsh, W.F. (2012). *Organizational behavior and management in law enforcement.* Upper Saddle River, NJ: Prentice Hall.

O'Connell, P.E., & Straub, F. (2007). *Performance-based management for police organizations.* Long Grove, IL: Waveland.

Osborne, D., & Plastrik, P. (2000). *The reinventor's field book.* San Francisco, CA: Jossey-Bass.

President's Task Force on 21st Century Policing. (2015). *Final report of President's task force on 21st-century policing.* Washington, DC: Office of Community Oriented Policing Services.

Ratcliffe, J. (2016). *Intelligence-led policing*, 2nd ed. New York, NY: Routledge.

Reith, C. (1956). *A new study of police history*. London: Oliver & Boyd.

Silverman, E. (1999). *NYPD battles crime: Innovative strategies in policing*. Boston, MA: Northeastern University Press.

Silverman, E., Eterno, J., & Levine, J. (2012). Manufacturing low crime rates at the NYPD: Reputation vs. safety under Bloomberg and Kelly. *The Huffington Post*.

Skogan, W.G. (2008). Why reforms fail. *Policing & Society*, *18*(1), 23–34.

Stone, C., & Travis, J. (2011, March). Toward a new professionalism in policing. In *New perspectives on policing* (pp. 1–26). Washington, DC: National Institute of Justice.

Timothy, C., O'Shea, T.C., & Nicholls, K. (2003). Police crime analysis: A survey of US police departments with 100 or more sworn personnel. *Police Practice and Research*, *4*(3), 233–250.

Weisburd, D., & Braga, A.A. (Eds.) (2006). *Police innovation: Contrasting perspectives*. Cambridge: Cambridge University Press.

Wexler, C., Wycoff, M.A., & Fischer, C. (2007). *"Good to great" policing: Application of business management principles in the public sector*. Washington, DC: Department of Justice Office of Community Oriented Policing Services and Police Executive Research Forum.

Wiseman, J. (2011). *Strategic cutback management: Law enforcement leadership for lean times*. Washington, DC: National Institute of Justice.

5 Managing Change and Culture

Learning Objectives

1. Define change and identify the different types of change.
2. Understand the role and responsibilities of change agents.
3. Differentiate between planned and unplanned change.
4. Identify the characteristics of transformational leadership.
5. Recognize the characteristics of a dysfunctional organization.
6. Identify the sources of organizational change.
7. Comprehend Lewin's three-stage process of planned change.
8. Understand what is required to implement change.

Introduction

This chapter focuses on the process of managing organizational change and culture. Beginning with the Community Problem-Solving Policing Era in the 1980s and the emergence of strategic policing strategies in the 1990s, change and innovation have become a continuous part of life in policing. Presently many police executives are reengineering their organizations with flexible and adaptive operational strategies. They seek to create more effective organizations by experimenting with public safety strategies that work and rejecting those that do not. As a result, understanding and implementing organizational change has emerged as an essential feature of police leadership and administration. **Change** is defined as any alteration that occurs in an organization's structure, people, and practice (Zhao, 1996). It is a natural and inevitable factor in organizational life. Change is undertaken to improve an organization and prepare it for its future. Organizations that do not change become stagnant, unable to adjust to changing demands, and subject to one crisis after another. One of the more important measures of an organization's strength is its ability to adapt to and manage change. Unfortunately, many researchers have found that police departments can resist change, and police managers often have difficulty implementing new programs (Weisburd & Braga, 2006). Leadership is about creating and managing change.

Creating change involves the development of innovative approaches and putting them into practice. The development of organizational strategies such as Comp-Stat, Intelligence-Led, and Evidence-Based Policing are examples of a creative change

DOI: 10.4324/9781003459095-5

response to internal and external demands affecting police departments. They are also examples of a product of the acquisition of new knowledge obtained through systematic problem-solving and experimenting with new tactical approaches. **Sustainable change** is earned by unlocking the forces of creativity and innovation through the management of an organization's culture and human capital (Schermerhorn, 2005). The end result organizationally is the transformation of a department to a more effective performance level by change that maintains and sustains itself. It sustains for a significant period of time. For example, the New York City Police Department developed CompStat in 1994 and it is still in use in that department today.

Change is constant, we create it, and we can control it. Organizational change typically affects processes, technology, positions, and culture in an organization. A significant change to even one of these areas requires leadership, analysis, and planning. Change is not a single occurrence that can be accomplished by the issuance of policy and procedural changes. It is a continuous process that must be clearly thought out with due consideration given to the people needed to support it and make it happen. It is about leadership that is open, honest, and willing to engage in frequent communication and exchange of information. Otherwise, its impact will be cosmetic and short-lived.

For example, the change to Community Policing in the Tempe, Arizona, Police Department evolved in three phases: (1) the early planning phase, which began in the late 1980s; (2) the start-up phase, which encompassed a Beat experiment conducted in the early 1990s; and (3) a department-wide implementation, which was launched after the Beat project ended. During this change process, the Tempe Police Department worked through a number of challenges. As a result the department evolved into a different and more responsive police organization in its service to Tempe's citizens. It changed from a reactive operational response mode to a proactive one centered on problem-solving; from an entirely centralized operation to a decentralized operation; from a department with minimal contact with the public to outreach to the public; from decision-making based on subjective judgment to decisions based on analysis; and from strict control of sworn personnel to flexibility and support for decision-making. This transition took place over a 12-year period and is ongoing. The lesson learned from this effort is that changing police organizations requires time and patience because of the radical changes that it imposes on a police department previously accustomed to a professional reform style of policing (McEwen, 2002).

Individuals or groups who take responsibility for changing processes and organizations are known as **change agents**. These individuals are responsible for planning, coordinating, and developing the change process. They are the catalysts who make things happen. Change agents are proactive innovative managers who anticipate the need for change and take deliberate actions to initiate a program of planned change within their organization. They are alert for organizational performance gaps between desired and actual outcomes. These individuals take responsibility for the analysis and resolution of problems or issues confronting their organization, coordinating the development of a planned response, and facilitating the collaboration of personnel involved in the change process.

However, the experience in policing is that organizational change has usually occurred as a reactive response, forced on many departments by external events or internal crises that demand change (Maguire et al., 2003). Policing today is facing challenging times involving crises of legitimacy in part to the ubiquitous presence of video cameras that have displayed before the American public the very best and worst of police conduct (Sparrow, 2016). Pressure from various sources such as the media, political structure, federal government consent decrees, changing crime conditions, community problems, civil disorder, political action groups, organizational crises, and other damaging events are all-too-familiar motivators for police organizational change. Henry (2002, pp. 31–32) claims that this pressure for change often results in an inadequate response by police administrators that he identified as "**cookie cutter management**." It is the tendency for police managers to find some policy or practice that another police department has successfully used and appropriate it. These administrators press the borrowed practice down on their department as if it were a cookie cutter or template. This practice is motivated by the subjective belief that "what works for others will work for us." Unfortunately, this activity often lacks systematic problem-solving, planning, careful implementation, and assessment. Managers involved in this borrowing process fail to appreciate the differences between the originating department and their own. This approach is doomed to fail. Suppose the factors that create the demand for change are not perceived and understood by the department's executive team and systematically analyzed. In that case, the change will become an externally imposed quick fix that underscores the leadership failure of the department's executive team.

Another aspect of externally imposed change is that administrators under the pressure of the demand for organizational change respond by selecting the easiest way out of the stressful situation. Simon (1997) referred to this as **satisficing**. It occurs when an administrator feels pressured to appear decisive and does not take the time to fully identify and analyze the problem or issue generating the demand. These individuals seek to handle the demand quickly with a good enough solution that offers the slightest uncertainty and risk for themselves or their organization. Unfortunately, this type of decision-making usually resolves day-to-day surface issues only and fails to consider the long-term impact on the department. Satisficing is a primary source of the managerial dictum that holds that "Yesterday's solutions are often the source of today's problems." It perpetuates organizational mediocrity and maintains the department's status quo.

Police Culture

A significant source of resistance to change is often the department's culture. An **organization's culture** is a shared system of beliefs, attitudes, values, traditions, and modes of behavior held and practiced by organizational employees (Schein, 1990; Dessler, 2004, p. 38). It reflects what the department and its members believe in as an organization and justifies what its employees do. Police culture teaches police officers about acceptable behavior and the explanatory reasons why officers act the way they do (Sparrow, 2016, p. 36). In many departments, culture maintains and perpetuates conformity to the established acceptable ways of doing things, the **status quo**. Status quo bias is often at the heart of resistance to change (Bratton & Tumin, 2012); people like to do what they have always done. If a department's culture is improperly understood and managed, it will work against organizational change.

A police department's culture consists of behavior patterns, such as ceremonial events, continuous behavioral activity, and official and unofficial written and spoken ways of doing things. Organizational culture reflects how employees treat each other, what they brag about, the job-related stories they tell, what members wear, and the types of behavior in which they consistently engage. For example, the culture of a small

30-person municipal police department, where most things are handled informally and formal ceremonies are non-existent, is quite different from that of a sizable multilevel state police agency. In an address before a management class at the Southern Police Institute, a Florida police chief of a 38-employee police department defined his 38-person department as a team. He described his leadership style as one designed to foster teamwork and mutual respect for all people who come in contact with his department and work there. He claimed that he consistently seeks to shape the values that support positive internal and external departmental relationships. This cultural perspective differs from that found in many multilevel bureaucratically administered agencies.

In his classic study, Skolnick (1993) outlined the characteristics of the working personality of police. He noted three outstanding features: the exercise of authority, pressure to produce, and suspicion while on patrol. These features were also related to police solidarity (the code of silence) and the use of force. Similarly, Reiner (2010) noted the "core characteristics" of police culture: a conservative, mission-oriented, isolated, masculine, pessimistic outlook that was the foundation of their worldview. He noted the existence of a cop "code of silence" and an "us versus them" mentality that the "thin blue line" separated officers from citizens. Within the culture, officer typologies exist—enforcers, optimists, and "Dirty Harrys." As a result, the police seek excitement on the job, have a cynical outlook on life in general, tend to be suspicious of others, are socially isolated, strongly support fellow officers, are politically and morally conservative, and reflect masculinity.

One interview-based study supports Reiner's conclusions about police culture. It revealed the existence of four dominant police organizational culture characteristics: The police family, us versus them, masculinity, and subcultural differences (Brough, Chataway, & Biggs, 2016). The police family view comes from the shared experiences of officers that contribute to the view that no one else can understand them and the pressures they face. Both "looking after each other" and "backing each other up" were core values (Brough, Chataway, & Biggs, 2016, p. 31). The "us versus them" theme had two components—the public and senior management officials. Both sources failed to recognize and support police officers. Masculinity involves feeling "better to look tough than soft" (Brough, Chataway, & Biggs, 2016, p. 32). Subcultural differences exist between police units with different and specific operational roles and responsibilities. The participants noted that a "drinking culture" declined, although they noted its beneficial role in reducing stress and granting the opportunity to debrief events with other officers. They also note a CYA ("cover your ass") culture—safety requires officers to check with superiors before taking action. This aspect of the police culture emphasizes control—"formality, enforcement of rules, compliance with procedures, a hierarchical structure, and clear lines of decision-making authority" (Brough, Chataway, & Biggs, 2016, p. 34). An additional aspect of police culture is a preoccupation with danger and potential death maintained by commemorating the officers killed in the line of duty (Sierra-Arevalo, 2019).

Campeau (2015) questioned these findings with two additional aspects of police culture: solidarity and mission. Officers stated that they were less likely to seek excitement because it could lead to actions violating official policy. Public visibility of their activities sponsored this viewpoint. Results from an online survey of American police officers reported their endorsement of the use of force and less support for procedural justice. Line officers from larger departments strongly supported these aspects, possibly due to their exposure to occupational and organizational strains. However, Black officers were less likely to support these views than White officers (Silver, Roche, Bilach, & Ryon, 2017, pp. 1293–1294).

Results from the analysis of survey data on the use of force examined how police culture influences police behavior. It determined that workgroups that valued aggressive behavior were more likely to generate more citizen complaints but not official sanctions. Workgroups expressing high distrust in their departments evidenced increased use of force, as did individual officers who favored aggressive patrol tactics (Ingram, Terrill, & Paoline, 2018, pp. 800–801; see also Terrill, Paoline, & Manning, 2003).

Survey research examined the extent to which officers held a warrior (police as crime fighters) or guardian (police working with the public on crime prevention) mindset. The results indicated that officers with the guardian mindset emphasized communication and interaction with citizens and less support of force misconduct, while officers with the warrior mindset held opposite viewpoints. The findings indicated that adopting the guardian mentality could lead to more positive community outcomes (McLean, Wolfe, Rojek, Alpert, & Smith, 2020, p. 1112).

Cordner (2017) surveyed 89 police agencies on police perspectives on culture. The research covered several significant aspects of culture. The officers exhibited a favorable opinion of the public, but 60 percent of respondents agreed that in some jurisdictional sections it was "more useful to be aggressive than courteous" (Cordner, 2017, p. 14). Loyalty to fellow officers should have a high priority. However, over 85 percent believed it would be serious or very serious for an officer not to report a use of force incident. Seventy-three percent strongly or very strongly supported community policing (Cordner, 2017, pp. 15–16).

Regarding supervision styles, most officers felt respected, were encouraged to provide input, and received help with personal development and problems (Cordner, 2017, p. 16). However, the officers felt that higher-level police executives were less supportive and successful in directing the organization and measuring police performance. Good work was not recognized or rewarded, but poor work was not penalized (Cordner, 2017, pp. 17–18).

Regarding demographic differences in these assessments, younger police stressed a need for more solidarity and physical toughness and perceived less support and respect from the public. Black officers were more likely to support their administration and the use of community policing and thought that misconduct was a serious issue. Female officers agreed with these perceptions and were less likely to support the need for physical toughness on the job. Hispanic officers shared the beliefs of their Black and female peers. Surprisingly, officer education did not influence these perceptions (Cordner, 2017, p. 19). Cordner concluded that "police culture is not necessarily problematic, it is not monolithic, and it is substantially organizational, not simply occupational or a matter of individual personal differences" (Cordner, 2017, p. 21).

Survey research by Paoline and Gau (2018) also questioned the monolithic nature of police culture, noting attitudinal differences among police officer respondents. A study of two departments reported similar findings. While the officers expressed support for aspects of traditional police culture (importance of maintaining safety and order, not shirking work or responsibilities, the value of experience, and verbal facility), they did not display "warrior values" (cynicism toward the public, rush to judgment, preoccupation with coercive tactics, indifference to rules and regulations, and deep skepticism toward science) (Willis & Mastrofski, 2017, p. 96).

A study of Texas police chiefs examines their work culture. It reported four distinct cultures: service-oriented chiefs favored community policing and procedural justice; peacekeeper chiefs emphasized order maintenance but also supported community policing; law and order professionals supported all four dimensions but stressed law enforcement and order maintenance; while lay-lows expressed below-average support for the four dimensions (Ingram, Paoline, Rockwell, & Azimi, 2023, p. 257). However, Gross's (2023) case study of three police chiefs demonstrates how they overcame the limitations of police culture and that reform based on procedural justice is possible.

Types of Change

Organizational change results from either planned or unplanned efforts. **Planned change** occurs when administrators identify a problem or issue, diagnose it, develop a solution, and implement it. This should be a continuous process that occurs in all organizations as they endeavor to be more effective. Continuous improvement requires a commitment to organizational learning (Senge, 1990). This process is usually a series of planned steps that involves problem identification and analysis, solution development, an implementation process, and evaluation. Another type is **incremental change**. This type of change seeks to improve existing ways of doing things by building upon existing organizational systems and practices to better align them with demands upon the organization. The objective is to achieve improved performance by making planned but limited change. Common incremental changes involve changing unit heads, developing new procedures, closing unit performance gaps, and improving outcome results.

Unplanned change occurs as a reaction to intense external pressure usually brought about by crises (Welsh & Harris, 2008). Pressure for change can come from both external and internal organizational forces. Police administrators need to be sensitive to the driving forces in their environments (crime, politics, the media, labor issues, economic events, and employee issues) that necessitate change. Organizations must be flexible enough to adjust to the need to change. A consistent event that creates change in policing is the replacement of the department's chief executive. This is a political decision that usually occurs after an election when the newly elected mayor wants to appoint a chief of his or her choosing. It can also occur if the department has been judged negatively and comes under extreme pressure to change because of community unrest, excessive use of deadly force, officer misconduct, scandal, or other wrongdoing that led to dramatic incidents publicized by the media (Swanson, Territo, & Taylor, 2005). For example, the City of Baltimore's mayor fired the city's police commissioner, claiming that a change in leadership was required, following a recent spike in homicides weeks after an unarmed Black man, Freddy Gray, died of his injuries in police custody that resulted in civil disturbances and destruction of property.

In the last two decades there has emerged in policing a form of leadership that is **transformational** in nature, focused on changing reactive departments to proactive ones. It involves an organizational reengineering process that is led from the top and designed to change operational strategies, tactics, and organizational effectiveness. Transformational police executives proactively create and implement the strategic redirection of their departments in order to meet the changing demands of their operational environments effectively. This leadership style is built around changing a department's vision, mission, values, goals, engagement, empowerment, accountability, outcomes, and evaluation. Transformational leaders seek to change their organizations from reactive organizations to open-system, adaptive-learning organizations.

Transformational Process

James MacGregor Burns (1978) first defined **transformational leadership** as a process in which leaders and their followers help each other to rise to a higher level of morale and motivation. Leaders of the **transformational change** model state what they expect in others while appealing to their followers' higher ideals and values. They are change agents who take on the responsibility of revitalizing their organizations. They define the need for change, create new organizational visions, mobilize commitment to those visions, and ultimately transform their organization. Transforming an organization requires change that involves new ways of thinking about strategy, structure, people, and outcomes. Transformational leaders start with the existing organization and redesign and reengineer it to achieve higher levels of accomplishment. The common characteristics of transformational leaders are:

They identify themselves as change agents. Their professional and personal image is to make a difference by transforming their organization.

They are courageous individuals. Courage is not stupidity. These are prudent risk takers, individuals who take a stand.

They believe in people. They are not dictators. They are powerful, yet sensitive of other people, and ultimately they work toward the empowerment of others.

They are value-driven. They can articulate core values and exhibit behavior entirely congruent with their value positions.

They are lifelong learners. They are able to talk about mistakes they had made and what they have learned from these.

They show a fantastic appetite for continuous self-learning and development.

They modify their behavior to reflect new knowledge and insights.

They have the ability to deal with complexity, ambiguity, and uncertainty.

They are able to cope with and frame problems in a complex, changing world. These individuals are capable of dealing with the cultural and political side of the organization, as well as the structural and human aspects. They are entranced by the world of ideas.

They are visionaries. They are able to dream and to translate those dreams and images so that other people could share them.

(Tichy & Devanna, 1990, pp. 271–280)

Transformational leaders reject the traditional view that police organizations operated in a stable and predictable environment that can be controlled through procedures and policy. They perceive of their organizations as open learning systems that exist in complex, demanding environments. They understand that, as conditions in society, security, community interrelationships, and people change, the need for modification in strategy, organizational structure, processes, and function increases. Their change efforts involve the effective use of information, analysis, problem-solving, and the development of flexible operational strategies to meet public safety needs and align their organizations with the challenges they face. Police administrators who are transformational leaders seek to create learning organizations focused on effective performance, crime prevention, community engagement, information management, managerial accountability, ethics, and the control of crime in many police and sheriff departments across this nation. Learning organizations create, acquire, transfer, and apply knowledge to modify performance and achieve improved outcomes (Senge, 1990).

Successful transformational change depends on the leader's ability to get others to see and understand a different organizational vision and commit to it. They seek to mobilize people within and outside the organization to accept and work toward achieving change. Lastly, they institutionalize these changes through a planned process to sustain them over time. The critical difference is that transformational leaders make significant changes and evoke fundamental changes in their organization's primary political and cultural systems (Tichy & Cohen, 1997). Instead of maintaining the status quo, these police executives seek to change it and direct their departments to develop more effective ways to face today's and tomorrow's challenges. They are leading a change within policing that emphasizes a greater focus on crime reduction, professionalization, developing knowledge, and moving toward more data- and information-based problem-solving (Ratcliffe, 2008, p. 187).

Dysfunctional Organization

Unfortunately, numerous organizations undertake change and commit substantial resources to the change effort but fail to create significant sustainable change (Kotter, 1996).

The history of police reform is filled with examples of highly publicized changes that promised much but failed to achieve a lasting impact on police culture and value orientations. Recently the deaths of unarmed minority citizens at the hands of police have commanded national headlines and brought protesters and civil disorder to the streets in Baltimore, Ferguson, New York, and elsewhere (Walker, 2005). It should come as no surprise, given studies showing that police culture and value orientations changed little during this period (Cohen, 2017). These organizations often end up facing crises and become dysfunctional. By then, their ability to achieve desired change is significantly reduced, and even after heroic efforts they often decline into a crisis management mode. This bleak appraisal occurs in many police departments whose efforts to implement organizational change have failed.

A **dysfunctional organization** fails to serve its original purpose. Instead, it expends efforts and resources to maintain its existence (Balthazard, Cooke, & Potter, 2006). Dysfunctional organizations eventually become victims of the driving forces in their environment. They respond and react to these forces moving from one crisis to another, but never attempt to control or change their organization. Typical development in dysfunctional organizations is administrative inattention to employee needs and effectiveness, resulting in lower morale, employee accomplishment, and disengagement. There are three stages through which organizations become dysfunctional. These stages and their contributing characteristics are:

STAGE ONE

1. The organization lacks a clear sense of direction.
2. The organization lacks vision, goals, objectives, or outcomes.
3. Performance expectations are unclear and variable.
4. The organization lacks intelligence gathering and analysis.
5. There is a lack of planning.
6. There is a lack of problem-solving and innovation.
7. There is a failure to make crucial decisions.

STAGE TWO

1. There is a communication breakdown between administration and line operations.
2. There is a failure to focus on the department's primary mission.
3. There is low employee morale.
4. The department acts in a purely reactive mode.
5. There is high personnel turnover.

STAGE THREE

1. Management by crisis becomes the norm.
2. The organization is locked into the status quo.
3. Resources are limited.
4. Officers are demotivated.
5. Powerful vested interests protect their turf, causing internal conflict.
6. Employees have feelings of abandonment and disengagement.

It is not necessary that all of these characteristics exist at each stage. However, as the dysfunctional aspects of the organization become more pronounced, the department loses it sense of direction and its employees become demoralized and disengage. The absence of leadership in the dysfunctional organization generates a sense of abandonment in employees. Operationally, people give up and only do what is necessary to get by. Everyone is worried about themselves and their unit, to the overall detriment of the department. Employees are not team members but a group of people who show up and handle the day-to-day workload and crises. A common theme in the dysfunctional organization is management by crisis and there always is a crisis.

Sources of Change

Each organizational problem or issue, whether it is the result of factors in the external environment, such as an increase in incidents of violent crime, or internal pressure resulting from labor unrest or inadequate unit performance, has the potential to create the need for change. However, the most crucial challenge facing administrators is how managerial intervention recognizes, understands, influences, or resolves the factor(s) necessitating change. Some problems are quickly resolved, while others are much more complicated. As a result, problem identification, analysis, and solution development and implementation are essential managerial elements in a planned change process. Yet, despite disciplined and careful environmental scanning, police organizations still become victims of unplanned change. There are two primary sources of organizational change: external or internal.

External sources of change are factors outside an organization's control that have the power to affect the organization. The external environment is the context in which an organization operates. Police departments have had change imposed on them from the outside because of external forces such as legislation, court decisions, media pressure, political decisions, commissions of inquiry, the federal government, pressure groups, changing crime patterns, and high-profile incidents (Greenberg & Flynn, 2004). These external forces often trigger an unplanned response to the crises they create. Change implemented in response to crisis is highly risky, but often occurs.

Organizations will find themselves victims of externally imposed change if they do not have subsystems designed to monitor key environmental indicators that will eventually influence them. Ongoing intelligence gathering, crime and incident data analysis, external relationship building, and stakeholder analysis (newspaper analysis, community surveys, callback programs, community dialogue meetings) can be used to identify areas and trends to which the department will need to respond. External indicators can serve as benchmarks for identifying the relative position and reputation of the police organization in the eyes of citizens.

It is the responsibility of the department's leadership to identify threats to the department's present and future status and then decide to take actions to neutralize or lessen their impact. Assessing the external environment includes monitoring the following:

Community crime and quality-of-life issues.
Special population or area needs.
Special events needs.
Potential crisis areas.
Levels of community crime and violence.
Political impact issues.
Media relations.
Community support systems.
Probation and parole population.

Internal sources of change are factors found within the organization. Monitoring these is easier for administrators, because they are under their control. Put simply, the internal environment of the organization is all that is within the organization. Organizations are composed of people, structure, patterns of behavior, and processes. People are an organization's most important asset, because they perform all activities necessary for the department to fulfill its mission. A department can have the best structure and well-planned operational strategies, but without trained, proficient, and motivated people it will not be able to accomplish anything. Thus, employees are critical to the success of any change effort. Change will only succeed if an organization's employees are willing to change their work behavior and task accomplishment by more efficient and effective performance. Employee change is concerned primarily with values, attitudes, motivation, skills, competence, and on-the-job behavior.

Organizational structure is another internal area of concern. The structure is either formal or informal. **Formal structure** defines employee roles, organizational subdivisions, and their place in the organizational hierarchy of authority. It also contains rules and procedures that govern role behavior (Bolman & Deal, 1993). Over time, changes in organizational structure are needed to improve the effectiveness of the organization's response to changing demands. The **informal organization** is the interlocking social network of relationships that governs how people work together. It consists of the informal connections and relationships between organizational employees through which to accomplish work. It complements the formal organizational structure and processes. **Organizational processes** are all the activities required for the organization to function. In policing, they involve administration, operations, and support services. The administrative process creates goals, objectives, policy and procedures, performance outcomes, and regulations and oversees operational performance. All of these can create the need for change and internal conflict in some instances. However, conflict created by change can be both functional and dysfunctional.

Functional conflict is a positive factor that can energize people, lead to goal-oriented behavior, and create higher levels of achievement, awareness, and understanding. Under the right conditions, it has the potential to generate creative problem-solving and produce adaptive change. **Dysfunctional conflict** is harmful because it disrupts organizational performance and goal accomplishment. Problems occur in police organizations because many administrators do not recognize the interdependencies of their organizations' internal change areas (Barnett & Carroll, 1995). However, the conflict created by change is not all bad. A certain amount of organizational conflict is normal and healthy. Under the right conditions, it can generate creative problem-solving and produce adaptive change. Since change is synergistic and cumulative, changing one area often leads to changes in others. Common interrelated internal organizational targets for change include:

Tasks: elements of work required to achieve the organization's mission, objectives, and strategy and job designs of individuals and groups.

People: their commitment, competencies, and the human resource system that supports them.

Culture: the organization's values, beliefs, and norms guiding individual and group behavior.

Technology: the operations and information technology used to support intelligence analysis, information distribution, work performance, and outcome achievement.

Structure: the configuration of the organization, lines of authority, task responsibility, and communication.

(Schermerhorn, 2005, p. 473)

The Process of Change

Effective change agents are problem-solvers, strategic thinkers, and decision-makers. How they think and make decisions is critical to their effectiveness. All organizational actions are contingent on decision-making. Good managers develop their ability to perceive problems and create solutions to resolve them. This ability is based upon **strategic thinking**. Strategic thinkers are flexible decision-makers who seek to understand the totality of the forces affecting the problems they are confronting while at the same time maintaining a focus on their mission and objectives. They are multidimensional thinkers who seek to understand the relationships existing in the whole organizational system rather than looking at the organization and its environmental relationships as the sum of its individual parts. Strategic thinking requires that managers examine the context, interrelationships, assumptions, and the potential impact of a situation or problem. This type of thinking enables change agents to develop an understanding of all sides of the complex issues involved in the organizational change process.

The capacity to think and analyze systematically is unquestionably necessary for police managers. To make appropriate decisions in today's public safety environment, law enforcement managers must possess a broad professional knowledge base, analytical skills, and the ability to make sound judgments. The ability to recognize organizational problems clearly and understand their potential meanings and relationships concerning persons and things is a critical managerial skill. It demands that managers must learn to see interrelationships rather than linear cause/effect sequences. This process requires diagnosis.

Diagnosis

The change process begins by identifying what is known or suspected about a problem, issue, or organization requiring change. The diagnosis aims to identify data, knowledge, and information about the problems and issues that are potential targets for change. A **diagnosis** should serve two critical functions. One, it begins the change process by identifying that a problem or issue does exist. Two, it should clarify the problem or issue needing change and suggest what type of change is required. Accurate diagnosis ensures managers have the information needed to develop intervention strategies based on root causes rather than symptoms (More, Vito, & Walsh, 2012). Diagnosis sets the stage for identifying the change target and the strategy required for its implementation. The following questions should guide this information gathering and analysis:

1.   What are the problems/issues?
2.   What is the evidence for clarifying these targets for change?
3.   What part(s) of the organization are affected?
4.   What type and level of change does the analysis suggest?

A diagnosis should draw information from a variety of sources, such as: (1) performance observations, (2) crime and disorder information, (3) crime and place analysis, (4) employee interviews, (5) questionnaires, (6) critical incident reports, and (7) record analysis. A proper diagnosis should identity conditions that require change, and suggest the appropriate strategy for implementing the change.

There are four stages to diagnosis:

1.   Problem identification.
2.   Isolation of primary and secondary causes of the problem.
3.   Identification of the current response to the issue.
4.   Development of a potential solution to the problem.

(Goldstein, 1990)

An excellent example of how to conduct a diagnosis has been an integral part of problem-oriented policing (POP) since its inception. The basis for POP is the belief that police organizations must develop systematic processes for examining and addressing problems. The POP approach to diagnosing and correcting problems uses a four-stage process called SARA (Scanning, Analysis, Response, and Assessment), which is an appropriate diagnostic technique:

1.   *Scanning* is the process of identifying a problem or issue.
2.   *Analysis* is learning the problem's causes, scope, and effects.
3.   *Response* is the implementation of a planned action(s) to alleviate the problem, and developing an appropriate and effective solution to the problem.
4.   *Assessment* is the determination of the effectiveness of the response.

(Scott, 2000, p. 15)

A successful diagnosis and change strategy will identify the areas of change, provide clear and realistic targets for measuring success, and appeal to the long-term interests of organizational stakeholders. The change process must address changes that will make the organization more effective. It should communicate the need for these changes as well as their purpose. It should answer employee questions and gain their support. Once people understand why change is needed and what is expected, they often strive to achieve it. The first step of the change process should identify the direction in which the organization is going.

Too often, efforts to improve an organization specify only one or two elements, such as structure and unit command, ignoring performance changes and employee competencies required to take place. For example, in one police department several years ago, a chief publicly declared that the agency was now engaging in Community Policing. Community Policing slogans were on the side of patrol vehicles, and a new community-oriented mission statement was stated. However, the identification of duties, training, accountability, and procedural support for the change was never discussed or implemented. A change in name only resulted in creating internal distrust, resistance, and friction in the department.

Police departments are organic organizations composed of dynamic interrelationships among people performing various functions and tasks necessary to achieve the organization's mission. To anticipate and identify the need for change, police managers should continuously scan and understand their department's internal and external environment for factors calling for organizational change. They need to:

1. Recognize the indicators that signal the need for some planned change.
2. Plan and implement the required change via a planned strategy.
3. Regulate the change strategy implementation by monitoring, evaluating, and managing the process.

(More et al., 2012, p. 355)

Kurt **Lewin** (1947) developed a planned **change process with three major elements**. These are:

1. **Unfreezing the status quo** (Creating Dissatisfaction with the Status Quo and Acceptance of the Change Model).
2. **Changing to a new state** (Mobilization + Alignment Process).
3. **Refreezing the new state** (Institutionalization & Measurement).

Unfreezing involves getting the organization ready for change by having its members confront the present reality to recognize the need and lessen their resistance to it. It involves creating dissatisfaction with the present state of the organization and a desire for a change to improve things. It is accomplished by confronting the inertia the organization's status quo has on the way the department functions and changing the existing culture that supports it. Unfreezing begins when support for current values and behavior is withdrawn, and old ways are no longer desirable or acceptable. It requires breaking down the beliefs, values, customs, traditions, and culture that support the current performing methods so that the employees are ready to accept change (Schein, 1985). During unfreezing, leaders must overcome individual resistance and group conformity to the status quo. Good administrators utilize organizational analysis to scan the internal and external environments for potential problems and initiate planned change before a crisis occurs (Yukl, 2006).

Changing occurs when the planned change process is implemented, and the forces against it are overcome. The change process is designed to reduce or resolve the target issue or problem. It should introduce new performance behaviors and cultural outlooks into the vacuum created during the unfreezing of the status quo. The change process is the responsibility of the department's executive team. Without top management sponsorship, implementation efforts will be strongly resisted and ineffective. Significant change occurs only when members of the organization identify with and accept new ideas, approaches, performance behaviors, and relationships. The mere introduction of change does not ensure its acceptance. The process must be carefully managed and evaluated for successful implementation (Hersey & Blanchard, 2012).

Refreezing occurs when the new change process is institutionalized in the organization and its employees. It becomes the new way or standard operating procedure for doing things. The change becomes stabilized when the forces for change overcome resistance. The mechanics of planned change are the same for organizations as for people, because changing people is the critical variable in changing the structure or function of any organization. CompStat is an excellent example of the planned change process. Crime strategy meeting leaders facilitate the unfreezing process by inducing a certain amount of stress in unit commanders to make them recognize their performance issues and why they should change their tactics. During these meetings, commanders are exposed to new ideas, values, skills, and tactics through ongoing strategic diagnosis and dialogue. Change begins when the commanders give credence to these ideas, values, and tactics and translate them into their problem-solving tactics. Once new ideas, values, skills, and behaviors are implemented to elicit appropriate reinforcements (internal or external rewards and punishments), the refreezing occurs when unit commanders accept, identify with, and internalize the change.

While there is great value in being aware of the unfreezing-changing-refreezing theory and understanding its dynamics, good administrators know that using this knowledge effectively requires a tremendous effort that is not easily accomplished. Yet, the three-stage change process applies to small and medium-sized police departments and large law enforcement agencies.

Implementing Change

For change to be adopted, it must be implemented. It will only happen after the desired change process is put into action, translated into reality, and become everyday practice. Implementation requires careful planning and development. One way to start this process is to begin by asking some simple planning questions.

1. Where are we going?   Defined by goals/objectives/outcomes
2. How do we get there?   Identified by strategy/tactics
3. What is our blueprint for action?   Created through an action plan
4. How do we know we are on track?   Planned controls/feedback
5. How do we know we did it?   Measurement of impact/outcomes

Step 1: Develop Goals, Objectives, and Outcomes

The first step in implementing a planned change process is describing what is to be accomplished through developing and communicating the *goals, objectives, and outcomes* that everyone in the organization can understand, believe in, and strive to obtain. It should inform all organization members about expected accomplishments resulting from the change process. It should guide the process, identify accomplishments, and provide the justification and approach for the change effort by answering the questions "Where are we going?" and "Why should we do it?" This step functions in many different ways. It defines expectations from change and its proposed accomplishments, helps spark motivation, keeps changes aligned, and provides a basis to evaluate how the change process is doing. It specifies a rationale for the changes the organization will have to make. In this manner, a sense of purpose is established. It should build trust, collaboration, interdependence, motivation, and mutual responsibility for success (Stoner, Blanchard, & Zigarmi, 2007). In Great Britain, the first Principle of Law Enforcement for the newly created London Metropolitan Police (1829) stated, "The basic mission for which the police exist is to prevent crime and disorder, as an alternative to their repression by military force and severity of legal punishment" (Reith, 1956).

The long-term challenge to organizational revitalization is the extent to which the change process is accepted and implemented. Senior leadership must retain the responsibility for creating the change vision and strategy. Delegating all of the responsibility for this step is not desirable. Implementation efforts can be strongly resisted and ineffective without top management sponsorship and oversight. Often, the chief or a small group of commanding officers should create the initial plan. From there, the management team and stakeholders can refine the process.

Recently a police chief was appointed to a department with a long adversarial relationship with its community. Citizens saw the police officers as aloof, disrespectful, and quick to use force. The political structure and the community demanded this change. In his first statements to his officers and the community, the new chief expressed his belief that "a safe community is a partnership effort and everyone has a role in it." In this manner, he was beginning to articulate a collaborative vision that all elements of the community, as well as the police department, were responsible for public safety. He was setting the direction for the community and the department to change how they work together, support and respect each other. The chief executive's beginning statement helped set the stage for the redirection of the department and the acceptance of the chief's efforts by the department's employees and community.

Step 2: Communicating the Change Process

Once the change process develops, it must be communicated to the organization. **This communication** should be designed to inform organizational members of the change and why it is necessary. The need for change should be relatively easy to communicate, and it should establish a clear direction for employees to follow. A helpful rule of thumb is that if the reason(s) for the change cannot be communicated to someone in five minutes or less and get a reaction that signifies both understanding and interest, this part of the implementation is not yet completed (Galbraith & Lawler, 1993). During this process, a sense of urgency must be created to tell each other, "Let's go. We need to change things" (Kotter & Cohen, 2002). The basis for a sense of urgency is the creation of dissatisfaction with the organization's status quo. Kotter (1996) found that over half of the organizations he observed have never been able to create enough urgency to overcome resistance to change. He found that without dissatisfaction, people will not participate in the change effort, and it will fail. Unfortunately, many managers often underestimate how hard it can be to drive people out of their comfort zones. During the 1990s, numerous police executives attempted to implement community and problem-solving policing in their departments, but failed at changing their organizations. Many of these efforts were inadequately planned, disregarded the police officer culture, and met with mixed success because the officers involved were satisfied with the status quo and refused to change because they saw no need to change (McElroy, 1992; Sadd & Grinc, 1996).

The more successful change efforts begin with the leadership group facilitating a frank discussion of potentially unpleasant facts about the department and its performance results. A primary objective of this discussion is to get employees to face the actual outcomes of their efforts and create a high urgency for change. It can be accomplished by:

1.   Communicating information about potential crises or threats to the organization and its members.
2.   Provide employees with factual data about organizational performance—what they are accomplishing, instead of what they say or think they are.
3.   Engaging in frank discussion and dialogue about organizational problems, tactics, and strategy.
4.   Setting realistic performance expectations that will create the desire to change.

The above elements evolved as part of the 1994 CompStat crime-strategy meetings by NYPD Commissioner William J. Bratton and his command staff (Henry, 2002). CompStat made NYPD's then 76 precinct commanders and their officers accountable for the city's crime rate. During the face-to-face communication at these meetings, a collaboration between executive-level, operational, and staff managers was established, real-time data on crime and community problems were presented and analyzed, consistent dialogue and diagnosis about tactics and strategy took place, and performance expectations were set. In these face-to-face meetings, a comprehensive, continuous analysis of crime, current crime conditions, and community problems became integral parts of the communication dialogue that consistently evaluated the department's performance and identified changes needed to strategy and tactics. These meetings focused the attention of the department's executive team and operational commanders on developing crime prevention and control strategies. CompStat created an organizational climate in which change and collaboration were constant (Bratton & Knobler, 1998; Maple, 1999; Bratton & Tumin, 2012).

Kim and Mauborgne (2003), in their analysis of Bratton's role as a change agent with many successful police organizational turnarounds, identified this stage in the change process as the "**cognitive hurdle**." The objective is to get vital organizational members, such as unit commanders, to confront their performance reality, create dissatisfaction, and achieve agreement on the causes of the current organization's problems and the need for change. It can be accomplished by putting operational managers face to face with performance problems and issues to create dissatisfaction with inadequate performance. The dialogue during this activity should identify inadequate performance results, analyze them, and develop ways to address these problems through the collaborative efforts of the managerial group. It is also designed to identify successful performance results and how they were achieved. Kim and Mauborgne claim that Bratton's successful turnarounds of different police departments are textbook examples of "Tipping Point Leadership" (Kim & Mauborgne, 2003).

William J. Bratton, Police Executive Career

- 1983 **Chief**, Massachusetts Bay Transit Authority Police.
- 1986 **Chief**, Massachusetts Metro District Community Police.
- 1990 **Chief,** New York City Transit Police.
- 1993 **Commissioner,** Boston Police Department.
- 1994 **Commissioner,** NYPD.
- 2002 **Chief of Police,** LAPD.
- 2014 **Police Commissioner,** NYPD.

"Tipping Point Leadership" theorizes that in any organization, once the beliefs and energies of a **critical mass** of people are engaged, conversion to a new idea will spread like an epidemic, bringing about fundamental change very quickly. The theory suggests that such a movement can be unleashed only by change agents who are dissatisfied with the current state of affairs and who make unforgettable and unarguable calls for change. These leaders concentrate their efforts and resources on what matters and mobilize the commitment of the organization's key players while silencing the most vocal naysayers (Gladwell, 2000). Kim and Mauborgne claim that Bratton did all of these things in each of his organizational turnarounds.

However, it is insufficient to provide data or identify performance failures. An honest dialogue and analysis of what is happening, as opposed to what should or could be happening, must occur. These efforts must establish the employees' dissatisfaction with the organization's present reality, the need for change, and a sense of urgency to bring about the change. Once this happens, employee motivation can be directed into a focused organizational improvement effort.

Step 3: Creating a Guiding Coalition

The next step in implementing the change is for the leader to identify critical organizational personnel needed to implement the new direction successfully. These individuals must accept and believe in the change and make it happen. They constitute the change effort's **guiding coalition** because they have enough power to lead the change (Kotter, 1996). They are the organization's critical mass. This group should include formal and informal stakeholders from all levels and units who must be involved in the change process. A **stakeholder** is any person, group, or unit with a legitimate interest in the problem or issue and its resolution. Some stakeholders will provide essential cooperation; others may provide potentially fatal opposition. If the change process is to be successful, the critical mass of relevant individuals, groups, and organizational elements must be involved. Otherwise, the project may face insurmountable difficulties due to inadequate information, resources, or cooperation. Police officers have a long history of using passive resistance and diversion to resist organizational change efforts. When identifying the critical mass, the following questions should be considered:

- Who are the individuals and groups vital to the change effort?
- How do we include these individuals in the process?
- How can we develop a sense of ownership for the process in these individuals?
- What actions and results can be expected from this group?

A guiding coalition or **critical mass** consists of employees who possess the vital skills, power, and influence needed for the implementation of the desired change. Once the beliefs and energies of this critical mass of people are engaged, conversion to a new idea will spread, bringing about fundamental change very quickly (Gladwell, 2000; Henry, 2002). The change agent is responsible for identifying these individuals and getting them to accept the new direction and make it happen. If not, they must be neutralized or removed from hindering the process.

Leaders who wish to change their organizations must understand their people, the political context of their organization, and their organization's culture. As a result, change agents often find themselves in continuous communication and negotiation with potential coalition members and employees to win them over and motivate them to support the new organizational direction. It is important to remember that not all persons and groups are motivated similarly. People will differ in how willingly they will be influenced and accept change. Membership in an organization's critical mass is not restricted to any rank, position, or organization level. They are essential because they are critical stakeholders in a position to influence the support of the more significant body of organizational employees. An external critical mass of community stakeholders, political and elite powerbrokers, and the media must be identified and won over to support the department's new direction.

A common approach for developing the guiding coalition is to start with a strong core of believers. At first, this core may be limited to a handful of people leading the effort. It then grows over time as respected, reputable individuals who can lead from various sectors within the organization are identified. Finding the right blend of strengths and interests pays great dividends toward future success. Coalition members should lead by example. They should embody the values of the vision for change and actively work to enhance the change process organization-wide.

Step 4: Implementation of the Change

Implementing a change involves putting the change process into operation supported by the modification of the organization's policies, procedures, culture, performance regularities, values, and climate to enable the adoption of new practices and role behaviors required to complete the change. It entails designing and activating activities with the best chance of achieving the desired change(s). It involves the identification of a planned sequence of behavioral actions that must be accomplished if the change is to achieve its goals and objective(s). The sequence of actions must be consistent with the goals, objectives, current information, resources, and needs of the change process. The sequencing of these action steps must be realistic, logical, and achievable. Monitoring this process should be designed to provide feedback on progress or roadblocks. The change agent and guiding coalition can then adjust the implementation process to respond to the issues identified in the evaluation process. The successful implementation will require the emergence and reinforcement of a new culture supporting the leader's vision and the organization's revitalization. The employees' culture, attitudes, values, motivation, and behavior patterns must change at this stage. As noted earlier, organizational culture is a system of shared beliefs, values, and meanings that develop within an organization and guide its members' behavior. It reflects the fundamental values organizational members share and how these values express themselves in their behavior (Dessler, 2004). Organizational culture theorists believe that formal rules, authority, and procedures designed to govern behavior do not restrain the personal preferences of employees (Kotter & Heskett, 1992). Instead, the organization's cultural norms, values, beliefs, and firmly held assumptions control employee behavior (Lucas & Kline, 2008). Thus, culture is considered the hidden meaning behind behavior. Culture can function as a help or hindrance to the implementation of change, because it is the basis for how organizational members perceive and feel about their organization, its leadership, and their work. Change agents should observe and understand it to implement change successfully.

The concept of culture is essential when attempting to manage organization-wide change. Many of the organizational changes in policing have not been successful, because they failed to address the organizational cultural norms of the employees involved. For example, during the early efforts to adapt to Community Policing, there was strong resistance. This problem is one of the reasons why many strategic planners now place as much emphasis on identifying organizational values as they do on mission and vision. In his first "turnaround" of the NYPD, Police Commissioner William J. Bratton used a cultural diagnostic to identify the cultural assets, obstacles, operating culture, core identity, and values that must guide the revision of the department's vital organizational systems to institutionalize a new high-performance culture (Bratton & Knobler, 1998, p. 215).

Implementation and Organizational Culture

The implementation of change cannot be dealt with independently of organizational culture, because the organization's culture will play an essential role in shaping and reinforcing the employees' acceptance or resistance to the change. Management of an organization's culture during the implementation process involves establishing a clear direction for the change process and maintaining appropriate supporting values daily by the department's management team. In an organization with a strong culture, core values are intensely held, maintained, and widely shared among members. The more members believe in and accept the organization's core values, the greater their commitment to them and the stronger the culture. A strong culture will have a more significant influence on the behavior of its members, because it creates a climate of intense internal behavioral control. For example, in World War II, Japanese soldiers committed suicide rather than surrender and admit defeat. Surrender and defeat represented their national duty's failure and their culture's disgrace. An increasing body of research indicates that a strong positive organizational culture is associated with ethical organizations and successful organizational performance. However, a robust negative culture can serve the opposite goal and create an organization where deviant behavior is condoned and protected (More et al., 2012).

Culture serves four essential organizational functions.

1. It provides a sense of identity to members and increases their commitment to the organization or their work group (a sense of belonging).
2. It provides a way for employees to interpret the meaning of organizational events and the external environment in which the organization exists (a way to make sense of the demands of everyday life).
3. It reinforces the organization's core values (everybody knows what counts and the right way to behave).
4. It serves as a behavioral control mechanism for organizational members (if they do not conform to the behavioral norms, they are outsiders or outcasts).

The guiding coalition must know and understand the fundamental beliefs and values that form their culture to understand or predict how organization members will behave during the change process. One way to analyze organizational culture is to envision the organization as having two stages. One serves as its public front stage that contains the image its members want to portray to the outside world. This public image often represents an ideal state the organization wants or wants others to think they have achieved. The othe stage, the inner stage, contains the actual organization, the internal world for organizational members to see, never to be disclosed to outsiders. It is the arena of reality where things are done according to the pragmatic methods developed by workers to handle daily challenges, not the ideal procedural way. The closer these two stages correspond, the more positive the organizational culture. However, the wider apart they are, the more we can expect to find internal dissension, conflict, and deviant behavior. Through culture maintenance and adjustment, managers keep their units focused on the mission and protect the organization and the individual officer from liability.

Change agents should understand their organization's cultural system and the factors that create and sustain it. Value-based management actively identifies, develops, communicates, and enacts shared values. Organizational values serve a variety of purposes, including:

1. Setting forth the department's philosophy of policing.
2. Stating clearly what a department believes in.
3. Identifying in broad terms the overall goals of a department.
4. Serving as the basis for developing policies and procedures.
5. Serving as the parameters for organizational flexibility.
6. Providing the basis for operational strategies.
7. Providing the framework for officer performance.
8. Serving as a basis to evaluate the department.

(USDOJ, 2003)

Organizational values, reward systems, rules, and policies should support a positive organizational culture. **Value-based management** has a significant impact on ethics and organizational integrity. All organizational managers are responsible for value-based management. How well the culture operates to support a change process and organizational performance objectives will depend upon the strength of the organization's core values and the manager's role in maintaining them. However, in some organizations, individual managers may claim they support specific values, but their actions contradict these statements. When this occurs, conflict, distrust, and unethical behavior can result.

Shared positive values promote loyalty, a willingness to change, personal effectiveness, consensus on goals, and a sense of ownership for the organization and its people. They form the foundation for mobilizing commitment to the manager's vision. Thus, all managers must maintain a positive culture within their work units. Developing a solid ethical organizational culture is the primary responsibility of every manager. However, they must always model what they want in what they say and do. Employees watch and judge their managers every day. In addition to clarifying positive core values, managers must continue communicating and reinforcing them through their observable actions.

Value-based management will assist in developing the department's redirection, institutionalization, and sustainability. This process can be accomplished by restructuring the following organizational elements to support the proposed change process:

- Selection and advancement systems.
- Managerial communication systems.
- Organizational policy and procedures.
- Decision-making and problem-solving processes.
- Accountability systems.
- Measurement and follow-up systems.
- Reward and discipline systems.

Step 5: Maintaining Dynamic Equilibrium

A well-managed change process must be able to adapt to and incorporate itself into the organization's daily routine. However, most organizations' problem is managing innovation and change while responding to the need for stability. Keeping these two opposing demands in balance is known as **dynamic equilibrium** (Smith & Lewis, 2011). This concept implies that administrators must maintain organizational stability, that is, perform the daily tasks of policing the community and providing public safety while creating change. They must strive to maintain a sense of order while performing day-to-day responsibilities while initiating and managing the change process. It requires that change be well managed. The essential elements of dynamic equilibrium are as follows:

Dimensions of Dynamic Equilibrium

1. Change agents must be adaptable to meet external challenges and changing internal conditions.
2. At the same time, **stability** must be maintained to facilitate the achievement of current performance levels, goals, and objectives. The organization must maintain its basic day-to-day processes.
3. Enough **cohesion** must be present to ensure an orderly change in either method (means) or goals (ends).
4. Enough **innovation** must allow the organization to initiate change when conditions warrant it proactively.

Step 6: Overcoming Resistance

Change is constantly accompanied by resistance. People often resist change because they fear what will happen to them and what they may lose. Change agents and administrators need to recognize and understand the causes of employee resistance to deal with it effectively. Resistance is a form of feedback that change agents can use to adjust the change process to fit situational needs and goals. Beer (1988) identified the following factors that form the basis for employee resistance when change occurs. He claims that employees fear a loss of:

1. **Power**—change involves the loss of power and control by some individuals in the organization.
2. **Competence**—change requires new competencies and skills that make the old ones obsolete. New ways of doing things create a loss of confidence. Employees often feel devalued by this and fearful of the new skills they must learn.

3. **Relationships**—changes in organizational arrangement typically will require new relationships and therefore make obsolete old networks.
4. **Rewards**—major changes threaten some individuals' tangible and intangible rewards. New ways demand that management align the reward and change structure.
5. **Identity**—managers and employees for whom work is central to their concept of self are particularly subject to loss of self-esteem during change. For example, many patrol officers believed that Community Policing lowered the self-esteem that they derived from the crime-fighter role.

A principle of modern management holds that individuals closest to a situation should have the authority and discretion to make decisions regarding situations they are involved in. This concept is known as **empowerment**. It is the process of unleashing the power of people and focusing their knowledge, experience, and motivation to achieve positive outcomes (Randolph & Blanchard, 2007). Executive managers should encourage line management decision-making and command accountability while tolerating mistakes during the change process. Empowering this decision-making and accountability will encourage participation and involvement in the change process. It will create a broader acceptance and participation of organizational members.

Unfortunately, many law enforcement agencies have evolved into complex policy and procedural systems designed to protect the organization by controlling employee behavior and preventing mistakes. This attribute is particularly true of traditionally managed organizations that have created a rule or policy each time a mistake or problem has occurred. However, those employees who fail to change and continue to resist cannot be ignored. Their immobilization must be analyzed and addressed. They may become willing participants in the change process through training, communication, and participation. If not, they must be disciplined or removed from their position. The sanction will depend upon the form and gravity of the employee's resistance.

Step 7: Measurement of Progress

Lastly, leaders should always measure what they are trying to accomplish. How will they know if they have accomplished anything if they do not evaluate it? Establishing appropriate quantitative and qualitative performance measures will help link the change process to specific outcomes. Hard data is necessary for the assessment of managerial strategies and outcomes. Monitoring, measurement, and evaluation are keys to managerial success. They determine if you are accomplishing what you set out to do.

All elements of the change process should be conducted with evaluation in mind. Feedback systems and measurable objectives should always be part of organizational plans. Administrators should avoid setting unrealistic and unattainable expectations by developing a strategy that incorporates realistic and attainable objectives as system elements. Goals and objectives (outcomes) should be established to provide the change agent with a way to assess progress accurately, cite success, identify strategies that work, and refocus resources as needed. Leaders must develop appropriate baseline measures that record conditions before implementing change should be identified to make a before-and-after comparison of relevant changes.

All performance measures should also relate to the agency, program, and operational unit mission and goals. The design and implementation of evaluations depend upon the specific intended purpose they serve. Always measure what matters and what gives you the information that you need. All else is a waste of time, budget, and organizational resources.

Attributes of Failed Change

There has been sufficient research in policing to tell us what contributes to failure in the change process.

- Lack of sustainable leadership.
- Change is imposed from the top or outside without a compelling reason or desire established inside the organization.
- Leaders think that announcing the change is the same as implementing it.
- Lack of planning involvement and understanding of the change process by those affected throughout the organization.
- A clear, concise vision that excites people about the future has not been developed or communicated. Vision is the primary ingredient for effective change leadership. It gives people direction, alignment, and inspiration to create change.
- No sense of urgency to overcome the status quo bias.
- Lack of employee support and union resistance.
- Mid-level managers and supervisors are not included in planning, are unprepared for role changes, and are unsupportive.
- Organizational systems aren't aligned with the change.
- Supporting process and structural changes not considered or made.
- Organizational culture is non-supportive.
- New program introduced by a special unit, not integrated into the whole organization. This unit becomes the organization's "Innovation Ghetto" (Grant & Toch, 2012).
- Overall effort is too much, too fast.
- Change process is not measured, evaluated, or adjusted as needed.

Conclusion

Police administrators must know that change is a constant reality in today's public safety environment. They are expected to handle planned as well as unplanned change. Change agents should be future-oriented strategic thinkers. They must anticipate the need for change and be willing to do what is needed to bring it about. The success of any change initiative will depend on the desire and ability of the organization's leadership team to implement the change and the willingness of employees to accept the change. To be successful as change agents, administrators must understand the internal (organizational) and external (environmental) factors pushing for change. It is important to remember that people change what they do because they come to believe that it is a worthwhile thing to do. Creating the environment for change to take hold is a primary task of the department's leadership team.

The primary change process requires unfreezing the current organizational status quo, moving it to a new state, and refreezing the change to make it permanent. The dynamics of planned change involve pressure on, and arousal of, the leadership team to take action, diagnosis of the issue(s) or problem(s) involved, collection of data and identification of the real problem, development of a solution, implementation, and evaluation of the results.

Police administrators have a responsibility to assess the impact of a planned change. If the change effort proves beneficial, it should be institutionalized through positive reinforcement techniques using the above organizational tools. Police managers need to acquire an understanding of and appreciation for their role in the change process. One thing is certain. Now and in the future, police administrators will be spending more of their time initiating, implementing, and managing planned change.

KEY TERMS

Adaptability
Change
Change agents
Changing to a new state
Cognitive hurdle
Cohesion
Communication
Competence
Cookie cutter management
Critical mass
Diagnosis
Dynamic equilibrium
Dysfunctional conflict
Dysfunctional organization
Empowerment

External sources of change
Formal structure
Functional conflict
Guiding coalition
Identity
Incremental change
Informal organization
Innovation
Internal sources of change
Lewin's three-stage process
Organizational culture
Organizational processes
Planned change
Power
Refreezing the new state

Relationships
Rewards
Satisficing
Sources of change
Stability
Stakeholder
Status quo
Strategic thinking
Sustainable change
Transformational change
Transformational leadership
Unfreezing the status quo
Unplanned change
Value-based management

References

Balthazard, P., Cooke, R., & Potter, R.P. (2006). Dysfunctional culture, dysfunctional organization: Capturing the behavioral norms that form organizational culture and drive performance. *Journal of Managerial Psychology, 21*(8), 709–732.

Barnett, W.P., & Carroll, G.R. (1995). Modelling internal organizational change. *Annual Review of Sociology, 21*(1), 217–236.

Beer, M. (1988). *Leading change.* Cambridge, MA: Harvard University Press.

Bolman, L.G., & Deal, T.E. (1993). *Reframing organizations: Artistry, choice, and leadership.* San Francisco, CA: Jossey-Bass.

Bratton, W., & Knobler, P. (1998). *Turnaround: How America's top cop reversed the crime epidemic.* New York, NY: Random House.

Bratton, W., & Tumin, Z. (2012). *Collaborate or perish: Reaching across boundaries in a networked world.* New York, NY: Crown Business.

Brough, P., Chataway, S., & Biggs, A. (2016). "You don't want people knowing you're a copper!" A contemporary assessment of police organisational culture. *International Journal of Police Science & Management, 18*(1), 28–36.

Burns, J.M. (1978). *Leadership.* New York, NY: Harper & Row.

Campeau, H. (2015). "Police culture" at work: Making sense of police oversight. *British Journal of Criminology, 55*(4), 669–687.

Cohen, R. (2017). The force and the resistance: Why changing the police force is neither inevitable nor impossible. *University of Pennsylvania Journal of Law and Social Change, 20*, 105.

Cordner, G. (2017). Police culture: Individual and organizational differences in police officer perspectives. *Policing: An International Journal, 40*(1), 11–25.

Dessler, G. (2004). *Management: Principles and practices for tomorrow's leaders.* Upper Saddle River, NJ: Pearson.

Galbraith, J.R., & Lawler, E.E. (1993). *Organizing for the future: The new logic for managing complex organizations.* San Francisco, CA: Jossey-Bass.

Gladwell, M. (2000). *The tipping point: How little things can make a big difference.* New York, NY: Little, Brown.

Goldstein, H. (1990). *Problem-oriented policing.* New York, NY: McGraw Hill.

Grant, J.D., & Toch, H. (2012). *Police as problem solvers.* New York, NY: Springer Science & Business Media.

Greenberg, S., & Flynn, E.A. (2004). Leadership and managing change. In W.A. Geller & D.W. Stephens (Eds.), *Local government police management* (pp. 67–84). Washington, DC: International City/County Management Association.

Gross, N. (2023). *Walk the walk: How three police chiefs defied the odds and changed cop culture.* New York, NY: Henry Holt & Co.

Henry, W. (2002). *The CompStat paradigm: Management accountability in policing.* New York, NY: Looseleaf Press.

Hersey, P., & Blanchard, K. (2012). *The management of organizational behavior.* Englewood Cliffs, NJ: Prentice Hall.

Ingram, J., Paoline, E., Rockwell, A., & Azimi, A. (2023). Police chief culture: A view from the top. *Police Quarterly, 26*(2), 245–273.

Ingram, J., Terrill, W., & Paoline, E. (2018). Police culture and officer behavior: Application of a multilevel framework. *Criminology, 56*(4), 780–811.

Kim, W.C., & Mauborgne, R. (2003). Tipping point leadership. *Harvard Business Review, 81*(4), 60–69, 122.

Kotter, J. (1996). *Leading change.* Boston, MA: Harvard Business School Press.

Kotter, J., & Cohen, D.P. (2002). *The heart of change.* Boston, MA: Harvard Business School Press.

Kotter, J., & Heskett, J.L. (1992). *Corporate culture and performance.* New York, NY: Free Press.

Lewin, K. (1947). Frontiers in group dynamics: Concept, method, and reality in social science: Social equilibria and social change. *Human Relations, 1*(1), 5–41.

Lucas, C., & Kline, T. (2008). Understanding the influence of group dynamics on organizational change and learning. *The Learning Organization, 15*(3), 277–287.

McElroy, J.E. (1992, January 15). Judging community policing: Three views. *Law Enforcement News.*

McEwen, T. (2002). *Evaluation of community policing in Tempe, Arizona, Final Report.* Institute of Law and Justice, Washington, DC: National Institute of Justice.

McLean, K., Wolfe, S., Rojek, J., Alpert, G., & Smith, M. (2020). Police officers as warriors or guardians: Empirical reality or intriguing rhetoric? *Justice Quarterly, 37*(6), 1096–1118.

Maguire, E.R., Zhao, J., & Hassell, K. (2003). Structural change in large police agencies during the 1990s. *Policing: An International Journal of Police Strategies & Management, 26*(2), 251–275.

Maple, J. (1999). *The crime fighter.* New York, NY: Doubleday.

More, H.W., Vito, G.F., & Walsh, W.F. (2012). *Organizational behavior and management in law enforcement.* Upper Saddle River, NJ: Prentice Hall.

Paoline, E., & Gau, J. (2018). Police occupational culture: Testing the monolithic model. *Justice Quarterly, 35*(4), 670–698.

Randolph, A., & Blanchard, K. (2007). Empowerment is the key. In K. Blanchard (Ed.), *Leading at a higher level* (pp. 67–86). Upper Saddle River, NJ: FT Press.

Ratcliffe, J. (2008). *Intelligence-led policing.* Portland, OR: Willan.

Reith, C. (1956). *A new study of police history.* London: Oliver and Boyd.

Reiner, R. (2010). *The politics of the police.* Oxford: Oxford University Press.

Sadd, S., & Grinc, R. (1996, February). Implementation challenges in community policing: Innovative neighborhood-oriented policing in eight cities. *National Institute of Justice, Research in Brief.* Washington, DC: National Institute of Justice.

Schein, E.H. (1985). *Organizational culture and leadership: A dynamic view.* San Francisco, CA: Jossey-Bass.

Schein, E.H. (1990). Organizational culture. *American Psychologist, 45,* 109–119.

Schermerhorn, J.R. (2005). *Management.* Hoboken, NJ: John Wiley.

Scott, M.S. (2000). *Problem-oriented policing: Reflections of the first 20 years.* Washington, DC: DOJ, Office of Community Oriented Policing Services.

Senge, P. (1990). *The fifth discipline: The art & practice of the learning organization.* New York, NY: Doubleday.

Sierra-Arevalo, M. (2019). The commemoration of death, organizational memory, and police culture. *Criminology, 57,* 632–658.

Silver, J., Roche, S., Bilach, T., & Ryon, S. (2017). Traditional police culture, use of force, and procedural justice: Investigating individual, organizational and contextual factors. *Justice Quarterly, 34*(7), 1272–1309.

Simon, H.A. (1997). *Administrative behavior: A study of decision-making processes in administrative organizations.* New York, NY: Free Press.

Skolnick, J. (1993). *Justice without trial.* New York, NY: Macmillan.

Smith, W.K., & Lewis, M.W. (2011). Toward a theory of paradox: A dynamic equilibrium model of organizing. *Academy of Management Review, 36*(2), 381–403.

Sparrow, M. (2016). *Handcuffed: What holds policing back, and the keys to reform.* Washington, DC: The Bookings Institution.

Stoner, J., Blanchard, K, & Zigarmi, D. (2007). The power of vision. In K. Blanchard (Ed.), *Leading at a higher level* (pp. 21–36). Upper Saddle River, NJ: FT Press.

Swanson, C.R., Territo, L., & Taylor, R.W. (2005). *Police administration: Structures, processes, and behavior.* Upper Saddle River, NJ: Prentice Hall.

Terrill, W., Paoline, E., & Manning, P. (2003). Police culture and coercion. *Criminology, 41*(3), 1003–1034.

Tichy, N.M., & Cohen, E. (1997). *The Leadership engine: How winning companies build leaders at every level.* New York, NY: HarperCollins.

Tichy, N.M., &. Devanna, M.A. (1990). *The transformational leader.* New York, NY: Wiley.

USDOJ. (2003). *Principles of good policing: Avoiding violence between police and citizens.* www.USDOJ.gov/CRS.

Walker, S. (2005). *The new world of police accountability.* Thousand Oaks, CA: Sage.

Weisburd, D., & Braga, A.A. (Eds.) (2006). *Police innovation: Contrasting perspectives.* Cambridge: Cambridge University Press.

Welsh, W.N., & Harris, P.W. (2008). *Criminal justice policy and planning.* Newark, NJ: Lexis Nexis.

Willis, J., & Mastrofski, S. (2017). Understanding the culture of craft: Lessons from two police agencies. *Journal of Crime & Justice, 40*(1), 84–100.

Yukl, G. (2006). *Leadership in organizations.* Upper Saddle River, NJ: Prentice Hall.

Zhao, J. (1996). *Why police organizations change.* Washington, DC: Police Executive Research Forum.

6 Strategic Analysis

Learning Objectives

1. Define strategic analysis.
2. List the elements of organizational direction.
3. Identify what is a SWOT analysis.
4. Describe what are threats and opportunities.
5. Describe what are strengths and weaknesses.
6. Define strategic management.
7. Identify organizational success factors.
8. Describe how to diagnose internal capability.
9. Explain how to use the five frames of reference.
10. List the critical elements of each frame of reference.

Introduction

Strategic organizations have a clear sense of purpose that guides them in the utilization of their resources and capabilities in the fulfilment of their mission (Banner & Gagné, 1995). Their strategic direction is based upon accurate and timely intelligence that provides managers with the knowledge upon which they base their decisions. Setting operational priorities and deciding on strategy are intelligence-driven activities (Ratcliffe, 2016). In order to fulfill these responsibilities, managers must have a clear understanding of the forces that affect their organization and its capacity to respond to these demands (Bryson, 2011). Police departments use crime analysis to identify patterns and relationships between crime data and other relevant data sources to prioritize and target their operational activity (Cope, 2004). This chapter will discuss the interdependence of the police organization and its environment.

Organizations are subjected to both internal and external environmental forces. Managers need to be sensitive to the driving forces that necessitate change in their resource utilization and operational strategies. They must be administratively flexible to adjust to the changing demands confronted by their organization. To accomplish this responsibility, managers must become aware of, understand, and strategically analyze the forces that affect their ability to fulfill their mission.

DOI: 10.4324/9781003459095-6

Leading Change

Are police executives prepared to take the steps necessary to implement change? Several issues surround this problem.

A survey of Canadian police officers revealed their feelings about implementing new crime prevention strategies. They believed that their lack of success originated with a lack of buy-in from officers, communication regarding the change, leadership support, the direction of the change, resources, adaptiveness, and person-job fit for the initiatives (Kayal, Huey, Blaskovitz, & Bennell, 2020, p. 129).

Survey results from interviews with 23 Swedish police chiefs examined how they dealt with change initiatives. These leaders received pressure from superiors and subordinates that reflected conflicting demands. They identified three leadership roles: overseeing performance (as an operations manager), formulating strategy and exercising authority, and facilitating a good work environment (Haake, Rantatalo, & Lindberg, 2015, p. 7). These chiefs tended to side with their subordinates than their superiors' demands for change. They listened to their people to maintain relationships (Haake et al., 2015, p. 13).

Hoover (2010) advocates for using a **strategic communication plan** to guide the implementation of new operations. The plan packages a core message that reflects the department's overall strategy, values, purpose, and mission. The aim is to persuade internal and external stakeholders to support the initiative (Hoover, 2010, p. 17). The strategic communication plan must include a rationale statement that makes the case for change. It identifies potential communication as well as implementation problems. It expresses the organization's core values to identify how the change fits into them. A guiding coalition must guide the change and identify the goals of the enterprise (Hoover, 2010, pp. 18–19).

It is also essential for police leaders to manage change. One key factor is the psychological contract with employees—"the shared beliefs and expectations staff have of their employer, and the beliefs and expectations the employer has of their staff" (White & Robinson, 2014, p. 259). Based upon interviews with British officers, Smith (2019) concluded that, unlike other technical aspects of the job, there is no formal selection process to identify leaders of change in policing. Police leaders must have sound operational training, but they also need the tools to manage change—business analysis, business process design, and analysis of case studies (Smith, 2019, pp. 164–165). The absence of such preparation for change management leaves police chiefs to seek their own education on the subject—as evidenced by the experience of William Bratton in his stints as the head of the NYPD and LAPD (see Bratton, 2021). The following sections address how police leaders can be prepared to manage change.

Strategic Analysis

Strategic analysis begins with the continuous assessment of the department's external operational demand and internal response capabilities. It seeks to build a comprehensive and accurate picture of the department's efforts to serve the community by answering the following questions.

1. How effective is our present strategy and tactics?
2. What are our organization's strengths, weaknesses, opportunities, and threats?
3. How efficient are we?

4.   What strategic issues does the department face?
5.   What should the department do to respond to these issues?

A strategic analysis provides a structured way for gathering and analyzing relevant information to support strategic decisions (Henry, 2002). It makes sense that, when managers act on timely information, their organization's effectiveness will increase. A department's strategic analysis should analyze the forces that affect it, their underlying causes, and evaluate the manner in which these are responded to. It enables the department to view the entire organization and evaluate its relationship to its internal and external environments. It should provide the department with an overview of the current and long-term issues affecting or likely to affect it (Ratcliffe, 2016).

Strategic analysis involves the systematic process of collecting, analyzing, and disseminating timely and accurate information about crime and disorder problems, the conditions that generate them, as well as organizational capability. It should also involve analysis of other police-related issues, including socio-demographic, spatial, and temporal factors that impact crime and disorder. This process serves three essential functions:

1.   Analysis of crime data in order to allocate resources and deploy personnel.
2.   Discovery of crime and suspect relationships, as well as information for investigations.
3.   To learn the reasons and conditions causing criminality, and to inform policy-makers about these reasons and conditions for further policies.
                                                                    (O'Shea & Nicholls, 2003)

Knowledge obtained from this analysis is the basis upon which operational commanders develop strategies to apprehend criminals, reduce crime and disorder, and enhance crime prevention and evaluation (Boda, 2005; Ratcliffe, 2016). The department's command team should work closely with operational commanders to understand their informational needs and make intelligence gathering and its distribution effective. In strategic policing, the process of gathering, analyzing, and acting upon timely intelligence develops the police department into a **learning organization** that assesses, evaluates, and adapts its operational responses to the demands of its environment (Senge, 1990; Walsh, 2001).

To obtain this information a department needs to create an information-gathering and processing system that will provide accurate and timely data (intelligence) about crime and community public safety issues. Data are observations and measurements about crime, disorder and alarms, persons, places, and events (Groff & Lockwood, 2014; Ratcliffe, 2016). What is needed is fluent and specific data about crime conditions and an adequate spatial analysis system which is capable of engaging and identifying local and global spatial factors that affect crime conditions (Adderley & Musgrove, 2001; Hillier, 2004). This information should be collected daily, analyzed, categorized, and mapped and disseminated to operational commanders in order to identify new or changing crime patterns or threats to public safety. All levels of the department should be involved in this process. Former Deputy Chief Jack Maple (1999, p. 97), one of the creators of NYPD's CompStat, asserts that the department's front-line officers are critical information gathers who should be trained to gather information beyond what is needed to fill out reports. The ideal would be that every line officer in the department have information gathering at the forefront of his or her mind. The objective is for a department to develop enough information to provide operational commanders and administrators a clear understanding of the factors that affect current and future public safety issues and their ability to respond effectively to these driving forces.

Accurate and timely intelligence requires that administrators understand and be sensitive to the driving forces in their organizational environments (crime, politics, media, labor, economic events, employee capabilities, and issues) that impact the department and necessitate change. Strategically, they must be flexible enough to adjust organizational strategies, resource allocation, and tactics to respond to these driving forces. To accomplish this objective, departments need to develop the capability to gather and analyze a variety of information in order to understand the forces that affect them. The systematic gathering of information, its analysis, and evaluation of its relevance to the department's strategic objectives is the foundation of successful strategic policing. The United Kingdom's National Intelligence Model (NCPE, 2005) recommends that following analytical techniques as necessary for the basis for informed police decision-making:

- *Crime pattern analysis*—trend identification and hot-spot analysis.
- *Demographic/social trend analysis*—assessment of the impact of socioeconomic and demographic changes on criminality as well as population shifts and homelessness.
- *Market profiles*—assessment of the criminal market for a commodity such as drugs or prostitution.
- *Criminal business profiles*—used to determine and understand the business model and techniques employed by offenders or organized crime groups.
- *Risk analysis*—assesses the scale of risks or threat posed by offenders or organizations to individual potential victims, police, and the public.
- *Target profiles analysis*—to understand the lifestyles, networks, criminal activities, and potential interdiction points in the life of a targeted offender.
- *Operational intelligence assessment*—evaluation of information collection to inform decision-making about an existing operation.
- *Results analysis*—process used to evaluate the effectiveness of law enforcement activities.

One way to achieve this is for the department to monitor and analyze the department's operational demand, changing environment, and response capabilities continually. It makes sense that, when police departments make decisions and act on relevant information and analysis, their organization's effectiveness will increase. Operational tactics developed through CompStat crime strategy meetings, for example, are based upon information that has been analyzed and integrated into a comprehensive format that can be used as the basis for police resource allocation and deployment. Strategic policing is based upon a structured way for gathering and analyzing relevant information to support operational decisions (Henry, 2002). This analysis should go beyond current situations and carefully assess the underlying causes of emerging public safety trends so that new and better ways to respond to these factors can be identified (Goldstein, 1990).

The department's analysis of its environment is a proactive instead of a reactive approach to organizational leadership. It is a process that leads to an understanding of the demands that are and will affect a department in the present and in the future. The driving forces that exist in a department's environment can affect a department's ability to achieve its mission, overcome performance problems, and be valued by the community it serves. These driving forces are often complex and usually are the result of a variety of factors. For example, the police shooting of 18-year-old Michael Brown in August 2014 in Ferguson, Missouri, generated clashes between the police and demonstrators that mirrored past, larger-scale riots in multiple U.S. cities. These demonstrations reflected long-held feelings of perceived racial injustice as well as strongly held views of policing and our justice system that transcended the incident and generated demands that were out of control of the local police department (Holland, 2014).

Defining the Environment

An organization's environment is defined as the internal and external elements that have the potential to affect all or part of the department's ability to fulfil its mission. Organizational leaders who have a clear understanding of their environment are better able to focus their department's resources on critical areas that demand its attention. This intelligence allows managers to align their department's internal capacity with its external demands. **Strategic alignment** is the linking of an organization's internal resources, capabilities, strategy, and tactics with the demands of its external environment. The goal is to achieve effectiveness and realization of desired outcomes through the strategic management of people, processes, and inputs (Kaplan & Norton, 2006). While some police managers may feel comfortable with their own subjective capacity to diagnose the agency's problems intuitively, a far more realistic and beneficial approach is for the leadership team to support their experiential insights with factual data obtained thorough systematic analysis.

Strategic alignment requires the development of data and analysis that enhances management's understanding of their department's operational capabilities, as well as its opportunities, and threats. A standard information-generating device used in strategic business organizations is the **SWOT** assessment. It is an information-gathering technique conducted to provide information that will assist in identifying the organization's operational strengths and weaknesses as well as its opportunities and threats. Strengths and weaknesses are *internal factors* that constitute the capability of the organization to respond to its present and future demands. Opportunities and threats are *external factors* that increase demands for public safety and services that affect the value of the department to the community (Bryson, 2011). The purpose of this analysis is to identify those critical areas of service demand and potential problems that the department must respond to in order to maintain its effectiveness and efficiency.

Police departments do not function in isolation; they are affected by a variety of driving forces in their environment. These factors must be identified and understood so that a department's objectives, and tactics, can be assessed and revisited based on their relevance to changing demands. The task of evaluating strategic effectiveness and initiating corrective adjustments is both the end and the beginning of the strategic administration cycle (Thompson & Strickland, 1998). **Strategic management** is the process of formulating, implementing, and evaluating strategies that enable the organization to achieve its objectives (Schermerhorn, 2005) (see Figure 6.1).

A properly conducted strategic assessment is similar to constructing a balance sheet where organizational strengths and opportunities represent assets and organizational weaknesses, and threats represent liabilities. This activity is based upon the managerial principle that effective strategy making must aim at producing a good fit between a department's capability and its external demands. The department's leadership needs a clear understanding of its capabilities, its deficiencies, external opportunities, and threats

FIGURE 6.1 Strategic Management Process

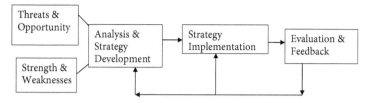

they are facing. Otherwise, the task of conceiving strategy and setting direction becomes at best a chancy proposition based upon subjective guesswork and is doomed to fail.

Internal Capability

An organization's internal capability consists of key functions (**strengths**) a department does well or an organizational asset that provides enhanced ability to achieve objectives and mission fulfillment. Analyzing a department's capabilities will lead to the identification of the organization's **core competencies**. These are the areas that the department has or does exceptionally well. For example, they may include having close positive relationships with minority community leaders, motivated patrol officers, expertise in crime scene processing, good crime prevention tactics, crime analysis techniques, and investigative skill sets. These competencies are part of the department's knowledge base that has developed through experiential learning, training, education, and creation of employee skill sets. They are capabilities that are rare, difficult to develop, and are not easily replaced because of the advantage they give the organization (Prahalad & Hamel, 1990).

Organizational capabilities can take any of several forms, such as:

Human capital—The quality of a department's employees measured in terms of their knowledge, education, training, skills, expertise, and performance accomplishments. For example, the department is noted for having well-trained, committed, and motivated employees serving in key operational areas. Technological expertise and training enhances employees' ability to provide quality service to the community (Dessler, 2012). The department's investigators perform at a high level that is reflected in a very favorable clearance rate.

Physical assets—A department's physical plant, equipment, vehicles, state-of-the-art computer hardware, and technology create a sense of organizational pride and assist the work process. Physical systems are evaluated, maintained, and updated on a regular basis.

Leadership—Managerial knowledge, development, leadership skills, and/or the collective learning and expertise of the leadership team are all strengths. The department's mission and values are supported by all employees. Executive management mentors and develops employees who are identified as future leaders.

Valuable intangible assets—The department's value as observed from the community's perspective. Value is assessed in terms of department's reputation, employee loyalty, positive work climate, community orientation, citizen support, cooperative managerial team, organizational culture, learning processes, and its ability to provide a safe community. The department has earned a high level of trust from the citizens it serves.

The capacity of a department to respond successfully to the demands of the external environment can take a variety of forms. They may be specific skills and/ or expertise. For example, the ability of the command staff to create crime strategy meetings that bring a variety of internal resources together to engage in problem identification, analysis, and response. The regularity with which employees from different parts of the organization engage in teamwork; support each other; pool their knowledge, expertise, and skills in solving problems and achieving organizational performance goals are prime strengths. The effectiveness of this collaborative effort can create performance levels not otherwise achievable by a single unit. Taken together, a department's skills and expertise, its leadership, its collection of assets, its capabilities, and its achievements determine its ability to deliver services and respond to changing external demands.

When conducting a strategic assessment, managers can evaluate a department's capabilities by observing them in action and measuring their impact. For example, the operational activities and tactics the department uses to achieve its goals and objectives should be monitored and evaluated as to their implementation and outcomes. Dedication and motivation of employees can be evaluated by observing how they perform their day-to-day work-related activities, noting how many employees are willing and able to achieve a high level of accomplishment in the performance of their duties. These assessments must be both objective and realistic. It is common for some managers to say "Our employees are dedicated" or "Our community-based operations are the best" without offering any concrete evidence or data to support this assessment. In order for the strategic assessment to have validity, all evaluative statements should be backed up with hard evidence. Objective data speak loud and clear as to what is actually happening.

Anything that detracts from the department's ability to perform its mission is a disadvantage (*weakness*) that must be addressed. Examples are inadequate management practices, such as failing to hold employees accountable, lack of leadership development, failure to provide direction, poor decision-making or problem-solving, high turnover rate, and poor morale. It may be something a department lacks, like a crime analysis capability, does inadequately, such as recruitment and training, or a condition that puts it at a disadvantage, such as budget reductions, low wages, and a poor benefits package. Any one of these will have the potential to affect the department's ability to maintain effectiveness and fulfil its mission.

Once a department's internal capabilities are identified, they need to be carefully evaluated by the leadership team. The importance of each factor should be determined by its impact on the department's ability to respond to external demands and fulfill organizational priorities. Some weaknesses may prove fatal to the department over time if they are not addressed, such as a failure to recruit quality employees. Employee quality directly affects the department's current and future capability to fulfill its mission and earn the community's support. Others may be easily corrected or offset by the department's strengths. For example, employee ability can be enhanced by a properly developed and conducted training program. The degree to which any of these factors affect a department's ability to fulfill its mission and delivery services determines its *criticality rating*. This rating is a numerical assessment with an assigned rating range from 1 (low criticality) to 5 (high criticality) for each factor, based upon an evaluation of its organizational impact. Areas of high criticality need to be addressed quickly by the department's executive team.

External Demand

The purpose of an external assessment is to examine the environment outside the department and to identify the opportunities and threats that exist there. This assessment seeks to develop information that will identify factors in the external environment that affect the department's ability to serve the community. These factors involve crime, community, economic, political, legal, social-demographic, or technological issues. This information should be systematically complied, analyzed, collated, mapped, and disseminated to the department's administrative and operational commanders. This process is the basis for the creation of the intelligence data that will be the foundation for the development of operational strategies and tactics in strategic policing. Ratcliffe (2003) suggests that the application of information analysis should be used as a rigorous decision-making tool to facilitate crime reduction and prevention through effective policing strategies. It is an analytically driven, objective process based upon hard data instead of the intuitive managerial feelings.

Identifying and paying attention to external demands—coupled with ongoing intelligence gathering, external relationship building. and stakeholder analysis—can identify areas and trends to which the department will need to respond. Stakeholder information can be obtained through newspaper analysis, community surveys, callback programs, and community dialogue meetings. This information can also be used to identify potential organizational success factors (Avinash & Nalebuff, 1991). It is important to remember that external factors are not under organizational control, while internal factors normally are.

Success factors are the things a department must do or the areas it must pay attention to for it to excel in addressing the demands of its external environment. These include such activities as assessment of crime conditions, crime control, identification of special population issues, planning for and management of special events, traffic control, crises, and risk management, building public trust, obtaining political support for the department, relations with the courts and prosecutor's office, and media image. Paying attention to these factors and responding to them appropriately enhances the value of the department in the eyes of its community and stakeholders. Thus, external indicators can serve as benchmarks for identifying the relative position and reputation of the police organization in the eyes of citizens, as well as the law enforcement profession (Moore, Thacher, Dodge, & Moore, 2002).

An external environmental scan should always pay specific attention to "**stakeholders**." Stakeholders are persons who have a direct interest in what is done by the department (e.g., citizens of the community, community leaders and spokespersons, local government organizations, and elected officials). This definition should be considered in the broadest possible terms. The concept of stakeholders is not limited to those outside the department; all members of the police organization are also included in this definition, because they have a direct interest in what the department does. Managers must decide who to involve, how to involve them, and how to solicit input from those who are not directly involved in daily contact with the department but are important to the mission of the department. Organizational executives must receive input from and consider the effect of their decisions and operations on their stakeholders. This is part of the political nature of the police executive's role (Osborne & Plastrik, 1997).

In addition to demand factors there are conditions, people, organizations, or situations in the external environment that can or will work to the department's benefit or advantage. Examples of these are positive political relationships, a supportive city manager, community partnerships, organizational partnerships, cooperative ventures, a good local employment pool, economy, and educational support systems. The factors most relevant to a department are those that offer support and aid toward mission fulfillment and organizational effectiveness. Those factors that can enable a department to advance beyond the limits of its internal constraints and achieve professional benefit must be identified and taken advantage of.

Corporate sponsorship of training scholarships for the development of department employees is one example. Annually, the International Association of Chiefs of Police awards the Michael Shanahan Award for Excellence in Public/Private Cooperation to recognize an agency's outstanding achievement in the development and implementation of public/private cooperation in public safety. Outreach and dialogue with representatives of new immigrant groups to promote mutual understanding is another example of developing information and knowledge about potential service demand.

Threat factors are external forces that threaten, or will threaten, the effectiveness and capability of the department. These can be in the form of increases in violent crime, potential crisis, competition from other police agencies for personnel, civil unrest, tax revenue shortfalls and community/political pressure groups, increased drug trafficking, political interference, community quality-of-life conditions, and organized criminal activity. External threats may pose no more than a moderate degree of hardship, or they may be so imposing as to make a department's capability and outlook quite weak. Management's task is to identify threats to the department's present and future status, prioritize these as to the criticality of their potential effect on the department, and then decide on what strategic actions should be taken to neutralize or lessen their impact.

Departments need to focus on external factors whose indicators exhibit they will become potential problems. These indicators need to be monitored. When patterns of criminal activity indicate an acceleration of incidences, appropriate response strategies must be developed and implemented. As part of its ongoing threat analysis function, police departments should have a crime analysis unit capable of providing an assessment of the broader patterns and ecology of community crime trends. Threat analysis requires that the department develop the capability to rapidly identify and understand the broader trends of criminal behavior in order to develop an effective crime control capability.

A basic premise of strategic police management is that a department should formulate strategies to take advantage of opportunities and strengths to overcome or reduce the impact of threats and weaknesses. For this reason, gathering intelligence, identifying, monitoring, and evaluating external opportunities and threats are essential to the success of the department's efforts.

A strategic analysis is therefore more than an exercise in making lists. In addition to identification of demand factors, it involves evaluating a department's response capabilities and drawing conclusions about how best to deploy its resources in light of the department's internal and external situation. Analysis of the above factors and prioritization of their impact on the department constitutes the beginning of both a strategic analysis and planning process.

Analyzing the Internal Environment

Diagnosing an organization's capacity to respond to its environmental demands requires that the executive team and all unit managers use their analytical skills to evaluate their organization's operational capability. Organizational performance issues are often complex, changing, and ambiguous. It is more advantageous to analyze organizational capacity by using different frames of reference as diagnostic tools. A frame of reference is an analytical tool that can be used by managers to evaluate an organizational element (Daft, 2002).

Described below are five **frames of reference** that managers can use to diagnose an organization's internal capacity (Bolmam & Deal, 1991). Each frame identifies a specific reference point and its core components. When these frames of reference are used together, they form an analytical framework that can be used to evaluate the organization or a specific performance problem. They provide the evaluator with a complete set of analytical perspectives that can be used to identify and evaluate the variety of factors that contribute to an understanding of internal organization.

Frames of Reference

Structural Frame

The **Structural Frame's** focus is the form and design of the organization. Its primary concern is how the organization, and its subunits, are structured, fit and synchronize their work to achieve the department's mission. Large-scale police departments are structurally complex because they combine a centralized authority system with a variety of specialized units. Smaller organizations tend to be more generalist in nature and thus less of a diverse structure. Structural analysis assesses the relationship between performance and organizational structural elements such as mission, goals, objectives, chain of command, span of control, unit size, formal roles, task specialization, job descriptions, unit outcome objectives and measures, policy and procedures. It should be remembered that organizational structure is a tool created to accomplish the mission, not blocks of unchanging granite once formed and never changed.

Organizational structures develop as the result of the need to accomplish a variety of tasks to fulfill the department's mission. It changes as police executives seek to find solutions to organizational problems through creation or disbanding of operational units. As the responsibilities of organizations and the external demands they confront become complex and grow, specialization increases, and organizational divisions and subunits are created. This development can be haphazard and result in inefficient organizational structures, overlapping of responsibilities, and lack of strategic alignment if it is not periodically evaluated.

A common misconception of some administrators is their belief that the way to improve organizational performance is simply a matter of creating standardized operating procedures. This perspective perceives the organization as a rational, objective, orderly system that can be controlled exclusively through policy and procedures (Morgan, 1997). Departments of this type often evolve into command-and-control-dominated organizations. Their internal structure becomes etched in stone and emerges as the primary organizational control mechanism. It is a serious matter if the chain of command is violated or procedures are challenged. Unfortunately, this is not realistic and hinders the way these organizations respond to the complex demands of their environment.

Today's law enforcement organizations face a fluid external environment that demands flexibility in organizational arrangement and strategy. A prime example of this new reality is the development of multijurisdictional task forces, cross-functional units, and special purpose units to address mutual public safety issues that cross jurisdictional boundaries.

Organizations that exist in a stable environment or have a singular purpose, with highly specific and measurable goals, can structure themselves tightly through written procedures and detailed checklists (e.g., McDonald's Corporation, prisons, and jails). The objective of this type of organizational structure is to control error and ensure a uniform product is produced. A Big Mac should be the same product in Akron, Ohio, as well as in Miami, Florida. However, the service area problems faced by police officers in these two cities are varied and diverse, demanding different strategies and tactics by their police departments. Environmental analysis, operational flexibility, and commander empowerment are essential for organizations to address changing conditions and threats. Unit structures will need to change over the life of an organization. Organizational leaders who fail to understand this run the risk of their organizations becoming stagnant and ineffective.

The use of the structural frame of reference as an analytical tool requires that managers seek to identify and analyze the structural factors that impact positively or negatively on the department's performance. If structural changes are required, these must be considered in relation to their impact on the organization's effectiveness and the other frames of reference. For example, a change in operational tactics may require employee input, retraining, a change of supervisors, and acceptable methods of performance.

It is a common practice when a crisis or a threatening incident occurs for some managers to call for reorganization, more rules, and centralization of decision-making in order to restore their control. However, too much reliance on rules, procedures, and managerial control can create a rule-bound organization. In this type of organization, people do not engage in problem-solving and creative decision-making; they follow the rules. They continue to meet current operational problems with the standard operating procedures designed to resolve past issues. These organizations maintain their status quo and remain locked in the past.

Insufficient understanding of the structural factors can result in role confusion, duplication of effort, conflict, and costly mistakes. A balance must be achieved between the need for structure and the need for organizational flexibility. The manner in which a manager creates this balance is one of personal choice, based upon need, experience, and analysis of the realities of the organizational situation. Remember, organizations are not blocks of granite cemented together, but tools to accomplish a mission (purpose). A way to address this problem is to start with the identification of what is to be accomplished and then restructure the organization to achieve this outcome. Below are several questions that will assist in conducting a structural analysis.

STRUCTURAL FRAME ANALYTICAL FACTORS CHECKLIST

Is the department (unit's) **Mission** clear and understood?
Have **Goals and Objectives** been **clearly** defined?
Are **Measures of Performance** defined and understood?

Does our current **Structure** contribute to mission accomplishment?
Has **Accountability** been clearly established in policy, job descriptions, and reality?
Are **Job Descriptions** clear and current?
Has **Position-Based Authority** been established?
Is the **Chain of Command** appropriate?
Is the **Span of Control** appropriate?
Is there a current **Policy,** or does it need to be written?
Are the operating **Procedures** clear?
Are outcomes being **Measured and Evaluated**?

Human Resource Frame

The analytical focus of the **Human Resource Frame** is the department's management of its personnel resources and polices. This frame of reference is treated more in depth in Chapter 9 of this text. Human resource management is a critical factor in creating and maintaining organizational effectiveness. Police departments can do many things right, but if they hire the wrong people, or do not prepare employees to perform properly or motivate them, they will not be effective employees. People produce results. The human resource perspective requires that a good fit be made between the organization's objectives and the people required to achieve them.

Today, there is a growing emphasis on "knowledge workers" and the importance of human capital. A **knowledge worker** is someone whose mind is a critical asset to the organization (Drucker, 1988). In strategic policing it signifies how officers think, use, analyze information, and engage in problem solving. Their performance is a product of how well they apply the core body of knowledge of policing in their daily tasks. **Human capital** refers to the quality of the knowledge, education, training, skills, and expertise of an organization's employees (Dessler, 2007). This is a qualitative assessment of the department's employees' skill set and intellectual abilities. On regular basis, strategic organizations actively modify their performance to reflect new knowledge, insights, and assessment of environmental driving forces (Senge, 1990). These departments analyze the variety of situations they confront, encourage their employees to practice independent problem-solving, and apply a diverse body of technical and analytical skills to resolve the driving forces that affect them. Organizations who seek to engage in strategic policing must actively develop the intellectual capabilities, information usage, and skill sets of their employees to accomplish their objectives. In strategic-focused police organizations, effectiveness depends more on the intellectual capabilities of their employees than any other factor.

Police employees apply a complex body of knowledge in their work. This knowledge base is obtained through continuous education, training, occupational experience, and information analysis. Knowledge workers are self-starters who engage in continuous learning. They place a great emphasis on their competency and professional accomplishments (Schermerhorn, 2005). Thus, a critical executive skill is the ability to manage the human intellect and convert it into productive organizational activities (Walsh, 1998). A core belief of this frame of reference is that people who feel they are prepared to engage in meaningful work and are respected in the workplace will give their knowledge, talent, and commitment to their organization. This frame of reference focuses managerial attention to the **competency, commitment,** and **teamwork** of their people.

Leadership, management style, job analysis, employee selection, education, training, placement, empowerment, personnel and organizational development, networking, consultation, employee involvement, relationships, and self-managed work teams are analytical elements of this frame of reference. However, it should be remembered that employees are not the only source of organizational problems and/or solutions. Managers will often blame organizational problems on poor selection, employee motivation, lowered standards, or poor training. They fail to recognize that the human element is but one factor contributing to problematic conditions. The dominance of these beliefs can lead managers into believing that all their problems can be resolved through changing employees, discipline, or training. Unfortunately, it is never that easy.

Every organizational manager, from the chief (CEO) to the sergeant (line management), is responsible for the competency, commitment, and development of their employees. Mentoring, counseling, training, and developing employees are basic managerial tasks. Management failure to address human resource needs can lead to incompetent employees, diminished creativity, little if any commitment, and communication breakdowns. Managers that treat their employees badly and with little regard will develop a conflicting or combative workforce that can make the lives of all involved miserable. Organizations that experience this form of conflict often break into warring camps that are divided into management versus operational personnel, them and us, line and staff (Reuss-Ianni, 1983). They become organizations in crisis.

A primary responsibility of a department's leadership team is to institute human resource policies and practices that produce employees with the competencies and commitment capable of achieving the department's goals and objectives. The following are several questions that will assist in a human resource analysis.

HUMAN RESOURCE FRAME ANALYTICAL FACTORS CHECKLIST

What kind of **leadership** style does this organization and/or strategy need?
What type of **people** should be **selected** for this assignment?
What are our employees' **competency levels**?
How **committed** are our employees?
What types of **training and development** do our employees need?
How should our people **be developed** for the department's future needs?
How should individual performance be **evaluated**?
How should **unit performance** be evaluated?
How much **empowerment and discretion** should employees have?
How do our employees **communicate** between themselves and others?
What kind of **teamwork** exists in this organization?

Political Frame

Politics and conflict are a normal reality of organizational life. Different groups and individuals within organizations develop agendas to satisfy their own needs and wants. In many organizations powerful vested interests will resist any change that affects them. The more likely change becomes, the more fiercely and vocal these negative influencers will fight to protect their positions (Kim & Mauborgne, 2003). The political frame of reference identifies and analyzes conflicting groups and individuals who are competing for power and control within and without a department. Its focus is the way people use power, build alliances, and engage in conflict and either hinder or assist the department to achieve its mission.

This frame of reference emphasizes that managers should clearly understand the political context and power networks of their organizations. They need to identify the individuals internally and externally who hold positions that will affect the accomplishment of organizational goals and objectives and understand their impact on the organization. Managers need to know how to productively confront, use, and manage power and conflict. Conflict analysis, tactics of conflict creation and/or control and power are tools that can be used to resolve interpersonal and organizational problems. Organizational conflict must be managed before it involves the breakdown or disruption of normal operational activities to a point where individuals or groups experience real difficulty in working with one another (More, Vito, & Walsh, 2012).

Power is the ability to influence the behavior and attitudes of others (Luthans, 2002). Individuals hold power because of their positional authority, individual expertise, control of rewards and punishments, alliances and networks, control of organizational symbols, and personal attributes. Knowing how to use power is a skill that managers should develop if they wish to be successful. However, using power inappropriately can result in failure for both the organization and the manager.

Conflict is not always destructive and it does not always have to be resolved. Conflict can be used as a tool to force employees to face a situation or problem, deal with it, and develop innovative approaches to problem-solving. It can be used to challenge the status quo and reduce complacency. If conflict is a normal organizational occurrence, then managers must understand it and learn to use it to their advantage (Afzalur, 2002).

It is also important to remember that one does not have to be in a position of authority to have power and influence over others. There are many individuals within and without organizations who possess different power bases that they use to affect the ability of others to achieve their goals. Individuals who understand and use power best will see their ideas implemented and their influence extend beyond their immediate area of control. Constructive use of power is necessary for the creation of effective organizations.

Managers who fail to understand the Political Frame of Reference will be ignoring an important aspect of organizational life. However, overuse of power as a management tool will increase conflict and prevent task accomplishment. It can lead people to feel they are being manipulated or devalued and result in their being cynical, pessimistic, and combative. Managers are often expected to balance and manage inevitable trade-offs and to equitably negotiate and integrate their organization's interests with those of others within and without the organization (Buchanan, 2008). Accomplishing this task requires expertise (technical knowledge), analytic ability (critical thinking), and interpersonal and group dynamics skills (personal power). Network-building and team-building skills have become a necessity for managerial effectiveness because of the complexity of many contemporary organizations and the demands placed on them by stakeholders (Schermerhorn, 2005).

The first step in developing successful work relationships is to identify those individuals who hold power and resources inside and outside the organization. Next is to determine what differences and similarities exist between the people whose cooperation is needed by the manager; for example, differences in goals, values, position, pressure, and working styles. Then try to understand what the basis of these differences and similarities are so that the relationship with the person needed to accomplish objectives can be strengthened.

Effective managers consider those on whom they are dependent as potential allies, even when they may at first appear to be adversaries. Unofficial and informal networks evolve within organizations as employees develop methods to work together, achieve goals and objectives. These networks are often based upon the **exchange theory** that involves employees bargaining for assistance, resources, and information needed to accomplish their jobs and is the basis of this exchange. Thus, mutually beneficial alliances are developed between individuals by their identifying what each exchange member might have to offer that they need or want (Stojkovic, Kalinich, & Klofas, 2012). The basis for network building is the **law of reciprocity**; that is, that one good deed deserves another. The primary way managers extend their influence through networks is by providing resources, information, and services to others in exchange for resources, services, and information they require. The Political Frame checklist below contains a number of questions that will assist with this analysis.

POLITICAL FRAME ANALYTICAL FACTORS CHECKLIST

How is power **distributed and used** in the organization?
Who are the **power holders** in this organization?
Who are the important **stakeholders outside** of the organization?
Whose **cooperation** is needed?
Whose **compliance** is needed?
What are the **conflict relationships** that exist within this organization?
What are the **sources of conflict**?
What **networks** should be developed?

Cultural Frame

An organization's shared values, beliefs, assumptions, perceptions, norms, artifacts, and accepted ways of behaving make up its culture (Ott, 1989). An organization's culture is passed from one generation of employees to another one through stories, rituals, myths, and day-to-day conversations. A department's history and traditions are the source of these stories, values, rituals, and myths. They form the basis of the department's belief system about how one should act as a member of the organization. The importance of an organization's culture is that it provides a sense of meaning and purpose for the way employees look at, attempt to understand, and work within their everyday world.

The critical point of analysis within this frame of reference is not the actual behavior of people, but what the behavior means to the members of the organization involved. The reasons why people act in a specific manner can be found in their values and the meanings they attach to their behavior. These beliefs, values, and acceptable modes of behavior are learned through the process of organizational socialization and are often expressed as rationalizations for behavior.

Managers who understand the importance of culture appreciate the power of an organization's vision, values, rituals, ceremonies, and stories. They use these to create a set of shared beliefs that help to shape their department's self-image. Many police organizations have developed strong organizational cultures based on meaningful rituals, traditions, and visions of what is their actual function. Organizational symbols can also be used to camouflage or distort. The certified police officer may be incompetent because of a lack of training after the certification was originally achieved. The training officer may give out test questions and answers during mandatory training sessions. The organization that states "Our People Come First" in its value statement might actually treat its workers terribly. There may be one set of rules and behavioral boundaries for managers, and another for employees. The "mission statement" on the wall may mean nothing at all. All of which can create a culture of distrust and conflict within an organization.

Organizations have been described as having two stages—one in front and one in the back of the curtain that divides them from the public (Goffman, 1959; Manning, 1997). The front stage projects the image the department wants to display to outsiders. They want outsiders to believe this is the real organization. However, only insiders, the organization's employees, get to see and know the real world hidden backstage—what the organization truly is and how it operates behind the front stage. In well-managed ethical organizations, there should be little difference between these two stages, but in organizations that lack integrity and ethical accountability there is a vast difference between the two.

For example, Sex Crimes and Special Victims Units are created by departments to handle the investigation of all rapes and attempted rapes, sexual batteries, and cases of a sexual nature. The Special Victims Section of the City of New Orleans Police Department consists of the Sex Crimes Unit, the Child Abuse Unit, and the Domestic Violence Unit. An investigation conducted by the City of New Orleans Office of Inspector General found that the department's investigators assigned to the Special Victims Section had questionable documentation for investigations. Detectives ignored reports of sex crimes, failed to follow up on reported sexual abuse cases, and routinely failed to provide documentation of sexual investigations, often writing up questionable case files. According to the report of the 1,290 sex crime incidents assigned to the unit's five detectives, from 2011 to 2013, only 179 (14 percent) included supplemental reports showing that they were properly pursued and investigated. In 450 cases with initial investigative reports filed by the detectives, 271 (60 percent) did not include documents showing that there was any additional follow-up (Quatrevaux, 2014). This report disclosed the huge discrepancy between what this unit was created to do and what it actually did.

For change to take place in an organization, managers must understand its cultural values and whether or not these could support behavior such as what was disclosed by the New Orleans Inspector General's report. However, this can be difficult for insiders to do because their organization's cultural system is very much a part of their psychological makeup. Organizational change agents must be able to stand outside of their organization's cultural value system, analyze it, and understand from without if their intervention is to succeed. Remember, from a cultural perspective, what is real is real, whether in fact it is real or not.

CULTURAL FRAME ANALYTICAL FACTORS CHECKLIST

What is the true **vision of this organization** and its members?
What are the **values, beliefs, history, and traditions** of this organization?
What **image (front and back stage)** does the organization present?
How are **accountability and ethics maintained** in the organization?
What are the **acceptable modes of behavior** in the organization?
What **values drive employee performance**?
Is there a different **ethical standard** for managers and officers?

Technology Frame

This frame of reference's focus is the manner in which information is obtained and processed. Organizational technology refers to the tools or processes used by organizations to transform data and raw information into useful and actionable intelligence. This information becomes the basis for strategic decision-making, strategy development, and the deployment of personnel and resources. Intelligence is not simply the collection of information; it is what is produced after the collected data is evaluated and analyzed (Peterson, 2005).

Operational managers, supervisors and officers, investigators and special unit officers should be trained to gather, receive, and disseminate time-sensitive and accurate crime and community problem information. This information is the foundation for crime analysis, strategy development, and outcome evaluation. The ability to make effective use of timely and accurate intelligence is linked to the department's technology systems that are used to collate, analyze, and present raw crime data. Teamwork and systems thinking should be employed between operational commanders, crime analysts, investigators, supervisors, and officers. They must work together to make intelligence gathering and distribution effective. For example, the primary data component of NYPD's CompStat is a database that contains daily crime counts, by precinct, for seven major crimes. To gain timely information and intelligence about these crimes in New York City, the department's executive team required every precinct to create its own "crime information center" to collate information on crime events, their location, suspects, and fugitives (Maple & Mitchell, 1999; Henry, 2002).

We exist in a technological age. Information gathering and processing is the lifeblood of an effective organization. Failure to engage the organization's environment in a structured manner to gain **accurate and timely intelligence**, to employ technology (tools/process, GIS systems) to process this information, and to distribute it to those who need it, will eventually victimize the organization and result in mission failure.

TECHNOLOGY FRAME ANALYTICAL FACTORS CHECKLIST

What are our **information needs**?
Where do we obtain this **information? (Sources)**
How will this **information be processed**?
Who needs this information?
Who will be responsible for it?
When do they need it?
How will it be **distributed** to those who need it?
What do our **management information systems** tell us?
How is information used to **solve problems**?
What **technology** do we have and need?

Conclusion

Taken together, the analytical tools described in this chapter can be employed by police administrators to analyze the environmental forces affecting their organization. Strategic analysis can provide timely information and differing perspectives and understanding of these forces. The subtlety is finding the right balance between the external and internal elements. Changes in one area inevitably reverberate through the other areas. Factors such as strengths or weaknesses that affect one frame of reference, if ignored, may distort or undermine the analysis. The process described above is an example of "**systems thinking**," because its focus is the whole organizational environment instead of its isolated parts (Senge, 1990). Systems thinkers strive to understand all the factors that affect their organization and how these relate to their problem-solving analysis. They are not fragmented thinkers, but individuals who know and understand the interconnectivity of the many factors that affect their organization. In strategic policing, all department managers should be systems thinkers. The concept underlying this type of thinking is the understanding that nothing in the organization stands alone, it must always be considered part of a greater whole.

Organizations are complex systems that involve a number of intertwined parts. The separate parts of the system do not exist, nor function, in isolation from each other. Managers need to understand the pattern of relationships that exist within and without their total organization and how these impact on their ability to function effectively (Banner & Gagné, 1995). An event in one part of the system can, and often does, have system-wide effects. Thus, managers must understand and learn to reinforce or change these relationships effectively. Unfortunately, managers usually focus on isolated parts of the organizational system instead and then wonder why their efforts at solving problems and effecting change fail.

KEY TERMS

Accurate and timely intelligence	Law of reciprocity	Strategic management
Commitment	Leadership	Strength
Competency	Learning organization	Structural frame
Core competencies	Physical assets	Success factors
Cultural frame	Political frame	SWOT
Exchange theory	Power	Systems thinking
Frames of reference	Stakeholders	Teamwork
Human capital	Strategic alignment	Technology frame
Human resource frame	Strategic analysis	Threat factors
Knowledge worker	Strategic communication plan	Valuable intangible assets

References

Adderley, R.W., & Musgrove, P. (2001). Police crime recording and investigation systems. *Policing, 24*(1), 100–114.

Afzalur, R.M. (2002). Toward a theory of managing organizational conflict. *International Journal of Conflict Management, 13*(3), 206–235.

Avinash, D., & Nalebuff, B.J. (1991). *Thinking strategically: The competitive edge in business, politics, and everyday life.* New York, NY: W.W. Norton & Co.

Banner, D.K., & Gagné, E.T. (1995). *Designing effective organizations: Traditional and transformational views.* Thousand Oaks, CA: Sage.

Boda, R. (2005). *Crime analysis and crime mapping.* Thousand Oaks, CA: Sage.

Bolmam, L.G., & Deal, T.E. (1991). *Reframing organizations: Artistry, choice, and leadership.* San Francisco, CA: Jossey-Bass.

Bratton, Bill. (2021). *The Profession.* New York, NY: Penguin Press.

Bryson, J.M. (2011). *Strategic planning for public and nonprofit organizations: A guide to strengthening and sustaining organizational achievement*, 4th ed. San Francisco, CA: Jossey-Bass.

Buchanan, D.A. (2008). You stab my back, I'll stab yours: Management experience and perceptions of organization political behaviour. *British Journal of Management, 19*(1), 49–64.

Cope, N. (2004). Intelligence led policing or policing led intelligence? *British Journal of Criminology, 44*(2), 188–203.

Daft, R.L. (2002). *The leadership experience,* 2nd ed. Orlando, FL: Harcourt.

Dessler, G. (2007). *Human resource management,* 11th ed. Upper Saddle River, NJ: Pearson Prentice Hall.

Dessler, G. (2012). *A framework for human resource management,* 7th ed. Upper Saddle River, NJ: Pearson Prentice Hall.

Drucker, P. (1988). The coming of the new organization. *Harvard Business Review, 66* (January), 45–53.

Goffman, E. (1959). *The presentation of self in everyday life.* New York, NY: Doubleday.

Goldstein, H. (1990). *Problem-oriented policing.* New York, NY: McGraw Hill.

Groff, E.R., & Lockwood, B. (2014). Criminogenic facilities and crime across street segments in Philadelphia: Uncovering evidence about the spatial extent of facility influence. *Journal of Research in Crime and Delinquency, 51*(3), 277–314.

Haake, U., Rantatalo, O., & Lindberg, O. (2015). Police leaders make poor change agents: Leadership practice in the face of major organisational reform. *Policing and Society,* 1–15. doi: 10.1080/10439463.2015.1099653.

Henry, V.E. (2002). *The Compstat paradigm: Management accountability in policing.* New York, NY: Looseleaf Law Publishing.

Hillier, B. (2004). Can streets be made safe? *Urban Design International, 9*(1), 31–45.

Holland, S. (2014). *Obama on Ferguson: U.S. "has more work to do" on race relations.* Washington, DC. www.Reuters.org

Hoover, C. (2010, August). The strategic communication plan. *FBI Law Enforcement Bulletin,* 16–21.

Kaplan, R., & Norton, D. (2006). *Alignment: Using the balanced scorecard to create corporate synergies.* Boston, MA: Harvard Business Press.

Kayal, H., Huey, L., Blaskovitz, B., & Bennell, C. (2020). If it's not worth doing half-assed, then it's not worth doing at all: Police views as to why new strategy implementation fails. *Police Practice and Research, 21*(2), 117–133.

Kim, W.C., & Mauborgne, R. (2003, April). Tipping point leadership. *Harvard Business Review,* 60–69.

Luthans, F. (2002). *Organizational behavior,* 9th ed. New York, NY: McGraw-Hill.

Manning, P.K. (1997). *Police work: The social organization of policing,* 2nd ed. Long Grove, IL: Waveland.

Maple, J., & Mitchell, C. (1999). *The crime fighter.* New York, NY: Doubleday.

Moore, M., Thacher, D., Dodge, A., & Moore, T. (2002). *Recognizing value in policing: The challenge of measuring police performance.* Washington, DC: Police Executive Research Forum.

More, H.W., Vito, G.F., & Walsh, W.F. (2012). *Organizational behavior and management in law enforcement.* Upper Saddle River, NJ: Prentice Hall.

Morgan, G. (1997). *Images of organization,* 2nd ed. Thousand Oaks, CA: Sage.

NCPE (2005). *Guidance on the national intelligence model.* Wyboston, UK: National Center for Policing Excellence on behalf of ACPO.

O'Shea, T., & Nicholls, K. (2003). Police crime analysis: A survey of US police departments with 100 or more sworn personnel. *Police Practice and Research, 4*(3), 233–250.

Osborne, D., & Plastrik, P. (1997). *Banishing bureaucracy: The five strategies for reinventing government.* Reading, MA: Addison-Wesley.

Ott, J.S. (1989). *The organizational culture perspective.* Pacific Grove, CA: Brooks Cole.

Peterson, M. (2005). *Intelligence-led policing: The new intelligence architecture.* Washington, DC: Bureau of Justice Assistance.

Prahalad, C.K., & Hamel, G. (1990, May–June). The core competencies of the corporation. *Harvard Business Review,* 79–91.

Quatrevaux, E.R. (2014). *A performance audit of the New Orleans police department's uniform crime reporting of forcible rapes.* Baton Rouge, LA: Office of Inspector General.

Ratcliffe, J. (2003). Intelligence-led policing. *Trends and Issues in Crime and Criminal Justice, 248.* Canberra: Australian Institute of Criminology. www.aic.gov.au.

Ratcliffe, J. (2016). *Intelligence-led policing,* 2nd ed. New York, NY: Routledge.

Reuss-Ianni, E. (1983). *Two cultures of policing: Street cops and management cops.* New Brunswick, NJ: Transaction Books.

Schermerhorn, J.R. (2005). *Management,* 8th ed. New York, NY: John Wiley.

Senge, P.M. (1990). *The fifth discipline: The art & practice of the learning organization.* New York, NY: Doubleday.

Smith, R. (2019). The "police change manager": Exploring a new leadership paradigm for policing. *International Journal of Police Science & Management, 21*(3), 156–167.

Stojkovic, S., Kalinich, D., & Klofas, J. (2012). *Criminal justice organization: Administration and management,* 5th ed. Belmont, CA: Wadsworth.

Thompson, Jr. A., & Strickland, A.J. (1998). *Strategic management concepts and cases.* New York, NY: McGraw Hill.

Walsh, W. (1998). Policing at the crossroads: Changing directions for the new millennium. *International Journal of Police Science and Management, 1*(1), 17–25.

Walsh, W. (2001). CompStat: An analysis of an emerging police managerial paradigm. *Policing: An International Journal of Police Strategies & Management, 24*(3), 347–362.

White, V., & Robinson, S. (2014). Leading change in policing: Police culture and the psychological contract. *Police Journal: Theory, Practice, and Principles, 87*(4), 258–269.

7

Strategic Planning

Introduction

In recent years, the need for efficiency and effectiveness in managing police agencies and their programs has increased. Pressures such as decreasing fiscal resources, increased demands for service, and citizen involvement have led to greater scrutiny of police operations. Developing and implementing a strategic plan can help police administrators address such concerns.

Through strategic planning, an organization attempts to anticipate future events and control its destiny. By analyzing its strengths and weaknesses, the organization can avoid future problems and ensure success in achieving its goals. Strategic planning represents a different way of managing police departments. It can serve as the basis for problem-solving. Rather than responding to crises at the last moment, agencies can anticipate difficulties and develop plans to deal with them beforehand. To deal with a crime problem, agencies must have valid information about where and when it occurs and then develop a response. Strategic planning can help police departments identify and mobilize available resources and apply them to community needs. It attempts to maximize opportunities and minimize threats to the organization.

Strategic planning has made a comeback in recent years. It is tied to participatory and **Total Quality Management** (TQM) (see Couper & Lobitz, 1991; Manning, 1995; Hoover, 1996; Kurz, 2006). It is a way to mobilize the organization, recognize the importance and contributions of line staff personnel, and tap into the community's resources. Strategic planning is also related to the "**Open Systems Model**", because it recognizes the crucial role of internal and external environments in reaching organizational goals (Munro, 1971).

DOI: 10.4324/9781003459095-7

In policing, strategic planning is enjoying a renaissance for several reasons. One is the shift to Community Policing. Its title infers a partnership between the police and the people they serve. This partnership improves the quality of life in the community through introducing strategies designed to enhance neighborhood solidarity and safety (Trojano-wicz & Bucqueroux, 1990). Community Policing requires that police departments initiate and adopt proactive strategies and tactics to repress crime, fear, and disorder within local neighborhoods. Citizens are expected take a proactive stance in helping the police and other government entities identify their public safety needs and policy. Agencies committed to Community Policing perform their traditional duties of law enforcement, order maintenance, and service, and additionally solve community problems. Therefore, officers and agencies must do more than just focus on crime control. They must anticipate social and law enforcement concerns before they become problems. Strategic planning is a tool to accomplish these tasks, as well as revealing the road the organization should take to work with the community to achieve higher levels of satisfaction and safety.

In addition, Community Policing calls for a decentralized approach to policy development. The aim is to better protect citizens by allowing officers to adjust their responses to serve the community best. Decentralization forces the department to partner with citizens dealing with crime, disorder, and quality-of-life issues (Wasserman & Moore, 1988). It empowers both police officers and community members to take an active stance and become accountable and responsible for the crime problems that plague a community.

A second related change that supports strategic planning is problem-oriented policing. This policing strategy enables the police to develop a systematic process for examining and addressing the problems that the public expects them to handle. Problems are identified through a strategic process that engages in data analysis, identification, and assessment of the current police response, evaluating the adequacy of existing authority and resources, engaging in a broad exploration of alternative responses to the problem, weighing the merits of these alternatives, and choosing from among them. This planning process focuses on a problem in a long-term, comprehensive manner, rather than as a series of separate incidents to be resolved via arrest or other police action (Goldstein, 1990).

Schism (2017, p. 50) identifies six key steps in strategic planning;

1. **Preparation**: Leadership must identify and include stakeholders who wish to move the department forward.
2. **Assessment**: The plan must assess the performance of employees at all levels.
3. **Creation**: This step involves the identification of issues and the determination of goals and objectives to address them.
4. **Implementation**: Resources must be acquired along with gaining support for the planning process.
5. **Communication**: Publication and dissemination of the strategic plan to all concerned stakeholders.
6. **Evaluation**: The success of the strategic plan must be assessed.

However, there are several impediments to developing strategic planning in policing. These include:

1. Lack of up-front training in planning for operational managers.
2. Reluctance to "let go" of control by middle and senior managers.

3. Aspects of the processes for planning and evaluation did not match police skills, knowledge, and activities.
4. Good planning models (or exemplars of "best practice") were not readily available to operational police.

(Hann & Mortimer, 1994)

Criticisms of strategic planning include that it is time-consuming and too demanding of human resources for many departments to undertake. Yet, these problems are not insurmountable. Strategic planning is a meaningful part of new policing strategies. For example, the Durham, New Hampshire, Police Department—a small agency with 19 sworn officers serving a fluctuating population comprising 8,700 full-time citizens and 12,000 students of the University of New Hampshire—found that the process benefited their department in the following areas:

1. **Community perceptions and needs**. The Durham Police Department decided to treat its constituents as partners and customers. Like any business, it needed to identify its constituents' needs, to know how to meet them, via a community safety survey.
2. **Building community partners**. Community members often have questions about police services and how they're delivered. When constituents are familiar with police services, they are more likely to be supportive. The One-Day Community Planning Session has built solid community-police partnerships. Officers indicate that the respect and cooperation they receive from the community has significantly improved since the strategic planning process was launched several years ago.
3. **Internal agency improvements**. Officers' responses to the agency's Internal Survey informed the chief more effectively about his officers' views and needs so that he could adequately respond (Kurz, 2006).

Elements of Strategic Planning

Planning is a primary step in the process of management. It attempts to mobilize organizational members and their resources toward achieving stated goals. An effective strategic plan answers the fundamental question, "What is the purpose of our organization?" Planning sets goals for the organization and maps out the methods to achieve them. It helps determine how to obtain resources and commit them to goal attainment. It directs organization members and channels their activities in the right direction. It measures progress toward meeting organizational goals. As a result, they can be rewarded, or changes can be made to correct and direct their efforts constructively.

Strategic planning requires focusing on what is essential for the organization, by holding discussions among crucial decision-makers and implementing these decisions through specific decisions and actions. It has three primary goals:

To build teamwork: People should be productive and enjoy their work and understand their role in the organization.

To strengthen communication and empower each staff member to help shape the culture and values of the organization.

To identify the tools people need to do the job, including resources, training, development, and recognition.

(Denhardt, 2000, p. 206)

Strategic planning does not just result in a document; it helps build the organization and develop teamwork.

The Process of Strategic Planning

As a process, strategic planning requires that the organization's leader be inclusive. Members of both the organization and the community participate. Their joint input is essential to creating the plan. The *process* involves systematically examining the organization and its environment by those who have a stake in its success (Gordon, 2005, pp. 3–4).

Internally, strategic planning requires democratic, participatory management. It brings the members of an organization together to discuss the strengths and weaknesses of their organization, where they would like to go, and how best to get there. It cannot function in an authoritarian organizational structure. Thus, the process of goal construction also promotes reaching a consensus.

It is not always a smooth process. Consensus must be built. It cannot be achieved through coercion. Strategic planning recognizes that conflicts exist within organizations. The process attempts to promote compromise by bringing disagreements into the open. As Gordon notes, "It is better to invite and resolve conflict early in the discussion and decision-making stages than to confront it while trying to implement the final plan" (Gordon, 2005, p. 10). For example, the Louisville Police Department completed a strategic planning process to implement Community Policing that included "Citizens Against Police Abuse"—a group formed in response to several civilian shootings by officers. The inclusion of groups critical of police operations is the recognition they are present and have a voice to be heard. They cannot be ignored, cowed into submission, or co-opted. Inclusion of the community in a meaningful way in the strategic planning process provides an agency with an avenue for establishing, regaining, or increasing police legitimacy (Aden, 2013).

The strategic planning process must have the support of internal and external partners from the police department. These partners should include:

INTERNAL

- **Department and city leaders**. Organizational change cannot be achieved without strong support from the top. The police chief and the mayor must support the plan. So should other political and civic leaders.
- **Departmental personnel**. The plan must be developed with the full involvement of the people who will be most responsible for implementing it: supervisors, officers, and unsworn personnel—all department members. There must be consensus on the mission and objectives among those carrying out the plan.

EXTERNAL

- **Active community leaders**. The plan must be developed in partnership with the community it serves.
- **Interagency partners**. They include active community members and staff from other government agencies.

(Gordon, 2005, pp. 18–20)

Thus, the strategic planning process requires that these partners be brought together for consultation to construct, implement, and change the plan.

The Outcomes of Strategic Planning

As a document, the strategic plan provides a long-term guiding vision and steps for practical, short-term action.

- **One outcome is a document that specifies the actions required to achieve future goals based on the information generated during the planning process**. It can build a bridge between the community and law enforcement agencies and help them to understand and work with each other. It creates an outline that all parties have agreed to, thus clearing the way for action.
- **It builds upon identifying the police agency's current strengths and weaknesses—** What works and doesn't work within an agency, with intra-governmental relations, and within the community.
- **It offers a robust, central, guiding vision**. Without it, an organization cannot adjust when change demands it. The mission statement develops new strategies and shows when to discontinue old ones.
- **Success is gauged, and progress toward it is measured**. The goals and objectives define direction from the beginning of the program. They provide standards against which budgeting, work plans, hiring, promotion, deployment, organizational structure, and all other implementation elements are tested. They are used to keep the community and law enforcement agency on track and ensure effectiveness and efficiency.
- **It provides a vehicle to build consensus within an organization**. Strategic planning is a democratic process. It provides a method to establish and build consensus within and outside the organization. Strategic planning has become a crucial part of the "empowerment model." It urges organizations to be more open in their deliberations and to welcome input.
- **It offers specific strategies for the near-term completion of tasks**. The manager can engage in strategic planning at all levels of the organization. It applies to the organization as a whole and specific programs and policies. It is a management tool to guide operational strategies throughout the organization.
- **It assigns specific responsibilities for tasks and results**. It builds an accountability process that determines whether tasks are undertaken and whether the desired outcomes are achieved. Evaluation is a crucial component of strategic planning. Valid outcome measures and a computerized information system must be established to capture data regularly and routinely. These data must be analyzed and serve as a feedback loop for operational performance. With data, reports become valuable and valued. Personnel are more likely to capture information used to generate reports.

With all these positive elements in mind, it is necessary also to consider the limitations of strategic planning.

What Strategic Planning Is Not

Gordon identifies some of these limitations (2005, pp. 10–11):

- **It is not a substitute for leadership**. It cannot prescribe specific courses of action that ensure success. The leader can use strategic planning to make change by building and mobilizing support for initiatives. But these initiatives must reflect consensus. Strategic planning is democratic. It is the hallmark of participatory management. A strategic plan with attainable goals, coupled with a realistic strategy, provides the membership of an organization with a clear vision of the leader's charted course. Developed with representation throughout the organization, it promotes the allegiance of the organization's members.

- **It is not a panacea for resolving organizational or community conflicts.** Strategic planning can structure and routinize community input. However, problems must be resolved through the active participation of department and community members.
- **It cannot increase scarce resources.** But it can promote sharing of resources to accomplish organizational goals and thus build unity across the organization. It can break down the tendency of organizational subunits to go their way. It calls for a flexible approach to managing organizational resources.
- **It is not a one-time endeavor.** To maintain flexibility, an organization must analyze the past, scrutinize the present, and prepare for the future. It is an ongoing process.
- **The final plan is not an endpoint.** It must be disseminated to local interest groups, explained, and promoted if it is to be embraced and supported by those who expect to implement it and those affected by it. Failure to get a commitment at all levels of the organization will doom the strategic plan to failure. Input must be sought and obtained from all levels of the organization, since they will be responsible for implementing the plan.
- **The final plan is a tool, not a task.** Strategic planning will develop the organization's future but does not stop there. It moves on to a series of action steps that will guide future activities (Denhardt, 2000, p. 37).
- **The final plan is not unalterable or carved in "stone."** Assumptions must be continually questioned if the plan is to be flexible and accurate.

The strategic plan is meant to be used, not saluted or placed on a shelf and forgotten. It is a guide for action and a directive for the entire organization. It should change to meet the changing conditions that the organization will face.

Strategic Planning Methodology

In recent years, many different strategic planning models have been developed. Each is unique in its own right, but contains the same primary element of management-for-results orientation. Here is an example of a basic approach (see Garner, 2005; Bryson & Alston, 2011).

1. Determine the Problems Facing the Organization

Determine the scope of the planning effort:

A. **Time frame**: What is the period for the plan?
B. **Focus**: What are your objectives? How can they be prioritized?
C. **Geographic area**: What geographic area is your organization responsible for?

Having a shared understanding of expectations is crucial as the plan develops. A budget and a reasonably detailed work plan should be prepared. The work plan will help to keep the project on schedule.

2. Scan the Environment

(S.W.O.T. — "Strengths, Weaknesses, Opportunities, and Threats")

The SWOT analysis identifies a "tension field" that acts as a lens that brings together opposing developments, focuses on their effects, and offers direction to the organization (Seagrave, 1993).

It should consider such questions as (Garner, 2005, p. 15):

A. **Past, present, and future**: What has happened in the past? Where is the organization now? What is likely to happen during the time frame of the plan?
B. **Comparative information**: What is happening nationally? Internationally? Within the state or region?
C. **Opportunities and constraints**: What advantages and obstacles to the plan's goals exist in the immediate environment?

What must the department do in response to the issues it faces?

The stages in the process follow this pattern, leading from the SWOT to the development of the strategic plan:

1. *The search for information and ideas*: Assess the immediate situation regarding strengths and weaknesses and future opportunities and threats.
2. *Synthesis*: Find generalizations and patterns. This leads to an agenda of strategic issues to be managed.
3. *Selection*: Set priorities for action by assessing the options in terms of stakeholders affected and resources required, and then implement the selected strategies.

Nutt and Backoff stress that this process should focus on key stakeholders, not just senior managers (Nutt & Backoff, 1992, p. 157). In Greensboro, North Carolina, Chief Aden personally invited citizen stakeholder groups that had not traditionally worked with each other or collaborated with the police department, including the Chamber of Commerce, East Carolina University (students and administrators), the Vidant Medical Center, Neighborhood Association boards, the Greenville Property Management Association, the NAACP, the Southern Christian Leadership Council, the Human Relations Council, and several non-profit organizations (Aden, 2013, pp. 29–30).

Typically, the environmental scan is a "needs assessment." A needs assessment pays specific attention to "stakeholders." Stakeholders are persons who are directly interested in what the organization does (e.g., the community, local government organizations, and local elected officials). This definition must be interpreted in the broadest possible terms. Strategic planners must decide who to involve, how to involve them, and how to solicit input from those not directly involved. Planners must receive input from, and consider the effect on, their stakeholders.

Needs assessment focuses on collecting information from various sources and analyzing the data to determine what problems the organization should address. It asks and answers the question, "What must be done?" Potential sources of information for police departments include community residents, the business community, city and county governments, other law enforcement agencies, the judicial system, healthcare providers, schools, and churches. Surveys and questionnaires distributed to these various groups can produce valuable information. Community meetings are another excellent source of information. Here, citizens can voice their concerns and provide ideas they may or may not state on a survey or questionnaire. Both sources should be used.

This analysis involves scanning the organization's environment for signs of change. Strategic planning enables an organization to cope better with change and to take maximum advantage of it. It also includes an internal scan of the strengths and weaknesses of the organization. With Community Policing, a usual starting point is a citizen attitude survey of the police and problems in the community.

The environmental scan should be both external and internal to the organization. Strengths and weaknesses are addressed in the Internal Analysis. Opportunities and threats are examined in the External Analysis.

- **The internal analysis** is a "resource audit"—an evaluation of the strengths and weaknesses regarding each strategic issue. They are subject to influence and change. To ensure a complete listing, make a direct comparison to other cities and counties.

Here, the strengths and weaknesses of the organization are evaluated. The resources the organization can bring to bear on the issues identified in the external analysis are determined. The critical question is: "What can we do, and what do we do well?"

Creating key performance indicators is a crucial element in this. Here are some examples of information that may be useful to an organization's internal assessment (Zurcher & Hudak, 1987):

- Number of police per capita.
- Non-sworn employees as a percentage of the total.
- Number of calls for service.
- Response time.
- Number of crimes against persons.
- Number of hazardous traffic violation citations/arrests.
- Number of driving-while-intoxicated arrests.
- Population density.
- Number of neighborhood watch programs.

The information compiled will identify what the organization can use to solve the selected problem.

Warren (2012, p. 39) identifies several symptoms of organizational problems to consider, including:

- Poor business practices.
- Lack of written or conflicting policies and standard operating procedures.
- Lack of required skill sets in the employee workforce.
- Redundancy of effort.
- Areas of undue risks experienced.

- Ethical transgressions and violations of rules and regulations.
- Morale issues.
- Mission creep.
- Major personality conflicts.
- Areas of disruptive or aggressive internal competition.
- Poor individual or team performance levels.

These issues must be addressed to unite and bring together members of the organization in support of the strategic plan.

The line officers on the street are another valuable source of information that should not be overlooked. Officers acutely know of the problems and needs existing on their beat. Soliciting information from the line officer also provides a secondary benefit. It allows the officer to be an integral and active participant in the strategic planning process. When the time comes for implementation, consulted officers will have a sense of ownership and be more likely to support any transition (Toch, 1980; Durivage, Barrette, Montcalm, & Laberge, 1992).

In his internal scanning effort, Bratton hired a management firm to conduct a "cultural diagnostic" of the NYPD. This tool determines the cultural factors impeding performance and the corrective values used as principles for organizational change. The method defines the cultural assets, obstacles to change, inherited core identity, projected core identity, and the values that must guide revising critical organizational systems to institutionalize a new, high-performance culture. They surveyed nearly 8,000 police officers and found:

- At its highest levels, the primary aim of the NYPD was not to bring down crime but to avoid criticism from the media, politicians, and the public. "Nobody ever lost a command because crime went up. You lose a command because the loudest voices in the community don't like you, or because of a bad newspaper story, or because of corruption."
- The greater the distance from headquarters, the lesser the trust from one rank to the next. Exclusion was the rule. Creativity was actively discouraged. "I have 300 assassins in my unit."
- Police officers believed the department had not backed them up, even when their actions were warranted.
- The department was structured to protect its good name (and the careers of its senior executives) rather than to achieve crime-fighting goals.
- The Internal Affairs Bureau was intent on tripping up officers for minor infractions rather than rooting out real corruption.
- The mayor and commissioner had voiced strong support for the department, but officers were waiting to see what they would both do.
- They found a wide disparity between statements by the bosses and what the officers believed the bosses wanted.
- Officers felt they were in a "twilight zone", where staying out of trouble (and thus keeping their bosses out of trouble) was more important than reducing crime rates.

(Bratton & Knobler, 1998, pp. 215–216)

BOX 7.1:   NYPD Internal Scan

CONSIDERED BY OFFICERS AS MOST IMPORTANT TO THE DEPARTMENT

1. Write summonses.
2. Hold down overtime.
3. Stay out of trouble.
4. Clear backlog of radio runs.
5. Report police corruption.
6. Treat bosses with deference.
7. Reduce crime, disorder, and fear.

CONSIDERED BY OFFICERS AS MOST IMPORTANT TO THEMSELVES

1. Reduce crime, disorder, and fear.
2. Make gun arrests.
3. Provide police services to people who request them.
4. Gain public confidence in police integrity.
5. Arrest drug dealers.
6. Correct quality-of-life conditions.
7. Stay out of trouble.

The internal analysis is thus structured to tap the opinions and perceptions of the departmental staff. In the Durham, New Hampshire, Police Department, officers rated each agency's functions (administration, first-line supervision, patrol, vehicle and equipment maintenance, computerization, and accreditation). The officers also rated each component's effectiveness, philosophy, leadership, policy development, and support to other components. They wrote responses to open questions such as:

1.   What would you change about this function if you were the chief of police?
2.   What challenges does this function currently face, and will it face in the future?

In this manner, the internal analysis provides valuable information while sponsoring a sense of ownership and belonging among department staff. Their opinions are solicited and treated with respect.

- **The external analysis** pinpoints critical threats and opportunities the external environment poses. It forces the organization to remedy the tendency to look at internal forces while planning. External indicators can serve as benchmarks for identifying the relative position of the organization. Trends that are occurring elsewhere could affect the organization in the future. External factors are usually uncontrollable. They include national and international trends (social, political, and demographic changes), actions of other governmental bodies, and technological change. This analysis should have a future (rather than a past) orientation.

Cohen and Brand have identified four aspects of the external environment of public agencies:

- **The political environment**: the legislative branch, the executive branch, the judicial branch, interest groups, and the political views of the broad public and the various politically active elites.
- **The economic environment.**
- **The social environment**: the sphere of interaction between the organization and the community at large.
- **The technological environment**: the technologies used or produced by the agency. In police work, This includes things like automatic weapons, improved communications, and DNA evidence.

(Cohen & Brand, 1993, pp. 61–66)

Regarding police departments, it is helpful to identify and get information on crime trends:

- What is the trend?
- What is its background?
- What is the probability of the trend occurring?
- What will be the magnitude of its impact?
- Does it provide an opportunity or pose a threat to the organization?

(Zurcher & Hudak, 1987, p. 27)

Once this information is obtained, the trend must be interpreted in terms of its magnitude and the probability it will occur. With this information, high-impact/high-probability trends will be scrutinized. With information from the needs assessment, it will provide the basis for the action plan to be addressed later in the strategic planning process.

3. Develop a Mission and a Vision Statement

The **mission statement** of an organization reflects its essential purpose. It should seldom change. Such statements should be concise, but encompassing enough to withstand the changes wrought by time and the environment. It reflects the central purpose of the law enforcement agency.

The mission statement communicates the organization's purpose to various audiences and forms the basis for goals, objectives, and strategies (implementation plans) (Gordon, 2005, p. 26). These statements describe what the strategic plan should do for the organization and the community. It also describes the target population and outlines the general approaches to change.

- A mission statement should convey, articulate, and reinforce the long-term view of where the law enforcement agency and the community want it to be. It creates a desired future to serve as the basis for developing goals, objectives, and strategies.

The mission statement concisely accounts for what is expected because of strategy development and implementation. It is a prelude to developing goals, objectives, and strategies. For example, here is a mission statement from the Greenville (NC) Police Department:

> *The Greenville Police Department exists to enhance public safety and quality of life, in partnership with ALL people in OUR community, by preventing crime with honor and integrity.*
>
> (Aden, 2013, p. 31)

The mission statement provides a focus for the strategic planning enterprise. It is a brief statement of the agency's long-range plan.

Values are also an essential part of this process. They are the defining characteristics of an organization's culture that foster the mission statement. They ensure that persons within the organization will appropriately respond to issues.

Values are the defining principles that embody the philosophy of the law enforcement agency that guides its operation. They represent enduring beliefs about what is suitable, sound, and desirable. They are standards of conduct that members of the department believe in. They guide behavior by communicating standards of conduct to all organization members (Community Policing Consortium, 1998, p. 1).

A values statement should:

- Set high standards for excellence
- Reflect high ideals
- Be based upon sound philosophy
- Inspire commitment
- Be proactive and positive
- Be communicated clearly
- Integrate the unique qualities and competencies of the organization.

(Community Policing Consortium, 1998, p. 2)

For example, consider the **values statement** from the Boston Metropolitan Police (Box 7.2).

BOX 7.2:   Boston Metropolitan Police Values

- The Metropolitan Police Department exists to protect and serve the public.
- The department and its members will maintain the highest ethical standards of conduct.
- We will treat all citizens with dignity, respect, and courtesy.
- We will safeguard each citizen's rights to free expression, movement, and constitutional liberty while within the Metropolitan District Commission jurisdiction.
- We will use only minimum necessary force when performing our lawful duties.
- In applying the law, we will exercise discretion with consistency and equitableness.
- We are committed to giving each employee the authority to make decisions and to hold them accountable for their actions.
- The Department is committed to creating a productive and satisfying environment that its members can be proud of.

(Bratton & Knobler, 1998, p. 137)

4. Develop Goals, Objectives, and Strategies

Goals and objectives are used interchangeably. Both are statements about intended future affairs—how you intend things to be. However, goals and objectives are inherently different. Goals are broad, vague statements intended to provide organizational direction. Objectives are detailed, results-oriented, measurable, and time-specific. Strategies are the steps in the action plan—who must do what and when to implement the designed changes. They also identify resources needed to carry out the plan step by step.

Goals

Goals are generalized statements of where an organization wants to be. They define the primary directives of the strategic plan. They are broad, visionary, projected outcomes viewed from a long-term perspective. Goals should be based on external and internal analyses. They should build upon strength while negating a weakness. Goals are few, concise yet not specific, and non-quantitative. Law enforcement goals address societal problems unlikely to be solved immediately. They tend to be permanent (Community Policing Consortium, 1998, pp. 1–2).

Law enforcement goals include four significant desired outcomes:

1.   A reduction in the incidence of crime.
2.   The repression of criminal activity.
3.   The regulation of non-criminal conduct.
4.   The provision of services.

Under community policing, departmental goals include:

1.   A reduction in the fear of crime.
2.   A reduction in social and physical disorder.
3.   Strengthening of community involvement.
4.   The empowerment of employees and citizens.

Goals should be attainable yet ambitious to make an organization and its people grow. **Stretch goals** are a part of the motivational technique known as Strategic Intent. It calls for the organization's leader to create unattainable, "stretch" goals and then challenges everyone to develop methods to attain them. Stretch goals challenge organizations to forgo incremental change in favor of "reinventing" the standard ways of doing business. They require that we do more than maintain the current rate of progress. They call for us to improve upon it. Yet, they should be realistic (based on trend data and research findings) and plausible. There should be a reasonable probability of their achievement with integrated effort and commitment. Stretch goals are objectives or performance targets used to evaluate the effectiveness of program strategies.

At the NYPD, Bratton said that they would take back the city "block by block." Over a two-year period, Bratton proposed to achieve a dramatic decrease in crime ("Ten percent the first year. Fifteen the next. Twenty-five percent in two years"). Several chiefs responded, "Can't be done." They thought they were already doing everything possible to bring down crime, and anything more was out of the question. "Dramatic? No. You can have decreases. Crime goes down 2 to 4 percent annually, and we can continue that trend. But 10 percent? No chance." Bratton wanted people who were "not only going to think differently but who were willing to go through walls to do it" (Bratton & Knobler, 1998, pp. 201–202).

The issue surrounding using stretch goals is whether to use the goal as a motivational tool or as a valid standard for performance measurement. Garner (2005, p. 18) suggests the use of **SMARTER goals**. Well-defined goals should be:

- **Specific**: Goals must be clear and specific. They should represent what the program is trying to accomplish and accurately measure successful operations.
- **Measurable**: There is no way to gauge progress if the goal is not measurable.
- **Acceptable (or attainable)**: Again, goals must be realistic. Some effort and stretching are always in order, but goals should neither be too high nor too low so they become meaningless.
- **Realistic (or relevant)**: The goals should represent and mirror the vision and mission of the program.
- **Timely**: Goals must have start and end points and be clear.
- **Extend** the capabilities of those working to achieve them.
- **Rewarding** the organization and its members.

Goals must have a basis in fact and have a reasonable expectation of occurrence. They should represent the desired impacts of the program or policy. Cohen and Eimicke do not favor setting numerical performance targets. They find it "more useful to work on improving the day-to-day performance of work processes" (Cohen & Eimicke, 1995, p. 165).

However, it is impossible to implement all of the goals established in a strategic planning process. Several alternatives will likely be proposed, since many actors are at the table. The goals generated by the process require prioritization according to their feasibility. It may be impossible to implement some goals, because they are politically impossible or they require more resources than are possible to commit. Choices must be made concerning the methods of solving a particular crime problem.

Objectives

Goals need to be further defined and quantified into objectives. **Objectives** set performance targets over time and act as "benchmarks" that aid decision-making and evaluate progress. They are the specific, measurable targets set for each goal. They define the actions needed to achieve each goal. They must be stated as briefly as possible and immediately understandable. Objectives are outcome-oriented statements of what a program intends to achieve for the community.

Objectives should be:

- Action-oriented: It starts with "to" followed by an action verb.
- Specific: States a particular result to be accomplished.
- Time-limited: Specifies a defined time frame for completion.
- Quantifiable: Presents a measurable standard of achievement.
- Realistic: Designates a feasible, attainable outcome.

Objectives should be cost-effective and consistent with available resources. They should provide a return on time, funding, facilities, and people investment. All stakeholders should support them (Community Policing Consortium, 1998, p. 1).

Strategies

Strategies are the step-by-step means by which an organization reaches its goals. They are programs, events, operations, and projects for the organization to accomplish its objectives. They are the "action steps" that help managers assign tasks and allocate resources to be successful. A strategy can be assigned to someone to be carried out. They represent specific approaches and help define what is to be accomplished. The effort should include some innovative or original ideas if they are likely to be effective.

Each proposed strategy should address the following issues:

- Cost.
- Personnel requirements.
- Agencies and organizations involved.
- Time frame.
- Impact.
- Legal implications.

The development of this information will lead to the listing and elimination of strategies. Here, feasibility is the key—figuring out which strategies have a chance of being implemented.

Contingency plans should also be considered. Fallback positions are used if the initial strategy is unsuccessful or the environment shifts.

Strategies bridge the gap between results and the specific tasks required to accomplish them. Implementing a specific strategy is less important than meeting the greater aim or goal. You should leave room for them to be changed, dropped, or implemented differently.

Here is a brief example of developing strategies. These elements are used in Community Policing when the goal is to reduce crime and the fear of it. When designing strategies for objectives, you should consider the steps taken by every level of the organization, and strategies to strengthen the response of the community and outside agencies.

STRATEGIES FOR REDUCING CRIME AND THE FEAR OF CRIME

- **Crime response.** It includes everything concerning a specific crime (i.e., prioritization of calls for service, backup response, report-taking, criminal investigations, warrants, arrests, district attorney prioritization/caseload, incarceration policies, probation, and parole management, etc.).
- **Problem-solving to reduce crime.** Methods for addressing chronic crime problems that elude the traditional, incident-based approach. Problem-solving addresses the specific elements that allow crimes to occur and aims to prevent crime by eliminating root causes. Examples: Hot Spot analysis and response; civil action against owners of crack houses; prioritization/use of information received through drug hotlines; intervention by code enforcement at sites where environmental factors lead to crime; development of new ordinances to help address chronic problems.
- **Crime prevention.** Crime prevention removes the opportunity for crime to occur. One method often promoted here is Crime Prevention Through Environmental Design (CPTED). CPTED encourages involvement by citizens and changing the physical environment. They take responsibility for public places and watch over them.

- **Early intervention**. This approach entails sponsoring and developing long-range approaches to reduce the conditions that breed crime (i.e., root causes, including domestic violence, reaching youth at risk for delinquency and drug abuse, etc.). Familiar approaches include the Police Athletic League (PAL), Drug Abuse Resistance Education (DARE), and Gang Resistance Education (GREAT). With such direct involvement by police departments, partnerships should be established with other governmental and civic agencies, schools, and churches.

The goals, objectives, and strategies provide the organization with an outline of programs, services, facilities, and staff funded under the plan—a blueprint for the budgeting process.

5. Develop an Action Plan

This plan shows who is responsible for the strategies when it should be done, and how it will be paid for (if direct costs are involved). The action plan will serve as a basis for monitoring implementation, but it must be flexible. It can include a month-by-month calendar showing what is to happen at each point in the implementation process. It can list all the strategic actions (relating to several issues and objectives) for which each key actor is responsible. It can include an overall budget for the implementation effort.

The implementation plan takes the strategic planning process to the level of individuals. It assigns specific responsibilities for programs and strategies. Individuals and groups within the organization are drawn into the plan. It forms the basis for personnel assignments and performance measures. They are lengthy. They often list the strategies and then list the corresponding official or agency with the primary responsibility for that effort.

The plan translates the vision or mission into practice. Everyone can understand its actions, cost, and achievements.

An integral part of the implementation plan is a timeline that breaks down each action into interim steps for completion. It permits easier tracking of progress toward achieving goals and objectives. Outlining interim steps also facilitates making mid-course adjustments that might be necessary in response to changing conditions or information.

The implementation plan should also identify who will oversee, coordinate, and evaluate progress toward achieving goals and objectives. It should also include provisions for gathering and incorporating public input from area residents and businesses to determine whether actions produce the desired effect within the community.

Costs are a significant element of a strategic plan. Even if no new personnel or equipment is required, such elements' "in-kind" costs should be listed.

6. Implementation

The key to strategic planning is that it is action- rather than planning-oriented. It allocates scarce resources to solve critical issues. Thus, the implementation phase is crucial. It depends upon the process of constructing the strategic plan. If this process has gone well, there should be a broad consensus about the key issues, how the external environment will affect the community in the future, and the key strengths and weaknesses. New coalitions of business, government, and community members will be formed with a commitment to specific strategies. Much of the success of the strategic plan comes from the process that developed it. Coalitions can develop to guide the implementation process. However, there must be a direct link between implementing the strategic plan and the budget cycle to ensure that funds are available to carry it out.

Once the action plan is in place, it must be merged into the organization's programs, policies, and daily operations. The best plan will be useless to the organization unless carried out effectively.

Implementation can be made much easier by involving employees in the planning process as much as possible. Strategic planning can pull an organization together and give it a common purpose if all employees feel involved. If done correctly, employees will know what is expected of them. They will understand what the organization is trying to achieve and how their work fits the overall picture. Communication between management and employees will improve by actively participating in the process, and team building will occur. Employees will develop a sense of ownership in the plan that translates into enthusiasm and support.

7. Monitoring and Updating

Successful strategic planning requires a continuing review of actual accomplishments compared to the plan. A specific individual or organization conducts monitoring. The monitoring system should track time and other resources expended versus resources allocated. It should keep track of changes in key actors and their assignments. Monitoring keeps the plan on target by accommodating adjustments as circumstances and the environment change. The environment should continue to be scanned to ensure that unforeseen developments do not sabotage the adopted plan or that emerging opportunities are not overlooked. This effort continuously renews the Strategic Plan, so it continues to develop and does not become static. New strategies should be developed periodically to ensure the plan adjusts to changing conditions. Developing new strategies should include substantial involvement by the original stakeholders.

As implementation proceeds, managers must check progress periodically. Here, the key questions are: (1) "Is the plan being implemented as designed?" and (2) "Is the plan achieving the intended results?" To accomplish this step, supervisors will monitor and evaluate the plan's success based on how well the objectives are being met as measured against the established performance criteria. If the results are as intended, the process continues. However, corrective action must be taken if the process is not producing the intended results. The manager should also document what changes were made and for what reason. Flexibility is paramount. Documenting such alterations will allow the planning and evaluation process to continue.

8. Evaluation

The impact of the plan must be evaluated. The evaluation is a research design focusing on program outcomes (Vito & Higgins, 2015). Plans should provide personnel with a clear definition of the desired outcomes and allow as much discretion as possible to achieve them. Also, outcomes should not be confused with the process. Again, partnership, problem-solving, arrest, and investigation are all processes that can achieve outcomes, but they are not outcomes in themselves.

Evaluation assesses the effectiveness of the plan. For the changes introduced with Community Policing to become permanent, it is necessary to recognize and reward new aspects of organizational performance. The criteria for recruitment, performance evaluation (individual and departmental), management, and training must be developed.

9. Dissemination

The plan must be widely disseminated. The plan should be available throughout the organization, community leaders, and other agencies. The plan can be promoted in the media.

An examination of strategic planning in American law enforcement agencies revealed how this method was implemented. This research was based on a telephone interview survey of 289 and site visits to seven law enforcement agencies (Zhao, Thurman, & Ren, 2008). As a result, a model of four types of strategic planning in police departments was constructed along a grid.

Model 1 was an in-depth one with limited application—rank involvement was high, but the extent of application was low. It was characterized by efficient use of limited resources and experimentation with change in a few selected divisions. Their objectives reflected the department's needs and were thus designed to gain the support of employees. Measures of effectiveness were easier to develop (Zhao et al., 2008, p. 21).

In the second model, the top administration fully controlled the planning process. Dissemination of information about the plan was restricted, making it difficult for employees to learn about it. This model fails to achieve the consensus-building effort at the heart of strategic planning. Employees do not support implementing such a model (Zhao et al., 2008, p. 22).

Top administration in the third model included divisions in the planning process and developed specific goals and measures to assess effectiveness. Yet, line officers were still uninformed about the plan. It created a consensus among division commanders and demonstrated departmental priorities to the external community (Zhao et al., 2008, p. 23).

The fourth model contained the elements of true strategic planning. Implementation of the plan was department-wide, and all employees were held accountable. It became the agency's daily plan for operations and represented a proactive, inclusive approach to implementation. Consensus about the department's direction spread across all department levels (Zhao et al., 2008, p. 23).

Example: United Kingdom's National Policing Plan, 2003–2006

Following the passage of Britain's Police Reform Act of 2002, the first annual National Policing Plan was published. It was developed in consultation with several internal (the Association of Police Officers, the Association of Police Authorities) and external (members of the National Policing Forum) stakeholders.

It was designed to provide a single place where the government's priorities, plans, and performance indicators could be found. It provided a sense of strategic direction for the police service as shared by the police and all its key stakeholders—in and outside government. The plan contains priorities for police service plus performance indicators to test the success of police actions.

Overall priorities for the period 2003 to 2006 were established:

- Tackling antisocial behavior and disorder.
- Reducing the volume of street, drug-related, violent, and gun crime in line with local and national targets.

- Combating serious and organized crime operating across force boundaries.
- Increasing the number of offenses brought to justice.

The National Policing Plan uses a strategic planning format similar to the one presented here. This plan provides an overall framework for local British police agencies to follow. As we see in Box 7.3, the plan sets goals and objectives. The goals are broad and set direction, while the objectives are narrow, specific, and measurable. The objectives set the benchmarks by which police performance can be measured and determine the effectiveness of crime-reduction methods.

BOX 7.3:   Setting Goals and Objectives—Thames Valley Policing Authority (UK)

GOAL: REDUCING CRIME

This means working with our partners, including our local communities, to prevent crime, including drug-related crime, by addressing the causes of crime as well as actual incidents of crime.

OBJECTIVES

Domestic burglary: Achieve a 14.5 percent reduction in offences compared to 2002/2003 by 2004–2006.

Vehicle crime: Achieve a 17 percent reduction in offences compared to 2002/2003 by 2004–2006.

Robbery: Achieve a 27 percent reduction in offences compared to 2002/2003 by 2004–2006.

Source: *Thames Valley Police Authority Strategic Plan, 2003–2006*, pp. 11–12.

www.thamesvalley.police.uk

Conclusion

Strategic planning is a proactive management approach that can help an agency determine whether its services respond to the needs of the citizens. It can shape the delivery of services. It is also a means of facilitating participation, communication, and systematic decision-making within the organization.

We have reviewed a general framework to develop a strategic plan. Its preparation requires the organization and its employees to engage in participatory management.

Strategic planning makes it possible for the organization to respond to change. Will the organization let change control it, or will it attempt to control its destiny? Strategic planning offers a tool to gain a semblance of control over future direction.

KEY TERMS

Goals	Open Systems Model	S.W.O.T. Analysis
Internal Scan	SMARTER Goals	Total Quality Management
Mission Statement	Strategies	Values Statement
Objectives	Stretch Goals	

References

Aden, H. (2013, October). Inviting the community into the police strategic planning process. *The Police Chief*, 28–31.

Bratton, W., & Knobler, P. (1998). *Turnaround: How America's top cop reversed the crime epidemic*. New York, NY: Random House.

Bryson, J., & Alston, F. (2011). *Creating your strategic plan*. San Francisco, CA: Jossey-Bass.

Cohen, S., & Brand, R. (1993). *Total quality management in government*. San Francisco, CA: Jossey-Bass.

Cohen, S., & Eimicke, W. (1995). *The new effective public manager: Achieving success in a changing government*. San Francisco, CA: Jossey-Bass.

Community Policing Consortium. (1998). *A staircase to strategic planning*. Washington, DC: Community Policing Consortium.

Couper, D.C., & Lobitz, S.H. (1991). *Quality policing: The Madison experience*. Washington, DC: Police Executive Research Forum.

Denhardt, R.B. (2000). *The pursuit of significance: Strategies for managerial success in public organizations*. Prospect Heights, IL: Waveland Press.

Durivage, A., Barrette, J., Montcalm, L., & Laberge, M. (1992). Analysis of organizational culture: A key to strategic planning. *Canadian Police College Journal, 16*, 94–134.

Garner, R. (2005, November). "SWOT" tactics—Basics for strategic planning. *FBI Law Enforcement Bulletin*, 17–19.

Goldstein, H. (1990). *Problem-oriented policing*. New York, NY: McGraw-Hill.

Gordon, G.L. (2005). *Strategic planning for local government*. Washington, DC: International City Management Association.

Hann, J., & Mortimer, B. (1994). Strategic planning and performance evaluation for operational policing. *Criminal Justice Planning & Coordination Conference Proceedings*.

Hoover, L.T. (1996). Translating total quality management from private sector to policing. In L.T. Hoover (Ed.), *Quantifying quality in policing* (pp. 1–22). Washington, DC: Police Executive Research Forum.

Kurz, D.L. (2006). *Strategic planning: Building strong police-community partnerships in small towns*. Alexandria, VA: IACP.

Manning, P.K. (1995). TQM and the future of policing. *Police Forum, 5*, 1–5.

Munro, J.L. (1971, November/December). Towards a theory of criminal justice administration: A general systems perspective. *Public Administration Review*, 621–631.

Nutt, P.C., & Backoff, R.W. (1992). *Strategic management of public and third sector organizations: A handbook for leaders*. San Francisco, CA: Jossey-Bass.

Schism, R. (2017, May). Strategic planning: A key component of organizational success. *The Police Chief*, 48–50.

Seagrave, J. (1993). Obtaining information for the corporate strategy: The Vancouver police department telephone survey. *Police Studies, 16*, 147–156.

Toch, H. (1980). Mobilizing police expertise. *Annals of the American Academy of Political and Social Science, 45*, 53–62.

Trojanowicz, R., & Bucqueroux, B. (1990). *Community policing: A contemporary perspective*. Cincinnati, OH: Anderson.

Vito, G.F., & Higgins, G.E. (2015). *Practical program evaluation for criminal justice*. New York, NY: Taylor & Francis.

Warren, G.A. (2012, March). Is your agency an integrated strategic management system? *The Police Chief*, 38–41.

Wasserman, R., & Moore, M.H. (1988). *Values in policing*. Washington, DC: National Institute of Justice.

Zhao, J., Thurman, Q., & Ren, L. (2008). An examination of strategic planning in American law enforcement agencies. *Police Quarterly, 11*(1), 3–26.

Zurcher, J., & Hudak, D. (1987, February). How to build a crystal ball: Strategic planning for police agencies. *The Police Chief*, 24–31.

8 Strategic Operations

DOI: 10.4324/9781003459095-8

Learning Objectives

1. Describe Strategic Policing.
2. Identify how to conduct community needs to determine accountability.
3. Identify the steps in the strategic management process.
4. Analyze and review the implementation and effectiveness of Community-Oriented Policing (COP).
5. Analyze and review the implementation and effectiveness of Problem-Oriented Policing (POP).
6. Analyze and review the implementation and effectiveness of Hot Spot Policing.
7. Analyze and review the implementation and effectiveness of CompStat.
8. Analyze and review the implementation and effectiveness of Intelligence-Led Policing (ILP).
9. Analyze and review the implementation and effectiveness of Focused Deterrence programs.
10. Analyze and review the implementation and effectiveness of Smart Policing.
11. Review the research findings on Traffic Stops—Racial Profiling, Veil of Darkness.
12. Review the research findings on Stop, Question, & Frisk (SQF).
13. Review the research findings on Crisis Intervention Teams (CIT).

Introduction

Many law enforcement organizations struggle to adapt to the demanding, complex, and external environment in which they exist. Police agencies are balancing consistency and predictability with adaptation and change. Most police leaders recognize the fluid context in which their departments operate (Batts, Smoot, & Scrivner, 2012). They are developing organizational strategies to meet these challenges different from the patrol-dominated ones created to address 19th- and early 20th-century conditions. As a result, there is a fundamental rethinking of how the police are operationalizing their response to the complex crime and disorder needs of the communities they serve. These current changes represent a strategic shift in the basic "business" of policing (Kelling & Bratton, 1993).

The present challenge for police leadership during this era requires police executives to think, manage, and lead strategically. Strategic management is

> the continuous process of determining the mission and goals of an organization within the context of its external environment and its internal strengths and weaknesses, formulating, and implementing strategies, and exerting strategic control to ensure that the organization's strategies are successful in attaining its goals.
>
> (Parnell, 2014, p. 14)

Police organizational reforms such as Community-Oriented Policing, Problem-Oriented Policing, CompStat, Intelligence-Led, and Smart Policing reconsider how police operational services are delivered. As a result, concerned police administrators are consistently seeking to discover better ways to manage their organizational resources and reinvent their organizations. This process involves systematic searching for and testing of new methods of police operations to serve communities. Police organizations are restructuring by changing their goals and objectives, core functions, incentives, accountability, distribution of power, and cultures to achieve a more effective public safety impact. The long-term result of these efforts is a redefinition of organizational effectiveness. Effectiveness is now measured in outcomes instead of statistical outputs that focus on tasks performed instead of results achieved. It is hoped that this process will lead to improved ways to create community security and safety, and also that operational services will be better managed and problem-solving will emerge as an essential operational technology. Strategic management will test the intellectual skill set of all police employees to its total capacity as creativity emerges as a primary organizational asset. This transformation demands that police executives meet these challenges by actively engaging the process of designing effective organizations to ensure that it occurs by intention, not by chance.

This redefinition of policing holds that an effective organization initiates and reshapes its operational service delivery in ways that will facilitate the fulfillment of its primary mission while increasing public value (Moore, 1995). It accomplishes its mission by understanding and adapting to the demands of its environment through the creation, acquisition, and transformation of information. This transformation of information creates intelligence data that serve as the basis for police managers successfully to plan, initiate, reshape, and evaluate their operational strategies in ways that promote effectiveness (Tilley, 2003).

This redefinition constitutes a strategic shift in policing. According to this new operational paradigm, the primary function of police administration and leadership is to engage, analyze, and respond actively to the needs of the external environment with internal resources and capabilities. If we consider this new perspective valid, we need to identify the operational processes currently being developed and employed by policing to enhance its effectiveness.

The Strategic Policing Process

Strategic policing is built upon four interrelated elements: (1) a shared sense of direction, (2) creativity, (3) commitment, and (4) accountability. Successful strategically managed organizations have a shared sense of direction present throughout the organization. This direction is defined by the organization's vision and mission statements, values, operational objectives, and performance. A vision that is actively practiced and shared by organizational members creates excellence, commitment, and effectiveness by focusing the entire organization on what must be accomplished. These are the desired outcomes the department wishes to achieve. In this manner, effectiveness becomes a core value in the high-performance agency. In this type of organization, operations are structured to maximize the use of organizational assets. Through constant managerial communication and teamwork, people know what is expected of them and what they must do to be effective. Lastly, they are held accountable for their effectiveness. A critical success factor is managerial commitment to the development and maintenance of a positive organizational culture that values both creativity and accountability.

New ideas come from within or outside the police organization. Whatever their source, the purpose for developing new operational tactics is improved performance. Ideas on their own cannot create an effective organization. Without accompanying changes in disseminating information, problems are identified and solved, employees are empowered, projects are created, and problem-solving teams develop strategies and plans. Only the potential for improvement exists. If the department's leadership wishes to encourage creativity, they must ask themselves this fundamental question: "How do we utilize the intellectual capacity and experience of our people?" Creativity is the basis for effective tactics.

People are the organization. Without their commitment to the mission and goals of the department, nothing will ever be accomplished. However, not everyone will agree with the organization's dominant or proposed new strategy. Fortunately, total agreement among all members of an organization is not required to change its direction. As we noted earlier in Chapter 4, the individuals who are needed are the organization's **critical mass**. The critical mass comprises individuals who because of their positions, personal charisma, skill set, and leadership ability exert the most power and influence over the other employees and organization.

For example, middle managers and supervisors define and shape a department's operational reality. They have the responsibility and power to convert the executive's vision and the organizational mission into operational behavior, performance, and outcomes. The true measure of their leadership is influence. They need to be made full partners in the development of the new organizational vision and believe in the direction it is setting. They are the managers who translate the department's mission, plans, objectives, policy, and procedures into day-to-day operations and outcomes. A critical number of these individuals constitute the department's critical mass. They are needed to commit to the organization's direction so that the strategies and operational tactics necessary are developed and implemented.

Architects of the strategic transformation must build on such time-tested strengths of middle management as these: close relationships with beat officers; breadth of organizational vision (vis-à-vis first-line officers and sergeants); knowledge of departmental culture (including agency strengths, weaknesses, and receptivity to innovation); the know-how to get things done without undermining resource commitments to preexisting programs; and attention to detail (Travis, 1995).

However, a significant problem for strategic leaders seeking to create more effective organizations is this: What should they do with managers who either do not support the new direction or are incapable of learning new skills? Judgments about who is working for the organization's success and what works must be objective and grounded in data, not subjective feelings. The follow-up, feedback, assessment, and evaluation at crime strategy meetings are critical factors in effective strategic management. Empowering managers and holding them accountable for achieving results is one way to create the means to assess effectiveness and to identify and remove incompetent ones. Middle managers and supervisors must be involved in the planning process and be provided with a clear mandate, authority, and responsibility to create and implement operational tactics. They should be prepared and trained for their new roles. While they must be held accountable for desired outcomes and provided with performance feedback, mistakes made in the attempt to advance organizational performance should be tolerated, not punished. The balance between eliminating and retraining individuals who fail to perform well must be maintained (see Kelling & Bratton, 1993; Oliver, 2000; Vito, Walsh, & Kunselman, 2005).

Earlier in this text, we noted that organizational culture is the hidden energy that moves people to act. It provides meaning for what people do and why they do it. Effective organizations promote shared values, beliefs, assumptions, perceptions, norms, and behavior patterns that support performance quality and effectiveness. All members of the organization share a robust organizational culture that values examples. Managerial behavior must model the behavior desired by the organization, as it attempts to introduce new ideas. Reward systems must be based on supporting positive norms and behaviors. Policies and procedures must hold individuals accountable for performance.

Leaders can affect organizational culture in several ways. They communicate the vision of the organization—where it has been (past), where it is now (present), and where it is going (future). Through their day-to-day actions, they can reinforce the values the organization considers essential. They model the actions they wish to see subordinates exhibit. These values are integral to achieving the operational strategies promoted by the leader (Yukl, 2013, p. 287).

Accountability is established through an internal assessment process that gives managers the authority but also assesses the effectiveness of their strategies and tactics developed to address operational problems and conditions. In this manner, the department responds to the environmental conditions that spawn crime and disorder. External monitoring should consider such issues as the following (see Yukl, 2013, p. 297):

1. What do the citizens of the community need and want?
2. What is the reaction of citizens to the department's current practices and services?
3. How will the department be affected by changing population demographics (e.g., aging, diversity) among the citizenry?
4. How will the department be affected by national and international events?

The answers to these questions will provide the information necessary to assist mangers with their strategy formulation.

Strategic managers must also consider how to achieve performance objectives in light of the situation they face and the organizational resources that are available to them. The department's organizational strategy should unite managerial and employee decision-making and actions into a coordinated and compatible pattern. Strategies can be both proactive (intended) and reactive (adaptive)—a combination of planned activities or "on-the-spot" reactions to changing and unanticipated conditions. Strategic managers must be flexible—shape and alter their tactics as events transpire and operational demands change.

The following elements of the strategic management process must be completed before a strategy is formulated (Yukl, 2013, p. 299; Parnell, 2014, p. 2;):

1. *External Analysis*: Requires an analysis of the opportunities and threats in the external environment.
2. *Internal Analysis*: Determination of the organization's strengths and weaknesses in its internal environment. Identify the "core competencies" (the technical expertise and application talents) of the department.
3. *Strategy Formulation*: The strategy should be developed by matching the organization's strengths and weaknesses with the opportunities and threats provided by the external environment. Evaluate the need for a significant change in strategy and identify promising approaches to deal with the problems ascertained. Anticipate the likely outcomes of potential strategies.
4. *Strategy Execution*: Implementing the strategy developed.
5. *Strategic Control*: Assess performance and make adjustments if the strategy is not achieving the desired outcome.

It must also be stressed that a strategy can be altered to meet changing conditions. Flexibility to meet changes in the external environment is crucial.

The strategic decisions made by the department's executive (chief, director, or sheriff) and their command staff should follow the steps listed above, accompanied with a thorough consideration of the internal and external factors facing the police organization. While a strategy should be based upon knowledge of the past and present, it must also attempt to anticipate future conditions and concerns. It should take advantage of the opportunities presented and balance them against the threats posed by the external environment. The process involves choice and trade-offs between immediate and long-term outcomes (see Parnell, 2014, p. 10).

New strategies and tactics developing in policing have been created in response to the failure of the "standard model of police practices" (National Academy of Sciences, 2004, p. 223). This model consists of a "one-size-fits-all" approach of reactive methods to deal with crime by:

Increasing the size of police agencies.
Random patrol across all parts of the community.
Rapid response to calls for service.
Generally applied follow-up investigations.
Generally applied intensive enforcement and arrest policies.
(National Academy of Sciences, 2004, p. 224)

In sum, this was the standard model developed during the early 20th-century's professional reform movement. Its primary focus is on the tasks of policing rather than strategies and tactics designed to identify and solve the problems that lead to crime (Goldstein, 1990). In response to the shortcomings of the standard model, several new strategies have been developed under the strategic policing process: (1) Community Policing, (2) Problem-Oriented Policing, (3) CompStat, (4) Intelligence-Led

Policing, and (5) Smart Policing. You were introduced to most of these strategies in Chapter 1. Here, we will briefly define each model and focus on the research on their implementation and effectiveness.

Community Policing

As introduced in Chapter 1, **Community Policing** constitutes the first attempt to challenge the organizational tactical orthodoxy that emerged during the reform era. It attempts to increase the interaction between police and the community through a process of collaboration and consultation, leading to partnerships between the police and community residents. Community is recognized as a required, crucial partner and participant in the production of public safety that policing needs in order to be successful. The hope is that the quality of life in the community will improve due to the introduction of collaborative strategies designed to enhance neighborhood safety. The police and community citizens are expected to work together to address problems of disorder and crime.

Typically, Community Policing provides identifiable officers who know their assigned patrol area and its residents. The assumption is that the community and its patrol officers will develop a mutually supportive bond. They are encouraged to get close to citizens on their beats and better understand their needs and desires. It is hoped that the officers will develop a sense of territorial responsibility for their patrol beat and partnership with its residents. Due to this close collaboration, officers can genuinely relate to the communities they serve and better understand and identify local problems. Hopefully, this will feed their creativity and enable them to solve problems before they become major criminal incidents. Under Community Policing, the police are not supposed to be insular, self-contained, or otherwise cut off from the communities they serve and from where their true power resides (Skolnick, 1999). Measures of success in Community Policing include:

- Improved community quality of life.
- Problem-solving.
- Resident fear reduction.
- Decreased incidents of disorder.
- Increased resident satisfaction with police services.
- Increased crime prevention.

Community Policing also assumes that, because of their development of a collaborative relationship with their communities, police departments will adopt proactive strategies that will repress crime, fear of crime, and disorder within neighborhoods. In addition, it assumes that citizens in a community who partner with their police officers will take a proactive role and help the police set and implement these strategies. Through this exchange process, citizens have input into the determination of police priorities. As a result, every community should be policed in accordance with neighborhood needs and values (see Trojanowicz & Bucqueroux, 1994; Kelling & Coles, 1996). Community Policing rejects the traditional, bureaucratic, policing model that promotes one service delivery strategy for all communities. Instead, it features a decentralized approach designed to provide citizens with tailor-made protection to meet the needs of diverse communities (see Reiss, 1992). Strategically, it attempts to align police operations and community needs.

This decentralization process also seeks to give the line officer a more significant role in decision-making. Thus, it promotes a change in organizational operations away from the "top-down" approach typical in law enforcement organizations. Community Policing is, therefore, more flexible, decentralized, and (hopefully) more humane, due to the input sought from community members and line officers. Officers and the department must commit to collaborative problem-solving partnerships with citizens (Wasserman & Moore, 1988, p. 5). Police officers and citizens in the community are empowered to take an active stance and become responsible and accountable for community problems.

Community Policing shifts the focus of police work from answering random calls for service to the identification, responding to, and resolving of community problems (Peak & Glensor, 2002). Departments thus have the responsibility to perform traditional duties of law enforcement, order maintenance, and service in addition to engaging in community problem-solving (see Rosenbaum, 1998). Police tactics include establishing a proactive response to maintaining order and dealing with quality-of-life offenses in communities (see Goldstein, 1993). Under Community Policing, operational officers are viewed as intelligent agents able to react intellectually and analytically to citizen concerns. Operational officers are expected to engage community citizens and anticipate their social and law enforcement concerns before they become community problems.

Through its emphasis on police/community partnerships, Community Policing restores the legitimacy of the police in the public's esteem. By making operations transparent and visible to the public, police accountability and procedural justice are stressed. It is a social service approach to fuel community safety and security. The assumption is that getting to know a community and its citizens and solving its problems will be more effective than traditional, reactive, single-incident, call-for-service-driven law enforcement. The ultimate goal is for the police and the community to solve problems before they become crimes. Community Policing officers must directly engage in actual, proactive crime prevention.

Implementing Community Policing

Evaluations of Community Policing programs have focused upon the impact of specific programs limited to certain areas. Research on Community Policing has examined the internal effects of these programs on the operations of departments, including the job satisfaction and related attitudes of police officers working in Community Policing programs. The strengths and weaknesses concerning Community Policing have been documented by this research. In most cities, Community Policing has been developed as a program or project rather than a full-blown, department-wide strategy (Skolnick & Bayley, 1988).

Research on the Innovative Neighborhood Oriented Policing Project (INOP) revealed the strengths and weaknesses of Community Policing. For example, in the city of Louisville, Kentucky, site interviews revealed that police administrators and officers believed their INOP project had been very effective in reducing fear in the target areas. However, community residents were less sure about these accomplishments. Across all eight Louisville sites, the authors uncovered several suggestions for departments seeking to establish Community Policing. For example, they noted that before the implementation of Community Policing there is a need for extensive training. Patrol officers in all eight INOP sites had little understanding of the goals of the

INOP projects or Community Policing that their police departments were seeking to accomplish (Sadd & Grinc, 1994, p. 31). Officers resisted Community Policing because it redefined the role of the patrol officer from crime-fighter to problem-solver (Sadd & Grinc, 1994, pp. 40–41). The need for training was also evident for community residents so they understood what the department was doing and trying to accomplish in the community. In all eight INOP sites, community leaders and residents complained that the police did not adequately inform or educate them about the goals and objectives of Community Policing. They also stressed the vital need for interagency involvement so that Community Policing is not an isolated change within city government.

These results mirror the findings of other studies of Community Policing. In their literature review on Community Policing, Lurgio and Rosenbaum consolidated research findings over an 18-year period covering 11 cities (Lurgio & Rosenbaum, 1994). They concluded Community Policing has exerted a positive influence on both the police and on citizens' views of the police. Police reported increases in job satisfaction and motivation, a broadening of the police role, improved relationships with co-workers and citizens, and greater expectations regarding community participation in crime prevention efforts. Citizens felt that Community Policing officers were more visible, helpful, polite, and effective on a variety of job activities (see Hayeslip & Cordner, 1987; Greene, 1989). In Madison, Wisconsin, Wycoff and Skogan (1994) found that even senior officers supported Community Policing. Madison officers also reported that increased contacts with citizens led to an increase in citizen requests for assistance. Wycoff (1988) also reported that four Community Policing strategies tested in Houston and Newark, New Jersey, appeared to reduce citizen fear of crime, improve citizens' views of crime and disorder problems in their neighborhoods, and improved evaluations of the police.

As previously noted, Community Policing recognizes the role of public and private institutions and organizations in combating crime in partnership with the police. This proposed change proved challenging to achieve. In 1989, a representative survey of police chiefs in cities of more than 25,000 revealed that 67 percent had implemented Community Policing programs in the last three years. However, Zhao, Thurman, and Lovrich (1995, p. 20) found that the departments with the most significant interest in training and education were more likely to implement Community Policing programs. Their factor analysis of the responses revealed three impediments to implementing Community Policing (organizational, community, and transitional). The mean ratings revealed that police agencies were more concerned with internal administrative barriers than obstacles in their community. The dominant factors were resistance from middle management and line officers. Departments with high correlations on these factors were less likely to implement Community Policing. In another analysis, these authors discovered that, between 1993 and 1996, interest in Community Policing rose while identifying implementation impediments. However, they concluded that the institutionalization of Community Policing was far from certain (Zhao et al., 1999).

An assessment of the implementation of Community Policing in several U.S. cities revealed that cities that received federal funding under the Crime Control Act of 1994 (that also established the Office of Community Policing Services) and that had city manager forms of government were primarily likely to implement Community Policing (He, Zhao, & Lovrich, 2005). However, further analysis of this data set determined that police chiefs largely maintained their operational priorities within the dictates of the professional model of policing (emphasizing crime-fighting) over those of Community Policing. As local crime rates increased, police agencies emphasized crime-fighting over providing services and order maintenance (Zhao, He, & Lovrich, 2006, pp. 715–716).

Walsh's (1994) survey of Northeastern first-line police supervisors revealed problems in the implementation of Community Policing. Notable was a lack of support and understanding from patrol supervisors and officers assigned to traditional patrol operations separated from the Community Policing unit. In addition, group discussion sessions revealed that these supervisors felt that operational personnel considered community-oriented policing as "soft policing" or not "real" police work and that Community Policing lacked legitimacy because the purpose of the program, personnel authority, and duties were not clearly specified nor training adequately provided. As a result, the feeling among the supervisors was that the program was temporary and would be disbanded when the funding ended.

However, a small portion of this sample offered a different perspective on their programs. These supervisors said their chief's leadership is the driving force behind the shift to Community Policing. They claimed that Community Policing has reduced service calls and has gained significant support throughout the department and community. In each department, the chief established external political and community support for the program before installing it. They also worked closely with the program supervisors to ensure it became correctly installed. Many of these supervisors were having problems balancing their traditional control orientation with the autonomy needs of their officers. Although administrators supported team building and employee participation, their behavior was control-oriented. For example, they expressed fear that the officers' familiarity with community members and operational freedom may lead to deviations from their department's standards of behavior and give management an excuse to end the program.

Similarly, police managers enrolled at the Southern Police Institute were asked to identify obstacles to the implementation of Community Policing, whether they could be overcome, and if Community Policing would help solve the problems facing their department. Overall, their responses indicated that they had "adopted the philosophy of community policing but were unwilling to make the organizational changes necessary to support it" (Vito, Walsh, & Kunselman, 2005, p. 18). They identified community involvement as the greatest hindrance to the adoption of Community Policing, but also offered methods such as strategic planning and new forms of performance evaluation to deal with implementation issues. They were particularly hopeful about the potential that Community Policing held for the line officer. However, they were reluctant to accept their role in the implementation process and assert the development of Community Policing as something other than a specialized unit in their departments.

Likewise, Bradstreet's (1997) interviews with a group of 20 patrol sergeants from the Austin Police Department (in Texas) led to several recommendations concerning the implementation of Community Policing. To ensure its acceptance, these sergeants advocated working in teams, the freedom to choose and tailor projects to fit officers' styles, tying Community Policing to police traditions, and working directly with citizens.

Finally, Gianakis and Davis (1998) conducted a survey of Florida law enforcement agencies and found that Community Policing took a variety of forms. They discovered that all the agencies employed some variety of Community Policing but, even when structural change occurred, the impact on existing policies and systems was minimal. Many of the organizations in this survey instituted Community Policing by changing the officers' role rather than the organization. The most common variant used was restructuring of patrol operations through the creation of decentralized sub-stations (Gianakis & Davis, 1998, p. 489).

Yet, research on Community Policing programs in six cities revealed that resistance to change may be an overrated threat (Weisel & Eck, 1994). At least two-thirds of officers felt that Community Policing is here to stay. A positive view of Community Policing is held regardless of years of service, education, race, sex, and experience in fixed beat areas. Several organizational approaches were shared across the Community Policing sites, including using participatory management, seeking input from line-level staff, changing promotional practices to reinforce officer involvement, changing performance evaluation systems to support Community Policing, and providing formal training for personnel. An interview-based study with Cleveland, Ohio, officers engaged in Community Policing determined that they had positive views toward the program and the communities it served. They noted that "good people" lived in the neighborhood and wanted something done about crime. The study also found "no ascertainable pattern" between the race of the officer, their attitudes toward the Community Policing program, and the racial composition of the neighborhood (Ammar, Kessler, & Kratcoski, 2007, p. 319).

A study of attitudes toward Community Policing in a small Southern city between 2002 and 2005 found that, while the police built neighborhood partnerships, there were no significant changes in the fear of crime or satisfaction with the police expressed by the citizenry. However, citizens who had direct contact with the police had higher levels of satisfaction and a lesser fear of crime (Lord, Kuhns, & Friday, 2009). Burruss and Giblin (2014) found that centrist forces in organizations (publications, the professionalization of law enforcement, and other law enforcement agencies) aided the implementation of Community Policing. They help an organization become familiar with the nature of an innovation.

Overall, these findings suggest that researchers of Community Policing programs must closely examine how community police units are integrated into the department's organizational structure and how the department's culture contributes to or hinders this operational reform. Community Policing must not lead to creating what Toch and Grant (1991, p. 65) termed "innovation ghettos" that isolate the people in them and minimize the service they provide. However, evidence is lacking that Community Policing was ever implemented to promote structural changes in police departments (Maguire, 1997; Maguire & Katz, 2002).

Several issues raised by these studies serve notice to departments who are planning a move to Community Policing. First, there is a clear need to conduct training sessions for both police officers and citizens on the meaning and nature of Community Policing. The nature of the process and the benefits to be gained should be fully specified and recognized. Similarly, a clearly defined relationship should be established between police departments and other agencies to address the community problems that are related to crime but know no jurisdictional boundaries. Finally, the most crucial element is a working relationship with the community. Community leaders must be identified, their support obtained, and partnerships maintained if Community Policing is to achieve its potential for meaningful change.

Garcia (2005) questioned whether COP programs were stigmatized in policing. She argued that COP norms were incongruent with the crime-fighting function valued in most organizations. Their emphasis on social service functions might lead to the shaming of COP. Her analysis of data from a national survey of officers found that a COP assignment did not affect the status of participants as "real police officers" (Garcia, 2005, p. 76). However, those officers who volunteered for COP duty did report a loss of status (Garcia, 2005, p. 78).

Effectiveness of Community Policing

In their review of research on the effectiveness of policing methods, the Committee to Review Research on Police Policy and Practices (National Academy of Sciences, 2004, p. 234) noted that Community Policing lowers the fear of crime in communities when the level of interaction between citizens and officers increases. Using police community stations and citizen contact patrols raised direct community involvement. However, reducing the fear of crime was not evident across all socioeconomic groups. The research also determined that, if the police evidenced respect toward citizens, they were more likely to obtain compliance for their requests (National Academy of Sciences, 2004, p. 235).

These research findings were upheld by studies that followed this report. In the most comprehensive evaluation of a Community Policing program, Skogan (2006) reviewed 12 years of data on Chicago's Community Policing program (**Chicago Alternative Policing Strategy—CAPS**). Unlike other departments, Chicago implemented Community Policing city-wide, dividing the city into beats. The CAPS program attempted to mobilize community members to partner with the police to prevent crime. In Chicago, Community Policing allowed residents to address crime and disorder problems by securing ties to police and public officials (Lombardo & Lough, 2007, p. 132). Skogan (2006) analyzes explicit data from two aspects of CAPS: one effective (beat meetings—open forums for neighborhood residents and officers assigned to it) and one less so (district advisory committees comprising selected community leaders and police officials). In particular, Skogan's (2006) analysis reveals a differential effect for CAPS by race. African Americans were most involved in the program, and their neighborhoods benefited from it most of all, while White residents did not seem to need it. Latino communities lacked participation due to language and economic barriers. Latino households were too involved in work to participate. Skogan notes (2006, p. 317) that beat officers "adopted very traditional problem-solving strategies, including high-visibility patrol, aggressive stops and field interrogations, and undercover operations." They also made referrals to other city agencies in 63 percent of the beats in the study.

In their reanalysis of data from the CAPS evaluation, Lombardo, Olson, and Staton (2010) determined that residents in areas served by the program had higher opinions of the ability of the police to fight crime than residents in matched comparison group neighborhoods. Overall, the CAPS experience documents that police departments need to tailor their approaches and responses to specific communities regarding their socioeconomic background to be effective in implementing Community Policing.

An analysis of the effect of Community Policing on crime showed that one jurisdiction registered a significant decline in the level of violent and property crimes in the area served by the program (Connell, Miggans, & McGloin, 2008). The research also determined that the officers working under this program were committed to implementing Community Policing. Also, the Community Policing program was implemented within a single unit, not adopted by the entire department. A similar study determined that Community Policing had an indirect effect on crime (Xu, Fiedler, & Flaming, 2005). It also found that citizens' fear of crime and perceived quality of life were significant predictors of the level of citizens' satisfaction with police performance.

Tillyer (2018) examined the impact of Community Policing on arrests, using official, national-level data on policing and crime. He found that the structure of Community Policing affected the results. Departments that simply created a COP unit or reported a single COP activity did not influence arrests. However, those agencies who conducted a greater number of COP activities made COP a part of their mission statement, and partnered with the community had a heightened likelihood of violent crime arrests—although the nature of the data could not exactly specify what operations were conducted (Tillyer, 2018, p. 547).

These goals are vital to the Community Policing strategy—meeting citizens' demands for police services and promoting feelings of safety in the community. The core idea of Community Policing encourages individual agencies to adapt it to meet the circumstances they face. Thus,

> community policing is a philosophy that promotes organizational strategies which support the systematic use of partnerships and problem-solving techniques to proactively address the immediate conditions that give rise to public safety issues such as crime, social disorder, and fear of crime.
> (Scheider, Chapman, & Schapiro, 2009, pp. 697–698)

In this chapter, we will also review how Community Policing was combined with other strategic policing strategies.

Problem-Oriented Policing

Many departments use Community Policing within a framework of **Problem-Oriented Policing** (POP) to enact it. Problem-Oriented Policing recognizes that the role of the police as law enforcers is overrated. Noted police scholar Herman Goldstein (1990) suggested that, if the police are serious about controlling crime, they must analyze the daily problems they address. Problem-Oriented Policing requires that the police develop a systematic process for identifying, examining, and managing the issues the public expects them to handle. It requires identifying these problems in more precise terms, researching each problem, documenting the current police response, assessing its adequacy and the adequacy of existing authority and resources, engaging in a broad exploration of alternatives to present responses, weighing the merits of these alternatives, and choosing from among them (Goldstein, 1979).

The heart of Problem-Oriented Policing is the **SARA model**. It directs police officers to engage in the following four basic steps in the problem-solving process (Goldstein, 1990):

- *Scanning*: Identify recurring problems and how they affect community safety.
- *Analysis*: Determine the causes of the problem.
- *Response*: Seeking out, selecting, and implementing activities to solve the problem.
- *Assessment*: Determine if the response was effective or identify new strategies.

This method encourages the police to adopt operational tactics to reduce or eliminate the problem that is the major contributor to the crime in question. As defined in San Diego (Capowich & Roehl, 1994, pp. 127–128),

> POP emphasizes identifying and analyzing problems (criminal, civil, or public nuisance) and implementing solutions to resolve the underlying causes of the problem. It emphasizes proactive intervention rather than reactive responses

to calls for service, resolution of root causes rather than symptoms, and use of multiparty, community-based problem solving rather than a unilateral police response. POP focuses on a long-term, comprehensive problem rather than handling the situation as a series of separate incidents resolved via arrest or other police response.

In San Diego, the police focused upon street robberies. Research determined that calls for service did not decrease over the one-year period. Yet, the indicators revealed that the POP approach improved the circumstances for those who use the Community Policing stations and reduced the police workload at these stations. However, the role played by citizen groups in this project was limited.

Cordner and Biebel (2005) interviewed officers engaging in Problem-Oriented Policing in San Diego, CA—a department devoted to the approach. Their analysis gives insight into implementation issues associated with the process. They determined that the officers tackled small-scale problems—particularly drug and disorder problems. Regarding the SARA model, POP initiatives flowed from observations and complaints rather than data analysis or a sophisticated scanning process. The research was informal and limited, originating from small-scale, reactive, incident-oriented problem-solving approaches. Officers did not expect that analysis would lead to effective responses to problems. Officers focused on the response aspect of POP, but relied upon their personal experience and the advice of fellow officers rather than developing imaginative responses through consultation with research results. As a result, they used such traditional responses as targeted enforcement by uniformed patrol officers and directed or saturation patrol tactics. These officers explained that their lack of creativity was tied to their reliance on their experience with traditional responses and time pressures to develop a response. They were too busy answering calls to brainstorm creative responses. However, these officers reported that their efforts were successful, with over half of the problems eliminated and 83 percent showing that the problem was reduced in severity (Cordner & Biebel, 2005, p. 170). They felt that POP was an excellent way to respond to community concerns. To improve the process, they suggested: (1) supervisors needed to be more supportive of POP efforts, (2) using more group meetings for brainstorming, (3) more direct POP mentoring in the field, and (4) more POP support from crime analysts (Cordner & Biebel, 2005, p. 173).

A study of POP implementation in Colorado Springs, CO, also revealed several implementation problems and issues. First, the external partners of this department did not appear to play a central and collaborative role in problem identification. Second, record-keeping was inconsistent and made it difficult to identify effective responses. Third, the assessment of the effectiveness of the responses was negligible. Officers typically did no evaluation or just a shallow one (Maguire, Uchida, & Hassell, 2015, p. 87). Finally, as with COP, POP is a function of specialty units rather than routinely practiced by all officers. Although POP has registered success in several instances, these findings highlight that the ideal implementation of this reform has been difficult to achieve, possibly due to a lack of resources and proper training.

Elsewhere, research on POP reports positive results. In both Newport News (VA) and Baltimore County (MD), officers concentrated on underlying causes of crime. They collected information and enlisted the support of public and private agencies. As a result, both crime and fear of crime were substantially reduced in both areas (Eck & Spelman, 1987). In a systematic review of POP research findings, Weisburd and his colleagues (2010) conducted a meta-analysis of more than 5,500 articles and reports (resulting in finding ten methodologically rigorous studies) and concluded that POP had an overall modest but statistically significant impact upon crime and disorder. The overall percent change in crime and disorder recorded by the studies was over 44 percent (Weisburd, Telep, Hinkle, & Eck, 2010, p. 162). The National Academy of Sciences (2018, p. 247) review of proactive policing concluded that Community Policing leads to modest improvements in the public's view of policing and police in the short term.

Hot Spot Policing

Another tactic of strategic policing that has been extensively researched is known as **Hot Spot (or place-based) Policing**. A hot spot is a small geographic location where the rate of crimes per square foot is higher than that of the surrounding areas. Thus, the hot spot is a valuable way to determine where police should focus their efforts to solve a crime problem. This tactic represents a shift from person-based policing to place-based policing. It has emerged as a central feature of cutting-edge law enforcement (Weisburd & Lum, 2005). While evolutionary, it demands radical changes in data collection, the organization of police activities, and the overall worldview of the police, which sees their primary task as catching criminals (Weisburd, 2008).

Crime hot spots are also examined to determine the day of the week, time of day and hours when crime calls are concentrated (Sherman, 2009, pp. 157–158). Besides the clustering of crime events, Hot Spot Policing analyses consider such variables as facilities (bars, churches, apartment buildings), site features (lack of guardianship, inept or improper management, presence of valuable items), offender mobility (factors influencing target selection by offenders—gender, race, age, experience, crime type), and target location (places that present acceptable risks and gains) (Braga, 2005, p. 319). A *hot spot* is a "micro" place that can be seen in its entirety by the human eye at one location on the ground (Sherman, 2009, p. 158).

In the 1980s, policing researchers narrowed the geographical area focus of their analysis to small high-crime areas within neighborhoods. The best-known study was conducted by Sherman and Weisburd in Minneapolis (Sherman & Weisburd, 1995). This study examined data on over 300,000 calls to Minneapolis police city-wide over a year and found that a few hot spots accounted for nearly all calls to the police. These areas, some as small as street intersections, were exceptionally high in predatory crimes such as robbery, rape, and auto theft. These findings suggest specific locales are more susceptible to crime. Presumably, further examination of these areas might provide tips on how to prevent offenses from occurring. Community problem-solving techniques may reduce crime and disorder substantially if risks at these locations are stable. If places run high risks only temporarily, such strategies may not work.

Reviews of studies on the effectiveness of Hot Spot Policing are encouraging. A meta-analysis of five Hot Spot Policing experiments published between 1989 and 1995 determined that these interventions reduced calls for service in the target areas (notably for disorder offenses). Still, treatment effects for property and violence calls were minor and not statistically significant (Braga, 2005, pp. 333–335). Weisburd and Braga (2006, pp. 232–233) reviewed nine prominent studies of Hot Spot Policing (published from 1989 to 1999) and determined that "noteworthy crime reductions" were reported in seven of these analyses. The results also showed that, rather than a displacement of crime, there was a "diffusion of crime control benefits." The areas not served by the experiment also improved crime prevention and reduction. A meta-analysis of 25 Hot Spot Policing studies determined crime control gains with the policing operational interventions tested when compared to control areas. Once again, the diffusion of benefits for these methods was confirmed, rather than evidence of crime displacement (Braga, Papachristos, & Hureau, 2012).

Recent research results on Hot Spot Policing are also positive. In Lowell, MA, a randomized controlled trial of Hot Spot Policing registered strong results. The identified Lowell hot spots accounted for over 23 percent of the total calls for crime and disorder in 2004 (Braga & Bond, 2008, p. 583). The police interventions resulted in a 14 percent reduction in disorder/nuisance calls, a 29.4 percent increase in misdemeanor offenses, and a 21.5 percent reduction in calls for service compared to the control areas. Social disorder was eased at 14 out of 17 of the treatment areas (Braga & Bond, 2008, pp. 594–596). It was also noted that Lowell police commanders were continuously held accountable for results in the treatment areas via a CompStat-like system.

In Philadelphia, a hot spot study of Operation Safe Streets examined the impact of placing officers at 214 of the highest drug activity locations in the city—24 hours a day, seven days a week (Lawton, Taylor, & Luongo, 2005). The research findings determined that the police crackdown failed to significantly impact homicides, violent crimes, or drug crimes on a city-wide basis. However, localized analyses determined that it affected violent and drug crime and spatial diffusion of benefits rather than crime displacement (Lawton et al., 2005, p. 447). A meta-analysis of Hot Spot Policing studies determined that diffusion of benefits was a much more likely outcome than crime displacement (Bowers, Johnson, Guerette, Summers, & Poyton, 2011). The authors cautioned that crackdowns, especially for drug crimes, may have a short-lived effect and not constitute a long-term solution.

A second Philadelphia-based study, featuring an experimental design, examined the impact of the placement of 200 foot patrol officers upon 60 violent crime hot spots in the summer of 2009. The violent crime hot spots were foot patrolled for up to 90 hours per week. They benefited from a net effect of 53 fewer violent offenses during the experiment, outperforming the control areas by 23 percent (Ratcliffe, Taniguchi, Groff, & Wood, 2011, p. 818). This experiment reveals the potential of foot patrol as a practical element of a problem-oriented, place-based policing strategy to reduce violent crime. Further study on this experiment showed a complementary relationship between foot and car patrol in these areas. The research findings indicated that car patrol officers could concentrate on violent severe crime incidents, while foot patrol officers concentrated on order-maintenance activities (Groff, Johnson, Ratcliffe, & Wood, 2013, p. 136). Therefore, both types of patrol should be possible operational tactics in a violent crime prevention strategy.

A third Philadelphia-based study used an experimental design to compare the effectiveness of three approaches to Hot Spot Policing: Foot Patrol, Problem-Oriented Policing (POP), and Offender-Focused Policing (OF). OF was the most effective hot spot method, reducing violent crime by 42 percent and violent felonies by 50 percent compared to the control areas, with a diffusion of benefits to neighboring locations (Groff et al., 2015, p. 42). These findings support the conclusion that the police should focus on intervention with known offenders rather than conducting random pedestrian or traffic stops.

A study based in Dayton, OH, also achieved positive results. Even though the officers were unable to devote full-time attention to the hot spots, foot patrol resulted in fewer total crime incidents, but only the decline in disorder crimes reached statistical significance. Crime also declined in surrounding areas, once again confirming the displacement of crime benefits (Haberman & Stivers, 2018, pp. 264–265).

There are other issues surrounding the use of crime hot spots. The first is dosage. How long should the police patrol the hot spot? Reanalyzing data from the Minnesota Preventive Patrol Experiment, Koper (1995) attempted to determine the optimum time officers should spend in a hot spot to obtain the maximum deterrent effect upon crime. He found that a "dosage effect" existed. Police stops were most effective when they were 13 to 15 minutes long, and the impact deteriorated after that point and must be of some quality, not just driving by (Koper, 1995, p. 663). Therefore, there is a saturation point for Hot Spot Policing that ultimately weakens any deterrent impact. The policy recommendation from this study, known as the "Koper Curve" theory, is that "police could maximize crime and disorder reduction at hot spots by making proactive, medium length stops" and reduce the unnecessary time spent at these locations (Koper, 1995, p. 668). But, if this patrol is effective, a paradox may occur. The more crime police prevent, the more boring they may find patrolling. Yet, even if this happens, patrolling hot spots puts officers in an improved position to respond to emergency calls in these high-call-producing areas when they come in. The "Koper Curve" demonstrates that sitting on a hot spot for 8 to 24 hours daily is wasteful (Sherman, 2009, p. 159). An experiment conducted in Sacramento, CA, documented the effectiveness of the Koper Curve recommendations. The results showed that 15-minute, randomized visits to crime hot spots significantly reduced Part I crimes and calls for service (Telep, Mitchell, & Weisburd, 2014). Increased police presence of medium length and randomly timed may be the most effective dosage for Hot Spot Policing. One study suggests that shifting proactive police work to hot spot locations and away from low-crime areas could maximize crime prevention (Koper, Wu, & Lum, 2021, p. 396). In Great Britain, an experiment found that using police community support officers (PCSOs—uniformed but civilian police staff—aka "soft policing") also reduced crime at hot spots. The research determined that the more the PCSOs visited the hot spots, the greater the effect on crime and disorder without crime displacement to adjoining areas (Ariel, Weinborn, & Sherman, 2016, p. 311). Since they have fewer arrest powers, the mere visibility of the PCSOs accounted for this result.

A hot spot experiment in Las Vegas, Nevada, resulted in a 21 percent reduction in overall crime and calls for service (−25.7 percent overall and 34 percent for violent crime calls) (Corsaro, Engel, Herold, Yildrim, & Motz, 2021, p. 1). Additionally, the experiment noted an impact on violent crime related to patrol dosage. Street segments with chronic, persistent violent crime benefited from concentrated HSP dosage. It also supported the "Koper Curve"—that short (<15 minutes) and intermittent presence in high crime hot spots can reduce criminal activity (both total citizen requests and total criminal offenses) (Corsaro, Engel, Herold, Yildrim, & Motz, 2021, p. 15).

Second, what is the effect of Hot Spot Policing methods on community residents? A study of the impact of police focus on crime hot spots determined that order maintenance methods promulgated under the Broken Windows theory may have unanticipated effects. Hinkle and Weisburd (2008) found that in Jersey City, New Jersey, the fear of crime expressed by citizens increased even though crackdowns had lowered the crime rate. The increased presence of police in the area negatively impacted residents' perception of the area's safety. This finding underscores the necessity for the police to communicate with citizens and explain their methods to mitigate their fear and be effective (Hinkle & Weisburd, 2008, p. 510).

In addition, results from a telephone interview with respondents from two southeastern U.S. cities found that physical disorder, rather than social disorder, affected their opinions about the quality of life in their neighborhoods. These findings suggest that police efforts to reduce social disorder may not influence the quality of life in areas (Chappell, Monk-Turner, & Payne, 2011). Similarly, data from Jersey City, New Jersey, from a telephone survey of residents and an observational study of blocks determined that evidence of physical disorder affected their notions of social disorder in neighborhoods. Therefore, the police may wish to include methods to reduce physical disorder (like graffiti removal) when conducting Broken Windows Policing (Hinkle & Yang, 2014). Finally, an analysis of survey data from Washington State also determined that people have difficulty discerning their perceptions of physical disorder and crime. People who felt that their neighborhood was disorderly were more likely to make distinctions between disorder and crime (Gau & Pratt, 2010). However, one Hot Spot Policing study that considered community attitudes toward operations found no significant impacts on fear of crime, police legitimacy, collective efficacy, or perceptions of crime and disorder (Weisburd, Hinkle, Famega, & Ready, 2011).

Third, which patrolling strategy is most effective in policing hot spots? An experiment focusing on 83 hot spots in Jacksonville, Florida, used a Problem-Oriented Policing strategy and directed saturation patrol as the treatment over 90 days. Both treatments resulted in higher levels of self-initiated police activity and field stops compared to the control group area. The main finding was that the problem-solving intervention was associated with a 33 percent reduction in violent street crime. The research registered no statistically significant differences for property and other violent crimes, but declined in the problem-solving intervention areas (Taylor, Koper, & Woods, 2011, pp. 172–173).

A nine-month randomized control study examined the ability of directed patrol to reduce firearms crime in St. Louis, MO. The hot spot intervention reduced non-domestic firearm assaults but not firearm robberies (Rosenfeld, Deckard, & Blackburn, 2014, p. 445). A Hot Spot Policing experiment in Louisville, Kentucky, compared calls for service (CFS) across urban and suburban areas. Directed patrol of 12 to 15 minutes had a statistically significant impact on CFS and soft crimes across the locations (Schafer, Hughes, & Stelzig, 2019, p. 13). In suburban areas, directed patrol had marked success, especially a 40 percent decrease in car thefts from a city park (Schafer, Hughes, & Stelzig, 2019, p. 15). The findings show that the intervention strategy adopted for hot spots can make a difference.

Lawrence Sherman maintains that the concentration of crime in hot spots is more intense than among individual repeat offenders (Sherman, 1995). Such places have characteristics like those considered in the criminal careers of persons: onset, continuance, specialization, and desistance. The development of computerized geographical information systems (GIS) has made identifying hot spots routine among police departments. Like individuals with a long "rap sheet," high-crime locations have become targets of policing initiatives.

Hot Spot Policing has demonstrated great promise. In their review of the effectiveness of recent police strategies, Eck and Weisburd (2004, p. 57) determined that such focused policing efforts had the most substantial evidence of success. A meta-analysis of Hot Spot Policing studies was conducted on studies published on or before 2010 on police-led crime control efforts. The overall conclusion was that Hot Spot Policing generated small but noteworthy reductions in crime that also spread to other areas surrounding the targeted area. Problem-oriented tactics were especially effective. Studies that considered resident attitudes reported positive reactions to hot spot methods (Braga, Papachristos, & Hureau, 2014).

However, it is also evident that the police must do more than put "cops on the dots" and create strategies to change conditions in the hot spot locations (Casady, 2011, p. 2). Koper (2014) surveyed 305 agencies led by general members of the Police

Executive Research Forum in 2008 on Hot Spot Policing. The respondents indicated they focused on larger areas as hot spots rather than the prescribed focus on micro-places. However, policing efforts in these areas were effective. Koper (2014, p. 137) suggests that police could focus on micro-places within a broader context of regions and neighborhoods to be optimally effective. In addition, the survey results indicated that police efforts could be more effective by focusing attention on hot spots over extended periods, such as giving them daily attention. Koper (2014, p. 137) recommends creating "place-based data systems" to track crime trends, actors, social and physical features, and interventions at hot spots over time. The police respondents relied upon traditional methods to handle hot spots (patrol, enforcement, targeting offenders) rather than adopting situational crime prevention methods. One-half of the respondents stated that they regularly briefed patrol officers and detectives on hot spot operations, and only one-third communicated with problem groups in the hot spot area. While police agencies have adopted Hot Spot Policing as an operational tactic, some fine-tuning is required to determine the proper methods and dosage of patrolling. Still to be determined are how Hot Spot Policing operations affect perceptions of police legitimacy, if it will be effective in smaller cities and rural counties, and what the long-term impact of Hot Spot Policing upon crime rates will be (Weisburd & Telep, 2014). The National Academy of Science study on proactive policing (2018, p. 173) concluded that Hot Spot Policing strategies generated short-term crime reduction effects and avoided displacing crime into surrounding locations. Instead, these efforts produced a diffusion of crime control benefits to those areas.

CompStat

Developed and implemented by the New York City Police Department, **CompStat** is a managerial accountability system that focuses the department on proactive crime control. It is a goal-oriented, strategic management process that aims to control crime by holding police operational commanders accountable for organizational performance. It is a revolutionary strategic police management paradigm adopted by departments worldwide (Walsh, 2001; Henry, 2002; McDonald, 2002).

CompStat is a product of the innovative strategies and the dynamic management processes developed in 1994 under then New York City Police Commissioner William Bratton and continued by his successors Howard Safir, Bernard Kerik, and Raymond Kelly and Bratton again (Safir, 1997; Bratton & Knobler, 1998; Maple, 1999; Silverman, 1999; Giuliani, 2002, pp. 87–88; Henry, 2002). CompStat evolved from the New York City Police Department's weekly Crime Control Strategy meetings that began in January 1994. These meetings increased the flow of crime information between the agency's executives and the commanders of operational units. William Bratton and his command staff created these CompStat meetings to make his 76 precinct commanders and officers accountable for the crime rate (Silverman, 1999). From 1993 through September 2014, using the CompStat process, seven felony crimes in New York City (Murder, Rape, Robbery, Felony Assault, Burglary, Grand Larceny, and Grand Larceny Auto) have declined by about 77.8 percent (www.nyc.gov/html/nypd/downloads/pdf/crime_statistics/cscity.pdf).

Bratton challenged the New York City Police Department to "Take Back the City, Block by Block" and reduce crime. During his tenure as the head of New York City's Transit Police, he made Wilson and Kelling's Broken Windows theory the centerpiece of his operational tactics. Zero tolerance for graffiti, aggressive panhandling, fare beating, and public urination led to a literal and figurative cleanup of the crime-ridden subway system. He also used it as his "lynch-pin strategy" to "Reclaim the Public Spaces of New York" as NYPD Commissioner. Instead of concentrating on felony offenses, quality-of-life crimes (or "incivilities") became the primary target for law enforcement. Bratton thus publicly and passionately embraced crime reduction as the department's primary mission.

CompStat promoted and enforced administrative responsibility. It comprises a four-step process:

1. **Accurate and timely intelligence**: To reduce crime, you must know about it.
   - What type of crime is it (i.e., drug sales, robbery, burglary)?
   - Where is the crime occurring (i.e., areas, types of location)?
   - When is the crime happening (i.e., the day of the week, the hour of the day)?
   - Why is the crime happening (motive, i.e., drug-related shootings)?
2. **Rapid deployment**: CompStat's weekly crime statistics provide data allowing operational commanders to assess crime conditions and quality-of-life trends in their area of responsibility. Commanders can then decide how to use and deploy their resources as rapidly as possible to address these conditions.
3. **Effective tactics**: Commanders can use various operational tactics to address specific problems. What they develop, how, and what results are essential to the evaluation process at crime strategy meetings.
4. **Relentless follow-up and assessment**: The first three steps are only practical if commanders constantly follow up on operations and assess their results. If results are not what they should be, something needs to change. CompStat requires this activity of all operational commanders at all department levels.

The centerpiece of the CompStat process is the briefing. The briefings are a strictly New York–style melding of Total Quality Management (in this case, directly opening lines of communication between executive leaders and staff and precinct commanders and their staff) and Theory X (with the "boss" calling subordinates on the carpet in a most aggressive fashion). CompStat transformed the NYPD into a "learning organization" that used up-to-date crime information, processed it quickly, and acted upon it (O'Connell & Straub, 2007, p. 55). CompStat briefings played a crucial role in this transformation by "improving the flow of useful information across NYPD's large and traditionally opaque bureaucracy" (Sugarman, 2010, p. 172).

Bratton stressed accountability. He also gave precinct commanders increased discretionary power and resources to focus on departmental goals rather than maintaining their commands.

There are four levels of CompStat. Bratton created a system in which the police commissioner, with his executive core, first empowers and then interrogates the precinct commanders, forcing them to devise a plan to attack crime. But it should not stop there. At the next level down, it should be the precinct commander, taking the same role as the commissioner, empowering and interrogating the platoon commander. Then, at the third level, the platoon commanders should ask their sergeants, "What are we doing to deploy resources on this tour to address these conditions?" And finally, the sergeant at roll call should be doing the same thing. This process flows throughout the department until everyone is empowered, motivated, engaged, assessed, and successful. It can work in all organizations, whether it's 38,000 New York cops or Mayberry.

(Bratton & Knobler, 1998, p. 239)

All too often, other departments and police experts dismiss innovations in New York Police Department. They are considered untranslatable due to the city's size and the NYPD's resources. This misperception often leads to the fatal error of not examining and assessing the CompStat process. Yet, departments of all sizes have reviewed these principles and have adopted CompStat-like management processes.

CompStat empowers operational managers to focus, manage, and direct their unit's problem-solving process. They are held accountable for addressing the crime and disorder issues and trends associated with the CompStat data for their areas. Traditional, Community, and Problem-Oriented Policing strategies are integral to their operational tactics. A principal aim of the CompStat process is not just to displace crime, but to reduce it and create a permanent change in the community. CompStat is about crime statistics and control (Safir, 1997).

The underlying concept of CompStat is that police officers and police agencies can substantially positively impact crime and quality-of-life problems facing the communities they serve, if managed strategically. It presents police executives and managers with a new way of examining police organizations and police activities. It is radically different from the accepted concepts and practices that have guided police administration through most of its existence, and it points to new methods and strategies like those used by business managers that police agencies can use to fulfill their mission (Henry, 2002). CompStat emphasizes the vital link between information, operational decision-making, and crime control objectives (McDonald, 2002). However, as a management tool, its impact extends beyond crime-fighting and can apply to any organizational setting. Its strength is that a contingency management process is flexible enough to adapt to constantly changing conditions. It is strategic policing at its best.

Again, the vital heart of the process is the CompStat briefing. Besides analyzing crime information, the CompStat briefing provides four functions. First, it is the "master classroom for on-the-job training and coaching," with supervision supplied by top-level administrators who officers may never see on such a regular basis. Second, it is a place for "peer learning among middle managers" who can learn from the experience and thus spread the benefits of successful crime-fighting methods. Third, senior managers obtain a "regular overview of all operations and problems needing special attention" rather than a piecemeal approach. Finally, it gives "top brass a bully pulpit and a megaphone to send edicts across agency and a stage to recognize and honor outstanding performers at any rank" (Sugarman, 2010, p. 173).

In December 1999, Mayor Martin O'Malley established CitiStat, a program modeled on NYPD's CompStat paradigm in Baltimore. Unlike CompStat, CitiStat aimed to improve all governmental agencies' performance, not just the police department. Every two weeks, agency administrators presented findings on key performance and human resource indicators for review by the mayor's staff and at meetings with the mayor's office. While accounting for their performance, agency heads had the support to improve their operational performance (Henderson, 2003, p. 6). Mayor O'Malley believed the CompStat strategy could make government agencies more efficient and effective. While improving agency performance and accountability, CitiStat also aimed to increase efficiency in the use of resources and improve the quality and quantity of services provided to the citizens of Baltimore (Henderson, 2003, p. 12).

Behn has extensively examined the factors influencing the implementation and execution of the CitiStat process. Specifically, he lists six core drivers of CitiStat:

- The active engagement of the city's top executives;
- The breadth, depth, disaggregation, and "nowness" of the data plus the thoroughness of the analyses of these data;
- The perseverance of the questioning, feedback, and follow-up (which is more persistent than relentless);
- The consequences for both good, poor, and improved performance;
- The focus on problem-solving, continuous experimentation, and learning; and
- The institutional memory of the city's top executives.

(Behn, 2005, p. 301)

Behn believes that, individually, none of the drivers suffices to make CitiStat effective and that none are required. Behn notes that maps were essential for CitiStat analysis in the Baltimore Police Department. They summarize crime patterns and consider such questions as "How many burglaries occurred on a block during any given month or week?" or "How many robberies occurred at an intersection between 2:00 and 5:00 a.m. on the last five Saturdays?" (Behn, 2005, pp. 298–299).

Potential Problems in CompStat Systems

Behn also diagnoses the "seven big errors of PerformanceStat"—an assessment of implementation and operational difficulties with a process like CompStat. These errors are:

1. **No clear purpose:** What results are we trying to produce? What would a better performance look like? How might we know if we made some improvements?
2. **No one has specific responsibilities:** Requires the conversion of explicit purposes into specific responsibilities, like reaching specific performance targets.
3. Meetings are held irregularly, infrequently, or randomly.
4. No one person is authorized to run meetings.
5. **No dedicated analytic staff.** When dealing with crime, the following questions should be considered:
   a. What crimes were committed? Where? When? By whom?
   b. What have we done about them?
   c. What patterns can we detect?
   d. What strategies should we employ in the future in response to these patterns?
6. **No follow-up:** Did today's meeting build upon the problems identified, solutions analyzed, and commitments made at the previous meeting?
7. **No difference between the brutal and the bland:**
   The Brutal ("Gotcha"): NYPD's CompStat meetings were infamous for being tough, uncompromising with poor performers, and unsentimental affairs—aggressively demanding and sarcastically demeaning. O'Connell and Straub (2007, p. 88) assert that CompStat-like systems can devolve into a forum for negative reinforcement, subjecting field commanders to embarrassing or harassing questioning.
   The Bland: Mostly "show & tell," a series of PowerPoint slides presenting another glowing picture of the unit's latest accomplishments.

(Behn, 2008, pp. 3–6)

Behn also recommends that "PerformanceStat" meetings maintain open avenues of communication and that the system be interactive and supportive.

A source of the perception that CompStat can affect homicide rates is that homicides dropped sharply (84.3 percent) between 1993 and 2014 in New York City. Within CompStat, this result came from NYPD's "Quality of Life" initiative, Street Crimes Unit, and stop-and-frisk program that attempted "to remove guns from the street and to prosecute petty offenders with the hope of connecting them to more significant crimes" (Joanes, 1999–2000, p. 275).[1] However, this decline began in New York City before CompStat's implementation. Comparing homicide trends in other U.S. cities during this period, Eck and Maguire (2000, p. 232) concluded that the claim that CompStat accelerated the homicide decline was not supported by the data (see also Joanes, 1999–2000, p. 292). Yet, these authors also cautioned that it was possible, "given the complexity of homicide patterns, that the CompStat process had a subtle and meaningful but difficult-to-detect effect on violent crime in New York" (Eck & Maguire, 2000, p. 235).

CompStat meetings should be strategy sessions to analyze data to determine the problem's nature and develop operational methods to deal with it effectively. It should be a collaborative process. It is not the setting of crime rate targets that is the problem. The issue is how these targets motivate individuals and hold them accountable for performing operations as directed. Sample (2003, p. 27) reminds us that "under certain conditions, the process of measurement can affect the outcome of a measurement in unpredictable ways"—asking the question can dramatically skew the answer. Similarly, Tenbrunsel (2011, p. 61) describes how setting specific performance targets can affect how employees conduct the measurement process. Such goals can lead them to neglect other areas, take undesirable "ends justify the means" risks, be dishonest in their reporting, or engage in unethical behavior they would not otherwise do.

Eterno and Silverman (2006) believe that NYPD's CompStat process fell prey to some of these evils. Based upon their research and observation of CompStat in action, they identified several flaws. The most significant problem is that CompStat's focus on crime reduction can lead police to ignore their "most fundamental goal"—protecting legal principles and democratic rights (Eterno & Silverman, 2006, p. 221). In addition, this focus promoted the perception that CompStat was a numbers game that used fear to drive the process. Berated by high-level NYPD command officers, commanders feared presenting their crime information at CompStat meetings and "would do almost anything to escape the embarrassment of crime statistics going up" (Eterno & Silverman, 2006, p. 223). The commanders then used fear to drive their charges to make arrests and generate statistics to promote crime reduction. Thus, the rank and file typically viewed CompStat as a numbers game where they were required to make more arrests and issue more summonses. They were not motivated by the process to fight crime unless they were members of specialized crime units designed to address a particular problem, like drugs. Reducing crime at any cost can be an outcome in such an atmosphere.

In a survey and interview study of over 500 NYPD officers (at the rank of captain or above), Eterno and Silverman (2010) examined whether the CompStat process exuded pressure upon officers to record crime statistics in favorable ways—specifically, pressure to downgrade index crimes. The research group included Commissioner Bratton-initiated officers who served both before and after CompStat. The retirees from the CompStat era reported that they felt significant pressure to decrease index crime (Eterno & Silverman, 2010, p. 434). They also noted that the demand for integrity in crime statistics was significantly less in the CompStat era and that promotions were more likely to be related to demonstrated decreases in the crime rate (Eterno & Silverman, 2010, p. 442). Thus, pressure and fear may lead subordinates to cheat on statistics rather than develop inventive ways to reach performance targets. This possibility exists within any management strategy focused on performance-based outcomes. However, departments can manage this tendency by using management systems to prevent falsifying performance outcomes.

CompStat Effectiveness

Research by Braga and Weisburd (2010, p. 4) provides empirical evidence that "police can control crime hot spots without displacing crime problems to other places" by utilizing Problem-Oriented Policing and situational crime prevention techniques to address the "dynamics, situations and characteristics" of the location. To implement and manage a Hot Spot Policing program effectively, they recommend that police departments use a "CompStat-like accountability system that puts a premium on problem-oriented policing and community policing" (Braga & Weisburd, 2010, p. 243).

An examination of the impact of CompStat operations on homicide rates in New York City between 1990 and 1999 also considered the effect of cocaine use during the period. The analysis found that misdemeanor arrests were negatively related to gun-related homicides. This effect was statistically significant, even when related factors (sociodemographic characteristics, changing levels of police human resources, and changes in felony arrests) were controlled for. In addition, declining cocaine use was related to declining gun-related homicide rates. These two trends, including the NYPD's initiative to "take guns off the street," impacted gun-related homicides in the city (Messner et al., 2007, pp. 405–407).

Fagan, Zimring, and Kim (1998) considered the impact of order-maintenance policing on homicide rates in New York City. They examined the city's homicide rates from 1950 to 1996 and determined that the decline in gun-related homicides could not be explained entirely by mean regression. Order-maintenance policing could be responsible for this decrease, but precisely to what extent was open to question (Fagan et al., 1998, p. 1322).

Rosenfeld, Fornango, and Rengifo (2007) examined the impact of order-maintenance policing on New York City homicide and robbery rates between 1988 and 2001. Using a multivariate design that controlled for other pertinent factors, they reported a modest impact for order-maintenance policing on these crimes. However, they also concluded that these declines would likely have occurred without order-maintenance policing. Control measures such as socioeconomic disadvantage, racial composition, and immigrant population concentration were also significantly related to homicide and robbery declines (Rosenfeld et al., 2007, pp. 377–379). Yet, some noted impact shows the effectiveness of order-maintenance policing under CompStat.

An exhaustive analysis of the effectiveness of the CompStat program by Zimring (2012, p. 134) reveals that New York City experienced a decline in seven major crime categories (Homicide, Rape, Robbery, Assault, Burglary, Larceny, Auto Theft) that was greater than the nine other largest U.S. cities during the period 1990–2009. For these crimes, the average decline in New York was 63 percent during the 1990s and 45 percent after 2000 (Zimring, 2012, p. 139). Specifically, Zimring (2012, p. 147) attributes this crime drop to the effective use of hot spots emphases and tactics—"the most important of these is a data-driven crime mapping and control strategy management program with many of the elements of CompStat."

Using a CompStat system in the White Plains, New York, Police Department between 2002 and 2005 led to a 69 percent increase in arrests, resulting in a 32 percent decrease in crimes against the person and a 33 percent decrease in property crime. In addition, vehicle and traffic summonses rose by 81 percent, a 6.4 percent reduction in motor vehicle accidents (despite increased traffic flow) (O'Connell & Straub, 2007, p. 19).

Other studies of CompStat have been less conclusive. Harcourt and Ludwig (2006) analyzed crime data from New York and five other cities where a social experiment (MTO—Moving to Opportunity) had taken place to consider if violent crime was related to disorder (as noted by the Broken Windows hypothesis). They concluded that the crime rate reduction reported by Kelling and Sousa resulted from regression to the mean. The precincts that received intensive order-maintenance policing were also the ones with the largest increases and levels of crime during the city's crack epidemic (Harcourt & Ludwig, 2006, p. 315). The results of the MTO analysis found that disorder led to a crime rate decline when people moved to more advantageous neighborhoods. Examining county crime data from California, Worrall (2006) found a significant relationship between Broken Windows Policing and burglary rates. However, there was no evident impact on larceny-theft crimes in these areas. An analysis of Texas crime data from 1990 to 2004 on the 35 largest municipal police agencies found that Broken Windows Policing raised clearance rates for burglaries and auto thefts (less significant) but decreased clearance rates for larceny-theft (Jang, Hoover, & Lawton, 2008). An evaluation of the impact of CompStat policing on crime rates in Fort Worth, Texas, found an effect on property and total index crime rates, but violent crime rates did not decrease. The research recommended that the police focus on a particular crime using a CompStat approach (Jang, Hoover, & Joo, 2010).

The Committee to Review Research on Police Policy and Practices (2004, p. 185) noted in their literature review that the effectiveness of CompStat would be challenging to ascertain scientifically. Recent research on the impact of CompStat and its strategies in New York City has been mixed and qualified in its assessment of effectiveness (Rosenfeld & Fornango, 2014; Weisburd, Telep, & Lawton, 2014). CompStat remains in place in the NYPD despite a change in mayors (from Giuliani to Adams). All police commissioners following Bratton have retained the CompStat process as NYPD organizational strategy. In addition, it is a process manufactured and defined by police administrators with little guidance from academic intelligentsia and no governmental grant dollar support.

One lesson for administrators that has evolved out of the current development of strategic policing is that technology is not enough. It must support commanders and assist their response to used strategically respond to current and future problems in innovative ways. This response should be built upon collaboration and support between units of the organization to achieve commonly held goals. Technology can structure and analyze information. It then must be transformed into intelligence that can drive the development of tactics that effectively address community crime and public safety. However, the operational commander must have the leadership ability and training to use this intelligence to its maximum advantage.

Intelligence-Led Policing

Intelligence-Led Policing (ILP) emphasizes using information to guide police operations, anticipating future risks, and influencing decision-makers to prevent crime (Ratcliffe & Guidetti, 2008). Ratcliffe (2009, p. 176) defines Intelligence-Led Policing as:

> A law enforcement operational strategy sought to reduce crime through the combined use of crime analysis and criminal intelligence to determine crime reduction tactics that concentrate on the enforcement and prevention of criminal offender activity, focusing on active and recidivist offenders. This approach emphasizes information gathering through the extensive use of confidential informants, offender interviews, analysis of recorded crime and calls for service, surveillance of suspects, and community sources of information.

Originally used to identify crime prevention targets, Intelligence-Led Policing has become a management philosophy that can lead to collaborative and strategic solutions to provide public safety. ILP began in the United Kingdom in response to official reports that the police were not spending enough time targeting offenders to prevent crime. The generation of reliable crime information is the key to this approach. Ratcliffe (2014) offers two "laws of intelligence":

1. *The most reliable indicator of future criminal activity is current criminal activity.* Offenders will continue to exploit a criminal opportunity until they are stopped (Ratcliffe, 2014, p. 2).
2. *Intelligence that does not influence the thinking of a decision-maker is not intelligence.* Intelligence must guide meaningful action against crime (Ratcliffe, 2014, p. 3). Crime analysis can tell a decision-maker *what* is going on, and criminal intelligence can tell them *why* it is going on.

The basis of ILP is the creation of "**actionable intelligence**"—the generation of helpful information that can inform and guide operations to drive operational responses and for strategic planning against threats (Carter & Carter, 2009, p. 318). One example of actionable intelligence is creating operational information to combat international terrorist attacks and attacks from far-right, domestic extremists (McGarrell, Frelich, & Chermak, 2007, p. 149).

To summarize, ILP:

- Is designed to be a model for the business of policing.
- Aims to achieve crime and harm reduction and prevention and disruption of offender activity.
- Focuses on crime hot spots, prolific offenders, repeat victims, and active criminal groups.
- Employs a top-down management approach.
- Merges crime analysis and criminal intelligence to objectively direct police resources.
- Aids police resource prioritization decisions.

(Ratcliffe, 2016, p. 65)

Thus, ILP is a managerial model of evidence-based police resource allocation decisions featuring the prioritization of problems. ILP methods use the investigation to determine the existence and management of linked series of crime incidents (hot spots), the targeting of specific offenders, and the application of preventative measures to combat the crime problem. Ratcliffe has studied the implementation of ILP in police departments and identified several areas of concern. For example, in New

Zealand, he found that the police had difficulty recording crimes other than burglary and vehicle crime in their computer system. More time was spent on data entry than analysis (Ratcliffe, 2005, p. 442).

Another common problem was relying on line staff to use information to guide operations. The difficulty here that plagues other police innovations is that line officers are typically limited in their ability and opportunity to engage in proactive policing methods, because they are spending the bulk of their time responding to calls for service (Ratcliffe, 2005, p. 443). Besides performing data entry, crime analysts spent time generating administrative statistics like performance appraisals rather than developing tactical intelligence. Executive decision-makers failed to make the development of criminal intelligence a priority. When intelligence reports were provided, they were "rarely read and even more scarcely acted upon" (Ratcliffe, 2005, p. 448). In New Jersey, the state police adopted a more positive approach to ILP. Using a strategic, statewide approach to gang problems led to the arrest of 100 Bloods gang members on charges of racketeering, conspiracy, and drug distribution (Ratcliffe & Guidetti, 2008, p. 119). Darroch and Mazerolle's (2013) ILP implementation study underscored the importance of leadership in adopting this process. They analyzed the organizational factors that constrained or facilitated the adoption of Intelligence-Led Policing principles in New Zealand police departments. Tactical operations under ILP included directed patrols at hot spot areas, bail checks of active offenders, and targeting the routine activities of prolific offenders. They determined that successful implementation of ILP was related to several factors, including evidence of a transformational leadership style in the area—including the celebration of crime reduction as a goal, the existence of a "can do" organizational culture, support for partnerships and problem-solving, tolerance for experimentation and trial of novel approaches, openness to learning, a willingness to sponsor improvement and engage in innovation. The areas that promoted and supported ILP had an open management style where officers felt closer to their managers, were comfortable taking independent action, and thought they could influence their job in a team environment. The implementation and development of ILP in these New Zealand departments were not driven by top-level administrators but led by individual commanders at the area and district levels who focused on crime reduction within their local area. These local-area and district-level commanders represent the critical mass for organizational change.

McGarrell and colleagues (2007, p. 154) suggest that police departments could adopt ILP in the following manner. Focus on the most significant threat facing the community. Establish a multiunit, multiagency task force to meet regularly and be held accountable for effectively addressing the issue. Use the intelligence process to develop information to guide and assess operations, efficiently deploy resources, and evaluate performance to enforce accountability. Implemented in this fashion, ILP has the potential to disrupt, enforce, and prevent crime problems previously believed to be intractable. Yet, the police must avoid "institutional bullying" and ensure that ILP programs promote less bias and blanket discriminatory policing practices (Griffiths & Christian, 2015, p. 7).

Focused Deterrence

One criminological truth consistently supported by research is that a small percentage of offenders are consistently responsible for the majority of crime. A recent meta-analysis of offending studies confirmed this conclusion. It determined that 20 percent of all individuals in a population are responsible for 80 percent of all crime. In addition, youthful and adult offenders commit similar crimes, and females may account for a greater crime concentration than males (Martinez, Lee, Eck, & O, 2017, p. 11).

Focused deterrence strategies attempt to prevent offenders from committing specific types of crime—homicides and gang and drug violence. Also known as "pulling levers," this approach involves strategies to increase the risks faced by criminals and use new and effective methods to use traditional and non-traditional law enforcement tactics to communicate incentives and disincentives right at the targeted chronic offenders. The focused deterrence strategy focuses on high-risk offenders (Land, 2015, p. 515). They represent new and creative ways of using traditional and non-traditional policing to apply incentives and disincentives to offenders (Rowe & Søgaard, 2019, p. 120).

The focused deterrence approaches share several characteristics. first, they feature an interagency enforcement group across the criminal justice system. Second, the research identifies offenders and offender groups. Third, the use of "levers" specifically designed to provide special attention to deter particular types of crime and offenders. The goal is to inform the offenders that they are under surveillance and that punishment is forthcoming unless they cease their criminal activities. Fourth, the provision of services to encourage offenders to disengage from crime and support their efforts (Braga & Kennedy, 2020, p. 3). Thus, focused deterrence initiatives are a "form of advertising" featuring "call-ins" to invite known offenders to meetings and make them aware of the consequences of continuing their criminal careers (Braga & Kennedy, 2020, p. 42).

Examples of Focused Deterrence Programs

Boston, Massachusetts

In 1990, **"Operation Ceasefire"** was developed as an innovative approach to combat youth violence. It was designed as an interagency violence prevention program featuring law enforcement and social service resources to focus on a small number of gang-related offenders. The Ceasefire "pulling-levers"-focused deterrence strategy resulted in a two-thirds decline in youth homicide in the late 1990s. Soon after, the U.S. Department of Justice recognized this as an effective tool to prevent crime, and it has been applied in several cities across the country (Braga, Papachristos, & Hureau, 2014, p. 114).

Operation Ceasefire was developed to prevent violence by contacting gang members, telling them violence would no longer be tolerated, and supporting this message by "pulling every lever" legally when offenders committed violent crimes (Braga, Papachristos, & Hureau, 2014, p. 115). The crackdown uses various criminal justice actions, from federal prosecution, strict probation, and being assertive in targeting low-level street crimes. Studies show this intervention significantly reduced murders in Boston by 72 percent when controlling recurrent trends and other pertinent demographic factors (Makarios & Pratt, 2012, p. 228).

Indianapolis, Indiana

The Indianapolis program was created and implemented by multiple agencies forming a task force known as the Indianapolis Violence Reduction Partnership (IVRP).

Research on the effectiveness of IVRP focused on all homicides occurring in Indianapolis between January 1997 and June 2001 (Corsaro & McGarrell, 2009, pp. 63, 69). The results indicated a significant decline in Indianapolis homicides–34.1 percent following the IVRP initiative. Gang homicides declined by 38.1 percent after the IVRP, while non-gang homicides declined by 8.6 percent. Indianapolis experienced a decline in overall homicides after the implementation of IVRP, while comparable Midwestern cities did not experience a similar decline during this time frame (Corsaro & McGarrell, 2009, pp. 69, 77).

Minneapolis, Minnesota

Typically, Minneapolis has a low homicide rate; however, it steadily increased through the 1980s. Between 1994 and 1995, the annual number of murders increased from 59 victims to 97 victims. In 1996, homicides remained high at 83 victims (Kennedy & Braga, 1998, p. 264). In response to this problem, community leaders, law enforcement officers, corporate representatives, and government officials developed the Minneapolis HEALS Initiative (Hope, Education, Law, and Safety). They utilized the Police Executive Research Forum (PERF) and Harvard University researchers to review and analyze their homicide problem and establish much-needed preventive strategies (Kennedy & Braga, 1998, p. 264).

The Minneapolis HEALS project focused on gang violence utilizing a wide range of criminal justice activities focused on gangs. In the first week, a crackdown by city, county, and federal authorities targeted the "Bogus Boyz" gang—this gang sponsored street violence, including killing a young boy in a gun shootout. Under the initiative, gang members were charged with federal weapons offenses with possible federal prison sentences (Kennedy & Braga, 1998, p. 284).

Cincinnati, Ohio

In mid-1990, Cincinnati, Ohio, experienced a significant increase in homicides. Cincinnati averaged 41.3 murders per year from 1991 to 2000, but from 2001 to 2006 the yearly homicide average rose to 73.3 per year, with a peak of 88 homicides in 2006. Research revealed that gang members accounted for about three-quarters of murders from 2006 to 2007 as either victims or suspects (Engel et al., 2011, p, 404). In response, political leadership in Cincinnati joined efforts with law enforcement, medical professionals, academics, street advocates, and community and business leaders to form the Cincinnati Initiative to Reduce Violence (CIRV). This approach was modeled after Boston's Operation Ceasefire—a focused deterrence strategy to openly communicate the cost of violence to at-risk gang members (Engel et al., 2011, p. 404). CIRV was developed in 2007 after a sudden uptick in Cincinnati's fatal and non-fatal gun violence. CIRV aimed to identify and reduce homicides and gun-related violence conducted by group members. To address concerns that crime reduction would not be sustainable over time, CIRV leaders developed a comprehensive organizational design with an improved social service component to ensure the sustainability of homicide reduction. Thus, CIRV became a model for other cities and is considered a leading city of the National Network for Safe Communities (Engel et al., 2011, p. 412).

Local business executives and Procter & Gamble Company assisted in the formation of this comprehensive organizational structure, consisting of four Strategy Teams (i.e., law enforcement, community engagement, services, and systems) supervised by a Strategy Implementation Team reporting to the Governing Body. The CIRV was responsible for increasing the risks and costs of involvement in violence, providing alternatives to violence, and changing community norms toward violence (Engel et al., 2011, p 412).

Implementing CIRV resulted in a significant reduction in group-member-involved homicides in Cincinnati. However, the drop was not apparent in non-Gang-Member-Involved (GMI) homicides. There was also a lower-level decline in violent firearm incidents after implementing CIRV. Overall, gang member-involved homicides evidenced a statistically extensive decrease of 37.7 percent after 24 months and a 41.4 percent reduction 42 months after CIRV implementation (Engel et al., 2011, p. 430–431).

Lowell, Massachusetts

Lowell, Massachusetts, a small city 30 miles northeast of Boston, experienced increased violent crime. Between 1996 and 2005, Lowell had 23 homicides and 557 gun-aggravated assault incidents. Additionally, between 1996 and 2002, they averaged 63.1 incidents of serious assaultive gun violence per year (Braga et al., 2008, p. 138). Lowell officials initiated the pulling levers strategies to address the severe gun violence problem. It was highly concentrated among many gang-involved repeat offenders engaged in ongoing disputes.

A partnership was established with criminal justice organizations, community-based groups, and social service agencies, centering on prevention, intervention, and enforcement activities on gang members involved in violent encounters. This initiative was called "Safety First." The task force directed a traditional pulling levers deterrence strategy aimed at deterring violent behavior by gang offenders by contacting gangs, sending the message that violence would no longer be tolerated by using legally reachable sanctions when violence occurred (Braga et al., 2008, pp. 141–142).

New Orleans, Louisiana

From 2008 to 2012, New Orleans averaged 55 homicides per 100,000 residents. Furthermore, since the mid-1970s, New Orleans has sustained a citywide homicide rate significantly higher than 90 percent of all the U.S. As a result, city officials employed the Group Violence Reduction Strategy (GVRS) to address the situation and underlying forces that produce the continuing criminal homicide problem. The GVRS used the focused deterrence framework and interagency partnerships to sway ongoing citywide patterns of violence by using data-driven approaches and the use of street workers with gangs (Engel et al., 2011, pp. 472–473). It targeted gang violence in hot spots identified by researchers throughout the city for a "pulling levers" approach—targeting 158 individuals from 54 gangs (Corsaro & Engel, 2015, p. 479). Findings from an interrupted time series design revealed significant reductions in overall homicides (-17 percent), gang member-involved homicides (-32 percent), homicides with Black male victims (-26 percent), and both lethal and non-lethal firearms violence (-16 percent) (Corsaro & Engel, 2015, p. 496). The research showed that street-level outreach workers were not responsible for this decline in violence. Still, it was greatly enhanced by the level of cooperation evidenced by political and police officials in New Orleans and that "maintaining a clear focus on problem identification (gangs and groups) is vital to sustained success" (Corsaro & Engel, 2015, pp. 497–498). Compared to rates in high-trajectory homicide cities, New Orleans experienced a seventeen percent reduction in lethal firearm violence (–16 percent) (Corsaro & Engel, 2015, p. 496).

Stockton, California

Stockton implemented a pulling levers deterrence strategy called Operation Peacekeeper. The city averaged about 35 gun homicides per year from 1990 to 1997. In September 1997, the SPD assigned patrol officers to a new unit focused solely on violent gangs. The primary goal was to get the attention of the gang members and send a clear message. The Gang Street Enforcement Team (GSET) aimed at any illegal behavior by an active violent gang member, including driving without a license or registration, consuming alcohol in public, and peddling drugs. Over several months, the SPD collaborated with local, county, state, and federal law enforcement agencies already working on gang problems in San Joaquin County (Braga, 2008, p. 334).

Additionally, the SPD partnered with the clergy in neighborhoods with violent gun problems. This group provided an effective response to serious gun violence problems. Operation Peacekeeper aimed at stopping gun violence among the Stockton gangs. The faith-based partnership in the Peacekeeper plan provided a tool for transparency and accountability preferred by Stockton's minority community. Brunson notes that the participation of faith-based leaders contributed to implementing the Boston Ceasefire operation. He recommends that the police consider "unconventional groups" involvement when planning focused deterrence interventions (Brunson, 2015, p. 511).

Operation Peacekeeper significantly reduced gun homicides in Stockton. Stockton was the only California city to experience a statistically more significant decline when Operation Peacekeeper was in place. The program impact associated with Peacekeeper intervention differed from gun homicide trends in other midsize California cities (Braga, 2008, p. 340).

Focused Deterrence Program Results from Other Cities

Focused deterrence interventions have also targeted illicit street drug markets (DMIs). An evaluation of a program based in High Point, North Carolina, documented mixed results. Violent crime declined at a higher rate (18 percent) than in the areas of the city targeted by the program (12.8 percent). Yet, this result was considered a "significant, although modest, impact on violent crime" (Corsaro, Hunt, Hipple, & McGarrell, 2012, p. 192). A program in Rockford, Illinois, focused on drug markets. Research determined that non-violent offenses declined in the targeted Rockford neighborhood. Interviews with residents found they endorsed these findings and an increased willingness to work with the police to regulate neighborhood behaviors (Corsaro, Brunson, & McGarrell, 2013, p. 1098). An evaluation of a pulling levers, drug market intervention strategy in Peoria, Illinois, produced negative results (Corsaro & Brunson, 2013). There was no evidence of an impact on violent, property, drug, and disorder offenses or total calls for service in the targeted areas. A survey of residents showed that most did not know the program was in operation. Overall, a review of DMI research revealed that their ability to impact drug crime was reduced by implementation issues—specifically, a lack of community involvement (Braga & Kennedy, 2020, p. 31).

An evaluation of the Phoenix TRUCE project (a program modeled after Chicago's CeaseFire) uncovered mixed findings. Shootings increased during the program, but assaults and other forms of violent crime declined, as the program served more gang-involved clients who were recent victims of violence or were released from prison (Fox, Katz, Choate, & Hedberg, 2014). In Pittsburgh, the One Vision program failed to reduce violence. It did not affect homicide rates; aggravated and gun assaults increased in the three service areas (Wilson & Chermak, 2011).

Other programs designed to reduce violence have produced mixed results. In seven areas of the city, Chicago's CeaseFire program effectively reduced shootings (declines ranged from -16 percent to -27 percent), violence in hot spot areas (reductions ranged from -15 percent to -40 percent), and gang homicides were reduced in six of the seven city locations (Skogan, Hartnett, Bump, & DuBois, 2008). Additional research on Chicago's Group Violence Reduction Strategy reported a 23 percent reduction in shooting behaviors and a 32 percent reduction in gunshot victimization in targeted areas compared to those instances in control areas (Papachristos & Kirk, 2015). A similar approach in Chicago determined that gang members who attended a violence reduction strategy (VRS) call-in evidenced cooperation. The purpose of a VRS is to send a deterrent message to gang members about the violence raging in the city and "tell them, in no uncertain terms, to put down the guns" (Papachristos & Kirk, 2015, p. 526). Using propensity score matching techniques to make relevant comparisons between groups, the research revealed a VRS treatment effect—a 23 percent reduction in overall shooting behavior and a 32 percent reduction in gunshot victimization (Papachristos & Kirk, 2015, p. 551). A systematic review of research on 24 focused deterrence operations revealed a "statistically significant moderate effect on crime" (Braga & Kennedy, 2020, p. 31). In Detroit, Ceasefire research results were confounded by the implementation of similar crime reduction programs focusing on the reduction of gun violence. However, the Detroit findings revealed that serious violent crime declined following Ceasefire implementation, led by a 39 percent reduction in the 5th and 9th precincts (Circo et al., 2021, p. 125).

Implementation of Focused Deterrence Programs

A review of crime reduction programs in Chicago, Tampa, Topeka, and El Monte (CA), reported positive results. These programs had several common implementation elements:

1. By fostering shared information between members, Significant attention is building strong partnerships with other components of the criminal justice system, local government, the business community, neighborhood groups, and residents.
2. Each community had established regular processes for analyzing crime, feeding crime information to officers and managers, and building accountability for crime prevention and control into the department's mission.
3. Each department had decentralized policing services to focus on specific neighborhoods and reporting districts.
4. Clear leadership in each jurisdiction that continually emphasized the expectation that the police (working in concert with community partners) were responsible for preventing and controlling violent crime.

These programs featured working coalitions, a focus on local problems and resources, data-driven problem-solving, and focused deterrence interventions (Hipple, McGarrell, Klofas, Corsaro, & Perez, 2010, pp. 79–81). In general, the available evaluation literature on focused deterrence suggests both short-term and long-term area-wide impacts on crime (National Academy of Sciences, 2018, p. 175).

Braga and Kennedy (2020) identify several important implementation issues that can potentially restrict the effectiveness of focused deterrence programs: first, analysis of crime problems in a community tends to be shallow and relies on traditional approaches rather than thoughtful and customized responses; second, a weak organizational structure to oversee the teamwork aspects of the program across agencies and interested parties in the community; third, the absence of strategic planning principles to guide operations; fourth, lack of systematic data collection to assess the operations and effectiveness of programs (Braga & Kennedy, 2020, pp. 58–65). Attention to these issues can ensure the fidelity of focused deterrence initiatives.

Finally, we know focused deterrence strategies work are short-lived, and the success diminishes over time, and addressing the opportunity structures for the crime can lead to a decrease in crime without looking at the motivational inclination of a potential offender (Tillyer et al., 2010, pp. 982–983). Findings from the Kansas City focused deterrence program is one example of the limitations of this approach.

The Kansas City No Violence Alliance implementation resulted in an immediate reduction in homicides and gun-involved aggravated assaults (Fox & Novak, 2018). Homicide levels dropped to its lowest level in 42 years. However, at the end of the third year, overall homicide levels in the city (including gang-involved homicides) returned to its pre-program levels (Fox & Novak, 2018, p. 298). One problem was that the program failed to provide new services or providers overtime and simply relied upon existing resources. The police do not have the capabilities to provide social services. As Fox and Novak (2018, p. 303) conclude,

> until violence is uprooted at its source, nothing in our interim violence prevention reduction strategies can remain static; to improve our odds of decreasing violence, criminal justice policy makers and practitioners must remain at least aware, engaged with innovation, and responsive to systemic changes as its perpetrators.

Smart Policing

Another initiative that seems to meld police strategies is known as **Smart Policing**. The website for this approach (www.smartpolicinginitiative.com/) states the goal of Smart Policing is to build "evidence-based, data-driven law enforcement tactics and strategies that are effective, efficient and economical." The Bureau of Justice Assistance has sponsored several Smart Policing Initiatives (SPI) in several cities. These initiatives feature approaches based on Hot Spot Policing and focused deterrence, offender-based strategies (Coldren, Huntoon, & Medaris, 2013, p. 281). Several forecasting techniques have been used by policing experts (Perry, McInnis, Price, Smith, & Hollywood, 2013, p. xiv) that are features of Smart Policing. They include:

1. Methods for identifying locations with an increased risk for crime.
2. Methods for identifying individuals at risk for future offending.
3. Methods to match likely offenders with specific past crimes.
4. Methods for predicting victims of crime.

Making predictions is only the beginning of the process. The next step is the creation of initiatives aimed at crime prevention. The entire process is dependent upon the collection and maintenance of accurate data. Finally, again the assessment process (evaluation of the effectiveness of the implemented interventions) is recommended.

Several strategies have been determined effective. For example, a problem-oriented approach to convenience store crime in Glendale, Arizona, resulted in a 42 percent decrease in crime at targeted stores (White & Katz, 2013, p. 305). In Boston, Safe Street Teams identified and targeted hot spots of violent crime, resulting in a 17 percent reduction in violent crimes—particularly robbery and aggravated assault (Braga & Schnell, 2013, p. 351). In Lowell, Massachusetts, the police identified hot spots of property crime. Increased surveillance of these areas resulted in decreases in motor vehicle theft (61 percent), larceny (43 percent and 50 percent), and shoplifting (42 percent and 41 percent) (Bond & Hajjar, 2013, pp. 332–333). The LAPD targeted repeat violent offenders and gang members (Operation LASER) in its Newton Division—a hot spot of gun and gang-related, violent crime. Removing the targeted offenders resulted in a 5.2 percent decrease in monthly gun crime in the hot spot area (Uchida & Swatt, 2013, p. 297). These Smart Policing Initiatives have shown that evidence-based strategies can effectively reduce crime in neighborhoods with long-term problems (Joyce, Ramsey, & Stewart, 2013, pp. 366–367).

Targeting of gun violence in nine cities funded by the Smart Policing Initiative featured the following strategies:

- Targeting persistent gun violence hot spots.
- Targeting prolific offenders in persistent hot spots.
- Employing new technologies and advanced crime analysis.
- Engaging a wide range of collaborative partners.
- Conducting advanced problem analysis.

The results of the LASER program in Los Angeles were listed above. Efforts in other cities were also effective. In Boston, a problem-oriented strategy focused on micro-level hot spots was able to reduce aggravated assaults by more than 15 percent, violent crime by more than 17 percent, and robberies by more than 19 percent. Target enforcement of crime hot spots in Baltimore reduced homicides by 27 percent. In addition, a related focused deterrence intervention reduced non-fatal shootings in one neighborhood by 40 percent and a gun offender registry reduced gun-related reoffending risks among participants by 92 percent (Braga, Webster, White, & Saizow, 2014, pp. ii–iii).

Traffic Stops and Racial Profiling

Various researchers studied **racial profiling** involving multiple law enforcement agencies. The use of drug courier profiles regarding who was potentially trafficking drugs during the 1980s was used as part of the war on drugs (Kocieniewski, 2000). Since post 9/11, Middle Eastern citizens have been concerned about stereotypes as part of the war on terror (Bah, 2006). Yet, for the discussion of racial profiling with police departments, we are focusing here as it relates to traffic stops. Citizen concerns regarding the issue of racial profiling, especially during routine traffic stops, reached national exposure in the mid-1990s, involving the New Jersey and Maryland State Police along Highway I-70 (Harris, 2002). Several terms summarized minority citizens' reactions to being pulled over, including "Driving while Black or Driving while Brown (DWB)." One of the reasons why it is crucial to examine racial profiling as it relates to a traffic stop is because, for the past almost 25 years, the traffic stop has consistently remained the top reason for police-initiated contact (Langan et al., 2001; Eith & Durose, 2011; Harrell & Davis, 2020).

Before defining racial profiling, it is important to note that a person's race or ethnicity could be used as a legitimate part of the decision-making process by an officer if information regarding suspect description is shared that describes such visual characteristics. A collectively approved definition does not exist when defining racial profiling, and multiple definitions are available (Batton & Kadleck, 2004). For this textbook, the authors recommend using the American Civil Liberties Union (ACLU) (2009) definition, which defines racial profiling as a discriminatory practice targeting citizens for one of two reasons: (1) the citizen's race, ethnicity, religion, or national origin, or (2) the officer suspects criminal involvement. Two issues affect officers if an officer is engaging in racial profiling practices. First is the issue of creating a "self-fulfilling prophecy" (Batton & Kadleck, 2004), because of the use of various police enforcement strategies that result in the perspective that minority citizens are likely to be involved in criminal activity when, in reality, it is the use of specific police strategies that are more likely to occur in predominantly minority areas. Second is that the issue of racial profiling also negatively impacts public perception when it comes to general feelings regarding various law enforcement activities, and this would relate to the issues of procedural justice and legitimacy and then leads to diminished public trust, which can also impact officers' ability to combat crime that does occur in the community they serve (Batton & Kadleck, 2004).

During a traffic stop, it is also essential to consider the overall decision-making of the officer. It is also necessary to understand that a high percentage of traffic stops are conducted based on the officer's discretionary decision-making. Because of this discretionary action, three things could influence the officer's decision-making. First, when the officer makes a traffic stop, they rarely have definitive knowledge of the citizen. It means that most information regarding the background of the person stopped is obtained through background and license checks. It could result in a lot of information that the officer must try to process, which can be difficult. Because of this, an officer may use what's called a stereotypical shorthand in terms of specific factors to deal with the cognitive overload, which may, unfortunately, lead to developing an unconscious profile that includes specific demographic characteristics of the person stopped, including things like race, ethnicity, gender, and age (Smith & Alpert, 2007). Second, some officers may abuse their discretion during a traffic stop, which can include convincing the citizen to give them verbal consent to a search. What's important with such a verbal consent search is the officer is not "duty-bound" to search (Totman & Stewart, 2006, p. 1). The final issue is conducting a traffic stop for pretextual reasons to justify the officer's actions for stopping the citizen in the first place in terms of looking for greater criminal activity beyond traffic enforcement (Novak, 2004; Withrow, 2007; Gizzi, 2011).

A vital issue that prior researchers considered in the literature on racial profiling and traffic stops relies upon the outcome of the traffic stop in terms of how the traffic stop ends or what activities the officer conducted, and for purposes of our discussion of the prior literature on this area we are focusing on citations, searches, consent searches, and consent search requests. Typically, an officer gives a citation for an equipment or moving violation. It is necessary to consider who is given a citation, because it may indicate racial profiling, especially regarding giving a citation versus a verbal or written warning. Previous research on citations has shown that minority drivers are at no greater odds of a citation in comparison to White drivers (Novak, 2004), but several other studies do show evidence of racial profiling for minority citizens even when including both legal and extralegal factors (Ingram, 2007; Barnum & Perfetti, 2010; Tillyer & Engel, 2013).

Searches are necessary to study in racial profiling, because a search increases the invasiveness and gravity of the stop itself. Second is the officer's greater discretion in deciding to search. Previous research on the subject does show evidence of racial and gender bias. Both Black and Hispanic drivers had a higher likelihood that a search would occur (Moon & Corley, 2007; Barnum & Perfetti, 2010; Higgins et al., 2008, 2012). When considering gender, male drivers are more likely to be searched (Schafer et al., 2006; Moon & Corley, 2007; Higgins et al., 2008, 2012), but even then, amongst male drivers, it is once again Black and Hispanic male drivers who officers searched more than other racial groups (Schafer et al., 2006; Moon & Corley, 2007; Higgins et al., 2012).

When conducting a search, there are legal limitations on how it can take place, including meeting the legal requirement for probable cause (*Brinegar v. United States, 1949*). However, if the officer can get the citizen to consent to the search voluntarily, then the need for probable cause is eliminated (*Schneckloth v. Bustamonte, 19723*). Examining the use of consent searches is vital, because the officer is using their discretion, and it's necessary to understand if the officer is doing so in a biased manner. Prior studies on racial profiling and consent searches have provided conflicting results. Several studies did show evidence of racial profiling in terms of consent searches being more likely to be used against minority drivers (Schafer et al., 2006; Close & Mason, 2007; Roh & Robinson, 2009; Barnum & Perfetti, 2010; Rosenfeld, Rojek, & Decker, 2012; Briggs & Keimig, 2016;). One study showed that White drivers were more likely to have a consent search (Smith & Petrocelli, 2001), and other studies found no evidence of racial profiling in consent searches for both White and minority citizens (Ridgeway, 2006; Pickerill, Mosher, & Pratt, 2009; Fallik & Novak, 2012; Tillyer et al., 2012). Additionally, other studies have shown certain other contextual factors that increase the odds of a consent search, including male drivers, younger drivers, stops in predominately minority neighborhoods, and how a police department deploys their officers (Smith & Petrocelli, 2001; Schafer et al., 2006; Pickerill et al., 2009; Roh & Robinson, 2009; Barnum & Perfetti, 2010; Fallik & Novak, 2012; Tillyer et al., 2012; Briggs & Keimig, 2016).

The final key area related to consent searches is the officer requesting a consent search. The key difference here is the officer making such a request, because that further exposes the discretionary behavior of the officer without considering the citizen's decision to accept or refuse such a request. The consent search request is an understudied issue in racial profiling relative to other traffic stop outcomes. For a request to consent to search the driver, there is concern that the citizen questions the officer's real motivation for the stop (i.e., procedural justice and legitimacy) (Gau, 2013). Additionally, two other studies found that White drivers were more likely to be offended when an officer makes such a request (Gau, 2012) and that, unfortunately, minority citizens have come to accept such a tactic by law enforcement because of the historical mistreatment as it relates to racial profiling (Gau & Brunson, 2012. Another study showed that consent search requests of the driver were less likely in predominantly minority neighborhoods, and that finding could be due to officers being aware of who potentially lives in the area or the building of greater public support between officers and those living in those areas (Nowacki & Spencer, 2019).

The researchers' statistical analysis is the last aspect to consider in racial profiling research. There are various statistical techniques and methodologies that researchers have used. One specific statistical method this textbook's authors will use to discuss involving their prior research is propensity score matching (PSM). PSM allows the researcher to examine better some differences amongst a similarly situated/matched group. Using PSM would be important to racial profiling research because the traffic stop data would then only analyze traffic stops amongst matched drivers based on various independent variables, with the only key difference being the matched groups, and for racial profiling it would be the race or ethnicity of the driver. The authors' prior work shows, even amongst matched groups between White and minority drivers, there is still evidence of racial profiling, with minority drivers being more likely to still be at higher odds of all the prior traffic stop outcomes discussed in the previous paragraphs (Vito et al., 2017, 2018; Vito & Higgins, 2021; Waldspurger & Vito, 2023).

Veil of Darkness

Several theories have been applied to explain the officer's decision-making in the context of racial profiling and traffic stops. Covering all those theories will not be part of this textbook, but, for those who are interested, includes Donald Black's Theory of Law (1976, 1980), focal concerns theory, and the social conditioning model and illusory correlation, to name just a few. Given the rise of big data in policing along with previous recommendations made by Former President Obama's Task Force on 21st-Century Policing, we feel it is imperative to provide a strategy that law enforcement agencies could utilize right away to see if there is an issue of racial profiling in their department using the traffic stop data that they have already collected. We would also recommend, if possible, working with trained methodologists and statisticians, particularly those with a criminal justice and criminology background. Based on these things, the authors would recommend using the veil of darkness for such a theoretical approach using empirical data.

The veil of darkness (VOD) hypothesis is a way to identify if the police officer can see the driver's race when making stops in daylight compared to those made in darkness. The originators of the theory, Grogger and Ridgeway (2006), define VOD as:

> During the night, police have greater difficulty observing the race of a suspect before they actually make a stop. We refer to this as the "veil of darkness" hypothesis. The implication of the veil of darkness hypothesis is that the race distribution of drivers stopped during the day should differ from the race distribution of drivers stopped at night if officers engage in racial profiling. Thus, if travel patterns, driving behavior, and exposure to police are similar between night and day, then we can test for racial profiling by comparing the race distribution of drivers stopped during the day to the race distribution of drivers stopped during the night.
>
> (Grogger & Ridgeway, 2006, p. 878)

Utilizing VOD for police departments based on existing data is beneficial for two reasons. First, the VOD methodology creates a natural experiment where typically the researcher compares stops during the civil dusk intertwilight period. For any police department, that would be stops made during the evening hours between the earliest and latest hours throughout the year when the sun sets. The purpose of the civil dusk intertwilight time period is that daylight varies on each particular day, so that some stops occur in daylight while others occur in darkness. The second reason relates to the data necessary to test VOD at a minimum, which would include the race or ethnicity of the driver, the time when the traffic stop occurred, and then the date of the traffic stop. The only other thing to add to this data would be to get the information on the earliest and latest sunset during the civil dusk intertwilight period, which anyone can find online using the U.S. Naval Observatory Astronomical Applications Department (https://aa.usno.navy.mil/).

Since Grogger and Ridgeway (2006), a small but influential number of studies tested either the original VOD hypothesis or provided new key data pieces that could help with this theoretical explanation. The findings of prior research present mixed results, with several studies finding no evidence of racial profiling (Grogger & Ridgeway, 2006; Worden et al., 2012) and others finding evidence of racial profiling for either Black drivers or Black male drivers (Ritter & Bael, 2009; Ross et al., 2016; Taniguchi et al., 2017). Additional studies are highlighted below for their unique methodological contributions to the VOD literature.

Horrace and Rohlin (2016) expanded upon the VOD hypothesis using two different pieces of data. First was using only discretionary traffic stops to consider better the officer's decision-making in situations where the officer is duty-bound to conduct the traffic stop for traffic-safety, driving-related reasons. Second was the simulation of ambient lighting by considering the use of streetlights. The thought process was that perhaps stops made closer to darkness could still be impacted if the traffic stop occurred near streetlights, which could allow the officer to still see the race or ethnicity of the driver before making the traffic stop. Initially, the findings of this study did not show support for VOD, but increased the odds that a Black driver was stopped by 15 percent after including the streetlights.

Vito and colleagues (2020) added to the VOD literature from a statistical analysis standpoint using both PSM and coefficients testing. The utility of PSM was to use the VOD measure between stops in daylight and darkness as the treatment measure for the study, creating a matched sample of stops occurring in daylight vs. darkness to examine better how daylight may influence the officer's decision-making. The PSM findings did show that matched stops occurring in daylight are more likely to involve Black drivers. Using coefficients testing allowed the researchers to consider how daylight impacted the officer's decision-making based on the citation. Also, it found evidence of racial profiling, with Black drivers being more likely to be stopped in daylight for mechanical or licensing violations.

Stacey and Bonner (2021) sought to expand upon the VOD hypothesis based on prior methodological issues regarding coding-specific VOD measures seen in previous research. Here, two new sampling variations were recommended: (1) removing traffic stops based on the sunset for a particular day that occurs within 30 minutes near the beginning or end of civil dusk intertwilight, because it's harder to determine if these particular stops occurred in daylight or darkness; and (2) limiting the traffic stop data to stops that occur 30 days before or after daylight savings time, because this better controls for seasonal differences based on the difference in daylight along with who is driving on the road and potential traffic patterns. The authors of this textbook do wish to note that other VOD studies did this as well, but Stacey and Bonner (2021) made this the focus of this research regarding how such methodological measures could change the findings. Using both methodological approaches still resulted in evidence of racial profiling, but there was a slight difference in statistical significance based on the year for the data.

Vito and Woodward Griffin (in press) tested the VOD hypothesis using traffic stop data in a pre- and post-design surrounding the COVID-19 pandemic and considering how the vehicle make may also influence the officer's decision-making. The findings of that study did not show evidence directly of racial profiling when it comes to VOD. However, several results of the study did show evidence that could indirectly relate to racial profiling in terms of who was stopped based on such factors as vehicle profiling, showing that cars thought to be driven by Black drivers were more likely to be stopped. This finding indicates that VOD could also be related to an indirect measure of race where the officer may not necessarily see the driver's race but is stopping the car based on the premise that it is more likely to be driven by a Black driver.

Stop-Question-and-Frisk (SQF)

A police officer can briefly stop a person's freedom of movement if the officer reasonably suspects that the person stopped by the officer was involved in a criminal act. In addition, the officer may frisk the person if the officer has reasonable suspicion to believe that the person is a threat to the officer or that the citizen has a weapon. Both of these aspects form what is known as either a stop-and-frisk or, more specifically, a **stop-question-and-frisk** (SQF) in the landmark case of *Terry v. Ohio (1968)*. Two additional cases since *Terry* have also added legal constraints to what is allowed during a frisk. *Minnesota v. Dickerson (1993)* showed that any drugs found during a frisk must be excluded from the trial, because a frisk intends to look for weapons or other objects that may injure an officer and not allow for a "fishing expedition" for different types of criminal activity. If an unprovoked citizen runs away from officers, this could create reasonable suspicion that a temporary stop of the citizen is acceptable (*Illinois v. Wardlow, 2000*). Other pertinent factors in that case that the officer could consider as part of their decision-making was where the citizen fled from a known high crime area.

Many studies examining the use of SQF have involved the New York City Police Department (NYPD). The reason for this is that one of the reasons academics, politicians, and the NYPD gave for the decline in the crime rate in New York City from the 1990s through the 2000s relates to the use of SQF. Regardless of whether using SQF was part of other crime control strategies used during the period, there are still criticisms regarding racial or ethnic bias in disparities when it comes to whom SQF is used, along with the level of effectiveness when combating crime. Prior studies show racial or ethnic disparities regarding the use of SQF, with Black, Hispanic, and Latino(a)s facing higher rates of the use in comparison to Whites and additional explanation being viewed as "out of place," especially in highly segregated areas (Gelman et al., 2007; Ferrandino, 2015; Zhao et al., 2019). Previous research on why an officer conducted an SQF includes stops in high-crime areas, the type of crime incident, and furtive movements by the suspect (Avdija, 2014; Fagan & Geller, 2015).

Both academics and the citizens of New York have been critical of using SQF and whether it's a good crime control strategy, given racial or ethnic disparities in its use. Previous research has shown that SQF is ineffective at reducing crime in general or, more specifically, when considering the number of SQFs compared to the rates of burglary and robbery (Rosenfeld & Fornango, 2014; Ferrandino, 2015). Conversely, other studies did show that SQF reduced crime, which could also be seen within 300 feet of where the stop occurred, and that, for all racial groups, there was a reduction in the rates of violent crime and property crime because of SQF (Wooditch & Weisburd, 2016; Rosenfeld & Fornango, 2017;). Regardless of the findings showing support for or against SQF as a crime control strategy, criticism also exists because other cities throughout the U.S. also experienced a decline in crime during the same time frame that did not use SQF (Lenehan, 2017).

In *Floyd v. City of New York (2013),* the NYPD SQF practice was ruled unconstitutional and violated minority citizens' Fourth Amendment rights. Due to this decision, the NYPD's SQF strategy had to undergo reform, which involved both police administrators and community leaders coming together to come up with solutions. Following the Floyd decision, MacDonald and Braga (2019) analyzed NYPD SQF data. They found that hit rates and additional factors previously involving minority citizens and SQF had all decreased because of the court ruling. What's also necessary to understand following the Floyd decision or using SQF, in general, is NYC citizens' opinions on using SQF. Minority citizens may hold negative feelings towards the NYPD because of SQF. It causes them to question their overall feelings about the legitimacy of law enforcement, especially as the number of such stops increases for the individual (Tyler et al., 2014; Evans & Williams, 2017). Research determined that the use of force by NYPD was a rare event, but Black and Hispanic citizens were more likely to experience non-weapon force than Whites (Morrow, White, and Fradella, 2017, p. 382).

Other law enforcement agencies have also used SQF with similar findings, but it's essential to consider these other cities or countries because criminal justice/criminology is a social science discipline. In Boston, minority citizens were more likely to experience an SQF, and White police officers had a greater number of SQF stops when interacting with all racial groups. Additionally, when considering the officer's race in general, SQF was more likely when the race of the officer and citizen differed (Fagan et al., 2016). A comparison of SQF between London and New York found that the number of people present on a particular street did not impact the use of SQF, but that when special events took place this increased the number of SQFs (Ashby & Thompson, 2017). Gaston and Brunson (2020) showed that high-crime areas in the city of St. Louis were more likely to result in an SQF, but, even though high-crime areas were an important indicator that Black citizens were still more likely to have SQF occur regardless of the level of criminal activity that was present where the SQF occurred. Using a PSM analysis with a theoretical framework of focal concerns theory looking at SQF decisions in Illinois, results showed that matched Black citizens (vs. White citizens) and Black male citizens (vs. White male citizens) were less likely to consent to an SQF. Also, the decision-making of the officer in Illinois to conduct an SQF was impacted by the officer's perception of the citizen being viewed as blameworthy (i.e., the reason for a frisk being for violent actions, violent crime, evasive actions, or a suspicious bulge): a citizen making a verbal threat (i.e., protecting the community) or the officer having prior knowledge about the citizen (i.e., practical constraints and consequences) all increased the likelihood of an SQF (Vito et al., 2021). A meta-analysis of studies examining the effects of stop-and-frisk policing determined that persons subjected to this procedure had significantly higher odds of mental and physical issues, were more likely to hold negative attitudes toward the police, but had higher self-reported levels of crime and delinquency (Petersen, Weisburd, Fay, Eggins, & Mazerolle, 2023, p. 3). Furthermore, pedestrian stops were unlikely to lead to arrests or weapons seizures. Overall, the results question the effectiveness of pedestrian stops and their ability to impact crime. These findings are supported by research on the NYPD—one of the foremost departmental practitioners of SQF. In their surveys of police officers, officials, and community members, Eterno, Barrow, and Silverman (2016) reported negative aspects of SQF. Police managerial respondents complained of significant management pressure to conduct stops—especially during the Bloomberg/Kelly era of the NYPD (2002–2012) (Eterno, Barrow, & Silverman, 2016, p. 184). Rank and file officers could interpret this pressure as the need for quotas— pressure to document activity, and leading to community perceptions of police legitimacy (Eterno, Barrow, & Silverman, 2016, p. 191).

In their review of the NYPD studies, White and Fradella (2016, p. 29) concluded: "SQF can and should be a valuable crime-control tool for twenty-first century police departments—if the practice is retooled and managed in ways that rely on the proper exercise of discretion." Furthermore, the authors recommended that SQF procedures meet constitutional standards regarding reasonable suspicion, control possible abuses of police discretion, and be employed with an eye toward citizen concerns about procedural justice and legitimacy (White and Fradella, 2016, p. 8). Their guidelines include careful selection of personnel, training in constitutional stop-and-frisk practices, administrative procedures to prohibit racial profiling, proper supervision to hold officers accountable, and external oversight of police stop-and-frisk practices (Purdon et al., 2021, pp. 471–473).

Specialized Units

Specialized units usually handle the operations described in this chapter. Specialized investigation units focus on methods to solve serious crimes and develop cases for prosecution. There are several advantages to specialization (Leonard & More, 2000, p. 353):

- Definite, fixed investigative responsibility.
- Enhanced development of investigative skills.
- Facilitation of training in the latest investigative technologies and methods.
- Development of higher morale and pride in accomplishment.
- Stronger sense of identification with goals and investigative performance levels.
- More time for uniformed officers to patrol their areas.

Specialized units relieve police personnel of handling routine 911 calls to concentrate on a specific problem, such as violent crime, gangs, or drug trafficking. Typically, they are directed at deterring or suppressing crimes and apprehending offenders.

For example, Burke (2022) examined the performance of specialized drug enforcement units in Chicago from 2009 to 2019. He reports that Blacks and being in a high-crime neighborhood were positively associated with a drug arrest. This result may be due to a "principal-agent problem"; these findings may be because specialized drug units continued to make arrests when violent crime declined. This association calls for the command staff to reassess its resource allocations. It was also determined that body-worn cameras did not impact drug arrests (Burke, 2022, p. 8).

However, there are some disadvantages to specialized units (Leonard & More, 2000, p. 354):

- Internal communication of information is impeded and ineffective.
- Negative impact on the morale of uniformed officers.
- Increase in administrative and clerical workloads.
- Time delays in investigations.

Lack of communication and supervisory oversight is a common problem with specialized units. They can become silos by creating barriers, causing people in the same organization to work against each other and not share information (Lencioni, 2006).

One example of a runaway, specialized unit is the LAPD Ramparts scandal. Whistleblower Rafael Perez described widespread misconduct in the CRASH (Community Resources Against Street Hoodlums) unit. Perez claimed that many unit officers routinely planted evidence, manufactured probable cause, beat citizens, and abused citizens' due process rights (Kaplan, 2009, p. 61). Officers were trained to hide misconduct from superiors and to plant evidence to justify arrests and police shootings (Kaplan, 2009, p. 64). Johnson (2019) examined the Ramparts Commission's investigation for possible precursors to predict problems with specialized units. One of the critical organizational forces at work in this scandal was decoupling. When units decouple, they develop norms and objectives that conflict with the larger organizational entity. However, if the unit goals reflect the legitimate goals of the organization, their illegal efforts may be ignored or go unnoticed by the parent organization (Johnson, 2019, p. 83). This detachment is common for specialized units, and their actions are often hidden by the police code of silence and the distance between line staff and administrative officers. Within the LAPD, Ramparts officers were decoupled from the department and assumed a new identity under the CRASH unit. Inaction by superiors within the department allowed the unit's misdeeds to flourish and continue. The lesson of Ramparts is that supervisors must be attentive to the performance of specialized units and not ignore deviant or out-of-policy behaviors (Johnson, 2019, pp. 86–87; see also Mijares & McCarthy, 2021).

Crisis Intervention Team (CIT)

The deinstitutionalization movement of the 1960s shifted the treatment of the mentally ill from long-term hospitalization to independent, community-based environments. Unfortunately, the unavailability of such care left former patients to their own devices—ending up on the streets or criminal justice clients due to their engagement in such behaviors as bizarre, destructive, and violent behavior. As a result, the mentally ill population became a problem for the police to deal with, despite their lack of training to handle them. They function as "gatekeepers" between the existing mental health and criminal justice systems (Jennings & Hudak, 2021, pp. 484–486).

Traditionally, the police have three discretionary options when persons with mental illness (PwMI) cause a disturbance. The first response is to transport the person to a hospital. The second is to make an arrest. The third option is to resolve the problem informally. Eventually, another possibility was developed by the Memphis Police Department—the **Crisis Intervention Teams** (CIT) (Davidson, 2016). These teams include specially trained police officers, family advocates, and mental health consumer groups. Family members of PwMI also play a crucial role. When CIT officers arrive at a scene involving PwMI, they assume responsibility for the outcome (Jennings & Hudak, 2021, p. 492). The training is designed to help officers defuse volatile situations, de-escalate conflict, and seek out treatment options for PwMI. The de-escalation aspect is a crucial alternative to the police use of arrest or force, offering a "therapeutic tool" and providing time to seek out treatment (Pelfrey & Young, 2020).

Research on a CIT program in Akron, Ohio, noted that calls for service in PwMI cases increased along with higher rates of transport for treatment by CIT officers and no increase in arrests following CIT implementation (Teller, Munetz, Gil, & Ritter, 2006). A systematic review of 23 studies of CIT effectiveness determined these operations were successful in an integrated service model focusing on collaboration and shared knowledge of community resources by CIT officers and mental health practitioners (Kane, Evans, & Shokraneh, 2018). A study of 405 South Florida CIT officers revealed that most PwMI encounters resulted in diversion rather than arrest (Bratina, Carrero, Kim, & Merlo, 2020, p. 289). A CIT program in a Midwestern Sheriff's Office found no use of force in over 86 percent of PwMI calls for service (Willis et al., 2023, p. 167).

Selecting officers for CIT training is a crucial task. Research on CIT training in the Chicago Police Department determined that those officers who combined training with the opportunity to put their skills into practice expressed the most substantial support for the program (Morabito, Watson, & Drane, 2013, p. 432). CIT-trained officers in a Midwest department evidenced an increased understanding of PwMI, made fewer emergency detentions, and were more likely to transport persons for voluntary treatment (Hassell, 2020, p. 167). A comparison of the performance of CIT and non-CIT-trained officers found that trained officers were more likely to seek out and make referrals to mental health treatment centers for PwMI (Comartin, Swanson, & Kubiak, 2019, p. 255).

When the police deal with PwMI, the safety of the community must be the primary goal. Mental health professionals must realize that they should assist the officer in conflict resolution and recommending the appropriate treatment (Jennings & Hudak, 2021, p. 494). Peaceful conflict resolution and treatment of PwMI are stressed under the CTI model.

Conclusion

What do these strategies have in common, and how do they differ? First, they use the information to develop strategies and tactics to guide operations and meet the true purpose of policing—to prevent and respond to crime. Second, they also follow up to evaluate and assess the effectiveness of these operations to determine whether they have been effective and, if not, how to alter operations so they can improve. Third, they seek the support of and input from the community and recognize that citizens are in partnership with the police in crime prevention efforts. Fourth, they hold the police accountable for their performance.

They are not mutually exclusive and can be blended. For example, Willis, Mastrofski, and Kochel (2010) examined how police departments faced implementing both CompStat and Community Policing in their departments. They conducted surveys and visited five police departments to make observations. They addressed the problem of co-implementation by comparing CompStat and Community Policing operations on seven elements or aspects: (1) Mission, (2) Internal Accountability, (3) Decentralization of Decision-Making, (4) Organizational Flexibility, (5) Data-driven Problem Identification and Assessment, (6) Innovative Problem-Solving, and (7) External Accountability. They concluded that there was no integration between the two concepts regarding all aspects, except decentralization of decision-making and organizational flexibility. These last two concepts achieved a low integration. In their study, Community Policing attained some level of decentralization of decision-making to the neighborhood level but not to sergeants or beat officers. CompStat led to a territorial focus at the district level by delegating decision-making authority to district commanders (Willis et al., 2010, p. 976). Across the board, the two organizational reforms appeared to have an "additive effect." One compensated for the other by helping the organization respond more comprehensively to the diverse demands confronted in its environment (Willis et al., 2010, p. 977). Although officers viewed these reforms as complementary, they seemed to respond to different problems in the organizational external environment.

Willis (2013) also addressed the co-implementation issue by examining how the decision-making of first-line supervisors operated under CompStat and Community Policing. He analyzed data from focus groups conducted with 34 participants. Under CompStat, sergeants could address crime problems as they saw fit, with no specific directives from above—do something about crime. The sergeants used CompStat crime data to determine where and when to focus patrol resources—particularly in identifying crime hot spots. Beyond this, their ability to engage in problem-solving was limited. Community Policing tended to be the province of a specialized unit rather than implemented through permanent beat teams. Both reforms were hindered by the department's focus on handling 911 calls (Willis, 2013, p. 248).

Two management issues appear to affect the implementation of all of the strategic initiatives covered in this chapter. The first is loose coupling. Coupling refers to the degree to which organizational elements are linked, connected, related, or interdependent. Loose coupling is the problem when organizational elements are minimally connected (Maguire & Katz, 2002, p. 504). To ensure the success of any of the strategies discussed in this chapter, all levels of the police organization must be both informed and involved. The typical problem here is that the line staff (patrol officers) are not consulted and trained in the nuances of the chosen method. The result is that they do not implement the initiative correctly when left to their own devices. Their performance is the key to implementing any initiative and their input can help prevent errors. Detectives serving the area must also be informed. Area residents and organized groups must be aware of police operations to secure their support and to establish legitimacy. A Hot Spot Policing effort in the Trinidad and Tobago Police Service used "scaling up" (from specific hot spot locations to a district-wide focus) and "feeding back" (telling constables what they have done and its effect) to overcome the problem of loose coupling. Every two weeks, a district-level "COPstat" meeting was held with the officers doing the patrols (Sherman et al., 2014).

Second, community involvement is a crucial element of these approaches. The police must recognize that effective crime prevention is tied to the support of the community. Their eyes and ears are always present, and they naturally have a key stake and interest in the safety of their neighborhood and its surroundings. Like the beat officers, they must be kept informed about police operations in their area so they can contribute to their success. They also act as a barometer of the legitimacy of such operations and provide feedback on their appropriateness.

Third, the 911 issue is a particular hindrance to establishing these methods across the board. To prevent crime, police departments must find ways to divest themselves of their 911 burden. The citizenry has come to expect responses to 911 calls. They affect citizens' attitudes toward the police. However, to truly focus on crime problems, leaders must make human resources readily available to implement these different strategies. They are evidence-based, and recent research supports their effectiveness. Strategic policing is the wave of the future.

However, the National Academy of Sciences (2018, p. 301) noted the tendency of proactive approaches to generate large racial disparities when targeting high risk people or places – policy concern that must be addressed. Elements of these paradigms are summarized and presented in Table 8.1.

TABLE 8.1 Strategic Policing Strategies

Paradigm	Focus	Strategy	Implementation Issues	Effectiveness
Community Policing (COP)	Community partnerships to deal with problems of crime and disorder.	Decentralized approach. Use of beat patrol, substations, and "beat meetings" to get close to citizens and obtain their input.	Lack of support among police administrators and officers. The tendency toward partial implementation in specialized units and the creation of "innovation ghettos."	Improved relations and appreciation of citizens (by the police) and police (by citizens). Reduction in the fear of crime among some community residents. Some evidence is that COP lowers the crime rate.
Problem-Oriented Policing (POP)	Police are required to develop a systematic process to identify the nature and causes of crime problems, review, analyze, and select a response, and determine the effectiveness of the chosen response or establish new strategies.	Police should focus on identifying and solving problems. Proactive intervention is required, such as the use of Hot Spot Policing.	Police tend to engage in "shallow" problem-solving and use traditional methods of policing rather than develop innovations.	Hot Spot Policing has been found to result in crime reduction (with violent and drug offenses) with a "diffusion of crime control benefits" to neighboring communities. Reduction in calls for service.

Law enforcement agencies must consider the impact on public trust when proposing and implementing crime control strategies. The obligation is not only to reduce crime, but to do so humanely in a way that protects the rights of citizens. The absence of crime is not law enforcement's sole or final goal. Promoting and protecting public safety must be balanced with the dignity and rights of all (President's Task Force on 21st Century Policing, 2015, p. 13). Establishing and maintaining this balance is the hallmark of police professionalism.

KEY TERMS

Accountability
Actionable Intelligence
Chicago Alternative Policing Strategy (CAPS)
Community Policing
CompStat
Crisis Intervention Team

Critical mass
Focused deterrence
Hot Spot Policing
Intelligence-Led Policing
Operation Ceasefire
Problem-Oriented Policing
Racial Profiling

SARA Model
Smart Policing
Stop, Question, and Frisk (SQF)
Strategic Planning

Note

1. Joanes (1999–2000, p. 298) determined that the decrease in NYC's homicide rate was "well within the range of decreases observed in half of the seventeen largest U.S. cities" following the 1991 peak in NYC homicides.

References

American Civil Liberties Union (2009). *The persistence of racial and ethnic profiling in the United States*. New York, NY: ACLU National Office.

Ammar, N., Kessler, D., & Kratcoski, P. (2007). The interaction between a neighborhood's racial composition and officer race in community policing: A case study from the residential area policing programme (RAPP), Cleveland, Ohio. *International Journal of Police Science & Management, 10*(3), 313–325.

Ariel, B., Weinborn, C., & Sherman, L. (2016). "Soft" policing at hot spots – do community service officers work? A randomized controlled trial. *Journal of Experimental Criminology, 12,* 277–317.

Ashby, M., & Thompson, L. (2017). Routine activities and proactive police activity: A macro-scale analysis of police searches in London and New York City. *Justice Quarterly, 34*(1), 109–135.

Avdija, A.S. (2014). Police stop-and-frisk practices: An examination of factors that affect officers' decisions to initiate a stop-and-frisk police procedure. *International Journal of Police Science & Management, 16*(1), 26–35.

Bah, A.B. (2006). Racial profiling and the war on terror: Changing trends and perspectives. *Ethnic Studies Review, 29*(1), 76–100.

Barnum, C., & Perfetti, R. L. (2010). Race-sensitive choices by police officers in traffic stop encounters. *Police Quarterly, 13*(2), 180–208.

Batton, C., & Kadleck, C. (2004). Theoretical and methodological issues in racial profiling research. *Police Quarterly, 7*(1), 30–64.

Batts, A., Smoot, S., & Scrivner, E. (2012). *Police leadership challenges in a changing world. New Perspectives in Policing Bulletin*. Washington, DC: U.S. Department of Justice, National Institute of Justice.

Behn, R.D. (2005). The core drivers of CitiStat: It's not just about the meetings and the maps. *International Public Management Journal,* 295–319.

Behn, R.D. (2008). *The seven big errors of PerformanceStat*. Boston: Harvard University, John F. Kennedy School of Government.

Black, D. (1976). *The behavior of law*. New York, NY: Academic Press.

Black, D. (1980). *The manners and customs of the police*. New York, NY: Academic Press.

Bond, B.J., & Hajjar, L.M. (2013). Measuring congruence between property crime problems and response strategies: Enhancing the problem-solving process. *Police Quarterly, 16*(3), 323–338.

Bowers, K., Johnson, S., Guerette, R., Summers, L., & Poyton, S. (2011, 15 June). Spatial displacement and diffusion of benefits among geographically focused policing initiatives. *Campbell Systematic Reviews*. doi: 10.4073./csr.2011.3.

Bradstreet, R. (1997). Policing: The patrol sergeant's perspective. *Journal of Police and Criminal Psychology, 12,* 1–6.

Braga, A.A. (2005). Hot spots policing and crime prevention: A systematic review of randomized control trials. *Journal of Experimental Criminology, 1,* 317–342.

Braga, A. (2008). Pulling levers focused deterrence strategies and the prevention of gun homicide. *Journal of Criminal Justice, 36*(4), 332–343.

Braga, A.A., & Bond, B.J. (2008). Policing crime and disorder hot spots: A randomized controlled trial. *Criminology, 46*(3), 577–607.

Braga, A., & Kennedy, D. (2020). *A framework for addressing violence and serious crime.* New York, NY: Cambridge University Press.

Braga, A., Papachristos, A., & Hureau, D. (2012). *Hot spots policing effect on crime.* Oslo, Norway: The Campbell Collaboration.

Braga, A.A., Papachristos, A.V., & Hureau, D.M. (2014). The effects of hot spot policing on crime: An updated systematic review and meta-analysis. *Justice Quarterly, 31*(4), 633–663.

Braga, A.A., Pierce, G.L., McDevitt, J., Bond, B.J., & Cronin, S. (2008). The strategic prevention of gun violence among gang-involved offenders. *Justice Quarterly, 25*(1), 132–162.

Braga, A.A., & Schnell, C. (2013). Evaluating place-based strategies: Lessons learned from the smart policing initiative in Boston. *Police Quarterly, 16*(3), 339–357.

Braga, A.A., Webster, D.W., White, M.D., & Saizow, H. (2014). *SMART approaches to reducing gun violence: Smart policing initiative spotlight on evidence-based strategies and impacts.* Washington, DC: Bureau of Justice Assistance.

Braga, A.A., & Weisburd, D.L. (2010). *Policing problem places: Crime hot spots and effective prevention.* New York: Oxford University Press.

Bratina, M., Carrero, K., Kim, B., & Merlo, A. (2020). Crisis intervention training: When police encounter persons with mental illness. *Police Practice & Research, 21*(3), 279–296.

Bratton, W., & Knobler, P. (1998). *Turnaround: How America's top cop reversed the crime epidemic.* New York, NY: Random House.

Briggs, S. J., & Keimig, K. A. (2016). The impact of police deployment on racial disparities in discretionary searches. *Race and Justice, 7*(3), 256–275.

Brinegar v. United States, 338 U.S. 160 (1949).

Brunson, R. (2015). Focused-deterrence and improved police-community relations: Unpacking the proverbial "black box". *Criminology & Public Policy, 14*(3), 507–514.

Burke, P. (2022). Examining drug enforcement by specialized police units in Chicago, 2009-2019. *Journal of Criminal Justice, 81*, 1–9.

Burruss, G., & Giblin, M. (2014). Modeling isomorphism on policing innovation: The role of institutional pressures in adopting community-oriented policing. *Crime & Delinquency, 60*(3), 331–355.

Capowich, G.E., & Roehl, J.A. (1994). Problem-oriented policing: Actions and effectiveness in San Diego. In D. Rosenbaum (Ed.), *The challenge of community policing: Testing the promises* (pp. 127–128). Thousand Oaks, CA: Sage.

Carter, D., & Carter, J. (2009). Intelligence-led policing: Conceptual considerations for public policy. *Criminal Justice Policy Review, 20*(3), 310–325.

Casady, T. (2011). Police legitimacy and predictive policing. *Geography & Public Safety, 2*(4), 1–2.

Chappell, A.T., Monk-Turner, E., & Payne, B. (2011). Broken windows or window breakers: The influence of physical and social disorder on quality of life. *Justice Quarterly, 28*(3), 522–540.

Circo, G., Krupa, J., McGarrell, E., & De Biasi, A. (2021). Focused deterrence and program fidelity: Evaluating the impact of Detroit ceasefire. *Justice Evaluation Journal, 4*(1), 112–130.

Close, B.R., & Mason, P.L. (2007). Searching for efficient enforcement: Officer charac-teristics and racially biased policing. *Review of Law & Economics, 3*(2), 263–281.

Coldren, J.R., Huntoon, A., & Medaris, M. (2013). Introducing smart policing: Foun-dations, principles, and practice. *Police Quarterly, 16*(3), 275–286.

Comartin, E., Swanson, L., & Kubiak, S. (2019). Mental health crisis location and police transportation decisions: The impact of crisis intervention team training on crisis center utilization. *Journal of Contemporary Criminal Justice, 35*(2), 241–260.

Committee to Review Research on Police Policy and Practices. (2004). *Fairness and effectiveness in policing: The evidence*. Washington, DC: National Academies Press.

Connell, N., Miggans, K., & McGloin, J. (2008). Can a community policing initiative reduce serious crime? A local evaluation. *Police Quarterly, 11*(2), 127–150.

Cordner, G., & Biebel, E.P. (2005). Problem-oriented policing in practice. *Criminology & Public Policy, 4*(2), 155–180.

Corsaro, N., & Brunson, R.K. (2013). Are suppression and deterrence mechanisms enough? Examining the "pulling levers" drug market intervention strategy in Peoria, Illinois, USA. *International Journal of Drug Policy, 24*, 115–121.

Corsaro, N., Brunson, R., & McGarrell, E. (2013). Problem-oriented policing and open-air drug markets: Examining the Rockford pulling levers deterrence strat-egy. *Crime & Delinquency, 59*(7), 1085–1107.

Corsaro, N., & Engel, R.S. (2015). Most challenging of contexts: Assessing the impact of focused deterrence on serious violence in New Orleans. *Criminology & Public Policy, 14*(3), 471–505.

Corsaro, N., Engel, R., Herold, T., Yildrim, M., & Motz, R. (2021). Hot spots polic-ing in Las Vegas: Results from a blocked randomized controlled trial in chronic violent crime locations. *Journal of Experimental Criminology*, 1–19. doi:10.1007/s11292-021-09485-8.

Corsaro, N., Hunt, E.D., Hipple, N.K., & McGarrell, E.F. (2012). The impact of drug market pulling levers on neighborhood violence. *Criminology & Public Policy, 11*(2), 167–199.

Corsaro, N., & McGarrell, E. (2009). Testing a promising homicide reduction strategy: Re-assessing the impact of the Indianapolis "pulling levers" intervention. *Journal of Experimental Criminology, 5*(1), 63–82.

Darroch, S., & Mazerolle, L. (2013). Intelligence-led policing: A comparative analysis of organizational factors influencing innovation uptake. *Police Quarterly, 16*(1), 3–37.

Davidson, M. (2016). A criminal justice systemwide-response to mental illness: Eval-uating the effectiveness of the Memphis crisis intervention team training curric-ulum among law enforcement and correctional officers. *Criminal Justice Policy Review, 27*, 46–75.

Eck, J., & Maguire, E. (2000). Have changes in policing reduced violent crime? An assessment of the evidence. In A. Blumstein, & J. Waldman (Eds.), *The crime drop in America* (pp. 207–265). New York: Cambridge University Press.

Eck, J.C., & Spelman, W. (1987). Who ya gonna call? The police as problem-busters. *Crime & Delinquency, 33*, 31–52.

Eck, J.E., & Weisburd, D. (2004). What police can do to reduce crime, disorder and fear. *Annals, AAPSS, 593*, 42–65.

Eith, C., & Durose, M. R. (2011). *Contacts between police and the public, 2008*. Wash-ington, DC: U.S. Department of Justice.

Engel, R., Tillyer, M., & Cosaro, N. (2011). Reducing gang violence focused deter-rence: Evaluating the Cincinnati initiative to reduce violence. *Justice Quarterly, 30*(3), 403–439.

Eterno, J., Barrow, C., & Silverman, E. (2016). Forcible stops: Police and citizens speak out. *Public Administration Review, 77*(2), 181–192.

Eterno, J.A., & Silverman, E.B. (2006). The New York City police department's CompStat: Dream or nightmare? *International Journal of Police Science & Management, 8*(3), 218–231.

Eterno, J.A., & Silverman, E.B. (2010). The NYPD's CompStat: Compare statistics or compose statistics? *International Journal of Police Science & Management, 12*(3), 426–449.

Evans, D.N., & Williams, C.L. (2017). Stop, question, and frisk in New York City: A study of public opinions. *Criminal Justice Policy Review, 28*(7), 687–709.

Fagan, J., Braga, A., Brunson, R., & Pattavina, A. (2016). Stops and stares: Street stops, surveillance, and race in the new policing. *Fordham Urban Law Journal, 43*, 539–614.

Fagan, J., & Geller, A. (2015). Following the script: Narratives on suspicion in Terry stops in street policing. *University of Chicago Law Review, 82*(1), 51–88.

Fagan, J., Zimring, F.E., & Kim, J. (1998). Declining homicide in New York City: A tale of two trends. *Journal of Criminal Law and Criminology, 88*(4), 1277–1323.

Fallik, S., & Novak, K. J. (2012). The decision to search: Is race or ethnicity important? *Journal of Contemporary Criminal Justice, 28*(2), 146–165.

Ferrandino, J. (2015). Minority threat hypothesis and NYPD stop and frisk policy. *Criminal Justice Review, 40*(2), 209–229.

Floyd et al. v. City of New York et al., 959 F. Supp. 2d 540 (2013).

Fox, A.M., Katz, C.M., Choate, D.E., & Hedberg, E.C. (2014). Evaluation of the Phoenix TRUCE project: A replication of Chicago Ceasefire. *Justice Quarterly, 32*(1), 85–115.

Fox, A., & Novak, K. (2018). Collaborating to reduce violence: The impact of focused deterrence in Kansas City. *Police Quarterly, 21*(3), 283–308.

Garcia, V. (2005). Constructing the "other" within police culture: An analysis of a deviant unit within the police organization. *Police Practice and Research, 6*(1), 65–80.

Gaston, S., & Brunson, R. (2020). Reasonable suspicion in the eye of the beholder: Routine policing in racially different disadvantaged neighborhoods. *Urban Affairs Review, 56*(1), 188–227.

Gau, J.M. (2012). Consent searches as a threat to procedural justice and police legitimacy: An analysis of consent requests during traffic stops. *Criminal Justice Policy Review, 24*(6), 759–777.

Gau, J.M., & Brunson, R.K. (2012). "One question before you get gone . . . ": Consent search requests as a threat to perceived stop legitimacy. *Race and Justice, 2*(4), 250–273.

Gau, J.M., & Pratt, T.C. (2010). Revisiting broken windows theory: Examining the sources of the discriminant validity of perceived disorder and crime. *Journal of Criminal Justice, 38*(4), 758–766.

Gelman, A., Fagan, J. A., & Kiss, A. (2007). An analysis of the New York City Police Department's "Stop-and-Frisk" policy in the context of claims of racial bias. *Journal of the American Statistical Association, 102*(479), 813–823.

Gianakis, G., & Davis, G. (1998). Reinventing or repackaging public services? The case of community policing. *Public Administration Review, 58*(6), 485–498.

Giuliani, R. (2002). *Leadership*. New York: Hyperion Books.

Gizzi, M. C. (2011). Pretextual stops, vehicle searches, and crime control: An examination of strategies used on the frontline of the war on drugs. *Criminal Justice Studies, 24*(2), 139–152.

Goldstein, H. (1979). Improving policing: A problem-oriented approach. *Crime & Delinquency, 25,* 236–258.

Goldstein, H. (1990). *Problem-oriented policing.* New York: McGraw Hill.

Goldstein, H. (1993). *The new policing: Confronting complexity.* Washington, DC: National Institute of Justice.

Greene, J.R. (1989). Police officer job satisfaction and community perceptions: Implications for community-oriented policing. *Journal of Research in Crime and Delinquency, 26*(2), 168–183.

Griffiths, E., & Christian, J. (2015). Considering focused deterrence in the age of Ferguson, Baltimore, North Charleston and beyond. *Criminology & Public Police, 14*(3), 1–9.

Groff, E.R., Johnson, L., Ratcliffe, J.H., & Wood, J. (2013). Exploring the relationship between foot and car patrol in violent crime areas. *Policing, 36*(1), 119–139.

Groff, E., Ratcliffe, J., Haberman, C., Sorg, E., Joyce, N., & Taylor, R. (2015). Does what police do at hot spots matter? The Philadelphia policing tactics experiment. *Criminology, 53*(1), 23–53.

Grogger, J., & Ridgeway, G. (2006). Testing for racial profiling in traffic stops from behind a veil of darkness. *Journal of the American Statistical Association, 101*(475), 878–887.

Haberman, C., & Stivers, W. (2018). The Dayton foot patrol program: An evaluation of hot spots foot patrol in a central business district. *Police Quarterly, 22*(3), 247–277.

Harcourt, B.E., & Ludwig, J. (2006). Broken windows: New evidence from New York City and a five-city social experiment. *University of Chicago Law Review, 73*(1), 271–320.

Harrell, E., & Davis, E. (2020). *Contacts between police and the public, 2018 – statistical tables.* Washington, DC: U.S. Department of Justice Office of Justice Programs Bureau of Justice Statistics.

Harris, D. A. (2002). *Profiles in injustice: Why racial profiling cannot work.* New York: New Press.

Hassell, K. (2020). The impact of crisis intervention team training for police. *International Journal of Police Science & Management, 22*(2), 159–170.

Hayeslip, D.W., & Cordner, G. (1987). Effects of community-oriented patrol on police officer attitudes. *American Journal of Police, 6*(1), 95–119.

He, N., Zhao, J., & Lovrich, N. (2005). Community policing: A preliminary assessment of environmental impact with panel data on program implementation in U.S. cities. *Crime & Delinquency, 51*(3), 295–317.

Henderson, L.J. (2003). *The Baltimore CitiStat program: Performance and accountability.* Baltimore: University of Baltimore.

Henry, W. (2002). *The CompStat paradigm: Management accountability in policing.* New York: Looseleaf Press.

Higgins, G.E., Vito, G.F., & Walsh, W.F. (2008). Searches: An understudied area of racial profiling. *Journal of Ethnicity in Criminal Justice, 6*(1), 23–39.

Higgins, G.E., Vito, G.F., Grossi, E.I., & Vito, A.G. (2012). Searches and traffic stops: Racial profiling and capriciousness. *Journal of Ethnicity in Criminal Justice, 10*(3), 163–179.

Hinkle, J., & Weisburd, D. (2008). The irony of broken windows policing: A microplace study of the relationship between disorder, focused police crackdowns and fear of crime. *Journal of Criminal Justice, 36,* 503–512.

Hinkle, J., & Yang, S. (2014). A new look at broken windows: What shapes individuals' perceptions of disorder? *Journal of Criminal Justice, 42*(1), 26–35.

Hipple, N., McGarrell, E., Klofas, J., Corsaro, N., & Perez, H. (2010). Identifying effective policing strategies for reducing crime. In J. Klofas, N. Hipple, & E. McGarrell (Eds.), *The new criminal justice: American communities and the changing world of crime control* (pp. 69–82). New York: Routledge.

Horrace, W.C., & Rohlin, S.M. (2016). How dark is dark? Bright lights, big city, racial profiling. *Review of Economics and Statistics, 98*(2), 226–232.

Illinois v. Wardlow, 528 U.S. 119 (2000).

Ingram, J. R. (2007). The effect of neighborhood characteristics on traffic citation practices of the police. *Police Quarterly, 10*(4), 371–393.

Jang, H., Hoover, L.T., & Joo, H.J. (2010). An evaluation of CompStat's effect on crime: The Fort Worth experience. *Police Quarterly, 13*(4), 387–412.

Jang, H., Hoover, L.T., & Lawton. B.A. (2008). The effect of broken windows enforcement on clearance rates. *Journal of Criminal Justice, 36*(6), 529–538.

Jennings, W., & Hudak, E. J. (2021). Police response to persons with mental illness. In R. Dunham, G. Alpert, & K. McLean, *Critical issues in policing: Contemporary readings* (pp. 461–483). Long Grove, IL: Waveland Press.

Joanes, A. (1999–2000). Does the New York City police department deserve credit for the decline in New York City's homicide rates? A cross-city comparison of policing strategies and homicide rates. *Columbia Journal of Law and Social Problems, 33*(3), 265–311.

Johnson, A. (2019). Police organizational failure and decoupling: Identifying precursors to failure through the rampart commission. *International Journal of Police Science & Management, 21*(2), 81–90.

Joyce, N.M., Ramsey, C.H., & Stewart, J.K. (2013). Commentary on smart policing. *Police Quarterly, 16*(3), 358–368.

Kane, E., Evans, E., & Shokraneh, F. (2018). Effectiveness of current policing-related mental health interventions: A systematic review. *Criminal Behavior & Mental Health, 28*, 108–119.

Kaplan, P. (2009). Looking through the gaps: A critical approach to the LAPD's Ramparts scandal. *Social Justice, 36*(1), 61–81.

Kelling, G.L., & Bratton, W.J. (1993). *Implementing community policing: The administrative problem*. Washington, DC: National Institute of Justice.

Kelling, G., & Coles, C. (1996). *Fixing broken windows: Restoring order and reducing crime in our communities*. New York, NY: The Free Press.

Kennedy, D.M. (2011). *Don't shoot: One man, a street fellowship and the end of violence in inner-city America*. New York, NY: Bloomsbury.

Kennedy, D., & Braga, A. (1998). Homicide in Minneapolis. *Homicide Studies, 2*(3), 263–290.

Kocieniewski, D. (2000, November 29). New Jersey argues that the U.S. wrote the book on race profiling. *New York Times*, Section A, Page 1. Retrieved from www.nytimes.com/2000/11/29/nyregion/new-jersey-argues-that-the-us-wrote-the-book-on-race-profiling.html

Koper, C.S. (1995). Just enough police presence: Reducing crime and disorderly behavior by optimizing patrol time in crime hot spots. *Justice Quarterly, 12*(4), 649–672.

Koper, C.S. (2014). Assessing the practice of hot spots policing: Survey results from a national convenience sample of local police agencies. *Journal of Contemporary Criminal Justice, 30*(2), 123–146.

Koper, C., Wu, X., & Lum, C. (2021). Calibrating police activity across hot spot and non-hot spot areas. *Police Quarterly, 24*(3), 382–406.

Land, K. (2015). Something that works in violent crime control. *Criminology & Public Policy, 14*(3), 515–519.

Langan, P. A., Greenfeld, L. A., Smith, S. K., Durose, M. R., & Levin, D. J. (2001). *Contacts between police and the public: Findings from the 1999 national survey.* Washington, DC: U.S. Department of Justice.

Lawton, B.A., Taylor, R.B., & Luongo, A.J. (2005). Police officers on drug corners in Philadelphia, drug crime, and violent crime: Intended diffusion, and displacement impacts. *Justice Quarterly, 22*(4), 427–451.

Lencioni, P. (2006). *Silos, politics, and turf wars: A fable about destroying the barrier that turn colleagues into competitors.* San Francisco: Jossey-Bass.

Lenehan, R. (2017). *What "stop-and-frisk" really means: Discrimination & use of force.* Northhampton, MA: Prison Policy Initiative.

Leonard, V., & More, H. (2000). *Police organization and management.* New York: Foundation Press.

Lombardo, R. & Lough, T. (2007). Community policing: Broken windows, community building, and satisfaction with the police. *The Police Journal, 80*(2), 117–140.

Lombardo, R., Olson, D., Staton, M. (2010) The Chicago Alternative Policing Strategy: A reassessment of the CAPS program, *Policing: An International Journal, 33*(4), 586–606.

Lord, V., Kuhns, J., & Friday, P. (2009). Small city community policing and citizen satisfaction. *Policing: An International Journal, 32*(4), 574–594.

Lurgio, A., & Rosenbaum, D. (1994). The impact of community policing on police personnel: A review of the literature. In D. Rosenbaum (Ed.), *The challenge of community policing: Testing the promises* (pp. 147–163). Thousand Oaks, CA: Sage.

MacDonald, J., & Braga, A. (2019). Did post-Floyd et al. reforms reduce racial disparities in NYPD stop, question, and frisk policies? An exploratory analysis using external and internal benchmarks. *Justice Quarterly, 36*(5), 954–983.

McDonald, P.P. (2002). *Managing police operations: Implementing the New York Crime control model—CompStat.* Stamford, CT: Thomson.

McGarrell, E.F., Frelich, J.D., & Chermak, S. (2007). Intelligence-led policing as a framework for responding to terrorism. *Journal of Contemporary Criminal Justice, 23*(2), 142–158.

Maguire, E.R. (1997). Structural change in large municipal police organizations during the community policing era. *Justice Quarterly, 14*(3), 547–576.

Maguire, E.R., & Katz, C.M. (2002). Community policing, loose coupling, and sensemaking in American police agencies. *Justice quarterly, 19*(3), 503–536.

Maguire, E.R., Uchida, C.D., & Hassell, K.D. (2015). Problem-oriented policing in Colorado Springs: A content analysis of 753 cases. *Crime & Delinquency, 61*(1), 71–95.

Makarios, M., & Pratt, T. (2012). The effectiveness of policies and programs that attempt to reduce firearms violence: A meta-analysis. *Crime & Delinquency, 58*(2), 222–244.

Maple, J. (1999). *The crime fighter: How you can make your community crime free.* New York: Broadway Books.

Martinez, N., Lee, Y., Eck, J., & O, S. (2017). Ravenous wolves revisited: a systematic review of offending concentration. *Crime Science, 6*(10), 1–16.

Messner, S.F., Galea, S., Tardiff, K.J., Tracy, M., Buccarelli, A., Piper, T.M., Frye, V., & Vlahov, D. (2007). Policing, drugs, and the homicide decline in New York City in the 1990s. *Criminology, 45*(2), 385–414.

Mijares, T., & McCarthy, R. (2021). *The management of police specialized units*. Springfield, IL: Charles C. Thomas.

Minnesota v. Dickerson, 508 U.S. 366 (1993).

Moon, B., & Corley, C. J. (2007). Driving across campus: Assessing the impact of drivers' race and gender on police traffic enforcement actions. *Journal of Criminal Justice, 35*(1), 29–37.

Moore, M. (1995). *Creating public value: Strategic management in government*. Cambridge, MA: Harvard University Press.

Moore, M., & Stephens, D. (1991). *Beyond command and control: The strategic management of police departments*. Washington, DC: Police Executive Research Forum.

Morabito, M., Watson, A., & Drane, J. (2013). Police officer acceptance of new innovation: The case of crisis intervention teams. *Policing: An International Journal of Police Science & Management., 36*(2), 421–436.

Morrow, W., White, M., & Fradella, H. (2017). After the stop: Exploring the racial/ethnic disparities in police use of force during *Terry* stops. *Police Quarterly, 20*(4), 367–396.

National Academy of Sciences, Engineering, and Medicine (2004). *Fairness and effectiveness in policing*, W. Skogan & K. Frydll (Eds.). Washington, DC: The National Academies Press.

National Academies of Sciences, Engineering, and Medicine (2018). *Proactive policing: Effects on crime and communities*, D. Weisburd & M. Majmundar (Eds.). Washington, DC: The National Academies Press.

Novak, K.J. (2004). Disparity and racial profiling in traffic enforcement. *Police Quarterly, 7*(1), 65–96.

Nowacki, J.S., & Spencer, T. (2019). Police discretion, organizational characteristics, and traffic stops: An analysis of racial disparity in Illinois. *International Journal of Police Science & Management, 21*(1), 4–16.

O'Connell, P.E., & Straub, F. (2007). *Performance-based management for police organizations*. Long Grove, IL: Waveland Press.

Oliver, W.M. (2000). The third generation of community policing moving through innovation, diffusion, and institutionalization. *Police Quarterly, 3*, 365–388.

Papachristos, A.V., & Kirk, D.S. (2015). Changing the street dynamic: Evaluating Chicago's group violence reduction strategy. *Criminology and Public Policy, 14*(3), 525–558.

Parnell, J.A. (2014). *Strategic management*. Thousand Oaks, CA: Sage.

Peak, K., & Glensor, R. (2002). *Community policing & problem-solving: Strategies and practices*. Upper Saddle River, NJ: Prentice Hall.

Pelfrey, W., & Young, A. (2020). Police crisis intervention teams: Understanding implementation variations and officer-level impacts. *Journal of Police and Criminal Psychology, 35*(1), 1–12.

Perry, W.L., McInnis, B., Price, C.C., Smith, S.C., & Hollywood, J.S. (2013). *Predictive policing: The role of crime forecasting in law enforcement operations*. Santa Monica, CA: The RAND Corporation.

Petersen, K., Weisburd, D., Fay, S., Eggins, E., & Mazerolle, L. (2023). Police stops to reduce crime: A systematic review and meta-analysis. *Campbell Systematic Reviews, 19*, 1–42.

Pickerill, J. M., Mosher, C., & Pratt, T. (2009). Search and seizure. Racial profiling, and traffic stops: A disparate impact framework. *Law & Policy, 31*(1), 1–31.

President's Task Force on 21st Century Policing (2015). *Interim report of the President's task force on 21st-century policing*. Washington, DC: Office of Community Oriented Police Services.

Purdon, J., White, M., & Fradella, H. (2021). Reforming stop and frisk for 21st-century policing. In R.G. Dunham, G.P. Alpert, & K.D. McLean (Eds.), *Critical issues in policing* (pp. 461–483). Long Grove, IL: Waveland Press,

Ratcliffe, J. (2005). The effectiveness of police intelligence management: A New Zealand case study. *Police Practice and Research, 6*(5), 435–451.

Ratcliffe, J.H. (2009). Intelligence-led policing. In A. Wakefield & J. Fleming (Eds.), *The Sage dictionary of policing* (pp. 176–179). London: Sage.

Ratcliffe, J.H. (2014, March 14). Retrieved from Jerry Ratcliffe: Policing, criminal intelligence, and crime science, www.jratcliffe.net/papers.

Ratcliffe, J. (2016). *Intelligence-led policing*, 2nd ed. New York: Routledge.

Ratcliffe, J.H., & Guidetti, R. (2008). State investigative structure and the adoption of intelligence-led policing. *Policing, 31*(1), 109–128.

Ratcliffe, J.H., Taniguchi, T., Groff, E.R., & Wood, J.D. (2011). The Philadelphia foot patrol experiment: A randomized controlled trial of police patrol effectiveness in violent crime hotspots. *Criminology, 49*(3), 795–831.

Reiss, A.J. (1992). Police organizations in the twentieth century. In M. Tonry & N. Morris (Eds.), *Modern policing* (pp. 51–97). Chicago: University of Chicago Press.

Ridgeway, G. (2006). Assessing the effect of race bias in post-traffic stop outcomes using propensity scores. *Journal of Quantitative Criminology, 22*(1), 1–29.

Ritter, J. A., & Bael, D. (2009). Detecting racial profiling in Minneapolis traffic stops: A new approach. *CURA Reporter, 39*(1–2), 11–17.

Roh, S., & Robinson, M. (2009). A geographic approach to racial profiling: The microanalysis and macroanalysis of racial disparity in traffic stops. *Police Quarterly, 12*(2), 137–169.

Rosenbaum, D.P. (1998). The changing role of the police: Assessing the current transition to community policing. In J. Brodeur (Ed.), *How to recognize good policing* (pp. 3–29). Thousand Oaks, CA: Sage.

Rosenfeld, R., Deckard, M., & Blackburn, E. (2014). The effects of directed patrol and self-initiated enforcement on firearm violence: A randomized controlled study of hot spot policing. *Criminology, 52*(3), 428–449.

Rosenfeld, R., & Fornango, R. (2014). The impact of police stops on precinct robbery and burglary rates in New York City, 2003–2010. *Justice Quarterly, 31*(1), 96–122.

Rosenfeld, R., & Fornango, R. (2017). The relationship between crime and stop, question, and frisk rates in New York City neighborhoods. *Justice Quarterly, 34*(6), 931–951.

Rosenfeld, R., Fornango, R., & Rengifo, A.F. (2007). The impact of order-maintenance policing on New York City homicide and robbery rates: 1998–2001. *Criminology, 45*(2), 355–384.

Rosenfeld, R., Rojek, J., & Decker, S. (2012). Age matters: Race differences in police searches of young and older male drivers. *Journal of Research in Crime and Delinquency, 49*(1), 31–55.

Ross, M.B., Fazzalaro, J., Barone, K., & Kalinowski, J. (2016). *State of Connecticut traffic stop data analysis and findings, 2014–15*. New Britain, CT: Connecticut State Legislature, Racial Profiling Prohibition Project.

Rowe, M., & Søgaard, T. (2019). "Playing the man, not the ball": Targeting organised criminals, intelligence, and the problems with pulling levers. *Policing & Society, 30*(2), 120–135.

Sadd, S., & Grinc, R. (1994). Innovative neighborhood-oriented policing: An evaluation of community policing in eight cities. In D. Rosenbaum (Ed.), *The challenge of community policing: Testing the promises* (pp. 27–52). Thousand Oaks, CA: Sage.

Safir, H. (1997, December). Goal-oriented community policing: The NYPD approach. *The Police Chief*, 31–58.

Sample, S.B. (2003). *The contrarian's guide to leadership*. San Francisco: Jossey Bass.

Schafer, B., Hughes, T., & Stelzig, C. (2019). Hot spots across the metropolis: Evaluating hot spots directed patrol at city and suburban locations. *Justice Quarterly*, *38*(1), 1–23. doi: 10.1080/07418825.2019.1616804

Schafer, J.A., Carter, D.L., Katz-Bannister, A.J., & Wells, W.M. (2006). Decision making in traffic stop encounters: A multivariate analysis of police behavior. *Police Quarterly*, *9*(2), 184–209.

Scheider, M., Chapman, R., & Schapiro, A. (2009). Towards the unification of policing innovations under community policing. *Policing: An International Journal*, *32*(4), 694–718.

Schneckloth v. Bustamonte, 412 U.S. 218 (1972).

Sherman, L.W. (1995). Hot spots of crime and criminal careers of places. In J.E. Eck & D. Weisburd (Eds.), *Crime and place—Crime prevention studies*, vol. 4 (pp. 35–52). Monsey, NY: Criminal Justice Press.

Sherman, L.W. (2009). Hot spots. In A. Wakefield & J. Fleming (Eds.), *The Sage dictionary of policing* (pp. 157–160). London: Sage.

Sherman, L.W., & Weisburd, D. (1995). General deterrence effects of police patrol in crime "hot spots": A randomized control trial. *Justice Quarterly*, *12*(4), 625–648.

Sherman, L.W., Williams, S., Ariel, B., Strang, L.R., Wain, N., Slothower, M., & Norton, A. (2014). An integrated theory of hot spots patrol strategy: Implementing prevention by scaling up and feeding back. *Journal of Contemporary Criminal Justice*, *30*(2), 95–122.

Silverman, E.B. (1999). *NYPD battles crime: Innovative strategies in policing*. Boston: Northeastern University Press.

Skogan, W.G. (1994). The impact of community policing on neighborhood residents: A cross-site analysis. In D. Rosenbaum (Ed.), *The challenge of community policing: Testing the promises* (pp. 167–181). Thousand Oaks, CA: Sage.

Skogan, W. (2006). *Police and community policing in Chicago: A tale of three cities*. New York: Oxford University Press.

Skogan, W.G., Hartnett, S.M., Bump, N., & Dubois, J. (2008). *Evaluation of ceasefire-Chicago*. Washington, DC: U.S. Department of Justice, Office of Justice Program, National Institute of Justice.

Skolnick, J.H. (1999). *On democratic policing*. Washington, DC: The Police Foundation.

Skolnick, J.H., & Bayley, D. (1988). *Community policing: Issues and practices around the world*. Washington, DC: National Institute of Justice.

Smith, M. R., & Alpert, G. P. (2007). Explaining police bias: A theory of social conditioning and illusory correlation. *Criminal Justice and Behavior*, *34*(10), 1262–1283.

Smith, M. R., & Petrocelli, M. (2001). Racial profiling? A multivariate analysis of police traffic stop data. *Police Quarterly*, *4*(1), 4–27.

Stacey, M., & Bonner, H. S. (2021). Veil of darkness and investigating disproportionate impact in policing: When researchers disagree. *Police Quarterly*, *24*(1), 55–73.

Sugarman, B. (2010). Organizational learning and reform at the New York City police department. *Journal of Applied Behavioral Science*, *46*(2), 157–185.

Taniguchi, T.A., Hendrix, J.A., Levin-Rector, A., Aagaard, B.P., Strom, K.J., & Zimmer, S.A. (2017). Extending the veil of darkness approach: An examination of racial disproportionality in traffic stops in Durham, NC. *Police Quarterly*, *20*(4), 420–448.

Taylor, B., Koper, C.S., & Woods, D.J. (2011). A randomized controlled trial of different policing strategies at hot spots of violent crime. *Journal of Experimental Criminology, 7*, 149–181.

Telep, C.W., Mitchell, R.J., & Weisburd, D. (2014). How much time should the police spend at crime hot spots? Answers from a police agency-directed randomized field trial in Sacramento, California. *Justice Quarterly, 31*(5), 905–933.

Teller, S., Munetz, M., Gil, K., & Ritter, C. (2006). Crisis intervention team training for police officers responding to mental disturbance calls. *Psychiatric Services, 57*(2), 232–237.

Tenbrunsel, A.E. (2011, April). Ethical breakdowns. *Harvard Business Review*, 58–67.

Terry v. Ohio, 391 U.S. 1 (1968).

Tilley, N. (2003). Community policing, problem-oriented policing, and intelligence-led policing. In T. Newburn (Ed.), *Handbook of policing* (pp. 311–339). Cullompton, UK: Willian.

Tillyer, R. (2018). Assessing the impact of community-oriented policing on arrest. *Justice Quarterly, 35*(3), 526–555.

Tillyer, R., & Engel, R.S. (2013). The impact of drivers' race, gender, and age during traffic stops: Assessing interaction terms and the social conditioning model. *Crime & Delinquency, 59*(3), 369–395.

Tillyer, R., Engel, R., & Lovins, B. (2010). Beyond Boston. *Crime & Delinquency, 58*(6), 973–997.

Tillyer, R., Klahm IV, C.F., & Engel, R.S. (2012). The discretion to search: A multilevel examination of driver demographics and officer characteristics. *Journal of Contemporary Criminal Justice, 28*(2), 184–205.

Toch, H., & Grant, J. (1991). *Police as problem solvers*. New York: Plenum Press.

Totman, M., & Stewart, D. (2006). *Searching for consent: An analysis of racial profiling data in Texas*. Austin, TX: Criminal Justice Coalition.

Travis, J. (1995). *Managing innovation in policing: The untapped potential of middle managers: Research in brief*. Washington, DC: National Institute of Justice.

Trojanowicz, R., & Bucqueroux, B. (1994). *Community policing: How to get started*. Cincinnati: Anderson.

Tyler, T., Fagan, J., & Geller, A. (2014). Street stops and police legitimacy: Teachable moments in young men's legal socialization. *Journal of Empirical Legal Studies, 11*(4), 751–785.

Uchida, C.D., & Swatt, M.L. (2013). Operation LASER and the effectiveness of hotspot patrol: A panel analysis. *Police Quarterly, 16*(3), 287–304.

University of Cincinnati Policing Institute. (2009). *Implementation of the Cincinnati initiative to reduce violence (CIRV): Year 2 report*. Cincinnati, OH: University of Cincinnati.

Vito, A.G., Grossi, E.L., & Higgins, G.E. (2020). "Does daylight matter"? An examination of racial bias in traffic stops by police. *Policing: An International Journal, 43*(4), 675–688.

Vito, A.G., Grossi, E.L., & Higgins, G.E. (2017). The issue of racial profiling in traffic stop citations. *Journal of Contemporary Criminal Justice, 33*(4), 431–450.

Vito, A.G., Grossi, E.L., & Higgins, G.E. (2018). Analyzing racial profiling from traffic searches: Using focal concerns theory and propensity score matching. *Policing: An International Journal of Police Strategies & Management, 41*(6), 721–733.

Vito, A.G., & Higgins, G.E. (2021). Understanding the role of race, gender, and age in request to consent search drivers. *Journal of Ethnicity in Criminal Justice, 19*(3–4), 223–243.

Vito, A., Higgins, G., & Vito, G. (2021). Police stop and frisk and the impact of race: A focal concerns theory approach. *Social Sciences, 10*(6), 230–243.

Vito, G., Walsh, W., & Kunselman, J. (2005). Community policing: The middle manager's perspective. *Police Quarterly, 8*(4), 490–511.

Vito, A.G., & Woodward Griffin, V. (in press). Blinded by the night: An examination of the veil-of-darkness within traffic enforcement before and during the Covid-19 pandemic. In S. Ilvkovich, M. Kotlaja, J. Náskaly, & P. Neyroud (Eds.), *Policing during the COVID-19 Pandemic: A global perspective*. Abingdon: Routledge.

Waldspurger, E., & Vito, A.G. (2023). Understanding vehicle consent search requests through the use of the social conditioning model and illusory correlation. *International Journal of Police Science & Management, 25*(4), 1–15.

Walsh, W.F. (1994). Community policing: Analysis of the supervisor's role. In P.C. Kratcoski (Ed.), *Community policing* (pp. 141–152). Cincinnati: Anderson.

Walsh, W. (2001). CompStat: An analysis of an emerging police managerial paradigm. *Policing, 24*(3), 347–362.

Wasserman, R., & Moore, M.H. (1988). *Values in policing*. Washington, DC: National Institute of Justice.

Weisburd, D. (2008). *Place-based policing: Ideas in American policing series*. Washington, DC: Police Foundation.

Weisburd, D., & Braga, A. (2006). Hot spots policing as a model for police innovation. In D. Weisburd & A. Braga (Eds.), *Police innovation: Contrasting perspectives* (pp. 225–244). Cambridge, UK: Cambridge University Press.

Weisburd, D., Hinkle, J.C., Famega, C., & Ready, J. (2011). The possible "backfire" effects of hot spots policing: An experimental assessment of impacts on legitimacy, fear and collective efficacy. *Journal of Experimental Criminology, 7*(4), 297–320.

Weisburd, D., & Lum, C. (2005). The diffusion of computerized crime mapping in policing: Linking research and practice. *Police Practice and Research, 6*, 419–434.

Weisburd, D., & Telep, C.W. (2014). Hot spots policing: What we know and what we need to know. *Journal of Contemporary Criminal Justice, 30*(2), 200–220.

Weisburd, D., Telep, C.W., Hinkle, J.C. & Eck, J.E. (2010). Is problem-oriented policing effective in reducing crime and disorder? *Criminology & Public Policy, 9*(1), 139–172.

Weisburd, D., Telep, C.W., & Lawton, B.A. (2014). Could innovations in policing have contributed to the New York City crime drop even in a period of declining police strength? The case of stop, question, and frisk as a policing strategy. *Justice Quarterly, 31*(1), 129–153.

Weisel, D.L., & Eck, J.E. (1994). Toward a practical approach to organizational change: Community policing initiatives in six cities. In D. Rosenbaum (Ed.), *The challenge of community policing: Testing the promises* (pp. 53–72). Thousand Oaks, CA: Sage.

White, M. & Fradella, H. (2016). *Stop and Frisk: The use and abuse of a controversial policing tactic*. New York: New York University Press.

White, M.D., & Katz, C.M. (2013). Policing convenience store crime: Lessons from the Glendale, Arizona Smart Policing Initiative. *Police Quarterly, 16*(3), 305–322.

Willis, J.J. (2013). First-line supervision and strategic decision-making under CompStat and community policing. *Criminal Justice Policy Review, 24*(2), 235–256.

Willis, J.J., Mastrofski, S.D., & Kochel, T.R. (2010). The co-implementation of CompStat and community policing. *Journal of Criminal Justice, 38*, 969–980.

Willis, T., Kern, L., Hedden, B., Nelson, V., Comartin, E., & Kubiak, S. (2023). The impact of crisis intervention team (CIT) training on police use of force. *Journal of Offender Rehabilitation, 62*(3), 157–173.

Wilson, J.M., & Chermak, S. (2011). Community-driven violence reduction programs. *Criminology & Public Policy, 10*, 993–1027.

Withrow, B. L. (2007). When Wren won't work: The effects of a diminished capacity to initiate a pretextual stop on police officer behavior. *Police Quarterly, 10*(4), 351–370.

Wooditch, A., & Weisburd, D. (2016). Using space-time analysis to evaluate criminal justice programs: An application to Stop-Question-Frisk practices. *Journal of Quantitative Criminology, 32*, 191–213.

Worden, R.E., McLean, S.J., & Wheeler, A.P. (2012). Testing for racial profiling with the veil-of-darkness method. *Police Quarterly, 15*(1), 92–11.

Worrall, J.L. (2006). Does targeting minor offenses reduce serious crime? A provisional, affirmative answer based on an analysis of county-level data. *Police Quarterly, 9*, 47–72.

Wycoff, M.A. (1988). Benefits of community policing: Evidence and conjecture. In J.R. Greene & S. Mastrofski (Eds.), *Community policing: Rhetoric or reality?* (pp. 103–120). New York: Praeger.

Wycoff, M.A., & Skogan, W. (1994). Community policing in Madison: An analysis of implementation and impact. In D. Rosenbaum (Ed.), *The challenge of community policing: Testing the promises* (pp. 75–91). Thousand Oaks, CA: Sage.

Xu, Y., Fiedler, M.L., & Flaming, K. (2005). Discovering the impact of community policing: The broken windows thesis, collective efficacy, and citizens' judgment. *Journal of Research in Crime and Delinquency, 42*(2), 147–186.

Yukl, G. (2013). *Leadership in organizations.* Upper Saddle River, NJ: Prentice Hall.

Zhao, J., He, N., & Lovrich, N. (2006). Community policing: Did it change the basic functions of policing in the 1990s? *Justice Quarterly, 20*(4), 679–724.

Zhao, J., Lovrich, N., & Thurman, Q. (1999). The status of community policing in American cities. *Policing, 22*, 74–92.

Zhao, J., Thurman, Q., & Lovrich, N. (1995). Community-oriented policing across the U.S.: Facilitators and impediments to implementation. *American Journal of Police, 14*, 11–28.

Zhao, Y., Yang, T.C., & Messner, S. (2019). Segregation and racial disparities in post-stop outcomes: Insights from New York City. *Journal of Crime and Justice, 42*(4), 365–381.

Zimring, F.E. (2012). *The city that became safe: New York's lessons for urban crime and its control.* New York: Oxford University Press.

9 Human Resource Management

Learning Objectives

1. Describe and define human resource management in policing.

2. Identify and define the historical and institutional context of police human resource management.

3. Explain the beliefs supporting strategic human resource management.

4. Describe the relationship between human resource management and the law.

5. Identify the steps in the recruitment process.

6. Analyze the police selection process.

7. Identify the steps in the training and development of police officers.

8. Understand the discipline process in human resource management.

9. Identify the difference between negative and positive discipline in policing.

10. Analyze the issues associated with the implementation of police discipline.

11. Identify the steps required to create a positive work environment.

12. Examine the forces influencing the recruitment and retention of officers.

13. Consider the issues facing women and minorities in law enforcement.

Introduction

This chapter identifies and explains the concepts, techniques, issues, and problems associated with human resource management functions in policing. The term "**human resource management**" (HRM) refers to the functions, policies, and activities a police department employs to utilize its human resources (now and in the future) effectively. Policing is a labor-intensive endeavor. A department's most essential and valuable resource is its employees, both sworn and non-sworn (**personnel**), who do police work (Nowicki, 2003). The ability of a police department to fulfill its mission and provide effective services is directly related to the quality of its personnel and how they are recruited, selected, developed, and managed. This issue presents organizational administrators with the following challenges:

DOI: 10.4324/9781003459095-9

How should these critical resources be recruited, trained, developed, and managed?
What are effective policies and practices for managing human resources?
How should the department manage its human resources that will ensure organizational effectiveness?

The goal of human resource management is to maximize both employee and organizational potential. The term "human resource management" has the same meaning that "personnel administration" did many years ago. The different titles reflect the changing mindset of today's organizational leadership and their understanding of the strategic role of this function (Dessler, 2013). Critical human resource functions are **recruitment, selection, training, development**, and personnel management. However, a department's human resource process does not exist in a vacuum. Federal and state law, local charters and ordinances, political motives, jurisdictional size, community values, budgets, and the department's culture influence the administration of its human resources.

A unique problem police departments face in formulating human resource management policies and strategies is that they do not entirely control their human resource function. Authority over this function is divided between the department's chief executive and the following:

The mayor or city manager.
Personnel administrator.
Personnel department.
City council.
Civil Service Commission.
Department's staff.

As the above list indicates, various individuals and functional subdivisions are involved in the administration of police human resources. In many municipalities, there is a Human Resource Department under the jurisdiction's chief executive, city manager, mayor, or chief administrative officer, or it may be a civil service commission independent of any administrative office. The Human Resource administrative function is usually the responsibility of a separate bureau or division in large police agencies. In most departments, it is a subunit of administrative services. Typically, a department does not have final decision-making authority in selecting police officers and promotional candidates. These decisions by law are assigned to the department's political subdivision's (township, city, county, or state) administrative body responsible for human resources. Because of this, many state legislatures have created peace officer standards and training commissions (**POSTs**) empowered to establish statewide minimum personnel training certification standards that all police departments within the state must follow. These factors contribute to a view held by some police managers that they are not responsible for the HRM function. Nothing is further from the truth. Managers are responsible for understanding and interpreting the political subdivision's and department's personnel policies and procedures, creating and maintaining a qualified workforce, and developing their officers' skills and abilities. It is a critical responsibility, because decisions about people's capabilities determine an organization's performance capacity.

Historical Development

Human Resource Management (HRM) has evolved from an administrative function concerned only with the organization's needs to one emphasizing its employees' needs and strategic direction. In the early 20th century, **Scientific Management** concepts developed by Frederick W. Taylor (1856–1915) dominated managerial philosophy. He advocated that managers should take a scientific and objective approach to how a person would perform a job. Taylor believed that organizational productivity could be improved by using scientific methods to analyze workflow and structure it into easily performed tasks. He was convinced that the best way to do a job was to break it down to its smallest parts, specialize it, and train the worker to perform these tasks without thinking. This concept, known as "task specialization," it is designed to leave little opportunity for error because the worker is not required to make decisions, think, or use judgment or discretion. It was a production-oriented process grounded in bureaucratic, structural control, and the employee was considered just another factor in the production effort (Taylor, 1911). Taylor's influence is present today in using a **job task analysis** to analyze jobs, create job descriptions, and establish the **validity** of hiring decisions, testing, and performance appraisal standards for police departments. It is also reflected in the task specialization structure of many large urban police departments.

A shift to the importance of the employee's impact on organizational effectiveness emerged out of the **Hawthorne Studies** conducted by Elton Mayo and F. J. Roethlisberger during the 1920s to the 1940s. They discovered that employee productivity was affected by how a job is designed and structured and by human, social, and psychological factors. Employees' feelings, emotions, and sentiments were strongly influenced by their work conditions, such as group relationships, leadership styles, and support from management. These feelings could have a significant impact on productivity and organizational effectiveness. The findings of Mayo and Roethlisberger disclosed the individual's critical role within the organization and the impact of group dynamics on employee performance. Out of their research developed the **Human Relations School** of human resource management. This approach to management emphasized a shift in focus to the most vital of all organizational resources, the employee, and a more supportive approach to treating employees. It held that most employees desired a job worth doing and meaningful to them. Workers also desired safe and secure work conditions, adequate pay and benefits, job security, competent supervision, performance feedback, recognition for their efforts, advancement on merit, and fair treatment by the organization.

Building on the lessons of the past, **Human Resource Management** emerged during the period from the 1960s to the 1980s. It held that organizational goals and human needs are mutual and compatible and that one need not be treated at the expense of the other. It hypothesized that if organizations wish to maximize employee performance, they need to consider culture, morale, and the psychological environment as essential variables that affect their employees and their performance. These factors should be managed to impact the organization and its employees positively. Today, human resource management involves designing, planning, and implementing policies and systems to improve these factors.

Police departments today find themselves in a challenging and changing environment consisting of workforce diversity, technology, developing legal trends, community expectations, and new employee value systems that necessitate that organizations take a strategic approach to employee management. As a result, **Strategic Human**

Resource Management has emerged as the prevailing approach to achieving effective organizations (Dessler, 2013). Strategic human resource management is the art and science of linking a department's personnel management with its strategic goals and objectives to improve organizational performance and develop a culture that fosters commitment, learning, innovation, and flexibility. The department's administrative leadership is responsible for creating human resource policies and practices to produce employee competencies and behaviors needed to achieve its strategic objectives and enhance its human capital. The department's executive leadership team fulfills this responsibility by creating the strategic human resource process by developing an organizational philosophy and management practices that support the department's strategic direction. The department's strategic direction provides the framework that guides the design of specific human resource activities such as recruitment, training, development, and discipline. In this manner, an integrated framework should systematically link human resource activities with strategic needs. It means getting everybody in the department, from the top to the bottom, to do what is necessary to implement actions to enhance organizational effectiveness (Schuler, 1992).

Strategic human resource management links organizational effectiveness to the **development** and management of its people. It considers employees as organizational assets who, when effectively recruited, selected, trained, developed, and managed, will provide long-term commitment and service to the organization. This perspective holds that the management of human resources should be a perfect fit with the organization's strategic management. In this way, employee behavior and skill sets form the bridge between the department's strategic direction and the effectiveness of its performance. It seeks to create a work environment where employees are encouraged to develop and use their skills and abilities to the maximum extent. Thus, how an organization organizes its human resource functions significantly impacts what it can accomplish. This process involves answering the following key questions:

- What is our fundamental purpose? (mission)
- How do we accomplish this purpose? (identifying strategy and functions)
- What type of resources do we need? (human/budgetary/technological)
- What knowledge, skills, and abilities are required? (job analysis/learning systems)
- How do we acquire individuals with these KSAs? (recruitment and selection)
- How do we prepare these people for their roles? (training, development, and management)

HR Management and the Law

A fundamental value of our society is equality of opportunity and fair treatment for all individuals in the workplace. The broad goal of this perspective is to provide all Americans, regardless of race, age, gender, religion, national origin, or disability, an equal opportunity to compete for jobs for which they are qualified. Civil rights legislation has been passed at the federal and state levels to provide remedies for job applicants or employees who feel they have been victims of unfair discrimination. From a personal, organizational, and managerial perspective, police administrators must understand the rights and obligations of employers, job candidates, and employees. Ignorance of the law in this area has resulted in lawsuits and personal liability claims against police departments and their administrators. Briefly described below is important **equal employment legislation**.

EQUAL EMPLOYMENT LEGISLATION

1. **5th Amendment (1791)**—"No person shall . . . Be deprived of life, liberty, or property, **without due process of the law**." The government must follow the rules and established procedures in everything it does.
2. **13th Amendment (1865)** outlawed slavery and has been held by the courts to bar racial discrimination. Under this amendment, any form of discrimination may be considered an incident of slavery or involuntary servitude.
3. **14th Amendment (1868)** makes it illegal for any state to "make or enforce any law which abridges the privileges and immunities of citizens of the United States." This amendment guarantees equal protection of the law for all citizens and bars discrimination based on sex, race, or national origin.
   The 13th and 14th Amendments are the source of constitutional power for all subsequent civil rights legislation because they granted Congress the constitutional authority to enact legislation to enforce their provisions.
4. **Civil Rights Act of 1866** gives all persons the right to make and enforce contracts and benefit from the laws of the land.
5. **Civil Rights Act of 1871** granted all citizens the right to sue in federal court if they feel deprived of any rights or privileges guaranteed by the Constitution and laws.
6. **Equal Pay Act of 1963 (as amended 1972)** requires equal pay for equal work, regardless of sex; pay differences may be based on a seniority system, a merit system, a system that measures earnings by quantity or quality of production, or a differential based on any factor other than sex.
7. **Title VII of the 1964 Civil Rights Act**, as amended, prohibits employment discrimination based on race, color, religion, sex, or national origin. This Act covers all public and private employers of 15 or more persons. Title VII is the most critical federal EEO law, because it contains the broadest coverage, prohibitions, and remedies. This Act created the Equal Employment Opportunity Commission (EEOC) to ensure employers comply with its provisions.
8. **Age Discrimination in Employment Act of 1967**, as amended in 1986, prohibits discrimination and explicitly protects individuals over 40 years old unless an employer can demonstrate that age is a BFOQ (bona fide occupational qualification) for the job in question. Although the Act serves to protect more senior employees, it does not require an employer to hire or retain an individual who is not qualified. Police officers are involved with public safety; job fitness is a principal concern; age, therefore, is asserted as a BFOQ in this profession. Fitness for the job, rather than age, is the employment criterion and focus of the BFOQ analysis. If age is a reason for discharge or refusal to hire, it should be supported by empirical data that validates a BFOQ. This data can be provided only by assessment of the police officer's job-related abilities as they are impacted objectively by the age factor.
9. **Equal Employment Opportunity Act of 1972**, amended Title VII of the 1964 Civil Rights Act, and instituted the **Equal Employment Opportunity Commission (EEOC)**. The EEOC is responsible for receiving and investigating complaints from aggrieved individuals about job discrimination. When it finds reasonable cause for the complaint, it attempts to eliminate the discrimination through conciliation. If this fails, the EEOC can go to court to enforce the law.
10. **Pregnancy Discrimination Act of 1978** prohibits sex discrimination based on "Pregnancy, childbirth, or related medical conditions." It establishes that if an employer offers disability coverage, pregnancy and childbirth must be treated like any other disability.

11. **The Americans with Disabilities Act 1990** prohibits discrimination against a "qualified individual with a disability" concerning applications, hiring, compensation, advancement, training, or other terms, conditions, or privileges of employment. A qualified individual can perform a job's "essential" functions with or without accommodation.

12. **The Civil Rights of 1991** is an amendment to Title VII that holds that a violation exists when an employee demonstrates that race, color, religion, sex, or national origin was a motivating factor in an employment action. Eliminated is the defense that the employer would have reached the same decision without considering these forbidden factors. It also added compensatory and punitive damages to the remedies available to plaintiffs.

    This act directly impacts police department entry-level physical testing procedures. It was a common practice for these tests to adjust for differences in upper-body strength between men and women. This act makes it unlawful "to adjust the scores of, use different cutoff scores for, or otherwise alter results of employment-related test based on race, color, religion, sex, or national origin."

13. **Sexual Harassment**. Title VII of the Civil Rights Act of 1964 42 U.S. Code Section 703 states that harassment based on sex violates the act.

    Sexual Harassment is any repeated and/or unwelcome verbal or physical sexual advances, request for sexual favors, sexually explicit derogatory statements, or sexually discriminatory remarks made by someone in the workplace that is offensive or humiliating or interferes with the recipient's job performance. Or when

    1. Submission to such conduct is made either explicitly or implicitly a term or condition of an individual's employment.
    2. Submission to or rejection of such conduct by an individual is used as the basis for employment decisions affecting such individual or
    3. Such conduct has the purpose or effect of reasonably interfering with an individual's work performance or creating an intimidating, hostile, or offensive working environment.
    4. There are two ways to prove sexual harassment is present:

    Quid Pro Quo is when submission to or rejection of sexual harassment is used for employment decisions.

    Hostile Work Environment is when sexual harassment unreasonably interferes with an employee's work or creates an intimidating or offensive workplace. A hostile work environment can be formed by supervisors, co-workers, or non-employees (Freyss, 2004, p. 126).

    In *Meritor Savings Bank, FSB v. Vinson (109 S.Ct. 2399, 1986)*, the Supreme Court broadly endorsed the EEOC's position on sexual harassment. It indicated that employers should establish meaningful complaint procedures and head off sexual harassment charges before they occur. In 1998, the Supreme Court in *Oncale v. Sundowner Offshore Services (523 S.Ct. 75)* held that Title VII's protection against workplace discrimination "because of . . . sex" applied to harassment in the workplace between members of the same sex.

14. Family and Medical Leave Act of 1993 (FMLA)

    This Act requires employers to provide up to 12 weeks of unpaid job-protected leave to "eligible" employees for specific family and medical reasons. Eligible employees must have worked for the employer for at least one year and 1,250 hours over the previous 12 months.

Leave must be granted for the following reasons:

1. To care for the employee's child after birth or placement for adoption or foster care.
2. To care for the employee's spouse, son, daughter, or parent with a serious health condition.
3. From a serious health condition that makes the employee unable to perform the employee's job.

At the employee or employer's option, paid leave may be substituted for unpaid leave. Employees must provide 30 days advance notice of request whenever the reasons for the leave are "foreseeable."

Employers have the right to:

1. Require medical certification to support family leave made because of severe health considerations.
2. Require second and third opinions at the employer's expense.
3. Require a fitness for duty report before the employee returns to work.

During family leave, the employer must maintain the employee's health coverage under any group plan. Upon return, employees must be restored to their original or equivalent position with equivalent pay, benefits, and other employment terms.

15. The **Fair Labor Standards Act** (**FLSA**) establishes minimum wage, overtime pay, recordkeeping, and child labor standards affecting full-time and part-time workers in the private sector and in federal, state, and local governments. Employees who hold positions covered under the mandatory overtime provisions of the FLSA must be compensated with overtime pay or compensatory time for all hours worked over 40 in a single workweek. Special rules apply to state and local government employment involving fire protection and law enforcement activities, volunteer services, and compensatory time off instead of cash overtime pay.

The Office of Community-Oriented Policing Services claims that this new approach to training sets a foundation for life-long learning that prepares new officers for the complexities of policing today and in the future. It allows a department to tailor the program to its unique needs. First tested in the Reno Police Department and subsequently tested by five other agencies, the PTO program has produced outstanding results. New officers enter the field with problem-solving skills that are rarely seen at that career level. The officers also display remarkable leadership and willingness to partner with the local community to fight crime and disorder problems. COPS concluded that the PTO program produces officers with the necessary knowledge, skills, and attitude for today's law enforcement environment (www.cops.usdoj.gov/default.asp?Item=461).

RAND's Public Safety and Justice Unit's (Glenn et al., 2003) evaluation of police training in LAPD found that departments implementing the changes needed for community police training have found success through the following sequence:

1. At the leadership and command levels of the department, there has to be total adherence to and understanding of the community. It requires leadership by the chief executive and their staff, supplemented by well-crafted leadership training throughout the organization.

2. **Entry-level** and **field training** programs must be altered to reflect new training goals. The recruit and **in-service training** cadre must share the philosophy and goals of the department leadership and integrate them throughout training.
3. Promotion requirements should include training and a demonstrated understanding of community policing.
4. Such philosophical shifts as Community Policing are best introduced at the division or station level to engage line supervisors and the organization's informal leaders in training and field implementation.

RAND found that implementing the most effective training practices is not an overnight process. Significant investments are needed for training innovations. While specific innovations can be implemented without great cost in the short term, the most substantial changes for LAPD training will require a long-term leadership commitment and significant investment in resources, most notably time (Glenn et al., 2003).

Several issues associated with the field training process include:

Organizational orientation.
Socialization to the organization's culture.
Selection of field training officers.
Training of field training officers.
Supervision of FTOs and the program.
Evaluation process of FTOs and recruits.
Validity issues.

Specialized/In-Service Training

Besides meeting mandatory training required by each state's POST system, police departments should identify training needs, establish training objectives, select or develop a training program to meet the department's strategic objectives, deliver the training, and evaluate its effectiveness. Police departments are responsible for keeping their personnel up to date with new laws, technology, and revisions in their policies, procedures, rules, and regulations. Mandatory training may also be required to provide specialized training to specific groups of officers and to maintain certain types of technical certification. Specialized training includes supervised on-the-job training by the department, training mandated by governmental authority such as training for certification as a breathalyzer operator, and enhancement of the skills, knowledge, and abilities particular to a specialization such as crime scene processing (CALEA, 2006, 33.6). It raises several critical questions, such as:

*   What knowledge, skills, and abilities (KSAs) are required to address current or future department needs and strategies?
*   To what extent do employees and managers have the mandatory KSAs?
*   What is the most cost-effective way of ensuring adequate KSAs?
*   What is the role of employees and managers in this effort?
*   How can training and development outcomes be evaluated to improve these efforts?

All in-service training and development programs should be based on a needs assessment. A training **needs assessment** is conducted to identify what training is required to meet the department's and its employees' needs. There are various ways to conduct a needs assessment to identify the skills and knowledge necessary for effective performance. The first step involves a job analysis, a detailed study of a job to determine the skills required for effective performance. This analysis should generate a list of tasks and the knowledge, skills, and abilities associated with each task (Peak, Gaines, & Glensor, 2009). Another source of information is the department's existing information on job duties and responsibilities. These are usually found in the department's job descriptions, job specifications, and list of duties found in policy and procedure manuals. Reviewing the department's performance evaluation reports, lawsuits, and citizen complaints are additional sources of information about officer performance effectiveness and deficiencies. Last, officers and operational supervisors should be surveyed and interviewed for input on their training needs. Dessler (2006, p. 154) suggests that the following informational sources can be used to identify employees' performance deficiencies and training needs:

- Supervisor, peer, self, and 360-degree performance reviews.
- Job-related performance data.
- Supervisor observations.
- Interviews with employees and supervisors.
- Assessment of employee knowledge, skills, and abilities.
- Attitude surveys.
- Individual daily performance report.

Once training needs are identified, objective and measurable training objectives can be established. Instructional objectives should specify what employees can accomplish after completing the training program. The objectives provide the key focus for developing the training program and a benchmark for evaluating its success.

Training can be delivered through lectures, demonstrations, discussions, case studies, and online or computer-based instruction. Many training programs combine several of these methods. In-service training should be as meaningful as possible for the attendees. Training and development programs should be designed to meet the needs of adult employees. Adult learners bring experience to the learning process and will seek to participate in that process actively. Thus, managers and trainers must understand the following **Principles of Learning** for adults.

- **Motivation** is important for creating the participants' desire to learn. Trainees will be motivated to learn when they understand the relevance of the training to their work effort. Managers should explain the reasons for the training and how it relates to the employee's job performance.
- **Relevance and Transference** are enhanced when the training directly relates to work issues, problems, and employee needs. Issues and concerns relating to the training subject should be openly discussed, and employees' suggestions to resolve them. Content can be meaningful by summarizing the material and ensuring the program uses familiar job-related examples to illustrate key points (Wexley & Latham, 2002). The relevance of the training and its benefit for the department's employees should always be explained.
- **Repetition**. It is important to remember that people learn how they process information and retention levels at different rates. Repetition helps learning by allowing people to handle information at their own pace. Repetition can be accomplished through the use of lectures and practical exercises.

- **Feedback and Positive Reinforcement** help reduce errors, enhance motivation, and increase attention to standards. Feedback that includes periodic performance assessments and more frequent verbal critiques reinforces behavior and negative feedback to stop it (Berman et al., 2006, pp. 224–225).

Evaluations are a critical part of the training process. All training programs, upon completion, should be evaluated to measure their effectiveness and if they have achieved their objectives. Evaluation should take two forms. A **process evaluation** should address issues of instructor quality and content delivery. An **outcome evaluation** should assess the learning process's impact on the student: passing the final course exam, improved performance, and enhanced abilities and skills. These can be difficult to assess. Evaluators should be aware that trainees may evaluate a program highly because of the charisma of the instructor. Also, performance improvements may take time to develop, and the impact of the training may not be felt until sometime after the training program has been completed. Validity must be considered and addressed in all training evaluations.

Last, each department should develop an in-service training plan to maintain appropriate performance levels and delivery of their training programs. This plan should identify the department's training needs in terms of officers and units that require training. It should establish a timetable for the training. The training schedule should consider training, training needs, and personnel availability. This plan aims to ensure that all employees receive proper training. The training plan helps to ensure that sufficient officers are available for each assignment within the department (Gaines & Kappler, 2011).

Roll Call Training

A well-managed, appropriately planned **roll call training** program is a positive training supplement. Roll call training occurs 15 to 30 minutes before the beginning of a duty shift. This training aims to keep officers up to date and present new ideas and techniques between formal training sessions. Roll call is the time unit commanders use to prepare officers for their patrol shift. Sergeants assign officers to their beats to disseminate information about significant incidents occurring on previous shifts and wanted or dangerous persons and vehicles. Other matters may also be addressed, such as issuing court subpoenas, explaining new policies and procedures, and discussing shift and beat-related topics (Peak et al., 2009). Roll call training programs should be well structured and reflect the department's needs while being flexible enough to fit into a roll call setting.

Managerial Development

Management in a police department is a complex and challenging function. Managers face an array of responsibilities regarding personnel, unit effectiveness, and ensuring obedience to policies and procedures. They must ensure that their department and its employees comply with federal, state, and local laws, regulations, and community safety needs. All department sworn and non-sworn managers, regardless of their organization level, play an essential role in their department's effective and efficient operations. Police departments should, therefore, make a considerable commitment to both the initial and ongoing preparation and development of their managers because of the significance of their role in creating and maintaining the effectiveness and efficiency of the department. Without it, a department's operational effectiveness will quickly become stagnant and inert (O'Keefe, 2004). Traditionally, police supervisors and managers frequently are not provided with training after promotion and later are not provided with appropriate in-service training (Gaines & Kappler, 2011).

Managerial training differs by state and organizations in law enforcement. Training and development programs for managers should be designed to improve current or future performance by imparting knowledge, changing attitudes, or increasing skills. These programs vary by the agency size, with large departments usually conducting internal programs and smaller agencies using external training. The Commission on Accreditation for Law Enforcement Agencies (2006, 33.8.2) holds that managerial training should be commensurate with the position's duties and occur before or within the first year following promotion.

Training first-line supervisors is the initial step in developing a department's present and future management. All police managers begin their managerial careers at this rank. First-line supervisors function at the technical/operational level of the department and, as a result, make decisions that affect their subordinates, departmental effectiveness, and financial liability. This initial managerial training should establish a foundation upon which the development of future organizational leaders is based. Supervisory classes for newly promoted sergeants must provide enough technical knowledge and managerial techniques to understand their role and manage their assigned employees. It should be focused on the skill set, knowledge, specific policies, procedures, personnel, and operational responsibilities of the rank (O'Keefe, 2004). In-service supervisory training should be focused on management techniques and leadership issues.

Middle managers who are either lieutenants, captains, or civilian managers in administrative staff positions function at the managerial and administrative levels. Managers at this level create and interpret policies and procedures and translate the department's goals and objectives into the day-to-day tasks of their operational units. These managers organize, coordinate, and control department resources and personnel. They also evaluate supervisory accountability and unit performance (More, Vito, & Walsh, 2012). Promotional and in-service classes should be educationally based, reviewing new or specifically significant policies, procedures, and problems of the position but focusing heavily on the conceptual principles of change, critical thinking, problem-solving, and organizational leadership. Many departments utilize the 12-week Administrative Officer's Course at the University of Louisville's Southern Police Institute, the three-month police administration course offered by Northwestern University, or the ten-week FBI National Academy for middle-management developmental training. Besides these programs, managers can participate in various seminars, workshops, and retraining conferences that provide instruction on developments and critical law enforcement issues. These programs are provided by a variety of organizations such as the International Association of Chiefs of Police, the Southern Police Institute, the Institute for Law Enforcement Administration at the University of Texas, Dallas; Police Training Institute at the University of Illinois; the Justice and Safety Institute at Pennsylvania State University; the Federal Bureau of Investigation; and many in-state training programs such as the Department of Criminal Justice Training in Kentucky.

Discipline

Police departments are similar to other organizations' need to control employee behavior by maintaining **discipline**. They develop policies, rules, regulations, performance standards, and conduct to prevent and control undesirable behavior. Employees are human, mistakes are made, and problems arise. However, the public's trust is quickly lost because of improper police employee behavior, misuse of authority, and improper departmental handling of misconduct allegations (Peak, 2014). The test of a properly administered human resource process is not identifying how many problems are identified but how effectively the department addresses and prevents them. Unfortunately, the administration of police discipline is often a source of frustration and dissatisfaction for everyone involved. The most effective disciplinary system combines the reinforcement of the proper set of values in all employees with behavioral standards that are consistently and fairly applied (Swanson, Territo, & Taylor, 2005, p. 412). Policing requires a disciplinary process capable of serving the interests of the community, the officers, and the department fairly and equitably (Stephens, 2011).

The primary objective of discipline is to control behavior. It reflects the administrative goal to achieve maximum conformity with legal requirements, established policies, professional standards, and prevailing norms of conduct. Most organizations have implemented a formal policy or set of guidelines governing the application of discipline. A department's disciplinary process should include training, rewarding, counseling, and punitive actions in the interest of discipline. It is recommended that disciplinary procedures include:

1. A code of conduct and appearance that is made available to all department personnel.
2. Criteria for recognizing and rewarding employees, including letters of commendation, compensation, and awards for merit.
3. A written directive that prohibits sexual and other forms of unlawful harassment in the workplace and a means to report harassment.
4. Procedures and criteria for using counseling as a function of discipline.
5. Procedures and criteria for using training as a function of discipline.
6. Procedures and criteria for using punitive actions in the interest of discipline, including oral reprimands, written reprimands, loss of leave, suspension, demotion, and termination.
7. Specify the role of supervisors and the authority attendant to each level of supervision and command relative to disciplinary action.
8. Appeal procedures that specify initiation procedures, time frames, method of recording, and scope of the appeal process.
9. An employee notification process in dismissal cases that states the reason for dismissal, the effective date of the dismissal, and the status of fringe and retirement benefits after dismissal.
10. Procedures for maintaining records of disciplinary actions and specifying under what circumstances they should be purged.

(CALEA, 2006, p. 26)

Discipline can be negative and positive as well as confusing and conflicting. This lack of clarity and confusion results from the negative connotation many have attached to the word since our early childhood conditioning. It has led to the belief that the only purpose of discipline is punishment. **Negative discipline** means punishment. Punishment is used to eliminate undesirable work-related behavior or undesirable individuals from the organization. It is used to accomplish an organizational purpose, not a personal one. It punishes explicitly the offender and notifies other employees that the organization will not tolerate the sanctioned behavior. Examples of employee behavior that would be appropriate for this type of discipline include corruption, sexual harassment, civil rights violations, substance abuse, insubordination, absenteeism, abuse of power, and poor work performance. This area is fully discussed in Chapter 11. Forms of punishment may involve an oral or written reprimand, voluntary surrender of regular days off or annual leave, demotion, loss of salary, suspension, or dismissal. Some departments prefer losing normal days off, annual leave, or accumulated compensatory time instead of outright suspension. In this manner, the employee's family does not suffer from lost wages because of their infractions.

In cases of negative discipline, a department must identify what rule or procedure was violated, what performance standard was not met, or what duty was breached. Also, the employee knew and understood the rule, procedure, performance standard, or duty to establish incompetency or misconduct successfully. The department must conduct a fair and complete investigation to establish the facts in each case before discipline is taken. A department's policy and procedures manual should set forth its personnel policies, code of conduct, rules, directives, and standards of conduct. The more precise the "rules" are, the easier it is for employees to understand what is expected and for the department to discipline them if they violate those "rules." It is also essential for all employees to know that a failure to abide by the "rules" or to meet minimum standards of competence may result in disciplinary action. Employees must understand that everyone in the organization is held accountable for their behavior, and if sanctions are different for similar behaviors, they are appropriate for the circumstances (Stephens, 2011). Last, the punishment must fit the offense and the employee. Arbitrators and courts have reversed disciplinary punishment that they found to be excessively harsh or inappropriate based on the employment record of the offender.

Positive discipline reinforces appropriate performance or corrects performance deficiencies without punishment. It involves training and the use of techniques of attitudinal conditioning designed to ensure the employee's commitment to organizational norms, values, and procedures without invoking punishment. Discipline is positive when employees share a common purpose, practice self-discipline, and voluntarily follow the policies, procedures, rules, regulations, and performance standards established to promote order and facilitation of the organization's work. The need for negative discipline should be lessened through applying positive discipline and the example set by organizational managers who demonstrate, guide, and counsel their employees.

Some commonsense guidelines for the use of discipline include:

Always base disciplinary decisions on facts, not hearsay or "subjective opinion."
Make sure the evidence supports the charge.
Base employee-related decisions on legitimate job-related/objective criteria.
Treat all employees fairly and consistently.
Employees should be warned of the disciplinary consequences of their behavior.
Acts of misconduct should be fairly and adequately investigated.
Employee's due process rights must be protected.
Maintain the employee's right to counsel.
Apply policy, rules, orders, and penalties even-handedly.

Provide timely and accurate feedback on your decisions to employees.

Ensure the penalty is reasonably related to the violation and the employee's work history.

Be prepared to defend disciplinary decisions.

The burden of proof is always with the department.

First-line supervisors are the most important individuals in the disciplinary process, because they directly manage more employees than any other position in the department. Their role requires working closely with their employees and monitoring their performance and behavior. They are often the first managers to observe behavioral changes or signs of misconduct in the members of their unit. As a result, in many police departments, first-line supervisors are required to conduct the initial investigation into a citizen's complaint. While they are expected to follow the department's directives, discretion in their use of discipline enhances their ability to influence the future behavior of their subordinates.

Some essential concepts relate to all managers and administrators regarding using positive and negative discipline. They should always use a positive approach to their use of discipline. However, they should take appropriate action to address mistakes and misconduct as soon as they occur. Additionally, managers should never display their emotions and temper when disciplining employees. An unstable manager will quickly lose their authority and the employee's respect. Consistency in the manager's mode of supervision is important. The creditability, morale, disposition, and allegiance to the department displayed by managers will be imitated and repeated by their subordinates. Never over supervise in petty situations. It is a common fault among newly appointed sergeants. Praise and acknowledgment of good work should vastly overpower criticism. Remember: the department's employees are entitled to respect and consideration.

Employee Procedural Rights

The procedures that law enforcement administrators must follow to balance the rights of their employees and the department's disciplinary concerns have been established in case law. In *Garrity v. New Jersey (385 U.S. 493 1967)*, officers were arrested for fixing traffic tickets. When the officers were called in to be interrogated, they were properly informed that anything they said could be used against them in a criminal proceeding. They were also informed that they could refuse to answer any questions that they felt could incriminate them. However, they were warned about possible dismissal if they refused to answer questions. The officers answered the questions and were subsequently prosecuted and convicted for their crimes. They appealed to the United States Supreme Court, which held that "policemen, like teachers and lawyers, are not relegated to a watered-down version of constitutional rights." The court ruled that statements given by a police officer under threat of possible forfeiture of their job could not be used against the officer in a criminal prosecution.

Garrity establishes a set of protections that apply automatically whenever a police officer is questioned during a disciplinary investigation. Managers must:

1. Advise the officer that the purpose of the interview is to obtain information that will assist in determining whether disciplinary action is appropriate and that the answers furnished may be used in disciplinary proceedings against the employee.

2.　Advise the officer that the answers to the questions will not be used against the officer in criminal proceedings.
3.　Advise the officer that all questions relating to their performance of official duties must be answered fully and truthfully and that disciplinary action, including dismissal, may be taken if the employee refuses to answer.

If the above warnings are given, the employee must answer questions that directly affect the individual's job performance. Refusal to answer can result in the department taking disciplinary action, including dismissal. If the department, during a disciplinary investigation, insists that the officer answer questions beyond those limited by *Garrity*, and if they include areas of personal concerns, it is violating the employee's right to privacy.

Police departments have the right to question an employee about the discharge of their official duties during an internal investigation. However, the employee may have a right to be represented during any such questioning, either by a lawyer or a union representative. This representation must not be an attorney unless specifically established by local statute or collective bargaining agreement. The right to such representation was established by the Supreme Court in *Weingarten v. United States (420 U.S. 251, 1975)*. The Court established the following rules for representation in disciplinary interviews:

1.　The employee's right to request representation as a condition of participation in an interview is limited to situations where the employee reasonably believes the investigation will result in disciplinary action.
2.　The right is only activated upon the employee's request for representation.
3.　The exercise of the right may not interfere with the employer's legitimate needs.

Law enforcement employees are also entitled to the protection of the Due Process Clause of the Fifth Amendment to the United States Constitution. This clause states that "No person shall be deprived of life, liberty, or property, without due process of law." Tenured, non-probationary employees are considered to have property rights in their jobs (*Wilson v. Robinson 668 F.2nd. 380, 1981*). Procedural due process must be followed in discharge from employment, temporary suspensions without pay, demotions, and removing employees from premium pay special assignments. These process rights for police officers during a police hearing were established by the U.S. Supreme Court in *Morrissey v. Brewer (408 U.S. 471 1972)*.

In disciplinary action involving the possibility of these punishments, the following actions will protect the employee's due process rights.

1.　Employees must be notified that their job-related conduct or performance is unacceptable.
2.　The notice to the employee must clearly describe the specific instances of poor performance or unacceptable behavior that are the subject of the charge(s).
3.　The employee must have been informed explicitly of what s/he must do to conform to the employer's standards or policy.
4.　The employee was offered assistance to overcome the deficiencies. Assistance can take the form of informal training, counseling, or on-the-job instruction by the manager.
5.　The employee was informed of the consequences if s/he failed to improve their performance or conduct.
6.　The employee was given a fair opportunity to bring their conduct or job performance up to an acceptable level.

The actions recommended above are also in various forms in the **Police Officer Bill of Rights**. The Police Officer Bill of Rights varies from state to state, but, as of April 2015, 14 states have adopted versions of the Bill, and more are considering similar legislation. These all include protections to ensure that investigations remain private and confidential until they are closed, and discipline is administered. They also make sure that investigations are conducted in such a way as to afford officers due process rights and protection from overly biased supervisors and political influence.

Thus, it is a matter of law and employee rights that managers who will take disciplinary action against an employee ensure that they are correct in their decision and that the disciplinary process is followed correctly and legally. Any disciplinary action taken by a police department should be fair, firm, and appropriate for the degree and type of behavior or performance problem to which it is applied. The minimum due process requirements for discharging a police department employee include that the employee:

Be afforded a public hearing

Be present during the presentation of evidence against them and have an opportunity to cross-examine their superiors

Have an opportunity to present their witnesses and other evidence concerning their side of the controversy

Be permitted to be represented by counsel

Have an impartial referee or hearing officer presiding

Have an eventual decision based on the weight of the evidence introduced during the hearing.

(Peak, 2014)

To ensure that the **procedural rights** of the employee are protected, many police departments have incorporated a system of progressive penalties in their discipline procedures. This system is commonly known as **progressive constructive discipline** (PCD).

Progressive Constructive Discipline

The progressive constructive discipline process employs a graduating sequence of penalties, with each penalty level having greater severity. The theory is that discipline should start at the lowest appropriate level and work up to more significant penalties. It is based on the belief that repetition of infractions, misconduct, and serious offenses will eventually lead to the employee's termination. Termination of employment should occur when an employee has demonstrated that they are unwilling to respond to less drastic disciplinary measures. Termination is a last resort after the employee has been put on notice repeatedly and warned of the consequences of failing to comply. The severity of each process level is based on the employee's actions. This process does not imply a required sequence for all acts of employee misconduct. Serious offenses such as acts of brutality, accepting bribes, and drug use are subject to immediate suspension and possible discharge. The steps in the sequence of penalties are as follows.

The oral reprimand occurs during a discussion between the manager and the offending subordinate. The manager should inform the subordinate of their misconduct or poor performance and explain the correct behavior to the employee. The focus of this discussion should be on the problem, not the punishment of the employee. The objective is to eliminate misunderstanding and ensure the employee clearly understands what is required in this matter. Through communication and coaching, it is a way for managers to maintain desired performance and conduct standards.

In many departments, the manager who delivers an oral reprimand must briefly describe the incident and the conversation with the subordinate in their critical incident file. Some departments require the manager and the employee to initial this critical incident report. Usually, the report is kept out of the employee's official record or removed when the manager feels that the condition is corrected.

Written reprimand: This is a written notice on an official department form. A copy should be placed in the individual's personnel file. This step should be taken after previous oral reprimands have failed to correct the condition or the offense is severe enough to require it. Department policy directives, rules, and labor contracts will provide guidelines for using written reprimands. A good manager does not write up everyone, only those who deserve it. Those who deserve it are employees who have engaged in:

1. Serious misconduct.
2. Major violations of departmental rules.
3. A pattern of poor performance after performance consultations and coaching by the manager.
4. A continual behavioral pattern (i.e., lateness) after previous oral reprimands.

A written reprimand should contain:

1. The name of the employee it is addressed to and the name of the manager filing the written reprimand.
2. A descriptive statement of the problem, incident, behavior, or performance. The report should be a specific factual account. It should answer the following questions:
   When did it happen (time of the incident)?
   Where did it happen (exact location)?
   What happened (specific descriptive account)?
   What is wrong? Actions should follow a descriptive statement that may include a history of events, a description of a specific rule, policy, or performance standard, and an employee's behavior.
3. A description of what the employee must do to improve or correct their performance. This statement should describe the level of performance desired to fix the issue.
4. The consequences if the employee fails to improve or correct their performance. The consequences should include any future actions the manager will take if the employee continues to perform below standards.

Written reprimand meets the legal requirement of establishing notice for the employee. It should specifically inform the employee what is wrong in clear and concise terms. The written reprimand's purpose is not to punish, but to inform the employee of a problem and what must be done to correct it. The reprimand also tells the employee of the consequences for failing to correct the problem. The ultimate objective of this step in the process is for the employee to correct the condition before more severe punishment is necessary. In effect, it makes the employee master of their fate. If the employee takes corrective action, the manager has achieved what they desired, but, if not, the next step in the disciplinary process is attained.

Suspension: This order releases the employee from duty for a specific time. The days off should be designated in departmental policy and procedures. Suspension may either be with or without pay. The employee should receive a written notice of the cause for suspension, including the facts in the case and information regarding the employee's right to reply. Sometimes, employees may be offered the right to respond before suspension. However, immediate suspension is appropriate in specific circumstances of serious misconduct or the commission of a crime. For example, the manager should be able to suspend an officer who reports to work late and unfit for duty because of intoxication or substance abuse.

A suspension is not always used as a form of punishment. In some departments, suspension is used administratively to:

1. Provide a period of time for the organization to investigate an incident, such as the use of deadly force.
2. Allow time for an investigation of a suspected, but not fully substantiated, complaint of a serious act of misconduct.

Dismissal: This is a department's most severe punishment against an employee. It is used when lesser disciplinary steps have failed or when the employee's conduct violates public trust or department regulations. The manager involved in a discharge recommendation must have appropriate supporting documentation. Managers should always have sufficient documentation to support their disciplinary decisions. Disciplinary decisions should never be made because of arbitrary or subjective reasons. The manager must be able to support their decision with objective job-related criteria. Documentation would include:

1. Critical incident reports.
2. Department records.
3. Civilian complaints (if any).
4. Performance evaluations.
5. Reports of interviews or conferences.
6. Witness statements.
7. Work examples.

Departments must be able to tie their disciplinary actions with job-related activities fairly and equitably. Employees feeling arbitrarily punished because of vague, subjective interpretations of policy or rules are quick to file grievances. The subordinate seeking redress will rely on past performance appraisals to make a case. If unsuccessful at the grievance level, the subordinate will take the next step, usually appealing to a civil service commission or a court. At this point, the basis for the department's charges against the employee comes under scrutiny.

The principle underlying the evaluation of the appropriateness of a disciplinary action is referred to as **just cause**. Just cause has become a common standard in labor arbitration and is included in labor union contracts. A police department must prove just cause to sustain an employee's termination, suspension, or other discipline. Usually, the employer has the burden of proof in discharge cases or if the employee is wrong. To determine whether there is just cause for discipline, they should ask themselves the following questions:

Was the employee aware or should have been aware of the rules or standards they are accused of violating?

Is the rule or standard reasonable?

Did the department conduct a reasonable investigation into the employee's wrong-doing or misconduct?

Was the investigation conducted fairly and objectively?

Has it been established that the rule or standard was violated?

What mitigating or aggravating factors are present in the employee's work history?

Have comparable situations occurred in the past, and if so, how have the employees involved been treated?

(Freyss, 2004, p. 204)

The just cause test is important because the department must be sure that its corrective actions and punishment fit the employee's behavioral violation. Progressive discipline provides a documented history of actions designed to correct employee behavior, which is an advantage in lawsuits and arbitration.

Developing a Positive Work Environment

Police administrators must establish a **positive work environment** based on positive instead of negative discipline. Regarding human resource management, the department's operational managers must be problem-preventers and problem-solvers. Negative discipline should only be used when it is clear that other methods have failed or the subordinate's intentional behavior requires it. The following suggestions will assist departments in creating a positive problem-prevention work environment.

1. Set Boundaries

Setting boundaries involves letting employees know what is expected regarding their work performance and on-the-job conduct. To hold employees responsible for their behavior and performance, they must understand what is expected of them. Department managers must be trained to interpret and implement department directives, policies, rules, and regulations relating to employee performance and conduct. When managers translate regulations into action, they set boundaries and performance standards for their work groups. How this is accomplished will depend upon the development and training of the manager and their perception of their role.

The department's leadership must communicate its performance standards and acceptable behavior to all employees and explain the probable consequences of non-compliance. Besides directives, police rules, and procedures, this communication is accomplished through the spoken word and managerial action. Officers will test their organization to find out what the boundaries are. Most veteran administrators have experienced these tests on numerous occasions. Departments must let employees know what they will or will not tolerate on the job. It will not be accomplished overnight or at one roll call. It will be an evolving testing, monitoring, evaluating, and communicating process. The integrity of the department is established by the decisions managers make.

Employees should not doubt where their department draws the line on performance and conduct. If they do not, administrators may be constantly resorting to negative discipline. The results will be that the department's internal environment will be adversarial instead of positive. It will mean administrators will work harder, putting out disciplinary fires and accomplishing very little for the department.

2. Train Your Employees

Training is a positive form of discipline that should reinforce standards of performance. It assists administrators with maintaining standards and correcting performance problems. Training is a problem-prevention activity that is an essential responsibility of all department managers. While most departments schedule formal training for employees, managers cannot rely on these alone to maintain employee proficiency. All managers should use on-the-job instruction to train their employees.

An excellent method of on-the-job instruction is to manage by asking questions. This technique involves encouraging operational managers to ask employees questions after an incident where the manager observed their work performance. First, the manager should not offer direction unless the officers are genuinely incompetent. Letting the officers finish their assignment without interference signals they are trusted. Second, after the incident, ask questions such as: "Why did you handle that situation in that manner?" or "Do you always handle situations like this in that manner?" The elicited response will give the manager an idea of the employee's skill level and overall job knowledge. If the policy has not been followed correctly or the performance is poor, instruction can be given immediately.

Questioning employees how and why they do what they do is a form of testing. It will reveal the employee's strengths and weaknesses, but may also reveal weaknesses in policy and procedure. It is important problem-prevention information that will assist the department in developing reasonable procedures to govern behavior in the workplace and meet subordinate and departmental needs.

3. Give Feedback

Feedback has been called "the Breakfast of Champions" (Blanchard, 2007). Employees should be informed when their performance is or is not meeting standards. Feedback is a form of positive discipline that supports compliance with standards and initiates employee improvement measures. Recognition should support employee accomplishments, large or small. If a subpar performer improves, let the officer know that the department is aware of their efforts. If an employee develops an innovative approach to solving a problem, the manager should quickly recognize this type of risk-taking. Recognition is one of the most powerful and underutilized tools for establishing and maintaining high-performance levels.

Discipline can be positive, as in rewards and recognition, or negative, as in punishment. A positive work environment is characterized by employees sharing a common sense of purpose, practicing self-discipline, and voluntarily following the policies, procedures, rules, regulations, and performance standards established to promote order and facilitate the department's work. Employees should not doubt where their department draws the line on performance and conduct. Effective discipline requires consistently applying managers' rules, regulations, and operational procedures. Administrators should strive to create a positive work environment for their departments through establishing boundaries, training, and feedback.

▌ Recruitment and Retention of Officers

The recruitment and retention of officers is a significant problem for law enforcement agencies. Filling vacant positions and retaining experienced law enforcement officers needed to serve as leaders and train future candidates has become challenging for law enforcement agencies (Sun, Dockstader, Colden, Saizow, & Patterson, 2022). In 2020, the International Association of Chiefs of Police found that 78 percent of agencies struggled to recruit qualified candidates, with 75 percent reporting that recruiting is more complex than five years ago and 65 percent expressing that they had too few candidates applying to be law enforcement officers (Sun, Dockstader, Colden, Saizow, & Patterson, 2022).

Recruitment

Recruitment difficulties are the result of several factors. Younger workers may not be attracted to policing and will seek employment elsewhere. They may also face military call-ups. Budget crises can lead to lower levels of salary and benefits. The applicant pool might be reduced by illicit drug use, obesity, debt, and enhanced skill requirements of policing. The changing police roles, including counterterrorism, immigration enforcement, and cybercrime, may not attract applicants (Wilson, Grammich, Cherry, & Gibson, 2023, p. 19). Agencies recruit new candidates to mitigate the shortages while maintaining their depleted forces. While they compete for qualified candidates to fill vacancies, agencies must be competitive with hiring tactics and methods. To find recruits, law enforcement agencies should have a focused strategy that may include attending community events, job fairs, advertisements, and being active on social media. Reaching out to younger generations to recruit candidates may require adjusting to current trends (McCafferty, 2003). Departments should consider relaxing grooming and tattoo policies (Skaggs, Harris, & Montgomery, 2022, p. 472). Using new approaches should be the goal of recruiting programs (Wilson, Dalton, Scheer, & Grammich, 2010, p. xx).

Potential recruits may balk at entering police work when they realize the job is dangerous and the citizenry fails to support them. New generations are looking for more flexibility on the job and a comfortable work-life balance. Younger officers are moving further away from the military style of policing. A survey of Generation X officers found they were concerned about having a salary aligned with their educational background and having their ideas recognized in the work environment (Mineard, 2006, pp. 352–353). Millennials have an interest in more immediate needs (McCafferty, 2003).

Law enforcement agencies should rethink entrance requirements, possibly relaxing some prior drug use restrictions, review physical requirements, and focus more on candidate skills. Reducing the time in the selection process can retain more candidates throughout the process. Having mentors guide candidates through the process can ensure they remain on track. Providing support and technology to help candidates stay fit while in the process and opening the fitness training to current agency members could help with retention. Applicants should know where they stand within the process (Sun, Dockstader, Colden, Saizow, & Patterson, 2022). They can attract recruits by strengthening policies prohibiting harassment of women and people of color in the workplace (Wiseman, 2011). The ability to recruit women and minority group members depends upon their proportion in the population, high recruitment budgets, and the availability of higher pay (Jordan, Fridell, Faggani, & Kubu, 2009, p. 339).

Retention

A study of nationwide data determined that the law enforcement turnover rate was 10.8 percent in 2003 and 2008 (Wareham, Smith, & Lambert, 2015, p. 345). Law enforcement retention depends on a range of factors. Retaining an existing officer is far less expensive than hiring a new candidate. Some factors that may assist with retaining officers include increased pay and benefits, recognition of the work-life balance, support from command staff, funding for higher education, training, specialized positions, promotions, positive culture, and proper equipment (Andreescu & Vito, 2021). Without these elements and others, the challenge of retaining officers is difficult. When law enforcement officers are concerned about their agency, they may leave their agency or the profession altogether. Various forms of stress may also contribute to health-related concerns for law enforcement officers (McCarty, 2019).

Veteran officers voluntarily have resigned because of "burnout" resulting from the culmination of occupational frustrations and dissatisfactions related to traditional authoritarian management styles, organizational policies, departmental politics, lack of appreciation for their efforts, the system of internal discipline, pay and fringe benefits, relations with civic officials, court policies, and community expectations (Wilson, Dalton, Scheer, & Grammich, 2010). Interviews with 36 former police officers revealed their reasons for leaving the profession. Hilal and Litsey (2020, p. 80) found that the officers identified working for a poor supervisor as a significant factor. Supervisors can contribute to work stress and job satisfaction by failing to recognize personal issues such as work-life balance for officers. They also noted the failure to consider training requests, opportunities for special assignments and career advancement, and provide realistic options for light-duty assignments. Shift work contributed to stress, by limiting family time. Lack of support from administrators and low pay led some trained officers to leave for another agency paying higher salaries. Agencies can enhance compensation and use contracts and bonuses to retain candidates (Hilal & Litsey, 2020, p. 80). Reducing stress or burnout helps officers persevere through difficult times (McCarty, 2019). Survey results from mid-career Australian officers reported that, while they were satisfied with their career choice, they were dissatisfied with how the organization operated, particularly concerning performance evaluations and promotion (Chan & Doran, 2009, pp. 75–76).

Reminding officers about why they wanted to join the law enforcement profession in the first place could help with retaining officers and realigning their focus. Agencies should consider understanding why their officers joined the law enforcement profession, determine their motivations, and provide recognition for exceptional performance (Wilson, Dalton, Scheer, & Grammich, 2010). A survey of veteran officers found that they were motivated by the opportunity to help others, having some control over their work environment, and the team aspects of police work (Monk-Turner, O'Leary, & Sumter, 2010).

One way to obtain valuable information is to conduct "Stay interviews" with veteran officers who choose to remain in policing (Wilson, Grammich, Cherry, & Gibson, 2023, p. 13). Implementing flexible schedules or making remote work available could change policing functions. The Covid-19 pandemic has shown that there can be other ways to accomplish some of these schedules. Applying commonsense changes can improve retention while reducing the stress on officers (Wiseman, 2011). Agencies can also offer tuition reimbursement bonuses, provide more training, allow officers to work out on duty, grant exposure to different assignments, provide administrative support, and treat their officers respectfully (Wilson, Dalton, Scheer, & Grammich, 2010).

A survey conducted with new police hires and officers who voluntarily departed found they shared common issues. Recruitment and retention were affected by institutional support, operational standards and compensation, organizational transparency, and departmental leadership. Salary was noted as a significant factor in turnover, as well as the lack of opportunities for growth, unmet job expectations, inadequate feedback, insufficient recognition, and poor training and equipment (Skaggs, Harris, & Montgomery, 2022, p. 470). Recruits complained that field training officers were lazy and stressed responding to calls for service and that organizational cliques contributed to a lack of support among colleagues (Skaggs, Harris, & Montgomery, 2022, pp. 472–473). Addressing such concerns can help departments address both recruitment and retention problems.

Women in Policing

Over the last 50 years, female representation in policing has dramatically improved, tripling from 1971 to 1980 and doubling from 1980 to 2000 (Cordner & Cordner, 2011). Between 1995 and 2019, the percentage of women officers increased by only 3 percent, from 9.8 percent to 12.8 percent (Federal Bureau of Investigation, 1996, 2019). According to the National Center for Women & Policing (2002, p. 4), the percentage of women in large police agencies was 14.3 percent in 1999, 13.0 percent in 2000, and 12.7 percent in 2001. The FBI (2019) reported that, in 2019, the national percentage of women in law enforcement was 12.8 percent. The representation of women in supervisory and command-level positions within police agencies is even lower. In 2020, in local police departments serving 250,000 or more residents, about 16 percent of police chiefs were female. About 14 percent of full-time sworn officers and 11 percent of first-line supervisors across local police departments were female (Goodison, 2022). While programs such as affirmative action, as well as lawsuits and consent decrees, have increased the hiring of women into law enforcement agencies as police officers, the increase in the representation of women among supervisory ranks has been marginal.

Women face difficulties entering and then advancing in policing. Typically, they practice a style of policing that focuses on effective communication styles, increased de-escalation, especially during violent encounters, and significantly less excessive use of force. They have saved departments millions of dollars in costly litigation payouts, have less sustained allegations of excessive force, fewer citizen complaints, and are less likely to be involved in a shooting. For example, research from the San Jose Police Department and the San Francisco Police Department indicated men were two to three times more likely than female officers to be named in a citizen complaint for excessive use of force (Lonsway et al., 2002, p. 6). Data indicate that women officers are less likely to use excessive force, costing departments less in litigious payouts.

In policing, masculine symbols, images, and ideologies are routinely promoted—the police culture clings to the masculine crime-fighting ideal. Images and ideologies work to exclude women and reinforce the dominant hegemonic masculine cultural norms that permeate policy. Women officers who threaten the masculine cultural norms and standards will likely receive control and isolation from members of the dominant male organization (Shelley et al., 2011).

When asked about additional difficulties they may have experienced regarding balancing their personal and professional lives, women officers surveyed said that shift work added unnecessary stress and strain to their marriages. The shift work schedule did not allow for much time for them to spend with their spouse, and a promotion and new shift change would only add to that personal marital conflict. The issue of affordable, quality overnight childcare was also a significant barrier influencing women officers' decision to seek promotion. Most of these women reported being married to another officer within the department and explained how this dynamic complicated their ability to find childcare during the nighttime hours (Archibald & Hassell, 2009). Cordner and Cordner (2011) found that 40 percent of the women officers surveyed stated the male-dominated atmosphere of the profession failed to support female officers. They felt discriminated against in promotional considerations and pressured to demonstrate that they could handle the job (Cordner & Cordner, 2011, p. 217). Archibald and Hassell (2009) examined the barriers female police officers faced when considering promotion. They found that family responsibilities and a lack of confidence were the primary personal factors preventing women from considering promotion. The female respondents also noted that they would not be willing or interested in rearranging their shifts to accommodate a promotion.

Control and segregation perpetuate the marginalization of women officers—controlling and segregating women "through structured hierarchies implemented to secure the position of white males" (Shelley et al., 2011, p. 354). It takes place in several forms, including limiting women to inferior positions within the department and placing them at a severe disadvantage in obtaining the necessary experience required to participate in the promotion process. Men use offensive sexual humor, sexual harassment, and profanity to perpetuate the hegemonic masculine culture and segregate women from feeling included. Such harassment creates an environment that sends a clear message—women are not valued, appreciated, or included in the profession. Typically, women officers face workplace incivilities—behaviors that communicate disrespect through rudeness and prevent women from doing their jobs effectively (Rief & Clinkinbeard, 2020, p. 437). Female officers are treated as outsiders by the male-dominated police culture and are not treated equally with males (Rief & Clinkinbeard, 2020, pp. 442–443).

In policing, women are expected to be more compassionate, nurturing, and supportive, whereas men are expected to exhibit masculine traits such as toughness, being unemotional, and strength. When faced with the decision of how they should conform, they find themselves choosing between defeminizing themselves—reducing the feminine qualities and characteristics known to be female, or de-professionalizing themselves and disengaging themselves from the masculine features known to be associated with successful police officers (Shelley et al., 2011). This was described by Jacobs (1987) as women choosing to either "act like a lady" or become "one of the boys." They assimilate to the masculine characteristics of the job and defeminize themselves to be accepted and viewed as capable (Martin, 1979). A qualitative study of female officers in one department revealed that those who "played the game" by adopting masculine norms were valued and rewarded (Brown, Baldwin, Dierenfeldt, & McCain, 2020, p. 166). Women officers felt a greater need to prove themselves than their male counterparts.

However, "policewomen" often shy away from the masculine characteristics of the job, keeping their feminine traits and focusing on a service-oriented outlook towards policing (Martin, 1979). This choice can place women at a disadvantage. If women fail to adopt the masculine role, they risk being perceived as a threat to the men and rejected. If they choose the feminine role, they potentially reduce their opportunities for upward mobility. Interviews with women and minority job candidates in a northeastern police department revealed they viewed policing as a childhood dream, wanting to make a difference in the community, and that it was a good transition from the military to civilian work. Such motives could serve as recruitment advertising. Women also cited "legacy" as a reason—suggesting that former officers among families and friends might be a recruitment source (Gibbs, 2019, p. 210). A survey of officers from two Midwestern police departments revealed similar female motives for entering police work—notably, the desire to protect and serve the public, and to serve as a role model for other women (Clinkinbeard, Solomon, & Rief, 2021, p. 727).

Lonsway (2002) proposes six advantages to increasing women's employment within law enforcement agencies:

1.   Female officers are proven as competent as their male counterparts.
2.   Female officers are less likely to use excessive force.
3.   Female officers implement community-oriented policing.
4.   More female officers will improve law enforcement's response to violence against women.
5.   Increasing female officers' presence reduces sex discrimination and harassment within a law enforcement agency.
6.   The presence of women can bring about beneficial changes in policy for all officers.

(Lonsway et al., 2002, pp. 2–7)

Gender diversity within law enforcement agencies is a possible means to reform and a strategy to improve public confidence in the police. Women, considered effective communicators, tend to use de-escalation techniques instead of violence and use of force. In addition, they have proven adept at breaking down the walls of the macho police subculture.

Police agencies across the country must address the inequalities and low representation of women in leadership roles to improve their legitimacy and become more representative of the public they serve and the workforce in America. Changes must start at the organizational level, with agencies taking a deep look at their corporate culture and recognizing the damage that male-dominated, hypermasculine subcultures have on female officers. The first step to achieving this is to reevaluate the department's sexual harassment policies and the required training provided to all employees. To change the culture within police departments, departments must message a zero-tolerance policy for such behavior. Harassment training is federally mandated. However, increasing the exposure and emphasis on such training will help change the culture. Agencies must develop reporting procedures encouraging victims to feel safe from retaliatory behaviors and stereotypical judgments.

Police agencies must address their lack of family-friendly policies to entice and encourage a fair playing field for women in promotional settings. A big part of this should consider changes to the scheduling process. Examining alternative giving of schedules, agencies should also evaluate and assess their anti-nepotism policies and develop creative ways to manage nepotism without adversely affecting women officers married to other officers.

Best practices to ensure reporting of sexual harassment include:

•   Transparency: reporting, investigating cases, monitoring outcomes, and evaluating the effectiveness of policies.
•   Use of victim-informed guidelines: They must outline the reporting process, the measures taken to protect victims, punishment for offenses, and the steps and timeline for the investigation.

- Confidentiality: Using an outside agency to investigate cases is recommended to protect victims.
- Impartiality: Using an outside agency will also reduce the risk of favoritism and ensure that the department's culture will not affect the outcome.
- Safety: The victim must be protected from retaliation from the accused perpetrator.
- Accountability: All employees should be provided with information about the process and its operation. (Clinkinbeard, Solomon, & Rief, 2021).

The existence of such policies will establish what constitutes harassment and how it will be dealt with. The aim is to improve the institutional climate to prevent such incidents.

Todak (2023) interviewed 226 female officers who obtained a promotion about their experience in the process. They noted several problems faced by women seeking police promotions: gender biases held by the evaluators (cronyism in the "good ol' boys club"), difficulties by mothers attempting to balance the time pressures created by the demands of work, childcare, and studying for the exam. They were judged on their appearance rather than performance. Women lacked mentorship in preparing for the exam, while males did not. They felt they had to work harder to prove themselves. Finally, they were accused of "gender favoritism" in the promotion process (Todak, 2023, pp. 973–976).

Attention should be given to women's hurdles and barriers when balancing their work and home life responsibilities. Departments nationwide have begun implementing childcare facilities, or programs, within their agency to provide much-needed assistance to officers with children. San Diego Police Department established the first-of-its-kind childcare facility for SDPD officers after years of research and hard work. The facility was specifically designed for officers of the SDPD. It operates from 5 a.m. to 10 p.m., is open on holidays, charges half of what market value childcare costs, and pays childcare providers 15 percent more than standard (Pruss & Austin, 2022). Creating childcare facilities or partnerships with daycares to combat childcare hurdles could increase the number of women participating in promotional processes and seeking upward mobility.

Agencies must emphasize and adapt their recruitment and retention policies to attract more women to join the force. By increasing the percentage of female officers, agencies can begin to address the effects of tokenism and try to remove barriers preventing women from being promoted. Diversity management requires addressing the sources of discrimination and improving the work environment. Mentoring should be established for women officers to facilitate their qualifications for promotion and reach their full potential. Female officers should be a part of this mentoring process (Sabat & Mishra, 2010, pp. 375–376).

Minorities in Policing

The history of policing is one of alienation from minority communities. The police were viewed as the agents of a tyrannical system of racism and injustice—an *indelible impression* rooted in a long and bloody history of minority oppression (Williams & Murphy, 1990, p. 6). As a result, police departments now find it difficult to find and develop the level of support necessary to institute reforms in urban areas. Despite official measures to eliminate police brutality, resentment still exists. Typically, African Americans were the object of police attention and were not a part of police departments themselves.

Following the Civil War, Blacks joined several police departments in the South: Selma, Alabama (1867), Houston, Texas (1870), and Jackson, Mississippi (1871). By 1870, New Orleans had a police board with three Black members out of five and a police force that included 177 Blacks (Williams & Murphy, 1990, p. 8). In the North, Blacks were appointed in Chicago (1872), Washington, DC (1874), Indianapolis (1876), Cleveland (1881), and Boston (1885) (Williams & Murphy, 1990, pp. 8–9). Black police officers were not given the same duties and powers as their White counterparts. Typically, they worked in plain clothes, were assigned to Black neighborhoods, and were restricted in their ability to make felony arrests.

Following the successful passage and implementation of segregation policies, Blacks were dismissed or forced to resign from police departments. For example, New Orleans had only five Black officers by 1900, none by 1910, and did not appoint another until 1950 (Kuykendall & Burns, 1980, pp. 4–12). Since 1950, employment percentage gains have surpassed total police growth. In the 1960s, for every seven police officers added, one was Black; thus, Blacks were employed at a rate of growth higher than their numbers in the population. Despite this increasing rate and the stimulation provided by the passage of the Equal Employment Opportunity Act of 1972, their police presence in most American cities was lower than their percentage in the local population (Alexander, 1978).

This racial pattern was not limited to the South. Beginning in 1891, Alexander (1978) reveals that each successive generation of Black officers in the NYPD slowly increased, and they were eventually placed in high positions. Black representation in the NYPD peaked in 1974 and fell off after that. Blacks in the NYPD were confronted with bigotry, underrepresentation, polarization, and tokenism. A double standard was in place for Black officers, as well as females.

In 2020, about 12 percent of full-time sworn officers in local police departments were Black, and 14 percent were Hispanic. In local departments serving one million or more citizens, about 47 percent of full-time sworn officers were White, and 30 percent were Hispanic. About 47 percent of local police departments serving 250,000 or more residents were White, 38 percent were Black, and 13 percent were Hispanic (Goodison, 2022, p. 1). The percentage of full-time sworn Hispanic officers serving local police departments rose to 14 percent from 8 percent in 1997. From 1997 to 2020, the percentage of White local police officers decreased from 78 percent to 69 percent in 2020 (Goodison, 2022, p. 5).

A review of research literature from 2000 to 2020 revealed four areas affecting the hiring of minority and female officers: 1) organizational and external predictors, 2) motivations and attitudes, 3) effective recruitment strategies, and 4) screening process barriers (such as failure to provide complete personal information). Internal predictors reflect how the department affects the attraction of minority and female officers—including agency size, unionization, educational requirements, and involvement in community policing. External factors include minority political power and relations in the community. Minorities seemed motivated by the challenges of the job of policing as a long-term career opportunity (Donohue, 2021, pp. 487–493). Gustafson notes that diversity in local governments carried over to minorities in policing. His study of Law Enforcement Management and Administration Statistics (LEMAS) concluded there was a greater proportion of minorities in administrative positions where salaries were high (Gustafson, 2013, p. 719).

There is some evidence that Black officers view policing differently. Survey results from a midsized Florida department found that Black officers had concerns about how their peers treated minority citizens. Two-thirds of the Black officers believed that there were racial differences in how persons were policed. Half of them felt that the police were also biased by the income status of the citizenry (Gau & Paoline, 2020, p. 486).

These factors influence the hiring and retention of minority officers in policing. It has been suggested that agencies could conduct a targeted recruitment campaign in areas of the state where minorities reside. Recruiting materials could target groups or organizations where minorities are present (Williams & Higgins, 2023, pp. 462–463).

LGTBQ Issues in Policing

The LGTBQ community has traditionally been the target of hyper-policing (Gillespie, 2008; Colvin, 2012). A study based on a national cohort of gay and bisexual men revealed that Black and Latino/x men were more likely to report extreme police-related stress. Gay and bisexual men who experienced discrimination at the hands of the police were also more likely to experience stress (Bacchus, D'Angelo, & Grov, 2023, p. 95). Black queer men have reported elevated hostility from the police than younger White queer men (Meyer, 2022). Transsexual persons report significantly lower positive perceptions of the police (Serpe & Nadal, 2017, p. 292). Members of the LGTBQ community also report harassment, including sexual advances made by officers (Hodge & Sexton, 2020, p. 257). Other detrimental consequences of hyper-policing of the LGTBQ community include queer people underreporting crime and victimization (particularly in the case of hate crimes) and skepticism and mistrust of the criminal justice system (Girardi, 2022, p. 860). Interviews with LGTBQ citizens revealed that they would only call the police under select circumstances—violent encounters, severe harassment, and medical emergencies (Shields, 2021, p. 19). Furthermore, they believed that summoning the police could lead to more problems, dismissing their complaint and engaging in misconduct (Shields, 2021, pp. 19–20).

One police method to increase victimization reporting among the LGTBQ community adopted in Australia is to establish liaison centers. The main problem surrounding such efforts is visibility—LGBTQ persons must approach an officer to access protection (Dwyer & Ball, 2020, p. 277). This issue is compounded by the police's conservative culture and the ability of officers operating the program to be identified (Dwyer, 2019, p. 401). Such liaison programs have also been implemented in the U.S. (Buist, 2022, p. 899). In addition to the use of liaison officers, other potential methods to improve LGBTQ-police relations include better training for officers, involving sensitivity-based scenarios and encouraging LBGTQ officers to "come out" and share their experiences with their peers (Hodge & Sexton, 2020, pp. 257–259). An evaluation of a scenario-based training program reported positive results in attitudes toward LBGTQ persons (Israel et al., 2015). In addition, research from Australia reported that LBG officers had more positive attitudes toward LBGTQ persons and expressed greater satisfaction with police work (Miles-Johnson & Death, 2020, p. 266). Yet, such disclosures may be difficult for gay male law enforcement officers to make (Collins & Rocco, 2018).

Stressors also affect police officers who are LGTBQ. Burke (1994) interviewed 36 gay, lesbian, and bisexual officers and found that they felt pressured by the police macho subculture, rejection by their peers and citizens, and ridicule at work. These stressors presented risks to their mental health, ability to function as a police officer, and maintaining satisfying personal relationships (Burke, 1994, p. 201). However, a Canadian study of LGTBQ police officers revealed that attitudes toward them are changing. Interviews with these 21 officers showed they felt more inclusivity, as more of their numbers entered policing and were promoted. Most of the resistance they encountered came from officers over 50, often in the form of "microaggressions" (i.e., inappropriate jokes). Overall, they supported policing as a profession providing services to the community (Couto, 2018, p. 85). Another Canadian study found that lesbian and bisexual police officers felt welcomed in their department (Giwa, Colvin, Ricciardelli, & Warren, 2022, p. 107).

In addition, laws to promote diversity and inclusion in Great Britain positively affect the workplace experience of LGTBQ officers. A national survey of officers after the Macpherson inquiry documented that over 75 percent of LBG officers felt their supervisors supported them, 74 percent said they were satisfied with being a police officer, 82 percent stated they never experienced discrimination at work, and 79 percent were "out" at work (Jones, 2015, pp. 69–71).

Despite the problems faced in policing the LBGTQ community, some potential solutions exist, providing that both sides approach their differences positively. Changes can be implemented in the community and within departments as well.

Conclusion

This chapter discusses the human resource management function in police administration. Human resource management (HRM) refers to the functions, policies, and activities a police department uses to enhance the effective utilization of its human resources now and in the future. Strategic management of human resources is emerging as the prevailing approach to the development of effective police organizations. It is the art and science of linking a department's human resource management with its strategic goals and objectives to improve organizational performance and develop a culture that fosters commitment, learning, innovation, and flexibility. Recruitment, selection, training, discipline, and development of employees are critical human resource functions. However, these functions are influenced by federal and state law, local charters and ordinances, political motives, jurisdictional size, community values, and the department's culture. The department's administrative leadership creates human resource policies and practices that produce employee competencies and behaviors needed to achieve its strategic objectives.

A department's administrative leadership structures the human resource function through its philosophy and practices. The department's strategic direction should provide the framework that guides the design of specific human resource activities such as recruitment, training development, and discipline. Administrators must develop an integrated framework linking human resource activities with the department's strategic needs. The management of human resources should be coordinated with the control of the organization and its strategic direction. In this way, employee behavior and skill sets bridge the department's strategic direction and effectiveness. The department should create a work environment where employees are encouraged to develop and utilize their skills and abilities to the maximum extent and give specific attention to women, persons of color, and members of the LBGTQ community. Thus, how an organization organizes its human resource functions has significant consequences on what it can accomplish.

KEY TERMS

Deliberate indifference
Development
Discipline
Employee procedural rights
Entry-level training
Equal employment legislation
Field training
Hawthorne Studies
Human Relations School
Human Resource Management
Job task analysis
Just cause
Labor market
Multiple hurdle process
Needs assessment
Negative discipline

Organizational image
Outcome evaluation
Peace Officer Standards and Training Act (POST)
Personnel
Police Officer Bill of Rights
Police Training Officer Program
Positive discipline
Positive work environment
Pre-employment academies
Principles of Learning
Procedural rights
Process evaluation
Progressive constructive discipline

Public Safety Training
Academy Accreditation
Recruiter
Recruitment
Recruitment Plan
Roll call training
Scientific Management
Selection
Special Population Recruitment Plan
Specialized/In-service training
Strategic Human Resource Management
Training
Validity

References

Alexander, J. (1978). *Bluecoats, black skin: The black experience in the New York City police department since 1891.* Hicksville, NY: Exposition Press.

Alpert, G., & Smith, W. (1991). Beyond city limits and into the wood(s): A brief look at the policy impact of the city of *Canton v. Harris and Wood v. Ostrander. American Journal of Police, 10*(1), 19–40.

Andreescu, V., & Vito, G. (2021). Strain, negative emotions, and turnover intentions among American police managers. *Policing, 44*(6), 970–984.

Archbold, C.A., & Hassell, K. D. (2009). Paying a marriage tax: An examination of the barriers to the promotion of female police officers. *Policing: An International Journal of Police Strategies & Management, 32*(1), 56–74.

Bacchus, E., D'Angelo, A., & Grov, C. (2023). Experiences of police-related stress among a U.S. national cohort of gay and bisexual men. *American Journal of Community Psychology, 72,* 89–100.

Bayley, D., & Bittner, E. (1984, Fall). Learning the skills of policing. *Law and Contemporary Problems,* 35–59.

Beres, J. (Ed.) (2009). *Law enforcement recruitment toolkit.* Washington, DC: COPS/IACP Leadership Project Office of Community Oriented Policing Services, U.S. Department of Justice.

Berman, E.M., Bowman, J.S., West, J.P., & Van Wart, M. (2006). *Human Resource Management in Public Service.* Thousand Oaks, CA: Sage.

Berman, E.M., Bowman, J.S., West, J.P., & Van Wart, M. (2013). *Human resource management in public service.* Thousand Oaks, CA: Sage.

Blanchard, K. (2007). *Leading at a higher level.* Upper Saddle River, NJ: FT Press.

Brown, T., Baldwin, J., Dierenfeldt, R., & McCain, S. (2020). Playing the game: A qualitative exploration of the female experience in a hypermasculine policing environment. *Police Quarterly, 23*(2), 143–173.

Buist, C. (2022). LGBT rights in the fields of criminal law and law enforcement.. *University of Richmond Law Review, 54*(3), 877–900.

Burke, M. (1994). Homosexuality as deviance: The case of the gay police officer. *British Journal of Criminology, 34*(2), 192–203.

Chan, J., & Doran, S. (2009). Staying in the job: Job satisfaction among mid-career police officers. *Policing, 3*(1), 66–77.

Clinkinbeard, S., Solomon, S., & Rief, R. (2021). Why did you become a police officer? Entry-related motives and concerns of men and women in policing. *Criminal Justice & Behavior, 48*(6), 715–733.

Collins, J., & Rocco, T. (2018). Queering employee engagement to understand and improve the performance of gay male law enforcement officers: A phenomenological explanation. *Performance Improvement Quarterly, 30*(4), 273–295.

Colvin, R. (2012). *Gay and lesbian cops: Diversity and effective policing.* Boulder, CO: Lynne Renner Publishers, Inc.

Commission on Accreditation for Law Enforcement Agencies (2006). *Standards for law enforcement agencies.* Fairfax, VA: CALEA.

Community Oriented Policing Services, https://cops.usdoj.gov/.c

Cordner, G., & Cordner, A. (2011). Stuck on a plateau? *Police Quarterly, 14*(3), 207–226.

Couto, J. (2018). Hearing their voices and counting them in: The place of Canadian LGTBQ police officers in police culture. *Journal of Community Safety & Well-Being, 3*(3), 84–87.

Decicco, D.A. (2000). Police officer candidate assessment and selection. *FBI Law Enforcement Bulletin, 69*(12), 1–6.

Dessler, G. (2006). *A framework for human resource management.* Upper Saddle River, NJ: Pearson-Prentice Hall.

Dessler, G. (2013). *Human resource management.* Upper Saddle River, NJ: Pearson-Prentice Hall.

Dickerson, N. (2003). *Navigating the U.S. labor market: Trends and prospects for workers.* Washington, DC: U.S. Department of Labor.

Donohue, R. (2021). Shades of blue: A review of the hiring, recruitment, and selection of female and minority police officers. *Social Science Journal, 58*(4), 484–498.

Drucker, P. (2020). *On the profession of management.* Boston, MA: Harvard Business School Press, p. 24.

Dwyer, A. (2019). Queering policing: What is best practice within LGBTQ communities. *Current Issues in Criminal Justice, 31*(3), 396–411.

Dwyer, A., & Ball, M. (2020). "You'd just cop flak from every other dickhead under the sun": Navigating the tensions of (in)visibility and hypervisibility in LGTBI police liaison programs in three Australian states. *Journal of Contemporary Criminal Justice, 36*(2), 274–292.

Equal Employment Opportunity Commission (1978). *Uniform guidelines on employee selection procedures.* Code of Federal Regulations, 41 CFR Ch. 60. Washington, DC: Department of Labor.

Federal Bureau of Investigation (2019). *Crime in the United States.* Washington, DC: Federal Bureau of Investigation, Table 74.

Freyss, S.F. (Ed.) (2004). *Human resource management in local government: An essential guide.* Washington, DC: International City/County Management Association.

Fyfe, J.J., Greene, J.R., Walsh, W., Wilson, O., & McLaren, R. (1997). *Police administration.* New York, NY: McGraw-Hill.

Gaines, L.K., & Kappler, V.E. (2011). *Policing in America.* Waltham, MA: Anderson.

Gau, J., & Paoline, E. (2020). Equal under the law: Officer's perceptions of equitable treatment and justice in policing. *American Journal of Criminal Justice, 45,* 474–492.

Gibbs, Jennifer C. (2019) Diversifying the police applicant pool: motivations of women and minority candidates seeking police employment, *Criminal Justice Studies, 32*(3), 207–221. doi: 10.1080/1478601X.2019.1579717.

Gillespie, W. (2008). Thirty-five years after stonewall: An exploratory study of satisfaction with police among gay, lesbian, and bisexual persons at the 34th annual Atlanta pride festival. *Journal of Homosexuality, 55*(4), 619–647.

Girardi, R. (2022). "It's easy to mistrust police when they keep on killing us": A queer exploration of police violence and LGBTQ+ victimization. *Journal of Gender Studies, 31*(7), 852–862.

Giwa, S., Colvin, R., Ricciardelli, R., & Warren, A. (2022). Workplace experiences of lesbian and bisexual female police officers in the Royal Newfoundland Constabulary. *Women & Criminal Justice, 32*(1–2), 93–110.

Glenn, R.W., Panitch, B.R., Barnes-Proby, D., Williams, E., Christian, J., Lewis, M.W., Gerwehr, S, & Brannan, D.W. (2003). *Training the 21st century police officer: Redefining police professionalism for the Los Angeles police department.* Santa Monica, CA: RAND Public Safety and Justice.

Gomez-Mejia, L.R., Balkin, D.B., & Cardy, R.L. (2012). *Managing human resources.* New York, NY: Pearson.

Goodison, S. (2022). *Local police departments personnel, 2020.* Washington, DC: U.S. Department of Justice.

Gustafson, J. (2013). Diversity in municipal police agencies: A national examination of minority hiring and promotion. *Policing: An international Journal of Police Strategies & Management, 36*(4), 719–736.

Hilal, S., & Litsey, B. (2020). Reducing police turnover: Recommendations for the law enforcement agency. *International Journal of Police Science & Management, 22*(1), 73–83.

Hodge, J., & Sexton, L. (2020). Examining the blue line in the rainbow: The interactions and perceptions of law enforcement among lesbian, gay, bisexual, transgender, and queer communities. *Police Practice and Research, 21*(3), 246–263.

Hyland, S.S., & Davis, E. (2019). *Local police departments, 2016: Personnel.* Washington, DC: U.S. Department of Justice.

Israel, T., Harkness, A., Avellar, T., Delucio, K., Bettergarcia, J., & Goodman, J. (2015). LGBTQ-affirming policing: Tactics generated by law enforcement personnel. *Journal of Police & Criminal Psychology, 31,* 173–181.

Jacobs, P. (1987). How female police officers cope with a traditionally male position. *Sociology & Social Research, 72,* 4–6.

Jones, M. (2015). Who forgot lesbian, gay, and bisexual police officers? Findings from a national survey. *Policing, 9*(1), 65–76.

Jordan, W., Fridell, L., Faggani, D., & Kubu, B. (2009). Attracting females and racial/ethnic minorities to law enforcement. *Journal of Criminal Justice, 37,* 333–341.

Koper, C. (2004). *Hiring and keeping police officers.* Washington, DC: U.S. Department of Justice, National Institute of Justice.

Kuykendall, J., & Burns, J. (1980). The black police officers: A historical perspective. *Journal of Contemporary Criminal Justice, 1*(4), 4–12.

Langworthy, R. Hughes, T.W., & Sanders, B. (1995). *Law enforcement, recruitment, selection, and training: A survey of major police departments in the U.S.* Highland Heights, KY: ACJS.

Lonsway, K. A. (2002). *Hiring & retaining more women: The advantages to law enforcement agencies.* Beverly Hills, CA: National Center for Women & Policing.

Lonsway, K., Carrington, S., Aguirre, P., Wood, M., Moore, M., Harrington, P., Smeal, E., & Spillar, K. (2002). *Men, women, and police excessive force: A tale of two genders..* Beverly Hills, CA: National Center for Women & Policing.

McCafferty, F. (2003). The challenge of selecting tomorrow's police officers from Generations X and Y. *Journal of the American Academy of Psychiatry and the Law, 31,* 78–88.

Macan, T. (2009). The employment interview: A review of current studies and directions for future research. *Human Resource Management Review, 19,* 203–218.

Marenin, O. (2004). Police training for democracy. *Police Practice and Research, 5*(2), 107–123.

Martin, S. E. (1979). Policewomen and policewomen: Occupational role dilemmas and choices of female officers. *Journal of Police Science and Administration, 7*(3), 314–323.

Meyer, D. (2022). "So much for protect and serve": Queer male survivors' perceptions of negative police experiences. *Journal of Contemporary Criminal Justice, 36*(2), 228–250.

Miles-Johnson, T., & Death, J. (2020). Compensating for sexual identity: How LGB and hetrosexual Australian police officers perceive policing of LBGTIQ+ people. *Journal of Contemporary Criminal Justice, 36*(2), 251–273.

Mineard, T. (2006). Career satisfaction of Generation X law enforcement officers. *Police Journal, 79,* 343–357.

Monk-Turner, E., O'Leary, D., & Sumter, M. (2010). Factors shaping police retention: Does Herzberg's theory of satisfaction hold? *Police Journal, 83,* 164–180.

Niederhoffer, A. (1967). *Behind the shield: The police in urban society.* New York, NY: Doubleday.

Nowicki, D.E. (2003). Human resource management and development. In W.G. Geller & D.W. Stephens (Eds.), *Local government police management* (pp. 353–390). Washington, DC: ICMA.

O'Keefe, J. (2004). *Protecting the republic: The education and training of American police officers.* Upper Saddle River, NJ: Prentice Hall.

Peak, K. (2014). *Policing America: Challenges and best practices.* Upper Saddle River, NJ: Prentice Hall.

Peak, K.J., Gaines, L.K., & Glensor, R.W. (2009). *Police supervision and management: In an era of community policing.* Upper Saddle River, NJ: Prentice Hall.

Posthuma, R.A., Morgeson, F.P, & Campion, M.A. (2002). Beyond employment interview validity: A comprehensive narrative review of recent research and trends over time. *Personnel Psychology, 55,* 1–81.

Pruss, N., & Austin, L. (2022, June). 'The San Diego Police Department's childcare solution'. *Community Policing Dispatch.* Washington, DC: COPS Office, U.S. Department of Justice.

Raymond, B., Hickman, L., Miller, L., & Wong, J. (2005). *Police personnel challenges after September 11: Anticipating expanded duties and a changing labor pool.* San Monica, CA: Rand. www.rand.org/pubs/occasional_papers/2005/RAND_OP154.pdf.

Reaves, B.A. (2009). *State and local law enforcement training academies, 2006.* Washington, DC: Bureau of Justice Statistics, U.S. Department of Justice.

Reaves, B.A. (2012). *Hiring and retention of state and local law enforcement officers, 2008 statistical tables.* Washington, DC: Bureau of Justice Statistics, U.S. Department of Justice. www.bjs.gov/index.cfm?ty=pbdetail&iid=4514.

Rice, G.E., & Rizzo, T. (2014, August 23). Like Ferguson, area police departments lack racial diversity. *Kansas City Star.* www.kansascity.com/news/local/crime1282013.html.

Rief, R., & Clinkinbeard, S. (2020). Exploring gendered environments in policing: Workplace incivilities and fit perceptions in men and women officers. *Police Quarterly, 23*(4), 427–450.

Robbins, S.P., & Judge, T.A. (2013). *Organizational behavior.* Upper Saddle River, NJ: Prentice Hall.

Roberg, R., Kuykendall, J., & Novak, K. (2002). *Police management.* Los Angeles, CA: Roxbury.

Roberg, R., Novak, K., Cordner, G., & Smith, B. (2012). *Police & society.* New York, NY: Oxford University Press.

Ross, D.L. (2000). Emerging trends in police failure to train properly. *Journal of Police Strategies and Management, 23*(2), 169–193.

Rydberg, J., & Terrill, W. (2010). The effect of higher education on police behavior. *Police Quarterly, 13*(1), 92–120.

Sabat, S., & Mishra, S. (2010). Role of women in the management of the police organisation: A paradigm shift. *International Journal of Learning and Change, 4*(4), 365–377.

Schuler, R.S. (1992). Strategic human resources management: Linking people with the strategic needs of the business. *Organizational Dynamics, 21,* 18–32.

Serpe, C., & Nadal, K. (2017). Perceptions of police: Experiences in the trans* community. *Journal of Gay & Lesbian Social Services, 29*(3), 280–299.

Shelley, T., Morabito, M., & Tobin-Gurley, J. (2011). Gendered institutions and gender roles: Understanding the experiences of women in policing. *Criminal Justice Studies, 24*(4), 351–367.

Shields, D. (2021). Stonewalling in the brick city: Perceptions of and experiences with seeking police assistance among LGBTQ citizens. *Social Sciences, 10,* 1–27.

Skaggs, S., Harris, C., & Montgomery, L. (2022). The impact of police-community relations: Recruitment and retention concerns of local police agencies. *Policing, 16*(3), 462–475.

Stephens, D.W. (2011). *Police discipline: A case for change.* Washington, DC: U.S. Department of Justice, National Institute of Justice.

Sun, C., Dockstader, J., Colden, J., Saizow, H., & Patterson, Q. (2022). *Blueprint for law enforcement recruitment and retention in the 21st century.* Washington, DC: U.S. Department of Justice.

Swanson, R., Territo, L., & Taylor, R.W. (2005). *Police administration: Structure, processes, and behavior.* Upper Saddle River, NJ: Prentice Hall.

Taylor, B., Kubu, B., Fridell, L., Rees, C., Jordan, T., & Cheney, J. (2006). *Cop crunch: Identifying strategies for dealing with law enforcement's recruiting and hiring crisis.* Washington, DC: National Institute of Justice.

Taylor, F.W. (1911). *Principles of scientific management.* New York, NY: Harper & Row.

Thibault, E.A., Lynch, L.M., & McBride, B.R. (2010). *Proactive police management.* Upper Saddle River, NJ: Prentice Hall.

Todak, N. (2023). "A panel of good ol' boys": Women navigating the police promotions process. *American Journal of Criminal Justice, 48,* 967–983.

Vosburgh, R. (2006). The evolution of HR: Developing HR as an internal consulting organization. *Human Resource Planning, 30*(3), 11–23.

Wareham, J., Smith, B., & Lambert, E. (2015). Rates and patterns of law enforcement turnover: A research note. *Criminal Justice Policy Review, 26*(4), 345–370.

Wexley, K., & Latham, G. (2002). *Development and training of human resources in organizations*. Upper Saddle River, NJ: Prentice Hall.

Williams, F., & Higgins, G. (2023). A holistic approach to diversity in recruiting in state police agencies. *Journal of Criminal Justice, 46*(4), 450–467.

Williams, H., & Murphy, P. (1990). *The evolving strategy of policing*. Washington, DC: National Institute of Justice.

Williams, M., Bartlett, A., Zare, M., Custer, N., & Osman, M. (2023). Sexual harassment and abuse in law enforcement: Best practices for creating safety for female officers. *Police Journal*, 1–16.: 10.1177/0032258X231156714.

Wilson, J., Dalton, E., Scheer, C., & Grammich, C. (2010). *Police recruitment and retention for the new millennium: The state of knowledge*. Santa Monica, CA: RAND Corporation.

Wilson, J., Grammich, C., Cherry, T., & Gibson, A. (2023). Police retention: A systematic review of the research. *Policing, 17*, 1–20.

Wiseman, J. (2011). *Strategic cut back management: Law enforcement leadership for lean times*. Washington, DC: U.S. Department of Justice.

Cases

Albemarle Paper Co v. Moody 95 S.Ct. 2362, 1975.

City of Canton v. Harris 109 S.Ct. 1197, 1989.

Garrity v. New Jersey 385 U.S. 493, 1967.

Griggs v. Duke Power Co. 401 U.S. 424, 1971.

Meritor Savings Bank, FSB v. Vinson 109 S.Ct. 2399, 1986.

Morrissey v. Brewer 408 U.S. 471 1972.

Oncale v. Sundowner Offshore Services, 523 S.Ct. 75, 1998.

Segar v. Civilliti 25 FEP 1425, 1981.

Weingarten v. United States, 420 U.S. 251 1975.

Wilson v. Robinson 668 F.2nd. 380, 1981.

10 Measuring Police Performance

Learning Objectives

1. To understand the methods of police performance measurement at both the departmental and individual levels.

2. To discuss the differences between input, output, and efficiency measurement.

3. To distinguish between general, macro, and specific agency performance measures.

4. To understand the differences between success and performance indicators.

5. To learn the differences between baseline and target measures.

6. To understand the basic principles of police performance appraisals.

Introduction

Performance measurement is a critical strategic management tool. Creating appropriate quantitative and qualitative performance measures enables law enforcement managers to determine the effectiveness and efficiency of their activities. Performance measurement evaluates organizational accomplishments and identifies areas where improvement may be needed or where organizational assets should be directed. It can also provide a link between public priorities and budgetary decisions and a means for communicating with elected officials and the public about police performance. Above all, it is a primary tool for establishing the police department's credibility.

Monitoring, gathering data, measuring, and evaluating organizational activities are critical to determining managerial success. A department's managers must develop a performance measurement system that is valid, reliable, and capable of letting them know how effective their operations are. Establishing appropriate quantitative and qualitative performance measures can assist law enforcement managers in meeting the demands of their external environment by linking the use of resources to specific outcomes. If there isn't any hard data to support their managerial decisions and strategies, police managers are placed in the position of being "just another individual with an unfounded opinion." Monitoring, measuring, and evaluating organizational activities are keys to preventing this.

Kouzes and Posner identify performance measurement as a crucial aspect of organizational leadership. It also recognizes that "What Gets Measured Gets Done" allows leaders to influence outcomes by providing the tools for measuring progress.

DOI: 10.4324/9781003459095-10

They stress that organizational goals must reflect the organization's values—doing the things that mean something, not just those that "count" (Kouzes & Posner, 2012).

Performance measurement is the process of collecting, analyzing, and/or reporting information regarding performance to determine the extent to which a police organization accomplishes what is expected. The reasons behind its use include (1) establishing the police capacity to accomplish an objective and (2) monitoring the extent to which a department or program is accomplishing an objective (Mastrofski, 2003, p. 464). This chapter reviews the measures and issues surrounding police performance at departmental and individual levels.

What Should Be Measured?

Establishing appropriate quantitative and qualitative performance measures can assist law enforcement managers in determining the effectiveness of their operational activities. If they are not gathering and measuring data to support their managerial initiatives and strategies, they are placing themselves in the position of not knowing what they have accomplished.

Traditionally, police performance measures have been based upon such categories as (a) numbers and types of arrests, (b) clearance rates, (c) ratios of police to civilian resident population, (d) citations/parking tickets issued, (e) reports taken, (f) property recovered, (g) bars checked. These areas are considered objective, concrete and provide for easy measurement. They are collected in the normal course of business by police departments and are recorded not so much for measurement as for documentation for later use (Klockars, 1999; Sparrow, 2015). They are typically used to determine what is accomplished, how efficiently resources are allocated, or the quality or effectiveness of the resources used.

Several police scholars and expert practitioners offered their thoughts on this subject in an influential monograph from the National Institute of Justice, *Measuring What Matters* (1999). Most often, these policing experts stressed the need to collect data on measures other than Index Crimes to reflect the total functions of policing better. For example, Kelling (1999, p. 29) recommended that the police collect data on disorder: "Fighting disorder, by solving the problems that cause it, is one of the best ways to fight serious crime, reduce fear, and give citizens what they actually want from the police force." He believes that the police should move away from an emphasis on the UCR Index Crimes toward arrest and police response reports on the crimes that most concern the daily lives of citizens—drugs, parking and traffic, disorderly groups, auto larceny, prostitution or gambling, burglary, and robbery.

Skogan (1999, p. 51) offers suggestions on assessments of the quality of police service and of citizen encounters with police: "People who were stopped by the police are asked if they were given reasons for being stopped; if they were questioned, searched or breath-tested; and if they were arrested, prosecuted, or otherwise sanctioned." Moore and Poethig (1999, p. 153) concluded that "the police are a more valuable asset when viewed from the vantage point of trying to strengthen urban life than they are when viewed from the narrower perspective of reducing crime through making arrests." Measures of police performance should consider the totality of police performance activity and its impact on community safety to judge their effectiveness. The police, daily, deal with things other than crime: managing disorder in public places, reducing fear, controlling traffic and crowds, and providing various emergency services. These are a few activities they engage in to keep communities safe.

A related problem is the difficulty in measuring when the police prevent crime—when they act as "sentinels" rather than apprehenders. Nagin, Solow, and Lum (2015) constructed a mathematical model to estimate the distribution of offender opportunities and decision-making on their chances to victimize and their risk of apprehension. When police are effective in the sentinel role, they deter crime from occurring in the first place, negating the need for arrest. It is impossible to measure deterred crimes. They remain a challenge to performance management (Nagin et al., 2015, p. 93).

Why Measure Performance?

Generally, law enforcement managers are responsible for the evaluation of the following functions (Oettmeier & Wycoff, 1996; Behn, 2003):

1. **Administration**: to help managers make decisions about promotion, demotion, reward, discipline, training needs, salary, job assignment, retention, and termination. These measurements provide a **control function** and answer the question: *How can I ensure my subordinates do the right thing?*
2. **Guidance and Counseling**: to help supervisors provide feedback to subordinates and assist them in career planning and preparation, and to **improve employee motivation**: *How can I motivate line staff, middle managers, non-profit and for-profit collaborators, stakeholders, and citizens to do the things necessary to improve performance?*
3. **Research**: to validate selection and screening tests and training evaluations and to assess the effectiveness of interventions designed to improve individual performances. The purpose here is **evaluation**: *How well is my agency performing?*
4. **Socialization**: to convey expectations to personnel about both the content and the style of their performance and reinforce other means of organizational communication about the mission and values of the department. **Celebration** is the desire: *What accomplishments are worthy of the important organizational ritual of celebrating success?*
5. **System improvement**: to identify organizational conditions that may impede improved performance and to solicit ideas for changing the conditions. Success at this point can lead to **promotion**: *Convincing political superiors, legislators, stakeholders, journalists, and citizens that the agency is doing a good job.*
6. **Documentation**: to record the types of problems and situations officers are addressing in their neighborhoods and the approaches they take to them. Such documentation provides data-based analysis of the kinds of resources and other managerial support needed to address problems. It also allows officers the opportunity to have their efforts recognized. **Improvement** is the aim: *What should we do differently to improve agency performance?*
7. **Strategy**: examining the effectiveness of a project or program. **Learning** is the goal: *To know why something is working or not.*

However, judging the performance of law enforcement operations is more than a technical matter of choosing appropriate measurement criteria and methodologies. It involves controversial decisions about what we should do (*Function*) and how we should do it (*Process*). For example, if we have a location, a "hot spot," that generates numerous incidents of drug sales, assaults, robberies, disorderly conduct, and quality-of-life violations, the initial question faced by the command staff is: How should we address this problem? A quick, immediate way is to use a concentrated strike involving many officers to sweep the area and make several arrests. This tactic could cause a temporary displacement of the offenders and several traditional performance statistics (arrests) for the department. However, if the customers remain, the dealers will return, and the problems in the area will resurface. An alternative strategy would be to form a problem-solving team of officers under the direction of a team manager. The team should be charged with identifying the factors contributing to the problem and suggesting several responses to address these factors that will result in a long-term solution for this problem.

Whatever strategy is selected should not be based on a knee-jerk response to pressure from the community. Instead, it should be based upon a clear assessment of the intelligence about the location, agreement among the command staff regarding the desired methods and outcomes, and identifying appropriate tactics to accomplish them.

Accurate performance measurement requires the use of indicators that are both valid and reliable. *Valid measures* correctly capture the concept under consideration. For example, does a drop in reported burglaries indicate that a Citizen's Crime Watch program is effective, or have citizens stopped reporting burglaries because they have lost faith in their police and feel nothing will be done? *Reliable measures* yield the same result upon repeated applications. For example, do police officers use a form to record traffic stop information and classify the same events similarly?

Valid and reliable evaluation of police organizational performance requires:

1.   Clearly defined outcomes (goals and objectives).
2.   Fixed command accountability for the achievement of these outcomes.
3.   Identification of appropriate measurement data that will tell us how successful we are in achieving the outcomes.
4.   Creation of a reporting system that will monitor strategy implementation and impact.
5.   Managerial oversight through implementation, follow-up, and assessment.

However, several problems must be overcome to implement such an information system. First, the criteria to determine agency effectiveness are seldom established. Traditional standards of response time, crime rates, and arrest rates continue to be offered as benchmarks with which the public should assess agency accomplishments. These are not "one-size-fits-all" performance measures and are only appropriate with specific, clearly specified tactical responses. Second, the quality of data is often sorely lacking. For example, police in many jurisdictions were given the task of recording and collecting data about traffic stops to address racial profiling. Here are two examples of how this process can go wrong. State troopers in New Jersey were accused of "ghosting"—stopping a Black motorist, recording the facts of the stop, and then recording the plate number of a passing car driven by a White person (Skolnick & Caplovitz, 2001, p. 418). Another racial profiling study observed that the police did not record about 25 percent of the stops they made even though they used mobile data terminals in their cars to record traffic stop data (Meehan & Ponder, 2002, p. 420). Even when the data is accurate, the third and most damaging problem is failing to use the data to guide operations.

Performance measurement involves the selection of indicators, their measurement, transparency, and the auditing of efficiency and effectiveness (Fleming & Scott, 2008, p. 322). It can also provide a means for communicating with elected officials and the public about police performance. Above all, it is the primary tool for establishing organizational credibility and professionalism. In Australia, it is linked to "managing for outcomes" and showing "value for money" in the measurement and evaluation of government outcomes (Fleming & Scott, 2008, p. 323). As organizational managers, police administrators are confronted with several fundamental questions.

- What works?
- What criteria do we use to measure the performance and impact of ourselves, or people and the programs we create?
- How can we demonstrate to elected officials and citizens that our people, programs, and services are effective and efficient?

Although new policing strategies are being tested in many departments, the success of these efforts must be measured to prove their effectiveness. One reason for this perception is the difficulties administrators have in determining what measures should be used to determine the success of their programs. If a program increases the quality of life in a neighborhood, then measuring response time and arrest rates will not accurately measure program effectiveness. For example, measuring the impact of police tactics designed to reduce residents' fear levels in a community defies the simple quantitative measurement systems now used by many departments.

Police managers are responsible for the evaluation of either some or all of the following actions:

1. Individual performance.
2. Unit performance.
3. Project or program performance.
4. Divisional performance.
5. Organizational performance.

However, accomplishment of these tasks is often difficult to achieve. Their achievement requires more than a technical matter of choosing appropriate measurement criteria and methodologies; it involves controversial decisions about what the department and its personnel should be doing and how they should do it. Fleming and Scott (2008) recommend measuring the "complexity of police work" through a combination of product and process measurement (using both quantitative and qualitative data) to obtain a solid and accurate picture of a police organization's achievements (Fleming & Scott, 2008, p. 323).

One standard and readily available measure typically used to assess police performance is the crime rate—statistics reported to the FBI and published yearly in the *Uniform Crime Reports*. However, the reporting and recording of a crime is subject to the following chain of events:

1. A crime event occurs.
2. The victim observes it or someone else (the police directly or a neighbor).
3. The police are notified of the offense.
4. The police decide if the event is a crime and how (and whether) it is recorded.
5. Often, this decision is reviewed (and can be dismissed) at another point in the police hierarchy.

6.   The police decide which of the FBI Uniform Crime Reporting categories is appropriate.
7.   The statistics are made public.

(Seidman & Couzens, 1974, p. 458)

In this fashion, the validity of crime rates is attributable to three primary sources: factors influencing the reporting of the crime to the police, recording practices of the police themselves, and subsequent problems in the official presentation and interpretation of the UCR statistics.

Crime rate figures are also subject to victims' reporting practices. For example, victims are unlikely to report a crime to the police when:

1.   The victim consents or agrees to the act (drug use, gambling, and prostitution).
2.   The victim believes that the crime is trivial.
3.   The victim does not wish to embarrass the offender (relative, friend, acquaintance, fellow employee).
4.   The victim is in an embarrassing situation (the married man on a business trip whom a prostitute robs).
5.   The victim believes that nothing will be done.
6.   The victim is unaware of the crime due to the skill of the offender.

(McClintock, 1977)

Thus, selective reporting by victims can influence the accuracy of crime rates.

Measurement Criteria

Three levels of measurement are available to managers (Bayley, 1996):

1.   **Macro measures** are direct outcome measures that focus on overall agency indicators. Examples include agency-wide *crime rates, cases cleared, victimization rates, cost of services, and sustained complaints about employee behavior.* Most of these are valid, traditional measures of police performance. However, Bayley suggests the following indicators can also tell us how successful a police department is in providing public safety:

     •   Real estate values.
     •   Public utilization of common space.
     •   Community commercial activity.

2.   **General measures** are broad indicators of effectiveness based on the subjective reflection of people's impressions of quality, accomplishments, service levels, and participation in police activities. Examples of these measures include:

     •   Citizen perception of community safety.
     •   Citizen fear levels.
     •   Percent of citizens assisting in problem-solving activities.
     •   Satisfaction with police activities.
     •   Perception of police integrity.

3. **Specific measures** are designed to evaluate individual and unit performance and efficiency. These measures should be developed at all levels of the organization; however, they are essential for operational units. These include performance goals and measurement indicators that supervisors should establish to evaluate the success of operational personnel. Examples of these measures include:

   - Targeted crime rates in a specific geographical area.
   - Numbers of identified and resolved incidents of social or physical disorder.
   - Percentage of problems identified and resolved in an area.
   - Number of community meetings attended.
   - Numbers of specific performance outcomes achieved by the officer or unit (arrests, citations, incidents, and/or calls for service reduced, etc.).

In addition, performance measures must reflect the mission of the department and the operational unit. The design and implementation of the evaluation of a strategy will depend upon the specific purpose it serves and the outcomes it is expected to achieve. These will differ according to the particular strategy and the type of measurement information the manager needs (Stephens, 1996). Measures should focus on service delivery as opposed to internal operations. They can be developed only after identifying the mission, strategy, and tactics. Measures must reinforce department priorities and quality of service delivery. They should include the quality of work accomplished and the resources devoted to completing certain activities.

Police performance measures should include the following elements:

1. **Success indicator**: This defines the attribute to be measured—a characteristic used to calculate an output or outcome.
2. **Performance indicator**: This describes what is to be measured (i.e., number of arrests or percentage of crimes solved by arrest).
3. **Baseline**: This determines the initial level of measurement against which targeted progress and success are compared. A baseline includes both a starting date and/or starting level or value, and an end date and/or end level or value.
4. **Target**: The part of a performance measure that establishes the desired level to be reached in a defined period, usually desired to be an improvement over the baseline.
(Shane, 2007, p. 32)

The establishment of such elements is crucial but can be difficult. For example, West (2003) notes that one of the most controversial components of research on racial profiling by police during traffic stops relates to the "baseline" or comparison group. Researchers have struggled with determining whether agencies are engaging in racial profiling when making traffic stops without some measure of what the world would look like in the absence of it. Baselines used in these studies have included (1) the racial distribution of the area as defined by census tract data, (2) the racial distribution of persons of driving age in the area, (3) the racial distribution of licensed drivers in the area, (4) the racial distribution of drivers driving on the roadways, as determined by stationary observation, (5) the racial distribution of speeders driving on the roadways, and (6) the racial distribution of drivers involved in accidents (West, 2003, pp. 64–65). All of these measures served as proxies for the population of drivers who could have been stopped, but they were all imperfect. Consider steps 1 through 3 above. Do they consider the possibility that drivers who do not reside in the area will use roadways not in their neighborhood? Or will drivers outside the city under observation not use these roadways? For such reasons, criminologists have focused on what happens after the stop (search, citation, arrest) and compared the percentage rates between African-American and White drivers (Higgins, Vito, & Grossi, 2012). These are examples of the problems that must be faced when developing performance measures.

Some proposed measures of police organizational performance measures are summarized in Table 10.1.

TABLE 10.1 Measures of Police Performance

Issue	Elements	Measures
Community Security	Measures of disorder: 1. The vulnerability of its citizens to various crimes of violence. 2. The risk of property loss through theft or vandalism existing in the community. 3. The probability of being a victim of an accident on the highways of the community. 4. The extent of activities defined to be illegal existing in the community.	• UCR crimes reported to police. • Calls for service to police. • Location of the crime (addresses, parks, schools, public transit). — Facilitates GIS analysis for "hot spots" of crime. • Victimization surveys. • Accident investigation reports. • Fear of crime via community surveys: — How do people assess their victimization risk? — What is their perceived threat of crime in their neighborhood? — What actions do citizens take in response to their fear of crime? • Data from hospital emergency rooms (trauma, stabbings, gunshot wounds). • Focusing on observable behavior: — graffiti — junk, trash, and litter — vacant and boarded-up buildings — abandoned vehicles — public drug use, drinking, and gambling — street-level prostitution — verbal harassment on the street
Efficiency and the quality of police service delivery	Police response time. Workload (self-initiated activity). Handling of major events. Response to civil disturbances.	• When the call is received. • When the police unit is dispatched. • When the police unit reports arrival at the scene. • Number of calls for service per sworn officer. • Number of police-initiated actions in the field (pedestrian and traffic) per sworn officer. — number of cars stopped. — parking and traffic tickets issued. — suspicious subjects checked. — buildings checked. — field interview reports completed. — warrants (both checked and issued). • Traffic control (disbursement traffic). How much crime occurred? • Complaints on how the police handled the event.

TABLE 10.1 (Continued)

Issue	Elements	Measures
	Arrests: Demonstration that something has been done about crime; exercising control over a particular problem with an eye toward the issue of Legitimacy.	• Arrest reports. • Clearance rate: number of crimes cleared by arrest. • Should also address the "quality" of the arrest (that it was conducted in a manner consistent with legal due process requirements and held up in court). —conviction rate. • Use of weapons. • Authorized wiretaps.
Citizen Contacts	Traffic and street-level stops: Establishing accountability— requiring the police to act within the limitations of the law and rules established by governmental authority. Public satisfaction with police service.	• Citizen observation of police operations: Reported, sustained, not sustained, exonerated, or unfounded. • Number and disposition of citizen complaints against police officers. • Observation of video recordings. • Community surveys and call-in reports. • Adequacy of coverage of calls for service. • Crime victim satisfaction with police handling of cases. • Results of use of force complaints.
Legitimacy	Customer satisfaction. Business community satisfaction.	• Citizen/police contact survey. • Retail business survey.
Organizational Environment Officer Misconduct	Employee job satisfaction and morale (including perception of agency leadership). Absenteeism. Number of disciplinary actions/sworn officer. Community perceptions of police abuse. Using force & authority fairly & effectively.	• Officer survey. • Mean number of sick and family leave time taken by sworn staff. • Self-assessment form. • Community survey.
Cost of Police Services	Dollar cost/custodial arrest. Dollar cost/call for service answered. The dollar cost of police department/resident.	• Self-assessment form.

Sources: Note 1 at the end of this chapter for source details for Table 10.1[1]

Several factors can increase the likelihood of success of performance measures. The first is buy-in by middle management and first-line supervisors. They will do much of the assessment of the measures and the data collection procedures necessary to conduct the analysis. Second, a consensus on measures' meaningfulness and measurability must be established. This factor depends upon the reliability and validity of the measures and requires input from all levels of the organization to ensure such a result. The benchmarks for performance must be appropriate and measure success rather than failure. The evaluation process should include adopting a problem-solving approach for resolving identified deficiencies that indicate the need for improvement rather than levying punishment. Last, performance information systems require technical support to provide timely reports and follow-up analyses.

Evidence-Based Practice (EBP)

In management, **evidence-based practice** (EBP) enhances decision-making by thinking critically about the best available evidence. In policing, this process is accomplished by (Barends, Rousseau, & Briner, 2014, p. 2):

- **Asking**: Translating a crime problem into an answerable question.
- **Acquiring**: Systematically searching for valid evidence on the crime problem.
- **Appraising**: Critically assessing the quality and validity of the research evidence about the crime problem.
- **Aggregating**: Weighing the evidence to address the crime problem.
- **Applying**: Incorporating the evidence into the decision-making process.
- **Assessing**: Evaluating the effectiveness of the crime problem response utilized.

Evidence-based practice aims to improve the effectiveness of crime prevention policies and programs.

Multiple sources of information must be consulted to obtain data for evidence-based practice. Specifically, the sources are (Barends, Rousseau, & Briner, 2014, p. 4):

- **The Scientific Literature**: Findings from empirical studies published in criminological and criminal justice journals, reports, and books.
- **The Organization**: Crime data of all types is regularly collected by your department.
- **Practitioners**: Information based upon their professional experience and judgment of practitioners.
- **Stakeholders**: Members of the internal and external elements of the department – employees and citizens.

All accumulated evidence from this process must be critically reviewed for relevance and accuracy. No one source has priority over the others.

Sherman (2015, p. 21) offers ten ideas on how to build an evidence-based police agency:

1. Creating an EBP Unit as a resource for the entire agency.
2. Offering a comprehensive EBP training program for all agency members that will keep them updated on recent research findings.
3. Sending selected "Power Few" employees for academic degrees so they can conduct their own research for the agency.
4. Creating a permanent Central Registry of projects undertaken by the agency, including evaluation reports on them.

5. Announce an open invitation for projects.
6. Establish a peer-review process to review EBP projects before internal approval, registration, and publication.
7. Retaining "embedded" Ph.D. criminologists in the department to assist the entire process.
8. Maintain a public EBP website to disseminate department-generated information.
9. Creating "evidence cops" in the EBPU to review selected police practices to see how well they reflect external and internal evidence.
10. Offering annual prizes for the named authors of the best EBP projects.

The proposed process can generate information to guide EBP with the goal of turning police officers into problem-solvers to prevent crime and neighborhood deterioration (Brown & Brudney, 2003; Sherman, 2020).

Martin and Mazerolle (2015) list six broad methods for police leaders to achieve reform based on evidence-based practice.

1. Address the paucity of policing research by implementing strategic plans to generate an evidence base to assess performance accurately.
2. Allocation of 10 percent of the agency budget to support regular evaluations of police practices.
3. Train the next generation of staff to understand the police evidence base and run their own policy-based evaluations of their operations.
4. Engage government leaders in resource allocation decisions based on the results of performance evaluations.
5. Mothball age-old police practices that no longer work or cause harm.
6. Foster a sophisticated public that demands evidence-based practice.

Police leaders must develop a sophisticated information system based on valid performance measures to guide decision-making and police operations.

Evaluating Strategy

Strategy evaluation is the systematic attempt to examine strategy process, implementation, and impact. Managers need this information to judge the operational performance of their strategic initiatives and change how day-to-day activities are conducted. Ideally, strategic evaluation should focus on the effectiveness and efficiency of the strategy. It seeks to determine the answer to the following questions:

1. Did the strategy impact the problems or conditions it addressed?
2. To what extent was that impact (percent decrease, increase)?
3. Was the process and service delivery consistent with strategy design specifications?
4. What is the cost-benefit analysis of expanded resources to strategy outcomes?
5. Were organizational resources appropriately used?
6. Were targeted populations or neighborhood groups reached?
7. How did the officers perform?

Operational planning should always be conducted with evaluation in mind. It should be clear that evaluation is centered on identifying and measuring what has occurred instead of what should have happened. Measurable objectives must be incorporated into the feedback system that tests strategy. An action plan including the following system elements will allow managers to avoid setting unrealistic or unattainable expectations. Outcomes and objectives should be realistically set to provide the organization with a way to assess progress. Baseline measures (what conditions existed before operations began) should be identified to make possible before-and-after comparison of performance indicators. Individual measures should always be linked to unit and strategy outcomes.

Typically, evaluating an anti-crime strategy considers the level of crime that is prevented or controlled following its implementation. The baseline measures compare the crime level after a specific period during which the strategy was applied with what existed before the strategy was adopted. Also, tactics often have several aims. Multiple measures are usually appropriate because crime problems are not isolated incidents. For example, an attempt to move against an open-air drug market may attempt to reduce citizen fear of crime, community disorder, or even traffic-related problems. Different outcome measures are required to capture these elements.

As a result, the strategy selected to eliminate the drug market may have several measurable outcomes, including elimination of the distribution center, reduction of ancillary criminal incidents, stabilization of the neighborhood, reduction of citizens' fear, and increased use of neighborhood space by ordinary citizens. Operational strategies are expected to have an impact. The amount of the effect should be projected, planned for, and measured. Managers must identify measurement criteria that will accurately inform them of their accomplishments, both positively and negatively. Efficiency and legality are also important evaluation strategy issues. The cost-benefit (efficiency) analysis of operational strategies is necessary to evaluate the best use of resources. An operational strategy may be an efficient use of resources or a terrible waste. A planned strategy evaluation that provides data on implementation, resource use, and associated costs (direct and indirect) should provide the information needed to determine cost-benefit promptly. Operational managers must also ensure that their strategy meets appropriate legal and ethical standards. The ends do not justify the means.

Monitoring operational systems involves identifying deficiencies in strategy implementation and unidentified consequences that prevent strategies from delivering what they were initially designed to do or what makes them work. The analysis of monitoring data addresses the actual strategy process to its design and outcomes. Key factors in evaluating an operational program's performance involve describing the activities undertaken in implementing the strategy (process outputs) and the specification of objectives in measurable terms (impacts/outcomes). Data for monitoring purposes can be collected from four sources:

- Direct observation.
- Official records.
- Operational statistics.
- Interviews of officers involved and program participants (community surveys).

Efficiency analysis provides a framework for relating program cost to results. Cost-benefit analysis directly compares program outcomes to process output costs in monetary terms. This analysis requires that program costs and benefits be known, quantified, and transformed into a standard measurement unit. It should be remembered that the true outcomes of programs include spillover effects, which should be in any cost-benefit analysis. Spillover effects are unanticipated outcomes or issues created by implementing the strategy, for example, the cost of the unexpected need for additional community outreach meetings during the initial stage of the strategy's implementation. A well-defined impact model is essential to both program design and evaluation. However, every review must be tailored to the implemented strategy.

Naturally, when measuring police operational performance, outcomes generate the most concern. Political and community representatives and policy-makers want to know: Is the department accomplishing what it said it would? Did crime go down, was disorder reduced, and are citizens satisfied? It should also be understood that the strategy used to accomplish the outcome would influence the results we obtain. Thus, the strategy implementation process is also essential. Did we select the right people for the task? Were they appropriately trained? Did first-line supervisors do their assigned tasks? Was it efficient, effective, legal, and ethical? We need to know what parts of the strategy worked and which did not. So, we can avoid mistakes. To answer these questions, law enforcement departments should:

1. Take maximum advantage of the data they routinely collect by analyzing the patterns and trends (intelligence) they contain.
2. Analyze and disseminate this intelligence to operational commanders who need it in a timely and understandable fashion.
3. Look for cost-effective ways to enhance their routine data collection and intelligence analysis.
4. Undertake special measurements when the cost is not prohibitive and the need is substantial enough to warrant the extra effort.
5. Use intelligence data to support operational decision-making.
6. Employ GIS systems.
7. Use volunteers, senior citizens, or college students enrolled in research methods classes in nearby colleges to conduct telephone surveys focused on citizens' fear of crime, satisfaction with the department, and other topics.
8. Set realistic outcomes and objectives to provide the organization with a way to assess progress accurately, cite success, identify effective strategies, and refocus resources accordingly.
9. Remember to establish appropriate baseline measures to make a possible before-and-after comparison of relevant factors.

The measurement of effectiveness is concerned with outcomes rather than outputs. **Input measures** address the resources used to provide a particular service, such as the number of hours spent patrolling a specific area—human, financial, and in-kind assets. **Output measures** consider the quantity of the service delivered: number of arrests, total dollars collected in seized assets, and number of cases resulting in conviction (Shane, 2007, p. 27). **Outcome measures** describe results achieved. They compare the actual results achieved to those desired. Thus, they are concerned with measuring the effectiveness of the process used to achieve the desired outcome. It is insufficient to know that a change occurred; managers need to determine whether the strategy and tactics caused the observed change. Have crime incidents been reduced?

Do community residents feel safer? Is there an improvement in officer performance after they attend a training program?

Measures of efficiency consider the amount of resources used to achieve an output, like hours spent per arrest and the cost thereof. Efficiency is tied to doing more work in less time and at less cost. The measure of *committed time* is concerned with an officer's time on a particular call for service (the combination of response and handling time). The ratio of these times to the available time for patrol (i.e., duty hours minus lunch breaks, report writing, and other non-patrol time) represents the proportion of the officer's day devoted solely to dispatched calls for service (Vega & Gilbert, 1997).

The above categories are crucial elements of performance measurement. It is not just the number of arrests made, but the condition of the community after the arrests were made, that should concern us. Has the safety and security of the citizens in that community increased measurably because of the arrests? Have we displaced the problem to another place requiring a new strategy and resources? Last, performance measurement should not be an end but a pathway to a more effective law enforcement department. It is used best when it is a feedback mechanism to help decision-makers focus on goals, strategies, and resource allocation to accomplish the department's mission and improve service to the community.

One key question is: Can the police have an impact on crime? The research presented in Chapter 13 reveals that the answer is a resounding "Yes!" Many experts consider crime control the "Bottom Line" of policing, but they also note it should not be the sole indicator of output (Stephens, 1996; Moore & Braga, 2004). Another reason to develop different performance measures is to monitor and evaluate how police officers use their discretionary authority. The aim is to provide data to judge the quality of service provided by police officers. For example, citizens stopped by the police can be asked if they were given the reasons for the stop, questioned, searched, or breath-tested, and if they were arrested, prosecuted, or otherwise sanctioned. Judging citizen satisfaction with the quality of the service received from their police department is an essential element of police performance measurement (Skogan, 1999, p. 51).

Some innovative methods have been developed to measure the effectiveness of new policing initiatives. For example, Ridgeway and MacDonald (2014) have established a technique to compare police performance between neighborhoods through internal benchmarking. Rather than compare police performance in one city to another outside entity, internal benchmarking makes comparisons within the city in question. In this example, comparisons regarding the average level of satisfaction with the police, perceptions of racial profiling behavior by the police, and personal experience with racial profiling were made in each Cincinnati neighborhood to a weighted comparison group of similarly situated residents within the city using propensity score matching. The results showed that some neighborhoods stood out in contrast to the comparison neighborhoods regarding their dissatisfaction with police performance. These differences can guide and focus policy interventions where they are needed. The internal benchmark provides a method to scrutinize police performance in problem neighborhoods with a more accurate gauge that matches the unique characteristics of a department's community. The results could improve the professionalism of the police, produce more effective and humane practices, and improve citizen's perceptions of the police (Ridgeway & MacDonald, 2014, p. 160).

Similarly, Coleman (2008) surveyed Canadian police agencies to determine if they had strategic performance measurement systems in place congruent with the goals of Community Policing. The survey results showed that departments focused on outputs instead of outcomes as performance measures. Measures like the time taken to respond to non-emergency calls for service, the crime rate, and caseload per officer based on reported crime (and failing to take unreported crime into account) remained key features of police performance. A strategic performance measurement system should develop measurable outcome goals based on its mission while establishing internal measurement systems to hold employees accountable and ensure they are working toward achieving organizational goals (Coleman, 2008, p. 310).

The International Association of Chiefs of Police developed a new method to consider benchmarks—the Law Enforcement Benchmarking and Performance Analytics Portal (www.theIACP.org/benchmarking). The Portal provides information on comparative reports on such issues as budgeting, calls for service, sworn strength, complaints, use of force statistics, and median salaries (Phillips, 2017, p. 80).

Shane (2007, p. 44) reminds us that the purpose of developing police performance measures is to establish accountability for improving service delivery. The performance of public agencies is typically focused on "the three Es" of (1) Economy, (2) Efficiency, and (3) Effectiveness (Boland & Fowler, 2000, pp. 419–420). Measures of economy typically focus upon the fiscal cost per output measured—cost per case, cost per service type, and numbers and categories of staff involved. Efficiency measures concern the ratio of inputs to outputs, such as the percentage of crimes solved by arrest. Indicators of effectiveness attempt to measure the extent to which outcomes meet a perceived societal need. Such measures are challenging to develop and measure and are tallied qualitatively. The typical result of the attempt to measure police performance is the use of quantitative indicators that recognize the intangibility of outcomes while still providing valuable data on how agencies are handling the obligation to meet their goals while making the best use of public resources—an exercise in accountability that impacts resource allocation (Boland & Fowler, 2000, pp. 420–421).

Individual Performance Appraisal

The evaluation of police performance is also conducted at the individual level. The typical goal of an employee performance appraisal is to hold individual employees accountable and ensure that their actions align with their organizational position and the achievement of department goals. To do this properly, police managers must (1) clarify what is expected of their employees, (2) examine officer activities and performance accomplishments and compare actual performance with what is expected, (3) act on findings to improve officer performance, and (4) communicate findings under agency and regulatory policy (Shane, 2007, p. 20).

There are three primary uses for the information provided by individual police performance appraisals: (1) to provide data for administrative decisions, (2) for research, and (3) for counseling personnel (Landy, 1977, p. 4). The law requires that measurement indicators used in personnel evaluations be based on job-related criteria. This legal standard requires that a manager's performance evaluation decisions must relate to the employee's responsibilities (*Griggs v. Duke Power Co., 401 U.S. 424, 1971*). Creating measurement indicators that serve as the basis for performance appraisals must be based on a job analysis. In *Segar v. Civiletti (25 FEP 142, 1981)*, the federal courts defined a job analysis as:

> systematic detailed study of the content of a job so that one can develop an accurate description of what the job entails, the conditions under which the job is performed, and the knowledge, skills and abilities needed to perform that job

Conducting a job analysis includes five basic steps: (1) a review of the department's sources of information (policy, rules, procedures) on job duties and responsibilities, (2) analyze department records that will provide information on work demand and output, (3) obtain information from persons familiar with the job—both employees and their supervisors, (4) observe on-the-job performance, and (5) identify a comprehensive list of job-related tasks (Walsh & Donovan, 1990). A properly conducted job analysis will provide the answers to four basic questions:

1.   What should be done?
2.   What is being done?
3.   Who is doing it?
4.   How is it being done?

One of the leading experts in police administration, O.W. Wilson (1963), noted that police performance appraisal is a difficult task but should be conducted every six months.

Managers should know that individual attributes can affect their employee performance appraisal process. Barrick and Mount (1991) conducted a meta-analysis of 117 studies that examined the relationship between the "Big Five" personality dimensions (extraversion, emotional stability, agreeableness, conscientiousness, and openness to experience) and job performance. Police departments were one group included in this study. The conscientiousness dimension was determined to predict job performance across all occupational categories. Traits associated with conscientiousness (a strong sense of purpose, obligation, plan-oriented, organized, hardworking, achievement-oriented, and persistence) were essential to job performance. These authors concluded that "it is difficult to conceive of a job in which the traits associated with conscientiousness would not contribute to job success" (Barrick & Mount, 1991, pp. 21–22).

Criticisms of the performance appraisal process center on complaints it is based on inaccurate measures of performance, sponsors dysfunctional employee conflict and competition, overemphasizes holding individual employees responsible for poor performance and undervalues the overall work process in the organization, fails to recognize group contributions, and is a "Theory X" control device by management (Roberts, 2003, p. 89). Unfortunately, dissatisfaction with police performance appraisal appears to be the norm. An investigation of the constructs underlying performance appraisals in a medium-sized police department found no consistent pattern in this evaluation method (Falkenberg, Gaines, & Cordner, 1991).

Walsh (1990) researched how performance evaluation was used in small and medium departments by surveying 150 sergeants attending continuing education courses in police supervision. He found that the majority of these departments borrowed their forms and processes from other departments—a threat to their validity.

Higher-level administrators typically imposed personnel appraisal systems without supervisors' input. The administrators stressed the use of performance evaluation in their departments' personnel process but provided no training to supervisors regarding their use. Last, the evaluation criteria used by these departments were not the result of a formal job analysis as required by court decisions.

In the United Kingdom, sergeants were surveyed about their experiences and attitudes toward introducing the New Public Management (NPM) system implemented nationwide in the 1990s (Butterfield, Edwards, & Woodall, 2004). These sergeants were operational officers who had supervisory responsibilities for the performance appraisal of constables under their charge. Under the NPM, their roles became more managerial and less operational. Their duties were expanded to include the responsibility to supervise crime investigation, budgets, work planning, deployment of teams, and handling complaints from the public. They were subject to more scrutiny and experienced an increase in paperwork, including performance appraisals of the constables. These sergeants complained that this role transformation increased their workload, with little training in performing their new duties. Performance appraisals were considered necessary exercises that relied upon invalid data and measures. There was an emphasis on the selective use of outputs (as recorded on computer systems) at the expense of demonstrated outcomes of the service delivered (Butterfield et al., 2004, p. 407). The sergeants believed that performance indicators were selected because they were easily measured but not strategically advantageous— with no relevance to the detection and prevention of crime (Butterfield et al., 2004, pp. 408–409)—"The impact of the performance measures was that sergeants undertook those aspects of their work that were measured, relegating other work to secondary importance" (Butterfield et al., 2004, p. 411). The sheer volume of work, the nature of the performance measures, and the computer system under the NPM constrained the operational autonomy of the sergeants. Pressures for accountability backfired and led to frustration and inflexibility caused by centralized control over the sergeants. This "Neo-Taylorism" contributed to a division between line supervisors and their superiors.

Negative attitudes toward police performance evaluation have also been documented in a Canadian study of constables and sergeants ($n = 393$) in 15 municipal agencies. Most officers reported that they were appraised based on their personal traits and had little or no input on their performance evaluation. Few officers stated that they received informal performance feedback from their supervisors regularly. One-third of the respondents showed that they did not receive formal face-to-face feedback following their performance appraisal. The study found that little training was provided to police supervisors to conduct performance appraisals (Coutts & Schneider, 2004, pp. 76–78).

Several recommendations have been made to improve individual police performance appraisals (Walsh, 1990, p. 103; Coutts & Schneider, 2004, pp. 68–69):

1. A job analysis of each position should be conducted, and job data should match the place under evaluation. To be legally sound, performance appraisals should be job-related and based on performance behaviors rather than traits.
2. These matched criteria should then be retained as rating factors, and the others should be discarded and replaced after a review by a committee of representatives from all ranks in the department.
3. Employees should have meaningful input to the evaluation process to enhance perceptions of fairness and legitimacy. Direct participation by employees in the

performance appraisal process has been determined to be a crucial attribute in its acceptance and effective implementation.

4.   When employees are confident that the appraisal process is fair and impartial, they are more likely to accept the evaluation results, even when adverse. In addition, the validity of the assessment increases when employees contribute to the construction of performance measures. They provide information that may not be readily perceived or available to the rater (Roberts, 2003, p. 90).

5.   This committee should then develop a set of behavioral descriptions of unacceptable and outstanding performance based on their matched criteria ratings.

6.   Reviews should be conducted annually, documented, filed, and reviewed with every employee: "Comprehensive and effective participation within the performance appraisal process consists of joint rater-ratee development of a) performance standards, b) the rating form, c) employee self-appraisal, and d) rater participation in the interview" (Roberts, 2003, p. 91).

7.   To foster growth and development, a continuous feedback process based on two-way communication must occur between superiors and subordinate employees. Employees should be able to expect accurate, meaningful, and timely feedback about their performance.

8.   Supervisors should assess important, job-related aspects of performance, inform employees about their shortcomings, and offer suggestions for improvement. The officer in question should be permitted to protest the results (if appropriate) and sign the final report. Performance appraisal should sponsor the achievement of individual and organizational goals. If the employees have confidence in the appraisal process, they will use the information to systematically assess their performance (Roberts, 2003, p. 91). With feedback on performance, employees can make adjustments and receive positive reinforcement when they prove effective, thus leading to greater job satisfaction and improved performance that the organization desires.

Employee performance evaluation has an importance beyond that of an administration system. It should be a significant factor in the manager's approach to their role. It is integral to the manager's efforts to motivate, change, and monitor employee performance. It also benefits employees by letting them know what they will be held accountable for and what their manager thinks of their work.

The chief (or highest-ranking officer in the department) should conduct an annual inspection of the system to identify instances of supervisory rating error, determine the reasons for mistakes, and take appropriate actions to correct them. Senior mentors should be provided to raters to evaluate the appraisal process continually, and employees should also be a part of this review (Roberts, 2003, p. 95). Administrators should continuously evaluate the purpose and content of the appraisal, provide rater training regarding its proper and valid use, and ensure that these elements are consistent with organizational objectives to accurately evaluate meaningful officer performance (Lilley & Hinduja, 2006, p. 35). The key is to develop measures that capture essential job duties and responsibilities by balancing process, outcome, and group and individual performance standards (Roberts, 2003, p. 91).

Employee participation in the performance appraisal process is crucial to its acceptance and effectiveness. They are more likely to accept the system when they understand the process, agree upon its value orientations, agree with management on the measures developed and used, are confident in their validity, and perceive that the raters are unbiased (Roberts, 2003, p. 93). If employees believe the process is tainted by favoritism toward an "in-group," trust will be completely extinguished. A meta-analysis of 27 studies that analyzed the appraisal process determined a strong and stable relationship between employee participation and satisfaction with the evaluation results (Cawley, Keeping, & Levy, 1998, p. 626). The authors listed five ways to involve employees in the appraisal process: (1) offer them the opportunity to voice their opinions, (2) allow them to influence the process thus, (3) allow them to perform self-appraisals, (4) allow them to take part in its development, and (5) allow them to participate in goal setting as a part of the process (Cawley et al., 1998, p. 628).

How a negative appraisal is delivered is a vital part of the appraisal process. Roberts (2003, p. 94) counsels managers to take a "courtroom perspective" and question their beliefs about worker motivation, ability, and poor performance, assuming that the employee is "innocent until proven guilty" through a thorough analysis of all available information that may provide explanatory, mitigating, or extenuating factors that influenced the employee's performance.

Cederblom and Pemerl (2002, p. 132) suggest that agencies move from performance appraisal to performance management:

> Performance management is an umbrella of all organizational components and activities affecting individual, work group, and agency performance. A performance management system would include performance appraisal, and other components such as strategic plans, manager accountability, pay, promotion, training/development, and discipline.

Rather than pursuing numbers, departments should also evaluate how officers identify and resolve community safety issues by soliciting input from citizens. Such a system would promote problem-solving, Community Policing, and CompStat approaches to increase the relevance of police performance appraisals. A survey of 600 U.S. police organizations revealed that job satisfaction in agencies engaged in Community Policing increased. Job satisfaction was heightened because engagement in Community Policing improved performance appraisal methods by providing more training for raters, greater evaluative emphasis on officer development, and using a broad range of performance criteria (Lilley & Hinduja, 2007, p. 147). Police administrators should think of new ways to drive police performance through improved recording, reporting, and communication with an eye toward "big picture" organizational objectives (Cederblom & Pemerl, 2002, p. 138). This strategic approach to performance management evaluates all an officer does and links it to achieving departmental goals and objectives.

However, the promise that Community Policing will lead to changes in police performance evaluation appears limited (Lilley & Hinduja, 2006). Lilley and Hinduja (2007) conducted a content analysis of 1,474 individual rating items on 150 officer evaluation instruments from police departments across the United States. They examined these evaluation instruments for five appraisal ratings: (1) stakeholder focus, (2) officer role emphasis, (3) level of service expectation, (4) employee traits encouraged, and (5) type of motivation used. In addition, they surveyed 197 agencies engaged in Community Policing from LEMAS data for 1997 and also randomly selected more traditional departments. The results revealed that, although supervisors from the Community Policing departments placed greater emphasis on problem-solving and neighborhood crime and disorder in their assessment of officer performance, the content analysis of the evaluation instruments demonstrated no substantial difference from more traditional agencies in terms of focus, role emphasis, service effort, or any other variable

(Lilley & Hinduja, 2007, pp. 147–148). Although the Community Policing departments emphasized a different service delivery and performance evaluation level, these changes were yet to be reflected in their performance appraisal instruments. Overall, rating items were directed toward avoiding citizen complaints and maintaining conformity (i.e., personal appearance assessment) as an essential officer trait. Innovation was not valued over the prevention of unwanted officer behaviors. Lilley and Hinduja (2007, p. 148) conclude from their analysis that the primary objective of performance appraisals was to reduce the workload of management in the police bureaucracy.

In addition, NYPD's CompStat process has also revealed issues with performance measurement. A survey of 1,770 NYPD retirees in three separate waves determined that performance pressures under the CompStat system led many to manipulate crime statistics for their benefit (Eterno, Verma, & Silverman, 2014). Statistical analysis of crime reporting data found that the pressure to downgrade crime statistics was highest during the Bloomberg–Kelly era of CompStat in the NYPD. There was similar pressure to obey legal/Constitutional rules (Eterno et al., 2014, p. 16). The data show that, over time, the initially productive CompStat system morphed into a culture of "gaming numbers" to keep the crime decreases going (Eterno et al., 2014, pp. 18–19). The authors suggest that transparency in police agencies can remedy the pressure to manipulate performance measures.

Conclusion

Police performance should be gauged at both the organizational and individual levels. Agencies must do a credible job of both by establishing valid and reliable measures for each type of appraisal. The thoughts and feelings of employees at all levels should be a significant part of both processes to ensure the accuracy and legitimacy of the measures. Police organizations do not have a readily definable bottom line, and the intensive focus on several crimes and arrests may lead police agencies to lose sight of other important goals like equity, fairness, and justice (Maguire & Uchida, 2000, p. 506). Qualitative and quantitative measures should be included in these appraisals. Leaders play a crucial role in the performance evaluation process and should consider how they use this information with an eye toward the followers' need for autonomy, competence, and relatedness (Masal & Vogel, 2016, p. 226)

The benefits of performance evaluation outweigh the drawbacks of the process. Employees wish to know where they stand, and evaluations offer transparency, allowing employees to understand how their performance is viewed in the organization. They provide a regular method to recognize and reward top performance. The information helps to develop employees by assessing their strengths and weaknesses and building an organizational culture that promotes improvement and growth (Goler, Gale, & Grant, 2016). Valid performance measures should serve as a basis for promotion and rewards (Tengpongsthorn, 2017, p. 43). A survey of 308 U.S. police departments found that performance management systems effectively reduce crime (Pasha, 2017).

Measurement is the first step that leads to control and, eventually, to improvement. Studies have found that "When performance is measured, it improves. When performance is measured and compared, it improves further. When performance is measured, compared, and appropriately recognized and rewarded, it improves dramatically more" (Creech, 1995, p. 473). Performance measurement is not just about numbers. When assessing feelings about public safety, counting incidents of crime, numbers of arrests, victims of violent crime, or drug sales in a public park, numbers are not the end of the process. The bottom line begins a continuing process of problem-solving, evaluation, managerial oversight, and constant improvement. It is important to remember that performance measurement is not a one-time event but a continual improvement process.

KEY TERMS

Baseline	Macro measures	Specific measures
Evidence-based practice (EBP)	Measures of efficiency	Success indicator
General measures	Outcome measures	Target
Input measures	Output measures	
	Performance indicator	

Note

1. Alpert, G.P., & Moore, M.H. (1993). Measuring police performance in the new paradigm of policing. *Performance measures for the criminal justice system* (p. 109). Washington, DC: U.S. Department of Justice; p. 111; Bayley, D.H. (1996). Measuring overall effectiveness or, "Police-force show and tell." In L.T. Hoover (ed.), *Quantifying quality in policing* (p. 46). Washington, DC: Police Executive Research Forum; Cordner, G. (2020). *Evidence-based policing in 45 small bytes.* Washington, DC: National Institute of Justice; Davis, R.C., Ortiz, C.W., Euler, S., & Kuykendall, L. (2015). Revisiting "Measuring What Matters": Developing a suite of standardized performance measures for policing. *Police Quarterly*, 18(4) (pp. 489–492); Mastrofski, S.D. (1996). Measuring police performance in public encounters. In L.T. Hoover (ed.), *Quantifying quality in policing* (pp. 223–224). Washington, DC: Police Executive Research Forum; Moore, M.H., & Braga, A. (2004). *The "bottom line" of policing: What citizens should value (and measure!)* In *Police performance* (pp. 79–86). Washington, DC: Police Executive Research Forum; Ostrom, E. (1973). On the meaning and measuring of output and efficiency in the provision of urban police services. *Journal of Criminal Justice*, 98; Skogan, W.G. (1999). Measuring what matters: Crime, disorder, and fear. In R.H. Langworthy (Ed.), *Measuring what matters: Proceedings from the policing research institute meetings* (pp. 42–43). Washington, DC: National Institute of Justice and the Office of Community Oriented Policing Services, 1999; Stephens, D.W. (1996). Community problem-oriented policing: Measuring impacts. In L.T. Hoover (ed.), *Quantifying quality in policing* (pp. 103–108). Washington, DC: Police Executive Research Forum.

References

Alpert, G.P., & Moore, M.H. (1993). Measuring police performance in the new paradigm of policing. *Performance measures for the criminal justice system* (p. 109). Washington, DC: U.S. Department of Justice.

Barends, E., Rousseau, D., & Briner, R. (2014). *Evidence-based management: The basic principles*. Amsterdam, NL: Center for Evidence-Based Management.

Barrick, M.R., & Mount, M.K. (1991). The big five personality dimensions and job performance: A meta-analysis. *Personnel Psychology, 44*(1), 1–26.

Bayley, D.H. (1996). Measuring overall effectiveness or police force "show and tell". In L.T. Hoover (Ed.), *Quantifying quality in policing* (pp. 37–54). Washington, DC: Police Executive Research Forum.

Behn, R.D. (2003, September/October). Why measure performance? Different purposes require different measures. *Public Administration Review, 63*(5), 586–606.

Boland, T., & Fowler, A. (2000). A systems perspective on performance in public sector organizations. *International Journal of Public Sector Management, 13*(5), 417–446.

Brown, M., & Brudney, J. (2003). Learning organizations in the public sector? A study of police agencies employing information and technology to advance knowledge. *Public Administration Review, 63*(1), 30–43.

Butterfield, R., Edwards, C., & Woodall, J. (2004). The new public management and the UK police service. *Public Management Review, 6*(3), 395–415.

Cawley, B.D., Keeping, L.M., & Levy, P.E. (1998). Participation in the performance appraisal process and employee reactions: A meta-analytic review of field investigations. *Journal of Applied Psychology, 83*(4), 615–633.

Cederblom, D., & Pemerl, D.E. (2002). From performance appraisal to performance management: One agency's experience. *Public Personnel Management, 31*(2), 131–140.

Coleman, T.G. (2008). Managing strategic knowledge in policing: Do police leaders have sufficient knowledge about organisational performance to make informed strategic decisions? *Police Practice & Research, 9*(4), 307–322.

Cordner, G. (2020). *Evidence-based policing in 45 small bytes*. Washington, DC: National Institute of Justice.

Coutts, L.M., & Schneider, F.W. (2004). *Police officer performance appraisals: How good are they? Policing, 27*(1), 67–81.

Creech, R. (1995). Employee motivation. *Management Quarterly, 36*(2), 33–40.

Davis, R.C., Ortiz, C.W., Euler, S., & Kuykendall, L. (2015). Revisiting "Measuring What Matters": Developing a suite of standardized performance measures for policing. *Police Quarterly, 18*(4), 489–492.

Eterno, J.A., Verma, A., & Silverman, E.B. (2014). Police manipulations of crime reporting: Insiders' revelations. *Justice Quarterly, 33*(5), 1–25.

Falkenberg, S., Gaines, L., & Cordner, G. (1991). An examination of the constructs underlying police performance appraisals. *Journal of Criminal Justice, 19*(4), 351–360.

Fleming, J., & Scott, A. (2008). Performance measurement in Australian police organizations. *Policing: A Journal of Policy and Practice, 2*(3), 322–330.

Goler, L., Gale, J., & Grant, A. (2016, November). Let's not kill performance evaluations yet. *Harvard Business Review*, 90–94.

Higgins, G.E., Vito, G.F., & Grossi, E.L. (2012). The impact of race on the police decision to search after a traffic stop: A focal concerns theory perspective. *Journal of Contemporary Criminal Justice, 28*(2), 166–183.

Kelling, G. (1999). Measuring what matters: A new way of thinking about crime and public order. In R.H. Langworthy (Ed.), *Measuring what matters: Proceedings from the policing research institute meetings* (pp. 27–36). Washington, DC: National Institute of Justice & the Office of Community Policing Services.

Klockars, C.B. (1999). Some really cheap ways of measuring what really matters. In R. Langworthy (Ed.), *Measuring what matters: Proceedings from the policing research institute meetings* (pp. 195–214). Washington, DC: U.S. Department of Justice.

Kouzes, J., & Posner, B. (2012). *The leadership challenge.* San Francisco, CA: Jossey-Bass.

Landy, F.J. (1977). *Performance appraisal in police departments.* Washington, DC: The Police Foundation.

Lilley, D., & Hinduja, S. (2006). Officer evaluation in the community policing context. *Policing, 29*(1), 19–37.

Lilley, D., & Hinduja, S. (2007). Police officer performance appraisal and overall satisfaction. *Journal of Criminal Justice, 35*, 137–150.

McClintock, F.H. (1977). The dark figure of crime. In L. Radzinowicz, & M.E. Wolfgang (Eds.), *Crime and justice. Vol. 1, the criminal in society* (pp. 126–139). New York, NY: Basic Books.

Maguire, E.R., & Uchida, C.D. (2000). Measurement and explanation in the comparative of American police organizations. *Criminal Justice, 4*, 491–557.

Martin, P., & Mazerolle, L. (2015). Police leadership in fostering evidence-based agency reform. *Policing, 10*(1), 34–43.

Masal, D., & Vogel, R. (2016). Leadership, the use of performance indicators, and job satisfaction: Evidence from police services. *International Public Management Journal, 19*(2), 208–234.

Mastrofski, S.D. (1996). Measuring police performance in public encounters. In L.T. Hoover (Ed.), *Quantifying quality in policing* (pp. 223–224). Washington, DC: Police Executive Research Forum.

Mastrofski, S. (2003). Personnel and agency performance appraisal. In W. Geller (Ed.), *Local government police management* (pp. 447–486). Washington, DC: International City Management Association.

Meehan, A.J., & Ponder, M.C. (2002). Race and place: The ecology of racial profiling African American motorists. *Justice Quarterly, 19*(3), 399–430.

Moore, M.H., & Braga, A.A. (2004, Winter/Spring). Police performance measurement: A normative framework. *Criminal Justice Ethics*, 3–19.

Moore, M.H., & Poethig, M. (1999). The Police as an agency of municipal government: Implications for measuring police effectiveness. In R.H. Langworthy (Ed.), *Measuring what matters: Proceedings from the policing research institute meetings* (pp. 151–168). Washington, DC: National Institute of Justice & Office of Community Policing Services.

Nagin, D.S., Solow, R.M., & Lum, C. (2015). Deterrence, criminal opportunities, and police. *Criminology, 53*(1), 74–100.

Oettmeier, T.N., & Wycoff, M.A. (1996). Police performance in the nineties: Practitioner perspectives. In G.W. Cordner, & D.J. Kenney (Eds.), *Managing police organizations* (pp. 131–156). Cincinnati, OH: Anderson.

Ostrom, E. (1973). On the meaning and measuring of output and efficiency in the provision of urban police services. *Journal of Criminal Justice, 1*(2), 93–111.

Pasha, O. (2017). Can performance measurement best practices help to reduce crime? *Public Administration Review, 78*(2), 217–277.

Phillips, T. (2017, July). IACP working for you: Benchmarking and performance analytics: Your new tool for data-driven decision making. *The Police Chief*, 78–80.

Ridgeway, G., & MacDonald, J.M. (2014). A method for internal benchmarking of criminal justice performance. *Crime & Delinquency, 60*(1), 145–162.

Roberts, G.E. (2003). Employee performance appraisal system participation: A technique that works. *Public Personnel Management, 32*(1), 89–98.

Seidman, D., & Couzens, M. (1974). Getting the crime rate down: Political pressure and crime reporting. *Law and Society Review, 8*, 456–493.

Shane, J.M. (2007). *What every police executive should know: Using data to measure police performance*. Flushing, NY: Looseleaf Law Publishing.

Sherman, L. (2015). A tipping point for "totally evidenced policing": Ten ideas for building an evidence-based police agency. *International Criminal Justice Reviews, 25*(1), 11–29.

Sherman, L. (2020). Goldilocks and the three "Ts": Targeting, testing, and tracking for 'just right' democratic policing. *Criminology & Public Policy, 21*, 175–196.

Skogan, W. (1999). Measuring what matters: Crime, disorder and fear. In R.H. Langworthy (Ed.), *Measuring what matters: Proceedings from the policing research institute meetings* (pp. 37–54). Washington, DC: National Institute of Justice & Office of Community Policing Services.

Sparrow, M.K. (2015). Measuring performance in a modern police organization. *New Perspectives in Policing Bulletin*. Washington, DC: US Department of Justice, National Institute of Justice.

Stephens, D.W. (1996). Community problem-oriented policing: Measuring impacts. In L.T. Hoover (Ed.), *Quantifying quality in policing* (pp. 95–129). Washington, DC: Police Executive Research Forum.

Tengpongsthorn, W. (2017). Factors affecting the effectiveness of police performance in metropolitan police bureau. *Kasetsart Journal of Social Sciences, 38*, 39–44.

Vega, A., & Gilbert, M.J. (1997). Longer days, shorter weeks: Compressed work weeks in policing. *Public Personnel Management, 26*(3), 391–402.

Walsh, W.F. (1990). Performance appraisal in small and medium police departments. *American Journal of Police, 9*, 93–109.

Walsh, W.F., & Donovan, E. (1990). *Supervision of police personnel: A performance-based approach*. Dubuque, IA: Kendall Hunt.

West, A.D. (2003). Chicken little, three blind men and an elephant, and "racial profiling": A commentary on the collection, analysis, and interpretation of traffic stop data. *Journal of Forensic Psychology Practice, 3*(2), 63–77.

Wilson, O.W. (1963). *Police administration*. New York, NY: McGraw-Hill.

Cases

Griggs v. Duke Power Co., 401 U.S. 424, 1971.

Segar v. Civiletti, 25 FEP 142, 1981.

11 Maintaining Integrity and Professional Standards

Learning Objectives

1.	Describe police deviance, misconduct, and corruption.
2.	Identify the dimensions of police corruption.
3.	Describe the ways police departments can control officer deviance.
4.	Identify the characteristics of the Internal Affairs process.
5.	Describe the police inspection process.
6.	Describe police early warning systems.
7.	Describe the use of discipline to control deviance.
8.	Examine how consent decrees operate.

Introduction

This chapter discusses the maintenance of organizational integrity and **professional standards** in policing. Its objective is to provide an understanding of police **misconduct** and corruption, its causes, and organizational strategies for its prevention. Policing in a democracy requires high levels of integrity. Police officers are entrusted with powers and responsibilities that set them apart from their fellow citizens. When the police are corrupt and operate without integrity, their actions erode public confidence in the democratic principles they are sworn to protect.

Police **deviance** is a recurring occupational hazard. Police officers and their organizations throughout history have engaged in illegal and unethical activity (Reppetto, 1978; Monkkonen, 1981; Whalen & Whalen, 2014). There have been persistent incidences of corruption, misconduct, and violation of professional standards of conduct and the law by all ranks in policing. Instances of organized police corruption have been found in Boston, Chicago, New York, Detroit, Los Angeles, Miami, and Philadelphia (Norwicki & Punch, 2003). Traditionally, police deviancy has been viewed as a big city problem, but misconduct and corruption are potential problems for all departments, regardless of their size.

Throughout the history of policing, officers have been found to have engaged in various corrupt activities that include bribe-taking, extortion, protection of gambling, suppression of evidence, excessive use of force, tampering with evidence, perjury, and accepting graft. Receiving free meals, tickets, tips, and discounts is accepted in many departments but considered misconduct in others. Deviant activities will

DOI: 10.4324/9781003459095-11

thrive in departments where administrators and managers are negligent in preventing and detecting wrongdoing by subordinates. For example, the Los Angeles Police Department's investigation into corruption in its Rampart Area Division found that inadequate discipline, lax supervision, and a general culture of acceptance of mediocre performance created a climate where corruption flourished. This climate resulted from a lack of commitment, laziness, excessive tolerance, and the failure of the division's managers to hold officers responsible and accountable (Parks, 2000). When misconduct and corruption exist in a department they represent a failure of leadership, command accountability, policy, and discipline.

After extensive research into police corruption, Klockars (1999) concluded that policing is an occupation ripe with opportunities for misconduct of many types. Inappropriate and illegal behaviors exist in policing because it is a highly discretionary, coercive activity that routinely takes place in private settings, out of the sight of supervisors and witnesses. Policing involves the exercise of authority over citizens and thus requires a high level of ethics and integrity to be perceived as legitimate in the eyes of the public. Close contact with citizens, the monitoring and control of vice activities, and the discretionary power exercised by officers make policing a "morally dangerous occupation" (Barker, 2006). It is because police officers are charged with such essential responsibilities and power that their behavior must be monitored and controlled. A police agency noted for its integrity and transparency will have an occupational culture that supports the discipline of officers who violate the law and does not tolerate those who abuse the rights and privileges of their office (Klockars, Ivkovic, & Haberfeld, 2006).

Properly utilizing police power and discretion requires a strong sense of ethical awareness and adherence to norms of professional conduct. Integrity is more than just officers following the department's rules. It entails reflective, self-prescribed, and self-governing discretionary decisions involving ethical standards of conduct and individual rights (O'Keefe, 2004). **Integrity** is the normative inclination among police to resist temptations to abuse the rights and privileges of their occupation (Klockars et al., 2006). To a large degree, the public's image of the police is determined by the department's maintenance of standards of integrity and its actions in responding to allegations of corruption, violations of professional standards, and serious misconduct by the agency or its employees (CALEA, 2006). Public trust is maintained when the police perform their duties with fairness, equity, and integrity.

Democratic policing is citizen-focused policing that combines crime control and crime prevention with a welfare and service role. It fulfills the institutional responsibilities of enforcing law and ensuring public social order while following four fundamental principles (Bayley, 2001):

Police must be accountable to the law rather than to the government. The rule of law must govern police actions in a democracy.

Police must give top operational priority to servicing the needs of individual citizens and private groups. The most dramatic contribution police can make in a democracy is to become responsive to the needs of individual citizens instead of primarily serving the government's interest.

Police must protect human rights, especially those required for unfettered political activity, which is the hallmark of democracy. Democracy requires not only that the police be constrained by law but also that they make a special effort to safeguard activities essential to exercising democracy.

Police should be transparent in their activities. Police activity must be open to observation and regularly reported to outsiders.

These principles hold that the police should be accountable to the communities policed, the taxpayers who pay the bills, and the legal order governing their authority. Police organizations should not be closed, insular, or cut off from citizens and the communities from which their power derives. Sir Robert Peel noted that the ability of the police to perform their task depends on public approval of their existence, actions, and behavior and on the ability of the police to secure and maintain public respect (Lee, 1901).

Public confidence in the police depends on police officers demonstrating the highest levels of personal and professional standards of behavior. Each department employee's performance and conduct should reflect the goal of honorably and lawfully serving and protecting the public. Strategically, police administrators and managers must see themselves as part of an organizational system whose ultimate goal is to create an environment where each officer is challenged to do their best legally and ethically (Murphy & Caplan, 1991). The integrity of a police department depends on the personal integrity and discipline of each of its employees. Police administrators and managers are responsible for ensuring that they and their employees adhere to the law and a code of professional values, standards, and behavior. **Integrity** is the most essential characteristic and strength of a police department and its employees. In the eyes of the public it is the foundation of police legitimacy.

Defining Police Deviance, Misconduct, and Corruption

To understand and manage police deviance, it is essential to establish what it entails and who it involves. **Police deviance** includes activities inconsistent with expected norms, values, or ethics from both a societal and police perspective. **Police misconduct** violates accepted standards, departmental policies, and procedures (e.g., drinking alcohol on duty, not responding to calls for service, sleeping on duty, filing false reports). It is classified as follows:

Malfeasance is the performance of a prohibited, unjustified, harmful act or activity that violates the public trust (e.g., seeking a gratuity or using police resources for personal benefit).

Misfeasance is the wrongful performance of an ordinarily lawful duty or authority (e.g., conducting improper searches, selective enforcement, verbally abusing a citizen).

Nonfeasance is the failure to perform a duty when it is required (e.g., failure to file reports, improper stop and frisk, security breach).

Corruption involves an officer's misuse of police authority to do or not do something to derive personal gain for the officer or others (Bayley & Perito, 2011). Roebuck and Barker (1974) defined police corruption as any form of deviant, dishonest, improper, unethical, or criminal behavior by a police officer. It typically involves an officer taking bribes (Norwicki & Punch, 2003). Kleinig (1996, p. 166) suggests, "Police officers act corruptly when, in exercising or failing to exercise their authority, they act with the primary intention of furthering private or departmental/divisional advantage." Skogan and Meares (2004) propose that **types of corruption** can be understood according to their intention. Examples include abuse of authority, physical abuse (e.g., police brutality and excessive force), psychological abuse (most often in the context of police interrogations), and legal abuse (generally in the form of perjury to achieve an organizational goal or to protect corrupt practices). Kappeler, Sluder, and Alpert (1998) identify **police crime** as a separate category of corruption that occurs when the officer's behavior violates existing criminal statutes. Courtemanche (2011) warns that misconduct gets police officers fired; however, corruption results in the firing of police chiefs.

Corruption may be carried out for "personal gain" and organizational gain. The latter is known as **"noble cause"** corruption because it involves using inappropriate or illegal means to obtain legitimate ends, such as committing illegal searches to achieve an arrest and lying on the witness stand to establish probable cause for an arrest. Klockars (1980) labeled these noble cause activities as the "Dirty Harry Problem." The critical element in this form of corruption involves the misuse of official authority. The officer or officers involved believe that the good consequences (i.e., criminal convictions, removal of bad people from the community, suppression of drug sales) justify their inappropriate or illegal behavior.

Corruption can be an activity in which both an individual and an organization engage. For example, some police administrators foster a culture that tolerates excessive force, commonly known as "street justice," by their officers to maintain public order and respect for authority (Skolnick & Fyfe, 1993). In these instances, the desire to solve and control crime and teach bad guys a lesson may sometimes result in the officer violating a citizen's constitutional rights by making an illegal arrest, conducting overly broad searches, coercing confessions, or using excessive force as a form of retribution. Some police managers tend to avoid disciplining officers in these situations, especially when felony arrests and cases are solved due to these practices. However, methods of this type have resulted in the city of Chicago spending nearly $100 million on settlements and legal fees relating to a police commander's use of a torture ring during the 1970s to the 1990s that used electrical shock, burning, and mock executions to elicit confessions from suspects (USA Today, 2015).

Dimensions of Police Corruption

Corruption has been the target of numerous efforts to create typologies. Newburn (1999) synthesized a typology of police corruption based on the work of Roebuck and Barker (1974) and Punch (1985).

> In the corruption of authority, an officer receives some material gain due to their position without violating the law *per se* (e.g., free drinks, meals, services).
> "Kickbacks" are Receipts of goods, services, or money for referring business (e.g., recommendation of a lawyer to arrestees).
> Opportunistic theft: Stealing from arrestees, traffic accident victims, crime victims, and the bodies or property of dead citizens.
> Shakedowns: Acceptance of a bribe for not following through on a criminal violation, that is, not making an arrest, filing a **complaint**, or impounding property.
> Protection of illegal acts: Police protection of those engaged in illegal activities (e.g., prostitution, drugs, pornography) enabling the activity to continue operating.
> The fix: Undermining criminal investigations or proceedings (e.g., giving inaccurate or false testimony).
> Direct criminal activities: A police officer commits an actual crime violating departmental and criminal norms (e.g., committing a burglary on duty).

Internal payoffs: Entitlements available to police officers (holidays, shifts, allocations, days off, promotion) are bought, bartered, and sold.

"Flaking" or "padding": Planting of or adding to evidence (increasing the weight of a narcotics seizure from a misdemeanor to a felony level).

The Knapp Commission's (1972) investigation of the New York City Police Department identified two types of corrupt officers, "grass eaters" and "meat eaters." **Grass eaters** engaged in opportunistic corruption. They accepted bribes and gratuities that were offered to them but did not actively seek these out. **Meat eaters** sought gratuities and bribes proactively. They would attempt to obtain assignments in enforcement units that provided many opportunities for illegal payoffs, such as those that enforced gambling, prostitution, and narcotics laws.

Kane and White (2009, p. 745) developed a classification scheme of police misconduct based on a study of 1,543 New York City police officers who were involuntarily separated from the NYPD for career-ending activity from 1975 to 1996. They classified police misconduct into eight categories:

1. *Profit-motivated crimes*: All offenses, other than drug trafficking and whether on or off duty, in which the end or apparent goal of officers' wrongdoing was a profit.
2. *Off-duty crimes against persons*: All assaultive behavior, except for profit-motivated robberies, by off-duty officers.
3. *Off-duty public order crimes*: All offenses, other than drug trafficking or possession, against public order, including driving while intoxicated and disorderly conduct.
4. *Drugs*: Possession and sale of drugs and related conspiracies, as well as failing or refusing to submit to departmental drug tests.
5. *On-duty abuse*: All offenses by officers that involved the use of excessive force, psychological abuse, or discrimination based on citizens' membership in a class (i.e., gender, race, ethnicity, or sexual preference).
6. *Obstruction of justice*: Conspiracy, perjury, official misconduct, and all offenses in which the apparent goal was obstruction or subversion of judicial proceedings.
7. *Administrative/failure to perform*: Failure to abide by departmental regulations concerning attendance, performance, obedience, reporting, and other conduct not included in other offense types.
8. *Conduct-related probationary failures*: All misconduct-related terminations of probationary officers in which misconduct in types 1 to 7 was not specified, excluding simple failure.

Sherman (1974) took an organizational approach and classified police departments according to the level of pervasiveness of their corruption. **Type I** departments are characterized by small numbers of individual officers and groups of officers who engage in unorganized corruption. He identified these officers as rotten apples and rotten pockets. **Type II** departments contain pervasive, unorganized corruption in which most police officers are corrupt. Still, they have a little relationship in that no informal organization engages in corruption. **Type III** departments have pervasive organized corruption in which a hierarchical and authoritarian system exists to control corrupt activity involving individuals from not only within the department but also political figures.

Fyfe, Greene, Walsh, Wilson, and McLaren (1997, p. 461) suggest a series of questions to identify whether a department's corruption indicates individual employees (grass eaters) or a deeper systematic Type III organizational problem.

1. How many officers are involved in the corrupt activity?
2. How high up the chain of command does the corruption extend?
3. How many non-participating officers, community members, or other officials knew about the corrupt activity?
4. Did any non-participating persons who knew of this activity report it? If so, how long did it take, and under what circumstances did it occur?
5. Have previous attempts to report the misconduct gone unheeded?
6. Is corruption associated with an activity that visibly provides illegal goods or services for a large clientele?
7. Is the corruption associated with enforcing laws or administrative ordinances that are routinely ignored and have no support in the community?
8. Is the corruption associated with a law enforcement activity about which the agency has not formulated a clear policy?
9. Is the corruption consistent with some partisan end?

Controlling Deviance

The police chief executive and management team are responsible for their organization's integrity and controlling deviant employee behavior. Deviance, corruption, and misconduct undermine the integrity of the police officer and the department in the minds of the citizens they have sworn to protect. All too frequently, citizens' confidence in the police has been damaged by repeated acts of deviant police behavior reported in the media. Incidents of excessive use of deadly force, brutality, and corruption around the country have become daily news items, all of which contribute to the erosion of public confidence in their police. The broad range of behaviors identified as deviant or corrupt suggests that, when investigating and attempting to prevent these activities, it is essential to employ a targeted yet complex approach. This approach must focus not only on the most frequently occurring incidents of deviance but, more importantly, seek to control the multiple factors that combine to produce corrupt behavior and a culture of deviance in the department (Porter & Warrender, 2009).

Controlling employee deviance requires constant attention, data collection, and analysis, confronting the reality of practice, and holding all employees accountable. It also necessitates the development of a long-term, multifaceted strategy that includes speaking out, setting clear standards and policy, holding those in authority accountable, improving the use of discretion, promoting integrity through training, enlisting outside help, and tackling corruption and deviance robustly and proactively (Norwicki & Punch, 2003, p. 333).

Three major categories of standards define police behavior: ethical, organizational, and legal. **Ethical standards** are principles of appropriate conduct. Ethical behavior is an expression of these principles. For example, Northumbria Police U.K. (2015) states on its website that the department takes pride in all that they do, putting the citizens first and applying the principles of integrity and high-quality service in their six ethical principles. These principles are defined as:

Attentive—by listening to communities.
Responsive—by responding to the needs of the communities.

Reliable—by not letting people down.
Skilled—by having staff with the right tools to do the job.
Polite—to the public.
Fair—always in carrying out their duties.

Organizational standards can be formal and informal; they are derived from the department's policy, procedures, rules, and regulations (formal) and one's peers' (informal) expectations. The law officers represent **legal standards** sworn to uphold by due process, establishing the means officers may use to achieve good ends (Roberg, Novak, Cordner, & Smith, 2012, p. 291).

In 1979, the Commission on Accreditation for Law Enforcement Agencies (CALEA) was created through the joint efforts of the International Association of Chiefs of Police, the National Organization of Black Law Enforcement Executives, the National Sheriffs Association, and the Police Executive Research Forum to establish a body of professional standards for police agencies. CALEA developed an accreditation process based on these standards to allow law enforcement agencies to voluntarily demonstrate that they meet an established set of professional standards. **CALEA's** *Standards for Law Enforcement Agencies* and its Accreditation Programs have evolved as the accepted set of standards by which a police department can demonstrate commitment to professional excellence in law enforcement. The standards upon which the Law Enforcement Accreditation Program is based are acknowledged nationally as benchmarks for evaluating the professionalism of law enforcement agencies. Since the creation of CALEA, many individual states have established accreditation programs for their police departments.

CALEA's accreditation program expects accredited police departments to comply with the established set of professional standards and demonstrate that they:

Have a comprehensive, well-thought-out, uniform set of written directives.
Provide the necessary reports and analysis a Chief Executive Officer needs to make fact-based, informed management decisions.
Have a preparedness program so the agency is ready to address natural or man-made critical incidents.
Develop or improve the agency's relationship with the community.
Have a standard continuum that clearly defines authority, performance, and responsibility and strengthens the department's accountability.

(CALEA, 2006)

Recent research on police integrity and corruption over the last five to ten years has concluded that acts of police misconduct and corruption are not isolated activities engaged in by a few individual "grass eaters" or "bad apple" officers (Klockars et al., 2006). They are aspects of the influential organizational culture within police departments (Leuci, 2004; Courtemanche, 2011). The United States Department of Justice recommends that departments emphasize building internal systems that continually reinforce a culture of integrity by reflecting core values in its daily processes (U.S. Department of Justice, 2010).

An organization's culture is a shared system of beliefs, values, traditions, and behaviors that employees share (Schein, 1990). It manifests itself in the continuous patterns of employee behavior and official and unofficial ways of doing things. It is also reflected in how employees treat each other and those outside the department and the behavior they consistently engage in. Instead of focusing on individual officers' personal ethics and morality, departments should focus on creating an organizational value system that perceives integrity as the responsibility of every organizational member.

When individuals enter policing, they undergo a socialization process that begins in the training academy and continues in the department's field training program, intended to prepare them for police work. During this experience they acquire new ideas, beliefs, values, attitudes, motives, and norms and internalize these into their frame of reference by which they judge their world. This process helps recruits adapt to the police organization's definition of the world and its operations. When they undergo field training they are immersed in the day-to-day experiences of police patrol work. During this process they are mentored by their fellow officers and supervisors, who teach them about the organization's cultural system and the techniques of police work. These experiences provide the new officers with an understanding of their job, commonsense methodologies for handling police incidences, justifications, and rationalizations for dealing with the demands of their job.

These methodologies and rationalizations form the critical elements of the police culture that guide officers' behavior in performing their duties. Consequently, a police officer is a dynamic composite of past learning, socialization, and knowledge modified by current experiences. Research has consistently found that how officers adjust to their day-to-day operational experiences and rationalize their behavior are the most critical factors in developing good or bad individual police officer behavior (Brooks, 2010).

Training should prepare officers to handle the challenges of their jobs realistically. It should support the department's value system, policies, and procedures for controlling corruption and misconduct. The department's entry-level and in-service training should instruct officers on identifying and rejecting the corrupting influences they are exposed to. This training should contain instruction and analysis of past department cases involving corruption and misconduct, as well as how to address potential violations of professional conduct. Additionally, all department employees should clearly understand inappropriate behavior and performance consequences.

A department can establish a culture of integrity by developing a clear set of standards and values that define its expectations of professional conduct to its employees and citizens. These should then act as a guide for daily employee performance. For example, the 44-person Green Cove Springs Police Department in Florida defines its mission, purpose, and core values as follows:

MISSION

The Green Cove Springs Police Department is unwavering in protecting all people's lives, property, and rights by resolving issues and promoting peace in our community through partnerships and the continuous development of our organization and its members.

PURPOSE

The Green Cove Springs Police Department, in partnership with our community, is committed to protecting life and property, safeguarding order, and enforcing criminal laws through the continuous application of proactive policing practices. The members of your Police Department proudly carry out their duties by exhibiting a professional demeanor, exemplifying their commitment to public service and professional integrity.

CORE VALUES

S Safety: We are committed to providing safety within our community through continuous partnerships and problem-solving methods.
P Professionalism: We are committed to providing excellent service to our community in all our duties.
I Integrity: We are committed to unwavering legal, ethical, and moral standards.
R Respect: We value and promote human dignity in all our duties.
I Innovation: We are committed to continuously improving the services we provide to our community.
T Training: We are committed to leading through continuous education and development of our personnel and the agency.

The department's mission, purpose, and core values are displayed on its website, reflected in its policy and procedures, and used to evaluate its officers' performance. Once a department establishes these defining characteristics of the organization's culture, its policies and reward system should be structured to support these standards and values. In this manner, they become guiding tools of accountability that inform all department employees of what is expected of them.

All organizational managers should be responsible for maintaining integrity and accountability throughout the department. Developing and preserving a solid ethical organizational culture must become a primary responsibility of every department manager. In this manner, accountability will become the foundation upon which the department's culture and integrity rest—holding all managers and supervisors accountable and their employees represents the extension of accountability throughout the department. In addition to making clear the existence of positive core values, managers must continue to communicate and reinforce them daily through their example. To enhance its integrity, the department's redirection and culture of accountability must be institutionalized and sustained. This can be accomplished by maintaining a transparent climate supported by an Internal Affairs process, inspections, and discipline.

To institutionalize an ethical culture, the executive command team and managers should control and eliminate arrangements, discriminatory practices. They are breeding grounds for corruption and misconduct within the department. Fundamental changes will only occur after the culture of integrity is operationalized and sustained throughout the department. This can be accomplished by confronting managers with current conditions and creating dissatisfaction with the status quo. The chief executive must put the department employees face-to-face with the actual state of the organization's integrity. This can be accomplished by honest discussion and open communication about what is happening instead of what should be happening. Key managers need to come to a consensus about the cause of these problems and what needs to change in the department. Once the beliefs and energies of this critical organization mass are engaged, conversion to a new culture of integrity will spread, bringing about fundamental change very quickly (Gladwell, 2000).

This discussion should focus on three essential relationships: police to the community, management to officers, and officers to officers (Gaffigan & McDonald,

1997, p. 66). The objective is to create an understanding within the department of why change is necessary and to develop a sense of urgency to bring about the change. Employee motivation should then be directed into a focused organizational improvement effort. Chief executives can create a culture of integrity dissatisfaction in their organizations by:

1. Communicating information to its members about potential crises or threats to the organization's integrity.
2. Providing employees with objective data about organizational integrity. Informing them what is happening as opposed to what should be happening.
3. Engaging in frank discussion and dialogue about the organization's integrity and standards.
4. Setting realistic standards and expectations that will create the desire to change.
5. Holding all employees accountable for maintaining the department's integrity and standards of professional conduct.

The result is for the department to establish and sustain a culture of integrity, transparency, and adherence to professional standards. This transition will only be sustained if all department employees are aware of and held accountable for the highest standards of the police profession.

Internal Affairs

The function of **Internal Affairs** is to assist in maintaining the professional integrity of the department and to preserve public trust by inspecting and controlling, preventing, detecting, and investigating allegations of employee misbehavior and violations of professional standards. Differences in state and local law, collective bargaining, and organizational and political cultures make it impossible to create a one-size-fits-all approach to Internal Affairs (Courtemanche, 2011). Despite this, each police department should develop a system of inspection, internal control, and the capacity to deter, detect, and punish employee wrongdoing. The Internal Affairs section is responsible for conducting investigations and carrying out all assignments related to resolving issues of **integrity, misfeasance, malfeasance**, and **nonfeasance** by employees and professional standards (CALEA, 2006, p. 52). Minor violations of lesser importance are usually assigned to be investigated by supervisory personnel. However, all department members, from the chief down to the officers on patrol, are responsible for upholding the department's integrity (Fyfe et al., 1997). This function should be conducted in a fair, accessible, and transparent manner.

When a department employee is accused of misconduct or criminal activity, he or she should be subject to an honest and fair fact-finding process that uncovers the truth. In large police departments, this is the responsibility of a particular unit staffed by investigators with the rank of sergeant and above whose commander reports directly to the chief of police (CALEA, 2006). In smaller police departments, this function is usually carried out by a ranking officer or the chief executive (Thurnauer, 2004). Personnel assigned to Internal Affairs are either volunteers or individuals serving under the direction of the chief executive. Some departments require that individuals be assigned to Internal Affairs as part of their development for promotion to command rank.

Fyfe et al. (1997, pp. 472–473) identify three desirable outcomes from this assignment practice. First, Internal Affairs would be destigmatized and humanized, less isolated from the field, and no longer vulnerable to criticism. Second, it will become more objective because of the regular new blood entry into it. Third, over the long term, this assignment would fill the agency's top rank with personnel who have an understanding of and sympathy for the work of Internal Affairs and would, therefore, share its goals. This assignment's sensitive nature requires personnel selection to be based on established criteria. Internal Affairs investigators should have a reputation for integrity, knowledge of the law and employee rights, and proficiency in investigation, interviewing, and interrogation techniques (Norwicki & Punch, 2003).

Complaints

A primary feature of the Internal Affairs process is a procedure for dealing with complaints against police officers. This procedure must ensure that citizens can file a complaint directly with the police, that all misconduct allegations, regardless of their source, are reviewed and validated, and that an investigation is conducted if required. Procedures for registering complaints should be made available to the community through the media or the department's community relations programs and disseminated to all department employees (CALEA, 2006). From intake to final disposition, the complaint process should be straightforward to all involved. It should include a general description of the agency's categories to group complaints and the procedures for handling each category (U.S. DOJ, 2009). These descriptions and procedures should be in writing and easily accessible to the public. The procedures should provide guidelines regarding the types of complaints handled by Internal Affairs and the department's discipline process. It should also specify the nature of those complaints that should be brought immediately to the department's chief executive.

A complaint is one or more allegations by any person that an employee of the department, or the department itself, has misbehaved, as defined by the person making the allegation. Each event of alleged inappropriate behavior is an allegation, whether reported verbally or by other depiction (U.S. DOJ, 2009). Not all complaints are about police misconduct but may relate to how people feel about the police service they received, policing standards, operational guidelines, or policies. Such so-called service complaints will not always require an investigation but nevertheless warrant an effective and timely response, just like any other complaint. However, their information may provide the police department with a learning opportunity or an awareness of where change is needed (United Nations Office on Drugs and Crime, 2011).

Complaints that are best resolvable beyond the realm of the Internal Affairs function should be redirected to other department areas as the nature of the complaint dictates (e.g., supervisory issues, personal grievances, employee disputes, etc.). Complaints are a source of information for the department to evaluate employees' performance, identify areas of police misconduct, monitor police relations with the public, and identify the need for new or revised policies or improved training (Norwicki & Punch, 2003, p. 342). Thus, they are a critical data source for managing the department's external and internal environments.

Handling of Complaints

A responsive police department that desires to maintain its integrity will accept complaints in any form, whether by phone, mail, in person, email, or web. Anonymous complaints should be accepted. Departments run the risk of losing valuable community input if the complaint process is not clear and straightforward. The practice of discouraging people from making complaints or refusing to accept or record complaints should always be avoided. A failure to register a complaint should be considered neglect of duty, representing a disciplinary offense. The department should keep records of all complaints received. Each complaint should be tracked through to its final disposition. The person making the complaint should receive verification that the department has received it. The status of the complaint and its investigation should be communicated promptly to the complainant throughout the process. Departments should conduct regular inspections of this process to verify that complaints are being taken properly, procedures are being followed, and all employees adhere to the department's complaint policy and procedures.

During intake, the complaint should be classified to determine where, when, and how the complaint will be investigated and resolved. It is helpful to classify complaints into either of two categories: criminal or administrative. **Criminal complaints** are investigated quite differently from administrative complaints. Criminal misconduct involving violations of law may lead to prosecution. An administrative complaint may lead only to internal discipline or other corrective action. Administrative complaints can be further classified as personnel or service complaints. Personnel complaints address alleged misconduct by an employee. Service complaints address problems in the provision of service not linked to an employee's possible misconduct, such as a complaint that the agency's response times to public housing areas are routinely too long. A department will demonstrate transparency by disclosing its complaint statistics. This report should be published annually and contain the number and nature of the complaints received, the number of officers involved, and their disposition.

Credibility and transparency are essential in maintaining a department's integrity with the public and the department's employees. The employee(s) who is the subject of the complaint should be notified of the circumstances of the complaint. The department's policy and procedures should indicate when employee notification of a complaint should occur. Usually, the employee is notified the day the complaint is received. This can be done in several different ways. Providing the employee with a copy of any written complaint is preferable. Administrators may also have guidelines in collective bargaining agreements that have to be met concerning complaint procedures (Thurnauer, 2004).

Complaint Investigation

Once a complaint has been received, the next step is to determine whether the case requires investigation. The guiding principle should be that all complaints made by members of the public and all internal complaints of a serious nature, as determined by the agency, must be investigated. Internal affairs should be responsible for conducting all serious investigations, including but not limited to officer-involved shootings, suspected criminal activity, in-custody deaths, alleged constitutional violations, allegations of racial profiling or discriminatory policing or racial prejudice, dishonesty, drug use, sexual misconduct, cases handled for other jurisdictions, interagency cases, and cases referred directly by the agency head or command staff. Internal affairs should also conduct all administrative investigations of misconduct allegations that will likely result in litigation against the agency or its members. Unless there is a specialized unit to handle internal complaints of discrimination, sexual harassment, and other unlawful employment practices by employees, internal affairs should conduct such investigations (U.S. DOJ, 2009).

Internal Affairs investigations should be factually focused, timely, and free from conflict of interest, bias, prejudice, or self-interest. The extent of the investigation will vary from complaint to complaint, commensurate with the seriousness and complexity of the case. The department's policy and procedures should describe what the investigation should include and identify each step of the internal investigation. This guides the process and lets the subject of the complaint know what to expect (Thurnauer, 2004).

All complaints brought to internal affairs should require at least a preliminary investigation. **Preliminary investigations** are conducted to verify whether there is a need for a disciplinary or criminal investigation. This investigation should involve gathering critical statements or evidence if reasonably attainable. Its objective is to determine if the complaint should be further investigated and, if so, by whom. The advantage of conducting a preliminary investigation is that it can guide decision-making and prevent damage to the reputation of a police officer who is found to be innocent (United Nations Office on Drugs and Crime, 2011). Enforceable timelines for investigations are critical. The investigator should interview the complainant and witnesses within 24 hours of filing the complaint, preferably within 24 hours of the complaint being reported. This allows the investigator to get information from the complainant and witnesses. At the same time, it is still fresh in their minds before they have an opportunity to taint their memory by second-guessing, talking with other witnesses, speaking with an attorney, or even being contacted by the subject of the complaint. A thorough and complete interview also locks the complainant and witnesses into their statements and helps identify any discrepancies or embellishments that may occur.

An investigation is completed when all relevant information is acquired, and a finding in the case can be made. A **complete investigation** should occur where the allegations, if true, would likely result in formal discipline. If the investigation concludes that charges against an officer are not sustained, he or she should be notified in writing and the case closed. Regardless of whether charges are sustained, the allegation and disposition should be retained in the officer's personnel file, while the investigation record should remain with internal affairs (Fyfe et al., 1997, p. 472).

Likewise, a complete investigation should be considered if a preliminary review shows that an agency's policy, standard, or training may be a factor in unintended consequences apparent in the complaint. The commander should make any decision to proceed after the completed investigation of Internal Affairs with a written explanation in the file and notification to the complainant (U.S. DOJ, 2009). Many investigations do not require the expertise of Internal Affairs investigators. These cases can be investigated at the unit level.

There are four possible **dispositions** of complaints received:

Unfounded: The allegation is found to be false, or there is a lack of credible evidence to support it.

Exonerated: The allegation is true, but the action of the department member is consistent with department policy, justified and legal.

Not sustained: The investigation failed to disclose sufficient evidence to prove or disprove the allegation.

Sustained: The allegation is supported by sufficient evidence, and the department member's action(s) is inconsistent with the department's procedures, policy, or the law.

Once a disposition is rendered, the employee(s) involved and the complainant should be notified (CALEA, 2006, 52.2.8). The employee should be notified of the findings and, if sustained, told that he or she will be disciplined. In all cases, the subject officer should receive a complete copy of the investigative report (U.S. DOJ, 2009). Similarly, the complainant should receive written notification of the final disposition of the complaint and, at a minimum, the name and contact information of the commanding officer who can answer any questions (Noble & Alpert, 2009).

Internal Affairs Files and Confidentiality

Once the Internal Affairs process is complete, all documents and files must remain controlled by the Internal Affairs unit, if applicable, or the law enforcement executive who oversees Internal Affairs. These files should be kept separate from all other personnel files and always remain locked, accessible only to appropriately credentialed personnel. All files must remain confidential and retained for a period required by law or, if no law exists, for an appropriate length of time determined by the chief of police (CALEA, 2006).

Finally, executives and investigators should operate on the assumption that the public may review all written interviews, statements, and reports. All 50 states and the District of Columbia have public records laws. Some states have enacted multiple statutes, but generally, these laws enable members of the public to obtain documents and other public records from state and local governments. Although these laws are similar to the federal Freedom of Information Act (FOIA), significant differences exist between and among the laws. At the very least, every police chief and Internal Affairs unit commander must familiarize himself or herself with the FOIAs within his or her state, knowing what information is vulnerable to public inspection (U.S. DOJ, 2009).

Inspections

Police departments should conduct two types of inspections:

1. *Staff inspections* are conducted by those who do not have direct control but who are responsible for determining how well employees do their jobs.
2. *Line inspections* are conducted to see that tasks are performed satisfactorily by those directly controlling the employees and things being inspected.

The *staff inspection* is a system of reviews and audits conducted by administrators to analyze and monitor the alignment of the department's policy and procedures with unit and individual performance. It is a way to ensure that the department's units and personnel comply with policies and procedures and to discover potential problems before they negatively affect the department and its integrity. However, all department managers and supervisors are responsible for monitoring and inspecting the performance of their employees continually in order to ensure that their employees are acting by the rules, regulations, and policies of the organization as they relate to their assignments. These managerial monitoring audits, known as *line inspections*, are designed to identify and correct minor infractions by supervisors through coaching and on-the-job training. The complexity of line inspections varies according to the length of the chain of command and the number of employees the manager supervises.

They are a primary means of ascertaining employee fitness for duty that include, but are not limited to, the following, if applicable:

1. Uniforms.
2. Appearance.
3. Equipment.
4. Vehicles.
5. Firearms.
6. Personnel.
7. Facilities.
8. Performance.

Staff inspections complement and augment the line inspection function. They are designed to assess the effectiveness of operational procedures and report on their shortcomings. They can audit financial records, inventory agency property, inspect equipment, and conduct surveys. It is an excellent administrative practice for the police chief to schedule unit inspections periodically. Many departments have developed standardized checklists to be used in the inspection process to ensure uniformity. The unit to be inspected should receive advance notice of the inspection. These inspections address items that are, for the most part, a matter of record.

There are six objectives of a staff inspection:

- To determine whether the department's procedures and policies are being correctly implemented.
- To determine whether the department's procedures and policies are adequate to attain the department's goals and maintain its integrity.
- To determine whether the department's resources (such as personnel) are being used thoroughly and sensibly.
- To determine whether the department's resources are adequate to attain the department's goals.
- To discover any deficiencies in integrity, training, morale, or supervision; and
- To help operating line units plan their line inspections.

(Fuller, 2004, p. 68)

In large departments, staff inspections are generally the responsibility of a particular unit of supervisors; in smaller departments, they are conducted by individual managers. Unit commanders and individuals responsible for inspections should report directly to the police chief executive or agency head. In small agencies, staff inspection should be conducted by the chief executive. This oversight responsibility of the chief is particularly critical, as it validates the independence and objectivity of the inspection process (Thurnauer, 2004).

The effectiveness and integrity of the staff inspection process depend on the quality of personnel selected for this assignment. These individuals should be, at a minimum, first-line supervisors with extensive operational experience. Ideally, they should possess a strong sense of personal integrity, excellent analytical, communicative, investigative, and problem-solving skills, and the ability to operate with little or no supervision.

The culmination of a staff inspection is a written report to the chief executive that defines the inquiry results. It is not sufficient to provide data or announce performance failures. This report should contain clear and comprehensive communication about what is happening instead of what should or could be happening. It should also provide the chief executive with a list of recommendations to consider in order to correct the issue.

Early Warning Systems

During the late 1990s, police departments began using **early warning systems** to address issues of officer integrity proactively. Early warning systems are data-based management information systems designed to identify those officers who are becoming problematic and subject them to an intervention to correct their future performance. It is a commonly held managerial belief that a small number of officers causes most of a department's behavioral problems. These officers are known to their supervisors, peers, administrators, and residents of the areas in which they work (Goldstein, 1977, p. 171; Walker, Alpert, & Kenney, 2001). The purpose of these systems is to acquire performance information, document it, analyze it, and transfer the result of this analysis to operational managers in order to correct future behavior. This process is a strategic learning organization technique. Walker (2003, p. 30) identified the following goals and impacts of early warning systems:

GOALS AND IMPACTS OF EARLY WARNING SYSTEMS
The Individual Officer

- Improved Performance.
- Higher Standards of Accountability.

Supervisors

- Improved Supervisory Practices.
- Higher Standards of Accountability as Supervisors.

The Department

- Higher Standards of Accountability.
- Reduction in Litigation.
- Improved Community Relations.

It is hoped that early identification and intervention response will correct the problem and prevent the behavior from becoming a more significant issue for the department. Early intervention usually involves some combination of deterrence, counselling, or training. At the end of the 20th century, approximately 40 percent of all municipal and county police departments serving populations greater than 50,000 either had an early warning system or planned to implement one (Alpert & Walker, 2000). Early warning systems involve three distinct stages: selection, intervention, and a follow-up process of post-intervention monitoring. A list of recommended standards has not been established to select officers for inclusion in the program. However, most selection programs are designed to identify problematic officers based on a combination of factors that include a variety of behavioral criteria, such as:

1. Citizen complaints and commendations.
2. Discharges of firearms.
3. Use of force incidents.
4. Misconduct allegations.
5. Involvement in civil litigation.
6. A disproportionate number of resisting-arrest incidents.
7. Involvement in high-speed pursuits.
8. Use and abuse of sick leave.
9. Occurrence of incidents causing vehicular damage.
10. Preventable motor vehicle accidents.
11. Habitual lateness.
12. Ongoing poor performance or sudden poor performance.
13. Unusual behaviors.
14. Garnishment of wages.
15. Being the subject of a restraining order.
16. Reports of prisoner problems and complaints.
17. Unfavorable traffic and pedestrian stop data.

The department should track all complaints, justified or not, to identify officer behavior patterns. Analysis of complaint patterns provides objective data on types of officer discretionary behavior (Gaines & Kappeler, 2011). Those police departments using citizen complaints as an identifying criterion usually require three complaints within a given time frame, such as 12 months (Walker, Alpert, & Kenney, 2001). Research into the characteristics of officers who most frequently receive complaints disclosed that the number of arrests, officer age, and officer gender differentiated officers with high complaints. Female officers received fewer complaints, while younger officers were more likely to use force and received more complaints (Brandl, Stroshine, & Frank, 2001).

Selection and intervention consist of both specific and general deterrence. Specific deterrence occurs when an officer is selected for inclusion in the program, and his or her performance behavior is changed for the better. General deterrence assumes that the officers not selected will adjust their behaviors so that the system will not identify them. In addition, any counselling and training that is part of the intervention has the potential to correct officers' mistakes and help them improve their performance. The initial response in most systems involves a review by the selected officer's immediate supervisor. Some departments have command officers counselling the officers and assigning identified officers to training classes (Walker, Alpert, & Kenney, 2001). However, supervisors involved in the process should be trained in counselling techniques, and their efforts to change officer behavior should be documented. Once intervention is completed, the selected officers are monitored to determine if the effort has impacted their performance. Departmental monitoring programs vary as to time frame and formality and can be developed on a case-by-case basis. An adequately managed early warning system requires a commitment to accountability and a significant administrative and supervisory effort from the department. However, they can be effective in raising performance standards and improving the department's quality (Swanson, Territo, & Taylor, 2011).

The impact of early warning systems in Minneapolis, New Orleans, and Miami-Dade County discloses that, overall, the systems in these cities appear to have been successful at reducing citizen complaints against officers and other indicators of problematic police performance. In Minneapolis, for example, complaints against selected officers dropped by 67 percent within one year of the initial intervention. In New Orleans, the reduction was 64 percent. In comparison, in Miami-Dade, the number of selected officers having no use of force went from only 4 percent to at least 50 percent following the early warning intervention (Walker, Alpert, & Kenney, 2001).

Sustained Complaint

A complaint against an employee will be sustained when it is supported by sufficient evidence that the action(s) of the individual is not consistent with the department's procedures, policy, or the law. The department must then take disciplinary action. The chief of police should have unrestricted disciplinary power subject only to the general direction and approval of the jurisdiction chief executive officer to address employee misconduct (Fyfe et al., 1997). Discipline is imposed:

- To modify the employee's behavior.
- To set expectations for other employees.
- To maintain public trust by holding employees accountable.

Discipline aims to bring employees into compliance with established standards, guiding principles, and department core values. However, the department must adhere to state and local laws and collective bargaining agreements before discipline is enacted to ensure compliance with the employee's legal and contractual rights. All disciplinary actions should be fair, consistent, and flexible. The application of discipline should not be to select a penalty to fit the offense but to maintain the integrity of the department (Noble & Alpert, 2009).

Police departments use a variety of ways to handle disciplinary proceedings, such as review and disposition by the department's chief executive, administrative hearings, individual hearing officers, and police or civilian review boards. This process should include a procedure that allows for disposing of minor infractions that require formal action but are not severe enough to be heard before a formal board of discipline. In the disciplinary process, the corrective action is calculated according to the degree of misconduct, modified by the offender's prior record and the extent to which systemic defects in the department may have contributed to the offense. Each case should be judged on its own merits, with penalties depending on the circumstances (Norwicki & Punch, 2003).

Administrative hearings are quasi-judicial fact-finding proceedings. Conclusions are reached based on a preponderance of the evidence, not a guilty-beyond-reasonable-doubt standard. All parties involved should be aware of the rules for the hearing. The procedures include opening statements for both the accused and the department, as well as provisions for cross-examination and questioning of board members. The following rules should apply:

- The accused employee should be notified in advance of the charges.
- The accused employee should receive reasonable notice of the time and place of the hearing.

- The accused employee must have the opportunity to call witnesses, cross-examine opposing witnesses, and testify on his or her behalf.
- The hearing should be held before those who will decide the issues.
- The disciplinary hearing should close with a decision, accompanied by a statement summarizing the essentials of the proceedings and findings. If there are multiple charges, each charge should receive a separate finding. If the hearing finds that the employee should be charged, one of the following can be recommended:
  - Oral reprimand.
  - Written reprimand in the officer's personnel file.
  - Disciplinary transfer from a particular assignment.
  - Loss of time or annual leave instead of suspension.
  - Suspension with or without pay.
  - Monetary fines to be deducted from salary or pension payments.
  - Demotion in rank.
  - Pass over for promotion.
  - Removal from service.

Before the recommended disciplinary action is imposed, the employee should receive written notification of the hearing's outcome and the right to respond to the finding formally. CALEA Accreditation Standard No. 52.2.7 requires an agency to have a written directive specifying how an employee may be relieved from duty. The employee should be allowed to address the charges against him or her and request a reduction in any proposed disciplinary action (IAP, 2007). Once the chief of police reviews the employee's response and finalizes the proposed discipline, the chief may order the disciplinary action to be implemented. It is important to note that some union contracts require that, before any corrective action or termination takes place, the agency must demonstrate cause in determining whether management acted reasonably in its decision to implement discipline or termination (Noble & Alpert, 2009).

When an employee willingly follows agency policy, meets or exceeds expectations, and practices good judgment, it indicates effective discipline and self-monitoring. There may be many ways to accomplish this goal and to maintain positive relationships between the employee and supervisors through coaching, mentoring, and discipline.

Consent Decrees

A **consent decree** is a federal court decision aimed at promoting police reform. Typically, it results from an investigation by the U.S. Department of Justice (DOJ), keyed by misconduct allegations. They are legally authorized by Section 14141 of the Violent Crime Control and Law Enforcement Act of 1994, Public Law 103–322. The resulting lawsuit compels the police department to comply with the terms arising from the investigation. The implementation of a typical consent decree in a police department is as follows:

1. The community impacted by a department's practices calls for an investigation.
2. The DOJ opens an investigation into an unjust practice or pattern.
3. Once the investigation is complete, the parties involved can negotiate a settlement.

4.   The court approves the agreement and typically appoints a federal monitor—a single person—to track progress on the plan and provide regular reports on the department's performance against the agreed-upon metrics. The federal monitor employs a team that works with them, many of whom are subject matter experts, and sometimes includes people directly affected by unlawful practices.

(Vera Institute of Justice, 2023)

Police department consent decrees typically follow in the wake of high-profile police killings that generate public pressure to investigate. Following the death of Breonna Taylor, the Louisville Police Department was placed under a consent decree. So, too, were police departments in Baltimore (after the death of Freddie Gray), in Ferguson, Missouri (after the death of Michael Brown), and in Minneapolis (following the death of George Floyd). If appointed by the court, a monitor will track the police department or jail system's progress on meeting the benchmarks all parties agreed to before entering the consent decree. When police departments are involved, that process can include measuring tools such as community surveys, interviews, data on officer activities like stops or searches, and the number of complaints lodged against the department.

The monitor reports their findings to the court. As the department implements proposed changes, the DOJ remains engaged, approving policies, training programs, and implementation plans about the consent decree. The consent decree may also require the local government to allocate resources that allow the department to meet the benchmarks (Vera Institute of Justice, 2023). When sufficient departmental changes are noted, the DOJ declares substantial compliance and the decree ends (Chanin, 2015, p. 185).

Chanin (2016) examined the impact of consent decrees in five police departments: Pittsburgh, PA; Washington, DC; Cincinnati, OH; Prince George's County, MD; and Los Angeles, CA. Evaluation research requires identifying performance measures that validly reflect the outcomes of the implemented operation. In his analyses, Chanin (2015, p. 168) reviewed outcome data, including use-of-force incidents, citizen-based allegations of misconduct, officer disciplinary decisions, and civil litigation related to police misconduct, as well as FBI crime data. In Pittsburgh, the tracking of citizen complaints (including the use of force) against the department revealed a 48 percent increase following the consent decree (from 556 to 822) (Chanin, 2016, p. 79). Use of force allegations increased annually, by 30 to 75 percent (Chanin, 2015, p. 170).

In Washington, DC, Chief Cathy Lanier credited the consent decree with a dramatic shift in departmental culture (Chanin, 2016, p. 86). Deadly force events declined from 23.4 incidents per year to 13.1 following the memorandum of agreement (MOA) (Chanin, 2016, p. 88). Cincinnati experienced notable positive results, including reduced use of force incidents and allegations of abusive or unlawful behavior (Chanin, 2016, p. 91). Prince George's County did not provide the same level of data as the other departments Chanin studied. Yet, it appeared that the consent decree did not reduce the volume or nature of complaints in the county (Chanin, 2016, p. 98). In Los Angeles, the department registered reductions in use-of-force complaints and civil suits alleging deadly force problems following the consent decree (Chanin, 2016, pp. 104–105).

In sum, Chanin's analysis concluded that consent decrees had a "sustained positive effect in Cincinnati and Washington, D.C." (Chanin, 2016, p. 108). However, he also noted that better data on the use of force statistics, officer disciplinary decisions, and civil litigation results would allow a thorough and more complete assessment of the impact of consent decrees (Chanin, 2016, p. 109).

An analysis of the impact of consent decrees in the Los Angeles Police Department, the New Jersey State Police, and the New York City Police Department concludes that they did not reduce racial disparity in policing. However, consent decrees have the potential to increase transparency in policing by requiring the collection and public release of data (Kupferberg, 2008). However, Goh (2020) examined data on the number of persons killed by the police between 2000 and 2016. He concluded that federal intervention by the DOJ resulted in a reduction of these killings by 27 percent (Goh, 2020, p. 921). Powell, Meitl, and Worrall (2017) studied the impact of consent decrees in 23 jurisdictions and utilized the number of Section 1983 complaints filed following the consent decree as an outcome measure, indicating legally improved policing. The research results indicated that filing Section 1983 civil rights complaints may be reduced by as much as 43 percent after a consent decree is entered into (Powell, Meitl, & Worrall, 2017, p. 596).

The major problem with these assessments of the results of consent decrees is that the outcome measures are not tied to what was done under the court order. There are no commonly accepted measures of successful implementation, sustainability, or how to measure changes under consent decrees (Ostrowe, 2021, p. 129). What specific steps, policies, and operations were undertaken? What outcome measures validly fit those attempts? It is a problem surrounding evaluation research on police operations in general—a lack of specification about what departments did to address issues (see Vito & Higgins, 2014). Regarding the effects of consent decrees, other research questions involve the effectiveness and sustainability of specific components, what are the financial costs of the process, does the effectiveness change over time, and whether there is an interaction between system usage and officer training (Chanin, 2016, p. 110). Establishing an auditing system could remedy these problems (Jiao, 2021, p. 803).

Scott (2017, p. 608) lists several factors that limit the effectiveness of consent decrees in producing police reform and asserts that efforts to "curtail unconstitutional practices might not even suffice to eradicate other bad practices." Many other elements can conspire to promote bad police practices untouched by constitutional remedies—poor personnel, incompetent managers, bad policies, poor labor–management relations, responding to political pressure, lack of funding, officers with bad intentions, and inadequate training (Scott, 2017, p. 609). The critical actor in reform is the police chief. Chiefs can confront and attempt to change a dysfunctional organizational culture (Jiao, 2021, p. 802). Again, the Cincinnati police department is credited with embracing improved policing methods, sponsored by training and collaboration with the consent decree monitoring team (Scott, 2017, p. 611).

However, the ability of consent decrees to establish change is subject to question. Ostrowe (2021) reviewed 21 published studies on the impact of consent decrees. He concluded that the implementation of consent decrees often led to de-policing, increased crime, and difficulties sustaining reform—factors that question the benefits of the process (Ostrowe, 2021, p. 130). The financial costs of consent decrees to a city budget are also significant. Estimates place the cost of compliance in the tens or even hundreds of millions of dollars, depending on the size of the police department and the complexity of the agreement (Rushin & Michalski, 2021, p. 303).

Conclusion

Since the development of professional policing in the 19th century, police deviance, misconduct, and corruption have been persistent problems. Democratic policing requires high levels of integrity and transparency if the police are to earn the trust of those whom they are sworn to protect and serve. All too often throughout the history of policing, citizen confidence in their police has been shaken by the disclosure of incidents of significant corruption, excessive use of deadly force, brutality, and sexual misconduct. This has contributed to the erosion of the public's confidence in the integrity of policing. The police chief executive and his or her management team are responsible for controlling deviant employee behavior and maintaining department integrity.

Ethical, organizational, and legal standards govern police behavior. However, as this chapter has identified, there are numerous ways by which these standards have been violated. Control of deviance requires constant attention, collection, and data analysis, confronting the reality of practice and holding all employees accountable. Identifying a few "rotten apples" and individual punishments has proven to be an inadequate response to this problem. Departments must develop a long-term, multi-faceted strategy to tackle corruption and deviance proactively. All organizational managers should be responsible for maintaining a culture of integrity and accountability throughout the department. Accountability is the foundation upon which the department's integrity rests. The department's culture of accountability must be institutionalized and sustained. This can be accomplished by maintaining a transparency climate supported by an Internal Affairs process, inspections, and discipline. Consent decrees represent another method of promoting police reform.

KEY TERMS

Administrative hearing	Ethical standards	Organizational standards
CALEA's Standards for Law Enforcement Agencies	Grass eaters	Police crime
	Integrity	Preliminary investigation
Complaint	Internal Affairs	Professional standards
Complaint investigation	Legal standards	Staff inspection
Consent decree	Line inspection	Sustained complaint
Corruption	Malfeasance	Type of corruption
Criminal complaints	Meat eaters	Type I Department
Democratic policing	Misconduct	Type II Department
Deviance	Misfeasance	Type III Department
Dispositions	Noble cause corruption	
Early warning system	Nonfeasance	

References

Alpert, G., & Walker, S. (2000). Police accountability and early warning systems: Developing policies and programs. *Justice Research and Policy, 2*(2), 59–72.

Barker, T. (2006). *Police ethics: Crisis in law enforcement.* Springfield, IL: Charles C Thomas.

Bayley, D.H. (2001). Democratizing the police abroad: What to do and how to do it. In *Issues in international crime.* Washington, DC: National Institute of Justice.

Bayley, D., & Perito, R. (2011). *Police corruption: What past scandals teach about current challenges—Special report.* Washington. DC: United States Institute of Peace.

Brandl, S., Stroshine, M., & Frank, J. (2001). Who are the complainant-prone officers? An examination of the relationship between police officers' attributes, arrest activity, and assignment. *Journal of Criminal Justice, 29*(6), 521–529.

Brooks, L.W. (2010). Police discretionary behavior: A study in style. In R.G. Dunham & G.P. Alpert (Eds.), *Critical issues in policing: Contemporary readings* (pp. 122–142). Long Grove, IL: Waveland Press.

Chanin, J. (2015). Examining the sustainability of pattern or practice in police reform. *Police Quarterly, 18*(2), 163–192.

Chanin, J. (2016). Evaluating section 14141: An empirical review of pattern or practice police misconduct reform. *Ohio State Journal of Criminal Law, 14*, 67–112.

Commission on Accreditation for Law Enforcement Agencies (CALEA). (2006). *Standards for law enforcement agencies*. Fairfax, VA: CALEA.

Courtemanche Jr., R.D. (2011, November). Internal affairs: An evolution in organizational culture? *The Police Chief, 78*, 14–15.

Fuller, J. (2004). Staff inspection: A strong administrative tool. *The Police Chief, 71*(12), 66–72.

Fyfe, J.J., Greene, J.R., Walsh, W., Wilson, O., & McLaren, R. (1997). *Police administration*. New York, NY: McGraw-Hill.

Gaffigan, S.J., & McDonald, P.P. (1997). *Police integrity, public service with honor*. Washington, DC: U.S. Department of Justice.

Gaines, L.K., & Kappeler, V.E. (2011). *Policing in America*. Waltham, MA: Elsevier.

Gladwell, M. (2000). *The tipping point: How little things can make a big difference*. New York, NY: Little, Brown and Company.

Goh, L. (2020). Going local: Do consent decrees and other forms of federal intervention in municipal police departments reduce police killings? *Justice Quarterly, 37*(5), 900–929.

Goldstein, H. (1977). *Policing a free society*. Cambridge, MA: Ballinger.

International Association of Police (IAP). (2007). Resolutions adopted at the 114th annual conference. New Orleans, LA.

Jiao, A. (2021). Federal consent decrees: A review of policies, processes, and outcomes. *Police Practice and Research, 22*(1), 793–804.

Kane, R.J., & White, M.D. (2009). Bad cops: A study of career-ending misconduct among New York City Police Officers. *Criminology & Public Policy, 8*, 37–769.

Kappeler, V., Sluder, R.D., & Alpert, G.P. (1998). *Forces of deviance: Understanding the dark side of policing*. Prospect Heights, IL: Waveland Press.

Kleinig, J. (1996). *The ethics of policing*. Cambridge: Cambridge University Press.

Klockars, C.B. (1980). The dirty harry problem. *The Annals of the American Academy of Political and Social Science, 452*(1), 33–47.

Klockars, C.B. (1999). Some really cheap ways of measuring what really matters. In R.H. Langworthy (Ed.), *Measuring what matters: Proceedings from the policing research institute meetings* (pp. 195–214). Washington, DC: National Institute of Justice.

Klockars, C.B., Ivkovic, S.K., & Haberfeld, M. (2006). *Enhancing police integrity*. Dordrecht, NL: Springer.

Knapp Commission. (1972). *Report of the New York City commission to investigate allegations of police corruption and the city's anti-corruption procedures*. New York, NY: Bar Press.

Kupferberg, N. (2008). Transparency: A new role for police consent decrees. *Columbia Journal of Law and Social Problems, 42*(1), 129–163.

Lee, W.L.M. (1901). *A history of police in England*. London: Methuen.

Leuci, R. (2004). *All the centurions: A New York City cop remembers his years on the street, 1961–1982*. New York, NY: Harper Collins.

Monkkonen, E.M. (1981). *Police in America—1860–1920*. Cambridge: Cambridge University Press.

Murphy, P.V., & Caplan, G. (1991). Fostering integrity. In W.G. Geller (Ed.), *Local government police management* (pp. 239–270). Washington, DC: International City Management Association.

Newburn, T. (1999). *Understanding and preventing police corruption: Lessons from the literature: Home Office Research Series Paper 110*. London: Home Office.

Noble, J.J., & Alpert, G.P. (2009). *Managing accountability systems for police conduct: Internal affairs and external oversight*. Prospect Heights, IL: Waveland Press.

Northumbria Police U.K. (2015). *Our values at Northumbria police*, www.northumbria.police.uk/about_us/organisation/values/.

Norwicki, D.E., & Punch, M.E. (2003). Fostering integrity and professional standards. In W. Geller (Ed.), *Local government police management* (pp. 315–352). Washington, DC: International City Management Association.

O'Keefe, J. (2004). *Protecting the republic: The education and training of American police officers*. Upper Saddle River, NJ: Prentice Hall.

Ostrowe, J. (2021). Federal intervention of police under section 14141 – a state-of-the-art literature review. *Policing: An International Journal, 1*, 118–133.

Parks, B.C. (2000). *Board of inquiry into the Rampart area corruption incident*. Los Angeles, CA: Los Angeles Police Department.

Porter, L.E., & Warrender, C. (2009). A multivariate model of police deviance: Examining the nature of corruption, crime and misconduct. *Policing and Society, 19*(1), 79–99.

Powell, Z., Meitl, M., & Worrall, J. (2017). Police consent decrees and section 1983 civil rights litigation. *Criminology & Public Policy, 16*(2), 575–605.

Punch, M. (1985). *Conduct unbecoming: The social construction of police deviance and control*. London: Tavistock.

Reppetto, T.A. (1978). *The blue parade*. New York, NY: The Free Press.

Roberg, R., Novak, K., Cordner, G., & Smith, B. (2012). *Police & society*. New York, NY: Oxford University Press.

Roebuck, J.B., & Barker, T. (1974). A typology of police corruption. *Social Problems, 21*, 423–437.

Rushin, S., & Michalski, R. (2021). Police funding. *Florida Law Review, 72*(2), 277–330.

Schein, E.H. (1990). Organizational culture. *American Psychologist, 45*, 109–119.

Scott, M. (2017). Which way to better policing? *Criminology & Public Policy, 16*(2), 607–616.

Sherman, L.W. (1974). *Police corruption: A sociological perspective*. Garden City, NY: Anchor Press.

Skogan, W.G., & Meares, T.L. (2004). Lawful policing. *The Annals of the American Academy of Political and Social Science, 593*(1), 66–83.

Swanson, C.R., Territo, L., & Taylor, R.W. (2011). *Police administration: Structures, processes, and behavior*. Upper Saddle River, NJ: Prentice Hall.

Thurnauer, B. (2004). *Internal affairs: A strategy for smaller departments*. Washington, DC: International Association of Chiefs of Police.

United Nations Office on Drugs and Crime. (2011). *Handbook on police accountability, oversight and integrity*. New York, NY: United Nations.

USA Today. (2015, April 15). Deal set for Chicago police torture victims. *USA Today*, 3B.

U.S. Department of Justice, Office of Community Oriented Policing Services. (2009). *Standards and guidelines for internal affairs: Recommendations from a community of practice.* Washington, DC: Office of Community Oriented Policing Services, U.S. Department of Justice.

U.S. Department of Justice, Office of Community Oriented Policing Services and the Boston Police Department. (2010). *Enhancing cultures of integrity: Technical assistance guide.* Washington, DC: Office of Community Oriented Policing Services, U.S. Department of Justice.

Vera Institute of Justice. (2023, 12 5). Retrieved from www.vera.org/news/everything-you-need-to-know-about-consent-decrees.

Vito, G., & Higgins, G. (2014). *Practical Program Evaluation in Criminal Justice.* Amsterdam, NL: Elsevier.

Walker, S. (2003). *Early intervention systems for law enforcement agencies: A planning and management guide.* Washington, DC: Office of Community Oriented Policing Services.

Walker, S., Alpert, G., & Kenney, D.J. (2001). *Early warning systems: Responding to the problem police officer.* Research in Brief. Washington, DC: National Institute of Justice.

Whalen, B., & Whalen, J. (2014). *The NYPD's first fifty years: Politicians, police commissioners & patrolmen.* Lincoln, NE: University of Nebraska Press.

12 Creating Safe Communities

Introduction

All people wish to live safely, free from the threat of personal violence and loss of their property. Unsafe communities collapse because residents live in fear and remain behind locked doors without a sense of well-being or connection to their neighbors. Creating safe communities is the responsibility of a community's residents and civil authority, represented by the police. Creating safe communities represents a never-ending challenge to police because they can only provide public safety and crime control with the approval and cooperation of community residents. The 1829 Principles of Law Enforcement from London state that: "The ability of the police to perform their task depends on public approval of their existence, actions, behavior, and on the ability of the police to secure and maintain public respect" (Reith, 1956, p. 156). This principle received greater recognition with the establishment of Community Policing as a dominant philosophy and strategy of modern policing.

The goal of Community Policing is to engage community residents as equal partners with the police in addressing local crime and disorder problems. The primary aim of this partnership is to involve residents as active participants in identifying and preventing crime and other street-level revitalization efforts. It is hoped

DOI: 10.4324/9781003459095-12

that neighborhood residents and community institutions would share responsibility with the police for dealing with community safety issues. This strategy requires police departments to actively seek to collaborate with the community in a planned manner and to build partnerships of mutual trust. As COPS Office (2015) notes, this mutual trust between police and citizens is essential in a democracy. It is critical to the stability of our communities, the integrity of our criminal justice system, and the safe and effective delivery of policing services.

The police cannot achieve community safety if they lack the respect and trust of the people who live in the community they serve. Civil disturbances in Ferguson, Missouri; New York City; Baltimore, Maryland; Cleveland, Ohio; Oakland, California; and demonstrations in many other areas of the country because of controversial police encounters involving the killing of unarmed individuals have challenged the legitimacy of the police use of deadly force. These disturbances have also questioned the tactics used by police departments to provide community safety, especially in minority neighborhoods. They have contested the authority of the police and challenged their ability to provide public safety in inner-city African American communities.

Drawing upon his many years of street-level experience attempting to reduce gun violence in inner-city America, David Kennedy (2011) provides an insightful perspective to understanding police–minority relations. He theorizes that at the heart of the problem is a general distrust and misunderstanding that minority residents and police have of each other. These opinions derive from the racial history of our country and the unintended consequences of the recent criminal justice policy, the "War on Drugs." Minorities often believe that the police are uninterested in protecting them, fail to keep their communities safe, are rude, corrupt, abusive, lock up their young men, use excessive force, and have no regard for their lives (Carter, 2002; Kennedy, 2011). Police believe that the inner-city community tolerates violent crime and drug dealing because it is corrupt or too broken to stand up against it. They believe that Black-on-Black homicide is a symptom of persistent lawless behavior by Black people and is a product of their tolerance for criminal behavior (Braga & Brunson, 2015).

However, research in Chicago found that residents were intolerant of teenage deviant behavior. However, racial, ethnic, and socio-economic groups differed substantially in their beliefs about the legitimacy of law and the police. The study found that a higher proportion of Blacks (29 percent) and Latinos (31 percent) than Whites (19 percent) view legal norms as not binding. These findings found that Blacks appear more cynical toward or dissatisfied with the police because they are more likely to live where disadvantage is concentrated (Sampson & Bartusch, 1998).

Kennedy concludes that each side's perceptions and the resulting narratives are entirely plausible and make sense when viewed from either side, but both are wrong. Both positions undermine community norms against crime and for the law, preventing meaningful partnerships or community safety. What is true is that both sides deeply desire public safety, but these core misunderstandings block each from shifting toward this common goal. Sampson, Raudenbush, and Earls (1997) suggest that the capacity of neighborhood residents to protect themselves against serious violence necessitates achieving a standard set of goals and exerting control over youth and public spaces. They label this effort "collective efficacy." Creating and supporting the development of neighborhood collective efficacy is a worthwhile objective for police–community partnerships. Weisburd, Davis, and Gill (2015) argue for the relevance of informal social controls in place-based policing in their analysis of an innovative Smart Policing collaboration between the Brooklyn Park (Minnesota) Police Department and the Center for Evidence-Based Crime Policy at George Mason University that implemented a department-wide program in which police lead interventions to increase collective efficacy in hot spots. Their study highlights the importance of police–community collaboration to improve public safety and reinforce informal social controls and the emerging empirical evidence that social disorganization and collective efficacy may influence crime patterns at the micro-geographic level. This chapter examines the issues relating to the role of the police in collaborating with communities to develop safe neighborhoods through community partnerships. To understand the interrelationship between the police and the community, it is essential to identify those terms and concepts commonly used to define it.

Community Concepts

Understanding the dynamics of "community" is essential to preventing and controlling crime and disorder and fear of crime (Trojanowicz & Bucqueroux, 1994). The term "community" is a crucial analytical concept that is often undefined in policing literature. Many Community Policing advocates use "community" as an objective phenomenon that collectively speaks with one unified voice and set of values. Nothing could be further from the truth.

Community is a social construct that refers to a fixed place (geographically defined area) where people live in a relationship of mutual interdependence, interact, have a sense of belonging, and have psychological identification with a common locality. The interactions and behaviors in a community are based on shared expectations, values, beliefs, and meanings held by the people who live and interact there. Communities will vary based on size, location, degree of urbanization, social composition, and economic base. For the people who live there, it is their place, their home ground, and they feel connected. The concept also denotes all individuals, groups, and institutions within a specific geographic area. These include civil and governmental organizations, such as the police, responsible for delivering security and other services in that area. However, when residents' shared sense of belonging and values breaks down, any sense of community will cease.

Community analysis is concerned with the type, quality, and basis for the interaction of people in the community. A community is a social place where families, friends, workers, neighbors, community associations, clubs, civic groups, churches, temples, ethnic associations, and governmental agencies interact. A community can comprise a politically defined municipal area, an economic zone, a residential subdivision, an urban public housing area, a city block, and a psychologically defined area.

It is important to note that today's perception of community differs from the traditional view that describes community as a homogeneous place of little change that demands a high degree of conformity and is wary of strangers (Peak & Glensor, 2012). Today, we live in heterogenetic communities that are influenced by and subjected to consistent change because of their connectivity to the macro-society and world in which they exist. In these communities residents have little sense of relationship with one another, a minimal sense of belonging, or opinion that the community is a significant social group. Residents occupy a space in the community but are more closely related to larger macro-system attachments, such as work groups, professional societies, or other institutional associations, than to components of the local community. As a result, creating community partnerships with the active participation of residents is difficult unless there is a serious issue or problem that concerns their safety.

The term "neighborhood" is often used interchangeably with community. A **neighborhood** is a geographically smaller sublocation within a larger community where people live or work near each other, recognize their recurring closeness, and have a personal sense of identity with this place and one another. It is a place of intense interrelationships that include a sense of personal belonging because of geographical and physical characteristics, racial, ethnic, and kinship networks, and residents' emotional attachment. Neighborhoods are often distinguished by their common ties of family, ethnicity, social class, religion, and occupation. The structure of a neighborhood is people acting together because they want to and need to.

In Louisville, Kentucky, places like Newburg, Portland, the Highlands, and St. Matthews are considered neighborhoods. New York City's neighborhoods include Yorkville, East Village, Chelsea, Harlem, the Hasidic community of Crown Heights, and Greenwich Village. Urban residents construct "cognitive maps" in which they allocate distinctive places as "their own": It is their neighborhood. For example, when one of the authors was a NYPD detective in the Bedford-Stuyvesant section of Brooklyn, New York, he often found that one city block was populated with individuals who came from or had roots in the same area in the South. People from this area migrating to New York City sought family, friends, and support from individuals they knew or connected with. They settled next to this support system and formed a neighborhood within the larger community.

The intensity of neighborhood relationships depends on many factors, including geographical and physical characteristics of the community, ethnic and kinship networks, affective attachment of residents, building construction features, local facility usage, pedestrian and automotive traffic patterns, the amount of time residents spend in the area, and demographic patterns.

A community or neighborhood can also be considered an inter-actionable field where community-based organizational systems are linked. These systems are linked **vertically** through structural and functional patterns with the macro-system (government, economic, educational, and public services). Macro-system attachments sustain the community's economic and socio-political base. They provide job preparation, access to employment, and governmental support services. They are also linked horizontally through structural and functional patterns with the local community's various social units and subsystems. In a well-functioning **horizontal system**, community associations develop and provide a support place for residents. Horizontal community associations provide a unique tool where belonging is the primary motivation, people of all capacities are members, and creativity to address issues can be developed. Horizontal community associations are interdependent. For example, if an American Legion Post disbands, several community fundraising events they perform annually may also cease. As a result, programs supported by the Legion Post that serve the community, such as maintaining the local ballpark and school scholarships, will end. The interdependence of the local associations and the community's dependence upon their work is a critical factor in developing an effective community.

Crime-ridden, disorderly, and disorganized communities with an undeveloped sense of belonging often lack horizontal community associations and have limited ties to the macro-system. These are the communities characterized by housing dilapidation, high resident victimization and fear, violent crime, drug markets, street gangs, unemployment, visible disorder, public drinking, and high unemployment. Time also changes neighborhood use and the way people feel about their area. At night, people lock themselves in their homes, fear for their children, stay off the streets, and do not use public places. The police, by default, are the primary social service in these communities. Unfortunately, residents rarely engage helpfully with the police due to strained relationships, skepticism of the sincerity of the police, and fear of reprisals from local criminals when cooperating with the police (Skogan & Frydl, 2004).

The literature that describes disorganized crime-ridden communities tends to link these conditions exclusively to urban areas. However, suburban and rural communities are not immune. Rural areas with limited policing resources have been plagued with the ravages of crime accompanying addiction to oxycodone, heroin, production of methamphetamines, marijuana grow operations, and other controlled substances (Vito, Higgins, Walsh, & Vito, 2012).

Effective communities defend against crime and disorder through the interaction of private social control maintained by family, neighbors, and religious and local organizations. In these communities, residents are concerned for their area's overall condition beyond that of their own individual homes. They accept a certain amount of responsibility for what takes place in their community. Residents exercise some control over the disorderly behavior of youth and others and ensure that common areas are free of litter and debris. This collective efficacy allows residents to create a safe and orderly environment (Sampson et al., 1997; Sampson, 2012).

Collective efficacy is the capacity of neighborhood residents to protect themselves against serious violence by achieving a common set of goals and exerting control over youth and public spaces. They care for and are concerned about the survival of the area in which they live. Collective efficacy involves residents monitoring children and other persons in public areas, acting to prevent disorderly conduct, and confronting individuals who exploit or disturb public spaces. Thus, creating safe communities depends upon residents trusting each other and cooperating with themselves and with the police.

Kelling and Stewart (1989, p. 3) identified six characteristics that contribute to the defense of neighborhoods.

1. Individual citizens act independently or in association with police and criminal justice agencies.
2. Individual citizens act alone by engaging in activities to protect themselves, their property, and their neighborhood.
3. Private groups of citizens may act on their behalf to protect the neighborhood, its residents, and users by forming self-help groups to enhance community safety.
4. Formal private associations such as funded community activists and community development organizations implement and maintain neighborhood programs.
5. Commercial firms such as small shopkeepers and large corporations provide proprietary protective services. These security operatives often work closely with neighborhood police.
6. Public criminal justice agencies like the police operate independently to provide community safety.

This discussion highlights the importance of residential participation and involvement in creating safe communities. This is what Community Policing hopes to restore and maintain through the development of community partnerships. It also negates the image that the police are the only source of community safety that is always ready to respond to citizen activation. It holds that the community and its members must be ready to take responsibility for their security problems in partnership with their police. Developing police–community partnerships is critical in creating a community's collective efficacy. This form of collaboration ensures that residents have a voice in identifying problems and participating in developing and implementing solutions that will affect them. Collaboration occurs when the police, residents, individual stakeholders, community organizations, and special interest groups work together to obtain the resolution of a problem or issue.

A **community partnership** is a working relationship between the police, residents, residential groups, and social organizations in a neighborhood. Community partnerships are an organizational strategy designed to prevent and eliminate crime while assisting in creating secure communities. They are a planned, more intense collaborative relationship that is created to address serious crime and disorder issues in a community. These partnerships are designed to achieve trust and legitimacy by establishing a positive presence at community activities and events, participating in proactive problem-solving, and ensuring that communities have a voice and seat at the table working with officers (COPS Office, 2015). Effective community partnerships can achieve the following six results:

Accomplish what individuals alone cannot.
Prevent duplication of individual or organizational efforts.
Enhance the power of advocacy and resource development for the initiative.
Create more public recognition and visibility for the community policing initiative.
Provide a more systematic, comprehensive approach to addressing community crime and disorder problems.
Provide more opportunities for new projects.

(Rinehart, Laszio, & Brisco, 2001, p. 175)

When the concept of community engagement through a partnership is discussed, it should be remembered that the police are referring to a planned, coordinated strategy in which each partner's role, knowledge, and effectiveness are critical to its success. Individuals involved should be knowledgeable partners to assist in identifying community problems and developing solutions. Community partnerships are essential to the creation of safe neighborhoods.

Community safety is a generic term used widely by the police, academics, protestors, politicians, community workers, and others regarding reducing localized levels of violent crime and disorder. It also involves addressing residents' fear of crime and perceptions of safety. Community safety means varying things to different people at different times. Its focus alters as the nature of crime and antisocial behavior shifts. Crime and disorder, coupled with one's feeling of personal safety and potential victimization (fear), are the greatest threats to our sense of community. Residents' fear is shaped less by their knowledge of specific criminals or crimes than by their knowledge of dangerous and safe places in their community. Community safety is a byproduct of society's private control system that comprises family, neighbors, religion, education, and social relationships. However, the strains and pressures of today's world have weakened the impact of this system. This strain emphasizes the public control systems that constitute the criminal justice system and governmental organizations. The police are members of this system and have primary responsibility for personal and community safety. However, for the community residents to collaborate and form partnerships with the police, they must believe and trust in the legitimacy of their police department and approve of its efforts.

Legitimacy/Procedural Justice

The effectiveness of police operations depends upon the public's willingness to provide information and help the police (Maple & Mitchell, 1999; Walsh, 2001; Henry, 2002). Police leaders increasingly realize that citizens' perception of their legitimacy and use of procedural justice are necessary conditions for gaining community residents' support, and are worthy goals (Fischer, 2014). Police legitimacy and procedural justice are based on the belief that the police are entitled to call upon the public to comply with the law and their right to exercise power. This enables the police to control the behavior of citizens. The police need people to accept their decisions and follow the law voluntarily through obligation and deference to police directives (Neyroud, 2009). **Legitimacy** is present when citizens believe the police have moral authority to enforce the law and deserve respect and compliance with their initiatives (Fischer, 2014). Police need to consider and understand how the public's perceptions of legitimacy and procedural justice can affect a department's efforts to achieve its goals and citizen compliance.

People obey the law voluntarily when:

1. It is instrumental. It creates a credible risk that people will be caught and punished for their crimes.
2. They believe in the moral rightness of the law.
3. They believe in the legitimacy of the authority enforcing the law.

Community residents will accept police decisions when they believe they are legitimate and to the degree that they consider the decisions to be favorable and fair. Citizens are more willing to cooperate with the police by engaging in community activities, reporting crimes, or identifying suspects when they view police actions as fair and unbiased (Sunshine & Tyler, 2003). If they view the police as unfair and biased it can lead to alienation, dissatisfaction, defiance, and a lack of public cooperation. Thus, the legitimacy of the police is linked to public judgments about the fairness of the processes through which the police make decisions and exercise authority. If citizens believe that police actions are morally justified and appropriate to the circumstances, they are legitimate.

The police can build trust in the community and increase residents' respect for police authority by listening to community residents about the issues that concern them and responding to them. Citizens will cooperate with the police when they believe that police performance in fighting crime is effective and that there is a credible threat of punishment for the crime (Tyler & Fagan, 2008, p. 263). Satisfaction with police control of disorder is significantly related to citizens' overall satisfaction with crime prevention (Zhao, Tsai, Ren, & Lai, 2012, p. 414). Visibility is another factor in this process. When citizens see the police doing their job and providing quality service, legitimacy is enhanced (Hawdon, Ryan, & Griffin, 2003, p. 485; Maguire & Johnson, 2010). A police chief familiar who is with the concepts of legitimacy and procedural justice and the research behind these ideas, and who works to incorporate these concepts into the practices in his or her department, will generate feelings of goodwill and support for the police among the public. This result is not a mere public relations success but rather an essential component of ensuring the overall success of the police (Fischer, 2014, p. 4).

Legitimacy may also facilitate community order maintenance. A survey conducted by Wolfe (2011) found that persons exhibiting low self-control were more likely to hold negative perceptions of police procedural justice. Such persons may also be more likely to be treated unkindly by the police because they challenge police actions and decisions. However, the results also showed that if the police follow the tenets of procedural justice, they will gain voluntary compliance and lower levels of offending from people with low self-control (Wolfe, 2011, p. 72). For example, when the police arrested James Eagan Holmes, the person responsible for the mass shooting in Aurora, Colorado, on July 20, 2012, he told the police that he had also rigged his apartment with homemade explosives. He later stated that he told them this because they had treated him properly when he was arrested (Oates, 2016).

To summarize, there are three interrelated points concerning police legitimacy. First, to be effective in their public safety maintenance role, the police need voluntary public support and cooperation. Second, such collaboration is intimately linked to public perceptions of police legitimacy. Finally, police legitimacy is determined by public assessments of how the police exercise authority (Tyler, 2004). Tyler and Huo (2002) advocate developing a "process-based model of regulation" to promote procedurally fair treatment of citizens by the police. The aim is to obtain voluntary compliance with police decisions due to the fair treatment that citizens receive. Legitimacy is crucial to respectful and effective relations between the police and the communities they serve.

Order Maintenance: Broken Windows Policing

As noted earlier in this chapter, order-maintenance policing has become a source of tension between minorities and many urban police departments. This form of policing is an outcome of a theoretical position expressed in a 1982 *Atlantic Monthly* article by James Q. Wilson and George Kelling which suggested that targeting minor disorders could help reduce more serious crime and resident fear and prevent neighborhoods from becoming crime ridden. Police departments in the three most populous cities, New York City, Chicago, and Los Angeles, and many smaller cities throughout the United States have all adopted at least some aspect of Wilson and Kelling's theory, primarily through more enforcement of minor misdemeanor laws. As first proposed by Wilson and Kelling, the basic idea behind what is today known as the **Broken Windows** theory is that if the police engage in quality-of-life or order-maintenance policing, they could simultaneously impact serious crime and citizen fear and prevent communities from becoming unsafe. They stressed the importance of addressing and solving neighborhood problems to reduce the opportunity for crime and the fear of it among residents. The theory suggests that citizen fear, created by disorder, leads to weakened social controls, thus creating conditions where crime and disorder can flourish. The justification for this emphasis on public order crime is drawn from history, namely that in the past, the police had carried out such activities and that the community from which the police gained legitimacy saw these activities as essential police functions (Weisburd & Braga, 2006). The article's central theme was that the link between minor incidents and serious crimes is exemplified by the metaphor of what happens to an abandoned building. If this building has all its windows intact, it can sit vacant and undisturbed indefinitely. However, if one window is broken and not quickly repaired, more windows will be broken, and the building will eventually be destroyed (Wilson & Kelling, 1982; Maple & Mitchell, 1999). Community disorder creates quality-of-life issues that, like breaking an abandoned building's windows left unchecked, eventually lead to the breakdown of community controls. Sousa and

Kelling (2006) note that the policy implication is that if the police working with community residents manage minor disorders and maintain public order, the result will be a reduction in more serious criminal activity. This implication also implies that the police and the community should support each other and work together to achieve community safety.

William J. Bratton operationalized the Broken Windows theory when he was chief executive of the New York City Transit Police, the New York City Police Department, and the Los Angeles Police Department. He believes that taking care of minor quality-of-life offenses in a neighborhood, like fixing the abandoned building's windows, will eventually head off more serious crime. Take a fare beater, a low-level drug dealer, or a disorderly drunk off the street, and whatever criminal behavior he intended to engage in goes away with him. Bratton's strategist, Deputy Police Commissioner Jack Maple (1999), however, warned that while one arrest can interrupt an active criminal career, quality-of-life enforcement is only fully effective if the department actively has its officers seek to obtain information about other crimes from their arrestees. Police officers should also be empowered to collaborate with residents to deal with small stuff that matters to communities, and the serious stuff will be taken care of (Bratton & Tumin, 2012). Maple's strategic view was that all department members should become information gatherers. This information and the data normally gathered by a department should serve as the basis for strategy development.

However, accomplishing this redirection requires changes in departmental administration. Broken Windows operations should give local commanders the discretion to target areas and focus on minor offenses based on residents' complaints and practices of their communities. Thus, policing an area should not follow a department's traditional mode of imposed operations but should reflect the community's needs. This will require decentralizing control over personnel to allow them to concentrate on problem areas and engage in community-based problem-solving, responding to problems rather than incidents and making it possible for them to work directly with their counterparts in the community and other government service agencies, freeing them from the control of the chain of command (Wilson & Kelling, 1989). Kelling has reiterated these ideas, emphasizing that the concept of Broken Windows has always been "a tactic of community policing, highly discretionary, easy to abuse, but when conducted properly contributes enormously to the quality of urban life" and the sense of security that grows out of close interaction between community residents and the police to maintain order and reduce crime (Kelling, 2015, p. 628).

Again, Kelling (2015, p. 628) defined Broken Windows Policing (BWP) as "a tactic of community policing—highly discretionary, easy to abuse, but when conducted properly contributes enormously to the quality of urban life." The police and the citizenry must work together to maintain order and reduce crime. Research on the effectiveness of BWP is mixed.

Meta-analysis results questioned BWP's central premise that neighborhood disorder promotes crime. This review of 96 studies did not support the BKP thesis that disorder promotes aggression and fear of crime in neighborhoods (O'Brien, Farrell, & Welch, 2019).

A meta-analysis of 30 studies on the link between disorder and crime found that police operations had a modest reduction effect. The most significant impact was recorded for those interventions that featured changing social and physical disorder conditions (Braga, Welch, & Schell, 2015). Welch, Braga, and Bruinsma (2015, p. 456) concluded that these research findings support the idea that police departments should adopt a "community co-production" model rather than engaging in a "zero-tolerance policing" model—that has the potential to enrage citizens and does not seem to reduce crime. However, six studies from this analysis found that disorder policing operations failed to reduce fear of crime significantly (Weisburd et al., 2015a). Similarly, a longitudinal study of a Houston police department operation based on BWP produced mixed results. The operation did not significantly affect crime—only one crime pattern out of five registered a notable benefit (Zhao & Zhang, 2022, p. 17).

In his second term as NYPD Police Commissioner, William Bratton established neighborhood policing—a variation of Broken Windows Policing designed to increase police contact with citizens. An evaluation based on monthly data from 76 precincts from 2006 to 2019 reported mixed results. Research revealed that the operation did not reduce property or violent crime but temporarily increased citizen complaints against the police. The policy reduced misdemeanor arrests and proactive arrests—especially in the poorest neighborhoods (Beck, Antonelli, & Pineros, 2022).

A survey of Houston residents supports the BWP hypothesis concerning disorder and fear of crime (FOC). Respondents in disadvantaged areas perceived and reported higher levels of disorder and FOC. These feelings were aggravated by "legal cynicism"—the perception that the police cannot effectively prevent crime (Oh, Ren, & He, 2019, p. 9). In addition, survey results from Baltimore determined that Black and White residents perceive the presence of disorder differently. Thus, when performing BWP-based operations, the police must be cognizant of the "diversity of perceptions of disorder" that could fail to reduce crime but could undermine police legitimacy (Hinkle, White, Weisburd, & Kuen, 2023, p. 53). The research findings suggest that BWP should abandon a dragnet, zero-tolerance approach in favor of more targeted operations. Weisburd and Majmundar's (2018, p. 176) report on proactive policing echoed this conclusion, stating that "broken windows policing interventions that use aggressive tactics for increasing misdemeanor arrests to control disorder generate small to null impacts on crime."

In the 1990s, the New York City Police Department targeted quality-of-life offenses (QOL), such as subway fare beating, aggressive panhandling, sleeping on public benches, smoking marijuana in public, and graffiti painting, in a program that began with Commissioner William J. Bratton and Mayor Rudy Giuliani and continued through the next 25 years. This tactic has been identified with Broken Windows and order-maintenance policing. It is designed for use in neighborhoods and places plagued by serious crime problems and has also displayed an inability to control them.

Another example of this strategy is the **Hot Spot Policing** implemented in 2005 by the Lowell (MA) Police Department. It sought to improve social order in targeted high-crime areas (Hot Spots) and was intended to create broad crime-reduction results across the greater area (Braga & Bond, 2008). To be effective, this style of policing should not only involve reducing crime and disorder but also ways to facilitate community collective efficacy. Therefore, matching the policing style to conditions in a neighborhood represents only the first step. The second step should be for the officers to find ways to move the community toward developing a stronger, self-reliant community (Noland, Conti, & McDevitt, 2005).

Early research on the effectiveness of **Quality of Life** policing recorded mixed results. Sherman (1990) examined the effect of QOL policing on public drinking and parking violations to see if it also impacted robbery in Washington, DC. Although the operation failed to reduce street-level robberies, it enhanced citizen perceptions of safety in the area. A similar study reported the same results: Cracking down on liquor law violations (public drunkenness, possession of alcohol by minors) failed to impact burglary and robbery offenses (Novak, Hartman, Holsinger, & Turner, 1999).

Both studies focused on the enforcement of alcohol offenses, but QOL policing often focuses on broader acts of public disorder.

Katz, Webb, and Schaefer (2001) researched the effectiveness of Operation Restoration, a QOL operation in a Chandler, AZ, redevelopment district. Here, a specialized police unit focused on disorder crimes (prostitution, street-level drug dealing, loitering) and physical conditions (graffiti abatement, property inspections, trash and litter removal). The research determined that the operation impacted social and physical disorder. Public morals crimes (prostitution and public drinking) were reduced, and physical disorder calls for service decreased. Evidence of crime displacement was also present—traffic violations and drug calls for service increased in surrounding areas (Katz et al., 2001, pp. 857–858). The benefits of the operation were limited to the offenses it targeted.

One of the major policy issues is whether QOL policing has a deterrent effect, reducing disorder and enhancing public safety. A survey of 539 New York arrestees in 1999 revealed that they knew of the quality-of-life policing activities by the NYPD and that they had changed their behavior (about two-thirds) in the last six months. The deterrent effect was especially pronounced among those who had engaged in disorderly behavior (Golub, Johnson, Taylor, & Eterno, 2003).

Another serious criticism of QOL policing is that it "widens the net" for arrests, especially among minority groups. Further analysis of the 1999 NYC QOL arrestee sample addressed this question by comparing them to arrestees for index and drug felonies. The research found that widening the net did not occur. While most (90 percent) of the QOL arrestees were Black or Hispanic, so were most of the serious felony arrestees during this period. QOL policing did not increase the targeting of minorities, but it also did not reduce it (Golub, Johnson, Taylor, & Eterno, 2004, p. 41). One of the major complaints raised by activists about this form of policing is that it primarily targets people of color.

A meta-analysis of Broken Windows Policing studies confirms the effectiveness of the approach, particularly those designed to change social and physical disorder at particular places rather than an aggressive order-maintenance strategy (Braga et al., 2015). The studies report the ability of order-maintenance policing to reduce violent, property, drug, and disorder crimes. They concluded that these types of strategies police departments use to control disorder seem to matter, and this holds important implications for police–community relations, justice, and crime prevention. This analysis underscores the conclusion that police "should continue to engage in policing disorder tactics as a part of their portfolio of strategies to reduce crime" (Braga et al., 2015, p. 581).

The question of the effectiveness of Broken Windows Policing is tied to its implementation. Are operations carried out with an eye toward collective efficacy and procedural justice? Mears (2015, p. 620) notes two "curricula" surrounding such operations. First is the overt curriculum that emphasizes constitutional rights. Here, the message to citizens from the police is: We are working for your good and especially for the good of those who live in high-crime communities. We are fighting crime while respecting your freedom and autonomy. Our goal is to maximize freedom, freedom from crime and predation, and freedom from the state's arbitrary power. The second is the "hidden curriculum" of Broken Windows Policing which gives certain citizens the impression that they are a "special, dangerous, and undesirable class." A potential threat to civil liberties counterbalances the benefits of Broken Windows Policing. A constitutionally respectful implementation of operations must frame the desirable fruits of order maintenance if they are to be thoroughly enjoyed. Unfortunately, at the beginning of the 21st century, the NYPD focused more on increasing misdemeanor arrests than on situational crime prevention and enhancing social order.

In July 2014, the death in New York City of Eric Garner created a growing campaign against Broken Windows Policing. Garner, a 350-pound asthmatic, was committing a misdemeanor offense by selling untaxed cigarettes in a commercial area of Staten Island. A group of New York City police officers tried to arrest him. He resisted, and the officers brought the 350-pound asthmatic to the ground by pulling him down by his neck. Garner went into cardiac arrest and eventually died. Critics of Broken Windows Policing contend that this case illustrates the dangers of this form of policing, especially for minorities, and that public order policing is a racist assault on poor minority neighborhoods that criminalizes inoffensive behavior. They claim it leads to harassment of Blacks and Hispanics and antagonizes residents of high-crime neighborhoods while doing nothing to fight serious crime (MacDonald, 2014). Critics claim that police tactics fail to distinguish minorities who are ordinary working individuals from those who engage in criminal behavior. It is claimed that the application of Broken Windows encourages officers to stop and harass minorities indiscriminately. As a result, in many areas of the country, Broken Windows enforcement has lost the minority community's support because it is seen as an externally imposed measure targeting residents of their communities. Critics say applications of Broken Windows, such as the stop-and-frisk policy of New York City, stretched from Kelling's original design into a convenient rubric for intrusive policing measures. Many in the most affected communities complained that protection had felt like an occupation. This debate, while critiquing police practice, is also creating a dialogue between the police and community members regarding what is an acceptable policing crime-control strategy.

Creating Community Safety

The prior discussion of police tactics highlights that community safety is a product of how well two critical stakeholders, the residents and the police, work together and respect each other. In a free society, there must be a balance between civil authority and citizens. Communities will never develop as safe and secure environments if the residents do not own security. Police departments, depending upon the size of the area they serve, can help build community self-defense through legitimacy, procedural justice, consultation, collaboration, and partnership. These efforts aim for the police to support and increase the inherent strengths and self-governing capacities of neighborhoods that enable them to defend themselves against crime and disorder. Kelling and Stewart (1989, pp. 8, 9) maintain that the following principles shape that relationship.

1. Community self-defense against crime and disorder is primarily a matter of private social control supported, but never supplanted, by public police.
2. Because neighborhoods vary in their problems and capacity for self-help (their ecology of self-defense, collective efficacy), they are tailoring police tactics to specific neighborhoods.
3. Tailoring tactics to neighborhoods will require decentralizing police authority and tactical decision-making to lower levels of the organization and empowering sergeants and patrol officers to decide about the problems they will deal with and the tactics they will use to deal with those problems.

4. Precinct (police subdivisions) and beat (officer-assigned area) configurations must be changed to reflect community and neighborhood form.

5. In the most troubled neighborhoods, especially those now being ravaged by the problems associated with drugs and violent crime, police must at least seek authority from residents to act on their behalf. In neighborhoods that are most bereft of self-help capacities, in inner-city underclass areas, and in neighborhoods most plagued by lawlessness, it is tempting for police to operate independently and without community consultations. The problems are so acute and the resources so meager that consultations may appear inefficient and needlessly time-consuming. This serves neither the police nor the residents well. Deprived of community authorization, police are vulnerable to charges of both neglect and abuse. The willingness of police to fill in the gap and "do it themselves" deprives citizens of the kinds of experiences that American political philosophy suggests will lead them to "acquire a taste for order" and develop their capacities as citizens.

6. If it is believed that the function of police is to support and increase the inherent strengths and self-governing capacities of neighborhoods that enable them to defend themselves against crime and disorder, a priority of police in deprived neighborhoods is not only to gain authorization for police action but also to help develop capacities for community self-defense. Given the desperate circumstances of some inner-city neighborhoods, this will be a difficult task. It will be perilous for citizens to defend their neighborhoods. The risk can be justified only if police commit themselves to pervasive presence for long durations of time. Such presence must always support and encourage self-help.

7. In neighborhoods capable of self-help and governance, police activities should be designed and implemented to strengthen neighborhoods. Police, like other government agencies, should not do for citizens what citizens can do for themselves. There are reasons to believe that when government supplants self-help, the capacity of citizens for self-help diminishes.

8. Because different neighborhoods have different interests that conflict with each other, police will have to manage inter-neighborhood and intra-neighborhood relations. Neighborhoods require free commerce and penetration by strangers and other groups to thrive.

9. Police must understand that just as their task is to support the self-help capacities of neighborhoods when those capacities are used for appropriate ends, they must thwart the self-help capacities of neighborhoods when they turn petty, mean, and tyrannical. Police are well equipped for this. During the past two decades, "constitutional policing," resisted by many police but later embraced and incorporated by the great chiefs and police leaders of the era, has empowered police to withstand parochial pressure. This does not mean that police will not have to be vigilant in resisting inappropriate pressures; it means that police executives have moved to instill the values and policies that will help them maintain constitutional practice. Justice is as important as security in policing.

These principles guide considerations to be addressed during the development of police and community collaboration to build safer communities.

Community Collaboration

Collaboration begins when the police department, community organizations, and neighborhood residents agree to work together to achieve community safety. The central issue for establishing a collaborative community environment is to get residents and neighborhood institutions to share responsibility for creating a safe community with their police. Developing a collaborative effort should increase knowledge, understanding, trust, and cooperation between the police and the citizens they serve. They are also created to orient police toward a more proactive and strategic approach to developing community safety. Collaboration is a way for departments to develop a sensitivity to citizen expectations, gain information about public safety issues, maintain an open dialogue during times of crisis, and achieve goals. **Community collaboration** requires police executives and managers to master interpersonal and group process skills and develop a talent for recognizing and managing the potential of intensifying positive and negative community involvement in organizational practice and culture (IACP, 1999).

Collaboration involves:

1. Knowledge and understanding of the parties involved.
2. Responsiveness to the needs of the community.
3. Trust, respect, and understanding between partners.
4. Communication consisting of an open and direct dialogue.

Community collaboration requires that police departments develop knowledge and understanding about the areas and people they serve and become skilled at diagnosing the issues affecting these neighborhoods. Communities are complex interactional settings whose public safety needs are subject to the forces of change within our society. Departments should develop timely and accurate information about the constituencies within their communities beyond developing data on crime and quality-of-life issues. From a strategic management perspective, this knowledge's key value lies in its "strategic" use (Dean & Gottschalk, 2007). To strategically manage their organizations, police executives must identify and monitor the factors creating change in their communities to develop the knowledge to diagnose these issues, collaborate, set public safety objectives, and build partnerships. A department's leadership must also be administratively flexible to adjust their response to the changing nature of community needs.

One way to develop this knowledge is to create an accurate and timely **community profile** to define stakeholder constituencies and identify driving factors within their community. Developing and maintaining a community profile provides a structured way for identifying, gathering, and analyzing relevant information to support collaboration and problem-solving. A department's community profile should not only define the various elements that make up and define the community but also identify the forces within the community that affect it and their underlying causes. It will serve as a basis for diagnosing these factors and lead to a fuller understanding of the community and its residents. A community profile should be descriptive and inclusive enough to enable the department to understand its relationship with its external environment. It should be considered a living document, not a static item that never changes but is consistently updated.

Information needed for a community profile includes:

1. Description of the area population by race, ethnicity by number and percentage, and gender and age distribution.
2. Community institutions, religious and educational, and the contact persons for each.

3. Physical characteristics such as boundaries, parks and recreation areas, name and number of buildings, and streets.
4. Commercial properties, numbers of high-rise buildings, single-family units, transient lodgings, vacant and abandoned housing units, and population density.
5. Streets important to traffic and people movement. Alleyway, backyard, and roof-top conditions. Illegal and legal markets.
6. Location and identification of liaison for all correctional, confinement, treatment, and community-based assistance programs: Emergency family shelters, food banks, welfare services, and homeless shelters.
7. Listing by name of community service organizations and their contact persons:
   a. Professional associations
   b. Business associations
   c. Civic groups
   d. Fraternal associations
   e. Volunteer organizations for youths
   f. Daycare centers
   g. Ethnic associations
   h. Athletic clubs
   i. Homeowner associations
   j. Parent-teacher associations.
8. Governmental agencies: Fire, sanitation, ambulance services, code enforcement, highway and street department, labor and welfare departments.
9. Offense-prone population: Parole and probation clients, percentage of violent and property offenders, repeat quality-of-life offenders.
10. Gang/group activity: Leaders, number and identity, ethnic composition, colors and symbols, affiliations, and membership.

The information in the community profile should be integral to orientating new employees to the department and managers to their commands.

Police executives must also develop an understanding and responsiveness to the political, administrative, community, and justice constituencies' needs they serve. These include:

Mayors and city managers set agendas and give policy and program direction to police chief executives. Understanding these individuals and responding to their primary policy and program initiatives is essential for successfully managing the department's external environment and executive survival.

City and county council members are elected officials representing the entire community and having special interests in issues affecting their electoral districts and citizens. They will expect the department to be sensitive to their constituents' concerns. The department and council members must understand the legal boundaries that conscribe these relationships.

Different neighborhoods and subcommunities exist within most jurisdictions. The community profile must identify the different sub-neighborhoods and the majority ethnic and racial groupings that comprise these areas. The issues relating to immigration, the influx of new ethnic groups, and sizable increases in the population of present groups require the police to possess an operationally heightened degree of cultural awareness and tailor their response to a more varied set of subcultural needs. Subcommunities will have differing sets of leadership and concerns. Some are organized, have established formal leadership, and are vocal in expressing their concerns, while others are disorganized and fail to express their needs. Regardless of their ability to seek attention, all neighborhoods must be understood and receive attention equally. Formal leaders may include the pastor of a local church, an elementary school principal, or a civic association leader. Informal leaders are residents respected in the neighborhood who can influence opinion but do not hold formal leadership positions in local organizations. Developing collaborative dialogues with residents and their spokespersons helps departments realize potential issues and satisfy neighborhood differences and safety concerns.

The business community is the economic basis for a community. Leaders of significant businesses frequently wield substantial political power and can be mobilized for political and financial support, including resources. However, small independent businesses contribute to the social cohesiveness of neighborhoods, and their owners are often well respected by community residents. Destruction of these businesses during civil disturbances deprives residents of their services and economic contribution while creating hardships for residents.

Civil service commissions enforce civil service laws governing entry-level requirements, selection practices, promotional eligibility requirements, promotional practices, and discipline. Commissions also function as the appeal body for employees dissatisfied with discipline decisions. Police executives work with commissioners to revise archaic, cumbersome, and counterproductive laws and ordinances and educate them about the purposes and values of discipline practices.

State and federal legislatures recommend, draft, and debate to establish legislation to achieve public safety objectives. They ensure that crime and social legislation do not come forth that is damaging to public safety. The issues that pertain to law-making at the state level pertain with equal relevance to federal law-making.

Federal and state law enforcement agencies have locally based federal and state operations, including special task forces (FBI, DEA, ATF, INS, and DOJ). These agencies are essential partners in addressing community public safety issues.

(IACP, 1999)

Collaboration efforts must build upon mutual trust, respect, and two-way communication. For example, a police chief executive of a 45-person department in northeast Florida explained to one of the authors that he meets bi-weekly or weekly with 30 community leaders. Each of these individuals represents constituencies and residential groupings served by his department. During these meetings, the chief shares information, gains awareness of issues, and discusses factors of mutual concern. The meetings are a proactive way for the chief to become aware of issues and to address problems and community concerns with important stakeholders through direct dialogue, trust, and respect. Increasing stakeholder access to information and invitations to solve issues of mutual concern proactively enhances the development of a mutually beneficial collaborative alliance between the community and its police.

Community Partnerships

Community partnerships consist of a planned, structured working arrangement designed to address a specific issue or problem affecting the community's public safety. It involves a formal process beyond that of collaboration. Forming community problem-solving partnerships between the police and neighborhood stakeholders represents what the late Stephen R. Covey (2008) identifies as a paradigm shift in policing. The new mindset is about partnering for a sustainable civil society, representing a shift toward a community justice system for victims, offenders, the police, judges, and society. This shift requires everyone to be involved in creating safe and just communities. These relationships help facilitate trust between community members and police organizations (Skogan et al., 2002, p. 10).

Covey (2008) suggests that community safety solutions should come from various pockets of the community, not just from those whose formal role is to provide protection. He suggests that communities must leave behind reactive systems and initiate proactive ones. Police and community stakeholders collaborating in partnership can contribute to halting the spiral of crime and developing safer neighborhoods. When citizens become co-producers of public safety it changes how they perceive themselves, their neighborhood, and the organizations that serve their community (Morabito, 2010). This paradigm shift emphasizes the importance of developing collective efficacy and co-production of community safety.

Police agencies need to find ways to connect with members of the communities in which they serve through collaborative partnerships. Community partnerships can help develop ways to overcome citizens' negative perceptions of their police (Skogan et al., 2002, p. 3). Safer neighborhoods are created when police and locally credible community stakeholders work together in partnership in a focused and planned manner (Geller & Belsky, 2009). Many departments have implemented partnerships with minority residents to strengthen minority confidence in the police and to increase their willingness to take part in crime-prevention activities (Wehrman & DeAngelis, 2011, p. 52). These collaborative efforts connect minority communities with law enforcement and create beneficial relationships between officers and citizens. For example, the Chicago Police Department allied with Latino community members to educate citizens about the law to help them avoid involvement in criminal activity (Skogan et al., 2002, p. 12).

Building and sustaining partnerships with the community is an ongoing responsibility of the police chief executive. The sustaining quality between participants is trust. Citizen partners should be willing to:

1. Assume a sense of ownership for their community and its safety.
2. Provide the police with information about crime, criminals, and unsafe conditions.
3. Actively participate in community-based self-help activities that address sources of crime and disorder.
4. Be willing to join with the police and their neighbors to assist in the development of the community's collective efficacy.
5. Be willing to participate with their neighbors in seeking help from other governmental resources besides the police.

The focus of this collaboration is the deterrence of specific crimes, mobilization of residents, and the development of environments inhospitable to crime. However, building community partnerships takes time, planning, communication, intention, willing participants, and mutual respect. Potential community partners include:

Residents.
Police officers.
Police command staff.

Community youth.
Business leaders.
Social clubs and organizations.
Community organizations.
Governmental agencies.
Religious institutions.
Schools.
Elected or appointed officials.
Criminal juvenile agencies.
Media.
Drug and alcohol treatment facilities.
Informal community leaders.
Representatives of racial, age, and economic diversity.

Community Leader/Stakeholder Identification

The process of identifying potential partners requires careful thought. One of the first tasks of developing community partnerships is identifying the public safety problems/issues and ascertaining how many individuals and organizations are interested in resolving these issues. Those claiming to be a spokesperson or leader at a community meeting may only represent themselves and their ideas. However, successful partnerships need committed residents who can influence their neighbors and get things done. They need people who care about their community, want to solve its problems, and are willing to work on providing safety to their community. An excellent way to identify these individuals is to determine their involvement in addressing neighborhood problems to help their community improve. Individuals with a proven track record of leadership in working effectively with residents and residential groups to address problems have priority when building partnerships.

Community leaders are individuals who influence the attitudes and behavior of others within their community. They have a direct influence on those who are willing to listen to them. They can often affect segments of community life and assist police service delivery. These individuals usually fall into two leadership types: Acknowledged or appointed.

Acknowledged leaders are community-sanctioned grassroots persons living in the community whom residents respect and will most likely turn to in critical moments. Acknowledged leaders earn their position because residents often visit them when they need help with problems. They are part of the community's informal power structure (Miller, Hess, & Orthmann, 2014). Acknowledged leaders may include a pastor in a local church, a local team coach, or a small business owner. They may or may not have wide acceptance but may have the respect of a subgroup of residents and the potential to be community leaders.

Appointed leaders are individuals whose positions within the community are politically decided, designated, or set by official employment or prominence.

APPOINTED LEADERS' CHARACTERISTICS

1. They are usually chosen and appointed by persons outside of the community.
2. They may or may not have personal knowledge of the community's problems since they may or may not be community residents.

3. They may have to prove themselves as effective leaders.
4. They may have to work extra hard to gain the community's trust.
5. They may not be able to mobilize community residents.

(NCPC, 1986)

The police should enlist the help of both types of leaders in creating secure communities. Including only appointed leaders when creating community partnerships can cause a loss of community support. However, including only acknowledged leaders may deny needed access to local government service institutions and official resource networks available through appointed leaders' more formal contacts. The department's problem is determining how both leadership types can assist in solving community problems.

Successful partnerships enlist resident assistance in crime identification, prevention, and street-level problem-solving. The primary aim is to get citizens and community institutions to share the responsibility for dealing with crime and crime-related problems.

Successful community partnerships involve:

1. Stakeholders with a vested interest in the issue.
2. Chronic problem(s) that residents have a substantial stake in addressing and offer an opportunity for organizing, planning, and partnership building.
3. Informed and committed resident and police leadership.
4. Trust among and between partners.
5. Shared vision and common goals.
6. Expertise among partners to solve community problems.
7. Community organizations through which volunteers can work and be effective.
8. Organizations that can support local efforts and provide community residents with training, education, and technical assistance.
9. Teamwork strategies.
10. Open communication between participants and the police.
11. Motivated partners.
12. Sufficient means to implement and sustain the collaborative effort.
13. An action plan.

(Rinehart et al., 2001, p. 7)

The problem-solving process is likely to succeed with partnerships from committed and active partners. The most significant investment of time and resources should come from community volunteers and staff members of non-organizations. In this manner, community stakeholders take responsibility for resolving their problems with police assistance.

Problems that make developing partnerships difficult and can lead to failure include:

1. Non-existent communication between community participants and police.
2. Lack of informed and committed resident and police leadership.
3. Lack of community organizations through which neighborhood residents can take part.
4. The only community-based organizations are concerned with serving clients, not solving community problems.

5. Community residents are discouraged and feel their neighborhood is lost and powerless.
6. Whether a group of dedicated individuals can make the neighborhood viable again.

Implementing a Partnership

A department's first step when implementing a community partnership is identifying its goals. For the partnership to work on community problems or issues it must be identified and defined. This task begins with the selection of a target neighborhood and the analysis of its public safety issues. Selection benefits from analyzing various data sources and information from the department and the community. All aspects of the target problem or issue should be identified in priority order to be addressed by the partnership team. It is the **scanning** in problem-oriented policing. It involves:

- Identifying recurring problems of concern to the residents of an area and the police.
- Identifying the consequences of the problem for the residents and the police.
- Prioritizing those problems based on their impact on community safety.
- Analyzing the problems using a variety of data sources.
- Identifying community residents' perceptions of their safety and how they are affected by the problems in their area.
- Determining the frequency of problem occurrences and how long they have occurred.
- Selecting the problem(s) for the partnership to address.
- Developing outcome goals relating to the resolution of the problem.

Once accomplished, the next step is to identify key neighborhood stakeholders with the skill sets and knowledge needed to affect the problem or issue selected for the group to work on. Individuals need to be identified, approached, and asked if they are willing to be group members that will focus on community safety issues. An essential step in getting people interested and willing to join is identifying what expectations are and their benefits. Next, the department must convene the first meeting to define group objectives and task responsibilities clearly. Each group member should be assigned an essential task(s) and the time required to accomplish it. It is vital that each member of the partnership be transparent about their role, informed, feel included, and have a sense of ownership for the entire effort. Keeping track of problems and progress requires regular meetings, ongoing communication methods, and an evaluation process. Partnership members must build commitment and a sense of accomplishment.

Next, the group needs to develop an action plan to implement the partnership project and accomplish the desired objectives. The **action plan** is a working document that serves as a tool to guide the collaboration of group members as they implement the problem response. An action plan identifies *what* will be done, by *whom*, and *when*. The action plan should also identify how the partnership will know if actions have achieved the desired outcomes. Rinehart et al. (2001,p. 4) recommend that the action plan should:

- Specify what activities and tasks should occur.
- Identify who is responsible for each task.

- Establish the timeframe for accomplishing the task and when action will occur.
- Identify the resources needed to accomplish the tasks and how to acquire them.

This plan should be disseminated to all members of the partnership. It is a working document that should be changed as new information and the project evolves during implementation. The plan should be periodically reviewed regarding the actions' relevance and consistency with desired outcomes. The last step is to design a means to evaluate what has been accomplished. Establishing appropriate quantitative and qualitative performance measures will help link partnership actions to specific outcomes. Monitoring, measurement, and evaluation are the keys to partnership success. They let the partnership determine if they have accomplished what they set out to do.

Valid and reliable **evaluation** requires:

1. **Identification of measurable outcomes (goals);**
2. **Identification of measurable objectives (milestones, steps)** that will lead to the accomplishment of the desired outcomes; and
3. **A reporting system** for monitoring progress and maintaining **accountability;**
4. Assessment of **actual accomplishments** versus desired outcomes.

All partnership tasks should be conducted with evaluation in mind. Feedback systems and measurable objectives should always be part of action plans. Partnerships should avoid setting unrealistic and unattainable expectations by developing a strategy that incorporates realistic and attainable objectives as system elements. Goals and objectives (outcomes) should provide a way to assess progress accurately, cite success, and identify tasks that work. Baseline measures that record the conditions for establishing the partnership before implementing the change need identification to compare relevant changes over time.

Finally, all performance measures should relate to the partnership's vision, mission, and goals. The design and implementation of evaluations depend upon their intended purpose. Always measure what matters and what provides the information needed. All else is a waste of time, budget, and organizational resources.

Conclusion

"Community" refers to a specific geographical area and the individuals, organizations, and agencies who live and function within that area. Creating and maintaining safe communities is an essential police function. Crime-ridden, disorderly, and disorganized communities are places where people lock themselves behind closed doors, stay off the streets, and are afraid to use public places. However, the police cannot create safe communities without the residents' support, approval, and assistance. The 1829 *Principles of Law Enforcement* and the concept of police–community collaboration reinforce Community Policing. Community Policing seeks to engage the community by involving residents as active participants in identifying and preventing crime and disorder and other street-level revitalization efforts. This strategy requires police departments to actively seek to collaborate with the community in a planned manner, build partnerships, and develop mutual trust.

The capacity of neighborhood residents to protect themselves against crime and disorder requires the achievement of "collective efficacy." Collective efficacy involves residents monitoring children and other persons in public areas, acting to prevent disorderly conduct, and confronting individuals who exploit or disturb public spaces (Sampson et al., 1997). These activities depend upon residents trusting each other and cooperating with themselves and trusting and cooperating with the police. Creating and supporting the development of collective efficacy is a worthwhile aim of police–community partnerships.

As first proposed by Wilson and Kelling (1982), the Broken Windows theory hypothesizes that if the police maintain public order they could simultaneously impact serious crime, address the fear of crime, and establish safe communities. They stressed the importance of addressing and solving neighborhood problems to reduce the opportunity for crime and the fear of it among residents. Citizen fear, created by disorder, leads to weakened social controls, thus creating the conditions for crime to flourish. The justification for this emphasis on public order crime is drawn from history, namely that in the past the police had carried out such activities and that the community from which the police gained legitimacy saw these as essential police functions (Weisburd & Braga, 2006).

Community partnership is an organizational strategy designed to create a working relationship among the police, residents, residents' groups, and social organizations in a defined neighborhood. The strategy calls for developing a planned collaborative relationship between the police and residents to alter the nature of crime and antisocial behavior by building a neighborhood collective efficacy. However, for the community residents to collaborate and form partnerships with the police, they must trust and believe in the legitimacy of their police department and approve of its efforts.

The police are viewed as legitimate when citizens believe that the police have moral authority to enforce the law and deserve respect, compliance, and support. Community residents will be more willing to work with the police when they view them as legitimate and consider their enforcement decisions favorable and fair. The police must consider how the community's perceptions of their legitimacy and use of procedural justice can affect how they work with residents to address public safety issues. Procedural justice reflects the rational, neutral, and transparent decision-making of police officers. It involves the belief that the police use their coercive authority in a trustworthy fashion. Suppose the police intend to create collaborative partnerships with community residents. In that case, they must promote a culture of respect within their departments and clarify that mistreatment of citizens will not be tolerated. Police legitimacy is determined by public assessments of how the police exercise authority. Legitimacy is crucial to respectful and effective relations between the police and the communities they serve.

KEY TERMS

Acknowledged leaders	Community leaders	Legitimacy
Action plan	Community partnership	Neighborhood
Appointed leaders	Community profile	Quality-of-life policing
Broken Windows	Community safety	Scanning
Collective efficacy	Evaluation	Vertical systems
Community	Horizontal systems	
Community collaboration	Hot Spot Policing Strategy	

References

Beck, B., Antonelli, J., & Pineros, G. (2022). Effects of New York City's neighborhood policing policy. *Police Quarterly, 25*(4), 470–496.

Braga, A.A., & Bond, B.J. (2008). Policing crime and disorder hot spots: A randomized controlled trial. *Criminology, 46*(3), 577–608.

Braga, A.A., & Brunson, R.K. (2015). The police and public discourse on "black-on-black" violence. *New Perspectives in Policing Bulletin.* Washington, DC: National Institute of Justice: John F. Kennedy School of Government, Harvard University.

Braga, A.A., Welsh, B.C., & Schell, C. (2015). Can policing disorder reduce crime? A systematic review and meta-analysis. *Journal of Research in Crime & Delinquency, 52*(4), 567–588.

Bratton, W.J., & Tumin, Z. (2012). *Collaborate or perish: Reaching across boundaries in a networked world.* New York, NY: Random House.

Carter, D.L. (2002). *The police and the community.* Upper Saddle River, NJ: Prentice Hall.

COPS Office. (2015). *President's task force on 21st century policing implementation guide: Moving from recommendations to action.* Washington, DC: Office of Community Oriented Policing Services.

Covey, S.R. (2008). A whole new mind-set on fighting crime. *The Police Chief, 75*(12), 16–18.

Dean, G., & Gottschalk, P. (2007). *Knowledge management in policing and law enforcement: Foundations, structures, applications.* London: Oxford University Press.

Fischer, C. (2014). *Legitimacy and procedural justice: A new element of police leadership.* Washington, DC: U.S. Department of Justice, Bureau of Justice Assistance.

Geller, B., & Belsky, L. (2009). *A policymakers guide to building our way out of crime.* Washington, DC: U.S. Department of Justice, Office of Community Oriented Policing Services.

Golub, A., Johnson, B.D., Taylor, A., & Eterno, J. (2003). Quality of life policing: Do offenders get the message? *Policing, 26*(4), 690–707.

Golub, A., Johnson, B.D., Taylor, A., & Eterno, J. (2004). Does quality of life policing widen the net? A partial analysis. *Justice Research & Policy, 6*(1), 19–42.

Hawdon, J.E., Ryan, J., & Griffin, S.P. (2003). Policing tactics and perceptions of police legitimacy. *Police Quarterly, 6*(4), 469–491.

Henry, V.E. (2002). *The Compstat paradigm: Management accountability in policing.* New York, NY: Looseleaf Press.

Hinkle, J., White, C., Weisburd, D., & Kuen, K. (2023). Disorder in the eye of the beholder: Black and white residents' of disorder in high-crime street segments. *Criminology & Public Policy, 22*, 35–61.

International Association of Chiefs of Police (IACP). (1999). *Police leadership in the 21st century: Achieving & sustaining executive success: Recommendations from the President's first leadership conference.* Alexandria, VA, www.theiacp.org/Police-Leadership-in-the-21st-Century.

Katz, C.M., Webb, V.J., & Schaefer, D.R. (2001). An assessment of the impact of quality of life policing on crime and disorder. *Justice Quarterly, 18*(4), 825–876.

Kelling, G. (2015). An author's brief history of an idea. *Journal of Research in Crime & Delinquency, 52*(4), 626–629.

Kelling, G.L., & Stewart, J.K. (1989). Neighborhoods and police: The maintenance of civil authority. *Perspectives on Policing, No. 10.* Washington, DC: National Institute of Justice, John F. Kennedy School of Government, Harvard University.

Kennedy, D.M. (2011). *Don't shoot: One man, a street fellowship and the end of violence in inner-city America.* New York, NY: Bloomsbury.

MacDonald, H. (2014, December 17). How broken windows policing puts fewer men in prison. New York, NY: *Time Magazine.*

Maguire, E.R., & Johnson, D. (2010). Measuring public perceptions of the police. *Policing, 33*(4), 703–730.

Maple, J., & Mitchell, C. (1999). *The crime fighter: Putting the bad guys out of business.* New York, NY: Doubleday.

Mears, T. (2015). Broken windows, neighborhoods, and the legitimacy of law enforcement or why I fell in and out of love with Zimbardo. *Journal of Research in Crime & Delinquency, 52*(4), 609–625.

Miller, L.S., Hess, K.M., & Orthmann, C.H. (2014). *Community policing: Partnerships for problem solving.* Clifton Park, NY: Delmar.

Morabito, M.S. (2010). Understanding community policing as an innovation: Patterns of adoption. *Crime & Delinquency, 56*(4), 564–587.

National Crime Prevention Council (NCPC). (1986). *Preventing crime in urban communities: Handbook and program profiles.* Washington, DC: NCPC.

Neyroud, P. (2009). Legitimacy. In A. Wakefield & J. Fleming (Eds.), *The Sage dictionary of policing* (pp. 190–192). London: Sage.

Noland, J.J., Conti, N., & McDevitt, J. (2005). Situational policing. *FBI Law Enforcement Bulletin, 74*(11), 1–9.

Novak, K., Hartman, J., Holsinger, A., & Turner, M. (1999). The effects of aggressive policing of disorder on serious crime. *Policing, 22,* 171–190.

Oates, D.J. (2016, October 3). Discussion of the Aurora Colorado Mass Shooting. *Presentation at the Southern Police Institute former Aurora the Police Chief.*

O'Brien, D., Farrell, C., & Welch, B. (2019). Looking through broken windows: The impact of neighborhood disorder on aggression and fear of crime is an artifact of research design. *Annual Review of Criminology, 2,* 53–71.

Oh, G., Ren, L., & He, P. (2019). Social disorder and residence-based fear of crime: The differential mediating effects of police effectiveness. *Journal of Criminal Justice,* 1–11.

Peak, K.J., & Glensor, R.W. (2012). *Community policing and problem solving: Strategies and practices,* 6th ed. Upper Saddle River, NJ: Prentice Hall.

President's Task Force on 21st Century Policing (2015). *Final report of President's task force on 21st century policing.* Washington, DC: Office of Community Oriented Policing Services.

Reith, C. (1956). *A new study of police history.* Edinburgh, Scotland: Oliver & Boyd.

Rinehart, T.A., Laszio, A.T., & Brisco, G.O. (2001). *Collaboration toolkit: How to build fix and sustain productive partnerships.* Washington, DC: US Department of Justice, Office of Community Policing.

Sampson, R.J. (2012). *Great American city: Chicago and the enduring neighborhood effect.* Chicago, IL: University of Chicago Press.

Sampson, R.J., & Bartusch, D.J. (1998). Legal cynicism and (subcultural?) tolerance of deviance: The neighborhood context of racial differences. *Law & Society Review, 32*(4), 777–804.

Sampson, R.J., Raudenbush, S.W., & Earls, F. (1997). Neighborhoods and violent crime: A multilevel study of collective efficacy. *Science, 277,* 918–924.

Sherman, L. (1990). Police crackdowns: Initial and residual deterrence. In M. Tonry & N. Morris (Eds.), *Crime and justice: A review of research – Vol. 12* (pp. 1–48). Chicago, IL: University of Chicago Press.

Skogan, W., & Frydl, K. (Eds.) (2004). *Fairness and effectiveness in policing: The evidence.* Committee to Review Research on Police Policy and Practices. Committee on Law and Justice, Division of Behavioral and Social Sciences and Education. Washington, DC: The National Academies Press.

Skogan, W.G., Steiner, L., DuBois, J., Gudell, J.E., & Fagan, A. (2002). *Community policing and "the new immigrants": Latinos in Chicago.* Washington, DC: U.S. Department of Justice, Office of Justice Programs, National Institute of Justice.

Sousa, W.H., & Kelling, G.L. (2006). Of broken windows, criminology and criminal justice. In D. Weisburd & A.A. Braga (Eds.), *Police innovation: Contrasting perspectives* (pp. 17–97). Cambridge: Cambridge University Press.

Sunshine, J., & Tyler, T.R. (2003). The role of procedural justice and legitimacy in shaping public support for policing. *Law & Society Review, 37*(3), 513–548.

Trojanowicz, R., & Bucqueroux, B. (1994). *Community policing: How to get started.* Cincinnati, OH: Anderson.

Tyler, T.R. (2004). To better serve and protect: Improving police practices. *Annals of the American Academy of Political and Social Science, 593,* 84–99.

Tyler, T.R., & Fagan, J. (2008). Legitimacy and cooperation: Why do people help the police fight crime in their communities? *Ohio State Journal of Criminal Law, 6,* 231–275.

Tyler, T.R., & Huo, Y. (2002). *Trust in the law.* New York, NY: Russell Sage Foundation.

Vito, A.G., Higgins, G., Walsh, W.F., & Vito, G. (2012). The threat of methamphetamine use and production: Evaluation results from a Kentucky law enforcement program. *International Journal of Police Science & Management, 14*(3), 1–12.

Walsh, W. (2001). Compstat: An analysis of an emerging police managerial paradigm. *Policing: An International Journal of Police Strategies & Management, 24*(3), 347–362.

Wehrman, M.M., & DeAngelis, J. (2011). Citizen willingness to participate in police–community partnerships: Exploring the influence of race and neighborhood context. *Police Quarterly, 14*(1), 48–69.

Weisburd, D., & Braga, A.A. (Eds.) (2006). *Police innovation: Contrasting perspectives.* Cambridge: Cambridge University Press.

Weisburd, D., Davis, M., & Gill, C. (2015a). Increasing collective efficacy and social capital at crime hot spots: New crime control tools for police. *Policing, 9*(3), 265–274.

Weisburd, D., Hinkle, J., Braga, A., & Wooditch, A. (2015b). Understanding the mechanisms underlying broken windows policing: The need for evaluation evidence. *Journal of Research in Crime and Delinquency, 52*(4), 589–608.

Weisburd, D., & Majmundar, M. (Eds.) (2018). Proactive policing: Effects on crime and communities. New York, NY: National Academies Press.

Welch, B., Braga, A., & Bruinsma, G. (2015). Reimaging broken windows: From theory to policy. *Journal of Research on Crime and Delinquency, 52*(4), 447–463.

Wilson, J.Q., & Kelling, G.L. (1982, March). The police and neighborhood safety: Broken windows. *Atlantic Monthly,* 29–38.

Wilson, J.Q., & Kelling, G.L. (1989, February). Making neighborhoods safe. *Atlantic Monthly,* 46–52.

Wolfe, S.E. (2011). The effect of low self-control on perceived police legitimacy. *Journal of Criminal Justice, 39*, 67–74. Zhao, J.S., Tsai, C.F., Ren, L., & Lai, Y.L. (2012). Public satisfaction with police control of disorder crime: Does the public hold the police accountable? *Justice Quarterly, 31*(2), 394–420.

Zhao, J., & Zhang, Y. (2022). A longitudinal study of police differential response team impact on crime in Houston: A test of broken windows thesis. *Police Quarterly*, 1–26.

13 Future Challenges and Concerns

Learning Objectives

1. To understand the changing nature of policing.

2. To identify the issues driving change in policing.

3. To understand the factors involved in the use of deadly force.

4. To consider the relationship between organizational culture and good policing.

5. To identify the strategies for building community trust.

6. To identify the "Principles of Good Policing."

7. To examine the concept of legitimacy and how it affects the police organization and the community.

8. To consider how to deal with budgetary issues.

9. To analyze the values of the "new generation" of police officers and how they affect supervisory styles.

10. To examine the impact of Body-worn cameras (BWCs) and COVID-19 on policing.

11. To consider innovations for effective policing.

Introduction

The role of a strategic leader is to develop an organization that responds to the needs of the present and the future using the resources and capabilities of the organization. Understanding the present is difficult, but preparing for and projecting the future is challenging. If, however, as most strategic thinkers claim, the past and present are a forecast of the future, policing can expect to face continued significant challenges. Chuck Wexler, Executive Director of the Police Executive Research Forum (PERF) (2014), stated that policing in the 21st century changes more in a year than it changed in a decade a generation ago.

While still being accountable for traditional responsibilities such as calls for service and crime investigation, many departments have expanded their mission to include crime prevention, fear reduction, lowering crime rates, and creating effective communities. Rather than focusing on responding to crimes after they are

DOI: 10.4324/9781003459095-13

committed, today's best police departments are looking for ways to be proactive. Progressive departments emphasize data analysis, technology, and analytical projection to assist in developing crime-control strategies and tactics. These changes are not just about finding new ways to reduce crime; they go deeper into evaluating the primary mission of the police and re-examining what people want from their police (PERF, 2014).

Successful police executives drive organizational change using strategic management, an ongoing process that seeks opportunities to enhance operational efficiencies by identifying internal issues and external influences hindering organizational sustainability. It focuses on management's responsibility for addressing these issues by creating a customer-focused, high-performance learning organization (Charrier, 2004). Communities are demanding more accountability, transparency, and oversight of their police in response to negative perceptions of police use of deadly force while reducing budgetary resources. Many crime-control tactics used by the police that are based on Broken Windows theory are being challenged because of concerns of racial bias. Police use of force (especially deadly force) has become the catalyst of sustained protests, demonstrations, and municipal riots about the legitimacy of police treatment of minorities. These protests call for more excellent protection and rights for citizens, whether they are under suspicion or not. As a result, police departments face a more complex and changing environment than in the past.

Trust between law enforcement agencies and those they protect and serve is essential in a democracy. It is vital to the stability of our communities, the integrity of our criminal justice system, and the safe and effective delivery of policing services (PTF, 2015b). Recent events have exposed severe rifts in the relationships between local police and the communities they protect and serve. On December 18, 2014, President Obama signed an executive order establishing the Task Force on 21st Century Policing. The President charged the task force with identifying best practices and recommending how policing practices can promote effective crime reduction while building public trust. This chapter will discuss identified trends and conclude to guide police preparation for the future.

Issues in Police Management

American policing is at a critical juncture. Since the summer of 2014 the nation has seen a series of controversial cases, many of them captured on videos taken by the police, bystanders, or nearby security cameras of police officers using deadly force in questionable circumstances. These events have sparked protests and soul-searching among police executives across the country. While these incidents represent a small fraction of the millions of encounters that take place between the police and the public, their portrayal by the national media has galvanized negative opinions of police and launched a national movement around the slogan "Black Lives Matter." As a result, the controversies surrounding the use of force and perceived mistreatment of minorities are significant issues threatening police–community relationships in many areas and have undermined citizens' trust and conceptions of police legitimacy. Police leaders must address and resolve this issue of "trust" for both the present and future because this upheaval in our society is continuing and is unlikely to abate soon. This is a critical responsibility because policing embodies and represents the ideal of the rule of law that governs civilized society (Covey, 2011).

Use of Deadly Force

Beginning with the death of Eric Gardner in New York City and Michael Brown in Ferguson, Missouri, at least a dozen other controversial uses of **deadly force** have received nationwide and even international attention. In many of these cases the officer's **use of force** had already been deemed legally "justified," and prosecutors have declined to press criminal charges. However, this did not mean that the use of force observed in video recordings of these events looked right to the ordinary citizen. PERF (2015) concluded that a fundamental change in how the American people view the issue of police use of force was occurring. Police killed 1,329 civilians in 2023—an increase of 78 over 2022 (Mapping Police Violence, 2024). Zimring (2017, pp 228–235) estimates that 50 to 80 percent of the incidents where the police kill citizens are not necessary to safeguard police or protect other citizens from life-threatening force. Continuous shooting by the police after the danger has passed doubles or triples this death rate (Zimring, 2017, pp. 68–69). However, a time series analysis determined that the number of civilians fatally shot by the police did not increase or decrease in the 16 months following the shooting of Michael Brown and the Ferguson riots (Campbell, Nix, & Maguire, 2017, p. 14).

In his research on the use of force, Fyfe (2015, pp. 522–523) notes several determinants of police violence. Police–citizen interactions are uniquely urgent, involuntary, and public. Police cannot choose the times and places where they perform their services. They must deal with both the shock and substance of citizen problems as they occur. Many individuals who come to their attention do not seek or welcome it. Their actions occur in a public setting in circumstances beyond their control in front of audiences willing to show their disagreement and dissatisfaction with their efforts. Police must diagnose the situation and assess their potential response.

Unfortunately, he found it challenging to define the factors that led well-meaning police officers to make wrong use of force decisions. Fyfe (2015, p. 526) suggests that these decisions are often hastily considered and may be a product of what he identified as the "**split-second syndrome.**" This syndrome serves both to inhibit the development of greater police diagnostic expertise and to provide after-the-fact justification for unnecessary police violence. He theorizes that this syndrome is a product of the following assumptions.

First, it assumes that no two police problems are precisely alike. As a result, no principles may apply to diagnosing specific situations. Thus, no more can be asked of officers than they respond as quickly as possible to problems, devising the best solutions they can on the spur of the moment. Second, because of these stresses and time constraints, a high percentage of inappropriate decisions should be expected. Finally, because of these assumptions, "the sole basis on which any use of force by the police needs to be justified is the officers' perception of the circumstances prevailing at the instant when they decide to apply force" (Fyfe, 2015, p. 527). He concludes that the acceptance of this syndrome lends approval to unnecessary police violence and the inability to consider whether the situation could have led to a successful, non-violent conclusion. It fails the police to meet their highest obligation: protecting human life. Nobel and Alpert (2015, p. 578) contend that there are very few instances where police have to make split-second use of force determinations. They maintain that officers should be trained and encouraged to reduce the need to make split-second decisions and slow down the pace of the encounter.

Since Fyfe's work, several studies have examined the factors influencing the police decision to shoot. Geographic places can impact police shootings. A study of

Philadelphia police shootings (2015–2019) reported that the most important predictor of these events was the level of violent crime in the area. High-risk places may have a reputation for danger that affects the police's decision to shoot (Keller, Caplan, & Kennedy, 2023, pp. 114–115). A review of the literature on police use of force published between 2000 and 2010 (181 studies) found that citizen possession of a weapon (especially a firearm) was the most consistent risk factor (Mora, Terrill, & Foster, 2023, p. 21).

A scenario-survey-based study examined the factors and forces in the decision to shoot. Eight hundred officers from one department were engaged in the survey. The findings revealed that officers discerned differences and did not treat all situations identically. They were most concerned about suspects with a firearm in hand (rather than reaching for one) versus possessing a gun but not reaching for it. Aggressive physical resistance by subjects was a greater concern for officers than passive/verbal or defensive physical resistance. The suspect's race was not a factor, but several contextual factors emerged. Suspect impairment, agitation, a history of violence, the severity of the crime, the presence of bystanders, and a lack of officer backup were significant issues. Overall, the shooting situation was the most important factor to these officers (Terrill & Somers, 2023, pp. 69–70). Interviews with 218 police officers directly involved in shooting incidents (where at least one lethal round was aimed at a citizen) examined their decision-making. These officers said that they collected information about the situation at hand, plus information about the subjects involved. The information obtained from fellow officers on the scene changed their perceptions of the incident and subsequent decision-making (Pickering & Klinger, 2023, p. 49). Logistic regression analysis confirmed that situational factors (serving a warrant and the presence of multiple officers or subjects) explained firearm displays by officers. While male officers were more likely to draw weapons, there was no association between officer race and tenure. Additionally, officer injury cases were less likely to draw weapons (Riddell & Worrall, 2021, pp. 8–9). Interviews with officers from six midsized U.S. police agencies examined whether police use of force was related to a particular mindset among officers. The study found no support for this hypothesis. Officers were most concerned about suspects who were non-White, possessed a weapon, and demonstrated a high level of resistance. Given the failure to document the existence of a police mindset, scenarios featuring these factors were recommended as a training vehicle (Paoline, Terrill, & Somers, 2021, pp. 566–567).

Adams (2015, pp. 534–546) reached several conclusions about what research disclosed about police use of force:

> *Police use force infrequently.* Between 2002 and 2011, only 1.6% of residents with police contact reported that police threatened or used force, and only 1.2% of them stated that the police used excessive force during their exchange (Hyland, Langton, & Davis, 2015, p. 1).
>
> *Police use of force typically occurs at the lower end of the force spectrum, involving grabbing, pushing, or shoving.*
>
> *Use of force typically occurs when police are trying to make an arrest and the suspect is resisting.*
>
> *Using force is unrelated to an officer's characteristics, such as age, gender, and ethnicity.*
>
> *Use of force is more likely to occur when police are dealing with persons under the influence of alcohol or drugs or with mentally ill individuals.*

A small proportion of officers are disproportionately involved in use of force incidents.

The incidence of wrongful use of force by police is unknown.

The impact of differences in police organizations, including administrative policies, hiring, training, discipline, and use of technology on excessive use of force, is unknown.

Influences of situational characteristics on police use of force and the transactional nature of these events are largely unknown.

Bolger (2015) conducted a meta-analysis of 44 studies published between 2001 and 2011 in which he confirms these conclusions. Bolger (2015, p. 483) reported that police use of force was more likely in encounters involving serious offenses, a resistant suspect, an arrest decision, when citizens are in conflict, when more officers are present, and during a police-initiated encounter. These variables increase the probability that an officer will use force to subdue the suspect. In addition, minority, male, and/ or lower-class suspects were more likely to be the targets of police use of force. While male officers were more likely to use force than females, the effect size for gender was substantially less than the encounter and suspect characteristics (Bolger, 2015, p. 484).

Deadly Force Policies

Fridell (2015, p. 548) points out that police executives cannot eliminate the necessity for using force. However, they can optimize it by (1) adopting sound and effective policies, (2) implementing mechanisms to promote policy adherence and accountability, and (3) training to ensure that officers have the knowledge, skills, and judgment to act under agency policy. Early intervention systems and appropriate reward structures for critical incidents should help avoid problems (Walker, Alpert, & Kenney, 2000).

Several training programs offer the hope that police can become more restrained in their use of force. A study of the impact of de-escalation training in the Louisville Police Department revealed that the sergeant's receptivity to the training and who deemed it valuable to police work was the most significant outcome variable. These LMPD supervisors were more able to supervise the de-escalation skills of subordinates (Engel, Isaza, Motz, McManus, & Corsaro, 2022, p. 217). An evaluation of procedural justice training with Chicago police officers (N = 8480) resulted in a 10 percent reduction in complaints and an over 6 percent reduction in the use of force against civilians (Wood, Tyler, & Papachristos, 2020, p. 9819). The use of force training in a large U.S. city documented that the decision to use deadly force was influenced by resistance, ability, opportunity, and intent surrounding the incident. Female officers were more likely to recommend force and higher levels of force. In contrast, officers who adopted the guardian approach to policing were less likely to promote using force–recommended open-hand tactics (McLean, Alikhan, & Alpert, 2022, pp. 19–20). Results from a randomized controlled experiment using a firearms simulator determined that officers relied upon dispatched information when deciding to pull the trigger on ambiguously armed subjects. When information regarding the subject was correct, officers' performance improved—emphasizing the significance of dispatch information on the use of deadly force by the police (Taylor, 2020, p. 324).

Chief executives who wish to improve their use of force policies should begin by reviewing their department's current policies. These policies should meet all current legal standards and advise officers on what they may do in situations involving force. Policies are goal-oriented general statements of intent designed to assist department personnel through problems and to give direction to assist in mission accomplishment. Departments should:

- Establish policies that guide the most critical decisions made by personnel.
- Ensure personnel are trained in the policies and how to apply them.
- Hold personnel accountable for abiding by policy.
- Continually review policies to ensure that they respond to community needs and hold personnel properly accountable as new issues are identified.

(Fyfe, Greene, Walsh, Wilson, & McLaren, 1997)

Procedural justice requires that these policies be explained to the public so they understand the obligations and boundaries for officers' application of force. The department must also ensure through established policy and administration that credible investigatory procedures are followed in deadly force incidents. Criminal investigations are often subject to open-record laws following the determination that no prosecution will result. When this happens or by subpoena in a civil manner, it will be disclosed if the department made a thorough and unbiased effort in policing itself. Administrators should also cultivate strong professional relationships with all involved in this process. This includes the prosecutor, medical examiner, coroner, and the media. Departments should also seek to educate the public regarding the use of force policy. In communities that have experienced confrontations with the police, the public should be educated appropriately to behave during traffic stops and contact with the police. Educating at-risk groups may prevent the possibility of violent confrontations from occurring. The department's culture must be assessed and changed to support the policy.

For example, a study of seven police departments determined that police occupational attitudes influenced citizen complaints. Officers with negative attitudes toward management generated more complaints regarding discourtesy, use of force, and total complaints. Officers who believed that their departments' use of force policy increased the likelihood of receiving complaints got them. These variables, combined with belief in the traditional crime fighting or "thin blue line" role of the police, were the most potent predictors of citizen complaints about procedural unjust encounters with officers (Terrill & Paoline, 2015, p. 204). These findings imply that police managers should pay attention to the attitudes and grumblings of their officers (especially the line staff) rather than write them off because they play a significant role in how citizens perceive the legitimacy of police departments. In addition, an examination of self-reported use of force incidents from the Austin (TX) police department determined that high neighborhood crime levels impacted the use of force. In addition, citizen resistance was the most critical factor in elevated police force levels (Lee, Vaughn, & Lim, 2014, p. 497).

Several other changes in policy have also been considered as possible methods to reduce the misuse of deadly force. A study on the effect of police agency education requirements on racial differences was conducted in 235 large U.S. cities from 2000 to 2016. The results indicate that departments requiring at least an associate degree for entry-level jobs had lower rates of Blacks and unarmed persons killed by the police, as well as a more balanced distribution of police-related fatalities. The rate of police-related fatalities of Blacks was three times lower in agencies with education hiring requirements (Johnson, Johnson, Sabol, & Snively, 2022, p. 19). However, hiring more

Black officers did not appear to have an impact on police-related fatalities of Black citizens. A study of data from 2014 and 2015 on police shootings in the 100 largest U.S. cities found that increasing the number of Black officers would be an ineffective method of addressing the problem of Black citizen fatalities by the police (Nicholson-Crotty, Nicholson-Crotty, & Fernandez, 2017, p. 214).

The International Association of Chiefs of Police (IACP) has played a central role in the research, development, and creation of model policies and leading practices regarding the use of force by law enforcement officers. To support agencies, the IACP has created a single webpage with model policies and other publications that address issues related to law enforcement's use of force. Besides the IACP's resources, many other organizations, such as CALEA and state accreditation boards, have developed policies governing the use of force that could prove valuable to law enforcement agencies.

The Police Executive Research Forum (2016) has offered 30 principles for using force (see Table 13.1). For example, Principle No. 2 calls for the use of force policies to exceed the "objective reasonableness" standard established in the U.S. Supreme Court decision *Graham v. Connor*. As a result of this decision, departments issued policies directing officers to create a buffer zone of 21 feet when faced with potential danger any time a person within this area is armed with a knife. Unfortunately, the "21-foot rule" has been taught informally in police training academies, and sometimes it has morphed into an incorrect way of thinking. Instead of seeing the 21-foot rule as a general warning to think defensively and protect themselves when confronted by a person with a knife, some officers came to see the rule as a legal justification to shoot a person with a knife less than 21 feet away. So, instead of protecting officers' safety, the rule has been cited to justify using deadly force in incidents when other tactics might have resolved the situation without the use of deadly force (PERF, 2015).

The PERF guidelines call for extending this zone to give officers time to assess their options to resolve incidents without the use of force. They also advocate methods to "slow things down" and de-escalate situations—asking questions in a normal tone of voice while summoning additional resources, if necessary and possible. These principles aim to ensure that police use of force is proportional to the threat faced and to respect the sanctity of human life. Zimring (2020, p. 117) concludes that the problems in police shootings of civilians "are a mix of ineffective administrative controls, vague regulations, and the absence of administrative policy analyses and incentives for reducing death rates." Furthermore, he believes that police shootings are due to the failure of state and local governments to assert authority over the law enforcement use of deadly force (Zimring, 2020, p. 121).

Less Than Lethal Force Use

Police have always been encouraged to use **less than lethal force** to subdue suspects besides avoiding injury to themselves and to others. Data from a medium-sized police department revealed that Tasers were more likely to be used in response to verbal resistance or suspect flight and not when faced with physical resistance or threatened with a weapon. Police were more likely to use a Taser on non-White and male suspects—controlling for the level of resistance, call type, and other factors (Crow & Adrion, 2011, pp. 380–381). In their comprehensive review of a national study, Alpert and Dunham (2012, pp. 251–253) made the following recommendations regarding the use of a conductive energy device (CED—Tasers) by the police:

TABLE 13.1 PERF 30 Principles for Use of Force

1. The sanctity of human life should be at the heart of everything an agency does.
2. Agencies should continue developing best policies, practices, and training on use-of-force issues beyond the minimum requirements of *Graham v. Connor*.
3. Police use of force must meet the test of proportionality.
4. Adopt de-escalation as a formal agency policy.
5. The Critical Decision-Making Model provides a new approach to critical incidents.
6. Duty to intervene: Officers must prevent other officers from using excessive force.
7. Respect the sanctity of life by promptly rendering first aid.
8. Shooting at vehicles must be prohibited.
9. Prohibit deadly force against individuals who pose a danger only to themselves.
10. Document use of force incidents and review data and enforcement practices to ensure they are fair and non-discriminatory.
11. To build understanding and trust, agencies should issue regular reports to the public on using force.
12. All critical police incidents resulting in death or serious bodily injury should be reviewed by specially trained personnel.
13. Agencies need to be transparent in providing information following use-of-force incidents.
14. Training academy content and culture must reflect agency values.
15. Officers should be trained to use a Critical Decision-Making Model.
16. Use Distance, Cover, and Time to replace outdated concepts such as the "21-foot rule" and "drawing a line in the sand."
17. De-escalation should be a core theme of an agency's training program.
18. De-escalation starts with effective communication.
19. Mental Illness: Implement a comprehensive agency training program on dealing with people with mental health issues.
20. Tactical and mental health training must be interwoven to improve response to critical incidents.
21. Community-based outreach teams can benefit agencies' mental health response.
22. Provide a prompt supervisory response to critical incidents to reduce the likelihood of unnecessary force.
23. Training as teams can improve performance in the field.
24. Scenario-based training should be prevalent, challenging, and realistic.
25. Officers need access to and training in less-lethal options.
26. Agencies should consider new options for chemical spray.
27. An ECW deployment that is not effective does not mean that officers should automatically move to their firearms.
28. Personal protection shields enhance officer safety. They may support de-escalation efforts during critical incidents, including situations involving persons with knives, baseball bats, or other improvised weapons that are not firearms.
29. Well-trained call-takers and dispatchers are essential to the police response to critical incidents.
30. Educate the families of persons with mental illness on communicating with call-takers.

- If injury reduction is the primary goal, agencies should forbid the use of less than lethal weapons (OC spray and CEDs) on passive resisters. They should only be used as possible response alternatives to active threats of resistance.
- Multiple applications of CEDs should be prohibited when they prove ineffective or create an unacceptable health risk.
- CED policies should require officers to assess continued resistance after each standard cycle and limit their use to no more than three standard cycles of total activation time against the same subject.
- Following the use of a CED, officers should examine the suspect for signs of distress and have them medically examined at the earliest possible time.
- Training on these principles could lead to fewer problems with CED deployment.

Recent studies have examined the effect of official policies on the use of less than lethal force by police. An analysis of data from a national use of force study sponsored by the National Institute of Justice (NIJ) and administered by the Police Executive Research Forum (PERF) concluded that when the policies toward the use of CEDs were less restrictive they resulted in fewer police shootings (Ferdick, Kaminski, Cooney, & Sevigny, 2014, p. 351). Terrill and Paoline (2016) analyzed 3,340 use of force incidents from three agencies. They determined that the agency with the most restrictive less than lethal force policy used it less often than two other agencies with less restrictive policies. The resistance faced by the officer should be considered in Tasers' policy-making and training.

Dealing with police use of force (both lethal and less than lethal) is a continuing issue for police leadership and a challenge to police legitimacy. This problem has motivated an analysis of the actual use of force incidents and recruitment, policy development, organizational culture, and management of force applications. Unless how police officers use and are held accountable for the use of force is improved, police leadership will continue to be challenged by this issue. The past two years have taught us that community oversight in the age of the Internet is a powerful force. The public's demands for increased accountability and transparency will continue to work their will on our 18,000 police departments (PERF, 2015, p. 10).

School Resource Officers

The use of school resource officers (SROs) is an attempt to deal with school crime directly. SROs are sworn officers assigned to a particular school to provide order and guardianship. Thus, their mission is consistent with the tenets of community policing (Broll & Howells, 2019; Fisher, McKenna, Higgins, Maguire, & Homer, 2022).

A longitudinal study of a national survey of school principals examined the impact of three typical roles of school resource officers (low engagement, full triad, and reactionary). The research results determined that the presence of SROs reduced non-serious violent and property crimes when the officers engaged in all three roles. However, this engagement method led to increased crime reporting to the police. Although reactionary SROs were more effective in detecting incidents, they were more likely to handle offenses internally (Fisher & Devlin, 2020, pp. 1625–1626; Devlin & Gottfredson, 2018). The roles SROs assume affect how they respond to school incidents. Often, they become involved in student misconduct, not serious crime, and increase the probability of a "school-to-prison pipeline" (Martinez-Prather, McKenna, & Bowman, 2016). Therefore, the SROs' roles must be firmly established before implementation (McKenna & White, 2018, p. 465).

A study from a southeastern state questions whether SROs referred students to the juvenile justice system at a higher rate than their counterparts on the street. The results indicated that SROs were significantly less likely to refer juveniles to the system for minor offenses than were officers working outside schools (May, Barranco, Stokes, Robertson, & Haynes, 2018, p. 100). Similarly, an analysis of national victimization survey data reveals the impact of exclusionary discipline by schools. Expulsion increased youths' involvement with the criminal justice system because it exposed their delinquency to police—especially for males and Black youths (Hullenaar, Kurpiel, & Ruback, 2021, p. 1321). Thus, the research findings on SROs are mixed, but the roles they assume affect their acceptance and effectiveness.

Principles of Good Policing

Throughout the past two decades there has been a constant attempt to suggest ways of enhancing police legitimacy, reducing civil disobedience and incidents of violence between police and citizens, and improving the relationship between the police and the communities they serve. A powerful force affecting the solution of these problems is how police officers continue to view themselves as the frontline operatives who are soldiers in a "war against crime." This is a common perception held by citizens and officers and supported by the popular media. This perception took root and developed during the 20th-century's reform era that emphasized crime fighting as the primary task of police. However, research has consistently found that most day-to-day police work comprises community service, crime prevention, and maintaining order, not law enforcement per se (Crank & Langworthy, 1992, p. 344).

An underlying theme of the President's Task Force on 21st Century Policing addresses this issue by suggesting that the culture of policing must change. They advise that police can build trust and legitimacy in the eyes of the citizens they serve by embracing a culture of guardianship, not that of the warrior. In Plato's "Republic," the most significant power is given to **Guardians** who serve and protect democracy. Only those with the most impeccable character are chosen to protect democracy (PTF, 2015a, p. 11). The Task Force calls for policing to adopt a culture of guardianship that protects the dignity and human rights of all, to be protectors and champions of the Constitution. However, this cultural change and role rethinking will require the redirection of recruitment, training, leadership, significant budgetary resources, and commitment throughout policing to ensure that internal and external policies, practices, and procedures support this effort.

In 2015, the International Association of Chiefs of Police held a national policy summit on police–community relations as a result of events in Missouri, New York, and Ohio that strained community–police relationships. The report issued by the summit outlines a series of tangible strategies and steps for law enforcement executives to build trust in their communities. Those strategies include (IACP, 2015, p. x):

Recommended Strategy 1: Redefine policing in a 21st-century democratic society utilizing shared definitions of roles, responsibilities, and priorities. Understanding law enforcement's role in enforcing the rule of law, state laws/statutes, and municipal ordinances changes in our world requires adjustments to our approach to policing. Law enforcement leaders must lead in working with the community to define innovative ways to police in the 21st century.

Recommended Strategy 2: Strengthen and/or rebuild the capacity of police agencies to develop legitimate, sustainable relationships with their communities and unique segments within the community.

Recommended Strategy 3: Implement meaningful ways to define and measure success in community–police relationships as a community.

The US Department of Justice (2003, pp. 19–20) developed a set of principles of good policing, which it suggested can be the springboard for a department's culture change. They proposed a road to implementing the guardianship ideal:

- Police departments must preserve and advance the principles of democracy. All societies must have a system for maintaining order. Police officers in this country, however, must not only know how to maintain order but must do so in a manner consistent with our democratic form of government. Therefore, it is incumbent upon the police to enforce the law and deliver various other services in a manner that not only preserves but also extends precious American values. In this context, the police become the living expression of the meaning and potential of a democratic form of government.
- The police must respect and protect the rights guaranteed to each citizen by the Constitution. To the extent that each officer considers his or her responsibility to protect the constitutionally guaranteed rights of all individuals, the police become the most essential employees in the vast government structure.
- The police should place the highest value on preserving human life. Above all, the police department must believe that human life is our most precious resource. Therefore, the department, in all aspects of its operations, will place its highest priority on the protection of life. This belief must be manifested in at least two ways. First, the allocation of resources and the response to demands for service must prioritize those situations that threaten life. Second, even though society authorizes the police to use deadly force, such force must be justified under the law and be consistent with the philosophy of rational and humane social control.
- The police department believes crime prevention is its top operational priority. The department's primary mission must be the prevention of crime. Logic clarifies that preventing a crime is better than putting the department's resources into motion after a crime has been committed. Such an operational response should improve citizens' quality of life and reduce the fear generated by the reality and perception of crime.
- The police should involve the community in the delivery of its services. The police cannot achieve their mission without the support and involvement of the people they serve. Crime is not solely a police problem, and it should not be considered as such. Instead, crime must be responded to as a community problem. Thus, the police department needs to involve the community in its operations. This sharing of responsibility involves providing a mechanism for the community to collaborate with the police in identifying community problems and determining the most appropriate strategies for resolving them. It is counterproductive for the police to isolate themselves from the community and not allow citizens the opportunity to work with them.
- The police are accountable to the community they serve. Police departments also are not entities unto themselves. Instead, they are a part of government and exist only to serve the public, to which it must be held accountable. An essential element of accountability is openness. Secrecy in police work is not only undesirable but unwarranted. Accountability means being responsive to the problems and needs of citizens. It also means managing police resources in the most cost-effective way. It must be remembered that the power to police comes from the consent of those being policed.

- Police departments should be committed to professionalism in all operations. The role of the professional organization is to serve its clients. The police department must view its role as serving the community's citizens. A professional organization also adheres to a code of ethics. The Law Enforcement Code of Ethics must guide the police department. A profession polices itself. The police department must maintain a system to promote the highest level of discipline among its members.

- The police department will maintain the highest standards of integrity. Society invests in its police with the highest level of trust. The police, in turn, enter a contractual arrangement with society to uphold that trust. The police must always be mindful of this contractual arrangement and never violate that trust. Each member of the police department must recognize that he or she is held to a higher standard than the private citizen. They must recognize that, besides representing the department, they also represent the law enforcement profession and government. They are the personifications of the law. Their conduct, both on and off duty, must be beyond reproach. There must not be even a perception in the public's mind that the department's ethics are open to question.

- Recognizing that society is undergoing massive changes, police agencies face a significant challenge. The essence of that challenge is to respond to problems created by social change while providing the stability that holds a society together during a period of uncertainty.

- By setting forth a clear set of values and articulating what it believes in, the police department has a foundation to guide itself. Such a foundation also allows for organizational flexibility. In addition, a set of values provides the community with a means of assessing its police department without becoming involved in technical operations. Value statements serve as the link between the ongoing operations of a police department and the community's ability not only to participate but also to understand the reason for police department strategies.

These **principles** challenge police leadership to come to terms with the changing environment in which their organizations live, and their legitimacy is being challenged. Meeting this challenge is necessary if a department wishes to develop a strategic approach to the factors in our society that are affecting policing today and tomorrow.

Legitimacy

As defined earlier in this text, police legitimacy is at the heart of the problem of reducing violence between police and citizens. This has been and will continue to be an issue all police leaders will face because it shapes the behavior of citizens toward their organizations. **Legitimacy** is present when citizens believe the police have moral authority to enforce the law and deserve respect and compliance with their initiatives (Gau, 2013, p. 760). People will voluntarily obey the law when they support it and believe in the legitimacy of the authority enforcing it. Thus, they will accept police decisions when they believe they are legitimate and to the degree that they consider the decisions favorable and fair. If they view the police procedures and practices as discriminatory and unfair, the results will be alienation, dissatisfaction, defiance, and a lack of public cooperation. The legitimacy of the police is linked to public judgments about the fairness of processes through which the police decide and exercise authority. If citizens believe that police actions are morally justified and appropriate to the circumstances, they are legitimate.

Satisfaction with police control of disorder is significantly related to citizens' overall satisfaction with crime prevention (Zhao, Tsai, Ren, & Lai, 2012, p. 414). Visibility is another factor in this process. When citizens see the police doing their job and providing quality service, legitimacy is enhanced (Hawdon, Ryan, & Griffin, 2003, p. 485; Maguire & Johnson, 2010). Citizens cooperate with the police when they believe that police performance in fighting crime is effective and that there is a credible threat of punishment for crime (Tyler & Fagan, 2008, p. 263). In a free society, citizen cooperation and trust are necessary to accept the police.

Kane (2005) studied variations in violent crime arrest rates in New York City (1975–1996) to determine if they could be explained by indicators of compromised police legitimacy (official misconduct and over-policing). Increases in police misconduct predicted increases in violent crime within precincts marked by high levels of disadvantage. It was recommended that police administrators pay specific attention to the use of aggressive methods in such neighborhoods because they may aggravate the level of violent crime in communities stressed by extreme disadvantage (Kane, 2005, p. 492).

These conclusions are supported by a study of calls for service following a use of force incident in Milwaukee, WI. Following the widely publicized police beating of Frank Jobe, an unarmed Black man, 911 calls to the police declined dramatically by an estimated 22,000 calls over one year. It is possible that publicized cases of police violence not only threaten police legitimacy but also the very safety of a community (Desmond, Papachristos, & Kirk, 2016).

Promoting legitimacy may also facilitate order maintenance. A survey conducted by Wolfe (2011) found that persons exhibiting low self-control were more likely to hold negative perceptions of police procedural justice. Such persons may also be more likely to be mistreated by the police because they challenge police actions and decisions. However, the results also showed that if the police follow the tenets of procedural justice, they will gain voluntary compliance and lower levels of offending from people with low self-control (Wolfe, 2011, p. 72).

Procedural Justice

Legitimacy is bound to **procedural justice**. Procedural justice concerns the officer's rational, neutral, and transparent decision-making. It provides tangible evidence that the police can be trusted to use their coercive authority in a trustworthy fashion (Gau, 2013, p. 760). As a social psychological construct, procedural justice is grounded in citizen perceptions and the actual behavior exercised by the police (Gau, Corsaro, Stewart, & Brunson, 2012, p. 333).

To demonstrate procedural justice, the police should explain their views and behavior when working with the community before deciding on a course of action to resolve problems, providing evidence of their neutral and objective decision-making and intention to treat people in a like manner with dignity and respect. For example, in the City of Boston, the police received praise and support for releasing a video of their killing of a knife-wielding man under terrorist surveillance. The police released the video to representatives of the African American community and the public while explaining their reasons for taking the action they did in this case (Marcelo, 2015).

There are several factors related to citizen perceptions of procedural justice in policing. First is the quality of police decision-making. Do the police accurately apply the law, and are their decisions based on the facts? Do they try to understand these facts in a situation before acting? Do they give honest explanations to citizens for their actions? In similar situations, do the police consistently apply rules to different people and treat them the same? The second factor is the quality of treatment by the police. Do they take into account people's needs and concerns? Do they respect and show concern for the rights of citizens? Do they treat people with dignity and respect (Dai, Frank, & Sun, 2011, p. 160)?

Procedural justice is also tied to moral principles (Bayles, 1990). The first principle is impartiality or neutrality (Dolan, Edlin, Tsuchiya, & Wailoo, 2007, p. 160). Officer decisions should be made without bias or self-interest. The second principle is allowing citizens to be heard, present information, and support their position. "Citizen voice" means that people affected by an official decision should contribute to the process (Dolan et al., 2007, p. 160). Third, actions should be transparent (Dolan et al., 2007, p. 161). Officers should give the reasons for their actions to citizens. The fourth principle involves adherence to formal justice—consistency, adherence to precedent, and conformity to rules (Dolan et al., 2007, p. 162). Fifth, decisions should be made based on accurate information (Dolan et al., 2007, p. 160). Sixth is the reversibility of the decision. Citizens should have a right to be heard and appeal the outcome of the decision (Dolan et al., 2007, p. 160).

Police administrators should understand that they have more control over how their officers treat citizens than they have over crime. When citizens feel that the police represent their values, they identify and cooperate with them (Sunshine & Tyler, 2003, p. 543). For example, Wells (2007, p. 615) surveyed three groups of citizens who had contact with the police: victims of crime, drivers involved in traffic accidents, and drivers who received citations. The results showed that measures of procedural justice (professionalism, competence, contact-specific behaviors) were strongly related to positive citizen ratings of officer performance across all three groups. Operating with an eye toward procedural justice enhances police authority and legitimacy.

Research findings support the conclusion that how the police operate affects public perceptions of legitimacy. Gau (2013) analyzed data from the National Police–Public Contact Survey to examine whether consent searches affected citizens' attitudes of legitimacy toward the police. Consent searches give the police an expedited way to check vehicles for contraband. However, consent searches can cause citizens to question officer motives for the traffic stop and damage their perceptions of procedural justice and police legitimacy. On this basis, Gau (2013, p. 760) recommended that police executives examine the frequency of consent searches in their departments and have written policies to evaluate this approach. She also endorses conducting focus groups with officers and community stakeholders to examine their feelings about requests for consent searches during traffic stops to determine how the process can be conducted in a manner that does not damage citizen perceptions of legitimacy. Police as guardians must be sensitive to citizens' judgments regarding the fairness of a procedure and maintain control over their behavior. Widespread use of stop and frisk leads to questioning of procedural justice and thus undermines police legitimacy. When such methods are used, the police must adhere to strict standards of professionalism and make sure that equity and fairness are paramount.

Most of this research and the recommendations of the federal reports suggest that police leaders must "promote a culture of respect within the department and clarify that mistreatment of citizens will not be tolerated within the organization" (Gau & Brunson, 2010, p. 274). **Communication** is a significant implementation factor in the accomplishment of this suggestion. A department's leadership team must work at informing and guiding their personnel in understanding these concepts, objectives, and performance indicators. A meta-analysis of studies on police legitimacy confirms this conclusion. It found that regardless of the crime strategy promoted by the police, it was positively affected by the "adoption of a dialogue that actively operationalizes the key principles of procedural justice to advance citizen perceptions of legitimacy" (Mazerolle, Bennett, Davis, Sargeant, & Manning, 2013, p. 266). Citizens' perceptions of procedural fairness by the police may overcome the influence that hostile neighborhoods and social environments have upon this assessment—particularly among citizens who have been victimized (Nix, Wolfe, Rojek, & Kaminsky, 2015, p. 632). The essence of procedural justice is that when citizens see the police administering the law neutrally and professionally, they can gain the community's trust even when they are not giving people exactly what they want (Fischer, 2014, p. 41). Citizens' perceptions of fairness determine their satisfaction with police encounters, whether they will obey the law, and trust and work with the police in the future (Rosenbaum et al., 2011).

The final report of the **President's Task Force on 21st Century Policing** (2015a) warned police leaders that unless they understand how the operational nature of their departments interrelate with the communities they serve and gain collaboration and support for their methods, their departments will never be able to provide true public safety. Specifically, as noted above, this requires a change in police culture from the crime-fighter **warrior** self-image to that of democratic guardians who value citizens' dignity and human rights. This rethinking of the role of police in a democracy requires leadership and commitment across law enforcement organizations to ensure internal and external policies, practices, and procedures that guide individual officers and make organizations more accountable to the communities they serve (President's Task Force on 21st Century Policing, 2015a, p. 2.).

Community expectations and needs play a significant role in developing what police departments should do now and in the future. For example, despite the absence of documented success, random preventive patrol and the use of 911 systems are a continued core of police operations in most of the nation's police departments. Citizens have come to expect a rapid response to their calls for service, and police departments are now chained to satisfying this expectation. Police departments engaging primarily in the strategies and tactics (i.e., Community Policing, CompStat, etc.) we have presented in this text because they are expected to do so by the "sovereigns" in their institutional environment and their actions contribute to "myth-building" processes (Crank, 2003, p. 189). **Sovereigns** are actors whose views can significantly impact the police organization. They include individuals from federal, state, and local law enforcement agencies, national and local media, law enforcement employees and community organizations, medical providers, and elected representatives (Matusiak, 2014, p. 9). For example, it is accepted by all the sovereigns listed above as a fact that "Community policing is the 'right way' to do police business because its underlying values of building positive linkages to the community are taken for granted." They link the organization to its broader societal context (Crank, 2003, p. 193). This position also reflects that, as the most visible agents of local and state government police in a democracy, they are expected to ensure domestic security and safety. However, if improperly used or uncontrolled they become subversive of the system they are sworn to protect.

The implementation guide for the President's Task Force on 21st Century Policing (2015b, pp. 2–3) contains several underlying themes on which specific recommendations for the future of policing are based.

1. **Change the culture of policing**. In a republic that honors the core of democracy, the most significant amount of power is given to Guardians. This calls for law enforcement to protect the dignity and human rights of all and to be the protectors and champions of the Constitution. This rethinking of the role of police in a democracy requires leadership and commitment across law enforcement organizations to ensure internal and external policies, practices, and procedures that guide individual officers and make organizations more accountable to the communities they serve.

2. **Embrace community policing as a philosophy and a way of doing business**. The commitment to working with communities to tackle the immediate and longer term causes of crime and joint problem-solving reduces crime and improves quality of life. It also makes officers safer and increases the likelihood of individuals to abide by the law.

3. **Ensure fair and impartial policing**. Procedural justice is based on four principles: (1) treating people with dignity and respect, (2) giving individuals "voice" during encounters, (3) being neutral and transparent in decision-making, and (4) conveying trustworthy motives. Besides practicing procedural justice, understanding the negative impact of explicit and implicit bias on police–community relations and then taking constructive actions to train officers and the community to recognize and mitigate are vital factors.

4. **Build community capital**. Trust and legitimacy grow from positive interactions based on more than just enforcement interactions. Law enforcement agencies can achieve trust and legitimacy by establishing a positive presence at community activities and events, participating in proactive problem-solving, and ensuring that communities have a voice and seat at the table when working with officers.

5. **Pay attention to officer wellness and safety**. Police officers face many threats and stresses that directly impact their safety and well-being. Ensure officers have access to the tools that will keep them safe, such as bulletproof vests, tactical first aid kits, and training. Promote officer wellness through physical, social, and mental health support.

6. **Technology, both new and emerging, is changing how we police**. It improves efficiency and transparency, raises privacy concerns, and has a significant price tag. Body-worn cameras, less than lethal use of force technologies, communication, and social media require a legal and pragmatic review of policies, practices, and procedures. These policies, practices, and procedures should be developed with input from the community and constitutional scholars.

Survey research supports the commonsense premise that if officers are the subject of procedural justice they are more likely to treat citizens fairly and respectfully. It is a strong message to police administrators: If you want your officers to exercise procedural justice, you must "walk the walk" and practice it with your subordinates. A study of two police departments revealed that officers did not respond to the administration's efforts to promote procedural justice when it was pushed from above with a distinct lack of accountability (Worden & McLean, 2018, p. 165). Perhaps administrators need procedural justice training as much as officers (Donner & Olson, 2020, p. 402). Results from a cross-national survey of officers determined that peers had a greater impact on procedural justice beliefs than did supervisors (Peacock et al., 2023, p. 386). Similarly, a Chicago-based survey (with focus group interviews) determined that when supervisors engaged in internal procedural justice (fairness in job assignments, transparency in promotions, and disciplinary processes), officers modeled their behavior on procedural justice when dealing with citizens (Van Craen & Skogan, 2017, p. 18). The study gives further support to the significance of the supervisor's role in sponsoring trust in citizens by officers (Van Craen & Skogan, 2017, p. 15). Together, these studies assert that the entire department must engage in engendering procedural justice beliefs and exercising them.

Body-Worn Cameras (BWCs)

Body-worn cameras (BWCs) offer several distinct advantages to the police and the public. The perceived benefits of BWCs include:

- BWCs can increase transparency and promote citizens' views of police legitimacy.
- The use of BWCs can improve the behavior of both police officers and citizens.
- BWCs can improve evidence for arrest and prosecution and expedite citizen complaints or lawsuits.
- BWCs can provide opportunities for police training (White, 2014, pp. 6–7).

Camera data can reveal what occurred during a police stop—evidence that others can readily review.

A study in 2019 based on viewing 1,100 BWC videos from a municipal police department monitored police performance. Overall, treatment by officers was related to socio-economic status and gender. While citizens were treated civilly, officers tended to discriminate against Blacks and people experiencing homelessness. However, they received higher performance scores when dealing with women and persons with mental health issues (James & James, 2023, p. 22).

Research also examined the attitudes of police officers toward BWCs. A survey of Orlando, FL officers found that they supported using BWCs. They believed the cameras were comfortable, would benefit their behavior, and would reduce citizen complaints against the police (Jennings, Fridell, & Lynch, 2014). Qualitative research from a southern city found that officers generally approved adopting BWCs to establish police accountability. However, they also believed they would need to overcome negative perceptions of the police (Falik, Deuchar, & Crichlow, 2020, p. 270). An observational study of 555 LAPD police–citizen encounters determined that BWCs positively impacted citizens' perceptions of procedural justice (McCluskey et al., 2019, p. 230). An analysis of three departments revealed their attitudes toward BWCs. Officers from all three departments became more comfortable with the cameras but were more skeptical about their impact on citizens (Gaub et al., 2016, p. 292).

A survey of police command-level officers revealed their attitudes toward deploying BWCs. These supervisors felt that BWCs could potentially restrain the employment of necessary force in citizen encounters. They also believed that the promotion of BWCs is fueled by public distrust of the police and that the media will use the data produced to embarrass them (Smykla, Crow, Critchlow, & Synder, 2016, p. 440). However, Williams (2021) found that citizens supported using BWCs because they could protect both the police and civilians.

However, there are several sources of police resistance to the employment of BWCs. A survey of police departments revealed several sources of resistance to using BWCs. Andreescu and Kim (2022) found that departments with a higher percentage of citizen complaints about the use of force cost concerns and states with solid police unions were more likely to resist BWC adoption. A qualitative study of specialty unit officers revealed that BWCs were worthwhile when investigating complaints, but they also offered several caveats on their use. They felt that BWC results could be used in "fishing expeditions" to get them into trouble when viewed by persons unfamiliar with their operations. Officers also noted that BWCs might not be appropriate in close-quarter and nighttime engagements, undercover work, surveillance operations, and operations involving shared work with Federal agencies (Gaub, Todak, & White, 2018, p. 150). Kyle and White (2017) found that officers' primary concern about using BWCs was organizational justice—specifically, how the data could provide evidence to judge performance. They also found that females and higher ranking officers had more positive attitudes toward their use (Kyle & White, 2017, p. 78).

A study based on LEMAS data revealed several factors influencing the use of BWCs. Agencies in counties with higher levels of concentrated disadvantage or a high proportion of young males were more likely to adopt BWCs. Residents in such areas are more likely to hold negative attitudes toward the police. Therefore, the use of BWCs could improve feelings of legitimacy. In addition, agencies with previous experience of adopting technologies (like vehicle cameras), having a foot patrol policy, and requiring more than a high school degree for employment were more likely to use BWCs (Lawshe, Zimmerman, & Stowell, 2022, pp. 744–745).

BWCs have impacted police officer behaviors. Boivin and Gendron (2022) conducted an experiment revealing that officers who reviewed body-worn camera footage wrote more accurate reports than those who failed to do so. The results suggest that reviewing body-worn camera footage will reduce subjectivity in police reports and complement other forms of evidence. A related study examined the activation rates for BWCs. BWC activation rates over ten months were 73 percent, but cameras were not activated in 25 percent of the incidents (Boivin, Poirier, & D'Elia, 2022, p. 113). Females and senior officers were less likely to trigger their BWCs. A randomized controlled experiment on BWCs found that their use decreased officer-initiated activity but increased the likelihood of police use of force while reducing complaints for incidents where they were used (Huff, Katz, & Hedberg, 2022, p. 266). Finally, an experiment examined the impact of body-worn cameras on self-initiated foot patrols and traffic stops. The findings reported no differences between police officers who were assigned cameras and those who were not. The results indicate that body-worn cameras did not lead to de-policing and deter police activity (Bennett, Bartholomew, Baxter, Champagne, & Schuler, 2022, p. 15).

Similarly, another experiment assessed citizen attitudes toward NYPD officers employing BWCs. The study found no significant differences in citizen perceptions of the NYPD regarding neighborhood safety, how complaints were handled, how requests for assistance were handled, or whether they had been stopped by the police (Braga, MacDonald, & Barao, 2021). Finally, a study of LEMAS and Fatal Encounters data suggested that BWCs could reduce the number of fatalities attributable to the police. Such reductions ranged from 22 to 29 percent. However, the authors cautioned that these findings were limited by several threats to validity (Miller & Chillar, 2022, pp. 748–750). The research documented a "civilizing effect" for BWCs based on national adoption from 2007 to 2016. Alda (2023, p. 426) found suggested reductions of 13.5 percent and 14 percent in complaints (about 30 complaints/year). After the seventh year of adoption, there was a more significant effect for BWCs—a 47 percent complaint reduction. Survey research on Albany, NY officers revealed that proactive officers were more supportive of BWCs and their ability to improve their professional growth. However, their direct experience with BWCs did not alter their views on this innovation (Cochran & Worden, 2023, p. 35).

A study of BWC activation examined the factors influencing their use based on 146,601 incidents in Phoenix, AZ. Katz and Huff (2023) determined that departmental policy was the most significant factor in BWC activation rates. These rates increased from 40 percent to 73 percent after policy implementation, and requiring activation when mobilized increased the odds of activation rates by 315 percent after the policy was announced and 295 percent after the policy went into effect (Katz & Huff, 2023, p. 328). Several individual factors were also at work. Officers were less likely to activate BWCs during subject/vehicle stops but were more likely to activate them in incidents involving arrest and the use of force (Katz & Huff, 2023, p. 328). Female officers were less likely to activate BWCs than were males; differences existed at the precinct level, and there was a 44 percent reduction in activation with every unit increase in the Hispanic population (Katz & Huff, 2023, pp. 330–331). Understanding such variation in departmental use of BWCs could improve their effectiveness.

Several recommendations are offered before BWCs are adopted by police departments. Petersen (2022) warns that reliance on body-worn camera footage to establish transparency needs to be increased. A systems-wide approach based on outcomes of police review, prosecution, and court decisions is required to establish the validity of such evidence and accountability. Kyle and White (2017) recommended that before BWCs are adopted, administrators should consider three factors. First, they should not "jump haphazardly" to use them due to their implications in employee review and supervision. Second, they should carefully address the need for this policy change. Third, their viewing by officers could help them learn from the mistakes of their peers (Kyle & White, 2017, p. 80). Regarding their implementation, BWCs can require a "substantial commitment of finances, resources, and logistics" (White, 2014, p. 9). BWC videos must be properly stored and secured for possible future use.

Demir (2023) made several policy recommendations based on his randomized study of citizens' attitudes toward BWCs. First, officers should tell citizens when the cameras are being used. Doing so increases their feelings of legitimacy and procedural justice (see also Souza, Miethe, & Sakiyama, 2018). This step may also increase the effectiveness of BWCs because officers might be more likely to activate them. Finally, police supervisors should regularly audit BWC footage to monitor their effect on officers and citizens (Demir, 2023, p. 334).

COVID-19

Seven hundred and twenty-nine officers died from COVID-19 between 2020 and 2021. The majority of deaths occurred in the Southern U.S., and most were recorded by officers who were White, male, and older (Boydstun & Wells, 2023, p. 1). Based on their review, Boydstun and Wells (2023, pp. 11–13) offered several recommendations. First, departments should provide officers with the resources to prevent COVID-19 infection, possibly establish training partnerships with health agencies on prevention methods, and encourage officers to get vaccinated. Second, they should encourage exposed and infected officers to stay home until they are cleared to work and provide them with resources to conduct work from home. Finally, providing mental health support to relieve stress and increase the workforce's ability to deal with absences would be helpful.

The COVID-19 pandemic created a unique opportunity for police departments and researchers to consider what is necessary in law enforcement. Crime patterns changed during the pandemic. A study based in Buffalo, NY determined that there were gradual and permanent increases in gun violence (non-fatal and gang-related violence) and an abrupt and temporary increase in the number of fatal shootings during the COVID-19 pandemic (Kim & Phillips, 2021, p. 8). Traditional law enforcement actions require close contact with citizens, including face-to-face communication/contact, which would violate most recommendations of the CDC in terms of protecting both individuals and stopping the spread of the virus. Based on these issues and the need for law enforcement to still have close contact with the public, especially when it comes to protecting the public from violence and disorder, three types of police activity could be examined during the pandemic, including reactive policing (i.e., making arrests), precautionary policing (reducing the enforcement of offenses that are misdemeanors and also officer-initiated contact), and proactive policing (i.e., traffic stops which are officer initiated) (Maskaly, Ikovich, & Neyroud, 2021; Nix, Ivanov, & Pickett, 2021). Additionally, the majority of police departments (53 to 78 percent) implemented some policy changes because of the novel Coronavirus, specifically with traffic stops because that is the most common form of police–citizen contact (Alexander & Ekici, 2020; Lum, Maupin, & Stoltz, 2020a, 2020b; Maskaly et al., 2022; Shjarback & Magny, 2022).

Given the pandemic's circumstances, various researchers have considered how the pandemic has impacted multiple forms of police activity. Both police traffic stops and the number of arrests decreased in different police departments during the pandemic, along with a general shift in enforcement practices with less use of traditional law enforcement strategies (Alexander & Ekici, 2020; Lum et al., 2020a, 2020b; Demir & Cassino, 2022; Jahn, Simes, Cowger, & Davis, 2022; Maskaly et al., 2022; Shjarback & Magny, 2022). However, there was evidence of biased policing still being present, with minority citizens or those living in SES-disadvantaged areas being more likely to be subjected to police activity (Bruner, 2020; Li, 2020; Southall, 2020; Kajeepeta, Bruzelius, Ho, & Prins, 2022; Petenko, 2022). This is not surprising because it supports Laufs and Waseem's (2020) systematic review of police behavior during natural disasters and public health emergencies, which found that in order to gain compliance during such events police resort to biased policing. We are only four years removed from the government shutdown because of the pandemic and what that meant for law enforcement. It does allow police administrators an excellent opportunity to consider what was necessary for the law enforcement officers to be doing and how this could result in changes in the future that would show a better use of time and resources to serve the public in terms of what is necessary and what works to protect them.

Budgetary Issues

A constant administrative problem that will directly impact departmental strategic redirection and the above suggestions both now and in the future is **budgetary issues**. The ability of the police department's leadership to redirect and use its resources and assets is determined by the political subdivision's budget. The budget directly impacts the police executives' ability to provide public safety and accomplish their goals. Because of several years of economic downturns on municipal tax bases, police executives, past, present, and future, have had to continually deal with fewer and fewer budgetary resources and be more creative with what they have been given. In an analysis of the economic impact on police agencies, the Police Executive Research Forum (2010, pp. 11–13) reported:

- Nearly a quarter of American cities surveyed have cut public safety budgets.
- Over one-third of the agencies that applied for COPS officer hiring funding reported an operating budget drop of more than 5 percent between 2009 and 2011.
- Nearly 12,000 police officers and sheriff's deputies will be laid off.
- An estimated 28,000 officers and deputies in 2010 have faced week-long furloughs.
- Some departments have stopped responding to all motor vehicle thefts, burglar alarms, and non-injury motor vehicle accidents.
- Departments also report decreases in investigations of property crimes, fugitive tracking, a variety of white-collar crimes, and even low-level narcotics cases.

In 2010, a PERF study found that nearly half (47 percent) of the responding agencies it surveyed showed that budget cuts had already caused or will cause changes in the services they provide to their communities. In response to their financial environment, many agencies have significantly reduced their staffing, training expenditures, and services to the community. The effects of such reductions will influence the capacity of law enforcement departments to provide services in the same ways as they have in the past, all of which will hurt a department's ability to serve the community now and in the future.

The National Institute of Justice (2011) has provided several suggestions for police leaders facing budget cutbacks, noting that circumstances call for **strategic management**. They suggest that police leadership (National Institute of Justice, 2011, pp. ii, 6–8):

- **Think long term**: Develop a strategic plan with a long-term timeframe.
- **Do not just cut costs; look for revenue opportunities**: Departments may charge user fees for some specialized services provided.
- **Invite innovation**: Turn this threat into an opportunity to find cost-effective methods.
- **Focus on what is kept rather than what has been cut**: Plan what you do with your retained funds. Budget for outcomes.
- **Allocate budget dollars to your top goals**.

Many of the cost-saving budgetary adjustments discussed in various studies suggest organizational transformation through strategic, operational strategies, partnerships, and problem-solving techniques to proactively address the immediate conditions that give rise to public safety issues such as crime, social disorder, and fear of crime. The three tenets of Community Policing—community partnerships, organizational transformation, and problem-solving—are of increased importance when facing budget cuts that reduce the number of officers on the streets. The National Institute of Justice (2011) also recommends that the NYPD's CompStat and Maryland's StateStat establish accountability in budgeting and performance. Tying goal accomplishment to available funding and command responsibility is a strategic management issue that must be dealt with now and the future in policing.

Recognizing and accepting the impact of this economic reality is a more important reason for developing strategic management practices to ensure the effective and efficient delivery of police services. Police nationwide will need to evaluate, adapt, and redevelop how they do their job to ensure appropriate levels of public safety.

Recruitment/Retention

In addition to dealing with the impact of the financial crises, departments are also faced with the challenge of recruiting qualified individuals to fill their ranks. Although recruitment was addressed in Chapter 9, it is identified here because it is a continuous problem for both the present and future of policing. Organizations must identify and hire the right people to maintain current and future performance levels. Shifting societal demands have created a demand for individuals who are critical thinkers and problem-solvers. These new officers represent the department's future. Unfortunately, current issues with police legitimacy and media coverage of demonstrations against the police use of force have resulted in qualified individuals no longer considering a police career.

However, it has also been found that the present generation of police recruits has attributes distinctly different from those of their predecessors. Labelled "**Millennials**," these individuals are considered "conscientious and independent in their thinking while also more tolerant of differences than those of other generations" (Batts, Smoot, & Scrivner, 2012, p. 3). They are not necessarily working for money but are noted for their altruism, which creates a desire to make the world a better place and give back to society via a team-oriented approach to work (Malcolm, 2016). These individuals can multitask, articulate their career values, use technology, and value diversity. They place a greater value on balancing work and family, experiencing comfort with questioning authority, challenging the traditional chain of command, demanding ongoing performance feedback, expecting transparency and timely outcome measures that show what is working, and relying on instant feedback from electronic communication and social networking. This generation also requires a management style distinctly different from the traditional methods used in the past. Police leadership must understand, utilize, or lose them to the organization (Batts et al., 2012, p. 4).

Traditional police managers and supervisors may view this new generation as "whiners," and their managerial methods may cause problems. Several questions arise from this potential conflict (Batts et al., 2012, pp. 10–11):

- Are they a generation that expects to be empowered and make too many demands for information and feedback?
- Is it equally likely that they are seeking clarification of roles and responsibilities but in ways perceived as challenges that make supervisors uncomfortable?
- Do they want a lucrative, easy ride, or are they seeking meaningful work and the opportunity to advance?
- Are they "risk adverse" and hesitant to go "hands-on" or use sensible risk management?
- Do they expect ongoing accolades for work, or are they seeking honesty and authenticity from their superiors?
- Does their questioning of rules mean actual resistance, or do they wish to understand the rules and learn the history of why they exist?

These factors suggest the need for changes in management style that encourage managers to engage in dialogues with their subordinates that will explain, instruct, and mentor rather than autocratically issue orders and expect unquestioning (or uncaring) compliance. This challenge requires reevaluating current supervisory training and development practices and management techniques discussed earlier in this text.

Internal Organizational Legitimacy

Just as in community relationships, **internal organizational legitimacy** is also tied to fairness within the workplace. Employees are more willing to follow organizational rules when they believe they are legitimate. Perceptions of organizational fairness create a "reservoir of support" that is vital to organizational survival during a crisis. It is linked to the use of open and participatory forms of leadership and the fairness of resource allocation procedures within the organization. Legitimacy provides a framework to evaluate procedures as just or unjust. Studies show that exercising legitimate authority with subordinates promotes positive outcomes and feelings in employees (Keyes, Hysom, & Lupo, 2000). Employees should be involved in developing the department's vision and mission to gain support and accountability. The organization's internal procedural justice begins with transparently creating its core values and developing its policies, protocols, and decision-making processes (President's Task Force on 21st Century Policing, 2015b, p. 13).

The department's leaders should model the way for their employees by engaging in actions and behaviors that promote organizational legitimacy. Modern law enforcement leaders will have to become more adaptive in order to stay relevant. They need to be self-aware of who they are and what they believe and value and act upon them while interacting with others. They should use their identification with their employees to create meaningfulness at work. This leadership style can become the basis of the organization's culture. **Authentic leaders** are guided by values based on "what is right and fair" for themselves and for organizational personnel. In this manner, the organizational values of their employees model those demonstrated by their leader. The leader's ethical behavior sends a solid message to followers that affects what they attend to, what they think, how they construct their roles, and how they behave. The authentic leader raises optimism and builds upon individual strengths rather than drawing attention to weaknesses. By sponsoring positive emotions, the authentic leader promotes positive behaviors such as creativity, coping with adversity, commitment, satisfaction, handling stress, providing motivation, and promoting quality performance.

Blader and Tyler (2003) note several aspects of procedural justice that affect employees regarding how their organization treats them. For example, employees wish to see that decisions made at work are unbiased and impartial. They wish to be treated fairly in evaluations and promotions regarding their dignity and rights. Fairness promotes feelings of inclusion and group importance. These perceptions have a formal and informal basis. Formal sources of procedural justice spring from the official rules, policy, and procedures of the department, are structural and are often constant across time, situations, and individuals. Informal bases of procedural justice in organizations are more dynamic, based on the perceptions of the employees, their supervisor, and their relationships (Blader & Tyler, 2003, pp. 114–115). This research shows how people are treated within their organization affects their treatment of organizational clients.

The Ferguson Effect

The "**Ferguson Effect**" refers to a perceived negative response to the performance of law enforcement officers due to increased scrutiny and bad publicity in the media. This effect is alleged to extend to two areas of policing: (1) The police are disengaging from vigorous activities (or even arrests), and thus crime rates are increasing, and (2) The lack of desire by police officers to collaborate with community members to prevent crime (see MacDonald, 2016, pp. 57–59). In addition, it has been suggested that such "de-policing" is attributable to changes in the law, departmental policies, implementation of new policing strategies, civil suits, the establishment of consent decrees on departments, and line-of-duty deaths (see Oliver, 2015).

A study by Nix and Wolfe (2015) was recently conducted to determine the effect of bad publicity on officer motivation. Their survey of 567 officers found that officers were less motivated because of negative publicity and also expressed less self-legitimacy (the confidence they have in themselves as law enforcement officers). This is unfortunate, because officers who view their authority as legitimate are more likely to engage in positive behaviors for their department and the community they serve, such as observing fairness in procedures. The best way for departments to counter bad publicity is to provide organizational justice for officers (Nix & Wolfe, 2015, p. 102). Subsequent analysis of these data also demonstrated that deputies who felt that their supervisors practiced organizational fairness were less likely to lack motivation, perceive more on-the-job danger, believe their colleagues feel adverse effects of Ferguson, and that citizens were less likely to support them (Nix & Wolfe, 2016). Again, how officers are treated by their departments affects the nature of their job performance.

Rosenfeld (2015) examined whether events in Ferguson affected crime rates in St. Louis, MO. He found no credible effect on homicides, a mixed result for violent crimes, but a temporal (but not causative) effect upon property crimes. He cautions police departments to monitor fluctuations in the crime rate and to apply evidence-based practices to any problems that occur. Similarly, a time series analysis of police officers killed in the line of duty found no evidence of a Ferguson Effect for the period August 2014 (following the shooting of Michael Brown in Ferguson, MO) to March 2016 (Maguire, Nix, & Campbell, 2016).

Legitimacy envelops the police organization and the communities they serve—both externally and internally. The findings on legitimacy confirm that how people are treated directly relates to their expectations and performance within the department and the community. Sponsoring the feeling of legitimacy among all concerned will affect not only how police agencies are perceived but also how they perform. Organizational justice and self-legitimacy are essential predictors of willingness to engage with the community. Treatment and support within law enforcement agencies can trump negative publicity in the media.

Effective Policing

Besides what has been identified above, the continuing challenge facing police leadership is the need to provide an effective public safety level for the community they serve both today and tomorrow. The general theme of this book is that a fundamental rethink is taking place in the manner by which this challenge is accomplished. We have entitled this organizational redirection strategic policing. **Strategic policing** is a continuing process of enhancing the effectiveness of a police department through its use of the latest information and analysis techniques to develop targeted, innovative strategies to address public safety issues (Moore & Stephens, 1991).

Many of today's police leaders base their organizational stewardship on leadership perceptions that emerged from demands of the Reform Era of policing when operational environments were more straightforward and based on the principles of Scientific Management. This leadership paradigm holds that organizational effectiveness can be achieved solely through the control or motivation of organizational personnel instead of changing processes and structure. It created top-down bureaucratically controlled organizations locked into providing public safety through three operational strategies: Random patrol, rapid response to calls for service, and reactive post-event investigation. The current environmental reality of policing is complex and demands a new proactive paradigm. Today's public safety issues and limited police resources have created the need for a strategic redirection in both leadership and administration that will affect the present and future operations of police organizations.

A consistent finding that has emerged out of the police operational experimentation and research of the past 20 years is that effective policing requires police leaders to think strategically and use a variety of tactics, treat and supervise their organization more purposefully and humanely, collaborate with the citizens they serve, and achieve legitimacy by upholding democratic principles. Citizens expect their police departments to be professional, accountable, transparent, and self-monitoring (Walker & Archbold, 2014). However, this raises the question: Can police leaderships develop and sustain an effective response to the driving forces their organizations are facing with their current level of capabilities, personnel, and resources?

The research noted throughout this book establishes that effective police organizations can and must adapt to their environment. Strategic police leadership requires that executives proactively develop and implement an organizational direction that allows their departments to meet the demands of their operational environments. Experience informs us that this can be accomplished by departments acquiring, creating, and transforming information into intelligence that they disseminate to all operational decision-makers within their organization. This intelligence-generating process provides operational decision-makers with timely and accurate intelligence to evaluate and prioritize community needs. This becomes the basis for planning and developing operational tactics and management practices to meet changing demands. Departments engaging in this process continually evaluate their strategies, tactics, objectives, and accomplishments in crime strategy meetings. Properly conducted, these meetings should override the tactical compartmentalization of traditional policing and have the entire department take ownership for problem identification, developing problem solutions, and tactical response. In this manner, strategically managed police departments become, in practice and accomplishments, learning organizations that engage in:

- Systematic problem-solving.
- Experimentation with new approaches.
- Learning from their own experiences and past practices.
- Learning from the experiences and best practices of others.
- Transferring intelligence quickly and efficiently throughout the organization.
- Engaging in continual dialogue, double-loop learning, and operational flexibility.

In these organizations, the chief and leadership team continually seek to understand the internal and external relationships with the department. They actively promote creativity and proactive policing while empowering their operational commanders to solve problems at all levels of the organization and develop problem-oriented tactics to help prevent and solve crime. Strategic management prevents these departments from becoming status-quo, crisis-driven organizations through in-depth information gathering, analysis, strategy and tactical formulation, and assessment based on real-time data.

Strategically managed departments also engage the community and rely on both police and non-police resources in their problem-solving efforts. They reinforce or change the department's operations to respond to driving forces through planning, communication, networking, and strategy development. **Strategic leaders** establish an organization-wide shared vision, mission, objectives, outcomes, and culture that has meaning for all department members and mobilizes their commitment. This redirection is shifting the dominant principle of organizational control from supervision and management to strategic leadership and organizational learning.

Conclusion

Effective police organizations are led by individuals who set direction for today and tomorrow. Their community service delivery is value driven based on objectives and outcomes that reflect the department's vision of effectiveness. Command accountability is established and practiced within the parameters of ethics and professional standards. Within these organizations **continuous improvement** is achieved through ongoing measurement, evaluation, analysis, and dialogue. An effective police organization is an adaptable department that can anticipate change and restructure its operational strategies to respond to these anticipated needs. It engages in a continuous process of determining what is required of the department and what must be done to accomplish it effectively. Administrators continually ensure that their organization's capabilities fit the demands of its current and future environments.

The issues raised in this chapter address these concerns and provide information on how they can be effectively managed. The foundation upon which traditional police organizations can be transformed into strategically focused ones is based on the following tasks:

1. Creation of a strategic vision.
2. Mobilization of commitment.
3. Institutionalization of change.
4. Measurement of progress.

It should be remembered that a department's vision, objectives, strategy, and execution are never final. Elements of the strategic management process involve evaluating performance, monitoring environmental changes, and making adjustments. Follow-up, assessment, and ongoing searches for ways to improve are normal managerial activities. What happens to crime and the quality of safety in a community is always a product of the department's organizational learning and strategic thinking (More, Vito, & Walsh, 2012). These changes will not be easily accomplished because they call for a radical change in how police agencies have traditionally operated. This is the challenge for the future—using strategic management concepts to guide police leadership, management, and community engagement.

KEY TERMS

Authentic leaders	Internal organizational	Sovereigns
Budgetary issues	legitimacy	Split-second syndrome
Communication	Legitimacy	Strategic leaders
Continuous improvement	Less than lethal force	Strategic management
Deadly force	Millennials	Strategic Policing
Effective police	President's Task Force on	Trust
organizations	21st Century Policing	Use of force
Ferguson Effect	Principles of Good Policing	Warrior
Guardians	Procedural justice	

References

Adams, K. (2015). What we know about police use of force. In R.G. Dunham & G.P. Alpert (Eds.), *Critical issues in policing: Contemporary readings*, 7th ed. (pp. 532–546). Long Grove, IL: Waveland Press.

Alda, E. (2023). The effects of differential timing in the adoption of BWCs on civilian complaints. *Policing: An International Journal, 46*(2), 418–440.

Alexander, D.C., & Ekici, N. (2020). *Survey: COVID-19's impact on LE operations*. San Francisco, CA: Police1. Retrieved from www.police1.com/coronavirus-covid-19/articles/survey-covid-19s-impact-on-le-operations-JmGm4beDhdAHhrE5/.

Alpert, G.P., & Dunham, R.G. (2012). Policy and training recommendations related to police use of CEDs: Overview of findings from a comprehensive national study. *Police Quarterly, 13*(3), 235–259.

Andreescu, V., & Kim, D. (2022). Drivers of police agencies' resistance to body-worn camera adoption. *International Journal of Police Science & Management, 24*(4), 437–452.

Batts, A.W., Smoot, S.M., & Scrivner, E. (2012). *Police leadership challenges in a changing world*. Washington, DC: Harvard Kennedy School; National Institute of Justice.

Bayles, M. (1990). *Procedural justice: Allocating to individuals*. Dordrecht, NL: Kluwer Academic Publishers.

Bennett, R., Bartholomew, B., Baxter, S., Champagne, H., & Schuler, E. (2022). The effects of body-worn cameras on self-initiated police encounters. *Police Quarterly*, 1–22. doi: 10.1177/10986111221123798.

Blader, S.L., & Tyler, T.R. (2003). What constitutes fairness in work settings? A four-component model of procedural justice. *Human Resource Management Review, 13*, 107–126.

Boivin, R., & Gendron, A. (2022). An experimental study of the impact of body-worn cameras on police report writing. *Journal of Experimental Criminology*, 747–764. doi:https://doi.org/10.1007/s11292-021-09469-8.

Boivin, R., Poirier, B., & D'Elia, M. (2022). Activate compliance: A multilevel study of factors associated with activation of body-worn cameras. *Criminal Justice Review, 47*(1), 103–118.

Bolger, P.C. (2015). Just following orders: A meta-analysis of the correlates of American police officer use of force decisions. *American Journal of Criminal Justice, 40*, 466–492.

Boydstun, J., & Wells, M. (2023). A review of COVID-19 deaths among law enforcement officers in the United States. *The Police Journal: Theory, Practice, and Principles*, 1–20. doi:10.1177/0032258X231164577.

Braga, A., MacDonald, J., & Barao, L. (2021). Do body-worn cameras improve community perceptions of the police? Results from a controlled experimental evaluation. *Journal of Experimental Criminology*, 1–32. doi:doi.org/10.1007/s11292-021-09476-9.

Broll, R., & Howells, S. (2019). Community policing in schools: Relationship building and the responsibilities of school resource officers. *Policing, 15*(2), 701–715.

Bruner, B. (2020, September 22). *Traffic stops in Columbus plummet amid COVID-19.* Retrieved from The Columbus Dispatch: www.dispatch.com/story/news/coronavirus/2020/09/22/traffic-stops-in-columbus-plummet-amid-covid-19/42676991/.

Campbell, B., Nix, J., & Maguire, E. (2017). Is the number of citizens fatally shot by the police increasing in the post-Ferguson era? *Crime & Delinquency*, 1–23. doi:10.1177/0011128716686343.

Charrier, K. (2004). Strategic management in policing: The role of the strategic manager. *Police Chief, 71*, 60–70.

Cochran, H., & Worden, R. (2023). Police culture and officer's receptivity to body worn cameras: A panel study. *Policing: An International Journal, 46*(1), 24–39.

Covey, S.M.R. (2011). Policing at the speed of trust. *The Police Chief, 78*(10), 58–70.

Crank, J.P. (2003). An institutional theory of police: A review of the state of the art. *Policing, 26*(2), 187–207.

Crank, J.P., & Langworthy, R. (1992). An institutional perspective of policing. *Journal of Criminal Law & Criminology*, 338–363.

Crow, M.S., & Adrion, B. (2011). Focal concerns and police use of force: Examining the factors associated with Taser use. *Police Quarterly, 14*(4), 366–387.

Dai, M., Frank, J., & Sun, I. (2011). Procedural justice during police–citizen encounters: The effects of process-based policing on citizen compliance and demeanor. *Journal of Criminal Justice, 39*, 159–168.

Demir, M. (2023). Effect of awareness of body-worn cameras on procedural justice, police legitimacy, cooperation, and compliance: Findings from a randomized controlled trial. *Journal of Experimental Criminology, 19*, 311–341.

Demir, M., & Cassino, P.P. (2022). The effect of COVID-19 on police activities: Traffic stops, arrests, and use of force. *Criminal Justice Review*, 1–9.

Desmond, M., Papachristos, A., & Kirk, D. (2016). Police violence and citizen crime reporting in the black community. *American Sociological Review, 81*(5), 857–876.

Devlin, D., & Gottfredson, D. (2018). The roles of police officers in schools: Effects on the recording and reporting of crime. *Youth Violence and Juvenile Justice, 16*(2), 208–233.

Dolan, P., Edlin, R., Tsuchiya, A., & Wailoo, A. (2007). It ain't what you do, it's the way that you do it: Characteristics of procedural justice and their importance in social decision-making. *Journal of Economic Behavior & Organization, 64*, 157–170.

Donner, C., & Olson, D. (2020). Fair treatment in policing: Testing the relationship between internal and external procedural justice. *Journal of Criminal Justice, 43*(3), 393–408.

Engel, R., Isaza, G., Motz, R., McManus, H., & Corsaro, N. (2022). De-escalation training receptivity and first-line police supervision: Findings from the Louisville Metro Police study. *Police Quarterly*, 201–227. doi:10.1077/10986111211019834.

Falik, S., Deuchar, R., & Crichlow, V. (2020). Body-worn cameras in the Post-Ferguson era: An exploration of law enforcement perspectives. *Journal of Police and Criminal Psychology*, 35, 263–273.

Ferdick, F.V., Kaminski, R.J., Cooney, M.D., & Sevigny, E.L. (2014). The influence of agency policies on conducted energy device use and police use of deadly force. *Police Quarterly*, 17(4), 328–358.

Fischer, C. (2014). *Legitimacy and procedural justice: The New Orleans case study*. Washington, DC: Police Executive Research Forum.

Fisher, B., & Devlin, D. (2020). School crime and the patterns of roles of school resource officers: Evidence from a national longitudinal study. *Crime & Delinquency*, 66(11), 1606–1929.

Fisher, B., McKenna, J., Higgins, E., Maguire, E., & Homer, E. (2022). The alignment between community policing and the work of school resource officers. *Police Quarterly*, 25(4), 561–587.

Fridell, L.A. (2015). Use-of-force policy, policy enforcement, and training. In R.D. Dunham & G.P. Alpert (Eds.), *Critical issues in policing: Contemporary readings*, 7th ed. (pp. 548–566). Long Grove, IL: Waveland Press.

Fyfe, J.J. (2015). The split-second syndrome and other determinants of police violence. In R.G. Dunham & G.P. Alpert (Eds.), *Critical issues in policing: Contemporary Readings*, 7th ed. (pp. 517–531). Long Grove, IL: Waveland Press.

Fyfe, J.J., Greene, J.R., Walsh, W., Wilson, O., & McLaren, R. (1997). *Police administration*. New York, NY: McGraw-Hill.

Gau, J.M. (2013). Consent searches as a threat to procedural justice and police legitimacy: An analysis of consent requests during traffic stops. *Criminal Justice Policy Review*, 24(6), 759–777.

Gau, J.M., & Brunson, R.K. (2010). Procedural justice and order maintenance policing: A study of inner-city young men's perceptions of police legitimacy. *Justice Quarterly*, 27(2), 255–279.

Gau, J., Corsaro, N., Stewart, E.A., & Brunson, R.K. (2012). Examining macro-level impacts on procedural justice and police legitimacy. *Journal of Criminal Justice*, 40, 333–343.

Gaub, J.E., Choate, D.E., Todak, N., Katz, C.M., & White, M.D. (2016). Officer perceptions of body-worn cameras before and after deployment: A study of three departments. *Police Quarterly*, 19(3), 275–302.

Gaub, J., Todak, N., & White, M. (2018). One size doesn't fit all: The deployment of police body-worn cameras to specialty units. *International Criminal Justice Review*, 30(2), 136–155.

Hawdon, J.E., Ryan, J., & Griffin, S.P. (2003). Policing tactics and perceptions of police legitimacy. *Police Quarterly*, 6(4), 469–491.

Huff, J., Katz, C., & Hedberg, E. (2022). A randomized controlled trial of the impact of body-worn camera activation on the outcomes of individual incidents. *Journal of Experimental Criminology*, 18, 247–272.

Hullenaar, K., Kurpiel, A., & Ruback, R. (2021). Youth violent offending in school and out: Reporting, arrest, and the school-to-prison pipeline. *Justice Quarterly*, 38(7), 1319–1341.

Hyland, S., Langton, L., & Davis, E. (2015). *Police use of nonfatal force, 2002–11*. Washington, DC: Bureau of Justice Statistics.

International Association Chiefs of Police. (2015). *National policy summit on community–police relations* Alexandria, VA: IACP.

Jahn, J.L., Simes, J.T., Cowger, T.L., & Davis, B.A. (2022). Racial disparities in neighborhood arrest rates during the COVID-19 pandemic. *Journal of Urban Health*, 99(1), 67–76.

James, L., & James, S. (2023). Using body-worn cameras to investigate predictors and the outcomes of police–community interactions. *Police Quarterly*, 1–27. doi:https://doi.org/10.1177/10986111231169788.

Jennings, W., Fridell, L., & Lynch, M. (2014). Cops and cameras: Officer perceptions of the use of body-worn cameras in law enforcement. *Journal of Criminal Justice*, 42, 549–556.

Johnson, T., Johnson, N., Sabol, W., & Snively, D. (2022). Law enforcement agencies' college education hiring requirements and racial differences in police-related fatalities. *Journal of Police and Criminal Psychology*, 1–21. doi:10.1007/s11896-022-09534-6.

Kajeepeta, S., Bruzelius, E., Ho, J.Z., & Prins, S.J. (2022). Policing the pandemic: Estimating spatial and racialized inequities in New York City police enforcement of COVID-19 mandates. *Critical Public Health*, 32(1), 56–67.

Kane, R.J. (2005). Compromised police legitimacy as a predictor of violent crime in structurally disadvantaged communities. *Criminology*, 43(2), 469–498.

Katz, C., & Huff, J. (2023). The Achilles heel of police body-worn cameras: Understanding the factors that influence variation in body-worn camera activation. *Justice Quarterly*, 40(3), 315–336.

Keller, T., Caplan, J., & Kennedy, L. (2023). The influence of the environment on officer-involved shootings. *Homicide Studies*, 27(1), 97–119.

Keyes, C., Hysom, S., & Lupo, K. (2000). The positive organization: Leadership legitimacy, employee well-being, and the bottom line. *The Psychologist-Manager Journal*, 4(2), 143–153.

Kim, D.-Y., & Phillips, S. (2021). When COVID-19 and guns meet: A rise in shootings. *Journal of Criminal Justice*, 73, 1–11. doi:https://doi.org/10.1016/j.jcrimjus.2021.101783.

Kyle, M., & White, D. (2017). The impact of law enforcement officer perceptions of organizational justice on their attitudes regarding body-worn cameras. *Journal of Crime and Justice*, 40(1), 68–83.

Laufs, J., & Waseem, Z. (2020). Policing in pandemics: A systematic review and best practices for police response to COVID-19. *International Journal of Disaster Risk Reduction*, 51, 101812.

Lawshe, N., Zimmerman, G., & Stowell, J. (2022). Examining the spacial distribution and contextual correlates of body-worn camera adoption in the USA. *Policing*, 16(4), 731–751.

Lee, H., Vaughn, M.S., & Lim, H. (2014). The impact of neighborhood crime levels on police use of force: Examination of micro and meso levels. *Journal of Criminal Justice*, 42(6), 491–499.

Li, W. (2020, June 2). *Police arrested fewer people during Coronavirus shutdowns – even fewer were white*. Retrieved from The Marshall Project: www.themarshallproject.org/2020/06/02/police-arrested-fewer-people-during-coronavirus-shutdowns-even-fewer-were-white.

Lum, C., Maupin, C., & Stoltz, M. (2020a). *The impact of COVID-19 on law enforcement agencies (wave 1)*. Alexandria, VA: IACP.

Lum, C., Maupin, C., & Stoltz, M. (2020b). *The impact of COVID-19 on law enforcement agencies (wave 2)*. Alexandria, VA: IACP.

MacDonald, H. (2016). *The war on cops: How the new attack on law and order makes everyone less safe*. New York, NY: Encounter Books.

McCluskey, J., Uchida, C., Solomon, S., Wooditch, A., Connor, C., & Revier, L. (2019). Assessing the effects of body-worn cameras on procedural justice in the Los Angeles Police Department. *Criminology, 57,* 208–236. doi:org/10.1111/1745-9125.12201.

McKenna, J., & White, S. (2018). Examining the use of police in schools: How roles may impact responses to student misconduct. *American Journal of Criminal Justice, 43,* 448–470.

McLean, K., Alikhan, A., & Alpert, G. (2022). Re-examining the use of force continuum: Why resistance is not the only driver of use of force decisions. *Police Quarterly,* 1–26. doi:10.1177/10986111211066353.

Maguire, E.R., & Johnson, D. (2010). Measuring public perceptions of the police. *Policing, 33*(4), 703–730.

Maguire, E.R., Nix, J., & Campbell, B.A. (2016). A war on cops? The effects of Ferguson on the number of U.S. police officers murdered in the line of duty. *Justice Quarterly, 35*(5), 739–758.

Malcolm, H. (2016). Millennials value happy workplace over better pay. *USA Today,* p. 4B.

Mapping Police Violence. (2024, January 18). *Mapping police violence*. Retrieved from https://mappingpoliceviolence.org/.

Marcelo, P. (2015, June 18). Boston praised for releasing video in police killings. *AOL. Com,* www.aol.com/article/2015/06/18/boston-praised-for-releasing-video-in-police-killings/21198105/.

Martinez-Prather, K., McKenna, J., & Bowman, S. (2016). The school-to-prison pipline: How roles of school-based law enforcement officers may impact disciplinary actions. *Journal of Qualitative Criminal Justice and Criminology, 4*(2), 244–272.

Maskaly, J., Ikovich, S.K., & Neyroud, P. (2021). Policing in the COVID-19 pandemic: Exploratory study of the types of organizational changes and police activities across the globe. *International Criminal Justice Review, 31*(3), 266–285.

Maskaly, J., Kutnjak Ivkovich, S., & Neyroud, P. (2022). A comparative study of the police officer views on policing during the COVID-19 pandemic in the United States. *Policing: An International Journal, 45*(1), 75–90.

Matusiak, M.C. (2014). Dimensionality of local police chiefs' institutional sovereigns. *Policing and Society: An International Journal of Research and Policy,* 1–18.

May, D., Barranco, R., Stokes, E., Robertson, A., & Haynes, S. (2018). Do school resource officers really refer juveniles to the juvenile justice system for less serious offenses? *Criminal Justice Policy Review, 29*(1), 89–105.

Mazerolle, L., Bennett, S., Davis, J., Sargeant, E., & Manning, M. (2013). Procedural justice and police legitimacy: A systematic review of the research evidence. *Journal of Experimental Criminology, 9,* 245–274.

Miller, J., & Chillar, V. (2022). Do body-worn cameras reduce citizen fatalities? Results of a county-wide natural experiment. *Journal of Experimental Criminology, 38,* 723–754.

Moore, M., & Stephens, D. (1991). *Beyond command and control: The strategic management of police departments*. Washington, DC: Police Executive Research Forum.

Mora, D., Terrill, W., & Foster, J. (2023). A decade of police use of deadly force research (2000–2010). *Homicide Studies, 27*(1), 6–33.

More, H.W., Vito, G.F., & Walsh, W.F. (2012). *Organizational behavior and management in law enforcement*. Upper Saddle River, NJ: Prentice Hall.

National Institute of Justice. (2011). *Strategic cutback management: Law enforcement leadership for lean times*. Washington, DC: U.S. Department of Justice.

Nicholson-Crotty, S., Nicholson-Crotty, J., & Fernandez, S. (2017). Will more black cops matter? Officer race and police-involved homicides of black citizens. *Public Administration Review, 77*(2), 206–216.

Nix, J., Ivanov, S., & Pickett, J. T. (2021). What does the public want police to do during pandemics? A national experiment. *Criminology & Public Policy*, 545–571.

Nix, J., Pickett, J., Wolfe, S., & Campbell, B. (2017). Demeanor, race, and police perceptions of procedural justice: Evidence from two randomized experiments. *Justice Quarterly, 34*(7), 1154–1183.

Nix, J., & Wolfe, S.E. (2015). The impact of negative publicity on police self-legitimacy. *Justice Quarterly, 34*(1), 84–108.

Nix, J., & Wolfe, S.E. (2016). Sensitivity to the Ferguson effect: The role of managerial organizational justice. *Journal of Criminal Justice, 47*, 12–20.

Nix, J., Wolfe, S.E., Rojek, J., & Kaminsky, R.J. (2015). Trust in the police: The influence of procedural justice and perceived collective efficacy. *Crime & Delinquency, 61*(4), 610–640.

Nobel, J., & Alpert, G. (2015). State-created danger: Should police officers be accountable for reckless tactical decision making? In R.G. Dunham & G.P. Alpert (Eds.), *Critical issues in policing: Contemporary rings*, 7th ed. (pp. 567–582). Prospect Heights, IL: Waveland Press.

Oliver, W.M. (2015). Depolicing: Rhetoric or reality? *Criminal Justice Policy Review, 28*(5), 437–461.

Paoline, E., Terrill, W., & Somers, L. (2021). Police officer use of force mindset and street-level behavior. *Police Quarterly, 24*(4), 547–577.

Peacock, R., Wu, Y., Ivkovic, S., Sun, I., Vinogradac, M., & Vinogradac, V. (2023). The distinct role of peers and supervisors in shaping officers' just and unjust interactions with citizens. *Criminal Justice and Behavior, 50*(3), 374–391.

Petenko, E. (2022, January 9). *The pandemic tanked traffic stops in 2020 – but racial disparities remained, data shows*. Retrieved from VTDigger: https://vtdigger.org/2022/01/09/the-pandemic-tanked-traffic-stops-in-2020-but-racial-disparities-remained-data-shows/#:~:text=But%20there's%20little%20evidence%20that,two%20racial%20groups%20in%20place.

Petersen, K. (2022). Looking at the big picture: Using systems theory to understand the impact of body-worn cameras on police accountability. *Crtiical Criminology*, 860–878. doi:https://doi.org/10.1007/s10612-022-09613-4.

Pickering, J., & Klinger, D. (2023). Shooting and holding fire in police work: Insight from a study informed by the Binder and Scharf model of deadly force decision-making. *Homicide Studies, 27*(1), 34–54.

Police Executive Research Forum (PERF). (2010). *Is the Economic downturn fundamentally changing how we police?* Washington, DC: Police Executive Research Forum.

Police Executive Research Forum. (2014). *Future trends in policing*. Washington, DC: Office of Community Oriented Policing Services.

Police Executive Research Forum. (2015). *Re-engineering training on police use of force*. Washington, DC: Police Executive Research Forum.

Police Executive Research Forum. (2016). *Use of force: Taking police to a higher standard—30 guiding principles*. Washington, DC: Police Executive Research Forum.

President's Task Force on 21st Century Policing (PTF). (2015a). *Final report of the President's task force on 21st century policing*. Washington, DC: Office of Community Oriented Police Services.

President's Task Force on 21st Century Policing. (2015b). *President's task force on 21st century policing, implementing guide.* Washington, DC: Office of Community Oriented Police Services.

Riddell, J., & Worrall, J. (2021). Predicting firearms and CEW displays as police officers' response to resistance. *Journal of Criminal Justice, 72,* 1–11. doi:10.1016/j.jcrimjus.2020.101775.

Rosenbaum, D.P., Shuck, A., Lawrence, D., Harnett, S., McDevitt, J., & Posick, C. (2011). *Community-based indicators of police performance: Introducing the platform's public satisfaction survey.* Washington, DC: National Police Research Platform, National Institute of Justice.

Rosenfeld, R. (2015). *Was there a "Ferguson Effect" on crime in St. Louis?* Washington, DC: The Sentencing Project.

Shjarback, J., & Magny, O. (2022). Cops and COVID: An examination of California officers' perceptions and experiences while policing during a pandemic. *Policing: An International Journal, 45*(1), 59–74.

Smykla, J., Crow, M., Critchlow, V., & Synder, J. (2016). Police body-worn cameras: Perceptions of law enforcement leadership. *American Journal of Criminal Justice, 41,* 424–443.

Southall, A. (2020, November 30). *Scrutiny of social-distance policing as 35 of 40 arrested are Black.* Retrieved from The New York Times: www.nytimes.com/2020/05/07/nyregion/nypd-social-distancing-race-coronavirus.html.

Souza, W.H., Miethe, T.D., & Sakiyama, M. (2018). Inconsistencies in public opinion of body-worn cameras on police: Transparency, trust, and improved police–citizen relationships. *Policing: A Journal of Policy and Practice, 12*(1), 100–108.

Sunshine, J., & Tyler, T.R. (2003). The role of procedural justice and legitimacy in shaping public support for policing. *Law & Society Review, 37*(3), 513–548.

Taylor, P. (2020). Dispatch priming and the police decision to use deadly force. *Police Quarterly, 23*(3), 311–332.

Terrill, W., & Paoline, E.A. (2015). Citizens' complaints as threats to police legitimacy: The role of officers' occupational attitudes. *Journal of Contemporary Criminal Justice, 31*(2), 192–211.

Terrill, W., & Paoline, E.A. (2016). Police use of less than lethal force: Does administrative policy matter? *Justice Quarterly.* doi:10.1080/07418825.2016.1147593.

Terrill, W., & Somers, L. (2023). Viewing firearm danger through the lens of police officers. *Homicide Studies, 27*(1), 55–76.

Tyler, T.R., & Fagan, J. (2008). Legitimacy and cooperation: Why do people help the police fight crime in their communities? *Ohio State Journal of Criminal Law, 6,* 231–275.

US Department of Justice, Community Relations Service. (2003). *Principles of good policing: Avoiding violence between police and citizens.* Washington, DC: Department of Justice.

Van Craen, M., & Skogan, W. (2017). Achieving fairness in policing: The link between internal and external procedural justice. *Police Quarterly, 20*(1), 3–23.

Walker, S., Alpert, G.P., & Kenney, D.J. (2000). Early warning systems for police: Concept, history, and issues. *Police Quarterly, 3*(2), 132–152.

Walker, S., & Archbold, C. (2014). *The new world of police accountability,* 2nd ed. Newbury Park, CA: Sage.

Wells, W. (2007). Type of contact and evaluation of police officers: The effects of procedural justice across three types of police–citizen contacts. *Journal of Criminal Justice, 35,* 612–621.

White, M. (2014). *Police officer body-worn cameras: Assessing the evidence.* Washington, DC: Office of Community Oriented Policing Services.

Williams, M. (2021). Explaining public support for body-worn cameras in law enforcement. *Police Practice and Research, 22*(6), 1603–1617.

Wolfe, S.E. (2011). The effect of low self-control on perceived police legitimacy. *Journal of Criminal Justice, 39,* 67–74.

Wood, G., Tyler, T., & Papachristos, A. (2020). Procedural justice training reduces police use of force and complaints against officers. *National Academy of Sciences in the United States of America, 117*(18), 9815–9821.

Worden, R., & McLean, S. (2018). Measuring, managing, and enhancing procedural justice in policing: Promise and pitfalls. *Criminal Justice Policy Review, 29*(2), 149–171.

Zhao, J.S., Tsai, C.F., Ren, L., & Lai, Y.L. (2012). Public satisfaction with police control of disorder crime: Does the public hold the police accountable? *Justice Quarterly, 31*(2), 394–420.

Zimring, F. (2017). *When police kill.* Cambridge, MA: Harvard University Press.

Zimring, F. (2020). Police killings as a problem of governance. *Annals of the Academy of Political and Social Sciences, 687,* 114–123.

Index

Page numbers in *italic* indicate a figure and page numbers in **bold** indicate a table on the corresponding page.

For Product Safety Concerns and Information please contact our EU
representative GPSR@taylorandfrancis.com
Taylor & Francis Verlag GmbH, Kaufingerstraße 24, 80331 München, Germany

www.ingramcontent.com/pod-product-compliance
Ingram Content Group UK Ltd.
Pitfield, Milton Keynes, MK11 3LW, UK
UKHW011457240425
457818UK00022B/880